D1623125

Children's
Seashore House

Handbook of
Developmental Disabilities

Resources for Interdisciplinary Care

Edited by

Lisa A. Kurtz, MEd, OTR/L, BCP
Director of Occupational Therapy
Associate Director for LEND Training, University Affiliated Program
Children's Seashore House
Assistant Clinical Professor of Occupational Therapy
Thomas Jefferson University
Philadelphia, Pennsylvania

Peter W. Dowrick, PhD
Co-Director, University Affiliated Program
Children's Seashore House
Associate Professor of Psychology in Pediatrics
University of Pennsylvania School of Medicine
Philadelphia, Pennsylvania

Susan E. Levy, MD
Clinical Attending in Pediatrics
Children's Seashore House
Clinical Associate Professor of Pediatrics
University of Pennsylvania School of Medicine
Philadelphia, Pennsylvania

Mark L. Batshaw, MD
Physician-in-Chief
Children's Seashore House
Chief, Division of Child Development and Rehabilitation
Children's Hospital of Philadelphia
W. T. Grant Professor of Pediatrics and Neurology
University of Pennsylvania School of Medicine
Philadelphia, Pennsylvania

AN ASPEN PUBLICATION®
Aspen Publishers, Inc.
Gaithersburg, Maryland
1996

Library of Congress Cataloging-in-Publication Data

Handbook of developmental disabilities : resources for
interdisciplinary care / edited by Lisa A. Kurtz ... [et al.].
p. cm.
Includes bibliographical references and index.
ISBN 0-8342-0786-9
1. Developmentally disabled children—Rehabilitation—Handbooks,
manuals, etc. 2. Developmentally disabled children—Care—
Handbooks, manuals, etc. 3. Child development deviations—
Handbooks, manuals, etc. I. Kurtz, Lisa A.
[DNLM: 1. Child Development Disorders—rehabilitation—handbooks.
WS 39 H2354 1996]
RJ138.H335   1996
618.92—dc20
DNLM/DLC
for Library of Congress
95-46367
CIP

Editorial Resources: Jill Berry, Amy Myers-Payne

Library of Congress Catalog Number: 95-46367
ISBN: 0-8342-0786-9

Printed in the United States of America

1 2 3 4 5

Table of Contents

Contributors

Jodie M. Ambrosino, MA
Referral Coordinator and Clinical Specialist, Department of
  Pediatric Psychology
Children's Seashore House
Philadelphia, Pennsylvania

Susan E. Ansul, MA
Pediatric Psychology Clinician
Children's Seashore House
Philadelphia, Pennsylvania

Marleen Anne Baron, MA, CCC/sp
Acting Director, Speech/Language Pathology, Division of
  Communication Disorders
Children's Seashore House
Philadelphia, Pennsylvania

Mark L. Batshaw, MD
Physician-in-Chief
Children's Seashore House
Chief, Division of Child Development and Rehabilitation
Children's Hospital of Philadelphia
W.T. Grant Professor of Pediatrics and Neurology
University of Pennsylvania School of Medicine
Philadelphia, Pennsylvania

Doré Blanchet, MS, OTR/L
Director, Pediatric Program, Good Shepherd Rehabilitation
  Program
Allentown, Pennsylvania

Nathan J. Blum, MD
Associate Director, Child Development Program
Children's Seashore House
Assistant Professor of Pediatrics
University of Pennsylvania
Philadelphia, Pennsylvania

Cynthia Borda, RPh, MBA
Director of Pharmacy
Children's Seashore House
Philadelphia, Pennsylvania

Jennifer Buzby-Hadden, MEd, LDTC
Director of Early Intervention and Related Programs
ATCO Child Development Center and
Children's Seashore House
Philadelphia, Pennsylvania

Lynette E. Byarm, MS, OTR/L, BCP
Coordinator of Clinical Education, Department of
  Occupational Therapy
Children's Seashore House
Philadelphia, Pennsylvania

Sean Casey, BA
Clinical Specialist
Children's Seashore House
Philadelphia, Pennsylvania

David E. Cohen, MD
Associate Professor of Anesthesia
University of Pennsylvania
Director of Pain Management, Department of Anesthesia
  and Critical Care Medicine
Children's Hospital of Philadelphia
Philadelphia, Pennsylvania

Anna-Maria DaCosta, MD
Clinical Attending in Pediatrics
Children's Seashore House
Clinical Assistant Professor of Pediatrics
University of Pennsylvania
Philadelphia, Pennsylvania

Beth A. Delaney, BA
Primary Therapist, Bio-Behavioral Unit
Children's Seashore House
Philadelphia, Pennsylvania

Johanna E. Dietz-Curry, MS, PT
Senior Physical Therapist
Children's Seashore House
Philadelphia, Pennsylvania

Hillary S. Domers, MSW, MA, LSW, ACSW
Social Worker
Children's Seashore House
Philadelphia, Pennsylvania

John P. Dormans, MD
Pediatric Orthopedic Surgeon, Division of Orthopedic
  Surgery
Children's Hospital of Philadelphia
Philadelphia, Pennsylvania

Peter W. Dowrick, PhD
Co-Director, University Affiliated Program
Children's Seashore House
Associate Professor of Psychology in Pediatrics
University of Pennsylvania School of Medicine
Philadelphia, Pennsylvania

Ann-Christine Duhaime, MD
Pediatric Neurosurgeon
Children's Hospital of Philadelphia
Associate Professor of Neurosurgery
University of Pennsylvania
Philadelphia, Pennsylvania

Peggy S. Eicher, MD
Co-Director, Pediatric Feeding Program
Children's Seashore House
Assistant Professor, Department of Pediatrics
University of Pennsylvania
Philadelphia, Pennsylvania

Laura Fus-Rowe, MA, CCC/SLP
Pediatric Speech-Language Pathologist
Children's Hospital of Wisconsin
Department of Speech and Hearing Disorders
Milwaukee, Wisconsin

Sonia V. George, MD
Fellow in Developmental Pediatrics
Children's Seashore House
Philadelphia, Pennsylvania

Lesley Austin Geyer, MA, OTR/L, BCP
Assistant Director of Occupational Therapy
Children's Seashore House
Philadelphia, Pennsylvania

Angelo P. Giardino, MD, MSEd, FAAP
Vice President, Ambulatory and Managed Care
Children's Seashore House
Clinical Assistant Professor of Pediatrics
University of Pennsylvania
Philadelphia, Pennsylvania

Linda Gibson-Matthews, PhD
Clinical Psychologist, Private Practice
Wyndmoor, Pennsylvania

Amy S. Goldman, MS, CCC/SLP
Project Director
Pennsylvania's Initiative on Assistive Technology
Institute on Disabilities, University-Affiliated Program
Temple University
Philadelphia, Pennsylvania

Shirley A. Harris-Carlson, PsyD
Psychologist, Feeding Disorders Program
Children's Seashore House
Philadelphia, Pennsylvania

Ada Dorothy Hayes, MD
Medical Director
Children's Seashore House
Philadelphia, Pennsylvania
Child Development Center
Atlantic City, New Jersey
Assistant Professor of Pediatrics
University of Pennsylvania
Philadelphia, Pennsylvania

Linda Hock-Long, MSSS
Child Development Program Manager
Children's Seashore House
Philadelphia, Pennsylvania

Karen M. Hudson, MSW, LSW
Social Work Supervisor
Children's Seashore House
Philadelphia, Pennsylvania

James L. Karustis, MA
Fellow in Pediatric Psychology
Children's Seashore House
Philadelphia, Pennsylvania

Kelly Kates, MA
Outpatient Therapist
Children's Seashore House
Philadelphia, Pennsylvania

Lee Kern, PhD
Assistant Professor
Department of Pediatrics
University of Pennsylvania
Philadelphia, Pennsylvania

MaryLouise E. Kerwin, PhD
Co-Director, Pediatric Feeding Program
Children's Seashore Houses
Assistant Professor, Department of Pediatrics
University of Pennsylvania
Philadelphia, Pennsylvania

Dana I. Klar, MPA
Coordinator of Special Projects, Department of Pediatric
    Psychology
Children's Seashore House
Philadelphia, Pennsylvania

Carol A. Knightly, MA, CCC-A
Acting Director of Audiology
Children's Seashore House
Philadelphia, Pennsylvania

Kathleen Ryan Kuntz, RN, MSN, CRRN
Nursing Education Director
Children's Seashore House
Clinical Instructor, School of Nursing
University of Pennsylvania
Clinical Instructor in Pediatrics
Thomas Jefferson University
Philadelphia, Pennsylvania

Lisa A. Kurtz, MEd, OTR/L, BCP
Director of Occupational Therapy and Associate Director
 for LEND Training
University Affiliated Program
Children's Seashore House
Assistant Clinical Professor of Occupational Therapy
Thomas Jefferson University
Philadelphia, Pennsylvania

Joseph S. Lalli, PhD
Assistant Director, Biobehavioral Unit
Children's Seashore House
Assistant Professor of Behavioral Psychology in Pediatrics
University of Pennsylvania
Philadelphia, Pennsylvania

Mary F. Lazar, PsyD
Developmental Neuropsychologist
Children's Seashore House
Philadelphia, Pennsylvania

Winifred Lloyds-Lender, PhD
Postdoctoral Fellow, Department of Pediatric Psychology
Children's Seashore House
Philadelphia, Pennsylvania

Susan E. Levy, MD
Clinical Attending in Pediatrics
Children's Seashore House
Clinical Associate Professor of Pediatrics
University of Pennsylvania School of Medicine
Philadelphia, Pennsylvania

David F. Lewis, PT, MBA
Vice President for Patient Care Services
Children's Seashore House
Philadelphia, Pennsylvania

Audrey E. Mars, BS, RN, MD, FAAP
Fellow in Developmental Pediatrics
Children's Seashore House
Philadelphia, Pennsylvania

Sandra M. McGee, PT
Assistant Director of Physical Therapy
Children's Seashore House
Philadelphia, Pennsylvania

Sheryl J. Menacker, MD
Division of Ophthalmology
Children's Hospital of Philadelphia
Clinical Associate, Division of Ophthalmology
University of Pennsylvania
Philadelphia, Pennsylvania

Gretchen Meyer, MD
Fellow in Developmental Pediatrics
Children's Seashore House
Philadelphia, Pennsylvania

Edward M. Moss, PhD
Director, Outpatient Neuropsychology
Children's Seashore House
Clinical Associate, Department of Pediatrics
University of Pennsylvania
Philadelphia, Pennsylvania

Kathleen H. Murphey, MS
Director of Child Life
Children's Seashore House
Philadelphia, Pennsylvania

Sandra J. Okino, OTR/L
Occupational Therapist
United Cerebral Palsy Association
Swarthmore, Pennsylvania

Mary L. Osborne, PhD
Clinical Assistant Professor of Pediatrics
University of Medicine and Dentistry of New Jersey
Robert Wood Johnson Medical School
New Brunswick, New Jersey

John M. Parrish, PhD
Head, Section of Pediatric Psychology and Behavioral
 Pediatrics
Children's Seashore House
Associate Professor of Psychology in Pediatrics and
 Psychiatry
University of Pennsylvania
Philadelphia, Pennsylvania

Lynn S. Paterna, MS
Alaska's Autism Intensive Early Intervention Coordinator
Center for Human Development, University-Affiliated
 Program
Anchorage, Alaska

Thomas J. Power, PhD
Co-Director, Attention Deficit Hyperactivity Disorder
 Evaluation and Treatment Program
Children's Seashore House
Clinical Assistant Professor of Clinical Psychology in
 Pediatrics
University of Pennsylvania
Philadelphia, Pennsylvania

Jerilynn Radcliffe, PhD
Assistant Professor of Clinical Psychology in Pediatrics
University of Pennsylvania
Philadelphia, Pennsylvania

Lynn Reynolds
Medical Illustrator
Ars Medica
Doylestown, Pennsylvania

Joan Rhodes, MSW, AMFT
Social Worker
Children's Seashore House
Philadelphia, Pennsylvania

Stephanie R. Ried, MD, MA
Assistant Professor, Department of Rehabilitation Medicine
  and Pediatrics
University of Pennsylvania
Philadelphia, Pennsylvania

Shirley A. Scull, MS, PT
Director of Physical Therapy
Children's Seashore House
Philadelphia, Pennsylvania
Adjunct Clinical Assistant Professor, Institute for Physical
  Therapy Education
Widener University
Chester, Pennsylvania
Adjunct Assistant Professor, Department of Physical
  Therapy
Philadelphia College of Pharmacy and Science
Clinical Assistant Professor, Department of Orthopedic
  Surgery and Rehabilitation
Medical College of Pennsylvania and Hahnemann
  University Graduate School
Philadelphia, Pennsylvania

Nancy L. Hale Sills, MSS, LSW
Senior Social Worker and Coordinator of Cochlear Implant
  Program
Children's Seashore House
Philadelphia, Pennsylvania

Carla A. Stokes, MEd
Developmental Neuropsychology Fellow
Children's Seashore House
Philadelphia, Pennsylvania

Valerie Wolf Shopp, MSW
Senior Social Worker and Student Program Coordinator
Children's Seashore House
Philadelphia, Pennsylvania

Cynthia B. Solot, MA, CCC/SLP
Senior Speech-Language Pathologist
Children's Seashore House
Philadelphia, Pennsylvania

H. Lynn Starr, MD
Attending Pediatrician
Behavioral Pediatrics Section, Division of Child
  Development and Rehabilitation
Children's Seashore House
Children's Hospital of Philadelphia
Instructor in Pediatrics
University of Pennsylvania
Philadelphia, Pennsylvania

Bridget A. Taylor, MEd
Predoctoral Intern
Children's Seashore House
Philadelphia, Pennsylvania

Symme W. Trachtenberg, MSW, LSW, ACSW
Director of Social Work
Children's Seashore House
Clinical Associate in Pediatrics
University of Pennsylvania
Philadelphia, Pennsylvania

Jocelyn I. Trachtenberg
Student
University of Delaware
Newark, Delaware

Suzanne Vender, MA, CCC/SLP
Speech/Language Pathologist
Children's Seashore House
Philadelphia, Pennsylvania

Paul P. Wang, MD
Clinical Attending in Pediatrics
Children's Seashore House
Assistant Professor of Pediatrics and Neurology
University of Pennsylvania
Philadelphia, Pennsylvania

Karen M. Ward, EdD
Associate Professor
Department of Psychology, University of Anchorage
Director, Center for Human Development, University-
  Affiliated Program
Anchorage, Alaska

Mary Lisa Wright, OTR/L
Clinical Specialist in Assistive Technology, Department of
  Occupational Therapy
Children's Seashore House
Philadelphia, Pennsylvania

Children's Seashore House: An Historic Perspective

From its founding, during the summer of 1872 in Atlantic City, New Jersey, the Children's Seashore House has had a full and rich history of serving children with disabilities. The original incorporators came from the ranks of Philadelphia's wealthy families who had been associated with The Children's Hospital of Philadelphia and were aware of the hospital's desire to have a permanent convalescent facility for children who needed long-term care. This group of committed citizens took it upon themselves to move ahead with the venture in Atlantic City. During that first summer, 27 children were provided care and the program was deemed a success.

THE EARLY YEARS

At first, the program operated only during the summer months. Children came principally from Philadelphia's urban areas, and were transported by train. However, after only a few years, it became clear that the needs of the children remained during the winter months, and that it was hard to keep a group of staff together operating only three or four months of the year. As a result, Dr. William H. Bennett, Physician-in-Chief of

Children's Seashore House, was instrumental in founding St. Christopher's Hospital for Children in Philadelphia. For the first few years the St. Christopher's program would close down in the summer months and the patients would move to the Children's Seashore House in Atlantic City. Those patients who were still there when the Children's Seashore House closed for the season would return to St. Christopher's for the winter. This continued until St. Christopher's began year-round operations in 1877. For the Children's Seashore House permanent, year-round operations were not established until 1909. From its early beginnings the Children's Seashore House has been linked to Philadelphia's two acute-care hospitals devoted exclusively to the care of children, a tradition which continues to exist today.

The medical problems of children treated during the early years were primarily related to diseases of the bone and joints, but also included infant diarrhea, respiratory diseases, and post-surgical care. Social conditions for children living in urban areas at that time in history were, for the most part, very poor. Hence, there was a need for an institution like the Children's Seashore House.

Dr. Bennett believed firmly in treating each child in the context of their family and built cottages for "children and their nursing mothers." The cottage system, which began around the turn of the century, was dealt a severe blow by the hurricane of 1944 which destroyed many of the cottages. The cottage system was gradually eliminated, but the commitment to a high degree of family involvement has continued.

The Children's Seashore House Atlantic City location was thought to provide a superb environment for the treatment of children with disabilities. There was a belief that the sea air and saltwater had a curative effect on the children. Medical treatment often included immersion in saltwater-filled tubs, a sort of "marine medication." Wealthy vacationers also sought the beneficial effects of the sea air and saltwater and would stay in the hotels along the boardwalk. Recognizing the value of treating children with disabilities, each hotel had a collection box in their lobby. Proceeds went to support the children who were cared for at Children's Seashore House, just a short stroll down the boardwalk.

DECADES OF CHANGE

The transition from a program that was principally convalescent in nature to one that focused on the complex medical and rehabilitative needs of children began during the tenure of Dr. Edward Z. Holt, Physician-in-Charge from 1919 to 1949. Advances in surgery, infectious diseases, neonatology, and intensive care resulted in the survival of children, many of whom were left with chronic illnesses and multiple disabilities. These children required competent health care professionals to deal, not only with their medical problems, but also their psychosocial and educational needs within the context of the family. The next three and a half decades, through the mid 1970s, concentrated on building multidisciplinary programs for these children and developing academic affiliations with The Children's Hospital of Philadelphia and the University of Pennsylvania.

In 1974, after many years of planning, The Children's Hospital of Philadelphia moved to the campus of the University of Pennsylvania. It was at this time that the Children's Seashore House made its first entry into Philadelphia, and opened a 12-bed unit within The Children's Hospital, a hospital within a hospital. The unit was conceived to be a transitional care unit for children who required rehabilitative care, parent teaching or were otherwise not yet ready to return home. Over the next 15 years the unit expanded to 26 beds. This growth took place at a time when the health care system was beginning its first attempts to minimize costs through programs of utilization review. The Philadelphia unit fared better than the main hospital in Atlantic City because increasingly complex medical problems were better managed in immediate proximity to the emergency medical services available at The Children's Hospital. Active planning for the consolidation of inpatient services in a new building adjacent to, and connected with, The Children's Hospital began in 1980 and was completed in 1990. While the main inpatient facility was closed, the freestanding outpatient center was expanded to serve the children of Atlantic City and the surrounding counties.

The move to the University campus has enabled Children's Seashore House to serve more children as well as to build many new teaching and research programs. The relationship with The Children's Hospital is complementary and nonduplicative. Each institution concentrates on what it does best, The Children's Hospital in the acute medical and surgical arenas, and Children's Seashore House in the developmental and rehabilitative needs of children. This combination of resources for children has produced a powerful synergy.

WHAT OF THE FUTURE?

The Children's Seashore House is preparing for the certain outcome that health care funding will be reduced. To be more accurate, the rate of increase will likely be reduced. What will this mean for a small, specialty hospital with an academic mission? To talk to some, the outlook is bleak. To me, the route to survival will include the building of an integrated-delivery network for children with disabilities, along with the development of a comprehensive approach to managing their medical care, rehabilitation, and education by utilizing existing funding in these separate streams.

The current experience of a family with a child with special needs can be compared to the sensation of being in an automobile traveling down the highway at 50 miles an hour. Every time the child and family move between providers, or cross into a different stream of funding, it is like hitting a speed bump without warning. The result is a bone-jarring thud that rattles everyone in the car. The system of the future should be one in which needed services are managed by a single-care manager who has the ability to coordinate the multiple funding streams and providers.

Whether this will in fact be the future system is still unknown, but we at Children's Seashore House will be devoting significant energies to make it a reality. There is hope, I believe, for both an improved and more cost-effective system of care for children with special needs.

In the meantime, changes that are taking place in the health care industry are of epic proportion and the "watch words" for the future will be *resourcefulness* and *flexibility*. Change is not always readily welcomed, and today changes are being thrust on us in amounts that are almost indigestible. Our success, both as institutions and individuals, will be determined by how well we are able to adapt to this new era and deal with a more constant and continuing level of change. We are increasingly being asked to do more and take on a wider range of responsibilities. The era of the specialist is evolving into the era of the generalist. Hospitals across the country have been experimenting with the concept of multiskilled workers and the primary care practitioners of medicine are being catapulted into the front lines of medicine as coordinators of care for the population at large.

So how does this philosophy and prognostication apply to you, a clinician who cares for children with disabilities? The *Handbook of Developmental Disabilities* will help make your transition from specialist to generalist a little easier. As a comprehensive, easy-to-read reference guide to the issues faced by children with disabilities, it will provide you with information necessary to diagnose and treat. It will also help you identify resources that are available to meet the many and varied needs of children with disabilities.

I want to acknowledge and thank each and every person who has contributed to this book, and hope that it will make all of our collective jobs easier and more rewarding at a time that is becoming more challenging every day. In addition, my personal thanks to each of you who are helping to improve the lives of children with disabilities.

—Richard W. Shepherd
President and Chief Executive Officer
The Children's Seashore House
Philadelphia, Pennsylvania

With these issues in mind, we have developed this handbook as a comprehensive, edited reference text. It is intended to serve as a general sourcebook for pediatric service providers, including, but not limited to, professionals from physical therapy, occupational therapy, speech/language pathology, special education, regular education, psychology, medicine, nursing, nutrition, and social work. Our goal is to provide readers with practical, "nuts-and-bolts" solutions to the practice dilemmas typically encountered on a day-to-day basis when caring for children with special needs and to present this information in the form of easy-to-read outlines, flow sheets, graphs, tables, and checklists. Information is organized not around disciplinary boundaries but around functional themes typically encountered in the day-to-day practice of professionals from diverse backgrounds. We fully recognize the limitations in publishing what may be perceived as "cookbook" solutions to very complex clinical problems. Though not intended to replace the need for more scholarly textbooks that detail the theoretical premises upon which these clinical procedures are based, this handbook, we hope, will serve an important function because of its comprehensive and practical nature.

There are four main sections in the handbook. Part I presents a brief synopsis of the major diagnoses that make up the developmental disabilities (incidence, etiologies, key diagnostic and commonly associated features) and offers current references for obtaining further information.

Part II presents an interdisciplinary approach to pediatric assessment. Guidelines for referral for comprehensive developmental assessment are presented, along with checklists for developmental milestones in key functional perform-ance areas. The typical roles and functions of interdisciplinary team members are reviewed, along with the appropriate criteria for referral to each of these disciplines as well as to other professionals and medical subspecialists who might need to be consulted. Selected protocols for common clinical assessment procedures are included. Where possible, we have tried to include screening procedures that might be used by professionals who have limited training or experience in the specific area of assessment. This section ends with an overview of the appropriate use of empirically validated tools in the assessment of children and includes an extensive annotated review of commonly used tests for children.

Part III presents an overview of common interventions organized around themes such as interdisciplinary team processes, special education practices, developmental therapy approaches, mobility and ambulation, feeding and nutrition, medical and nursing care, functional skills training, splinting and casting, communication skills, applications of assistive technology, psychosocial management, and play and recreation for children with disabilities. We have tried to be as specific as possible in guiding readers to select appropriate intervention strategies and have included specific examples and references whenever possible.

In the Appendixes, we conclude with an extensive resource section listing professional organizations and agencies that can provide further information about children with disabilities, as well as a resource directory of suppliers that distribute products used in pediatric care.

Lisa A. Kurtz, MEd, OTR/L, BCP
Senior Editor

Acknowledgments

The successful publication of this handbook serves as a good example of the kind of interdisciplinary team process we endorse, and we are deeply indebted to the many individuals who lent their support to the project. We thank the Board of Trustees of the Children's Seashore House for promoting the handbook as one component of the hospital's strategic plan, thereby bringing the project to the attention of the entire hospital community and ensuring that there would be sufficient resources allocated to its production.

Over 70 contributing authors produced manuscripts that were subjected to considerable editorial revision to ensure that the book would be free of unnecessary redundancies, well organized, and consistent in its style of presentation. We appreciate not only the authors' knowledgeable contributions but also their tolerance for our editorial license. Lynn Reynolds produced the figures for the handbook, illustrating our concepts clearly and with style. Many other people, including professional and clerical staff at the Children's Seashore House and the Children's Hospital of Philadelphia, trainees, and friends and colleagues of our University Affiliated Program, offered their assistance in many ways far too numerous to list but no less appreciated. The project was supported in part by funding for a Maternal and Child Health LEND Training Project, MCJ-429308 from the Maternal and Child Health Bureau (Title V, Social Security Act), Health Resources and Services Administration, Department of Health and Human Services.

We gratefully acknowledge the efforts of our colleagues who agreed to review the manuscript for content, organization, and format and who provided us with critical feedback from the reader's perspective. They include Becky Austill, MS, OTR/L; Mary Ellen McCaffrey, PhD; Thomas Campbell, PhD; Susan V. Duff, MPT, OTR/L, CHT, BCP; Abigail Farber, MD; Laura L. Hayman, PhD, FAAN; Judith M. Levy, MSW, LCSW-C; Barbara Macks, MS, OTR/L; Margaret M. Mahon, PhD, RN, C; Donna H. Mueller, PhD, RD; Diane Sabo, PhD; Linda Townes-Rosenwein, PhD; and Lawrence Brown, MD

Special thanks are extended to Margaret Rose, who assisted with the technical aspects of producing this handbook and kept us focused on its completion. Her incredible organization and attention to detail, combined with her sustained good humor under stress, make her an absolute delight to work with.

Finally, we wish to thank the many children and families who challenge our beliefs and practices and, in doing so, enrich our lives.

Lisa A. Kurtz, MEd, OTR/L, BCP
Senior Editor

Part I

Scope of Pediatric Development Disabilities

Chapter 1

The Developmental Disabilities

Susan E. Levy

Purpose: to provide an overview of the range of developmental disabilities.

Table 1–1 lists developmenal disabilities along with their definitions, diagnoses, incidence, causes, means of diagnosis, associated features or disabilities, and key current references for further reading. It is meant to serve as a brief outline of types of disorders a practitioner may encounter, not an exhaustive discussion.

Table 1-1 Definitions of Developmental Disabilities

Developmental Disability Description	Incidence	Cause	Means of Diagnosis	Associated Disabilities/Feature	References
Learning disorder (LD): group of heterogeneous disorders resulting in school failure and/or academic difficulties Also known as • Reading disorder • Mathematics disorder • Disorder of written expression	2–10% of school-age children	Multifactorial: • Familial predisposition (especially dyslexia) • Association with genetic or metabolic syndromes (e.g., neurofibromatosis, Turner syndrome)	1. Achievement level is "substantially below" (>2 SD) cognitive ability (IQ) 2. Psychoeducational assessment to determine strengths and weaknesses	1. Motor incoordination 2. Behavior difficulty (e.g., ADHD, conduct disorder, oppositional defiant disorder, depressive disorders) 3. Language disorders (70–80%)	Shapiro and Gallico (1993), Capute and Shapiro (1995)
Attention deficit/ hyperactivity disorder (ADHD): patterns of abnormalities in attention, impulsivity, distractibility, and/or hyperactive behavior Also known as • Attention deficit disorder	3–10% of school-age children	No single or known cause. Possible causes: • Genetic (familial predisposition) • Biologic (e.g., fetal alcohol syndrome, lead) • Social	1. History—use of parent and teacher questionnaires 2. Psychological assessment—deficits in attention, organization	1. Other behavior difficulties (including conduct disorder, oppositional defiant disorder, depressive disorders) 2. Learning disorders (50–60%)	Blondis (1995)
Mental retardation (MR): characterized by general delay in acquisition of cognitive, language, motor, and social skills Classification: • Mild MR (IQ range 55–69) • Severe MR (IQ < 55)	2.5%	Multiple etiologies: • Genetic (chromosomal syndromes or disorders) and/or familial • Metabolic disorders • Perinatal: toxin exposure, intrauterine infection, injury • Idiopathic	1. History 2. Psychological evaluation with cognitive and social/ adaptive skills < 70	Prevalence increases with severity of MR: 1. Cerebral palsy 2. Sensory deficits: visual, hearing 3. Feeding problems 4. Psychiatric or pervasive developmental disorder 5. Seizure disorder 6. ADHD 7. Speech/language disorders	Batshaw (1993), Accardo and Capute (1995)

Developmental Disability Description	Incidence	Cause	Means of Diagnosis	Associated Disabilities/ Feature	References
Autism/pervasive developmental disorder (PDD): impairments in reciprocal social interaction, communication, imaginative activity; restricted repertoire of activities and interests. Onset during infancy or childhood	0.05%	Multiple etiologies, including • Familial predisposition • Genetic syndromes with increased association (e.g., fragile X, untreated PKU, Williams syndrome, others) • Other disorders with association: congenital rubella, infantile spasms, other • Rett syndrome (in females)	1. Psychological evaluation of cognitive, play skills 2. Medical evaluation (developmental pediatrics, neurology, and/or genetics) for etiology 3. Speech/language evaluation	1. MR (66%) 2. Behavior difficulties, including hyperactivity, aggression, self-stimulation, and self-injurious behavior	Mauk (1993)
Communication disorder: Also known as • Expressive language disorder • Mixed receptive-expressive language disorder • Phonological disorder • Stuttering	3–10%	Multiple etiologies; see *learning disorder* May be isolated (e.g., articulation disorder, stuttering) May be associated with other disorders, including anatomic anomalies (e.g., cleft palate), cerebral palsy, MR, autism, traumatic brain injury, others	1. History of acquisition of language milestones 2. Language screening tools 3. Formal assessment by speech/language pathologist and/or psychologist, using standardized test 4. Hearing evaluation	See *Cause*	Klein (1991), Montgomery (1992)

continues

Table 1–1 continued

Developmental Disability Description	Incidence	Cause	Means of Diagnosis	Associated Disabilities/ Feature	References
Cerebral palsy: nonprogressive disorder of movement and posture secondary to central nervous system injury or dysfunction occurring during the first 3–5 years of life Classification: • *physiologic:* spastic, dyskinetic, ataxic, mixed • *topographic:* diplegia, hemiplegia, quadriplegia	0.5%	Multiple etiologies (approximately 25% with no identifiable cause): • Prematurity-associated complications • Asphyxia • Prenatal abnormalities • Biochemical abnormalities (e.g., bilirubin encephalopathy) • Genetic causes • Environmental toxins • Congenital infections • Postnatal events	Interdisciplinary approach is necessary due to complex problems: 1. Historical review of problems 2. Physical examination, with emphasis on growth, musculoskeletal abnormalities, sensory deficits 3. Sensory screening 4. CNS investigations according to history and symptoms (e.g., EEG, head MRI) 5. Developmental evaluation: psychologist, developmental pediatrics 6. Speech/language evaluation (especially if oral motor dysfunction) for possible augmentative communication 7. Motor: physical and/or occupational therapy for motor function, mobility, activities of daily living	1. Cognitive impairment MR (>60%); learning disorders 2. Sensory deficits (hearing loss, visual impairment, strabismus) 3. Growth impairment and/or gastroesophageal reflux 4. Oral motor dysfunction/swallowing disorders 5. Constipation 6. Seizure disorders 7. Behavior and attentional disorders 8. Musculoskeletal abnormalities (e.g., scoliosis, dislocated hip, contractures)	Eicher and Batshaw (1993), Nelson (1995)

continues

Developmental Disability/ Description	Incidence	Cause	Means of Diagnosis	Associated Disabilities/ Feature	References
Myelomeningocele/spina bifida: disorder noted at birth, involving a midline defect of skin, vertebral arches, and neural tube. Complications include cerebrospinal fluid leakage, hydrocephalus (usually requiring shunt placement), Arnold–Chiari malformation (maldevelopment and downward displacement into the cervical spinal canal of parts of the cerebellum, 4th ventricle, and medulla oblongata), paraplegia	0.03% (live births)	Cause unknown: • Suggested polygenic mode of inheritance (higher recurrence rate in affected families) • Research suggests that certain environmental factors contribute to etiology (e.g., folic acid prenatal supplementation resulting in decreased prevalence)	1. Prenatal diagnosis: measurement of alpha-fetoprotein, ultrasonography 2. Evaluation for degree of neurologic impairment: paralysis (clinical evaluation); hydrocephalus (head CT or MRI)	Multiple associated deficits or problems: 1. Mobility: due to paralysis (varies from walking with assistive devices to nonambulatory) 2. Musculoskeletal: joint deformities (e.g., clubfoot), scoliosis 3. Bladder dysfunction 4. Bowel dysfunction 5. Skin breakdown 6. Obesity 7. Seizure disorders 8. Visual deficits (e.g., strabismus) 9. Cognitive deficits	Chauvel and Kinsman (1995)
Hearing impairment: acquired and congenital • *Conductive hearing loss:* due to abnormalities or damage to external or middle ear; maximum loss is 60 dB • *Sensorineural hearing loss:* due to damage or abnormalities of cochlea or auditory nerve	1% (profound hearing loss: 0.2%)	*Conductive:* • Middle ear infection (otitis media) or fluid accumulation *Sensorineural:* • 1/3 genetic; 1/3 acquired; 1/3 unknown • Genetic—>70 syndromes or chromosomal disorders associated with deafness; most autosomal recessive • Craniofacial anomalies (e.g., cleft palate)	1. History of language milestone acquisition, responsiveness to environment 2. History of risk factors: illnesses, prematurity, family history of hearing impairment, frequent ear infections 3. Hearing evaluation (audiometry, tympanometry); if no adequate results, consider BAER (brainstem auditory evoked response)	1. Many of the genetic causes have a range of associated other disabilities, including MR, visual impairment, hyperactivity 2. Depending on the severity of hearing loss, language function will be impaired, with inattention, speech dysfunction	Roizen (1995)

Table 1–1 continued

Developmental Disability Description	Incidence	Cause	Means of Diagnosis	Associated Disabilities/Feature	References
Hearing impairment: acquired and congenital (cont'd):		*Conductive (continued):* • Neonatal complications and prematurity (e.g., asphyxia, intracranial hemorrhage, ototoxic drugs) • Trauma • Infections and antibiotics (e.g., prenatal infection with rubella, cytomegalovirus)	4. Medical evaluation for etiology (as necessary); may include head CT or MRI		
Vision disorders: • Strabismus/amblyopia • Refractive errors • Ocular disorders (e.g., corneal clouding, glaucoma) • Visual impairment ("blindness")	• Strabismus: 2% • Other ocular disorders: 0.1% • Blindness: 0.06% • In population of individuals with developmental disabilities: 48–75%	1. Isolated ocular disorders, strabismus, or refractive errors (in otherwise asymptomatic child) 2. Association with other disorders, including • Congenital abnormalities (e.g., ocular colobomas in CHARGE syndrome; fetal alcohol syndrome) • Genetic and metabolic disorders (e.g., Tay–Sachs, Down syndrome) • Infectious diseases (prenatally acquired; including TORCH, syphilis) • Cortical visual impairment (e.g., secondary to vascular abnormality such as hypoxia) • Tumors • Traumatic injury	1. Pediatrician: screening acuity, cover test for alignment; ophthalmologic exam for red reflex, cornea, retina, optic nerve 2. Evaluation by pediatric ophthalmologist: clinical examination, optokinetic nystagmus, electroretinogram, visual evoked potential	Determined by other associated disorders No research confirmation that visual acuity or tracking abnormalities is associated with learning disorders	Menacker (1993), Hoon (1995)

Developmental Disability Description	Incidence	Cause	Means of Diagnosis	Associated Disabilities/ Feature	References
Behavior disorders: • *Conduct disorder (CD):* rights of others or societal rules are violated. Types include aggression to people/ animals; destruction of property; deceitfulness or theft; violations of rules • *Oppositional defiant disorder (ODD):* recurrent pattern of negativistic, defiant, disobedient, and hostile behavior toward authority figures	2–15%	• Multiple etiologies • Familial pattern • More common in children of biological parents with alcohol dependence, mood disorders, ADHD, or conduct disorders	1. History 2. Psychologic evaluation	1. Frequent school under-achievement 2. Psychosocial complications such as poor self-esteem, poor peer relations, poor frustration tolerance 3. Higher accident rates 4. Often associated with early onset of sexual behavior, use of illicit substances and/or alcohol	Zoccolillo (1992), Rey (1993)
Dual diagnosis: Psychopathology or behavior disorders associated with MR: • Self-injurious behavior • Aggression • Hyperactivity • Stereotypy • Anxiety • Depression	In those with developmental disabilities, may be 5–70%	• Biologic basis in a select population (e.g., Down syndrome, fragile X syndrome, Rett syndrome) • Combination of environmental and/or management factors	1. History of past function, skills, associated behavioral or emotional difficulties 2. Determination of frequency, duration, intensity, and antecedents of behavior in question 3. Referral to appropriate intervention (e.g., psychiatry, behavior psychology, neurology)	Specific syndromes may be more commonly associated with psychiatric symptoms, for example: 1. Down syndrome (dementia) 2. Fragile X (impulsivity, distractibility, atypical behavior) 3. Fetal alcohol syndrome (ADHD) 4. Cerebral palsy (emotional lability, irritability, impulsivity, hyperactivity, attention deficits) 5. Rett syndrome (stereotypic hand movements) 6. Autistic disorder (stereotypy, self-injury, aggression)	Lovell and Reiss (1993)

continues

Table 1–1 continued

Developmental Disability Description	Incidence	Cause	Means of Diagnosis	Associated Disabilities/ Feature	References
Developmental coordination disorder: impairment in development of motor coordination (not due to general medical condition such as cerebral palsy, muscular dystrophy)	2–6%	Varies; developmental lag in acquisition of fine motor and gross motor coordination	Not due to a discrete neurologic disorder	1. Associated disorders include phonological disorder, expressive language disorder, mixed receptive-expressive disorder 2. Lack of coordination may continue through adolescence and adulthood	Henderson et al. (1992)
Developmental delay: nonspecific term for children under 5 years of age with developmental skills below the level expected for age; should be reserved for preschool children with developmental quotients greater than 50	2–5%	Multiple etiologies; for approximately 80%, no specific cause identified; similar etiologies to mental retardation	1. History—review of medical and developmental history 2. Specific developmental assessment to determine levels of function	Same as for mental retardation	Levy and Hyman (1993)

REFERENCES

Accardo, P.J., and A.J. Capute. In press. In *Developmental disabilities in infancy and childhood*, 2nd ed., ed. A.J. Capute and P.J. Accardo. Baltimore: Paul H. Brookes.

Batshaw, M.L. 1993. *Pediatric Clinics of North America* 40:507–522.

Blondis, T.A. In press. In *Developmental disabilities in infancy and childhood*, 2nd ed., ed. A.J. Capute and P.J. Accardo. Baltimore: Paul H. Brookes.

Capute, A.J., and B.K. Shapiro. 1995. In *Developmental disabilities in infancy and childhood*, 2nd ed., ed. A.J. Capute and P.J. Accardo. Baltimore: Paul H. Brookes.

Chauvel, P.J., and S.L. Kinsman. In press. In *Developmental disabilities in infancy and childhood*, 2nd ed., ed. A.J. Capute and P.J. Accardo. Baltimore: Paul H. Brookes.

Eicher, P.S., and M.L. Batshaw. 1993. *Pediatric Clinics of North America* 40:537–552.

Henderson, L., et al. 1992. Reaction time and movement time in children with a developmental coordination disorder. *Journal of Child Psychology and Psychiatry and Allied Disciplines* 33:895–905.

Hoon, A.H. In press. In *Developmental disabilities in infancy and childhood*, 2nd ed., ed. A.J. Capute and P.J. Accardo. Baltimore: Paul H. Brookes.

Klein, S.K. 1991. Evaluation for suspected language disorders in preschool children. *Pediatric Clinics of North America* 38:1455–1468.

Levy, S.E., and S.L. Hyman. 1993. *Pediatric Clinics of North America* 40:465–478.

Lovell, R.W., and A.L. Reiss. 1993. *Pediatric Clinics of North America* 40:579–592.

Mauk, J.E. 1993. *Pediatric Clinics of North America* 40:567–578.

Menacker, S.J. 1993. *Pediatric Clinics of North America* 40:659–674.

Montgomery, J.W. 1992. Easily overlooked language disabilities during childhood and adolescence. *Pediatric Clinics of North America* 39:513–524.

Nelson, K. In press. In *Developmental disabilities in infancy and childhood*, 2nd ed., ed. A.J. Capute and P.J. Accardo. Baltimore: Paul H. Brookes.

Rey, J.M. 1993. Oppositional defiant disorder. *American Journal of Psychiatry* 150:1769–1778.

Roizen, N.J. In press. In *Developmental disabilities in infancy and childhood*, 2nd ed., ed. A.J. Capute and P.J. Accardo. Baltimore: Paul H. Brookes.

Shapiro, B.K., and R.P. Gallico. 1993. *Pediatric Clinics of North America* 40:491–506.

Zoccolillo, M. 1992. Co-occurrence of conduct disorder and its adult outcomes with depressive and anxiety disorders: A review. *Journal of the American Academy of Child and Adolescent Psychiatry* 31:547–556.

Chapter 2

The Syndromes

Mark L. Batshaw and Gretchen Meyer

Purpose: to describe the range of genetic and metabolic disorders.

Table 2–1 lists genetic and metabolic disorders of children along with their clinical features, associated deficits, causes, incidence, and inheritance. Current references are included for additional reading. The table may be used as a resource to guide practitioners to understand better the medical and developmental implications of genetic or metabolic disorders and facilitate the care of these children and their families.

Table 2–1 Description of Syndromes

Syndrome	Clinical Features	Associated Deficits	Cause	Incidence; Inheritance	References
Achondroplasia	Disproportionate short stature, large head, normal intelligence	Spinal cord compression, apnea, delays in motor milestones	Defect in fibroblast growth factor; localized to chromosome 4p	5–15/100,000; AD	Hecht and Butler (1990)
Aicardi syndrome	Infantile spasms, abnormalities of eyes, absence of corpus callosum	Poorly controlled seizures, severe MR, visual impairment	Unknown	Rare, XLD; lethal in males	Neidich et al. (1990)
Angelman syndrome	"Puppetlike" gait, characteristic facial appearance, microbrachycephaly	Paroxysms of laughter, MR, seizures	Deletion of chromosome 15q11–13 (maternal) or uniparental disomy	Rare	Saitoh et al. (1994)
Apert syndrome	Head misshapen, often with a high forehead and flat occiput; widely spaced eyes; syndactyly	Hydrocephalus, developmental delays, MR, hearing loss	Mutation in genes	1.5–1.6/100,000; AD	Cohen et al. (1993)
Batten disease (ceroid lipofuscinosis)	Progressive neurodegenerative disease beginning at 6–18 months	Seizures, microcephaly, MR, severe visual impairment	Unknown	1/100,000; AR	Boustany et al. (1988)
Brachmann de Lange (Cornelia de Lange) syndrome	Short stature, microcephaly, characteristic facial appearance, hypertrichosis	Autisticlike behaviors, language delays, feeding abnormalities, MR	Possible chromosome 3q mutation	1/10,000; probable AD	Kousseff et al. (1994)
CHARGE association	*C*oloboma, *H*eart defect, *A*tresia choanae, *R*etarded growth, *G*enital and *E*ar anomalies	Cleft lip/palate, facial asymmetry, MR	Unknown	Unknown; usually SP	Lin et al. (1990)

continues

Table 2-1 continued

Syndrome	Clinical Features	Associated Deficits	Cause	Incidence; Inheritance	References
Cri-du-chat syndrome	Catlike cry in infancy, pre- and postnatal growth retardation, MR, congenital heart defects, microcephaly, simian creases	Severe respiratory and feeding abnormalities in infancy, hypotonia, inguinal hernias	Partial deletion of short arm of chromosome 5	1/20,000	Wilkins et al. (1983)
Down syndrome	Hypotonia, flat facial profile, upwardly slanted eyes, small nose and ears, short stature, MR, simian creases, congenital heart disease	Atlantoaxial instability, ligamentous laxity, visual and auditory deficits, thyroid disease, premature senility	Trisomy 21 or, rarely, mosaicism or translocation	Variable, age related; SP, age related	Cooley and Graham (1991)
Duchenne muscular dystrophy (DMD)	Progressive pelvic muscle weakness and atrophy, with enlargement of thigh muscles, tight heel cords	Contractures, scoliosis, wheelchair dependence (usually by age 10–12 years); progressive weakness, pneumonia, EKG abnormalities	Mutation in dystrophin gene located on the short arm of X chromosome	1/3,300 in U.S.; usually XLR, rare AR form	Darras et al. (1988)
Facio-auriculo-vertebral spectrum (Goldenhar syndrome)	Hemifacial microsomia, ear anomalies, vertebral anomalies	Cardiac and renal anomalies; MR	Unknown	Unknown; usually SP, rare AD	Ignacio et al. (1993)
Fetal alcohol syndrome	Pre- and postnatal growth retardation; mild–moderate MR; microcephaly, small eyes with droopy eyelids; maxillary hypoplasia; long philtrum; joint abnormalities; congenital heart disease	Joint contractures, cardiac abnormalities, myopia, strabismus, hearing loss, dental malocclusion, eustachian tube dysfunction	Maternal ingestion of alcohol during pregnancy, particularly during first trimester	1% of newborns in Western countries; however, approximately 1/3 of infants prenatally exposed to chronic alcohol intake will have the disorder	Conlon (1992)

continues

Syndrome	Clinical Features	Associated Deficits	Cause	Incidence; Inheritance	References
Fragile X syndrome	Prominent jaw, large ears, large testes, mild connective tissue abnormalities	Behavior problems, hyperactivity, and autistic features common to both sexes; learning disabilities in females only; MR in males only	Defect in X chromosome	1/1,250 male births, 1/2000 female births; XL	Fisch (1993)
Galactosemia	Jaundice in newborn period, enlarged liver, vomiting, lethargy, and increased risk of serious infection	*E. coli* sepsis, cataracts, failure to thrive, ovarian dysfunction	Deficiency of enzyme galactose-1-phosphate uridyl transferase; located on chromosome 9p13	1/50,000–1/70,000; AR	Schweitzer et al. (1993)
Homocystinuria	Inborn error of metabolism associated with MR, dislocated lenses and increased risk of stroke	Skeletal abnormalities, osteoporosis, dislocation of optic lens, intravascular blood clots	Deficiency of the enzyme cystathionine beta-synthase; located on chromosome 21	less than 1/100,000; AR	Cacciari and Salardi (1989)
Huntington disease (Huntington chorea)	Choreic movement disorder and progressive neurological disease with dementia. Usual age of onset is 35–40 years but can present in juvenile onset form and as late as 60–65 years	Joint contractures, swallowing dysfunction, depression. Neurological deterioration, seizures, and speech abnormalities can be associated with juvenile onset	Defect in chromosome 4	1/18,000; AD	Clarke and Bundey (1990)

Table 2–1 continued

Syndrome	Clinical Features	Associated Deficits	Cause	Incidence; Inheritance	References
Hurler syndrome (Mucopolysaccharidosis I-H)	Short stature, progressive MR, coarse facial appearance, full lips	Visual and hearing deficits, progressive joint limitation, kyphosis, hernias, progressive cardiac failure	Deficiency of enzyme alpha iduronidase; located on chromosome 4	1/100,000; AR	Neufeld and Muenzer (1995)
Congenital hypothyroidism (cretinism)	Hoarse cry, large for gestational age, large tongue, umbilical hernia, floppy tone, MR	Growth retardation, delayed bone and dental maturation	Primary defect in development of thyroid gland, an inborn error of metabolism, or an abnormality of the pituitary gland or hypothalamus	1/4,000	New England Congenital Hypothyroidism Collaborative (1990)
Lesch–Nyhan syndrome	Progressive neurological disorder, self-injurious behavior, MR, progressive choreoathetoid cerebral palsy, excessive uric acid in blood	Urinary uric acid stones, kidney disease, mild anemia, arthritis, dysphasia, vomiting	Deficiency of enzyme HGPRT necessary for purine metabolism	1/100,000; XLR	Gibbs et al. (1984)
Lowe syndrome	Boys with bilateral cataracts at birth, physical and mental retardation, hypotonia, renal tubular dysfunction with proteinuria, glucosuria, metabolic acidosis, aminoaciduria	Kidney stones, glaucoma, growth failure, rickets	Defect in X chromosome (Xq24–26)	Undetermined; XLR	Kenworthy et al. (1993)
Maple syrup urine disease	Inborn error of amino acid metabolism presenting with vomiting, lethargy, and coma in the first week of life; urine smells like maple syrup	Acidosis, low blood sugar	Enzyme deficiency affecting branched-chain amino acids	1/125,000; AR	Kaplan et al. (1991)

Syndrome	Clinical Features	Associated Deficits	Cause	Incidence; Inheritance	References
Marfan syndrome	Tall, thin stature, spiderlike limbs, hypermobile joints, dislocation of lens, aortic aneurysm, usually normal intelligence	Joint instability, thoracic deformities, loss of vision	Abnormality in the fibrillin gene; located on chromosome 15q	1/10,000; AD	Lee et al. (1991)
Menkes syndrome	Small for gestational age, progressive neurological disorder, sparse abnormal hair; profound MR	Developmental regression, severe visual abnormalities, 12% live to 2 years	Defective uptake or transport of copper that may be due to an abnormality of cytochrome c oxidase	3/100,000; XLR	DiMauro et al. (1990)
Metachromatic leukodystrophy	Progressive neurological disorder, profound MR, loss of reflexes; rapidly fatal	Progressive loss of motor function, urinary tract infections, pneumonia	Deficiency of enzyme aryulsulfatase A	1/40,000; usually AR	Kolodny and Fluharty (1995)
Methylmalonic aciduria	Inborn error of organic acid metabolism leading to an abnormal accumulation of methylmalonic acid	Neutropenia, osteoporosis, infections, feeding abnormalities	Deficiency of enzyme methylmalonyl CoA mutase, or defect in cobalamin metabolism	Unknown; AR	Fenton and Rosenberg (1995)
Neurofibromatosis (type I, Von Recklinghausen disease)	Multiple "cafe-au-lait" spots on body; nerve tumors in body and on skin	Optic gliomas, glaucoma, macrocephaly, hypertension; learning disabilities/ADHD	Defect in chromosome 17q11	1/3,000; AD	Listernick and Charrow (1990)
Noonan syndrome	Short stature; congenital heart defects; webbed neck; widely spaced, downwardly slanting eyes; low-set ears; chest deformity	Coagulation defects, cryptorchidism, mild MR, motor delays	Multiple causes	1/1,000–1/2,500; AD	Noonan (1994)

continues

Table 2–1 continued

Syndrome	Clinical Features	Associated Deficits	Cause	Incidence; Inheritance	References
Osteogenesis imperfecta	Increased susceptibility to fractures that result in bony deformities; blue-colored sclera; translucent skin; normal intelligence; possible hearing impairment	Multiple bone fractures, tendon abnormalities, increased capillary fragility, neurological dysfunction, short stature	Underlying abnormality in the formation of collagen	1/30,000; usually AD, some AR families	Binder et al. (1993)
Phenylketonuria (PKU)	Inborn error of amino acid metabolism presenting with MR. Untreated patients often have blond hair and blue eyes; hyperactivity	Microcephaly, hand posturing, seizures	Deficiency of enzyme phenylalanine hydroxylase, located on chromosome 12	1/15,000; AR	Scriver et al. (1995)
Prader–Willi syndrome	Severe obesity, MR, small hands and feet, small genitalia; infants have poor tone, but it improves; short stature; behavior problems	Feeding problems in infancy; scoliosis, diabetes mellitus in second decade	Deletion of chromosome 15 (paternal) or uniparental disomy	1/10,000	Butler (1990)
Propionic acidemia	Inborn error of organic acid metabolism; recurrent episodes of vomiting, lethargy and coma	Developmental delays are common in those who survive	Deficiency of enzyme propionyl CoA carboxylase	Unknown, but rare; AR	Nyhan (1987)
Rett syndrome	MR, stereotypic hand wringing, autistic features, movement disorder	Loss of language skills and fine motor skills of hands, self-injurious behavior, seizures, constipation	Unknown	1/10,000; XLD; suspected lethal in males	Braddock et al. (1993)

Syndrome	Clinical Features	Associated Deficits	Cause	Incidence; Inheritance	References
(Congenital) rubella syndrome	Intrauterine growth retardation, MR, microcephaly, cataracts, sensorineural hearing loss, chorioretinitis, congenital heart disease	Glaucoma, hematological problems	Maternal infection with rubella prior to 17th week of gestation	1/10,000 in areas where vaccine is widely administered; higher in unvaccinated areas	Miller et al. (1982)
Russel–Silver syndrome	Short stature; skeletal asymmetry; small, incurved 5th finger; triangular facies	Cafe-au-lait spots, occasional renal anomalies, hypospadius, cognitive deficits in 50%	Unknown	Unknown; usually SP	Lai (1994)
Spina bifida (myelomeningocele)	Incomplete closure of the embryonic neural tube that results in a defect of the spine and paralysis below the level of the lesion; hydrocephalus	Depending on the level of the lesion: neurogenic bladder, fecal incontinence, cranial nerve abnormalities, orthopedic abnormalities	Decreased incidence with preconceptual folate intake	1/500–1/2,000; MF	Byrd et al. (1991)
Spinal-muscular atrophy (Werdnig–Hoffman syndrome)	Progressive respiratory failure and severe muscle weakness in infancy; normal intelligence; survival unusual past 2 years of age	Contractures, cardiomyopathy, respiratory infections, scoliosis	Deletion in chromosome 5q	4/100,000; AR	Wessel (1989)
Sturge–Weber syndrome	Tumor composed of blood vessels over half of face and in brain, intracranial calcifications, seizures	Progressive problems, hemiplegia, glaucoma	Unknown	Unknown; SP	Sujansky and Conradi (1995)

continues

Table 2–1 continued

Syndrome	Clinical Features	Associated Deficits	Cause	Incidence; Inheritance	References
Tay–Sachs disease	Progressive nervous system disorder, deafness, blindness, seizures; rapidly fatal, usually by 4 years	Feeding abnormalities, aspiration	Deficiency of enzyme hexosaminidase; located on chromosome 15	1/3,800 in Ashkenazic Jews; AR	Neufeld (1989)
Torsion dystonia (dystonia musculorum deformans)	Progressive involuntary movement disorder, normal intelligence	Contractures in affected limbs	Defect in chromosome 9q	1/20,000 in Ashkenazic population; AD or rare XLR	Wachtel et al. (1982)
Treacher Collins syndrome (mandibulofacial dystosis)	Characteristic facial appearance, malformation of external ear, flattened area near cheekbones	Choanal atresia, respiratory and feeding problems in infancy, obstructive apnea	Defect in chromosome 5q3	Unknown; AD; variable expressivity	Dixon et al. (1991)
Trisomy 13	Microphthalmia, cleft lip and palate, and polydactyly, dysmorphic appearance	Multiorgan system involvement; profound MR, visual impairment, cerebral palsy	Nondisjunction resulting in extra chromosome 13, rarely translocation	1/8,000 births; SP	Rodriguez et al. (1990)
Trisomy 18	Small for gestational age, low-set ears, clenched hands with overriding fingers, congenital heart defects	Feeding problems, aspiration, diaphragmatic hernia; most do not survive first year of life	Nondisjunction resulting in trisomy for chromosome 18	1/6,000; SP	Van Dyke and Allen (1990)
Tuberous sclerosis	Hypopigmented areas, acnelike facial lesions, infantile spasms, calcium deposits in brain	Malignancies, hydrocephalus, tumors of the heart	Defect on chromosome 9 or 16	1/10,000–1/50,000; AD; variable expressivity	Kwiatkowski and Short (1994)

Syndrome	Clinical Features	Associated Deficits	Cause	Incidence; Inheritance	References
Turner syndrome (XO syndrome)	Short stature; female; broad chest with widely spaced nipples; congenital heart disease; ovarian dysgenesis; usually normal intelligence	Thyroid abnormalities, diabetes mellitus, kidney abnormalities, learning disabilities	Chromosomal nondisjunction resulting in a single X chromosome	1/5,000	Saenger (1993)
VATER association (VACTERL association)	Vertebral defects, Anal atresia, Tracheoesophageal fistula, Esophageal abnormalities, radial abnormalities, Renal anomalies	Respiratory, cardiac and renal abnormalities can be severe	Unknown	Not known; usually SP, rare families with AR	Lubinsky (1986)
Velocardiofacial syndrome	Small stature, small mouth, cleft palate, slender-flexible fingers, cardiac defect	Mild intellectual impairment, conductive hearing loss, microcephaly	Microdeletion in chromosome 22q11	Unknown; AD	Goldberg et al. (1993)
Waardenburg syndrome	White forelock, unusual facial appearance, irises of different colors, confluent eyelashes	Congenital deafness of variable severity	Inherited	1/20,000–1/40,000; AD	Liv et al. (1995)
Williams syndrome (hypercalcemia-elfin facies syndrome)	Short stature, full lips and cheeks, periorbital fullness, hoarse voice, MR	Cardiac abnormality, renal abnormalities, contractures	Deletion on chromosome 7q11 (elastin locus)	1/10,000	Tome et al. (1990)
XYY syndrome	Tall stature, poor fine motor coordination, aggressive behavior	Slow nerve conduction velocities, learning disabilities	Chromosomal nondisjunction	1/1,000; SP	Stewart et al. (1982)

continues

Table 2–1 continued

Syndrome	Clinical Features	Associated Deficits	Cause	Incidence; Inheritance	References
Zellweger syndrome	Muscle hypotonia, absent deep tendon reflexes, absent psychomotor development, severe feeding problems, seizures, dysmorphic facial appearance, congenital heart lesions, enlarged liver	Multiorgan system involvement; profound MR	Absence of peroxisomes	1/25,000–1/50,000; AR	Zellweger (1987)

Note: AD = autosomal dominant, AR = autosomal recessive, MF = multifactorial, SP = sporadic, XL = sex linked, XLD = sex linked—dominant, XLR = sex linked—recessive.

REFERENCES

Binder, H., et al. 1993. Comprehensive rehabilitation of the child with osteogenesis imperfecta. *American Journal of Medical Genetics* 45:265–269.

Boustany, R.M., et al. 1988. Clinical classification of neuronal ceroid-lipofuscinosis subtypes. *American Journal of Medical Genetics* 5:47–58.

Braddock, S.R., et al. 1993. Rett syndrome: An update and review for the primary pediatrician. *Clinical Pediatrics* 32:613–626.

Butler, M.G. 1990. Prader-Willi syndrome: Current understanding of cause and diagnosis. *American Journal of Medical Genetics* 35:319–332.

Byrd, S.E., et al. 1991. Developmental disorders of the pediatric spine. *Radiologic Clinics of North America* 29:711–752.

Cacciari, E., and S. Salardi. 1989. Clinical and laboratory features of homocystinuria. *Haemostasis* 19:10–13.

Clarke, D.J., and S. Bundey. 1990. Very early onset Huntington's disease: Genetic mechanism and risk to siblings. *Clinical Genetics* 38:180–186.

Cohen, M.M., et al. 1993. An updated pediatric perspective on Apert syndrome. *American Journal of Diseases of Children* 147:989–993.

Conlon, C.J. 1992. New threats to development: Alcohol, cocaine, and AIDS. In *Children with disabilities: A medical primer*, 3rd ed., ed. M.L. Batshaw and Y.M. Perret, 111–136. Baltimore: Paul H. Brookes.

Cooley, W.C., and J.M. Graham, Jr. 1991. Common syndromes and management issues for primary care physicians: Down syndrome—an update and review for the primary pediatrician. *Clinical Pediatrics* 30:233–253.

Darras, B.T., et al. 1988. Direct method for prenatal diagnosis and carrier detection in Duchenne/Becker muscular dystrophy using the entire dystrophin cDNA. *American Journal of Medical Genetics* 29:713–726.

DiMauro, S., et al. 1990. Cytochrome c oxidase deficiency. *Pediatric Research* 28:536–541.

Dixon, M.J., et al. 1991. The gene for Treacher Collins syndrome maps to the long arm of chromosome 5. *American Journal of Human Genetics* 49:17–22.

Fenton, W.A., and L.E. Rosenberg. 1995. Disorders of propionate and methylmalonate metabolism. In *The metabolic and molecular bases of inherited disease*, 7th ed., ed. C.R. Scriver et al., 1423–1449. New York: McGraw-Hill Publishing Co.

Fisch, G.S. 1993. What is associated with the fragile X syndrome? *American Journal of Medical Genetics* 48:112–121.

Gibbs, D.A., et al. 1984. First trimester diagnosis of Lesch-Nyhan syndrome. *Lancet* 2:1180–1183.

Goldberg, R., et al. 1993. Velo-Cardio-Facial syndrome: A review of 120 patients. *American Journal of Medical Genetics* 45:313–319.

Hecht, J.T., and I.J. Butler. 1990. Neurologic morbidity associated with achodroplasia. *Journal of Child Neurology* 5:84–96.

Ignacio, R.J., et al. 1993. Severe axial anomalies in the oculo-auriculo-vertebral complex (Goldenhar). *American Journal of Medical Genetics* 47:69–74.

Kaplan, P., et al. 1991. Intellectual outcome in children with maple syrup urine disease. *Journal of Pediatrics* 119:46–50.

Kenworthy, L., et al. 1993. Cognitive and behavioral profile of the oculocerebrorenal syndrome of Lowe. *American Journal of Medical Genetics* 46:297–303.

Kolodny, E.H., and A.L. Fluharty. 1995. Metachromatic leukodystrophy and multiple sulfatase deficiency: Sulfatide lipidosis. In *The metabolic and bases of molecular inherited disease*, 7th ed., ed. C.R. Scriver et al., 2,693–2,739. New York: McGraw-Hill Publishing Co.

Kousseff, B.G., et al. 1994. Brachmann de Lange syndrome: 1994 update. *Archives of Pediatric and Adolescent Medicine* 148:749–755.

Kwiatkowski, D.J., and M.P. Short. 1994. Tuberous sclerosis. *Archives of Dermatology* 130:348–354.

Lai, K.Y.C. 1994. Cognitive abilities associated with the Silver-Russell syndrome. *Archives of Diseases of Children* 71:490–496.

Lee, B., et al. 1991. Cloning and analysis of the candidate fibrillin gene for Marfan syndrome [Abstract]. *American Journal of Human Genetics* 49:20.

Lin, A.E., et al. 1990. Central nervous system malformations in the CHARGE association. *American Journal of Medicine Genetics* 37:304–310.

Listernick, R., and J. Charrow. 1990. Neurofibromatosis type I in childhood. *Journal of Pediatrics* 116:845–853.

Liv, X.Z., Newton, V.E., and A.P. Read. 1995. Waardenberg syndrome type II: Phenotypic findings. *American Journal of Medical Genetics* 55:95–100.

Lubinsky, M. 1986. VATER and other associations: Historical perspectives and modern interpretations. *American Journal of Medical Genetics* 45:313–319.

Miller, E., et al. 1982. Consequences of confirmed maternal rubella at successive stages of pregnancy. *Lancet* 2:781–784.

Neidich, J.A., et al. 1990. Heterogeneity of clinical severity and molecular lesions of Aicardi syndrome. *Journal of Pediatrics* 116:911–917.

Neufeld, E.F. 1989. Natural history and inherited disorders of a lysosomal enzyme, beta-hexosaminidase. *Journal of Biological Chemistry* 264:10927–10930.

Neufeld, E.F., and J. Muenzer. 1995. The muco-polysaccharidoses. In *The metabolic and molecular bases of inherited disease*, 7th ed., ed. C.R. Scriver et al., 2465–2569. New York: McGraw-Hill Publishing Co.

New England Congenital Hypothyroidism Collaborative. 1990. Elementary school performance of children with congenital hyperthyroidism. *Journal of Pediatrics* 116:27–32.

Noonan, J.A. 1994. Noonan syndrome: An update and review for the primary pediatrician. *Clinical Pediatrics* 33:548–555.

Nyhan, W.L. 1987. Propionic acidemia. In *Diagnostic recognition of genetic disease*, ed. W.L. Nyhan, 36–41. Philadelphia: Lea & Febiger.

Rodriguez, J.I., et al. 1990. Trisomy 13 syndrome and neural tube defects. *American Journal of Medical Genetics* 36:513–516.

Saenger, P. 1993. Clinical review 48: The current status of diagnosis and therapeutic intervention in Turner syndrome. *Journal of Clinical Endocrinology and Metabolism* 77:297–301.

Saitoh, S., et al. 1994. Molecular and clinical study of 61 Angelman syndrome patients. *American Journal of Medical Genetics* 52:158–163.

Schweitzer, S., et al. 1993. Long-term outcome in 141 patients with galactosemia. *European Journal of Pediatrics* 152:36–43.

Scriver, C.R., et al. 1995. The hyperphenylalaninemias. In *The metabolic and molecular bases of inherited disease*, 7th ed., ed. C.R. Scriver et al., 1027–1046. New York: McGraw-Hill Publishing Co.

Stewart, D.A., et al. 1982. Summary of clinical findings of children with 47,XXY, 47,XYY, and 47,XXX karotypes. *Birth Defects* 18:1–5.

Sujansky, E., and S. Conradi. 1995. Sturge-Weber syndrome: Age of onset of seizures and glaucoma and the prognosis for affected children. *Journal of Child Neurology* 10:49–58.

Tome, S.A., et al. 1990. Temperament in Williams syndrome. *American Journal of Medical Genetics* 36:345–352.

Van Dyke, D.C., and M. Allen. 1990. Clinical management considerations in long-term survivors with trisomy 18. *Pediatrics* 85:753–759.

Wachtel, R.C., et al. 1982. Torsion dystonia. *Johns Hopkins Medical Journal* 151:355–361.

Wessel, H.B. 1989. Spinal muscular atrophy. *Pediatric Annals* 18:421–427.

Wilkins, L.E., et al. 1983. Clinical heterogeneity in 80 home-reared children with cri-du-chat syndrome. *Journal of Pediatrics* 102:528–533.

Zellweger, H. 1987. The Zellweger syndrome and related peroxisomal disorders. *Developmental Medicine and Child Neurology* 29:821–829.

Part II

Interdisciplinary Assessment of Developmental Disabilities

Chapter 3

Guidelines for Referral

Linda Hock Long

Purpose: to describe the purpose of developmental assessment, the benefits of a comprehensive interdisciplinary developmental assessment, criteria for referral, and national resources for obtaining early intervention services.

RATIONALE FOR DEVELOPMENTAL ASSESSMENT

Comprehensive developmental assessments serve three primary functions:

1. *Descriptive*—An initial comprehensive assessment provides baseline information regarding a child's level of functioning and areas of strength and weakness. Subsequent assessments document the trend of a child's development.
2. *Diagnostic*—An assessment can determine whether a child has a specific developmental disability or is at risk for having a developmental disability.
3. *Prescriptive*—If it is determined that a child is at risk for or has a developmental disability, the interdisciplinary assessment team can provide recommendations regarding the type of intervention that is indicated and the community resources needed to implement the plan.

While developmental screening is mandated by the American Academy of Pediatrics and federal legislation, there is no one specific method deemed to be the most effective. A comprehensive developmental assessment uses multiple data collection methods, including observation, interview, and standardized measures. Combinations of methods seem most effective for early identification, including identification of parental concerns and risk factors (e.g., family or medical history) and direct physical, neurologic, and developmental examination using a standardized screening tool. Once the presence of concerns has been identified by the clinician, referral for further developmental assessment should be made.

For developmental assessment of children, an *interdisciplinary team model* is the most effective. In addition to the family, the interdisciplinary assessment team is made up of professionals from at least two different disciplines (e.g., audiologists, developmental pediatricians, nutritionists, educators, occupational therapists, physical therapists, child psychiatrists, pediatric psychologists, speech/language pathologists, social workers). The members perform individual evaluations, meet to discuss evaluation results, formulate diagnoses and recommendations, and meet with the family to share findings. This model results in a more comprehensive understanding of a child's functioning than an evaluation by a single discipline. The interdisciplinary model is especially suited for developmental assessment due to the multiplicity of factors that influence the course of a child's development, including genetic, prenatal, perinatal, medical, cultural, ethnic, religious, and other psychosocial influences.

No single assessment instrument or method is completely free of bias. All contain at least some degree of error due to factors such as variations in administration of testing instruments or distracting environmental factors (see Chapter 7, subchapter "Guidelines for Use of Tests in Pediatrics"). But when multiple assessment methods are utilized, the effect of bias on assessment findings is likely to be reduced. The interdisciplinary model can provide findings that have greater validity due to its reliance on multiple, complementary data sources. Since the results of a developmental assessment may indicate that a child has a significant developmental disability with potential long-term implications for the child and family, it is imperative that findings be based upon assessment methods that are as valid and as comprehensive as possible.

In keeping with standards set forth by the Maternal and Child Health Bureau of the U.S. Department of Health and Human Services, it is important to remember that the family is an integral part of the interdisciplinary team. Family members provide valuable diagnostic information and are ultimately responsible for carrying out recommendations that are generated by the assessment.

SPECIAL CONSIDERATIONS

Referral Criteria

Referral for an interdisciplinary developmental assessment is indicated when

1. Developmental screening identifies possible delays or unusual features in a child's development.
2. A child has not attained developmental milestones within the expected range for chronologic age.
3. A child exhibits atypical, unusual, or nonsequential patterns of development or behavior.
4. A child demonstrates lack of progress or no longer displays previously achieved skills.
5. A child has a medical or physical condition (e.g., spina bifida, cerebral palsy, HIV/AIDS, inborn errors of metabolism, sensory impairment) that is known to be associated with developmental delay or disability.
6. A child exhibits behaviors such as inattentiveness, impulsivity, and level of activity that are not commensurate with chronologic age and that interfere with his or her ability to function appropriately.

Important Information To Provide the Interdisciplinary Assessment Team

The interdisciplinary assessment team will require the following information:

1. demographic data, including child's date of birth, place of residence, and names of parents/legal guardian; if a child is in foster placement, the names of the responsible child welfare agency and assigned social worker are essential
2. referent's observations, concerns, and questions
3. parents' or legal guardian's observations, concerns, and questions
4. brief prenatal, birth, and medical history
5. results of evaluations previously completed, including medical, laboratory, or other diagnostic studies (e.g., neurological evaluation, chromosomal studies,

MRI, CAT scan, metabolic and lead screening) or developmental (e.g., psychological testing)

6. types of therapeutic intervention that the child is currently receiving (e.g., early intervention; occupational, physical, speech/language therapy; psychotherapy)

7. description of preschool/educational services, including type of placement; academic, behavioral, and social functioning; special assistance provided, such as therapy services or resource room help

Resources for Comprehensive Developmental Assessments

Comprehensive, interdisciplinary evaluation services must be provided to assess a child's functioning, to identify a family's strengths and needs, and to determine whether eligibility requirements for services are met. Assessments are offered in a variety of settings:

- *Medical Settings:* Comprehensive assessment programs are often available through pediatric and general tertiary care institutions as well as community hospitals. Hospital-based programs vary in terms of the types of services offered. The interdisciplinary team can include general pediatricians, developmental pediatricians, neurologists, child psychiatrists, nutritionists, psychologists, physical therapists, occupational therapists, speech/language pathologists, social workers, audiologists, nurses, and/or special educators. In addition, hospital-based programs provide laboratory and other diagnostic testing as needed to aid in diagnosis.

- *Early Intervention Settings:* Statewide early intervention services are legislated by Public Law 99-457, Part H, Handicapped Infants and Toddlers Early Intervention Program. If a state chooses to accept federal funds for early intervention, certain requirements must be met. Public Law 99-457, Part H, specifies that it must provide a coordinated, comprehensive, multidisciplinary, interagency early intervention system. Among requirements of early intervention legislation are the following:

   1. Each state must develop a definition of *developmental delay* as well as the eligibility requirements that must be met for a child to receive services.

   2. A state agency known as the *lead agency* must take on the responsibility for implementing and monitoring the system. The state can use its discretion in appointing a lead agency. Lead agencies vary from state to state and are listed in Part IV, "Resource Directory."

- *Public Education Systems:* Once a child reaches three years of age, the local school district is responsible for providing resources for developmental and educational intervention.

Criteria for Selection of Referral Center/ Personnel

Several factors should be taken into consideration when selecting an assessment center and the specific personnel who will participate in the assessment. These may include

- age of the child
- specific diagnostic concerns
- cost

Chapter 4

Developmental Milestones

Purpose: to provide an overview of the progression of developmental skills in all the streams of development, with emphasis on the milestones of postural reflexes, locomotion, visual motor skills, oral motor development, prehension, self-care, language and speech, and cognition. The tables in this chapter should not be used to substitute for administration of standardized assessment tools to determine levels of function, but should provide the reader with a sense of the age-range of different functional skills in a given child.

TOOLS FOR DEVELOPMENTAL SCREENING

Susan E. Levy

A variety of standardized tools may be used to screen development (Glascoe 1991; Levy and Hyman, 1993). Selected examples are presented in Table 4-1.

Table 4-1 Developmental Screening Instruments

Type of Screening	Name of Tool	Description	References
General Screening	Batelle Developmental Inventory Screening Test	Screens multiple areas by combination of observation and history. Ages 0–8 yr.	Newborg et al. (1984)
	Denver II	Global screening (personal/social, fine motor/adaptive, gross motor). Scored as pass/fail questionnaire. Ages 0–6 yr.	Frankenberg et al. (1990)
	Developmental Indicators for Assessment of Learning—Revised (DIAL—R)	Screens fine/gross motor, expressive/receptive language, and cognitive/adaptive skills by direct observation. Ages 2–6 yr.	Mardell-Czudnowski and Goldenberg (1983)
	Infant Monitoring System	Screening by parent report (communication, gross/fine motor, adaptive, personal social). Ages 0–36 mo.	Bricker and Squires (1989)
	Revised Developmental Screening Inventory	Screens gross/fine motor, adaptive, problem-solving, and language skills. Ages 0–3 yr.	Knobloch et al. (1980)
Language Screening	Clinical Linguistic Auditory Milestones Scale (CLAMS)	Assesses receptive and expressive language by observation and parent interview. Ages 1–36 mo.	Capute et al. (1986)
	Early Language Milestone Scale	Assesses receptive and expressive language (pass/fail) by interview, observation, and test administration. Ages 0–36 mo.	Coplan (1984)
	Peabody Picture Vocabulary Test—Revised (PPVT—R)	Assesses single-word receptive vocabulary. Ages 26 mo. to adult.	Dunn et al. (1981)
	Receptive-Expressive Emergent Language (REEL)	Assesses receptive and expressive language age by parent interview. Ages 0–3 yr.	Bzoch and League (1971)

Source: From "Pediatric Assessment of the Child with Developmental Delay" by S.E. Levy and S.L. Hyman, *Pediatric Clinics of America*, 40, p 272. Copyright © 1993 by W.B. Saunders. Adapted by permission.

Table 4-2 continued

Age of Occurrence

Preterm	Newborn	1 Mo.	2 Mo.	3 Mo.	4 Mo.	5 Mo.	6 Mo.	7 Mo.	8 Mo.	9 Mo.	10 Mo.	Reflex
37 wk.	XXX	XXX	XXX										*Automatic walking/reflex stepping:* The newborn infant is held vertically, with the feet on a support, and the examiner moves the baby slowly forward. The infant begins to "walk," a movement characterized by high stepping with a regular rhythm.
28 wk.	XXX	XXX	XXX	XXX	XXX								*Palmar grasp:* The examiner places his or her index finger in the infant's palm, offering either light pressure or a distally moving stimulus. The infant responds by grasp of the finger.
28 wk.	XXX	XXX	XXX	XXX	XXX	XXX	XXX	XXX	XXX	XXX			*Palmar grasp:* The examiner places his or her index finger on the sole of the foot just distal to the metatarsal heads. The infant responds by flexing the toes, as if to grasp.
28 wk.	XXX	XXX	XXX	XXX	XXX								*Moro reflex:* While the infant is in a supine position either on a table or in the examiner's arms, support is briefly removed from the infant's head, allowing it to drop backwards through a small excursion. Alternately, the supported infant may be made to feel that the entire body is falling backward while the head remains supported. The normal response is abduction and extension of both upper extremities, with splaying of the fingers. This may be followed by a second "embrace" phase, in which the arms flex and adduct. Occasionally, the response may also occur in the legs.
20 wk.	XXX	XXX	XXX	XXX	XXX								*Asymmetrical tonic neck reflex (ATNR):* Neck rotation causes extension of the arm on the jaw side and flexion of the arm on the occiput side, assuming a "fencing" posture. Occasionally a similar response is seen in the legs, with trunk lateral curvature, concavity on the occipital side. The response may occur spontaneously or be elicited by the examiner's passively rotating the neck.

Reflex	Age of Occurrence											
	Preterm	Newborn	1 Mo.	2 Mo.	3 Mo.	4 Mo.	5 Mo.	6 Mo.	7 Mo.	8 Mo.	9 Mo.	10 Mo.
Symmetrical tonic neck reflex (STNR): Extension of the neck causes the infant to show increased extensor tone in the arms and increased flexor tone in the legs, as if to assume a hands-and-knees posture. Flexion of the neck has the opposite effect—the arms flex and the legs extend.							XXX	XXX	XXX	XXX		
Tonic labyrinthine reflex (TLR; never normal): Extensor tone is maximal in the supine position, including arching of the trunk, and extension, adduction, and plantarflexion of the lower extremities. Flexor tone is maximal in the prone position.												
Positive supporting reaction (never normal): From a position of vertical suspension, the soles of the feet are bounced onto the floor. The child's legs stiffen in extension, adduction, and plantar flexion to assume a standing posture in scissored position. The normal child begins to take weight when supported in standing at about 5–6 mo., but the limbs are slightly flexed and abducted.												
Associated reactions (never normal): Voluntary contraction of one limb, such as grasp, caused by overflow of tone to other areas of the body.												

AUTOMATIC RIGHTING AND EQUILIBRIUM REACTION

Shirley A. Scull

Table 4–3 shows milestones in the development of automatic righting and equilibrium reactions. Most of these reactions are not present at birth but emerge with maturation of the central nervous system on a fairly fixed schedule during the first year of life. The righting reactions orient the body in space so that the head is vertical and the eyes are horizontal, and they emerge with developing head control in the infant. The equilibrium reactions serve to protect the body from loss of balance when the center of gravity shifts outside the base of support. Their emergence in a developmental sequence allows for higher level gross motor skills to emerge, resulting ultimately in ambulation.

Table 4–3 Automatic Righting and Equilibrium Reactions

| Age of Occurrence | | | | | | | | | | | | Reaction |
1 Mo.	2 Mo.	3 Mo.	4 Mo.	5 Mo.	6 Mo.	8 Mo.	10 Mo.	12 Mo.	18 Mo.	24 Mo.	Life	
	Prone		Supine		Lateral							*Labyrinthine righting/optical righting:* The baby is held in space in prone suspension. The mature response is lifting of the head to 90° so the face is vertical and the eyes are horizontal. Supine righting may be tested on a pull-to-sit maneuver. Lateral righting is tested by holding the baby in vertical suspension and tipping him or her slightly to the side. The input from the labyrinths may be isolated from vision by blindfolding the infant.
			XXX	XXX	XXX	XXX	XXX	XXX				
							XXX	XXX	XXX	XXX		*Landau reflex:* When the child is held in ventral suspension, the head rights itself, followed by trunk extension and lower extremity extension until a full airplane posture is assumed. The components emerge from proximal to distal over this time frame.

Age of Occurrence

Reaction	1 Mo.	2 Mo.	3 Mo.	4 Mo.	5 Mo.	6 Mo.	8 Mo.	10 Mo.	12 Mo.	18 Mo.	24 Mo.	Life
Body righting acting on the body: Rotation of the thorax on the pelvis causes the body to roll so that it is in normal alignment. It is generally tested by passively rotating the child from the supine to the prone position. The more primitive reflex of neck righting, simulated by rotating the neck, also re-aligns the body but does not involve any trunk rotation.					XXX	XXX	XXX	XXX	XXX	XXX	XXX	
Protective extension/parachute reaction: The prone suspended infant is moved quickly, head first, toward a supporting surface. The arms extend immediately, with abducted and extended fingers and extended wrists, to prepare to take the body weight. The response may also be elicited in the sitting position by displacing the child sideways and backwards and seeing if he or she extends the arm to support the body. The forward response emerges at 6 mo., the sideways response at 8 mo., and the backward response at 10 mo.						XXX	XXX	XXX	XXX	XXX	XXX	XXX
Equilibrium reactions: Movement of the center of mass away from the base of support causes the trunk to curve and the limbs to extend and abduct to restore balance. The response may be tested on a tilt board by perturbing the patient from a static posture or by asking the patient to reach. The exact strategy used will vary among individuals and with the parameters used to elicit the response.						Prone	Supine	Sitting	Quadruped	Standing		

GROSS MOTOR SEQUENCES

Shirley A. Scull

Table 4-4 shows milestones in gross motor development.

Table 4-4 Gross Motor Milestones, Birth to Two Years

Position	Birth	2 Mo.	4 Mo.	6 Mo.	8 Mo.	10 Mo.	12 Mo.	15 Mo.	18 Mo.	2 Yr.
Supine	Physiological flexion Head to side ATNR	Arms more extended LE kicking ATNR	Symmetrical posture Head in midline Hands to knees	Symmetrical posture Transfers objects Plays with feet	Refuses to lie in supine					
Pull to sit	Head lag	Head lag	No lag and pulls with UEs	Tucks chin and pulls	Head leads					
Prone	Clears nose from bed LE flexion—pelvis high	Lifts head to 45° Elbows behind shoulders Legs "frogged" Pelvis lower to surface	Holds head at 90° Props prone, elbows under shoulders LEs adducted	Reaches on elbows Prone on extended arms Side prop Pivots in prone Commando crawls (7 mo.)	Assumes quadruped Rocks Creeps Kneels at support (9 mo.)	Creeps quickly	Moves in bear position	Most creeping discarded except stairs	Climbs onto adult chair, turns and sits	
Rolling			Rolls supine to side Rolls prone to supine (5 mo.)	Rolls supine to prone						

Position	Birth	2 Mo.	4 Mo.	6 Mo.	8 Mo.	10 Mo.	12 Mo.	15 Mo.	18 Mo.	2 Yr.
Sit	Sup-ported—head sags forward C-curve of back	Sup-ported—head bobs erect Poor trunk control	Sup-ported—head steady Upper thorax extended Lower spine rounded	Sits—hands propped forward Hips flexed >90° and abducted	Sits—hands free for play Gets to sitting from prone Lateral prop	Rotates in sitting Side-sits Legs disasso-ciated Quick transi-tions		Plays in squatting	Seats self in small chair	
Stand	Primary standing Automatic walking	Abasia Astasia	Takes weight—support at axillae	Stands and bounces—support at hands	Stands holding on—wide base Pulls to stand (9 mo.)	Cruises at furniture Lowers self to sitting Walks—2 hands held	Stands alone Takes first steps Steppage gait High guard Walks—1 hand held	Gets to stand in middle of floor Walks well Middle guard	Decreased base of support for walking Heel strike Low guard Runs stiffly Stairs—1 rail	Runs well Kicks ball forward Arm swing Stairs—mark time

VISUAL-MOTOR AND WRITING SEQUENCES

Lisa A. Kurtz

Table 4–5 shows milestones in the development of visual-motor and writing sequences.

Table 4–5 Visual-Motor and Writing Sequences, Age One to Nine Years

Approximate Age	Skill
12 mo.	Marks paper with crayon
15 mo.	Scribbles spontaneously
18 mo.	Imitates* stroke, nondirectional
2 yr.	Imitates vertical stroke
2 ½ yr.	Imitates horizontal stroke
	Imitates circle
	"Names" own drawing or scribble
	Holds pencil with thumb and fingers
3 yr.	Copies** horizontal stroke
	Copies vertical stroke
	Imitates cross
4 yr.	Copies cross
4 ½ yr.	Copies square
5 yr.	Copies oblique cross
	Copies triangle
	Draws recognizable face with eyes, nose, mouth
5 ½ yr.	Copies manuscript letters, numbers
	Prints own first name without model
	Copies last name
6 yr.	Prints all letters and numbers 0–9 without model
	Prints simple words without model
7–8 yr.	Prints or writes 3–4 word sentences
	Prints or writes short notes or messages
	Reversals are uncommon
9 yr.	Writes in cursive most of the time

Source: Adapted from Beery (1989), Furuno et al. (1984), Knobloch et al. (1980), Santa Cruz County Office of Education (1987), Sparrow et al. (1984).

Imitates = demonstration given.

**Copies* = from visual model, no demonstration given.

REFERENCES

Beery, K. 1989. *Developmental Test of Visual Motor Integration, 3rd revision*. Cleveland, Ohio: Modern Curriculum Press.

Furuno, S., et al. 1984. *Hawaii Early Learning Profile (HELP)*. Palo Alto, Calif.: VORT Corporation.

Knobloch, H., et al. 1980. *Manual of developmental diagnosis*. Rev. ed. New York: Harper & Row.

Santa Cruz County Office of Education. 1987. *HELP for Special Preschoolers: Assessment checklist: Ages 3–6*. Palo Alto, Calif.: VORT Corporation.

Sparrow, S.S., et al. 1984. *Vineland Adaptive Behavior Scales: Survey form manual, Interview Edition*. Circle Pines, Minn.: American Guidance Service.

SEQUENCES OF PREHENSION

Lisa A. Kurtz

Table 4–6 shows milestones in the development of sequences of prehension.

Table 4–6 Developmental Sequences of Prehension

Chronologic Age	Characteristic Prehension Patterns
1 mo.	Hands primarily fisted at rest
2 mo.	Hands open or loosely closed at rest
< 4 mo.	Involuntary grasp (rattle): hand closes around object upon contact with palmar aspect of hand; wrist tends to be flexed; thumb is not involved in grasp
3–4 mo.	Arms activate when toy is brought within sight; may contact toy with one or both hands; retains and glances at toy placed in hand Bilateral reach toward toys when lying in supine position
6 mo.	Palmar grasp (cube): actively grasps toy with fingers against palm; initially, object is closer to little finger than thumb, then moves toward thumb as grasp matures (6 mo.); thumb is adducted and does not assist in grasp; wrist continues to be flexed
6 mo.	Transfers objects adeptly from one hand to the other Rakes and contacts tiny object using extended fingers and whole-arm movement, does not secure object
6–7 mo.	Unilateral reach for objects when sitting
7 mo.	Wrist is straight during grasp of toy *Inferior scissors grasp* (pellet): successfully rakes tiny object into palm using flexion motion of all fingers; thumb is adducted
8 mo.	*Radial digital grasp* (cube): object is held with thumb opposing the fingers, space is visible between the thumb and palm Uses *index finger approach* to explore toys *Scissors grasp* (pellet): tiny object is secured between thumb and curled side of index finger; other fingers are relatively motionless during grasp
9 mo.	Wrist extends during grasp of toy *Inferior pincer grasp* (pellet): tiny object secured between pads of thumb and index finger; forearm rests on table for support Holds 2 blocks, one in each hand, and brings together at midline
10 mo.	*Three-jawed chuck grasp* (cube): object grasped precisely between thumb and 2 fingers; ring and little fingers not involved in grasp Can release toy purposefully, but with exaggerated extension of the fingers
12 mo.	*Superior pincer grasp* (pellet): tiny object is secured between tips of thumb and index finger; hand and arm are elevated above tabletop
12-18 mo.	*Fisted grasp* (crayon): holds crayon with whole hand, wrist slightly flexed, whole arm moves when scribbling
2–3 yr.	*Digital pronate grasp* (crayon): crayon is held with all fingers pointing downwards toward tip of crayon, forearm slightly pronated
3½–4 yr.	*Static tripod grasp* (pencil): pencil held with fingers in grasp approximating adult grasp; wrist is straight; grasped around proximal section of shaft (away from tip)

continues

Table 4–6 continued

Chronologic Age	Characteristic Prehension Patterns
4½–6 yr.	*Dynamic tripod grasp* (pencil): pencil held with precise opposition of fingers; MCP joints (proximal knuckles) are stable, allowing fine, localized movements of PIP joints (distal knuckles); grasped near point of pencil

Source: Adapted from Duff (1994), Erhardt (1994), Knobloch et al. (1980).

REFERENCES

Duff, S. 1994. Prehension through the lifespan. In *Functional movement development through the life span*, ed. D. Cech and T. Martin, 313–352. Philadelphia: W.B. Saunders.

Erhardt, R.P. 1994. *Developmental hand dysfunction: Theory, assessment and treatment,* 2nd ed. Tucson, Ariz.: Therapy Skill Builders.

Knobloch, H., et al. 1980. *Manual of developmental diagnosis.* Rev. ed. New York: Harper & Row.

ORAL-MOTOR REFLEXES AND SKILLS

Suzanne Vender

Tables 4–7 and 4–8 show milestones in the development of oral-motor reflexes and oral-motor skills, respectively.

Table 4–7 Oral-Motor Reflexes Milestones

Oral-Motor Reflexes	Age and duration
Rooting	0–4 mo.
Gag	0–adulthood
Phasic bite	0–4/6 mo.
Transverse tongue	0–6 mo.
Suckle/swallow	0–6 mo.

Table 4–8 Oral-Motor Skills Milestones from Birth to Two

Age	Oral-Motor Skills
0–1 mo.	Uses a suck or suckling pattern Sequences 2 or more sucks before pausing to breathe
3 mo.	Sequences 20 or more sucks from bottle Sucking or suckling soft solids Rooting and phasic bite beginning to disappear
4–6 mo.	Uses suck or suckling pattern with bottle Can be introduced to liquids via cup Can be introduced to cereals and purees Primitive phasic bite and release on soft cookie with emerging munching Tongue begins to lateralize
6–8 mo.	Uses suckling pattern with cup drinking, with wide jaw excursions and loss of liquid Upper lip assists with food removal Jaw movement is up/down and diagonal Beginning tongue lateralization if food is presented to side of mouth Given liquids, purees, ground table foods
9–12 mo.	True suck with vertical movements Longer sequences of suck/swallow that are more coordinated Controlled bite for soft solids Swallows ground or mashed table food Lips are active in chewing Chewing in vertical or diagonal/rotary pattern Transfers food from midline to sides of mouth
15–18 mo.	Suck, swallow, and breathing well coordinated Diagonal and rotary jaw movements are smooth, can chew with lips closed Upper incisors clean lower lip Meats and raw vegetables added to diet
19–24 mo.	Tongue used in sweeping motion to clean lips Swallows food with texture combinations Able to grade jaw opening Uses rotary chewing motions and can transfer food easily from center to sides

LANGUAGE AND SPEECH

Marleen A. Baron

Table 4–9 shows milestones in the development of language and speech.

Table 4–9 Language and Speech Milestones from Birth to Eight Years

Age	Skills
0–1 mo.	Reflexive smile to stimuli Startle response to loud sounds Quiets to familiar voice Vocal grunt, throaty noises, and frequent crying
2–3 mo.	Awareness of voices, visual and auditory stimuli Social smile and cooing to pleasant tones Searches for sound with eyes Laughs aloud and uses sounds like *p*, *b*, and *m*
4–5 mo.	Turns to his or her name Turns head to sound source Vocalizes to gain attention, express displeasure, and show eagerness Produces raspberries, squeals, and trills Shakes and bats at objects
6–7 mo.	Attention to music or singing Recognizes spoon or bottle as well as names of family members Understands "hi" and "bye bye" Likes mirror play Uses reduplicated babbling, e.g., "baba," "wawa" Imitates familiar sounds and produces some idiosyncratic words
8–9 mo.	Stops activity when name is called Gives an object, throws and drops objects Babbles with inflectional and rhythmic patterns Uses some gesture language Understands "no"
9–10 mo.	Pats mirror image and participates in speech such as "pat-a-cake" and " peek-a-boo" Parrotlike repetition of words and jargoning Responds to simple verbal requests with gesture
11–12 mo.	Enjoys rhymes and songs Responds to simple commands without a gesture Knows one body part Uses primitive play, e.g., using spoon as telephone Produces true words during sound play Beginning to use one word to convey whole ideas
13–15 mo.	Understands objects when named Points to several body parts Produces 4 to 7 words
15–18 mo.	May infer cause and effect Refers to self by name and uses some pronouns Occasionally produces 2-word utterances Understands up to 50 words Uses jargon

Age	Skills
20–24 mo.	Understands simple prepositions Points to pictures and enjoys being read to Produces 25–200 words by 24 mo. Uses one pronoun Full representational play Uses 2- and 3-word combinations Jargon disappears by 24 mo.
24–30 mo.	Listens to simple stories and nursery rhymes Understands concepts of "one," "little," and "on" Follows directions with 3 linguistic elements (e.g., "give me spoon") Identifies objects by function Uses articles, plural *s*, adjectives, and pronouns Uses 9–10 initial consonants and 5–6 final consonants
30–36 mo.	Identifies colors, understands turn taking Follows 2-step commands Understands "what" and "where" questions Rapid vocabulary expansion, about 900 words Asks questions; uses quantitative words; uses the verb *be* Carries on purposeful conversation Echolalia is extinguished by age 3
3–4 yr.	Understands up to 1,500 words by age 4 Understands time concepts Can group objects according to category Can recall 3–4 digits in a sequence Can follow commands with modifiers (e.g., "Walk slowly to the ____") Speech with 90% intelligibility in context Uses requests; answers questions logically Uses language for imaginative play Can relate events and experiences
5–6 yr.	Carries out complex commands Likes silly words and riddles Expressive vocabulary of 1,500–2,000 words Uses conjunctions and auxiliary verbs Can tell stories and articulate with 80% accuracy Egocentric speech is decreasing and social speech emerges Uses 6- to 8-word sentences
6–7 yr.	Understands 4,000 words Grammatic patterns resemble cultural models
7–8 yr.	Comprehension of 6,000–8,000 words Reading and writing at school Shares ideas and opinions using 2,500–3,000 words

Source: Adapted from Baron et al. (1993), Brown (1973), Zimmerman et al. (1991)

REFERENCES

Baron, M.A. 1993. *Development of communication skills.* Philadelphia, Pa.: Children's Seashore House.

Brown, R. 1973. *First language: The early stages.* Cambridge, Mass.: Harvard University Press.

Zimmerman, I.L. et al. 1991. *Preschool language scale-3.* The Psychological Corporation. San Diego, Calif.: Harcourt Brace Jovanovich, Inc.

ADDITIONAL SUGGESTED READINGS

Bzoch, K., and League, R. 1970. *Receptive-Expressive emergent language scale.* Baltimore, Md.: University Park Press.

Hedrick, D., Pratner, E., and Robin, A. 1984. *Sequenced inventory of communication development-R.* Seattle, Wash.: University of Washington Press.

COGNITIVE PROCESSES

Susan E. Ansul

Table 4–10 shows milestones in the development of cognitive processes.

Table 4–10 Cognitive Milestones, Birth to Five Years

Age	Skills
0–1 mo.	Social awareness; regards person, responds to voice, eyes follow moving person, anticipatory excitement Visually explores surroundings Regards/attends to visual and auditory stimuli, briefly retains object, searches with eyes for sound
2–3 mo.	Visually recognizes caregiver, social smile Reacts to disappearance of face Tracks objects (horizontal, vertical, and circular: follows with eyes, then turns head) Habituates to auditory and visual stimuli, shows preference for novel and more complex stimuli Localizes to sounds Inspects own hands, fingers hands in play Sustained regard for objects Object exploration/manipulation (attends to visual, auditory, tactile stimulation) Reaches for and grasps objects, carries to mouth, swats at objects Regards/approaches mirror image
4–5 mo.	Smiles and responds playfully to mirror image Discriminates familiar from unfamiliar people Shows eye–hand coordination in reaching, secures cube, uses both hands to secure object, retains object in each hand Bangs objects in play, transfers objects from one hand to another, mouths objects, holds 2 objects in one hand and reaches for third Regards small objects (e.g., pellet) Turns head after fallen object
6–7 mo.	Beginnings of object permanence: looks to where fallen objects disappeared Manipulates/explores parts of objects One-hand approach to secure objects, transfers adeptly Beginning understanding of cause/effect: pulls string to secure attached object (initially unintentionally) Imitates ringing bell
8–9 mo.	Emergence of stranger anxiety Object permanence: looks for and retrieves hidden objects Cause/effect: pulls string adaptively to secure object Looks at pictures in book Participates in cooperative games (e.g., peekaboo) Combines objects at midline Imitates actions with objects: push car, pat toy, and suspend ring Places 1 to 3 cubes in cup in imitation
10–12 mo.	Interest in container play; places beads in box, attempts to place shapes in shape sorter Turns pages in book Inserts pellet in bottle Attempts to imitate scribble Places peg in pegboard, places circle in 3-shape formboard
13–18 mo.	Places 9 cubes in cup, stacks two blocks in tower in imitation Spontaneously scribbles, then imitates crayon strokes Object permanence; finds toys following displacements Means/end causal relations (e.g., uses rod to obtain toy) Completes 3-shape formboard (reversed orientation begins at about 18 mo.)

Age	Skills
19–24 mo.	Stacks 6 to 8 blocks in tower in imitation Development of self-concept: identifies self in mirror, refers to self by name, uses pronouns Expressive language spurt: single words to 2- to 3-word utterances Attends to simple story Matches pictured objects; matches 3 colors Completes simple formboards
24–30 mo.	Builds train of cubes in imitation Imitates vertical and horizontal strokes Understanding of concept of "one" Recognition of basic shapes Understanding of simple spatial concepts (e.g., "in," "on")
30–36 mo.	Builds simple block structures (e.g., bridge, wall) Discriminates/matches simple pictured objects Understands concepts of "big/little" Understands spatial concepts (e.g., "up/down," "out," "under," "in front," "behind") Begins to identify colors, sorts objects by color Counts to at least three
3–4 yr.	Recalls 2 to 3 digits, simple sentences, and motor sequences Identifies gender Development of visual-perceptual skills: formboards to inset puzzles to interlocking puzzles Development of visual discrimination skills (e.g., patterns, same/different, incomplete pictures) Conceptual reasoning: recognizes categories (e.g., points to the animals), or classifies objects within group, sorts objects by color, shape, and size Relates temporal sequence of events Counts with one-to-one correspondence up to 5, counts in stable order, understands "more," understands number concepts/quantity (e.g., match same number of objects) Understanding of size concepts (e.g., matches, sorts, and arranges objects by size) Development of prewriting skills
4–5 yr.	Places simple pictures in sequence Understands time concepts Rote counting to 10 Further development of classification skills (e.g., groups by category, describes similarities and differences, and describes reasoning for classification/ categorization) Verbal reasoning skills (e.g., describes verbal absurdities—what's silly or wrong about this?) Development of readiness skills: reading, writing, and math

Source: Adapted from Bayley (1993), Knobloch et al. (1987), Sanford and Zelman (1981), Santa Cruz County Office of Education (1987).

REFERENCES

Bayley, N. 1993. *Bayley Scales of Infant Development: Second edition.* San Antonio, Tex.: The Psychological Corporation.

Knobloch, H., et al. 1987. *Manual of developmental diagnosis.* Hagerstown, Md.: Harper & Row.

Sanford, A., and J. Zelman. 1981. *The Learning Accomplishment Profile (LAP): Revised edition.* Winston-Salem, N.C.: Kaplan Press.

Santa Cruz County Office of Education. 1987. *HELP for Special Preschoolers: Assessment checklist: Ages 3–6.* Palo Alto, Calif.: VORT Corporation.

SELF-CARE

Lisa A Kurtz

Table 4-11 shows milestones in the development of self-care skills.

Table 4-11 Self-Care Milestones

Age*	Feeding	Dressing	Toileting	Grooming/Hygiene	Household/Community
1 mo.	Opens/closes mouth in response to food stimulus				
2 mo.					
3 mo.	Anticipatory facial response to bottle				
4 mo.	Pats bottle				
5 mo.	Holds bottle independently (5–6 mo.) Mouths and gums hard cookie				
6 mo.	Swallows strained/pureed food (3–6 mo.) Drinks from cup if held (6–8 mo.)				
7 mo.	Self-feeds cracker (7–8 mo.)				
8 mo.					
9 mo.	Finger feeds (9–12 mo.)				
10 mo.		Cooperates by extending arm/leg (10–12 mo.)			

Age*	Feeding	Dressing	Toileting	Grooming/Hygiene	Household/Community
11 mo.	Holds handle of cup while drinking (11–12 mo.)				
12 mo.	Brings filled spoon to mouth (12–15 mo.) but turns over		Indicates discomfort with soiled diapers (12–18 mo.)		
15 mo.	Scoops and brings spoon to mouth with spillage, forearm pronated (15–18 mo.)				
18 mo.	Chews semisolid foods Holds small cup with 1 hand Drinks from straw (18–24 mo.) Distinguishes edible/nonedible food (18–24 mo.) Brings spoon to mouth, forearm supinated (18–24 mo.)	Removes socks	Bowel control with adult regulation (18–24 mo.) Indicates need to eliminate bowel/bladder (18–24 mo.)	Partially washes hands (18–24 mo.)	
21 mo.					Turns knob to open door (21–24 mo.)
24 mo.	Uses glass, 2 hands	Unties and removes shoes (2–3 yr.)	Bladder control		Imitates housework
2½ yr.	Uses napkin (2½–3 yr.) Pours liquid from small container (2½–3 yr.)	Fastens large front buttons			Puts away jacket, toys (2½–3 yr.)
3 yr.	Feeds self independently with fork/spoon, little spillage	Snaps in front Unfastens buttons, front and side Unzips front zipper		Turns water faucets on/off	

continues

Table 4–11 continued

Age*	Feeding	Dressing	Toileting	Grooming/Hygiene	Household/Community
3½ yr.		Puts shoes on correct foot Knows front from back of clothing Unfastens buckle (3½–4 yr.)	Flushes toilet (3½–5 yr.)	Allows hair to be washed without fussing (3½–4 yr.) Blows nose into tissue (3½–4 yr.)	
4 yr.	Drinks from soda can or bottle	Removes pullover garment Fastens buckle Dons socks/shoes completely Dons pants	Arranges clothes to prepare for toileting	Runs brush/comb through hair Washes and dries hands and face effectively Brushes teeth effectively (4–4½ yr.)	Places dirty clothes in hamper Sets table with assistance
4½ yr.	Drinks from water fountain without help (4½–5 yr.) Serves self and carries tray in line (4½–5 yr.)	Fastens separating front zipper Inserts belt in loop Laces shoes (4½–5 yr.) Unfastens back zipper (4½–5 yr.)	Toilets independently without accidents (4½–5 yr.)		
5 yr.		Dons pullover garment	Wipes self after toileting Arranges clothes after toileting (5–6 yr.)	Bathes/showers when reminded (5–5½ yr.); Washes hair using fingers to massage Covers nose during sneeze (5–6 yr.)	Looks both ways before crossing street
5½ yr.	Uses knife for spreading (5½–6 yr.) Cuts with knife and fork (5½–6 yr.)	Unfastens back buttons Zips back zipper			
6 yr.		Ties bow Buttons back buttons (6½ yr.)		Cares for nose effectively Cleans/cuts fingernails Adjusts faucet temperature for bath	Initiates telephone calls to others

Age*	Feeding	Dressing	Toileting	Grooming/Hygiene	Household/Community
7 yr.				Styles hair (7½ yr.)	Knows value of coins
8 yr.				Washes ears Bathes/showers independently	Sweeps, mops, or vacuums floors
9 yr.					Uses stove or microwave independently (9–10 yr.) Uses household cleaning agents appropriately (9–10 yr.)
10 yr.		Ties necktie			
11 yr.					Counts change for purchase costing more than $1.00 (11–12 yr.)
12 yr.				Uses deodorant	Straightens room without reminders (12–15 yr.)

*Approximate age at which skills are expected.

Source: Adapted from Brigance (1978), Coley (1978), Furuno et al. (1984), Santa Cruz County Office of Education (1987), Sparrow et al. (1984).

REFERENCES

Brigance, A.H. 1978. *Inventory of early development.* North Billerica, Mass.: Curriculum Associates, Inc.

Coley, I.L. 1978. *Pediatric assessment of self-care activities.* St. Louis: C.V. Mosby Co.

Furuno, S., et al. 1984. *Hawaii Early Learning Profile (HELP).* Palo Alto, Calif.: VORT Corporation.

Santa Cruz County Office of Education 1987. *HELP for Special Preschoolers: Assessment checklist: Ages 3–6.* Palo Alto, Calif.: VORT Corporation.

Sparrow, S.S., et al. 1984. *Vineland Adaptive Behavior Scales: Survey form manual, Interview Edition.* Circle Pines, Minn.: American Guidance Service.

Chapter 5

Roles and Functions of the Interdisciplinary Team

Purpose: to describe the characteristic roles and functions assumed by selected members of the interdisciplinary team in caring for children with developmental disabilities and their families. Information pertaining to the theoretical frame of reference for each discipline is reviewed, along with a description of the minimal educational and certification requirements for professional practice. Suggested criteria for referral are designed to assist consumers and professionals when making informed decisions about the need to request additional services.

Outlines containing the typical components of an initial assessment appropriate for children with developmental disabilities are designed as a guide for professionals who may have limited experience in pediatrics. Furthermore, these outlines illustrate that there is often considerable overlap among the roles of the various disciplines. In practice, specific roles may vary depending on the philosophy of the center, the training of the clinicians, or the model of team collaboration that is used to organize the provision of care.

AUDIOLOGY

Carol A. Knightly

ROLES AND FUNCTIONS OF AUDIOLOGISTS

Audiologists specialize in the prevention, identification, and nonmedical management of hearing loss. The goal of the pediatric audiologist is to lessen the impact of hearing loss on language acquisition and consequently on the social, emotional, educational, and ultimately vocational status of the child. As with any disability, this goal is achieved through early iden-

tification and prompt intervention. The audiologist possesses the skills and technology necessary to identify hearing loss and initiate management as early as the newborn period.

The minimum requirements for entry-level practice as an audiologist include a master's degree in audiology, at least 350 clock-hours of supervised patient contact during the training period, a nine-month full-time clinical fellowship (CFY), and a passing score on a national certification exam. Audiologists who have successfully met these requirements are awarded the Certificate of Clinical Competence in Audiology by the American Speech-Language-Hearing Association and list the initials *CCC-A* after their names. It is typically during the CFY period that audiologists may choose to seek additional exposure or skill development in certain areas such as pediatrics or geriatrics, but the professional organization does not formally recognize specialization.

Permanent hearing loss that occurs after basic language proficiency has been established may result in intervention strategies different from those employed with prelingual hearing impairment. As a result, the audiologist frequently works in conjunction with other specialists familiar with the pediatric patient.

TYPICAL SERVICES PROVIDED BY AUDIOLOGISTS

Identification

The audiologist performs a variety of screening and diagnostic tests to identify hearing impairment. The audiologist may also refer the patient to other specialists, including the speech/language pathologist and the psychologist, to determine what, if any, impact the hearing loss has had on language and cognitive development. In addition, the audiologist may be in a position to refer the patient to other specialists, such as the developmental pediatrician or geneticist, since hearing loss may present as the most obvious sign of other related disorders.

Management

Management of the child with hearing loss requires amplification combined with appropriate language stimulation.

1. *Amplification:* The most effective way to lessen the impact of hearing loss is through the use of amplification, such as hearing aids or auditory trainers, since these methods provide the child with access to the speech spectrum. However, it is imperative to obtain medical clearance before fitting the child with amplification so that the physician has the opportunity to diagnose and treat any medical condition that may be responsible for the hearing loss.

2. *Language stimulation:* Amplification does not restore normal hearing ability, nor can it remedy language delay without the provision of other interventions. The child with significant hearing loss must also receive intensive language stimulation, regardless of the methodology employed (e.g., auditory/oral, manual, or total communication).

CRITERIA FOR REFERRAL TO AUDIOLOGY

Although a physician's referral is not typically required by the profession, individual insurance companies may require a physician's referral for reimbursement. The referral should include identifying information, reason for referral, medical diagnoses, and pertinent developmental history.

Children should be referred for an audiological evaluation whenever there is reason to suspect hearing loss—for example:

1. Infant presents with history that suggests high risk for hearing loss (American Academy of Audiology 1994).

2. Infant demonstrates inconsistent responsiveness to environmental sounds.

3. Child exhibits delay in the acquisition of speech/language skills at the expected ages.

4. Child demonstrates poor school performance relative to expected ability.

5. Child has had exposure to sudden-impact noise (e.g., firecrackers, gunshots) or high-level noise over a long period.

6. There is a family history of late-onset hearing loss or conditions associated with hearing loss (e.g., chronic renal failure, otosclerosis).

Advances in technology in recent years have increased the chances for survival of severely compromised newborns who are at risk for hearing loss. In 1982, the Joint Committee on Infant Hearing recommended identifying infants at risk for hearing loss through the use of seven criteria and suggested audiological follow-up of these infants until formal documentation of hearing sensitivity could be made (American Academy of Pediatrics 1982). In 1994, the Joint Committee issued an updated statement, expanding the indicators and making recommendations for assessment and management of infants with hearing impairment, including the goal of universal detection of and management for hearing loss by six months of age (American Academy of Audiology 1994). Neonates (birth-28 days) who should be considered at risk for hearing loss include those with the following conditions:

1. family history of congenital or delayed-onset childhood sensorineural impairment

2. congenital infection known or suspected to be associated with sensorineural hearing impairment, such as toxoplasmosis, syphilis, rubella, cytomegalovirus, or herpes

3. craniofacial anomalies, such as morphologic abnormalities of the pinna and ear canal, absent philtrum, low hairline

4. birthweight less than 1,500 grams

5. hyperbilirubinemia level exceeding indication for exchange transfusion

6. severe depression at birth, which may include infants with Apgar scores of 0–4 at 1 min. or 0–6 at 5 min.

7. prolonged mechanical ventilation for a duration equal to or greater than 5 days (e.g., persistent pulmonary hypertension)

8. ototoxic medications, including but not limited to the aminoglycosides (e.g., gentamicin, tobramycin, kanamycin, streptomycin) and loop diuretics used in combination with aminoglycosides

9. bacterial meningitis

10. stigmata or other findings associated with a syndrome known to include sensorineural and/or conductive hearing loss (e.g., Waardenburg syndrome or Treacher Collins syndrome)

Some children may pass an initial screening but require monitoring of hearing sensitivity to detect any delayed-onset hearing loss. In addition, some health conditions that may develop later may require rescreening. Infants (29 days–2 years) who should be considered at risk include those with the following conditions:

1. parent/caregiver concern regarding hearing, speech, language, and/or developmental delay

2. neonatal risk factors that may be associated with progressive sensorineural hearing loss (e.g., cytomegalovirus or prolonged mechanical ventilation)

3. head trauma, especially with loss of consciousness or skull fracture

4. children with neurofibromatosis Type II or other neurodegenerative disorders such as myoclonic epilepsy, Werdnig–Hoffman disease, Tay–Sachs disease, infantile Gaucher disease, Niemann–Pick disease, any metachromatic leukodystrophy, or any infantile demyelinating neuropathy

5. childhood infectious diseases known to be associated with sensorineural hearing loss (e.g., mumps, measles)

6. recurrent or persistent otitis media with effusion

7. eustachian tube dysfunction

8. family history of hereditary childhood hearing loss

9. ototoxic medications, including but not limited to the aminoglycosides (e.g., gentamicin, tobramycin, kanamycin, streptomycin) and loop diuretics used in combination with aminoglycosides

10. bacterial meningitis

11. stigmata or other findings associated with a syndrome known to include sensorineu-

ral and/or conductive hearing loss (e.g., Waardenburg syndrome or Treacher Collins syndrome)

SUGGESTED OUTLINE/FLOW SHEET FOR INITIAL AUDIOLOGICAL EVALUATION

The following should be considered for inclusion in an initial audiological evaluation. Actual tests and testing methods must be determined by the presenting diagnosis and the developmental age of the child.

- Demographic information
- Case history
  1. reason for referral
  2. pre-, peri-, postnatal complications/illnesses
  3. family history of hearing loss/illnesses associated with hearing loss
  4. childhood illnesses, including middle ear pathology
  5. parent/caregiver/teacher concerns
- Initial impressions
  1. craniofacial anomalies, preauricular pits or tags
  2. attentional behavior
  3. overall development
  4. interaction with parent/caregiver
  5. motor control/tone
  6. expressive/receptive language and speech patterns

- Assessment of middle ear function
  1. tympanometry
  2. physical volume measurements
  3. acoustic reflex thresholds
- Assessment of hearing sensitivity
  1. brainstem response audiometry
  2. pure tone air conduction thresholds/responses
  3. pure tone bone conduction thresholds/responses
  4. speech audiometry (detection, reception, recognition)
- Assessment of suspected retrocochlear pathology
  1. brainstem response audiometry
  2. acoustic reflex threshold and decay
  3. performance intensity functions for phonetically balanced word lists (PI-PB function)
- Summary and recommendations
  1. description of test procedures
  2. departure from standard procedures, if necessary, due to cognitive or physical limitations
  3. results of assessment
  4. recommendations for intervention (e.g., amplification, environmental adaptations)
  5. frequency of recommended follow-up
  6. referrals to other professionals for further evaluation/intervention

REFERENCE

American Academy of Audiology. 1994. Joint Committee on Infant Hearing—1994 Position Statement. *Audiology Today* 6:6–9.

American Academy of Pediatrics. 1982. Position statement 1982—Joint Committee on Infant Hearing. *Pediatrics* 70:496–497.

DEVELOPMENTAL PEDIATRICS

Susan E. Levy

ROLES AND FUNCTIONS OF DEVELOPMENTAL PEDIATRICIANS

A developmental pediatrician is a board-certified pediatrician who has completed three years of pediatrics residency followed by three years of a developmental pediatrics fellowship. The aim of the developmental pediatrics fellowship is to train the pediatrician for an academic career with skills in the diagnosis, assessment, management, and research of children with physical, cognitive, and behavioral disabilities. In addition, the developmental pediatrician is an advocate for children and families with disabilities within the medical community and provides input into legislative and resource planning.

Developmental pediatricians practice in multiple settings, including tertiary medical centers, university-affiliated programs, private practices, and community centers. They often serve as team leaders, with overall responsibility for integrating data from all medical and developmental caregivers and assisting the team to develop a coordinated and comprehensive plan for management of the child and family.

TYPICAL SERVICES PROVIDED BY DEVELOPMENTAL PEDIATRICIANS

1. *Diagnosis* and further evaluation of children with a history of delay or differences in acquisition of developmental milestones. Diagnosis includes developmental assessment and medical evaluation to determine if there is a medical or neurologic etiology.
2. *Medical management* of a range of developmental and/or behavioral disabilities. One example is medical complications of cerebral palsy, including poor growth, gastroesophageal reflux, constipation, spasticity, and seizures. Another

example is pharmacologic management of attentional difficulties in attention-deficit/hyperactivity disorder (via Ritalin or other medication) in conjunction with a behavioral and educational approach.
3. *Developmental evaluation* of children with chronic illness, genetic disorders, or metabolic disorders. Children with these complex disorders frequently require hospitalization or may have intercurrent illnesses that compromise development. The developmental pediatrician helps to monitor development and serves as a liaison with subspecialists (see Chapter 6) involved in managing the disorder.

CRITERIA FOR REFERRAL TO A DEVELOPMENTAL PEDIATRICIAN

Any child suspected of having a developmental disorder or difference may be referred for evaluation and/or management by a developmental pediatrician. Developmental disorders include developmental delay, mental retardation, communication disorders, learning disorders, attention-deficit/hyperactivity disorder, autism and pervasive developmental disorder, cerebral palsy, and behavior disorders (e.g., conduct disorder, disruptive behavior disorder, and oppositional defiant disorder). Children who have not been diagnosed with a specific developmental disorder may present for evaluation of delays in various aspects of development (e.g., fine motor, speech and language, gross motor) that may be associated with other medical disorders. Examples include neurofibromatosis (associated with learning and attentional disorders), metabolic disorders (with developmental delay or retardation associated with perturbations of control), and chronic illness such as bronchopulmonary dysplasia (chronic lung disease in former premature infants).

SUGGESTED OUTLINE/FLOW SHEET FOR INITIAL EVALUATION BY DEVELOPMENTAL PEDIATRICS

The following outline reflects the need to document the concerns of the referral source, details of past medical history and family history (to help determine medical factors or etiology), findings on physical and neurologic examination, and developmental screening or assessment.

- History
  1. demographics: name, date of birth, date of evaluation, chronological age, referrer
  2. chief complaint/ referral questions
  3. past medical history
     (a) birth history: maternal age, number of pregnancies, length of gestation, prenatal complications or exposures, delivery (neonatal events and complications, route of delivery, presentation, resuscitation), Apgars, duration of hospitalization and complications
     (b) general history: allergies, medications, growth, frequent illnesses such as otitis media, hospitalizations, seizures
  4. developmental history: recall of milestones (language, fine motor, gross motor, adaptive, social)
  5. educational history: current placement, past education, additional assistance
  6. previous formal evaluations (including sensory)
  7. family history: parental age, health, and educational attainment; siblings; family members with similar problems or other developmental disabilities.
  8. social history: family composition, supports
- Physical examination
  1. growth parameters (weight/height/head circumference)
  2. observations: demeanor, activity; behavior, spontaneous language
  3. HEENT: eyes, nose, mouth, throat
  4. chest: lungs; thorax shape; heart rate, rhythm, murmur
  5. abdomen: liver, spleen, masses
  6. genitalia
  7. spine: curvature
  8. skin: pigmented and other lesions
- Neurological examination
  1. mental status: alertness, orientation
  2. cranial nerves
  3. motor: muscle mass, strength, tone
  4. cerebellar function
  5. reflexes: deep tendon reflexes, primitive reflexes
- Developmental screening/assessment
- Summary
  1. summary of pertinent history examination findings
  2. conclusions: developmental and medical diagnoses
- Recommendations/plan
  1. suggested medical evaluations and/or treatment
  2. appropriate developmental interventions
  3. suggested follow-up

NURSING

Kathleen Ryan Kuntz

ROLES AND FUNCTIONS OF REHABILITATION NURSES

The pediatric rehabilitation nurse assists children with developmental disabilities, physical impairment, or special health care needs to attain a maximum level of functional ability, maintain optimal health, and adapt to a lifestyle that may be different from their peers'. The nurse cares for the child from the time of injury or diagnosis through to productive adulthood in collaboration with the interdisciplinary team. The goal is to promote not only the health and abilities of the child but the skills and abilities of family members as well.

The pediatric rehabilitation nurse cares for the child and family in a variety of roles and in settings that may include hospitals, rehabilitation facilities, residential facilities, clinics, day care agencies, home, and school. Typical roles include educator, caregiver, counselor, coordinator of care, advocate, researcher, and consultant.

Registered nurses are prepared for practice by graduation from an accredited program at the diploma, associate-degree, or baccalaureate level that includes didactic instruction and practical clinical experience. Following graduation and passing of a national examination for licensure, individuals will include the initials RN (registered nurse) after their names. Rehabilitation nurses function in both generalist and advanced-practice roles. The role of the rehabilitation nurse generalist is influenced by basic nursing preparation, continuing education, and experience. After a minimum of two years of experience caring for individuals with physical and developmental disabilities and special health care needs, registered nurses are eligible to take a national certification examination in rehabilitation. Individuals successfully passing this examination will include the initials CRRN (certified rehabilitation registered nurse) after their names. For advanced-practice roles in rehabilitation nursing, graduate preparation at a master's degree level or higher is needed. This educational attainment may be indicated after one's name, along with the level of licensure and/or certification (e.g., MSN, PhD).

Other levels of direct nursing caregivers include the licensed practical nurse (LPN) and the nurse assistant (NA). The LPN completes a 12-month education program leading to a diploma that includes didactic instruction and clinical experience. After completion of this program, this individual is eligible to take a national examination for licensure. The LPN provides direct care under the direction of a physician or registered nurse, within a defined scope of practice, to individuals who are medically stable, in situations not of risk. There is no current licensure of caregivers at the assistant level. The NA provides direct care under the direct supervision of a registered nurse, implementing the non-licensed aspects of patient care.

TYPICAL SERVICES PROVIDED BY THE REHABILITATION NURSE

1. performs activities that maintain and restore function and prevent complications and further loss
2. provides direct nursing care
3. directs the carryover of skills taught and practiced during therapies
4. coordinates the daily schedule of team activities
5. provides a therapeutic environment
6. educates the child and family
7. acts as a child and family advocate

CRITERIA FOR REFERRAL TO REHABILITATION NURSING

Children with physical and developmental disabilities and special health care needs may receive care by nursing personnel in a variety of settings. In most cases, care by the pediatric rehabilitation nurse is provided as part of a general referral to a rehabilitation program (inpatient or outpatient). Specific treatments or regimens may require a physician prescription (i.e., medication administration, lab tests, and invasive procedures such as catheterization). Referral to the advanced-practice nurse in the community can be initiated by an individual, a social service agency, or other health care professionals. In some cases, the pediatric rehabilitation nurse is involved in medical-legal consultation and is referred by an attorney at law. An initial assessment by the pediatric rehabilitation nurse will include an interview and physical assessment. The nurse then formulates nursing diagnoses, identifying physical, developmental, psychosocial, and functional care needs. The nurse develops a plan of care in collaboration with the child, family, and interdisciplinary team members. Utilizing outcomes identified in the plan, the nurse evaluates the effectiveness of nursing interventions toward achieving goals. The plan is revised as necessary to achieve desired outcomes.

Conditions or situations that would suggest the need for pediatric rehabilitation nursing services in the community include

1. an identified need for child and family education regarding physical and developmental disabilities and special health care needs
2. need for assistance in coordination of care (or case management)
3. need for someone to serve as an advocate for the child and family
4. need for a consultant to assist in determining the need for therapeutic services

SUGGESTED OUTLINE/FLOW SHEET FOR INITIAL NURSING ASSESSMENT

Pediatric rehabilitation nursing involves the assessment of the child's physical and developmental condition, identification of relevant etiologies or risk factors that may be associated with physical and mental status, self-care abilities, emotional responses to alterations in funcional ability and lifestyle, pain, alteration in self-concept, and individual and family coping issues. The exact nature of the child's disability or special health care needs varies widely. The nurse assesses changes in the child's condition and their relationship to resulting health problems. The general health history and physical assessment may be done in part by other members of the health care team when conducted in the hospital or rehabilitation facility.

- Demographic information
  1. name
  2. age
  3. race
  4. sex
  5. religion
  6. referral source
  7. informant
- Purpose for assessment and presenting concerns
- Current problem(s)
  1. date and manner of onset
  2. precipitating and predisposing factors related to onset
  3. description of problem characteristics
  4. course of problem and response to interventions
- Past medical history
  1. information regarding pregnancy, labor and delivery, birth
  2. previous illness, operations, or injuries
  3. allergies
  4. current medications
  5. immunizations
- Physical condition and ability
  1. general/overall health
  2. growth measurements (length/height, weight, head circumference)
  3. physiologic measurements (temperature, pulse, respiratory rate, blood pressure)

4. skin (color, moisture, turgor, risk for breakdown, hair texture and distribution)
5. eyes
6. nose
7. ears
8. mouth (dentition, mucous membranes)
9. sensory function (vision, hearing, taste, smell, touch)
10. nutrition (diet/texture(s), meal schedule, food preferences and restrictions, oromotor function, feeding behaviors, devices used, hydration)
11. chest/respiratory (airway, color, respiratory effort, secretions, breath sounds)
12. cardiovascular (heart sounds/rhythm/rate, skin temperature, edema, peripheral pulses, capillary refill)
13. gastrointestinal (food tolerance, bowel sounds, abdominal girth)
14. genitourinary/elimination (bladder pattern/program, urine characteristics, bowel pattern/program, stool characteristics, toileting skills)
15. gynecologic/sexuality (menarche, date of last menstrual period, regularity of cycles, discharge, sexual activity/concerns, contraception)
16. musculoskeletal (range of motion, muscle strength, means of mobility, transfer methods, exercise patterns, transportation issues)
17. neurologic (mental status, motor and sensory function, reflexes, seizure activity)
18. activity/rest/sleep (typical activity level, rest periods, nighttime sleep patterns)
19. mechanical/physical/environmental risk (apnea, central venous access device, intravenous access device, cast, wound/decubitus, burn, surgical incision, ventriculoperitoneal shunt, pain management, infections)
20. activities of daily living (bathing/washing, oral hygiene, grooming, dressing, skin care, level of independence)
21. development (fine/gross motor, communication, cognition/school level)

- Family/medical history
- Family/personal/social history

  1. socialization (play, affect/behavior, activities with peers, coping behaviors, substance abuse)
  2. family system (environment, family participation in care, special religious/cultural practices, family support network, family concerns)

- Knowledge of condition and treatment plan—education needs for discharge or independence (understanding of diagnosis/prognosis, expectation of treatment, level of ability in caretaking skills, knowledge/skills required, home equipment/services needed)
- Nursing diagnosis

  1. identification of needs of the patient and family
  2. related factors or etiology

OCCUPATIONAL THERAPY

Lisa A. Kurtz

ROLES AND FUNCTIONS OF OCCUPATIONAL THERAPISTS

Occupational therapists help children with physical, developmental, or behavioral disabilities to become more successful in their ability to perform meaningful activities of daily life. The goal of occupational therapy is to help the child function as independently as possible in the three basic skill areas that typically "occupy" a child's time. These include but are not limited to

1. *Self-maintenance skills*, including activities of daily living such as eating, dressing, toileting, personal hygiene, food preparation, and carrying out household chores and routines

2. *Play and leisure skills*, ranging from sensorimotor exploration of the environment, to symbolic play, to recreational crafts and formal games, all of which help the child to develop basic learning concepts, to develop reasoning skills, and to strengthen social skills while having fun

3. *Work-related skills*, including those skills, attitudes, and behaviors that allow the child to function successfully in school and to develop prevocational interests and abilities

Pediatric occupational therapists work in a variety of settings, including hospitals, schools, rehabilitation settings, early intervention programs, homes, community-based settings, and private practices, where roles may include those of consultant, direct service provider, educator, researcher, advocate, and community liaison.

Minimum requirements for practice as an occupational therapist include graduating from an accredited baccalaureate-degree program or basic master's degree program, completing at least six months of supervised fieldwork, and passing a national certification exam. Therapists who have met these qualifications use the initials *OTR* or *OTR/L* after their names. In addition, most states regulate practice as an occupational therapist through licensure or other means. Many occupational therapists choosing to specialize in pediatric therapy will obtain advanced training/professional preparation through graduate education or specialty certifications such as for neurodevelopmental therapy or sensory integration. Also, advanced certification as a pediatric occupational therapy specialist is available through the American Occupational Therapy Association and is indicated by the initials *BCP* (*board certified in pediatrics*). Minimum requirements for practice as an occupational therapy assistant include completing a two year associate-degree program and two months of supervised fieldwork, passing a national certification examination, and, in most states, obtaining licensure. The primary role of the occupational therapy assistant (COTA or COTA/L) is to carry out treatment plans that have been designed and are supervised by a registered occupational therapist (OTR or OTR/L).

TYPICAL SERVICES PROVIDED BY OCCUPATIONAL THERAPISTS

Supervised practice in purposeful activity designed to challenge skill development is the primary treatment modality used by occupational therapists. Therapy typically incorporates a variety of intervention strategies selected to ensure success in the activity. Examples of special intervention strategies commonly used by pediatric occupational therapists include

1. *Exercise* to strengthen weak muscles, increase mobility, and increase endurance for activity

2. *Adapted positioning and seating*, selected to ensure the child's comfort, prevent physical complications, and encourage more controlled head and arm movements

3. *Splints and casts*, used to relax excessive muscle tone, prevent deformity, or support or strengthen a weak limb (most typically the upper extremities)

4. *Adaptive aids and equipment*, including assistive technology devices, to compensate for disabilities that interfere with the performance of daily activities

5. *Training for independence in self-care*, including dressing, toileting, personal hygiene, functional and community mobility, feeding, and household skills

6. *Neurodevelopmental therapy* using therapeutic handling techniques to modify abnormal muscle tone and facilitate more normal patterns of active movement so that the child can benefit from sensorimotor feedback

7. *Sensory integration therapy*, which helps the child to use the senses of touch, vision, body awareness, and sense of gravity and motion to organize behavioral and motor responses better

8. *Cognitive and perceptual training*, often including the use of computer-assisted methods, which helps the child to compensate for problems with memory, judgment, spatial awareness, or conceptual learning

9. *Social skills training*, to develop skills in social communication, judgment, and negotiation

10. *Environmental adaptation* to ensure accessibility and to promote an optimal therapeutic or developmental milieu

11. *Prevocational skills training*

CRITERIA FOR REFERRAL TO OCCUPATIONAL THERAPY

Children with developmental disabilities should be referred to occupational therapy whenever there is reason to suspect impairment in the performance of daily tasks and routines, including self-care, play, recreation, social inter-

action, or the performance of school-related tasks. Depending on local regulatory guidelines or insurance requirements, referral from a physician may be necessary before the therapist can become involved. Referral should include identifying information, diagnosis and precautions, known medical/developmental/social history, and reason for referral. The initial occupational therapy evaluation will include a summary of findings and treatment recommendations, including objective long-term and short-term goals that reflect the reason for referral.

Conditions that suggest the need for referral to occupational therapy include

1. medical, developmental, social, or environmental situations that limit the child's ability to participate in normal daily routines

2. physical limitations that affect the child's ability to be mobile within the environment or that result in impaired upper extremity function

3. developmental level of performance in self-maintenance skills, play-leisure skills, or work-related skills that is less mature than expected, given cognitive ability to acquire those skills

4. qualitative difficulties in the performance of daily living skills that contribute to problems with frustration, attention, motivation, behavioral organization, or social interactions

5. parents' or other caregivers' need for assistance in learning strategies to encourage the child's independence in daily living tasks

SUGGESTED OUTLINE/FLOW SHEET FOR INITIAL OCCUPATIONAL THERAPY EVALUATION

The following outline suggests functional aspects of human performance that should be considered for inclusion in an initial occupational therapy evaluation. The reason(s) for referral and background medical/developmental/social history suggest those areas requiring formal assessment. When possible, empirically referenced assessment tools should be used to supplement clinical impressions of performance.

- Identifying/demographic information
- History leading to referral
  1. birth/medical history and diagnoses
  2. events leading to OT referral
  3. summary of other tests/consultations (e.g., IQ, vision, hearing)
  4. description of home/school environment
  5. description of current equipment/seating/orthotics
  6. parent/caregiver concerns and goals
- Description of evaluation methods
  1. review of records
  2. caregiver/child interviews
  3. play observation
  4. clinical assessment procedures
  5. standardized tests
- Behavioral observations
  1. mental status
  2. quality of social interaction
  3. cooperation/motivation for testing
  4. ability to communicate/follow directions
  5. attentional behavior
     (a) concentration
     (b) impulsivity/distractibility
     (c) perseveration/ability to shift focus
     (d) organizational approach to tasks
- Musculoskeletal examination
  1. appearance/presence of fixed deformities/skin integrity
  2. muscle tone
  3. active/passive range of motion
  4. manual muscle testing/functional strength
  5. endurance for functional tasks

- Examination of sensory systems
  1. sensory modulation (hyper/hyporeactivity)
  2. functional vision
     (a) acuity
     (b) ocular reflexes
     (c) visual fields
     (d) ocular fixation/tracking/saccades
     (e) visual guidance for reach
  3. somatosensory
     (a) kinesthesia/proprioception
     (b) tactile discrimination
        i. steregnosis/graphesthesia
        ii. texture
        iii. sharp/dull
        iv. hot/cold
        v. finger identification
  4. vestibular
     (a) stationary/dynamic balance
     (b) postrotary nystagmus
     (c) postural/gravitational insecurity, intolerance to movement
- Functional movement assessment
  1. reflexes (primitive/appropriate)
  2. spontaneous movement (prone/supine/quadruped/sitting)
  3. movement transitions (roll/pivot/pull-to-sit/stand)
  4. ambulatory status/wheelchair mobility
  5. transfers
  6. postural praxis
- Fine motor assessment
  1. hand preference
  2. prehension patterns
  3. tool use/object manipulation
  4. bilateral integration
  5. coordination (control/gradation/speed/dexterity)
  6. developmental level
- Cognitive/perceptual assessment
  1. adaptive skills—developmental level

2. visual perception
3. visual-motor integration/constructional praxis
4. concepts (color, size, shape, number, space, time, place, money, right-left, body awareness)
5. visual memory and visual-motor memory
6. problem solving/reasoning/judgment
7. functional reading/writing/math skills
- Personal-social skills
  1. communication/interaction style
  2. play/leisure interests
  3. self-care skills
     (a) feeding
     (b) dressing
     (c) personal hygiene
     (d) recreation
     (e) adaptation to home/school/community environments

- Summary
  1. synthesis of results
  2. functional levels of performance in occupational skill areas
  3. description of strengths/weaknesses
- Recommendations/plan
  1. appropriateness for occupational therapy
  2. plan of care
     (a) consultative/individual/group
     (b) treatment frequency/duration
     (c) planned intervention strategies modalities
     (d) caregiver education plan
  3. long-term objectives
  4. short-term objectives
  5. other recommendations
     (a) further testing/consultation
     (b) equipment
     (c) environmental adaptations

PHYSICAL THERAPY

Shirley A. Scull

ROLES AND FUNCTIONS OF PHYSICAL THERAPISTS

Pediatric physical therapists evaluate and treat physical disability due to disease, injury, and/or birth defect, with emphasis on impairments of movement that lead to functional limitations. The physical therapist treats patients with musculoskeletal problems, neurological deficits, or cardiopulmonary diagnoses. Examples of assessments include range of motion, muscle strength testing, and gait analysis. Short- and long-term goals that are age appropriate, functional, and measurable are developed for each patient. Reassessment should occur periodically to determine the patient's progress toward the goals.

Minimum requirements to practice as a physical therapist include an entry-level degree from an accredited program (most typically a master's degree), completion of six months of supervised fieldwork, and passing of the state licensure exam. Some therapists trained at the bachelor's level have been grandfathered into practice. Many therapists continue to pursue an advanced degree in some area that could include pediatric specialization. Others may enroll in continuing education courses leading to certification in neurodevelopmental therapy (NDT) or sensory integration (SI). Certification as a pediatric clinical specialist can be obtained by passing an additional application and examination procedure.

Physical therapist assistants (PTAs) have an associate degree from an accredited program and are registered or licensed by exam, depending on state laws. As the name implies, these individuals assist the physical therapist to carry out the therapeutic techniques. However, they are not permitted to assess the patient or practice without supervision.

TYPICAL SERVICES PROVIDED BY PHYSICAL THERAPISTS

Clinical services may include screening or more detailed evaluation, including standardized tests, depending on the purpose of the session. Treatment techniques are varied and include consultation, such as with school personnel, and parent/family education to carry over the therapy into the home setting. Play is often incorporated into the therapy session to interest the child in the activity. The therapist must be creative in engaging the child to achieve the rehabilitation goals.

The following are samples of interventions employed by physical therapists to achieve the rehabilitation goals:

1. passive or active exercise to maintain or increase range of motion
2. active or resistive exercise to increase muscle strength; may use manual resistance, free weights, equipment such as ergometers, or isokinetic dynamometers
3. training in functional skills such as bed mobility and transfers
4. developmental therapy designed to facilitate progress toward gross motor milestones with optimal movement quality
5. fabrication and use of orthotics or casts for positioning or functional activity
6. preparation and training in the use of prosthetics
7. modalities such as heat, cold, electric current, or whirlpool to decrease pain, improve flexibility, control pain, or promote wound healing
8. aquatic therapy for increasing flexibility and strength, decreasing pain, and ambulating in a partial weight-bearing environment
9. recommendations for adaptive equipment such as wheelchairs, ambulation aids, or standers
10. evaluation and adaptation of the environment to promote accessibility
11. postural drainage and percussion to clear the lungs of secretions and promote optimal air exchange
12. breathing exercises to improve use of respiratory muscles
13. aerobic exercise to improve cardiovascular endurance

CRITERIA FOR REFERRAL

Children with developmental disabilities should be referred for a physical therapy evaluation whenever the parent or physician suspects a delay in gross motor development or abnormal movement quality. In addition, children at risk for neuromotor dysfunction may be referred for screening and identification of abnormalities. Depending on state law and insurance company regulations, a physician's written referral may be needed. The referral should include diagnosis, precautions (especially weight-bearing restrictions), and reason for referral. If the family permits, the review of previous evaluations provides detailed information and decreases the likelihood of posing redundant questions regarding developmental history and so on to the parents.

Conditions that may benefit from physical therapy assessment and treatment include

1. cerebral palsy
2. spina bifida
3. developmental delay
4. high-risk infant
5. traumatic brain injury
6. scoliosis
·7. burns
8. juvenile rheumatoid arthritis
9. hemophilia
10. sickle-cell anemia
11. osteogenesis imperfecta
12. arthrogryposis
13. congenital or acquired limb deficiencies
14. orthopedic conditions—acute/chronic
15. cystic fibrosis

**SUGGESTED OUTLINE/FLOW SHEET
FOR INITIAL PHYSICAL THERAPY
EVALUATION**

- Musculoskeletal
  1. history and observation
  2. range of motion (active and passive)
  3. manual muscle test
  4. functional skills
  5. gait
  6. sensory
  7. special tests
     (a) leg length
     (b) posture
     (c) ligamentous laxity
     (d) regional diagnostic tests
- Neurorehabilitation
  1. tone
  2. range of motion (active and passive)
  3. primitive reflexes
  4. righting and balance reactions
  5. gross motor development
     (a) standardized tests = age-equivalent score or developmental quotient (DQ)
     (b) quality of movement

  6. functional skills
  7. gait
  8. equipment
  9. special tests
     (a) leg length
     (b) posture
- Cardiopulmonary
  1. heart rate
  2. respiratory rate
  3. O_2 saturation
  4. breathing pattern
  5. musculoskeletal status—trunk
  6. endurance
- Summary and recommendations: Impairments and functional limitations are analyzed to determine their impact on disability. Problems are identified and prioritized. Measurable long- and short-term goals are identified and given a time frame. Goal-oriented treatment plans are then suggested, including identification of treatment frequency, planned intervention strategies, and patient/family education. Equipment needed to accomplish the goals is identified and ordered.

PSYCHOLOGY

Linda Gibson Matthews

ROLES AND FUNCTIONS OF PSYCHOLOGISTS

Within the context of the interdisciplinary team, the role of the psychologist is to provide

1. a measure of the child's cognitive capabilities
2. differential analysis of those capabilities (e.g., verbal vs. nonverbal skills)
3. measures of academic achievement
4. measures of adaptive skill development
5. clinical impressions as well as formal indices of behavior

The goal of psychological assessment is then to interpret the above to identify, in conjunction with other disciplines,

1. those diagnoses that can best represent the child's functioning
2. additional areas, if any, in which assessment may be warranted
3. those educational, behavioral, and therapeutic services that are most appropriate to the child's needs

State licensure is required for use of the title *psychologist*, as well as for private practice. Licensure requirements vary from state to state but most typically include a PhD or PsyD from an American Psychological Association (APA)-approved or equivalent accredited graduate program, a predoctoral internship, a minimum of one additional year of field experience under direct supervision, and passing of the applicable state licensure exam. Requirements for practice as a certified school psychologist likewise vary somewhat from state to state but typically include a master's degree from an APA-approved or equivalent accredited graduate program followed by one year of supervised field experience. Individuals who have additionally passed the national certification exam may use the initials *NCSP* after their names. Three years of supervised experience are required for independent (unsupervised) practice as a school psychologist. Private practice by unlicensed certified school psychologists is typically limited to the scope of practice that would be expected within a school setting, such as psychoeducational assessment and consultation.

TYPICAL SERVICES PROVIDED BY PEDIATRIC PSYCHOLOGISTS

Psychological evaluation within a pediatric setting typically includes

1. interview and review of records to delineate referral issue(s), current status, and history, including the results of prior evaluations
2. observation, including both clinical impressions and structured measures of behavior
3. direct assessment of cognitive abilities and, where appropriate, of more specific learning, memory, achievement, and play skills
4. indirect assessment, via parent and/or teacher report, on formal measures of behavior and adaptive skill development

Instruments used for psychological assessment, particularly those used as measures of cognitive ability, are more comprehensive and provide for more detailed analysis than those typically used for developmental screening. Assessment within the context of a pediatric multidisciplinary team approach is most often designed to address developmental and/or behavioral issues, and measures of emotional functioning/status are therefore not routinely included.

CRITERIA FOR REFERRAL TO PEDIATRIC PSYCHOLOGY

Psychological evaluation can provide

1. a determination of current cognitive capabilities, strengths, and weaknesses, given a previously identified developmental disorder (e.g., Down syndrome)
2. a determination of postmorbid capabilities, strengths, and weaknesses following illness, injury, or trauma
3. differential diagnosis (e.g., autism vs. a developmental language disorder)
4. identification of a specific learning or other developmental disability

Referrals for psychological evaluation should include identifying information; developmental, medical, and social history; diagnoses; prior evaluation results and recommendations; interventions, current or past; and reason for referral. Referral for initial psychological evaluation is appropriate

1. when there is delay in a child's acquisition of developmental milestones, such as speech
2. when a child has been identified as "at risk" for developmental problems due to his or her prenatal and/or social history, such as in utero exposure to alcohol or cocaine
3. when a child has been diagnosed with a condition (e.g., Down syndrome) known to be associated with developmental delays
4. when a child has experienced illness or injury likely to influence his or her cogni-

tive development/functioning and/or behavior

5. when there are apparent discrepancies between a child's perceived level of ability and his or her school performance

6. when a child displays a decline/regression in skill development in the absence of a known cause

7. when a child displays behaviors that are atypical in quality or inappropriate to the child's chronological age or that interfere with the child's ability to function in line with his or her perceived capabilities

An initial psychological evaluation addresses the referral question through the assessment of appropriate developmental, cognitive, academic, and/or behavioral parameters and provides recommendations as to appropriate intervention strategies and resources.

SUGGESTED OUTLINE/FLOW SHEET FOR INITIAL PSYCHOLOGICAL EVALUATION

The following outline delineates those elements most typically incorporated in an initial psychological evaluation. The scope of the evaluation and those specific areas to be assessed are dictated by the referral question within the context of the child's age, estimated developmental level, and physical or other functional limitations. Empirically based instruments should be used to the extent possible and the results interpreted within the context of those clinical impressions formed.

- Identifying information
- Evaluation methods
  1. formal test measures (direct and indirect)
  2. parent/teacher/child interviews
  3. observations
  4. review of records
- Background information
  1. prenatal/birth/medical history and diagnoses
  2. familial/social history
  3. developmental and behavioral history
  4. intervention/educational history
  5. prior evaluations
- Behavioral observations
  1. quality of social interaction
  2. use of and responsiveness to spoken language
  3. nonverbal communication skills
  4. quality of motor functioning (gross and fine)
  5. degree of engagement/responsiveness to materials
  6. cooperation/motivation for formal test activities
  7. attention span, level of distractibility and impulsivity
  8. ability to transition/shift focus (both between and within tasks)
  9. organizational skills
  10. activity level
  11. atypical behaviors
- Cognitive assessment
  1. level of overall cognitive ability
  2. verbal abilities—general and specific
     (a) receptive/expressive
     (b) simple/complex material
     (c) concrete/abstract reasoning
  3. nonverbal abilities—general and specific
     (a) visual-motor integration, manipulative/pencil-and-paper tasks
     (b) visual perception
     (c) speed
  4. differential analysis
     (a) of verbal and nonverbal skills
     (b) of verbal vs. nonverbal skills
- Specific measure(s) of language abilities
  1. receptive language skills
  2. expressive language skills
  3. nonverbal communication skills (gesture, signing, augmentive)

- Specific measure(s) of visual-motor skills
  1. visual-motor integration (graphomotor) skills
- Specific measure(s) of memory and learning
  1. visual/verbal format
  2. simple/complex material
  3. short-/long-term memory
- Structured assessment of play (ages three years and under)
  1. developmental level
  2. quality/extent/duration
- Adaptive skills assessment
  1. communication skills
  2. socialization skills
  3. self-help skills
  4. motor skills
- Structured behavioral assessment
  1. direct observations/parent report/ teacher report
  2. general/specific areas of difficulty

- Summary and diagnostic impression
  1. synthesis of test findings
     (a) developmental levels
     (b) pattern of strengths and weaknesses
  2. clinical impressions
  3. diagnoses
  4. implications for functional/educational/ behavioral needs
- Recommendations
  1. educational/intervention program
     (a) type/size/structure
     (b) frequency
  2. other therapeutic services
     (a) type
     (b) frequency
  3. specific instructional strategies
  4. specific behavioral strategies
  5. indications for additional evaluations/ consultations
  6. need for follow-up

SPECIAL EDUCATION

Jennifer Buzby-Hadden

ROLES AND FUNCTIONS OF THE SPECIAL EDUCATOR

The special educator designs instructional programs that bring the child's unique needs and the learning task into close proximity with one another. The special educator may also take on the role of trainer, advisor, tutor, consultant, counselor, influencer, and/or mentor. Special education teachers work in a variety of settings including traditional classrooms within the school setting, community-based settings, rehabilitation settings, early intervention programs, and private tutoring settings. They may work with a variety of age groups from birth to age 21.

Minimum requirements for a training as a special educator include graduation from an accredited baccalaureate-degree program and at least one semester of student teaching under the direct supervision of a certified special education teacher. Certifications may vary from state to state for various specialty areas under the general heading of special education. For example, in New Jersey the following are specific certifications that may be obtained: teacher of the deaf, teacher of the visually impaired, and learning disabilities teacher consultant (LDT-C).

TYPICAL SERVICES PROVIDED BY THE SPECIAL EDUCATOR

For early intervention (birth to age three), the special educator is just one of many professionals that make up an early intervention team. The special educator helps children with physical and/or developmental disabilities and/or chronic illnesses to reach their maximum potential in the areas of learning and of interaction with the environment. The educator utilizes the modality of play to evaluate effectively the child's overall developmental status, especially in the areas of cognition and social-emotional development. The special educator is specifically trained to view the child as a "whole."

In preschool and school-age programs, special educators provide a range of services to support the child's progress in learning and essential life skills, including direct teaching or tutoring, curriculum design or modification, and parent support and training.

CRITERIA FOR REFERRAL

Early Intervention

Children may be referred for an early intervention evaluation by a variety of sources, including the primary care physician, an NICU, a high-risk follow-up clinic, and, most preferably, the parent. The special educator is just one of several members of the team. Children typically referred have either a known diagnosis (e.g., Down syndrome) or a high probability of being "at risk" (e.g., prematurity) or are demonstrating developmental delay. To provide the most comprehensive assessment, the special educator may ask the following questions of the parent/guardian:

1. How would you describe your child?
2. What does a typical day include?
3. What activities do you enjoy doing together?
4. What progress or changes have occurred?
5. What toys/activities are preferred by your child?
6. What does your child do well?
7. What goals do you have for your child within the next six months?
8. What are your most important family needs? (optional)
9. How can the early intervention program help you?

Preschool- and School-Age Special Education

Children who are not responsive to instruction, are disruptive in class, fail to make expected gains in a particular skill after repeated exposure to training, or have problems in reading, mathematics, language, writing, social adjustment, and/or motivation should be referred for a special education evaluation. The special educator may want to interview the child to gain the following information from the child:

- Interests
  1. favorite TV show
  2. favorite man/woman
  3. favorite sport/game
  4. pets
- School
  1. what you like most/least about school
  2. favorite subject/least favorite subject
  3. hardest/easiest subject
  4. what helps you learn

The special educator may also want to obtain the following information from the classroom teacher:

1. strengths/weaknesses of the child
2. description of learning styles (visual, auditory)
3. major areas of concern
4. expectations from the evaluation

SUGGESTED OUTLINE/FLOW SHEET FOR INITIAL SPECIAL EDUCATION EVALUATION

- Early intervention
  1. identifying/demographic information
  2. pertinent history
     (a) review of birth/medical history and diagnosis
     (b) review of developmental history
     (c) parental understanding/expectations

   3. child assessment
      (a) team composition
      (b) assessment tools used
      (c) special considerations for assessment
      (d) play observation
      (e) child's interaction with the environment
      (f) ability to calm in stressful situation
      (g) stranger anxiety
      (h) play schema with materials/toys
   4. summary
      (a) synthesis of results
      (b) developmental levels
      (c) description of strengths and weaknesses
      (d) goals for the individual family service plan
   • Preschool/school-aged
      1. demographic information
      2. reason for referral
      3. background/educational history
         (a) family composition
         (b) parental concerns/expectations of evaluation
      (c) has child been retained
      (d) grades on recent report cards
   4. classroom observation/teacher interview
   5. parent interview
   6. child interview
   7. review of school records
   8. description of child's behavior during assessment
   9. assessment procedures and results
      (a) general educational aptitude/achievement
      (b) receptive/expressive/written language development
      (c) reading fluency
      (d) reading comprehension
      (e) math skills—application and computation
      (f) spelling skills
      (g) visual motor/handwriting skills
      (h) auditory/visual memory
   10. summary
      (a) synthesis of assessment information
      (b) recommendations for remedial education

SPEECH/LANGUAGE PATHOLOGY

Marleen Anne Baron and Cynthia B. Solot

ROLES AND FUNCTIONS OF SPEECH/LANGUAGE PATHOLOGISTS

Speech/language pathologists are trained to diagnose and treat a wide variety of communication disorders in both pediatric and adult populations. They address issues relating to both language *competence* (knowledge of the system of rules by which meaning is represented in verbal symbols) and *speech* (the process of executing these symbols into audible form by respiratory, vocal, and articulatory movements). Speech/language pathologists serve in roles that include provision of direct therapy, performance of diagnostic evaluations, teaching, and research. In some settings, they may be referred to by other names (e.g., *speech therapist, speech clinician*).

There are a wide variety of therapy settings in which to obtain services. Public schools provide speech and language therapy for school-age and preschool children aged three to five years in every state. Most major hospitals have outpatient programs that serve children with speech and language disorders. A number of state health agencies sponsor community clinics. Other settings include university speech and language clinics and services provided by professionals in private practice. In some cases, services may be carried out in the client's home.

Minimum requirements for practice as a speech/language pathologist include a master's degree, passing of a national certification examination, and completion of a clinical fellowship year (CFY) that includes completion of nine months of supervised clinical practice following graduation. This process is required to obtain a certificate of clinical competence (CCC) awarded by the American Speech-Language-Hearing Association. A CCC is often necessary for employment and may be used as evidence of meeting state licensure requirements. Therapists who have met these qualifications use the initials CCC/SLP after their names. Graduate students should be carefully supervised by instructors with an MS or MA degree and CCC certification.

There are two types of licensure that speech/language pathologists generally hold. One is issued by the state board of examiners and is required for all work settings other than schools; the other is issued by the state board of education and is valid only in schools. Forty-four states currently regulate professional standards for speech/language pathologists and audiologists. These states require a master's degree, except for Georgia, which requires a baccalaureate degree.

Licensure may also be issued by the state board of education and is usually required of those who work in schools. Most, but not all, states require a master's degree for education licensure.

TYPICAL SERVICES PROVIDED BY SPEECH/LANGUAGE PATHOLOGISTS

Conditions commonly treated by speech/language pathologists include

1. problems with speech/phonological development secondary to structural abnormalities, developmental delay, or motor speech disorders

2. communication delays or abnormalities secondary to hearing impairment

3. language delays or disorders secondary to developmental delay, mental retardation, learning disabilities, pervasive developmental disorder, or congenital or acquired neurologic impairment

4. feeding and/or swallowing disorders

5. stuttering

6. inability to communicate orally, resulting in the need for augmentative communication systems

7. voice disorders secondary to problems with motor control, structural anomalies, or inadequate functional use of vocal/respiratory systems

Typical services provided by speech/language pathologists may include:

1. *evaluation* and *treatment* of the conditions listed above

2. prescription for and training in the use of *augmentative communication devices* to help the child to compensate for problems with oral communication

3. *cognitive retraining* following acquired brain injury to help the child compensate for problems with memory, judgment, conceptual learning, and expressive language

4. recommendations for specific techniques and/or equipment designed to improve functional *feeding skills*

5. *parent teaching/training* designed to help parents to appropriately stimulate their child and to provide models and opportunities for practicing communication goals

6. *consultation* to other interdisciplinary team members around diagnostic and treatment issues relating to communication and oral-motor skills

CRITERIA FOR REFERRAL

Children should be referred to a speech/language pathologist whenever there is reason to suspect a delay or impairment in communication skills, including receptive and expressive language functions, social use of language, speech articulation, oral-motor coordination, voice, fluency, hearing loss, or auditory processing. Children with oral-motor impairment affecting feeding or swallowing function are also appropriate for referral.

A communication deficit can exist in isolation or overlap with other disabilities. Although professional standards of practice do not require speech/language pathologists to obtain a physician referral to initiate treatment, this may be required for reimbursement by some insurance programs or required by the policies of a particular hospital or clinic. Referrals should include identifying information, diagnosis, reason for referral, and known medical, developmental, and social history. Initial speech/language pathology assessment will include comprehensive evaluation and treatment recommendations, including objective long-term and short-term goals that reflect the reason for referral.

Conditions that suggest the need for referral to a speech/language pathologist include

1. medical, neurological, developmental, or behavioral issues that limit the child's ability to acquire or use adequate communication skills
2. a developmental level of communication performance below expectancy, given cognitive ability to acquire those skills
3. physical limitations that affect the child's ability to acquire adequate oral-motor skills, influencing speech articulation and/or feeding skills
4. parents' or other caregivers' need for assistance in learning strategies to encourage and enhance the child's communication skills

The following is a list of danger signals of speech and language problems that suggest the need for referral for a speech/language evaluation. The earlier communication concerns can be identified, the better the chance that a disability may be avoided.

- Zero to six months
  1. Child does not respond to the sound of others talking.
  2. Child fails to turn toward a speaker who is out of sight.
  3. Child cries but makes no other sounds (e.g., cooing or comfort sounds).
- By one year old
  1. Child fails to respond or shows inconsistent responses to sound (environmental sounds and/or speech).
  2. Child has not started to babble, or child babbled, then stopped.
- By two years old
  1. Child does not understand or attend when spoken to.
  2. Child does not use words.
  3. Child does not respond when name is called.
  4. Vocabulary is not growing.
- By two and one-half years old
  1. Child does not combine words.
  2. Speech is largely unintelligible.
  3. Child has difficulty following commands or answering simple questions.
- By three years old
  1. Echolalia is still present.
  2. Child cannot comprehend *what* and *where* questions.
  3. Sentences are not used.
  4. Vocabulary is less than 100 words.
  5. Child uses gestures as a primary means of communication.
  6. Child cannot use speech to fulfill communicative functions (to acknowledge, describe, relate, inquire, assert).
  7. Child has limited intelligibility, even to parents.
- By four years old
  1. Child has unintelligible speech. (Child should have acquired a sufficient number of consonants and vowels to make speech intelligible 100% of the time.)

2. Child has poor language skills and difficulty formulating statements and questions; sentence structure is faulty.

3. Child has difficulty recalling the names of things.

4. Child has poor descriptive, narrative, conversational skills.

5. Child has difficulty learning concepts and/or sequences, such as numbers, colors, and the alphabet.

6. Child's language usage is deviant and not used appropriately for social interaction.

- By five years old
  1. Child cannot retain and follow verbal directions.

  2. Child has difficulty in school (learning concepts or sound–symbol relationships).

  3. Speech is characterized by many sound substitutions.

  4. Sentence structure is noticeably faulty.

  5. Child uses inappropriate word order in sentences.

  6. Child cannot describe an outing or event.

- At any age
  1. Child shows loss of previously acquired verbal language.

  2. Child has dysfluency or stuttering that interferes with communication and causes anxiety or frustration to the child or his parents. (Speech is marked by prolongations, repetitions, blocks, or rising pitch; vocal, respiratory tension, or other struggle behaviors are noted.)

  3. Speech has noticeable hypernasality or lack of nasal resonance.

  4. Pitch is not appropriate for the child's age and sex.

  5. Voice is monotone, extremely loud, largely inaudible, very hoarse, or of poor quality.

  6. Child has hearing loss to a significant degree.

7. Child needs to see the speaker to listen.

8. Child has short lingual frenulum.

9. Child is embarrassed/frustrated by his or her communication skills.

10. Child has difficulty with feeding skills.

SUGGESTED OUTLINE/FLOW SHEET FOR INITIAL SPEECH/LANGUAGE EVALUATION

The following outline suggests aspects of communication that should be considered for inclusion in an initial speech/language pathology evaluation. The reason(s) for referral and background medical/developmental/social history indicate those areas requiring formal assessment. When possible, standardized assessment tools should be utilized to supplement clinical impression of performance.

- Identifying information
- Background information
  1. diagnoses
  2. birth/medical/developmental history
  3. school and therapy history (when appropriate)
  4. events leading to referral
  5. summary of other tests and consultations (e.g., hearing, IQ)
  6. current equipment (e.g., augmentative communication systems, amplification, tracheostomy)
  7. home environment and communication (e.g., primary language used, bilingualism, cultural communication style)
  8. parent/caregiver concerns and goals
- Description of evaluation methods
  1. review of records
  2. parent/teacher/therapist/child interviews
  3. behavioral observations
  4. clinical assessment procedures
  5. formal tests

- Behavioral observations
  1. mental status
  2. quality and style of social interaction
  3. cooperation/motivation for testing
  4. attentional behavior
     (a) impulsivity/distractibility
     (b) concentration
     (c) perseveration and ability to shift focus in tasks
     (d) response style
     (e) functional hearing and listening
  5. quality of play
- Oral peripheral examination
  1. size, shape, and presence of oral structures (at rest and dynamically)
  2. oral-motor coordination for speech production and nonspeech movements
  3. strength
  4. range of motion
- Speech articulation
  1. intelligibility in spontaneous conversation (known/unknown contexts)
  2. phoneme production
     (a) spontaneous versus imitated production
     (b) sounds in isolation
     (c) sounds in discourse
     (d) language factors (i.e., syntax, semantics, prosody, pragmatics)
  3. systematic phonological analysis
     (a) error classification by distinctive feature
     (b) phonologic process
  4. stimulability for improvement
- Language
  1. receptive language
     (a) ability to follow/process directions and questions
     (b) vocabulary, concept acquisition, verbal reasoning
     (c) auditory skills, including verbal memory for digits, words, sentences

(d) comprehension of grammar
(e) comprehension of semantic relationships, including word relationships
  2. expressive language
     (a) vocabulary and concept use
     (b) grammar and syntax use (e.g., morpheme acquisition, length and complexity of utterance)
     (c) organization of discourse and narrative skills
     (d) word finding; naming skills
  3. pragmatics: social use of language (eye contact, turn taking, initiation of comments, cohesion, specificity, accuracy, and nonverbal aspects of communication)
- Assessment of communication deficits secondary to hearing loss
  1. should be preceded by audiometric evaluation and, as needed, amplification
  2. functional hearing/listening (with/without amplification)
  3. speech reading skills
  4. receptive and expressive language skills
  5. speech articulation
  6. vocal quality
  7. primary communication mode (spoken language, sign language, cued speech)
- Voice
  1. vocal habits (e.g., patterns of abuse or misuse)
  2. onset and course of the disorder
  3. clinical assessment of pitch (habitual pitch, optimal pitch, pitch range)
  4. loudness
  5. respiration (musculature, volume, breathing type, coordination, and efficiency)
  6. quality (e.g., hoarseness, harshness, cry, breathiness)
  7. resonance (nasal emission, nasality, facial grimace, voice quality)

8. areas of tension
9. motor-sensory function
10. instrumental evaluation of anatomical integrity and function of phonatory structures (nasometry, stroboscopy, endoscopy, spectrography, Visipitch)

- Fluency
  1. development/course of dysfluent behaviors
  2. family speaking style and environmental speaking demands
  3. situational variants that affect fluency
  4. duration/frequency of stuttering
  5. type of dysfluency (blocks, sound and/or word prolongations)
  6. physical concomitant behaviors, respiratory and phonatory anomalies associated with dysfluency

- Feeding skills
  1. examination of oral structures
  2. oral reflexes
  3. evaluation of stages of swallow (oral, pharyngeal, esophageal)
  4. tolerance for food textures and consistencies
  5. typical diet (textures and preferences)
  6. usual feeding utensils and methods

7. usual and optimal feeding position
8. motor control of body
9. presence of respiratory problems
10. presence of associated medical conditions (e.g., tracheostomy, tracheomalacia, reflux)

- Summary
  1. synthesis of results
  2. functional levels of performance
  3. strengths/weaknesses

- Recommendations/plan
  1. appropriateness for speech/language therapy
  2. plan of care
     (a) consultative/individual/group
     (b) treatment frequency/duration
     (c) planned intervention strategies/modalities
     (d) caregiver education plan
  3. long-term objectives
  4. short-term objectives
  5. other recommendations
     (a) further testing/consultation
     (b) equipment
     (c) modifications to the environment

SOCIAL WORK

Symme W. Trachtenberg

ROLES AND FUNCTIONS OF SOCIAL WORKERS

Social workers provide a wide range of services that are designed to support the social and emotional adjustment and functioning of the child with a developmental disability and his or her family. Intervention plans are highly individualized and occur within the particular child's medical, psychosocial, cultural, and educational context. Because of a unique ability to view the impact of disability from a holistic perspective, combined with skill in facilitating positive interpersonal interactions, it is often the social worker who functions in an integrative role as the coordinator of an interdisciplinary team of care providers.

Minimum requirements for practice as a clinical social worker include completion of a master's degree in social work from a university that is accredited by the National Council on Social Work Education. Advanced social work certification is available through the Academy of Certified Social Workers (ACSW) and requires two years of supervised clinical practice and passing of a competency examination. Many states require licensure to practice and/or secure third-party payment. Social workers who have been prepared at the bachelor's degree level may perform specified tasks at an entry level of practice, such as providing information and referral services.

TYPICAL SERVICES PROVIDED BY SOCIAL WORKERS

Although specific roles may vary according to the needs of a particular agency, typical responsibilities of the professional social worker may include

1. assessment of family needs and concerns in relation to care of the child
2. assessment of social adaptation and function of the child and family
3. provision of emotional support and encouragement to family members
4. provision of individual, family, or group counseling and education regarding the implications of disability and coping strategies
5. crisis intervention and referral
6. advocacy for the basic human rights and entitlements of the child and family, encouraging respect for individual differences that may be influenced by cultural diversity
7. assistance to the family and team in identifying resources for needed services
8. facilitation of communication and collaboration between the family and team members and community service providers
9. empowerment of families to understand public policy and entitlements, seek funding for needed services, access supportive community and national resources, and develop realistic plans to meet the long-term needs of the child (e.g., long-term placement, supported employment, wills and estate planning)

CRITERIA FOR REFERRAL TO SOCIAL WORK

Criteria for referral to social work vary according to a particular agency's policies and the availability of other related disciplines that may also provide psychotherapeutic intervention. However, referral should be considered for the following situations and concerns:

1. suspected child abuse or neglect
2. acute distress in family or child, with considered risk for suicide or serious mental illness
3. dysfunctional family system, with question of guardianship or of the safety of the living arrangement
4. child or family transition to new or changing set of circumstances (e.g., recent devastating illness or disability leading to questionable prognosis for life and/or function, or child with chronic illness or disability experiencing worsening symptoms or decreased functioning)
5. chronic stress from prolonged caregiving responsibilities
6. poor adjustment to disability and/or to the need for special services by child or family; this may manifest in a variety of ways, such as denial, anxiety or depression, over- or underinvolvement in care
7. parental difficulty with learning required training or provision of care
8. team concern about the family's ability to manage the needs of the child and to carry out agreed-upon team recommendations
9. assistance required by family, or other team members need assistance with referral, access, or funding for needed services

SUGGESTED OUTLINE/FLOW SHEET FOR INITIAL SOCIAL WORK ASSESSMENT

• Background information
    1. patient name, birth date, diagnoses, religion, ethnic origin

2. parents' names, birth dates, marital status, education, religion, occupation, financial condition, health, mental health
3. siblings/household members/others involved with child/family
4. insurance
5. collateral social services, therapeutic and financial resources

- Assessment
  1. perception of purpose for evaluation/treatment
     (a) parents
        i. goals
        ii. anticipated diagnosis (for initial diagnosis)
     (b) child (if applicable)
  2. expectation for outcome of evaluation/treatment
     (a) parents
     (b) child (if applicable)
  3. parents' current understanding of child
     (a) description of child (include premorbid condition if present condition's onset is post injury, post surgery, or post insult)
     (b) medical issues
     (c) developmental functioning
     (d) emotional needs
     (e) educational program
  4. family structure and dynamics
     (a) relevant family history
     (b) description of typical day (child with family)
     (c) family relationships
     (d) areas of family strength and support (financial, religious, marital, extended family relationships, friendships)
     (e) areas of family stress (housing, financial resources, illness/death of significant family member, significant life event (e.g., move, divorce, job change)

- Clinical impressions and summary: analysis of information from previous sections concerning family's ability to cope with their situation
- Social work plan: problem focused, and as agreed upon with child/family

Chapter 6

Roles of Specialists

Ada Dorothy Hayes

Purpose: to review the essential roles and functions of medical and related specialists who may participate in the care of children with disabilities or special health needs and their families.

Specialists usually take care of specific medical problems, not the whole child. The primary care physician is usually the coordinator of care and keeps all participants informed of relevant issues, thus allowing subspecialists to maintain optimal contributions to the child's care.

A child may be referred for ongoing care (e.g., seizures) or for a consultation in which the specialist renders an opinion. Reasons for referral include diagnosis, treatment, and assistance with management. Reasons for consultation include uncertainty about diagnosis or etiology, confirmation of diagnosis to maximize treatment, uncertainty about appropriate management or therapy, reassurance to family, assistance with long-term follow-up (anticipation of course and complications), and in some cases medical-legal consultation.

There are no regulations to prevent any physician from practicing a specialty (except insurance payments and malpractice claims). All physicians have either an MD (doctor of medicine) or DO (doctor of osteopathy). Individual states have varying requirements for the practice of medicine, but virtually all require some postgraduate training. Subspecialty postgraduate training is generally done beyond basic, general, or specialty training in areas such as pediatrics or surgery. Most specialists are either *board eligible* (they have completed the necessary training but have not passed the certifying exam) or *board certified* (they have passed the qualifying exams).

GENERAL GUIDELINES FOR REQUESTING AN EVALUATION BY SPECIALISTS

1. State the goals for the evaluation and provide appropriate background information.
2. Be aware of uncertainty and concerns of the patient and the family.
3. Keep the needs of the family in mind and support them in active decision making.
4. Ensure that appropriate information is received by both family and primary care physician.
5. Clarify the responsibility for various physicians and the patient and the family.
6. For some insurance plans and some specialists, a formal referral is needed.

STANDARDS FOR USE OF CONSULTING SPECIALISTS

The Committee on Standards of Child Health Care of the American Academy of Pediatrics (1979) has established the following guidelines for responsibility, etiquette, and ethics of referring consulting physicians:

- Responsibilities of referring physician
    1. initiate and determine timing of referral.
    2. choose consultant.
    3. identify specific concerns.
    4. establish level of confidence.
    5. prepare patient and family for consultant.

- Responsibilities of the consultant
    1. distinguish appropriate and inappropriate concerns.
    2. take the time to get complete history and address major concerns.
    3. avoid use of excessive technology.
    4. communicate specific evaluation, conclusions, and recommendations to both referring physician and patient and patient's family.

ROLES OF SPECIALISTS

Table 6–1 is not meant to be complete but describes some of the physician specialists most often seen by children with developmental disabilities.

Table 6–1 Role Delineations of Physician Specialists

Specialist	Role Delineation	Examples of Criteria for Referral

Cardiologist	• Role encompasses evaluation and management of diseases of the heart and circulatory system
	• Some clinicians are board-certified pediatric cardiologists
	• Assessment procedures
	  1. Electrodiagnostic procedures, including EKG, Holter monitoring
	  2. Ultrasound imaging (by echocardiography) with or without color Doppler to assess blood flow
	  3. Cineangiography (injection of radio-opaque material to visualize interior of heart and vessels)
	  4. MRI
	  5. Cardiac catheterization (invasive interventional radiologic procedure for diagnosis and treatment)
		1. Children with symptoms including cyanosis (blue color to skin and mucous membranes), heart murmur, failure to thrive, arrhythmia, and/or enlarged heart
		2. Children with conditions including congenital heart disease, particularly malformations that might be part of a general syndrome such velocardial facial (VCF) syndrome
		3. Children with Down syndrome; all should be referred at birth for a cardiac evaluation because of high incidence of cardiac malformation in this population, whether or not symptoms are present
		4. Older boys with Duchenne muscular dystrophy who may have an involvement in the cardiac system

Gastroenterologist	• Role encompasses evaluation and management of diseases of the GI (gastrointestinal) tract • Training includes fellowship and board certification as pediatric gastroenterologist • Specialized procedures 1. Endoscopy, which includes direct visualization of all parts of the GI tract from the esophagus to the rectum	1. Children with conditions including malabsorption, short bowel syndrome, need for enteral or parenteral nutrition, gastroesophageal reflux, chronic functional constipation, chronic diarrhea, peptic ulcer disease, failure to thrive, and other developmental disabilities with GI components such as spina bifida and myotonic dystrophy

continues

Table 6–1 continued

Specialist	Role Delineation	Examples of Criteria for Referral
Gastroenterologist (continued)	2. Biopsy—taking a tissue sample for microscopic evaluation (liver; GI tract during endoscopy) 3. Manometry (measurement of pressure)—anorectal or esophageal 4. pH probe (to check acidity in esophagus) 5. Gastrostomy placement with general surgery—percutaneous endoscopic gastrostomy (PEG)	2. Children with multiple disabilities, including cerebral palsy, failure to thrive, and poor eating habits, including difficulties with elimination 3. Children with feeding disorders, with and without failure to thrive 4. Children with symptoms including abdominal pain, nausea and vomiting, GI bleeding, chronic constipation, diarrhea, anorexia, failure to thrive, blood in the stools, jaundice, vomiting, and malabsorptions

Geneticist	• Role involves care for children and families with inherited disorders and genetic syndromes
	• Training includes fellowship and board certification
	• Evaluation usually involves a detailed family history and physical examination (with precise measurements: e.g., distance between the eyes, examination of palm prints)
	• Special tests
	  1. Chromosome evaluation (karyotype), specialized test identifying single genes or areas on chromosomes
	  2. Special enzymatic tests and a variety of very specialized investigative tests
		1. Children with congenital malformations, familial history of MR or genetic disease, chromosome abnormality, or a known or suspected syndrome
		2. Pregnant mothers over 35 years of age
		3. Children with minor malformation noted at birth that could be related to radiation, maternal drug or alcohol ingestion, or a genetic syndrome
		4. Adult patients who have survived pediatric genetic disease such as PKU and become pregnant
		5. Children with Down syndrome; all should be evaluated at birth to rule out translocation, which might predict a second child with Down syndrome in the same family
		6. Children with short stature such as those with Turner's syndrome and achondroplasia
		7. Children with other medical problems such as heart disease that may be associated with syndromes and have a specific pattern of inheritance

Neurologist	• Role encompasses evaluation and management of disorders of the brain and nervous system
	• Training includes residency in adult and/or pediatric neurology and board certification
	• Special procedures
	  1. EEG—brain wave test for study of seizures; EEGs may also be used to assess apnea and sleep problems
	  2. Electrodiagnostic procedures—EMG (electromyogram) and nerve conduction tests to study diseases of the motor unit (connection of the nerve to the muscle)
		1. Evaluation for etiology of developmental disability (macrocephaly, microcephaly, hypotonia, asymmetry, clinical features of neurologic disorder)
		2. Suspicion of new onset of seizures
		3. History of loss of developmental skills or plateau (R/O acute neurological disorder)

Specialist	Role Delineation	Examples of Criteria for Referral
Neurologist (continued)	3. Evoked potentials, which show the electrical manifestation of the brain's response to stimuli (includes visual, brainstem auditory and somatosensory evoked potentials) 4. Neuroimaging: ultrasonography (usually in neonates with an open anterior fontanelle) and MRI, CT, or PET scan	4. Disorders including CNS malformations, peripheral neuropathies, neuromuscular junction, stroke, movement disorder (e.g., tics, chorea, athetosis, dystonia), muscle diseases, hydrocephalus, cranial skeletal dysplasia and storage diseases, CNS malformations (e.g., spina bifida, holoprosencephaly), intracranial hemorrhage (secondary to arterial or venous malformations or prematurity with periventricular leukomalacia), progressive genetic metabolic diseases including the leukodystrophies, neurocutaneous syndromes (e.g., tuberous sclerosis and neurofibromatosis), Rett syndrome, CNS AIDS
Neurosurgeon	• Surgeon with specialized training in surgery on the brain and spinal cord. Some neurosurgeons have developed expertise in specific parts of the nervous system (e.g., spinal cord) • Training includes surgical residency, special fellowship in pediatric neurosurgery, and board certification	1. Acute hydrocephalus 2. Cranial synostosis 3. CNS malformations 4. Atlantoaxial subluxation and dislocation (as seen in Down syndrome) 5. Head trauma 6. Spinal trauma 7. Tumors of the brain 8. Cerebral palsy; many neurosurgeons will perform selective dorsal rhizotomies

Ophthalmologist	• Surgeon who specializes in evaluation and treatment of disorders of the eyes and vision
	• Training includes ophthalmology residency, (possible) additional training in pediatric ophthalmology, and board certification
	• Special procedures
	  1. Vision: electrophysiologic testing (electroretinogram [ERG]; visual evoked response [VER]); visual field testing
	  2. Direct and indirect ophthalmoscopy (visualization of retina and inside of orbit)
		1. Developmental disabilities with suspected impairment of visual acuity, strabismus (cross-eyed), or eye malformations
		2. Obstruction to the iris such as ptosis or cataract; children should be referred as soon as the defect is discovered to preserve visual acuity
		3. Prematurity; premature children should be followed routinely to evaluate the status of retinopathy of prematurity
		4. Suspected metabolic disorders such as Tay–Sachs disease; such children require retinal evaluation
		5. Abnormal appearance of the eye, such as a white pupil or cataract; ptosis covering the iris; cataracts; nystagmus; nonconvergent eye movements or wandering eye movements; symptoms of poor vision; and strabismus or crossed eyes

continues

Table 6–1 continued

Specialist	Role Delineation	Examples of Criteria for Referral
Orthopedist	• Specialized surgeon working with problems in the musculoskeletal system, especially bones and joints • Training includes 1 year of general surgery followed by orthopedic surgery residency and board certification. Some orthopedists may further subspecialize in hand surgery, back surgery, or pediatric orthopedics • Special procedures 　1. X-rays—film of hips, spine, extremities 　2. Myelogram of spine 　3. MRI of hips, spine, joints 　4. Surgical intervention	1. Discrepancy in limb length 2. Contractures (especially in CP) 3. Dislocations and subluxations of joints 4. Fractures, including "brittle bone disease" 5. Scoliosis 6. Malformations requiring reconstruction 7. Tibial torsion
Otolaryngologist (also known as otorhinolaryngologist or ear, nose, and throat [ENT] specialist)	• Surgeon with specialized training in diseases of the ears, nose, and throat • Training includes general surgery (1 year), specialized fellowship training in otolaryngology and specific training in pediatric otolaryngology; board certification • Special procedures 　1. Placement of tracheostomy (artificial airway) for children with lung disease (with or without assisted ventilation) or mechanical obstruction; reconstruction of trachea 　2. Myringotomy with the placement of tubes (in the eardrum), usually for chronic infections or fluid 　3. Tonsillectomy and adenoidectomy 　4. Audiologic surgery (e.g., cochlear implant) 　5. Reconstructive surgery of larynx, involving head and neck	1. Suspected impairments in the areas of hearing, breathing, or swallowing and the associated structures 2. Malformation of the ENT tract (e.g., cleft palate and other facial deformities) 3. Chronic otitis media 4. Laryngomalacia 5. Swallowing problems 6. Large tongue 7. Congestion of the upper airways 8. Chronic tonsillitis
Physical medicine and rehabilitation (PMR) specialist (also known as *physiatrist*)	• Special training in physical medicine and rehabilitation, including nonsurgical treatment of traumatic brain injury, back injuries, neuromuscular diseases, and other diseases leading to physical deficits. These specialists generally work with rehabilitation teams and may prescribe orthoses and prostheses • Training includes internal medicine or pediatrics residency, residency in PMR; board certification • Physiatrists are often part of specialist teams in multispecialty clinics serving such disorders as cerebral palsy, myelomeningocele, head trauma, and spinal cord trauma	1. Head trauma 2. Myopathies 3. Chronic pain 4. CNS disorders (cerebral palsy, myelomeningocele, and others) 5. Spinal cord trauma 6. Amputation 7. Other chronic diseases

Specialist	Role Delineation	Examples of Criteria for Referral

Physical medicine (continued)	• Specialized tests or treatment
	  1. electromyogram (EMG)
	  2. nerve blocks	

Plastic surgeon	• Surgeon who does both reconstructive and cosmetic surgery • Training includes general surgery residency followed by plastic surgery residency; specialization in pediatric plastic surgery is also available; board certification	1. Congenital head and neck deformities 2. Cleft lip and palate 3. Hand and limb deformities
Psychiatrist	• Adult or pediatric training in mental and emotional disorders • Training includes internal medicine or pediatric residency and/or psychiatric residency; board certification in child and adolescent psychiatry • Special techniques such as play therapy and structured interviews	1. Suspected impairment in the areas of emotion or thought process 2. Dementia 3. Behavioral problems 4. Adjustment disorders 5. Situational distress 6. Other specific psychiatric disorders

Pulmonologist	• Specialized training in diseases of the lungs and respiratory system
	• Training in pediatrics and pulmonary fellowship; board certification
	• Special procedures
	  1. Pulmonary function tests (PFTs), giving information about severity of lung disease
	  2. Spirometry
	  3. Oxygen saturation (pulse oximetry) and CO_2 monitor
	  4. Radiologic imaging: chest x-ray, chest MRI
		1. Symptoms such as asthma, allergies, apnea, aspiration syndromes, bronchopulmonary dysplasia, and compromised airways such as those seen in achondroplasia
		2. Severe cerebral palsy in children who are nonambulatory; such children are at risk for aspiration syndromes and would benefit from close follow-up by a pulmonologist

Radiologist	• Specialized training in diagnosing conditions by x-ray, computerized tomography (CT scan), MRI (magnetic resonance imaging) and other sophisticated technological methods • Some radiologists also do treatment on cancer patients • Training includes internal medicine or pediatrics residency, radiology residency with board certification and subspecialty certification • Special procedures 1. Diagnostic—procedures such as VCUG (voiding cystourethrogram), arteriograms, use of radio-opaque material to evaluate the GI tract, injecting radioactive material to evaluate organ function (e.g., renal scan for kidneys, Milk scan for GI tract)	1. Patients are referred by physicians who require further diagnostic evaluation for their disorder (e.g., CNS evaluation by MRI)

continues

Table 6–1 continued

Specialist	Role Delineation	Examples of Criteria for Referral
Radiologist (continued)	2. Neuroradiologic diagnostic procedures such as MRI, PET scanning, and MR spectroscopy 3. Interventional radiology—insert percutaneous gastrojejunostomy, acute stroke management, etc.	
Rheumatologist	• Training in diseases involving the joints and connective tissues • Training includes pediatric and/or internal medicine residency, fellowship in rheumatology, with subspecialization in pediatric rheumatology • Special procedures 1. Joint injection or aspiration	1. Conditions that suggest joint and connective tissue disorders: e.g., Down syndrome in young and adults who may be at high risk for rheumatoid disease
Pediatric surgeon	• Residency training in surgery, with special training in pediatric surgery; board certification	1. Congenital anomalies (e.g., diaphragmatic hernia) 2. Gastrointestinal disorders (e.g., severe gastroesophageal reflux requiring Nissen fundoplication) 3. Gastrostomy tube placement

Urologist	• Surgeon who is trained in caring for conditions of the urinary tract and kidneys
	• Training includes general surgery residency and urology fellowship; some are specially trained in pediatric urology; board certification
	• Special procedures
	  1. Urodynamics (pressure measurements)
	  2. Endoscopy (direct visualization)
	  3. Radiologic studies (e.g., VCUG) to visualize the urinary tract
		1. Disorders with neurogenic bladder such as spina bifida
		2. Traumatic brain injury
		3. Spinal trauma
		4. Congenital malformations

Table 6–2 describes some of the nonphysician specialists most often seen by children with developmental disabilities.

Table 6–2 Role Delineations of Nonphysician Specialists

Specialist	Role Delineation	Examples of Criteria for Referral
Registered dietitian	• Consultant for children with normal or special dietary needs; evaluates nutritional parameters such as height, weight, fat, iron stores, and caloric intake; may prescribe diets to help children gain or lose weight; also helps with formulation of special dietary formulas and gives advice about supplementary feeding	1. Disorders requiring special diets (e.g., PKU, carnitine deficiency, ketogenic diet) 2. Poor growth associated with chronic disorder and/or oral motor dysfunction, such as cerebral palsy 3. Obesity
Genetic counselor	• Specially trained individual (usually master's level) for counseling patients and family after a specific genetic diagnosis has been made; helps with explaining syndromes and associated medical, social, and developmental findings; also helps families decide about future pregnancies	1. Any child determined to have a specific genetic syndrome or disorder 2. Families in need of counseling about recurrence risk of children with developmental or medical disorders
Nurse practitioner	• Licensed nurse who has completed additional graduate training that allows him or her to perform examinations and procedures under the supervision of a physician; often function as "physician extenders" • Nurse practitioners practice in a number of subspecialty and general pediatric inpatient and outpatient settings, in conjunction with a physician	
Physician assistant	• Clinician who has completed 2 to 4 years of training in physical examination and treatment; usually works under the supervision of a physician as a physician extender; is licensed to practice in many states by the same board that licenses physicians • Physician's assistants practice in a number of subspecialty and general pediatric inpatient and outpatient settings, in conjunction with a physician	

REFERENCE

American Academy of Pediatrics. 1979. Pediatrics as a primary, secondary, and tertiary care specialty: Cost, and reimbursement implications. *Pediatrics*, 63, no. 4:659–662.

Chapter 7

Selected Clinical Assessment Procedures

ASSESSMENT OF PHYSICAL WELL-BEING

Kathleen Ryan Kuntz

Purpose: review basic clinical procedures for assessment of physical well-being in children with neurodevelopmental or special health needs; assessment of respiratory function, growth and nutrition, feeding/oral intake, rest/sleep, and skin is included.

Routine assessment of physical well-being is an important aspect of child health care. It is important for all children to have routine medical or nursing examinations at periodic intervals to monitor their health and well-being, even when parents or caregivers have no specific concerns. Because children with physical and developmental disabilities and special health care needs may be at greater risk for health problems than their nondisabled peers, it is especially important for all health care and education providers to be alert to physical signs that may signal a health concern requiring medical intervention. Table 7–1 presents recommendations from the American Academy of Pediatrics for periodic health assessments in children.

ASSESSMENT OF RESPIRATORY FUNCTION

Children with neurodevelopmental disabilities frequently have special problems related to respiratory function. Whether the etiology is a need for an artificial airway, immature lung tissue, restricted lung capacity, or a neuromuscular inability to support the respiratory effort, the respiratory assessment is key to monitoring adequate ventilation.

Features to be noted in a respiratory assessment are as follows:

- Oxygenation/ventilation
  1. color (skin, mucous membranes, nail beds)
  2. level of consciousness
  3. level of activity
  4. air movement with chest wall expansion

Table 7–1 Recommendations for Preventive Pediatric Health Care

	INFANCY[3]							EARLY CHILDHOOD[3]						MIDDLE CHILDHOOD[3]				ADOLESCENCE[3]										
AGE[4]	new-born[1]	2–4 d.[2]	1 mo.	2 mo.	4 mo.	6 mo.	9 mo.	12 mo.	15 mo.	18 mo.	24 mo.	3 yr.	4 yr.	5 yr.	6 yr.	8 yr.	10 yr.	11 yr.	12 yr.	13 yr.	14 yr.	15 yr.	16 yr.	17 yr.	18 yr.	19 yr.	20 yr.	21 yr.
HISTORY (Initial/Interval)	•	•	•	•	•	•	•	•	•	•	•	•	•	•	•	•	•	•	•	•	•	•	•	•	•	•	•	•
MEASUREMENTS Height & Weight	•	•	•	•	•	•	•	•	•	•	•	•	•	•	•	•	•	•	•	•	•	•	•	•	•	•	•	•
Head Circumference	•	•	•	•	•	•	•	•	•	•	•																	
Blood pressure												•	•	•	•	•	•	•	•	•	•	•	•	•	•	•	•	•
SENSORY SCREENING Vision	S	S	S	S	S	S	S	S	S	S	S	O[5]	O	O	S	S	O	S	O	S	S	O	S	S	O	S	S	S
Hearing[6]	S/O	S	S	S	S	S	S	S	S	S	S	O	O	O	S	S	O	S	O	S	S	O	S	S	O	S	S	S
DEV/BEHAV ASSESS[7]	•	•	•	•	•	•	•	•	•	•	•	•	•	•	•	•	•	•	•	•	•	•	•	•	•	•	•	•
PHYS EXAM[8] GENERAL	•	•	•	•	•	•	•	•	•	•	•	•	•	•	•	•	•	•	•	•	•	•	•	•	•	•	•	•
PROCEDURES[9] Hereditary/Metabolic Screening[10]	•↕																											
Immunization[11]	↕							↕						↕				↕			↕							
Lead Screening[12]							•	•			•																	
Hematocrit or Hemoglobin								↕	•↕					↕	•			•										
Urinalysis														•														
PROCEDURES—PATIENTS AT RISK Tuberculin Test[15]								*	*	*	*	*	*	*	*	*	*	*	*	*	*	*	*	*	*	*	*	*
Cholesterol Screening[16]														*	*	*	*	*	*	*	*	*	*	*	*	*	*	*
STD Screening[18]																		*	*	*	*	*	*	*	*	*	*	*
Pelvic Exam[18]																		*	*	*	*	*	*	*	*[16]	*[16]	*[16]	*[16]
Anticipatory Guidance[19]	•	•	•	•	•	•	•	•	•	•	•	•	•	•	•	•	•	•	•	•	•	•	•	•	•	•	•	•
Injury Prevention[20]	•	•	•	•	•	•	•	•	•	•	•	•	•	•	•	•	•	•	•	•	•	•	•	•	•	•	•	•
INITIAL DENTAL REFERRAL[21]												•																

continues

Table 7–1 continued

Source: From "Recommendations for Preventative Pediatric Health Care" by the American Academy of Pediatrics, 1995, *Pediatrics*, 96(2), 373–374. Reprinted with permission.

Note: • = to be performed; * = to be performed for patients at risk; S = subjective, by history; O = objective, by a standard testing method; <—> • = the range during which a service may be provided, with the dot indicating the preferred age. Special chemical, immunologic, and endocrine testing is usually carried out upon specific indications. Testing other than newborn (e.g., inborn errors of metabolism, sickle-cell disease, etc) is discretionary with the physician. These recommendations do not indicate an exclusive course of treatment or serve as a standard of medical care. Variations, taking into account individual circumstances, may be appropriate.

[1] Breastfeeding encouraged and instruction and support offered.

[2] For newborns discharged in less than 48 hours after delivery.

[3] Developmental, psychosocial, and chronic disease issues for children and adolescents may require frequent counseling and treatment visits separate from preventive care visits.

[4] If a child comes under care for the first time at any point on the schedule, or if any items are not accomplished at the suggested age, the schedule should be brought up to date at the earliest possible time.

[5] If the patient is uncooperative, rescreen within six months.

[6] Some experts recommend objective appraisal of hearing in the newborn period. The Joint Committee on Infant Hearing has identified patients at significant risk for hearing loss. All children meeting these criteria should be objectively screened. See the Joint Committee on Infant Hearing 1994 Position Statement (American Academy of Pediatrics. 1995. Joint Committee on Infant Hearing 1994 position statement. *Pediatrics* 95, no. 1:152–156).

[7] By history and appropriate physical examination; if suspicious, by specific objective developmental testing.

[8] At each visit, a complete physical examination is essential, with infant totally unclothed, older child undressed and suitably draped.

[9] These may be modified, depending upon entry point into schedule and individual need.

[10] Metabolic screening (e.g., thyroid, hemoglobinopathies, PKU, galactosemia) should be done according to state law.

[11] Schedule(s) per the Committee on Infectious Diseases, published periodically in *Pediatrics*. Every visit should be an opportunity to update and complete a child's immunizations.

[12] Blood lead screen per American Academy of Pediatrics (AAP) statement "Lead Poisoning: From Screening to Primary Prevention" (American Academy of Pediatrics. 1993. Lead poisoning: From screening to primary prevention. *Pediatrics* 92, no. 1:176–183).

[13] All menstruating adolescents should be screened.

[14] Conduct dipstick urinalysis for leukocytes for male and female adolescents.

[15] TB testing per AAP statement "Screening for Tuberculosis in Infants and Children" (American Academy of Pediatrics. 1994. Screening for tuberculosis in infants and children. *Pediatrics* 93, no. 1:131–134). Testing should be done upon recognition of high-risk factors. If results are negative but high-risk situation continues, testing should be repeated on an annual basis.

[16] Cholesterol screening for high-risk patients per American Academy of Pediatrics (AAP) statement "Statement on Cholesterol" (American Academy of Pediatrics. 1992. Statement on cholesterol. *Pediatrics* 90, no. 3:469–473). If family history cannot be ascertained and other risk factors are present, screening should be at the discretion of the physician.

[17] All sexually active patients should be screened for sexually transmitted diseases (STDs).

[18] All sexually active females should have a pelvic examination. A pelvic examination and routine pap smear should be offered as part of preventative health maintenance between the ages of 18 and 21 years.

[19] Appropriate discussion and counseling should be an integral part of each visit for care.

[20] From birth to age 12, refer to AAP's injury prevention program (TIPP) as described in "A Guide to Safety Counseling in Office Practice" (American Academy of Pediatrics. 1994. *TIPP: A guide to safety counselling in office practice.* Elk Grove Village, Ill.: Author).

[21] Earlier initial dental evaluations may be appropriate for some children. Subsequent examinations as prescribed by dentist.

5. thorax configuration, symmetry, and abnormalities
6. type of breathing (diaphragmatic, thoracic, abdominal)
7. respiratory rate/depth/rhythm
8. respiratory effort
9. use of accessory muscles
10. nasal flaring

- Airway
  1. natural or artificial
  2. patent
  3. noisy respirations without auscultation (wheeze, stridor)
  4. effective cough
- Secretions
  1. color
  2. consistency
  3. amount
- Breath sounds
  1. auscultation to all lung fields
  2. air movement or decreased aeration to areas
  3. wheeze, rales, coarseness
  4. change in breath sounds with cough
- Effect of treatment
  1. change in breath sounds with suctioning
  2. change in breath sounds with percussion and postural drainage
  3. change in breath sounds with respiratory treatment

ASSESSMENT OF GROWTH

Weight and height are important growth measurements and should be plotted on a growth chart, presented in Figures 7–1 to 7–8. Normally weight and height will remain within the same percentile range from measurement to measurement. Sudden increases or decreases in percentile should be further investigated.

Procedures for a growth assessment are as follows:

- Measurement of weight
  1. *Infants (birth to 24 months):* Undress completely, including diaper, and lay on a balanced infant scale. Protect the scale with a cloth or paper liner that is in place when the scale is balanced before obtaining weight.
  2. *Young children (two to five years):* Undress except for underpants and weigh on a standing scale. Some scales incorporate a pole that does not affect the weight measurement for the child to grasp to maintain his or her balance on the scale. *Alternative:* If the young child cannot be safely and accurately weighed on the standing scale, the adult should weigh himself or herself, then obtain a weight while holding the young child. The weight of the adult is subtracted to obtain the child's weight measurement.
  3. *Older children (5 years and older):* Remove shoes. Weigh, clothed, on a standing scale. If it is necessary to keep shoes/splints on so that child can stand, note this with measurement. *Alternative:* If the older child cannot be safely and accurately weighed on a standing scale, the use of a wheelchair or bed scale should be considered. With a wheelchair scale, a weight of the child's wheelchair is obtained; then a weight is obtained with the child in the wheelchair. The original weight of the wheelchair is subtracted to obtain the child's measurement. A bed scale allows the child to be in a recumbent position to be weighed. In each case, the scale should be balanced prior to weighing the child.
- Measurement of height
  1. *Infants (birth to 24 months):* Lay infant flat on a firm surface. Hold infant's head as legs are extended with gentle pressure. Make a mark at tip of heel with toes straight up and at vertex of head. Measure between marks with a

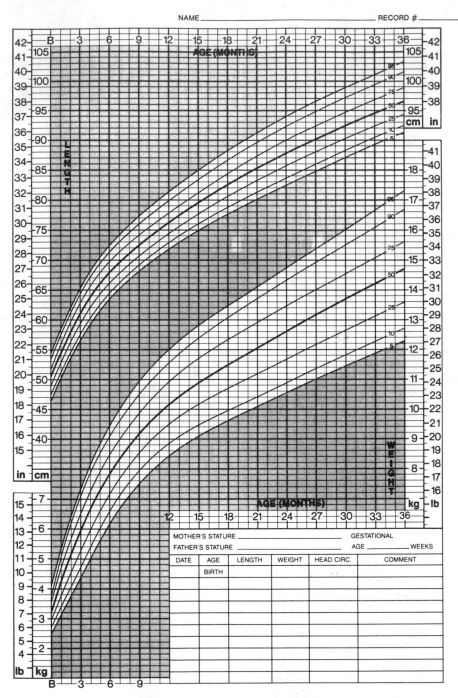

Figure 7–1 Physical Growth, Length and Weight by Age, NCHS Percentiles for Boys, Birth to 36 Months. *Source:* Used with permission of Ross Products Division, Abbott Laboratories, Columbus, OH 43216. From *NCHS Growth Charts*, © 1982 Ross Products Division, Abbott Laboratories. Adapted from: Hamill PVV, Drizd TA, Johnson CL, Reed RB, Roche AF, Moore WM: Physical growth: National Center for Health Statistics percentiles. AM J CLIN NUTR 32:607-629, 1979. Data from the Fels Longitudinal Study, Wright State University School of Medicine, Yellow Springs, Ohio.

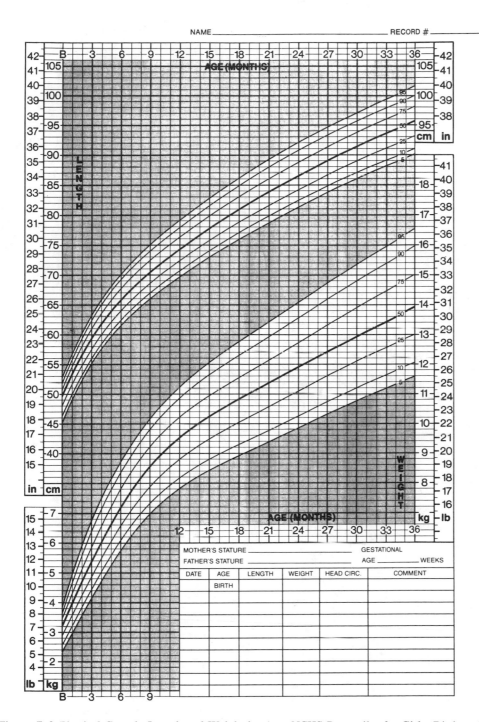

Figure 7–2 Physical Growth, Length and Weight by Age, NCHS Percentiles for Girls, Birth to 36 Months. *Source:* Used with permission of Ross Products Division, Abbott Laboratories, Columbus, OH 43216. From *NCHS Growth Charts*, © 1982 Ross Products Division, Abbott Laboratories. Adapted from: Hamill PVV, Drizd TA, Johnson CL, Reed RB, Roche AF, Moore WM: Physical growth: National Center for Health Statistics percentiles. AM J CLIN NUTR 32:607-629, 1979. Data from the Fels Longitudinal Study, Wright State University School of Medicine, Yellow Springs, Ohio.

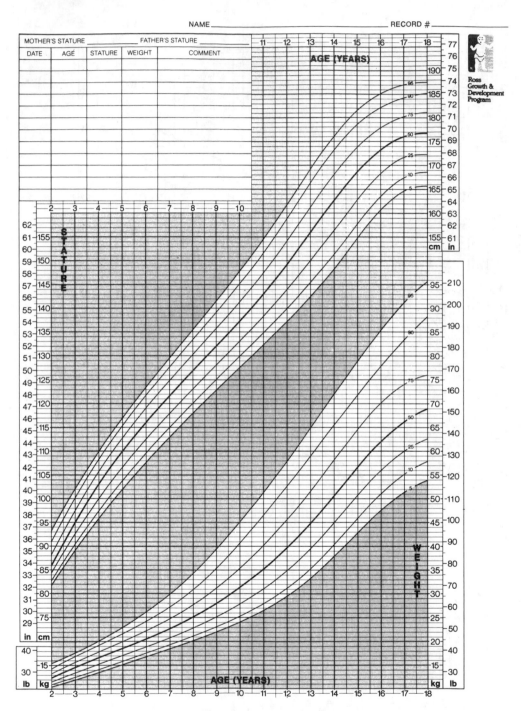

Figure 7–3 Physical Growth, Stature and Weight by Age, NCHS Percentiles for Boys, 2 to 18 Years. *Source:* Used with permission of Ross Products Division, Abbott Laboratories, Columbus, OH 43216. From *NCHS Growth Charts*, © 1982 Ross Products Division, Abbott Laboratories. Adapted from: Hamill PVV, Drizd TA, Johnson CL, Reed RB, Roche AF, Moore WM: Physical growth: National Center for Health Statistics percentiles. AM J CLIN NUTR 32:607-629, 1979. Data from the National Center for Health Statistics (NCHS), Hyattsville, Maryland.

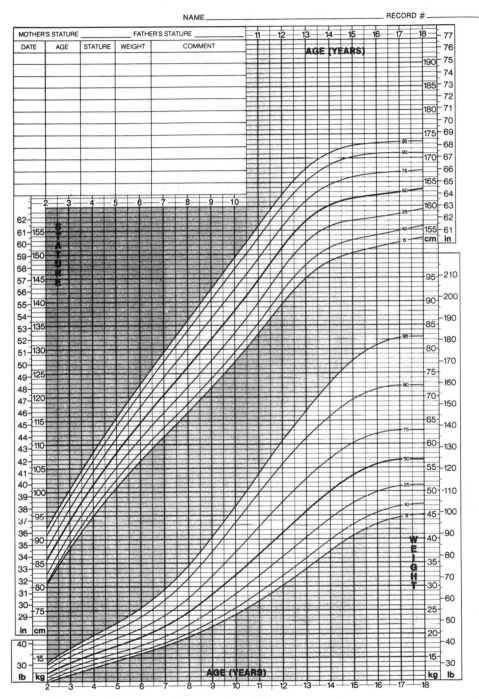

Figure 7–4 Physical Growth, Stature and Weight by Age, NCHS Percentiles for Girls, 2 to 18 Years. *Source:* Used with permission of Ross Products Division, Abbott Laboratories, Columbus, OH 43216. From *NCHS Growth Charts*, © 1982 Ross Products Division, Abbott Laboratories. Adapted from: Hamill PVV, Drizd TA, Johnson CL, Reed RB, Roche AF, Moore WM: Physical growth: National Center for Health Statistics percentiles. AM J CLIN NUTR 32:607-629, 1979. Data from the National Center for Health Statistics (NCHS), Hyattsville, Maryland.

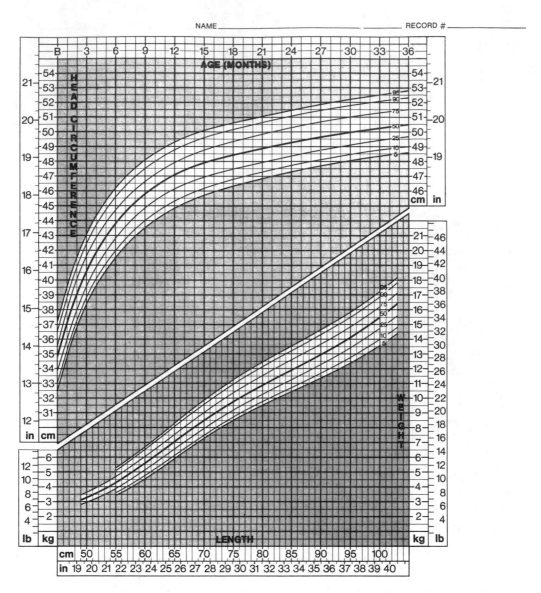

Figure 7–5 Physical Growth, Head Circumference by Age and Weight by Length, NCHS Percentiles for Boys, Birth to 36 Months. *Source:* Used with permission of Ross Products Division, Abbott Laboratories, Columbus, OH 43216. From *NCHS Growth Charts*, © 1982 Ross Products Division, Abbott Laboratories. Adapted from: Hamill PVV, Drizd TA, Johnson CL, Reed RB, Roche AF, Moore WM: Physical growth: National Center for Health Statistics percentiles. AM J CLIN NUTR 32:607-629, 1979. Data from the Fels Longitudinal Study, Wright State University School of Medicine, Yellow Springs, Ohio.

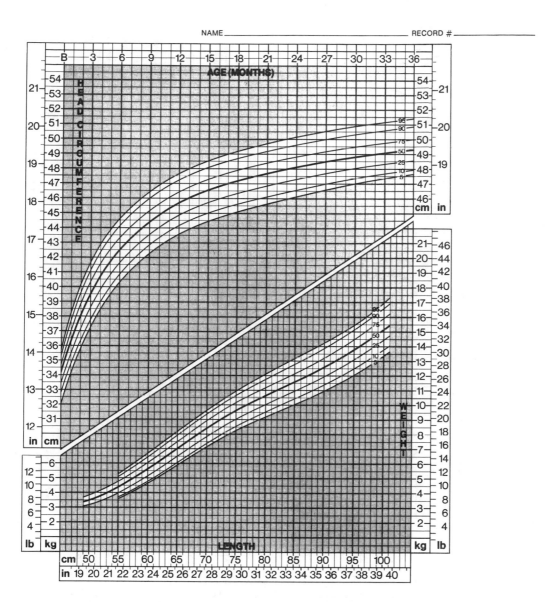

Figure 7–6 Physical Growth, Head Circumference by Age and Weight by Length, NCHS Percentiles for Girls, Birth to 36 Months. *Source:* Used with permission of Ross Products Division, Abbott Laboratories, Columbus, OH 43216. From *NCHS Growth Charts*, © 1982 Ross Products Division, Abbott Laboratories. Adapted from: Hamill PVV, Drizd TA, Johnson CL, Reed RB, Roche AF, Moore WM: Physical growth: National Center for Health Statistics percentiles. AM J CLIN NUTR 32:607-629, 1979. Data from the Fels Longitudinal Study, Wright State University School of Medicine, Yellow Springs, Ohio.

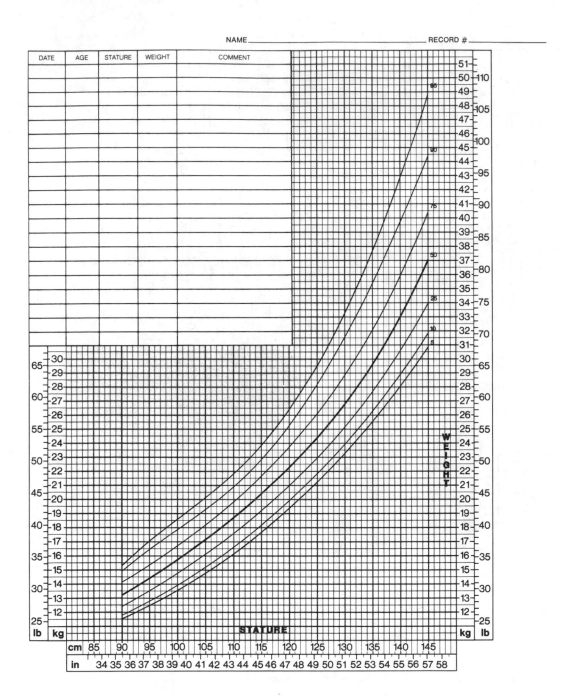

Figure 7–7 Physical Growth, Stature by Weight, NCHS Percentiles for Prepubescent Boys. *Source:* Used with permission of Ross Products Division, Abbott Laboratories, Columbus, OH 43216. From *NCHS Growth Charts*, © 1982 Ross Products Division, Abbott Laboratories. Adapted from: Hamill PVV, Drizd TA, Johnson CL, Reed RB, Roche AF, Moore WM: Physical growth: National Center for Health Statistics percentiles. AM J CLIN NUTR 32:607-629, 1979. Data from the National Center for Health Statistics (NCHS), Hyattsville, Maryland.

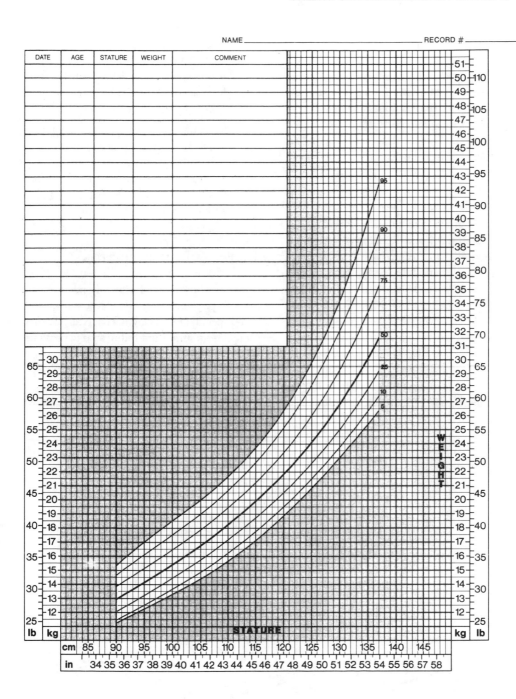

Figure 7–8 Physical Growth, Stature by Weight, NCHS Percentiles for Prepubescent Girls. *Source:* Used with permission of Ross Products Division, Abbott Laboratories, Columbus, OH 43216. From *NCHS Growth Charts*, © 1982 Ross Products Division, Abbott Laboratories. Adapted from: Hamill PVV, Drizd TA, Johnson CL, Reed RB, Roche AF, Moore WM: Physical growth: National Center for Health Statistics percentiles. AM J CLIN NUTR 32:607-629, 1979. Data from the National Center for Health Statistics (NCHS), Hyattsville, Maryland.

noncloth tape measure. *Alternative:* Use a length board that provides a firm, flat surface. Hold head firmly and gently against stationary end and move sliding plate until it comes against feet, noting measurement indicated (see Figure 7–9). This is the most accurate method of measurement.

2. *Young children (two to five years):* Have child stand up straight on a standing scale with a height measurement. Bring marker down to rest lightly on the head while straight out. Read measurement indicated. *Alternatives:* Use a stadiometer mounted level on a wall. The child should stand straight against the wall. Bring the flat portion of the stadiometer down to rest lightly on the head. Read measurement indicated (see Figure 7–10). This is the most accurate method of measurement. If the child is unable to stand, perform a length measurement as described for the infant. If

measurement is compromised by joint contracture, measure length of limb segments and note on the record. This is the least accurate method of measurement.

• Measurement of head circumference
1. Measure with paper or steel tape at greatest circumference, from slightly above the eyebrows and pinnae of the ears to occipital prominence of the skull (see Figure 7–11). Repeat measurement should agree within 0.2 cm.

ASSESSMENT OF NUTRITION

Nutritional problems frequently occur in children with physical and developmental disabilities and special health care needs. Nutritional assessment is an important initial step in providing health care and preventing problems.

Table 7–2 presents an overview of physical assessment procedures to determine adequacy of nutrition in children. These include growth

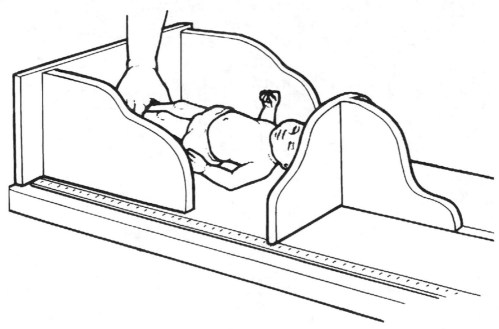

Figure 7–9 Use of a Length Board To Measure Infant's Height. *Source:* Copyright © 1996, Mark L. Batshaw, M.D.

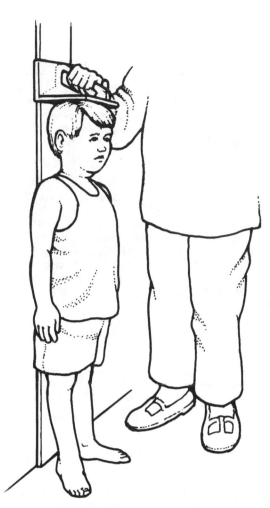

Figure 7–10 Use of a Stadiometer To Measure a Young Child's Height. *Source:* Copyright © 1996, Mark L. Batshaw, M.D.

2. problems with feeding (fatigue, poor suck, "spitting up," colic, irritability)
3. breast milk or formula
4. vitamin supplements
5. how infant communicates hunger
6. sleep-wake cycle
7. elimination patterns
8. breast milk:
   (a) length of time infant nurses
   (b) whether infant nurses on both sides at each feeding
   (c) usual diet of mother
   (d) concerns of mother
9. formula
   (a) type of formula
   (b) how formula is prepared
   (c) type of bottle/nipple
   (d) concerns of mother
10. solids
   (a) when introduced
   (b) how tolerated
   (c) textures

measurements, the procedures for which are described in detail in the previous section, as well as the assessment of a variety of other bodily signs.

Nutrition should also be assessed by interview of the caregiver and/or the child him- or herself. The following information should be obtained:

- Infants (birth to 24 months)
  1. weight gain of mother during pregnancy

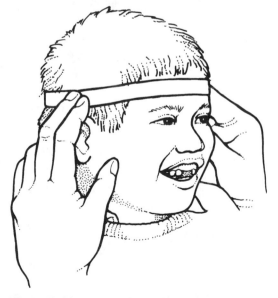

Figure 7–11 Measurement of Head Circumference. *Source:* Copyright © 1996, Mark L. Batshaw, M.D.

Table 7–2 Physical Assessment of Nutrition

Area	Signs of Adequate Nutrition	Signs of Inadequate Nutrition	Considerations with Developmental Disabilities
Overall growth	Height/weight/head circumference within 5th to 95th percentile; continues along same percentile measurement to measurement	Height/weight/head circumference below 5th or above 95th percentile; sudden increase or decrease in percentile	Child frequently is lower than 5th percentile. Monitor growth pattern on child's own curve
Sexual development	Sexual development as age appropriate	Sexual maturation may be delayed; possibly disruption in menses	Sexual characteristics may be premature or delayed
Skin	Elastic, firm, slightly dry; no lesions, rashes, altered pigmentation	Dryness, lesions, change in pigmentation, poor turgor, edema, delayed healing, decreased subcutaneous tissue, pallor	Nutritional issues often influence condition of skin. Immobility, bracing, splinting often contribute to skin breakdown
Hair	Shiny, firm	Dull, dry, thin, brittle, sparse	
Head	Evenly molded, facial features symmetrical, sutures fused by 12–18 months	Skull flattened, suture fusion delayed	Skull shape may be altered in infancy with prolonged hospitalization related to positioning
Neck	Thyroid gland not obvious on inspection; palpable in midline	Thyroid gland obvious to inspection	
Eyes	Clear, bright, shiny; membranes pink and moist	Dull; white or gray spots on cornea; pale membranes; burning, itching, sensitivity	Anemia may contribute to pale membranes
Nose	Smooth, intact nasal angle	Cracks, irritation at nasal angle	
Lips	Smooth, moist, no edema	Angular fissures, redness, edema	
Tongue	Deep pink, papillae visible, moist, taste sensation intact, no edema	Red, swollen, raw; decreased taste	Persistent extrusion reflex (tongue thrust) may contribute to delay in accepting solid foods
Gums	Firm, coral color	Spongy, bleed easily, receding	Condition of gums may be compromised by medication (e.g., Dilantin)

Area	Signs of Adequate Nutrition	Signs of Inadequate Nutrition	Considerations with Developmental Disabilities
Teeth	White, smooth, no spots or pits	Mottled enamel, brown spots, pits; defective enamel, caries	
Cardiovascular	Pulse and blood pressure within normal limits	Palpitations, rapid pulse, arrhythmia	Cardiovascular effects of medications should be considered
Gastrointestinal	Bowel habits normal for age	Constipation, diarrhea	Gastroesophageal reflux may contribute to loss of calories or food refusal. Constipation may be related to decreased muscle tone and physical activity. Diarrhea may be associated with neuro-genic bowel
Musculoskeletal	Muscles firm and well developed, joints flexible and pain-free, extremi-ties symmetrical and straight	Muscles atrophied, dependent edema, bleeding into joints, pain, beading on ribs	Muscle strength and joints may be affected by neuromuscular or rheumatic conditions
Neurological	Behavior alert and responsive; intact muscle innervation		

Source: From *Pocket Guide to Pediatric Assessment*, 2nd ed, by J. Engel, 1993, St. Louis, MO: Mosby-Yearbook. Copyright © 1986 by Mosby-Yearbook. Adapted by permission.

- Toddlers/young children
  1. food preferences
  2. balance of foods from all groups
  3. "food jags"
  4. snacks; type and frequency
  5. fluids
- Adolescents
  1. food preferences/dislikes
  2. choices for snacks
  3. quantity of food at meals/snacks
  4. frequency of meals/day
  5. dieting
  6. level of physical activity (sports, fitness)
  7. female—beginning menstruation; use of contraceptives

It is important to recognize that dietary practices are very personal. Efforts to give the "correct" answer can affect the accuracy of the assessment. Religious and cultural practices can also influence the child's diet and eating habits.

ASSESSMENT OF FEEDING

Many children with neurodevelopmental disabilities and special health care needs require specialized feeding procedures. Intolerance or safety concerns may indicate a need to administer enteral feedings. When providing nourishment in any form, it is important to preserve the feeding environment and behaviors as much as possible, providing a foundation in order to progress when the child's condition changes. For example, an infant receiving a nasogastric (NG) tube feeding is held during the feeding and offered a pacifier. In this way, an association is made between these nurturing behaviors and the pleasurable feeling of having hunger satisfied. Assessment of feeding behaviors is important to implement techniques that will foster the development of future skills. Features to be noted are as follows:

- Bottle feeding
  1. accepts stimulation to face and oral cavity without hyperactive gag reflex
  2. protective airway reflexes intact
  3. able to close mouth around nipple sufficiently to create suction
  4. able to express milk from nipple without overexertion
  5. coordinated suck/swallow/breathing pattern
  6. able to accept sufficient quantity before tiring
  7. able to retain fluid in stomach without reflux or regurgitation
- Spoon feeding/pureed foods (Note: in most instances, pureed foods or thickened liquids are managed more easily than liquids by individuals with decreased oromotor control)
  1. extrusion reflex (tongue thrust) decreased
  2. accepts spoon to mouth without hyperactive gag reflex
  3. able to close lips around spoon
  4. accepts/tolerates texture in mouth
  5. able to move food from front of mouth to back of mouth
  6. able to coordinate swallow/breathing pattern
- Increased textures/soft foods
  1. able to move food laterally side to side in mouth

  2. able to masticate foods of soft consistency
  3. able to move food from front of mouth to back of mouth
  4. able to coordinate swallow/breathing pattern
- Finger feeding/crunchy foods
  1. able to bite off from crunchy food
  2. able to move food to back molars and laterally side to side
  3. able to masticate food sufficiently and to mix with saliva to prevent crumbling
  4. able to coordinate swallow/breathing pattern
- Enteral feeding via nasogastric or gastrostomy tube
  1. able to tolerate tube and introduction of fluid to stomach without hyperactive gag reflex
  2. able to tolerate feeding administration at specified rate (continuous or bolus)
  3. able to retain fluid in stomach without reflux or regurgitation
  4. accepts nurturing feeding behavior associated with enteral feeding (e.g., non-nutritive sucking, holding, high chair, toddler chair, play with food stuff, tastes of food, sitting with peers at mealtime)
  5. low, or no, residual volumes prior to subsequent feeding

ASSESSMENT OF REST

Many children with physical and developmental disabilities and special health care needs require a different balance in activity and rest than their peers. Energy requirements may be higher due to increased work of the body to perform otherwise normal activities such as breathing, walking, and attending to instruction. Additional strength and energy reserves are necessary for wheelchair mobility and transfers. An assessment of activity/rest patterns is important to ensure adequate energy reserve. Features to be noted are as follows:

- Sleep
  1. child's usual bedtime
  2. child's usual morning awakening
  3. periods awake at night (frequency, duration)
  4. periods of nap during day (frequency, duration)
  5. total amount of sleep/day
- Activity
  1. description of child's usual day
  2. description of how child performs certain activities
  3. periods of increased and decreased activity alternating through day
  4. "short-cuts" child has developed to perform activities
- Fatigue
  1. amount/level of activity before fatigue noted
  2. response of child to feelings of fatigue
  3. actions that relieve feelings of fatigue

ASSESSMENT OF THE SKIN

Assessment of the skin should be an integral part of every health assessment. Many common physiologic problems have associated signs that are apparent on the skin (e.g., inadequate nutrition/hydration, contagious viral diseases). Children with physical and developmental disabilities and special health care needs are especially at risk for compromise to the skin due to issues of altered nutrition/hydration, pressure from immobility or splints/braces, and increased contact with bodily fluids (e.g., oral and tracheal secretions, incontinence of bowel and bladder, gastric contents at an ostomy site).

The skin consists of three layers:

1. *epidermis:* the outermost layer
2. *dermis:* underlies the epidermis; contains blood vessels, lymphatic vessels, hair follicles, and nerves
3. *subcutaneous tissue:* underlies the dermis, helps to cushion and insulate the body; contains sweat and sebaceous glands, which are important in the effects of thermoregulation and protection of skin from infection

Overall, the skin has four main functions:

1. protection against injury
2. thermoregulation
3. impermeability
4. sensation of touch, pain, heat, and cold

Assessment of the skin includes assessment of the nails and hair as well. Features to be noted are as follows:

- Skin
  1. color/pigmentation
  2. odor
  3. turgor
  4. elasticity
  5. dryness/moisture
  6. circulation
  7. areas of redness/lesions
     (a) primary lesions
        i. macule: small, flat mass differing from surrounding skin (e.g., freckle)
        ii. papule: small, raised solid mass
        iii. nodule: slightly larger solid, raised mass; deeper than papule
        iv. tumor: solid, raised mass; larger than nodule; may be hard or soft
        v. wheal: irregularly shaped, transient area of skin edema (e.g., hive, insect bite).
        vi. vesicle: small, raised, fluid-filled mass (e.g., cold sore, chicken pox)
        vii. bulla: raised, fluid-filled mass; larger than a vesicle (e.g., second-degree burn)

viii. pustule: vesicle containing purulent drainage (e.g., acne, impetigo, staphylococcal infection)

(b) secondary lesions

i. scale: thin flake of exfoliated epidermis (e.g., psoriasis, dandruff)

ii. crust: dried residue of serum, blood, or purulent drainage (e.g., eczema)

iii. erosion: moist lesion resulting from loss of superficial epidermis (e.g., ruptured lesion in varicella/chicken pox)

iv. ulcer: deep loss of skin surface; may extend to dermis and subcutaneous tissue (decubitus ulcer)

v. fissure: deep linear crack in skin (e.g., athlete's foot)

vi. striae: thin white or purple stripes, commonly found on abdomen; resulting from weight gain and loss

(c) purpuric lesions

i. petechia: small, flat, round, deep red or purplish mass

ii. ecchymosis: mass of variable size and shape; initially purplish, fading to green, yellow, then brown

• Nails
  1. color
  2. shape
  3. condition
  4. nail biting
  5. skin picking
  6. infection
  7. clubbing of fingers

• Hair
  1. distribution
  2. color
  3. texture
  4. amount
  5. quality
  6. signs of lice (eggs)

SUGGESTED READINGS

American Academy of Pediatrics. 1995. Recommendations for preventive pediatric health care. *Pediatrics*, 96(2), 373–374.

Engel, J. 1993. *Pocket guide to pediatric assessment.* 2nd ed. St. Louis: Mosby-Yearbook.

Faine, M.P. 1994. Dental nutrition concerns of children with developmental disabilities. *Infant-Toddler Intervention: The Transdisciplinary Journal* 4, no. 1: 11–24.

Hagelgans, N. 1993. Pediatric skin care issues for the home care nurse. *Pediatric Nursing* 19:499–507.

Pipes, P.L., ed. 1993. *Nutrition in infancy and childhood.* 5th ed. St. Louis: C.V. Mosby Co.

Pipes, P.L., and R.P. Glass. 1993. Nutrition and feeding of children with developmental delay and related problems. In *Nutrition in infancy and childhood*, 5th ed., ed. P.L. Pipes, 345–370. St. Louis: C.V. Mosby Co.

Wong, D.L., and L.F. Whaley. 1990. *Clinical manual of pediatric nursing.* 3rd ed. St. Louis: C.V. Mosby Co.

PROCEDURES FOR MUSCULOSKELETAL ASSESSMENT

Shirley A. Scull and Lisa A. Kurtz

Purpose: to describe clinical procedures commonly used to assess musculoskeletal dysfunction in children, especially limitations in flexibility and strength.

RANGE OF MOTION (ROM)

Range of motion is the arc of motion, measured in degrees of a circle, through which a joint can be moved. It may be *active* (patient performs motion without assistance) or *passive* (examiner moves limb to limit of motion).

Screening for active ROM is used to screen functional motion. Active ROM may be limited by *contracture* (loss of motion at a joint, often due to muscle tightness or joint adhesions), weakness, or pain. Screening is conducted by the upper extremity (UE) screen (Apley Scratch Tests, Hoppenfield, 1976), or Simon Says, in which the examinee is requested to assume the following positions (see Figures 7–12 through 7–19):

1. arms overhead
2. hands behind head
3. hands behind waist
4. elbows bent, palms up
5. arms straight out in front
6. prayer position
7. grasp
8. release

Lower extremity (LE) screening consists of

1. observing the patient walk
2. observing the patient stoop and recover (appropriate for over 15 months)

Screening for passive ROM is used to determine flexibility of a joint. The examiner applies light overpressure to determine end-feel.

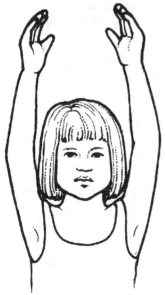

Figure 7–12 Active ROM Upper Extremity Screen, Arms Overhead Position. *Source:* Copyright © 1996, Mark L. Batshaw, M.D.

Figure 7–13 Active ROM Upper Extremity Screen, Hands Behind Head Position. *Source:* Copyright © 1996, Mark L. Batshaw, M.D.

Figure 7–14 Active ROM Upper Extremity Screen, Hands Behind Waist Position. *Source:* Copyright © 1996, Mark L. Batshaw, M.D.

Figure 7–16 Active ROM Upper Extremity Screen, Arms Straight Out in Front Position. *Source:* Copyright © 1996, Mark L. Batshaw, M.D.

Figure 7–15 Active ROM Upper Extremity Screen; Elbows Bent, Palms Up Position. *Source:* Copyright © 1996, Mark L. Batshaw, M.D.

Figure 7–17 Active ROM Upper Extremity Screen, Prayer Position. *Source:* Copyright © 1996, Mark L. Batshaw, M.D.

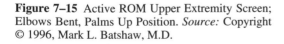

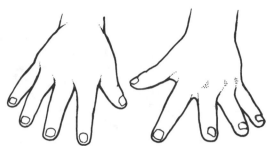

Figure 7–18 Active ROM Upper Extremity Screen, Grasp Position. *Source:* Copyright © 1996, Mark L. Batshaw, M.D.

Figure 7–19 Active ROM Upper Extremity Screen, Release Position. *Source:* Copyright © 1996, Mark L. Batshaw, M.D.

Table 7–3 shows normal values of range of motion for children over five years and for neonates (if different).

Some special ROM tests are

- Thomas test for hip flexion contracture (Figure 7 20)
- Ober test for tight iliotibial band (Figure 7–21)
- straight leg raising—hamstring length (Figure 7–22)
- popliteal angle—hamstring length (Figure 7–23)
- gastrocnemius test (Figure 7–24)
- test for intrinsic tightness (IP joints cannot be forced into flexion with MP joint fully extended; IP joints flex freely when MP joint allowed to flex; Figure 7–25)
- tests for extrinsic tightness
  1. IP joints flex freely when MP joint is extended; with MP joint flexed, it is difficult to flex IP joints
  2. long finger and thumb flexors: with the fingers and thumb in extension, measure the amount of active/passive wrist extension
  3. long finger and thumb extensors: with the fingers and thumb in flexion, measure the amount of active/passive wrist flexion

Table 7–3 Normal Values of Range of Motion

Normal Values (in Degrees)	Over 5 Years	Neonate Values (if Different)
Shoulder:		
Flexion	0–180	
Abduction	0–180	0–130
Extension	0–50	
External rotation	0–90	
Internal rotation	0–70	
Elbow:		
Flexion	0–140	30–140
Supination	0–90	
Pronation	0–90	
Wrist:		
Extension	0–70	
Flexion	0–70	
Finger:		
MCP flexion	0–90	
PIP flexion	0–120	
DIP flexion	0–60	
Hip:		
Flexion	0–120	30–120
Extension	0–20	–30
Abduction	0–45	0–70
Adduction	0–20	0–5
External rotation	0–45	0–90
Internal rotation	0–45	0–70
Knee:		
Flexion	0–135	20–135
Extension	0	–20
Ankle:		
Dorsiflexion	0–20	0–60
Plantarflexion	0–50	0–25
Inversion	0–20	
Eversion	0–10	

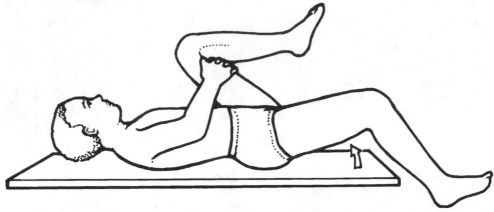

Figure 7–20 Thomas Test for Hip Flexion Contracture. *Source:* Copyright © 1996, Mark L. Batshaw, M.D.

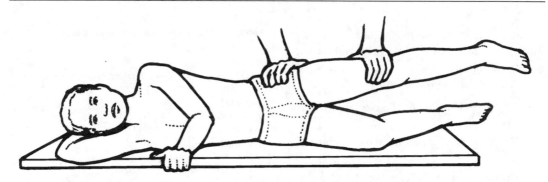

Figure 7–21 Ober Test for Tight Iliotibial Band. *Source:* Copyright © 1996, Mark L. Batshaw, M.D.

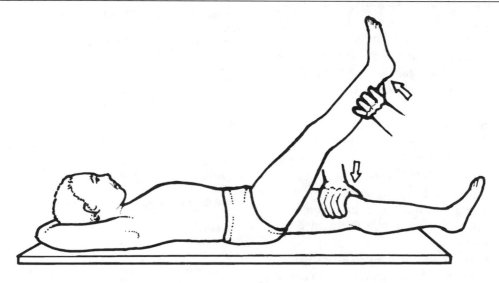

Figure 7–22 Straight Leg Raising—Hamstring Length Assessment. *Source:* Copyright © 1996, Mark L. Batshaw, M.D.

Figure 7–23 Popliteal Angle— Hamstring Length Assessment. *Source:* Copyright © 1996, Mark L. Batshaw, M.D.

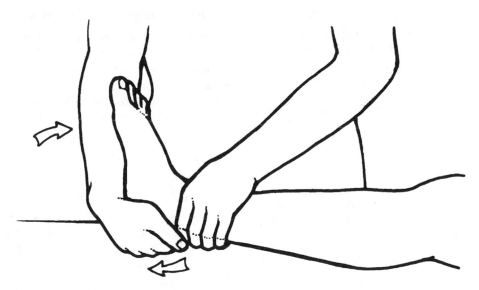

Figure 7–24 Gastrocnemius Test. *Source:* Copyright © 1996, Mark L. Batshaw, M.D.

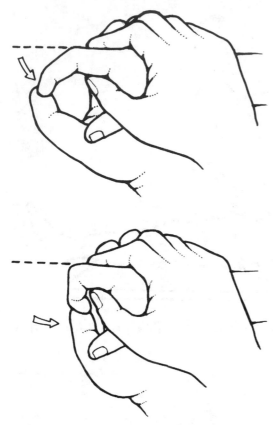

Figure 7–25 Test for Intrinsic Tightness, IP and MP Joints. *Source:* Copyright © 1996, Mark L. Batshaw, M.D.

Neonate's range of motion differs somewhat from that of older children. They are in physiological flexion. Although they have normal hip and knee flexion contractures, they have excessive ankle dorsiflexion. Their legs can be placed in frog position, with increased abduction and external rotation. In general, dorsiflexion is increased, and plantarflexion is decreased. Radiologic differences are

1. increased femoral angle of inclination
2. increased femoral anteversion
3. internal tibial torsion
4. varus posture of feet

The examiner should try to control the infant's behavioral state and avoid a crying infant if possible. The infant's head should be positioned in midline to avoid asymmetric tonic neck reflex. All motions should be symmetrical.

STRENGTH

Manual Muscle Testing

Strength is graded as follows on an ordinal scale based on the ability to move the limb against gravity and manual resistance:

- 5 (Normal): muscle contraction against gravity through full ROM with manual resistance that cannot break the force
- 4 (Good): muscle contraction against gravity through full ROM with moderate manual resistance
- 3 (Fair): muscle contraction against gravity through full available ROM
- 2 (Poor): muscle contraction with gravity minimized, such as on a powder board, through full ROM
- 1 (Trace): palpable muscle contraction without motion
- 0 (Zero): no palpable contraction

The examiner should start with a fair test for each muscle and move up or down the scale depending on results. Each grade may have a plus or minus to qualify further.

Recommended procedures for infant muscle testing are as follow (Connolly 1995):

- Test muscles in functional groups
- Grade grossly as normal/fair/zero
- Techniques
  1. observe spontaneous motion
  2. elicit and observe primitive reflexes
  3. elicit and observe righting and equilibrium reactions
  4. restrict limb in awkward position
  5. use sensory stimulation such as tickling
- Head and neck: sample tests
  1. visual tracking of toy
  2. pull-to-sit
  3. observe neck extension in prone

- Trunk: sample tests
  1. pull-to-sit
  2. strength of cry
  3. getting to sitting
  4. prone skills
- Upper extremities: sample tests
  1. arms flailing when excited or crying
  2. restrict arm overhead or across chest
  3. grasp reflex
  4. Moro reflex: look for symmetry
  5. pull-to-sit
  6. protective extension
  7. prone skills requiring weightbearing on arms
- Lower extremities: sample tests
  1. spontaneous kicking
  2. hold knees to chest
  3. tickle feet
  4. prone, with legs dangling over lap or edge of table
  5. Landau reflex
  6. crawling; creeping
  7. pull-to-stand

8. recurvatum in stance
9. stand and bounce

Dynamometry

Dynamometers are instruments designed to measure certain aspects of grip and pinch strength. Several different models are available. When considering normative values for strength, it is important to apply norms that have been developed for a particular model (see Tables 7–4 through 7–9).

Table 7–4 Hand Strength Norms, Elmed Vigorimeter

Group	Hand Strength Norms
Children	
3 years	0.12 kPa
5 years	0.3 to 0.7 kPa
7 years	0.4 to 0.8 kPa
Adolescents	0.4 to 1.2 kPa
Adults (F)	0.7 to 1.2 kPa
Adults (M)	0.8 to 1.3 kPa

Source: From Elmed Vigorimeter Company. Reprinted by permission.
Note: This instrument is available from Elmed Vigorimeter, 60 West Fay Avenue, Addison, IL 60101.

Table 7–5 Grip Strength Norms, in Pounds, Smedley Dynamometer

Age	Male/Right	Male/Left	Female/Right	Female/Left
6	9.21	8.48	8.36	7.74
7	10.74	10.11	9.88	9.24
8	12.41	11.67	11.16	10.48
9	14.34	13.47	12.77	11.97
10	16.32	15.59	14.65	13.72
11	18.85	17.72	16.54	15.52
12	21.24	19.71	18.92	17.78
13	24.44	22.51	21.84	20.39
14	28.42	26.22	24.79	22.92
15	33.39	30.83	27.00	24.92
16	39.37	36.39	28.70	26.56
17	44.74	40.96	29.56	27.43
18	49.28	45.01	29.75	27.66

Source: From Lafayette Instrument Company. Reprinted by permission.
Note: The Smedley Dynamometer is available from the Lafayette Instrument Company, Bypass 52 and N. 9th Street Road, Lafayette, IN 47902.

Table 7–6 Grip Strength Norms, in Pounds, Jamar Dynamometer Set at Second Position

Age	Hand	Males			Females		
		Mean	*SD*	*Range*	*Mean*	*SD*	*Range*
6–7	R	32.5	4.8	21–42	28.6	4.4	20–39
	L	30.7	5.4	18–38	27.1	4.4	16–36
8–9	R	41.9	7.4	27–61	35.3	8.3	18–55
	L	39.0	9.3	19–63	33.0	6.9	16–49
10–11	R	53.9	9.7	35–79	49.7	8.1	37–82
	L	48.4	10.8	26–73	45.2	6.8	32–59
12–13	R	58.7	15.5	33–98	56.8	10.6	39–79
	L	55.4	16.9	22–107	50.9	11.9	25–76
14–15	R	77.3	15.4	49–108	58.1	12.3	30–93
	L	64.4	14.9	41–94	49.3	11.9	26–73
16–17	R	94.0	19.4	64–149	67.3	16.5	23–126
	L	78.5	19.1	41–123	56.9	14.0	23–87
18–19	R	108.0	24.6	64–172	71.6	12.3	46–90
	L	93.0	27.8	53–149	61.7	12.5	41–186

Source: From "Grip and pinch strength: Norms for 6-to-19 year olds" by V. Mathiowetz et al., 1986. *American Journal of Occupational Therapy* 40, 705–711. Copyright 1986 by American Occupational Therapy Association. Reprinted by permission.

Table 7–7 Tip Pinch Strength Norms (Thumb Tip to Index Finger), in Pounds, B & L Pinch Gauge

Age	Hand	Males			Females		
		Mean	*SD*	*Range*	*Mean*	*SD*	*Range*
6–7	R	7.2	1.6	4–10	6.7	1.2	4–10
	L	7.1	1.4	5–11	6.1	1.5	3–10
8–9	R	8.6	2.2	6–17	7.6	1.4	5–10
	L	8.3	2.2	4–15	7.2	1.3	5–10
10–11	R	10.0	2.4	5–16	9.7	1.4	7–13
	L	9.5	2.3	5–16	9.4	1.7	6–12
12–13	R	10.5	2.5	5–14	10.6	2.2	6–17
	L	9.8	2.3	5–13	10.1	2.3	5–17
14–15	R	13.1	2.9	8–20	10.2	2.3	5–15
	L	12.6	3.0	6–18	9.5	2.4	4–17
16–17	R	15.0	2.7	11–21	11.9	2.3	9–19
	L	13.8	2.7	7–22	11.1	2.3	7–17
18–19	R	17.0	3.8	10–31	13.5	2.8	7–20
	L	16.1	3.8	11–29	13.4	2.9	8–20

Source: From "Grip and pinch strength: Norms for 6-to-19 year olds" by V. Mathiowetz et al., 1986. *American Journal of Occupational Therapy* 40, 705–711. Copyright 1986 by American Occupational Therapy Association. Reprinted by permission.

Table 7–8 Palmar Pinch (Thumb Pad to Pads Index/Middle), in Pounds, B & L Pinch Gauge

Age	Hand	Males			Females		
		Mean	SD	Range	Mean	SD	Range
6–7	R	10.0	2.2	5–13	9.0	1.7	6–12
	L	9.2	2.0	5–13	8.4	1.4	6–11
8–9	R	11.6	2.3	7–17	10.7	2.1	8–17
	L	11.2	2.8	6–16	10.3	2.2	6–20
10–11	R	13.9	2.7	7–21	13.5	2.2	11–22
	L	13.2	2.9	8–23	12.6	2.0	10–17
12–13	R	15.5	3.6	8–26	15.4	2.6	11–23
	L	15.1	4.1	8–23	14.2	2.8	10–20
14–15	R	19.2	4.2	11–28	15.6	3.3	9–26
	L	18.8	5.0	10–33	14.7	3.4	8–25
16–17	R	22.2	5.0	17–39	17.8	3.9	12–27
	L	20.3	4.1	14–31	16.6	3.9	10–26
18–19	R	23.8	4.3	17–34	20.2	3.3	10–26
	L	23.4	4.5	16–34	19.0	3.0	14–25

Source: From "Grip and pinch strength: Norms for 6-to-19 year olds" by V. Mathiowetz et al., 1986. *American Journal of Occupational Therapy* 40, 705–711. Copyright 1986 by American Occupational Therapy Association. Reprinted by permission.

Table 7–9 Key Pinch (Thumb Pad against Radial Side of Index between DIP and PIP), in Pounds, B & L Pinch Gauge

Age	Hand	Males			Females		
		Mean	SD	Range	Mean	SD	Range
6–7	R	11.3	2.0	7–16	9.6	1.5	6–12
	L	10.6	2.1	4–15	9.1	1.5	5–11
8–9	R	13.1	2.6	9–18	11.6	2.6	8–23
	L	12.2	2.5	8–20	11.3	2.1	8–21
10–11	R	15.3	3.1	9–22	14.2	2.1	11–21
	L	14.5	2.9	9–22	13.3	2.0	11–19
12–13	R	16.6	2.9	11–22	15.2	2.6	11–22
	L	15.6	2.8	10–21	14.1	3.0	10–23
14–15	R	20.9	3.8	14–32	15.6	2.5	12–22
	L	19.9	3.7	12–26	14.8	2.7	7–22
16–17	R	23.3	3.4	14–31	17.3	3.0	12–27
	L	21.8	3.6	13–30	16.6	3.1	11–25
18–19	R	23.5	4.1	17–34	18.1	2.4	12–23
	L	22.9	4.0	14–33	17.2	2.5	12–22

Source: From "Grip and pinch strength: Norms for 6-to-19 year olds" by V. Mathiowetz et al., 1986. *American Journal of Occupational Therapy* 40, 705–711. Copyright 1986 by American Occupational Therapy Association. Reprinted by permission.

GAIT ANALYSIS

Qualities of Gait for New Walker (12 Months of Age)

- General observations
  1. wide base of support
  2. increased time in double limb support
  3. staccato movements
- Arms
  1. high guard—shoulder abduction and elbow flexion
  2. no reciprocal arm swing
- Stance
  1. whole foot at foot contact
  2. loading response—no knee flexion wave or plantar flexion
  3. increased knee flexion and ankle dorsiflexion during midstance
  4. lacks heel rise and hip extension at toe off
- Swing
  1. steppage gait
  2. increased anterior pelvic tilt and pelvic rotation
  3. increased hip flexion, abduction, and external rotation
- Timing
  1. cadence = 120 steps/minute
  2. step length = 20 cm
  3. walking velocity = 60 cm/second

Qualities of Maturing Gait Components

- General observations
  1. base of support within lateral dimensions of trunk
  2. increased percent of single-limb stance as limb stability improves
  3. mature gait components present by 2½ years

- Arms
  1. down at sides
  2. reciprocal arm swing
- Stance
  1. heel strike present at foot contact, with knee extension
  2. loading response—knee flexion wave with plantarflexion
  3. knee extension at midstance
  4. hip extension and heel rise at toe off
- Swing
  1. hip flexion with knee extension during mid- and terminal swing, ankle dorsiflexion
  2. decreased steppage gait
- Timing
  1. cadence decreases
  2. step length increases, as limb length increases
  3. walking velocity increases

SPECIAL MUSCULOSKELETAL TESTS

- Leg lengths
  1. actual leg length—ASIS to medial malleolus
  2. apparent leg length—umbilicus to medial malleolus
  3. Galeazzi's sign—lying in supine with hips and knees flexed (hooklying) and check height of knees
  4. standing—site pelvic brims and PSIS from posterior view
  5. special x-rays may be ordered if discrepancy requires exact documentation
- Girth
  1. figure eight at ankle
  2. circumference in relationship to various bony landmarks
- Posture
  1. view anterior, posterior, and laterally against a plumb line or posture grid

2. forward head
3. trunk alignment
   (a) scoliosis screen—bend-over test
   (b) kyphosis
   (c) lordosis
   (d) pelvic tilt

(e) pelvic obliquity
4. lower extremity alignment
   (a) genu varus/valgus
   (b) rotational abnormalities
   (c) genu recurvatum
   (d) ankle pronation/supination

REFERENCES

Conolly, B. 1995. Testing in infants and children. In *Daniels and Worthingham's Muscle Testing*, 6th ed., ed. H.J. Hislop and J. Montgomery, 238–260. Philadelphia: W.B. Saunders Co.

Hoppenfeld, S. 1976. *Physical examination of the spine and extremities*. New York: Appleton-Century-Crofts.

Mathiowetz, V., et al. 1986. Grip and pinch strength: Norms for 6-to-19 year olds. *American Journal of Occupational Therapy* 40: 705–711.

ADDITIONAL SUGGESTED READINGS

Pedretti, L.W. 1990a. Evaluation of muscle strength. In *Occupational therapy practice skills for physical dysfunction*, 3rd ed., ed. L.W. Pedretti and B. Zoltan, 89–130. St. Louis: C.V. Mosby Co.

Pedretti, L.W. 1990b. Methods of evaluation and treatment for patients with physical dysfunction: Evaluation of joint range of motion. In *Occupational therapy practice skills for physical dysfunction*, 3rd ed., ed. L.W. Pedretti and B. Zoltan, 61–88. St. Louis: C.V. Mosby Co.

ASSESSMENT OF SENSATION: SENSIBILITY TESTING

Stephanie R. Ried

Purpose: to describe the importance of cutaneous and cortical sensation, considerations for assessment (e.g., age, testing environment), the types of functions of sensory modalities to be evaluated, and the techniques available to assess function.

GENERAL PRINCIPLES

Sensibility testing is important because information generated by the somatosensory system

1. provides critical information for effective motor performance
2. constitutes a very important protective mechanism that allows us to function safely in our environment

In the examination and interpretation of both cutaneous and cortical sensory functions, the age of the child is an important consideration. A complete examination is possible only in older children with adequate cognitive abilities. Usu-

ally a developmentally normal child of five or six years of age is able to participate in objective evaluation of pain, temperature, vibration, proprioception, two-point discrimination, graphesthesia, and topagnosis. It is especially important when evaluating younger children and infants to be patient and to make the child as relaxed and comfortable as is feasible. Awareness of behavioral changes concomitant with introduction of stimuli is critical in evaluating children who are developmentally under two years of age.

Testing should be done in a quiet environment to minimize distractions. The examiner should be alert for sounds made by the testing instrument before or during administration of the stimulus that may effect a change in behavior or cue the child to a change in stimulus.

Perceptions of heat, cold, deep pressure, and low-grade repetitive pressure are protective sensations that denote the ability to sense painful or potentially harmful stimuli to the skin or subcutaneous tissues.

Cortical sensory functions include stereognosis, graphesthesia, two-point discrimination, and topagnosis. These processes involve complex processing and require a higher level of attentiveness and cooperation on the part of the child. For this reason, tests of these functions are usually reserved for children five years or older, although the maturity and developmental level of the individual child must always be taken into consideration. In addition, intact cutaneous sensation and proprioception are prerequisites for testing these functions. In younger children, poor spontaneous function and visual monitoring while an extremity is used are suggestive of impairment. Impairment in these areas is usually associated with parietal lobe injury.

Peripheral sensory modalities include light touch and deep pressure, vibration and temperature sense, pain, and proprioception.

EXAMINATION TECHNIQUES

Peripheral Sensory Modalities

Light touch and deep pressure sensibility are felt to represent the extremes of the spectrum of cutaneous sensation. Light touch is necessary for fine discrimination and is perceived by receptors in the superficial skin layers. Pressure, on the other hand, is detected by receptors in the subcutaneous and deeper tissue and represents a form of protective sensation, warning of either deep pressure or low-grade repetitive pressure that might result in injury to the skin. In infants and very young children, light touch sensation may be assessed by observing the child's behavioral response to stroking of the extremities. The older child can verbalize whether he or she senses light touch. More precise measurements of light touch or deep pressure can be obtained by using the Semmes–Weinstein Pressure Aesthesiometer, which is composed of a series of 20 graduated nylon monofilament probes attached to a polymethylmethacrylate (Lucite) rod. Each probe is calibrated in terms of the force required to buckle that filament. The forces required for these probes to buckle ranges

from 0.0045 grams for the finest filament to 448 grams for the thickest filament. Deficits should be characterized by dermatomal distribution and relationship to nonimpaired areas.

Vibration sense (pallesthesia) can be grossly assessed even in very young children on the basis of the behavioral response to a tuning fork applied to a bony prominence. Range of responses may include a surprised facial expression, cessation of activity, or withdrawal. A more sensitive assessment can be done in older children by asking the child to close his or her eyes and by placing the handle of the tuning fork on a bony prominence and asking the child to indicate when the vibration is no longer felt by saying "stop" or holding up a hand. A 128-Hz tuning fork is used, and the base of the tuning fork is applied perpendicularly to the area with a pressure equal to its weight. This decreases variability of response due to differences in the pressure of application. In addition, the examiner may control for differences in vibration amplitude of the tuning fork, to some extent, by always hitting its prongs with sufficient force each time to cause the prongs to touch each other and emit a sound.

Temperature sense, though not usually assessed during routine clinical exam, should always be tested when pain sense is impaired. Both pain and temperature fibers travel within the spinal cord in the spinothalamic tract, from which fibers then extend to the thalamus and on to the cerebral cortex. Test tubes or cylinders filled with hot and cold water have been used to evaluate thermal discrimination, but this method is very gross and of limited value in serial assessments due to lack of control of the temperature of the water. Heat-transfer characteristics of different materials were used to develop the Minnesota Thermal Disks, which use copper and polyvinyl chloride disks to provide relatively constant thermal stimuli for cold and warm, respectively. Prior to beginning the assessment, the examiner should apply each disk to the skin and identify it verbally. These thermal disks do not allow measurement of precise thermal sensory threshold but, in general, are adequate to detect thermal deficiencies that could prevent a child from functioning safely in his or her environment and in addition provide a means for the objective comparison of thermal discrimination over time since the disks produce relatively constant thermal stimulation.

Pain is assessed by pinprick. This test evaluates the ability to sense superficial pain; it is regarded as the best measure of protective sensation and is also the most commonly used measure. In children, this modality should be saved for the end of the examination due to its noxious nature. The range of responses to a quick pinprick applied in a playful manner are variable and include change in facial expression, turning or moving away from the stimulus, cessation of activity, or crying. Withdrawal to pinprick (or touch) due to isolated distal spinal cord reflex activity may be mistaken for a voluntary response in children with spinal cord dysfunction. For this reason, it is important to observe the younger child for change in facial expression, level of alertness, and discomfort and to contrast this to the response to noxious simulation above the level of the spinal cord lesion. In older children, the child should be asked to discriminate between the sharp and dull sides of a pin. As in assessment of light touch, patterns of deficits should be noted, including dermatomal distribution (based on standard dermatomal maps), laterality, and proximal/distal gradients. Care should be taken not to break the skin, and each child should be tested with a new pin to limit the risk of infection.

Proprioception (kinesthesia) cannot be directly tested in younger children or those children with significant cognitive limitations, but some indication of disturbances/normality of function may be gained from observing the child's gait, posture, or sitting position. In the older child, this may be evaluated by a series of passive displacements of a single joint, with eyes closed, for which the child must identify the direction of the movement, either verbally or by pointing. The clinician must take care to control the amplitude of the displacement: for example, the passive kinesthetic threshold at the index finger is 5 to 10 degrees. Proprioception should be assessed in joints of the upper and lower extremities.

Cortical Sensory Functions

Topagnosis refers to the ability to localize the area of contact of tactile stimuli. With the eyes closed, the child should be touched and then asked to identify, either verbally or by pointing to the area, the areas touched. This localization differs from simple recognition of a stimulus because it represents a more integrated level of perception. Double simultaneous stimulation is an even more sophisticated assessment of localization, in which the child must recognize simultaneous touch of two areas. The child's inability to perceive touch in one of the areas is termed *extinction* and implies injury to the parietal lobe contralateral to the side on which the child failed to perceive the stimulus. This test is performed by having the child close his or her eyes and touching or tapping two areas, then asking the child where he or she feels it. Extremities, trunk, and face should be assessed.

Stereognosis refers to the ability to recognize familiar objects placed in the hand. After the child closes the eyes, a common object such as a coin or key is placed in the hand, then transferred to the other hand. The child is asked to identify the object. This assesses haptic recognition, or the ability to feel and recognize what is grasped using clues from the texture, temperature, size, shape, weight, and other features of the object. Moberg has used the term *tactile gnosis* to refer to the capacity to recognize an object solely by gripping or manipulation and refers to this to denote the functional sensibility necessary to perform many necessary daily activities.

Graphesthesia represents the ability to recognize letters or numbers written in the palm without visual clues. This can usually be tested in five year olds by drawing a circle or cross on the palm and by age eight years by the traditional method of tracing numbers in the palm for identification.

Two-point discrimination is classically felt to be the sensibility test that best addresses function because of its relation to fine tasks. This test is usually performed on the fingertips because they are most important in active exploration and tactile object scanning. It requires the child to recognize, with vision occluded, two closely approximated points of stimulation as separate. The examiner may use two dull points or a commercially available two-point discrimination instrument such as the Disk-Criminator or the Boley Gauge. The usual starting distance between the points is 5 mm. Researchers have found that 6 mm of two-point discrimination is required to wind a watch, whereas 15 mm is adequate for gross tool handling (adult norms).

This sense is particularly critical for reading Braille, which requires 2 mm of two-point discrimination. Because fingertip sensibility is highly dependent on motion, an assessment of moving two-point discrimination has been devised using the two-point discrimination instrument in a process similar to that employed in static two-point discrimination testing. In this dynamic test, the instrument is moved proximally to distally on the fingertip parallel to the long axis of the finger with the testing points side by side, and the child is required to discriminate the two points with progressively shorter distances between them.

SUGGESTED READINGS

Hunter, J.M., et al. 1990. *Rehabilitation of the hand*, 3rd ed., St. Louis: C.V. Mosby Co.

Dellon, A.L. 1988. *Evaluation of sensibility and re-education of sensation of the hand.* Baltimore: Williams & Wilkins.

Tan, A.M. 1992. Sensibility testing. In *Concepts in hand rehabilitation*, ed. B.G. Stanley and S.M. Tribuzi, 92–112. Philadelphia: F.A. Davis Co.

SENSORY SCREENING: VISION

Sheryl J. Menacker

Purpose: to describe methods commonly used to assess visual function in children with developmental disabilities.

Visual acuity may be formally assessed in both verbal and nonverbal children. Acuity charts with pictures or alphanumeric characters may be used even with young children who are nonverbal, as long as their level of interaction permits. Preferential looking acuity cards are used with less interactive children. Optokinetic nystagmus and electrophysiological testing is available to evaluate visual function when the inability to cooperate precludes a more refined assessment. (See also Chapter 8, section "Low Vision Management," for suggested methods to evaluate functional vision use.)

VISUAL ACUITY CHARTS

There are two types of visual acuity charts. With a *picture chart* (e.g., Allen Kindergarten Chart, Allen 1957), the child verbally names the pictures on the chart, both at a distance and near. Those who cannot (or will not) verbally identify pictures point to a figure on a hand-held near card, upon request.

An *alphanumeric chart* may be a conventional eye chart on which the child verbally identifies or points to letters and numbers, or an H, O, T, V chart—a distance visual acuity chart containing only the letters H, O, T, and V. This chart is shown to the child, and a large card with the same letters is placed on the child's lap. As each letter is presented on the distance chart, the child is asked to point to the appropriate character on the lap card. (Of course, if possible, the child may respond verbally rather than point to the card.) No familiarity with the alphabet is required (Jenkins et al. 1983).

PREFERENTIAL LOOKING VISUAL ACUITY CARDS

This technique relies on the fact that children will preferentially fixate on a boldly patterned striped target rather than an equally luminous blank target (Teller et al. 1986). Success rate of preferential looking acuity testing in children with developmental disabilities varies from 82% to 99% (Hertz and Rosenberg 1992; Hertz et al. 1988; Mohn et al. 1988).

Each acuity card contains a small peephole in the center, through which the examiner watches the child's eyes. A pattern of black and white stripes (gratings) is on one side of the peephole, and an equally luminous, blank gray target is on the other side. The black- and white-stripe widths become progressively thinner on successive acuity cards, creating finer gratings that require better visual resolution to see.

Testing proceeds as follows (Teller et al. 1986):

1. Child is seated on lap of adult. Examiner is seated facing child at a predetermined distance. Patch one eye for monocular testing.

2. Cards are presented to the child in order of wider to thinner stripe widths.

3. Examiner sees only the back of the card, without knowledge of whether the stripes on front are on the right or left.

4. Examiner watches child's eyes through the peephole, looking for movement to the right or left. From this, examiner guesses the location of stripes on card.

5. Examiner turns card 180 degrees and watches for child's eyes also to move in the opposite direction. If so, examiner then checks front of card to verify location of stripes.

6. Finest set of stripes for which child reliably produces this behavior is the grating visual acuity.

OPTOKINETIC NYSTAGMUS (OKN)

Optokinetic nystagmus is involuntary nystagmus (jerking motions of the eyes) induced by stripes on a rotating drum or other moving target. Vision necessary for OKN to be induced must at least allow the perception of fingers held in front of the eyes (Burde et al. 1985). By using successively thinner stripes on OKN testing targets, the examiner may estimate visual acuity. False negative response to OKN testing may be caused by inattention to stripes, inappropriate rate/distance of stripes, or abnormal oculomotor system (Hoyt 1986; Friendly 1989; Lewis et al. 1989).

ELECTROPHYSIOLOGICAL TESTING

Electrophysiological testing determines whether visual dysfunction is primarily ocular or cortical.

The *electroretinogram* tests the retinal function of the eye. It is particularly useful in testing for disorders such as retinitis pigmentosa. Equipment comprises electrodes affixed to face or body, a specialized computer, lights, and contact lenses for eyes. Testing involves flashing lights in the child's eyes under different conditions. Sedation may be necessary.

Visual evoked potential tests the neural pathway between the eye and the brain. Equipment comprises scalp electrodes, a specialized computer, a screen, and lights. To test gross visual function, the examiner flashes a bright light into the child's eyes. To estimate visual acuity, the examiner seats the child in front of a television screen on which patterns of checks or line waves are shown. A normal result may not predict normal visual acuity in the future; an abnormal result does not necessarily indicate that abnormal visual function will persist.

REFERENCES

Allen, H.F. 1957. A new picture series for preschool vision testing. *American Journal of Ophthalmology* 44:38.

Burde, R.M., et al. 1985. Nystagmus and other periodic eye disorders. In *Clinical decisions in neuro-ophthalmology*, ed. R.M. Burde and P.J. Savino. 197. St. Louis: C.V. Mosby Co.

Friendly, D.S. 1989. Visual acuity assessment of the preverbal patient. In *The eye in infancy*, ed. S.J. Isenberg, 48. Chicago: Year Book Medical Publishers, Inc.

Hertz, B.G., and J. Rosenberg. 1992. Effect of mental retardation and motor disability on testing with visual acuity cards. *Developmental Medicine and Child Neurology* 34:115–122.

Hertz, B.G., et al. 1988. Acuity card testing of patients with cerebral visual impairment. *Developmental Medicine and Child Neurology* 30:632–637.

Hoyt, C.S. 1986. Objective techniques of visual acuity assessment in infancy. *Australian and New Zealand Journal of Ophthalmology* 14:205–209.

Jenkins, P.F., et al. 1983. Preliterate vision screening: A comparative study. *American Orthopotic Journal* 3:91.

Lewis, T.L., et al. 1989. Optokinetic nystagmus in normal and visually deprived children: Implications for cortical development. *Canadian Journal of Psychology* 43:121–140.

Mohn, G., et al. 1988. Acuity assessment of non-verbal infants and children: Clinical experience with the acuity card procedure. *Developmental Medicine and Child Neurology* 30:232–244.

Teller, D.Y., et al. 1986. Assessment of visual acuity in infants and children: The acuity card procedure. *Developmental Medicine and Child Neurology* 28:779–789.

SENSORY SCREENING: HEARING

Carol A. Knightly

Purpose: to describe the methods used to assess hearing sensitivity in the pediatric population and the interpretation of audiological results.

A variety of methods may be used to assess hearing sensitivity in the child with developmental disability. Table 7–10 summarizes the methods that may be most appropriate for children at different ages or developmental levels. Access to a sound-treated audiometric booth is assumed, unless otherwise noted. The procedures also assume that equipment is calibrated to all applicable American National Standards Institute specifications. See Melnick (1991) for a review of instrument calibration. A glossary of definitions at the end of this section includes terminology that may be found in a typical audiological assessment report.

INTERPRETATION OF THE AUDIOGRAM

An audiogram is a graphic representation of a patient's hearing sensitivity. Refer to published guidelines for drawing audiograms (e.g., American Speech-Language-Hearing Association 1990).

Frequency is graphed along the abscissa (horizontal). Most sounds of the English language occur between 500 and 2,000 Hz. As a reference point, "Middle C" is 256 Hz.

Intensity is graphed along the ordinate (vertical). The range for "normal" hearing sensitivity is 0 to 15 dB HL. Average conversational loudness is 50 dB HL. Threshold of pain is 120 dB HL.

Hearing can be categorized in a variety of ways on the basis of the audiogram:

- Degree—may be predicted based upon pure tone average (PTA; Northern and Downs 1991)
    1. normal hearing sensitivity: 0–15 dB HL
    2. slight hearing loss: 15–25 dB HL
    3. mild hearing loss: 25–30 dB HL
    4. moderate hearing loss: 30–50 dB HL
    5. severe hearing loss: 50–70 dB HL
    6. profound hearing loss: 70+ dB HL
- Configuration (examples follow)
    1. *flat hearing loss*—All frequencies are affected equally so that function on au-

Table 7–10 Hearing Assessment and Screening

Assessment Tool*	0–6 Mo.	6 mo.–2½ Yr.	2½ Yr.	> 4 Yr.
BSRA (brainstem response audiometry)	Preferred method of assessment for this age group *Screen:* natural sleep or sedated; control run and repeatable tracings at 40 dBnHL (*pass*); if *fail*, refer for medical/otological eval. and complete BSRA *Complete BSRA:* natural sleep or sedated; tympanometry and latency-intensity function for wave V each ear; if response abnormal, perform bone conduction *Normal* = repeatable wave V at 20 dB nHL	See previous; appropriate if cooperation or developmental level not adequate for methods seen below	See previous; appropriate if cooperation or developmental level not adequate for methods seen below	See previous; appropriate if cooperation or developmental level not adequate for methods seen below
Screening audiometry	BOA screen (behavioral observation audiometry): response includes eye-blink, quieting, startle; if *pass*, refer for reevaluation at developmental age of 6 months	VRA (visual reinforcement audiometry) • In soundfield or with earphones • 10–30 dB HL accepted as "normal limits" • In soundfield, use warble tones or narrow band noise • Responses obtained in soundfield do not reflect ear-specific information ("better ear") • If fails, perform threshold search	Conditioned play audiometry • Under earphones • Pure-tone stimuli presented at 20 dB HL for frequencies 1,000, 2,000, and 4,000 Hz (does not require audiometric booth) • If fails, recommend second screening • Refer for full audiologic assessment if 2nd screening fails	Voluntary response: same guidelines as conditioned play, but use adult techniques to elicit response (e.g., hand raising)

continues

Table 7–10 continued

Assessment Tool*	0–6 Mo.	6 mo.–2½ Yr.	2½ Yr.	> 4 Yr.
Audiometric tone assessment		Visual reinforced audiometry (VRA) • As above, perform threshold search, using accepted procedures • Obtain unmasked bone conduction responses if possible	Conditioned play audiometry • Under earphones, perform threshold search, using accepted procedures • Responses obtained at a level of 15 dB HL or better are considered normal • Perform masked bone conduction testing if thresholds by air conduction exceed 15 dB HL	Voluntary response • As earlier, but use adult techniques to elicit response • Complete pure tone assessment
Speech audiometry			Use standardized tests for both speech reception threshold and word recognition ability; present word recognition tests at level of 40 dB SL if hearing sensitivity is within normal limits	As earlier
Immittance measurements	Required special higher frequency probe tone for accurate measurements	Tympanometry, physical volume measurements, acoustic reflex thresholds	Same	Same

*See glossary for definition of evaluation methods.

---

diogram is essentially flat horizontal line.

2. *high-frequency hearing loss*—Hearing sensitivity at frequencies lower than (approximately) 2,000 Hz is within normal limits, but thresholds at 2,000 Hz and above indicate hearing loss.

3. *low-frequency hearing loss*—Hearing sensitivity at frequencies higher than (approximately) 1,000 Hz is within normal limits, but thresholds at 1,000 Hz and below indicate hearing loss.

• Type

1. *sensorineural*—Air conduction symbols (i.e., thresholds) and bone conduction symbols do not deviate for a given ear by more than 10 dB. This type is usually present or greater in the higher frequencies.

2. *conductive*—Air conduction symbols fall outside the normal range, but bone conduction symbols are within the normal range. This type is usually flat or

low frequency in configuration and generally will not exceed 60 dB HL.

3. *mixed*—Both air and bone conduction symbols fall outside the normal range, but the symbols deviate by more than 10 dB, or the audiogram indicates a conductive hearing loss for certain frequencies and a sensorineural hearing loss for others. This type usually has a larger conductive component in the lower frequencies.

An audiogram form is shown in Figure 7–26. Audiogram codes are shown in Figure 7–27.

Figures 7–28 through 7–31 are representative audiograms. Figure 7–28 shows high-frequency sensorineural hearing loss in the right ear. This individual might perceive speech in the right ear as loud enough but "muffled," as the hearing loss would affect primarily the unvoiced consonants (e.g., *f*, *s*, *th*, *p*). Figure 7–29 shows flat conductive hearing loss in the left ear. This individual would perceive an overall decrease in the

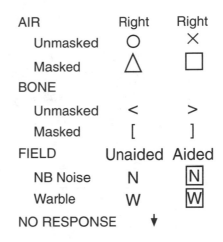

Figure 7–27 Audiogram Codes.

loudness of speech in the left ear. This degree of hearing loss (i.e., 35 dB HL, or "mild") is slightly worse than is experienced with the use of ear plugs. Figure 7–30 shows bilateral mixed

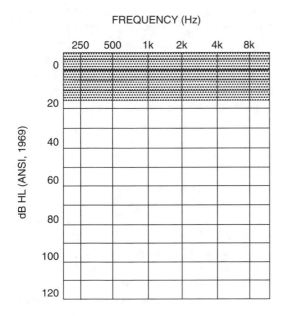

Figure 7–26 Audiogram Form.

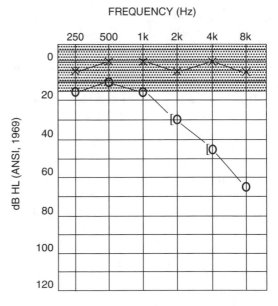

Figure 7–28 Audiogram Showing High-Frequency Sensorineural Hearing Loss in the Right Ear.

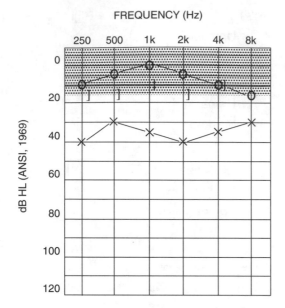

Figure 7–29 Audiogram Showing Flat Conductive Hearing Loss in the Left Ear.

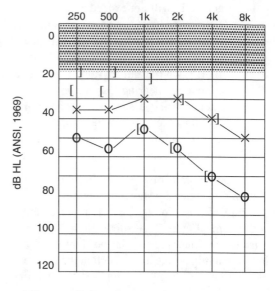

Figure 7–30 Audiogram Showing Bilateral Mixed Hearing Loss.

hearing loss. This individual generally would not perceive normal conversational speech in the right ear, as the hearing loss is of a degree greater than 50 dB HL. In the left ear, the individual would probably judge speech of normal conversational loudness as sounding like a muffled whisper. Figure 7–31 shows normal hearing sensitivity assessed in soundfield.

Figures 7–32 and 7–33 are representative brainstem response audiometry (BRSA) tracings. Figure 7–32 shows a normal latency-intensity function for a child age 2+ years (refer to Durrant and Wolf 1991 for further discussion regarding auditory evoked potentials). Figure 7–33 shows an abnormal BSRA tracing from a child with response absent below 50 dB nHL.

GLOSSARY OF AUDIOLOGIC TERMINOLOGY

Air conduction: method of delivering an auditory stimulus to an individual that uses air as the medium of conduction (e.g., earphones). This type of delivery involves the outer, middle, and inner ear.

Behavioral observation audiometry (BOA): elicits nonconditioned responses to various stimuli.

Bone conduction: method of delivering an auditory stimulus to an individual that uses bone as the medium of conduction (e.g., bone conduction vibrator placed on the skull). This type of delivery assesses the inner ear.

Brainstem response audiometry (BSRA, BSR, ABR, BSER): method of predicting hearing sensitivity that employs the principles of low-level EEG and computer averaging.

Conditioned play audiometry: method of assessing hearing sensitivity in which the response to a stimulus is in the form of a specific activity (e.g., placing rings on a peg).

Conductive hearing loss: hearing loss that results from dysfunction of the outer and/or middle ear in the presence of a normal inner ear.

Configuration of hearing loss: refers to the "curve" determined by the auditory thresholds graphed on the audiogram.

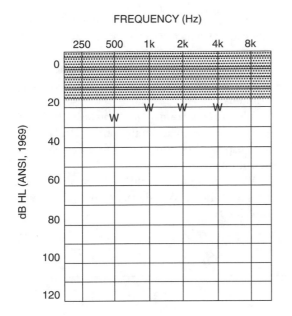

Figure 7–31 Audiogram Showing Normal Hearing Sensitivity Assessed in Soundfield.

Decibel (dB): unit of measurement of sound intensity (i.e., loudness). dB HL references the measurement to the average threshold of audibility of normal young adult ears. dB SL references the level to the individual's threshold of audibility.

Degree of hearing loss: predicts handicapping effect of the hearing loss, based upon the average of where most of the individual's responses fall. Anticipated handicapping effects were developed for adults and may not apply to children, depending on variables other than auditory threshold (e.g., existing language skills and listening environment).

Hertz (Hz): unit of measurement of the frequency (i.e., pitch) of a pure tone.

Immittance measurements: provide information relative to the status of the middle ear system, including compliance of the system and patency of pressure-equalization tubes, as well as information regarding cochlear function.

Masking: the introduction of noise to a nontest ear to prevent participation in assessment of the test ear.

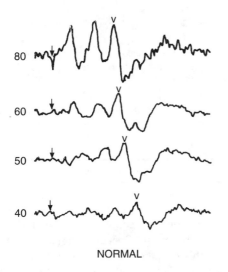

NORMAL

Figure 7–32 BRSA Tracing, Normal Latency-Intensity Function for Child Age 2+ Years.

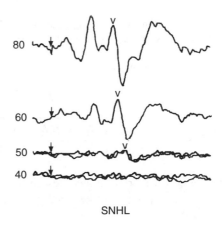

SNHL

Figure 7–33 Abnormal BRSA Tracing from Child with Response Absent below 50 dB nHL.

Mixed hearing loss: hearing loss that results from both conductive and sensorineural impairment.

Pure tone: the simplest form of sound. A single frequency.

Pure tone average (PTA): the value determined by adding the threshold values at two or three frequencies, usually 500, 1,000, and 2,000 Hz. Usually correlates very closely with the speech reception threshold.

Sensorineural hearing loss: hearing loss that results from pathology of the inner ear or pathology along the auditory nerve pathway.

Soundfield: implies delivering an auditory stimulus to an individual using speakers.

Speech reception threshold (SRT): the softest intensity at which a person can repeat a given word.

Threshold of hearing: the softest intensity at which a patient will respond to an auditory stimulus.

Visual reinforcement audiometry (VRA): employs operant conditioning procedures (stimulus-response-reinforcement) to assess hearing sensitivity.

Word recognition ability: a measure of a person's ability to understand speech at suprathreshold levels.

REFERENCES

American Speech-Language-Hearing Association. 1990. Guidelines for audiometric symbols. *ASHA* 32, suppl. 2:25–30.

Durant, J.D., and K.E. Wolf. 1991. Auditory evoked potentials: Basic aspects. In *Hearing assessment*, ed. W. Rintelmann, 321–381. Austin, Tex.: PRO-ED, Inc.

Melnick, W. 1991. Instrument calibration. In *Hearing assessment*, ed. W.F. Rintelmann, 805–844. Austin, Tex.: PRO-ED, Inc.

Northern, J.L., and M.P. Downs. 1991. *Hearing in children*. 4th ed. Baltimore: Williams & Wilkins.

ADDITIONAL SUGGESTED READINGS

American Speech-Language-Hearing Association. 1985. Guidelines for identification audiometry. *ASHA* 27:49–52.

American Speech-Language-Hearing Association. 1990. Guidelines for screening for hearing impairments and middle ear disorders. *ASHA* 32, suppl. 2:17–24.

Goldstein, B.A., and C.W. Newman. 1985. Clinical masking: A decision-making process. In *Handbook of clinical audiology*, 3rd ed., ed. J. Katz, 170–201. Baltimore: Williams & Wilkins.

Olsen, W.O., and N.D. Matkin. 1991. Speech audiometry. In *Hearing assessment*, ed. W.F. Rintelmann, 39–135. Austin, Tex.: PRO-ED, Inc.

Schwartz, D.M., and G.A. Berry. 1985. Normative aspects of the ABR. In *The auditory brainstem response*, ed. J.T. Jacobson, 65–97. San Diego: College Hill Press, Inc.

SPEECH/LANGUAGE MEASURES

Marleen Anne Baron

Purpose: to describe procedures commonly used to assess speech and language deficits or delays in young children.

Numerous standardized tests are available that allow the clinician to make comparisons with peers who have typical speech and language function (see section "Annotated Index of Tests," subsection "Speech/Language Tests," later in this chapter for review of a representative sample). When evaluating speech/language function, one should select tests to measure all parameters of communicative competency and not merely one aspect of language development.

For example, tests of single-word vocabulary knowledge should not be used alone to determine a child's linguistic function. Both receptive and expressive language skills need to be assessed and scored separately because some children exhibit a significant discrepancy between their comprehension and their ability to communicate verbally. Other skills that require careful assessment include pragmatic use of language for social communication, ability to comprehend spoken directions, ability to understand and use age-appropriate grammatical forms, concept formation, and ability to produce intelligible speech sounds.

Because of the complexity of communicative function in children, effective assessment requires the use of tests in combination with other procedures that yield qualitative information about the child's skills. Attempts to identify communication delays and impairments at early ages require the examiner to be familiar with normal milestones for language development, vocabulary acquisition, syntax acquisition (the way in which words are combined to produce meaning), speech sound acquisition, oral-motor control, cognitive development, and play skills. With this knowledge, parental report and direct observation of the child in less structured communicative and play contexts provide information useful in determining the existence of a problem and in making comparisons with language and speech behaviors of similarly aged children.

Definitions of terms frequently included in speech/language reports are included at the end of this section and may be used to assist other professionals in reading and interpreting these reports.

ADAPTATIONS OF ASSESSMENT PROCEDURES FOR CHILDREN WITH DISABILITIES

This section will discuss some clinical procedures and strategies that may prove helpful in assessing the speech and language skills of children who may be difficult to assess for a variety

of reasons. It is important to remember that even normally developing children may not acquire all communication skills according to a precisely predictable time line. Individual learning styles will influence development, and there are accepted ranges during which a child may acquire skills and still be considered within normal parameters. The population of children who present with delayed speech and language skills is extremely diverse with respect to communication, cognitive, developmental, behavioral, motor, medical, and cultural-social parameters. There will be occasions when formal standardized test procedures cannot be administered or when test procedures must be adapted. Creativity and clinical judgments are key elements to a successful diagnostic evaluation when working with young children, especially with children who are uncooperative, nonresponsive, hyperactive, or atypical. Tips that may be helpful for specific populations are described in the following sections.

Assessment of Receptive Language in the Active Preschooler

If the child is not yet ready to identify pictures on a picture vocabulary task or is noncompliant when asked to identify clinic materials, the following techniques may be used:

1. Have the child identify family members in photographs. Parents often have photographs in their wallets, and this activity may be more meaningful to the child than responding to unfamiliar clinic materials.

2. Ask families to bring favorite toys and books to the assessment so that the child may demonstrate language competency with familiar items.

3. Some young children are reluctant to follow noncontextual verbal directions or requests on command. Try to express verbal requests in a more pragmatic manner to elicit the desired response (e.g., ask the child to close the door, get the keys to lock the door, wipe the dirt off his or her

nose, tie his or her shoe, put the ball in his or her pocket, turn on the radio, turn off the light).

Assessment of Expressive Language in the Active Preschooler

If the child is shy or reluctant to respond verbally to formal expressive language measures, less confrontational techniques to engage the child in simple conversation may be more successful:

1. Encourage conversation during structured and unstructured play, especially if a sibling is available either to act as a model or to stimulate communicative interaction.
2. Concrete reinforcers, such as placing pegs in a form board, may be helpful in keeping the child's interest and in fostering compliance for formal testing.
3. The clinician may be able to obtain small samples of connected utterances if he or she asks casual but focused questions relating to specific test stimuli used in another format. For example, the stimulus *accident* on the Peabody Picture Vocabulary Test provides the opportunity to question, "What happened?" Similarly, on the Expressive One Word Picture Vocabulary Test, the clinician may ask for the *function* of a specific vocabulary stimulus (e.g., "What do you *do* with a scissors?" "Did *you* ever see a tiger?" "*Where?*").
4. The child functioning at a low developmental level may be more willing to name items that he or she has personal familiarity with than to name clinic materials.

Assessment of Language in the Child with Long-Term Hospitalization

Many children with complex medical needs spend large amounts of time living in hospitals or rehabilitation centers. Some children may have lived in hospitals their entire lives. Limited

opportunities for preverbal communicative activities (e.g., vocal play for the child with a critical airway) or the need to live in a confined environment, often without the typical opportunities for cognitive, social, and motor exploration, can significantly influence the development of speech and language skills. The child may lack familiarity with typical words used on standardized vocabulary measures but may be able to identify such items as *tracheostomy*. Attempts to assess the development of language must take into consideration the context in which exposure to language has occurred, using vocabulary that will be familiar to the child.

Assessment of Language in the Child with Suspected Pervasive Developmental Delay

Children with pervasive developmental delay (PDD) frequently exhibit atypical language development and usage patterns. It is especially important with this population to assess and interpret carefully all parameters of communication, especially social intent. The goal of assessment should be to determine functional competence with interactive communicative, not just linguistic, competency. Some linguistic patterns that are noteworthy for both diagnostic and therapeutic considerations will not be easy to quantify on standardized measures. Yet their occurrence needs to be stated and understood. The clinician should also attempt to modify atypical and impaired linguistic behaviors during the examination, since observing the child's responses to various therapeutic strategies will be helpful in planning intervention.

When appropriate, the clinician should collect spontaneous language samples in more than one context, as language interactions may vary according to the context in which they occur.

Children with PDD often use excessive echolalia long after it is developmentally acceptable. While this behavior is not measurable, a detailed description of its usage is warranted. The following behaviors should be considered:

1. immediate echolalia or delayed repetitions
2. single-word, phrase, or sentence echolalia

3. immediate repetition of heard language as a mechanism for improved processing and comprehension
4. echolalia without comprehension of the message
5. echolalia as a response or "space filler" to maintain interaction
6. speech clarity of echoed responses compared to spontaneous utterances
7. intonation patterns of echoed speech

The examiner may be able to alter and decrease the child's use of echoed speech by

1. using associated gestures and simple signs to facilitate comprehension of the spoken message
2. using an immediate concrete reinforcer to establish and increase use of appropriate responses
3. giving the child the correct response to a question before he or she has the opportunity to echo the question

The clinician should carefully observe and note the child's

1. eye contact with others
2. eye gaze to gain attention
3. eye gaze for gestures, body language, objects, and pictures
4. communicative intent
5. conversational participation
6. ability to initiate meaningful language
7. ability to be a listener and responder during conversation
8. ability to take turns during discourse
9. ability to ask and answer questions
10. ability to take turns during play
11. inflectional patterns

Many children with PDD have a facility for mastery of rote linguistic material, such as counting, recitation of the alphabet, identification of letters and numbers, reading, and recitation of songs, nursery rhymes, and commercials. However, in a child who exhibits a very uneven language development profile, these skills may represent splinter skills that occur without underlying comprehension of the concepts. It is important to recognize that these skills, which are often isolated and inflated, may not truly reflect the child's functional communicative ability. Further analysis of these rote skills may determine the child's degree of flexibility with the skill as well as the level of comprehension. For example, if the child can recite "Old MacDonald Had a Farm," the clinician might provide an unpredictable verse and note the child's response. Once the child has counted by rote, the clinician should determine if the child has mastered number-to-object correlation. If the child reads single words or simple sentences, the clinician can present correlating pictures and have him or her identify the correct associated visual stimulus.

Assessment of Children with Bilingual and Bicultural Backgrounds

The existence of a culturally diverse population within our society, often communicating through non-English languages and multiple dialects, presents many challenges to speech/language pathologists as they attempt to diagnose and treat communication disorders. Most speech/language pathologists practicing in the United States can expect to work with at least some children and families who speak a language that is unfamiliar to them. This can significantly influence the clinician's ability to interview family members to take a history, administer standardized procedures, or adequately interpret speech and language samples. Low test scores obtained by a bilingual child on a test that was normed primarily on monolingual, English-speaking children may not necessarily indicate a language disorder. Currently, few standardized measures for non-English-speaking bilingual children are available; most are designed for Spanish-speaking children. The *TVIP: Test de Vocabulario en Imágenes Peabody* (Dunn et al. 1986) is a Spanish version of the Peabody Picture Vocabulary Test that has been normed on monolingual Spanish-speaking children in Mexico and Puerto Rico. Mattes and Omark (1993) described other published speech and language instruments for bilingual populations.

Cultural differences in communicative style need to be further explored and appreciated by those professionals working with individuals with communication problems. In the absence of a trained speech/language pathologist who speaks the child's native language, this evaluation will require the assistance of an interpreter. Clinical findings need to be carefully framed when interpreting information and making judgments about linguistic deficits. Clinicians need to rely on the interpreter's assessment of grammatical usage, discourse organization, phonologic competency, and pragmatic style of interaction. The child's nonverbal communication, such as eye contact, facial expressions, and use of body language and gestures, needs to be viewed in terms of cultural attitudes. It will be helpful to observe the child's interactions with both parents and peers in low-structure situations, as communicative initiation may vary dramatically. Prior life experiences, semantic differences in the child's native language, and length of exposure to English need to be considered when drawing conclusions about the child's linguistic competency. At best, language assessment may provide only a gross estimate of a child's skills. Recommendations for remediation of suspected communication deficits also need to be sensitive to the family's cultural and linguistic background.

Other resources that may be helpful to speech/language pathologists working with bilingual populations may be found through Academic Communication Associates, 4149 Avienda de la Plata, P.O. Box 586249, Oceanside, CA 92058-6249, Tel.: (619) 758-9593.

Assessment of Oral-Motor and Speech Imitation Skills (see also Chapter 8, section "Therapeutic Feeding")

The preschooler who has not yet acquired spoken language or who exhibits significantly unclear articulation patterns should receive a thorough oral peripheral examination that examines the oral mechanism and assesses oral-motor

planning, speech and language stimulability, and imitation skills. The clinician may be required to make a differential diagnosis between delayed phonologic/articulation development, specific phonologic/articulation disorder, apraxia, and dysarthria. It is important to obtain this information without frightening or frustrating the child. This can be accomplished using the following techniques:

1. Young children enjoy turn-taking and imitation games. Allow the child to play with and explore your flashlight and tongue depressor.

2. Draw a happy face on the tongue depressor.

3. Allow the child to look in the parent's and examiner's mouth with both the light and the depressor first before the roles are reversed.

4. Give the child the tongue depressor as a souvenir.

5. Use bubbles, candles, powder, and single-ply tissue to assess blowing skills. Stimulation of the phoneme /p/ is often successful when accompanied by a visual aid. Practice /p/ production while blowing powder away from your palm or into a tissue.

6. Observe the child's drinking and chewing skills during snack time.

7. Use concrete reinforcers, such as a ring stack or peg board, to engage the child in direct imitation activity. Start with a gross motor action, such as jumping, clapping, or touching the head. The examiner initiates the action; the child imitates and then receives a reinforcer. Once the child feels comfortable with the format, which may only require one or two trials, the examiner can then target desired oral-motor acts and specific sounds for imitation.

MEASURES OF SPECIFIC SPEECH/ LANGUAGE FUNCTIONS

Tables 7–11 through 7–16 show selected measures of specific speech/language functions.

Table 7–11 English Consonant Sounds

Place of Constriction	Manner of Production								
	Stop–Plosive		Fricative		Nasal	Glide	Semivowel	Affricate	
	Unvoiced	Voiced	Unvoiced	Voiced	Voiced	Voiced	Voiced	Unvoiced	Voiced
Bilabial	p (pig)	b (big)			m (sum)	w (watt)			
Labiodental			f (face)	v (vase)					
Linguadental			θ (thigh)	ð (this)					
Lingua-alveolar	t (Tom)	d (dot)	s (see)	z (zoo)	n (sun)		l (lot)		
Linguapalatal			ʃ (shoe)	ʒ (measure)		j (yacht)	r (rot)	tʃ (choke)	dʒ (joke)
Linguavelar	k (coat)	g (goat)			ŋ (sung)				
Glottal			h (happy)						

Source: Adapted from Bloodstein (1983) and Owens (1988).

Table 7–12 Differential Diagnosis of Motor Speech Problems

Problem Area	Apraxia	Dysarthria	Functional Articulation Deficit
Language development	May be delayed but often within normal range	Usually delayed	None
Phonation	Normal	Incoordination of phonation and articulation, or of both with respiration, may be present	None
Movement of articulators	Vegetative function is normal. Normal movements except for speech, in verbal apraxia	Vegetative functions, such as swallowing and chewing, may be impaired. One or more muscle groups affected. Motor speech disorder associated with paralysis, paresis, or incoordination of the musculature involved in speech production	None
Neurological signs	"Soft" neurological signs; may exhibit difficulty with gait and fine motor coordination	Usually part of a more generalized neuromuscular disorder, such as cerebral palsy	None
Articulation	Deviant phonetic organization; problems in syllable structure, syllabification, speech sound selection, and syllable sequencing. Errors increase with increase in word length, especially substitutions, repetitions, additions	Errors are consistent and determined by the group of muscles affected; primarily errors of simplification (distortions, slightings, omissions)	Vowels are usually normal. Consonant errors are usually consistent
Prosody	Compensation for difficulties often results in intentional slow rate, pauses and even stress	Incoordination slows rate of speech	None
Imitative responses	May have more articulation errors than spontaneous speech production	Minimal or no change	Improves with practice
Associated problems	Language difficulties, frustration associated with inability to be understood, distractibility	Drooling, feeding difficulties	None

Source: Adapted from Darley et al. (1975), Nicolosi et al. (1989), and Thompson (1989).

Table 7–13 Estimated Sound Acquisition Ages

Sound	50% Mastery Age	75% Mastery Age	90% Mastery Age
Vowels		36 mo.	
Diphthongs		36 mo.	
n	24 mo.		24 mo.
m		24 mo.	28 mo.
p	24 mo.		28 mo.
h	24 mo.		28 mo.
t		24 mo..	32 mo.
k	24 mo.	36 mo..	32 mo.
f	24 mo.	36 mo..	36 mo.
w	24 mo.		40 mo.
ng	24 mo.		36 mo.
b		24 mo.	36 mo.
g	24 mo.	36 mo.	36 mo.
s	24 mo.		44 mo.
ye	28 mo.		32 mo.
d	28 mo.		36 mo.
hw	28 mo.		48 mo.
l	32 mo.	48 mo.	48 mo.
r	32 mo.		48 mo.
sh	36 mo.		48 mo.
ch	36 mo.		48 mo.
j	36 mo.	48 mo.	48 mo.
v	40 mo.		48 mo.
z	44 mo.		48 mo.
zh (rouge)	44 mo.		48 mo.
th	44 mo.		48 mo.
Double consonant blends		48 mo.	
Triple consonant blends		48 mo.	

Source: Adapted from Hedrick et al. (1975) and Powers (1971).

Table 7–14 Acquisition of Selected Pronouns

Pronoun	Approximate Age
my	12–18 mo.
me	18–24 mo.
it	12–18 mo.
he	24–36 mo.
she	24–36 mo.
your	24–36 mo.
we	30–48 mo.
you	30–48 mo.
they	30–48 mo.
our	36–60 mo.

Source: Adapted from Bangs (1989), Woolfolk-Carrow (1985), and Wiig and Semel (1976).

Table 7–15 Acquisition of Word Formation Rules

Word Formation Rule	Application	Approximate Age Range for 75% Acquisition
Regular noun plurals	"balls"	3.6 yr.
Present progressive tense	"hitting"	3.0 yr.
Conjunction	"and"	3.0 yr.
Comparative adjective forms	"smaller"	4.0 yr.
Superlative adjective forms	"fattest"	3.0 yr.
Negative forms	"not," "can't," "don't	4.0 yr.
Conjunctions	"when," "so"	4.0 + yr.
Question forms	"who," "what," "where"	4.0 yr.
Negative form	"isn't"	5.6 yr.
Adverb derivation	"easily"	7.0 yr.
Conjunction	"if…then"	7.0 + yr.

Source: Bangs (1989), Woolfolk-Carrow (1985), Miller (1981), and Wiig and Semel (1987).

Table 7–16 Language Sample Analysis

Stage	MLU*	CA**	Analysis
Presyntactic	N/A	<12 mo.	Child uses one-word utterances that label objects, people, or actions to express holophrastic "thoughts." Jargon may be quite prevalent.
Stage I	1.1–2.0	12–26 mo.	Child begins to use more than one word. No inflectional endings are used.
Stage II	2.0–2.5	27–30 mo.	Simple declarative and interrogative sentences are used. There is frequent omission of plurality, articles, auxiliary, and copula.
Stage III	2.5–3.0	31–34 mo.	Simple declarative and interrogative sentences are used. Past tense forms, if used, are generally irregular. There is often overgeneralization of irregular past tense forms. Articles are used inconsistently. Rudimentary prepositional phases appear.
Stage IV	3.0–3.75	35–40 mo.	Complex sentences begin to be used. Conjunctions are limited to "and" and "but."
Stage V	3.75–4.5	41–46 mo.	Continued development of complex sentences. Conjunctions are more varied and more frequent. Subordinate clauses are used more frequently. Relative clauses are embedded in positions other than end of sentence.

Source: Adapted from Brown (1973).
*Mean length of utterance.
**Chronologic age.

GLOSSARY OF SPEECH/LANGUAGE TERMINOLOGY

Apraxia: Difficulty planning and controlling muscular movements.

Articulation: The production of speech sounds.

Articulators: The lower jaw, lips, tongue, soft palate, and pharynx, which produce meaningful sounds by shaping the flow of air.

Consonant blends: Two or more consonant sounds spoken together, such as *sn*, *tr*, or *cl*.

Consonants: The sounds made by stopping or restricting the outgoing breath. Consonants can be described by place and manner of articulation.

Affricate: Consonant that begins as a stop but is expelled as a fricative. These include /tʃ/ as in chair and /dʒ/ as in judge.

Fricative: Consonant sound produced as the breath stream is forced out of the oral cavity. The breath stream is directed against one or more surfaces, including the hard palate, alveolar ridge, lips, and palate. This produces a continuous friction noise. /f/, /v/, /θ/, /ð/, /s/, /z/, /ʑ/, /ʃ/, /ʒ/, and /h/

Glide: Consonant sound produced by movement of an articulator, rather than produced with the articulator in a static position. /hw/, /w/, and /j/

Nasal: Consonant sound that results when the breath stream exits by way of the nasal cavity, as the velum or soft palate is in a lowered position. /m/, /n/, and /ɧ/

Semivowel: Consonant sound that is vowel-like in nature. The vocal tract is in a vowel-like position, then gradually changes to a position for the following vowel in the syllable. /r/ and /l/

Sibilant: Consonant with a fricative sound whose production is accompanied by a hissing noise. /s/ and /z/

Stop: Consonant sound produced by two phases, stop and plosive. In the stop phase, the nasal port is closed and the oral cavity is sealed at the lips, alveolar ridge, or velum, thus compressing air in the oral cavity. In the plosive phase, impounded air pressure in the vocal tract is released through the vocal tract. /p/, /b/, /t/, /d/, /k/, /g/

Alveolar or linguadental: Consonant sound made when the front tip of the tongue makes contact with the alveolar ridge behind the upper teeth for production of /t/, /d/, and /n/. Sibilants /s/ and /z/ are produced with the tongue in the same position but not quite in contact with the roof of the mouth.

Glottal: Consonant sound produced at the level of the vocal folds. Air is impeded at the glottis, but not enough to produce vibrations. /h/

Labiodental: Consonant sound produced when the lower lip rests against the upper teeth; air escapes between a slight space between the lip and teeth. /f/ and /v/

Linguadental: Consonant sound produced with the tongue between the upper and lower front teeth. /θ/, /ð/

Palatal: Consonant sound made when the center of the tongue makes contact with the

area in front of the highest point of the roof of the mouth. /ʃ/, /ʒ/, /dʒ/, /tʃ/, /j/, and sometimes /r/

Velar: Consonant sound made when the back midsection of the tongue makes contact with the area at the back of the roof of the mouth. /k/, /g/, and /ɧ/

Voiced: Consonant sound produced with vibration of the vocal folds.

Voiceless: Consonant sound produced without vibration of the vocal folds.

Diadochokinesis: The ability to execute rapid repetitive alternating movements of the articulators in speech.

Diphthong: Vowel-like speech sound produced by blending two vowels within a syllable.

Dysfluency: A break in the smooth, meaningful flow of language.

Dysarthria: Speech disorders caused by motor impairments of both voluntary and involuntary movements.

Grammar: Rules governing how words are combined in sentences.

Hypernasality: The voice sounds as if it is produced or resonated in the nose.

Inflection: The change in pitch of the voice, rising and falling to convey meaning.

MLU: Mean length of utterance, which increases as the child matures (Brown, 1973).

Morphology: How words are used to convey a message; the structural form of language, an aspect of syntax.

Phonology: The rules governing the structure, distribution, and sequencing of speech sound patterns.

Pragmatics: Language use within a communicative context, incorporating social parameters.

Resonance: The vibration of air in the throat and nasal cavities during speech.

Semantics: Meaning or content of language.

Stuttering: Disturbance of the normal fluency or timing of speech.

Syntax: The internal structure of language, involving the way words are put together in a sentence to convey meaning.

Vowels: The sounds associated with the letters *a, e, i, o, u,* and *y,* made by allowing air to pass through the nose or mouth without friction or stoppage.

REFERENCES

Bangs, T.E. 1989. *Language and learning disorders of the pre-academic child: With curriculum guide.* 2nd ed. Englewood Cliffs, N.J.: Prentice Hall.

Bloodstein, O. 1983. *Speech pathology: An introduction.* 2nd ed. Boston: Houghton Mifflin Co.

Brown, R.A. 1973. *First language: The early stages.* Cambridge, Mass.: Harvard University Press.

Darley, F., et al. 1975. *Motor speech disorders.* Philadelphia: W.B. Saunders.

Dunn, L.M., et al. 1986. *TVIP: Test de Vocabulario en Imágenes Peabody.* Circle Pines, Minn.: American Guidance Service.

Hedrick, D.L., et al. 1975. *Sequenced inventory of communication development.* Seattle: University of Washington Press.

Mattes, L.J., and D.R. Omark. 1993. *Speech and language assessment for the bilingual handicapped.* 2nd ed. Oceanside, Calif.: Academic Communication Associates.

Miller, J.F. 1981. *Assessing language production in children.* Baltimore: University Park Press.

Nicolosi, L., et al. 1989. *Terminology of communication disorders: Speech, language and hearing.* 3rd ed. Baltimore: Williams & Wilkins.

Owens, R.E., Jr. 1988. *Language development, an introduction.* 2nd ed. New York: Macmillan Publishing Co., Inc.

Powers, M.N. 1971. Functional disorders of articulation/symptomatology and etiology. In *Handbook of speech pathology and audiology*, ed. L.E. Travis, 837–875. Englewood Cliffs, N.J.: Prentice Hall.

Thompson, C. 1989. Articulation disorders in children with neurogenic pathology. In *Study guide for the handbook of speech-language pathology and audiology*, ed. J. Northern. Toronto: B.C. Decker, Inc.

Wiig, E.H., and E.M. Semel. 1976. *Language disabilities in children and adolescents.* Columbus, Ohio: Charles E. Merrill Publishing Co.

Woolfolk-Carrow, E. 1985. *Test of auditory comprehension of language—revised.* Allen, Tex.: DLM and Teaching Resources.

ADDITIONAL SUGGESTED READINGS

Bloom, L., and M. Lahey. 1978. *Language development and language disorders.* New York: Macmillan Publishing Co., Inc.

Carrow-Woolfolk, E. 1975. *Carrow Elicited Language Inventory.* Austin, Tex.: Learning Concepts.

Fisher, A., and J. Logeman. 1971. *Fisher-Logeman Test of Articulation Competence.* Geneva, Ill.: Houghton-Mifflin Co.

Gallagher, T.M., and C.A. Prutting, eds. 1983. *Pragmatic assessment and intervention issues in language.* San Diego: College Hill Press, Inc.

Gleason, J.B. 1985. *The development of language.* Columbus, Ohio: Charles E. Merrill Publishing Co.

Lahey, M. 1988. *Language disorders and language development.* New York: Macmillan Publishing Co., Inc.

Miller, J.F., and R. Chapman. 1981. Analyzing free language samples. In *Assessing language production in children*, ed. J. Miller. Baltimore: University Park Press.

Miller, N. 1984. Some observations concerning formal tests in cross-cultural settings. In *Bilingualism and language disability: Assessment and remediation*, ed. N. Miller. San Diego: College Hill Press, Inc.

Perkins, W.H., ed. 1983. *Dysarthria and apraxia: Current therapy of communication disorders*, vol. 2. New York: Thieme-Stratton, Inc.

Roseberry-McKibbin, C. 1994. *Multicultural students with special language needs: Practical strategies for assessment and intervention.* Oceanside, Calif.: Academic Communication Associates.

Semel, E.M., et al. 1987. *Clinical evaluation of language fundamentals—revised.* San Antonio, Tex.: The Psychological Corporation.

Shewan, C. 1988. Omnibus survey: Adaptation and progress in times of change. *Journal of the American Speech and Hearing Association* 30:27–30.

Templin, M., and F. Darley. 1969. *The Templin-Darley Test of Articulation.* Iowa City, Iowa: University of Iowa, Bureau of Educational Research and Service.

Vaughn-Cooke, A. 1986. The challenge of assessing the language of non-mainstream speakers. In *Communication disorders in culturally and linguistically diverse populations*, ed. O.L. Taylor. San Diego: College Hill Press, Inc.

PSYCHOEDUCATIONAL MEASURES: CURRICULUM-BASED ASSESSMENT

Thomas J. Power

Purpose: to describe the rationale for evaluating academic skills using curriculum-based assessment methods, contrast curriculum-based methods with traditional methods of academic assessment, and present examples of how these procedures can be used in assessing reading and math skills.

DEFINITIONS OF TERMS

Curriculum-based assessment (CBA): the evaluation of academic skills by assessing a student's performance using materials taken directly from his or her curriculum. This type of assessment is useful in selecting curricular materials that match the student's level of skill and in monitoring academic progress as well as evaluating the efficacy of specific academic interventions.

Instructional level: the curriculum level that is optimal for instructing a child. At the instructional level, the student is familiar with most elements of the curriculum, but the proportion of unfamiliar material is high enough to warrant the need for a teacher to assist with learning.

Instructional match: the matching of students with curriculum materials that are likely to maximize their level of attention, comprehension, and productivity.

Idiographic analysis: the comparison of a student's performance to his or her performance at other points in time to determine the child's progress in meeting instructional objectives.

Nomothetic analysis: the comparison of a student's performance to that of a large group of children of similar age and gender to determine the relative standing of the child in relation to his or her peers.

Progress monitoring: the assessment of changes in a child's academic skills relative to short- and long-term instructional objectives.

Probe: a sample of work taken from the child's curriculum that is used to conduct a curriculum-based assessment.

CHARACTERISTICS OF CURRICULUM-BASED ASSESSMENT

The methods of CBA are unique and can be differentiated from those of traditional assessment in several ways (see Table 7–17).

Table 7–17 Contrasting Methods of Academic Assessment

Feature	Curriculum-Based Assessment	Traditional Assessment
Test–curriculum overlap	Ensures overlap by using materials taken directly from curriculum	Assumes overlap by sampling items that presumably correspond to curriculum
Method of analysis	Idiographic (comparison within child)	Nomothetic (comparison to a group of children of similar age)
Link to intervention	Helpful in determining instructional match	Used to determine eligibility for special programs
Monitoring of academic progress	Sensitive to small changes in academic performance	Lacking in sensitivity to changes in academic performance
Psychometric properties	Reliable; moderate to high correlation with traditional methods	Reliable and valid measures of academic functioning

Overlap between Test Items and Curriculum

Traditional measures of achievement include a sample of items that presumably correspond to materials included in a child's curriculum. However, data have shown a relatively poor match between the items on achievement tests and the content of children's instructional curriculum (Jenkins and Panny 1978). With CBA, test–curriculum match is ensured by using materials taken directly from the child's curriculum.

Idiographic Method of Analysis

Standardized measures of achievement (e.g., Kaufman Tests of Educational Achievement, Wechsler Individual Achievement Tests) utilize a nomothetic or norm-referenced method of analysis (see also section "Guidelines for Use of Tests in Pediatrics" later in this chapter). Standardized measures have been used to make decisions regarding eligibility for services (e.g., special educational programming), but they generally are not helpful in assessing academic progress. Curriculum-based assessment employs an idiographic or within-subject method of analysis, which is very useful in monitoring academic progress.

Link to Intervention

Traditional measures of assessment provide information about a child's level of functioning in relation to peers but generally do not offer specific ideas about how to remediate the child's skills deficits. In contrast, CBA is very helpful in establishing an instructional match (Gickling and Thompson 1985). Using the methods of CBA, an examiner can determine which curricular materials are too easy, which are too hard, and which are appropriately challenging for the child. In addition, CBA can be useful in evaluating the effects of interventions employed to remediate academic skills deficits.

Appropriate for Continuous Progress Monitoring

Curriculum-based measurement procedures are easy to administer, score, and interpret, and thus it is efficient to use these methods repeatedly to monitor student progress. For instance, progress monitoring in reading can be accomplished by administering a one-minute reading probe once per week over the course of several weeks. In addition, CBA procedures have been shown to be sensitive to relatively small changes in academic performance over brief periods of time. In contrast, traditional assessment methods typically are lacking in sensitivity to changes brought about through academic intervention (Shapiro 1989).

Psychometrically Sound

The methods of CBA have been shown to be reliable and valid in assessing levels of academic skill. Test–retest reliability and inter-rater reliability coefficients are uniformly very high with these procedures. Also, the primary indices of CBA (i.e., number of words read correctly per minute; number of digits calculated correctly per minute) have been shown to correlate highly with standardized measures of academic achievement (Marston 1989).

ASSESSMENT OF READING

The assessment of reading using CBA procedures involves the administration of brief reading passages or probes to the child and the determination of the child's rate of oral reading. The following steps are employed:

1. Testing should begin by using passages from the book in which the child is currently placed. The examiner should select a passage from the beginning, a passage from the middle, and a passage from the end of the reading. For ease of administration and scoring, it is recommended that (1) the passages be retyped; (2) two copies be made, one for the child and the other for the examiner; and (3) running word counts be written in the righthand margin of the examiner copy.

2. For each passage, the child is asked to read aloud for one minute. The examiner

records errors of omission, substitution, and addition on the examiner copy. Each passage is scored for number of words read correctly and number of errors per minute.

3. After the child has read the three passages from a particular book, the examiner computes the median number of words read correctly and errors per minute. The median scores are then compared to guidelines that have been established for determining instructional level of functioning for each grade level (see Shapiro 1989).

4. Assessment of reading generally proceeds until the examiner identifies the highest reading level at which the child is instructional. The examiner follows the procedures described above in assessing the child's rate of reading at each reading level.

5. Once the examiner has determined the highest level at which the child is instructional, changes in curriculum can be made to achieve a more appropriate instructional match.

6. For progress monitoring, multiple reading probes are selected from the book that is one level higher than the child's current instructional level to assess progress in attaining long-term objectives (Fuchs 1989). One probe generally is administered each week during the period of progress monitoring. Progress is evaluated in relation to preestablished goals, developed on the basis of baseline data and classroom expectations, and reflecting rate of change in academic skills to be expected for students at a particular grade level.

ASSESSMENT OF MATHEMATICS

Assessing math skills is more complicated than assessing reading skills in that the content of the math curriculum at each grade level includes several arithmetic operations. For instance, in the third grade, children typically learn to add and subtract three- and four-digit numbers without regrouping, add and subtract two- and three-digit numbers with regrouping, and do word problems that require multiplying numbers from 3 to 9 (see Shapiro 1989). The following steps are used to assess math skills:

1. Testing should begin by assessing a child's ability to perform arithmetic skills in which he or she has recently been instructed. The examiner should develop three equivalent forms (each consisting of approximately 30 problems) for each arithmetic skill being assessed.

2. The child is given two minutes to work on each worksheet or probe. When the time limit expires, the examiner computes the number of digits calculated correctly per minute.

3. After the child has performed the three equivalent forms pertaining to a particular arithmetic skill, his or her median score is compared to guidelines established for determining instructional levels of performance (see Shapiro 1989). Other arithmetic skills in which the child has recently been instructed are assessed in the same manner.

4. Testing proceeds until the examiner identifies the most advanced skills in which the child is instructional for each type of operation (e.g., addition, subtraction, multiplication). For instance, if the child is at a level of frustration when performing addition problems involving three-digit by three-digit numbers with regrouping, the examiner might assess the child using problems involving fewer digits with regrouping. Because it is not feasible to assess the child's ability to perform each skill related to a particular type of operation, examiners are advised to select a sample of skills for assessment.

5. For progress monitoring, many equivalent forms of math worksheets are developed that include two or more arithmetic skills that the child is expected to master over the course of a specified length of

time. The child typically is administered one probe per week to determine progress toward meeting preestablished educational objectives.

Curriculum-based assessment methods have also been developed to assess spelling and written expression skills. For further information about the assessment of spelling and writing, the reader is referred to Shapiro (1989). Although CBA has been developed for use by educational professionals, these methods could be adapted by physical therapists, occupational therapists, and speech/language pathologists to assess a child's progress in meeting therapeutic objectives. For instance, a language pathologist could keep weekly records of number of articulation errors per minute in conversational speech to evaluate a child's progress in achieving treatment objectives.

CASE STUDY

Micah, an eight-year-old student in first grade, was referred to a child development clinic because of concerns about significant academic skills deficits and attention deficits. Upon evaluation, he was assessed as having a reading disorder as well as attention-deficit hyperactivity disorder. Micah was placed into a special education program at school. An initial assessment of Micah's academic skills revealed that he was essentially a nonreader; he was able to read approximately ten words in isolation, but he was at a frustrational level even in a preprimer or beginning first-grade reader.

For purposes of monitoring progress in reading, probes from the preprimer reader used in his school were chosen. During the baseline and intervention phases, Micah was administered a one-minute reading probe twice per week.

The results of progress monitoring are shown in Figure 7–34. During the baseline and intervention phases, rate of reading skill acquisition was determined by calculating an index of slope (see Good and Shinn 1990). During the 16-day baseline period, estimations of slope reflected an average weekly improvement of 1.8 words read correctly per minute.

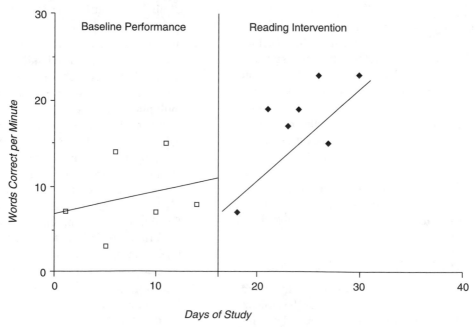

Figure 7–34 Case of Micah: The Effect of a Reading Intervention on Acquisition of Reading Skills.

Following the baseline phase, a reading intervention was introduced. The reading intervention involved use of the "folding-in" procedure (see Shapiro 1992), a flashcard approach that enables children to practice word recognition skills while experiencing high rates of success. The results showed that the reading intervention resulted in an improvement of 3.8 words correct per week, more than twice the rate demonstrated during the baseline phase. Thus progress monitoring procedures verified that the reading intervention was very successful in improving Micah's oral reading skills.

REFERENCES

Fuchs, L.S. 1989. Evaluating solutions: Monitoring progress and revising intervention plans. In *Curriculum-based measurement: Assessing special children*, ed. M.R. Shinn, 153–181. New York: Guilford Press.

Gickling, E.E., and V.P. Thompson. 1985. A personal view of curriculum-based assessment. *Exceptional Children* 52:205–218.

Good, R.H., and M.R. Shinn. 1990. Forecasting accuracy of slope estimates for reading curriculum-based measurement: Empirical evidence. *Behavioral Assessment* 12:179–193.

Jenkins, J.R., and D. Panny. 1978. Standardized achievement tests: How useful for special education? *Exceptional Children* 44:448–453.

Marston, D.B. 1989. A curriculum-based measurement approach to assessing academic performance: What it is and why do it. In *Curriculum-based measurement: Assessing special children*, ed. M.R. Shinn, 18–78. New York: Guilford Press.

Shapiro, E.S. 1989. *Academic skills problems: Direct assessment and intervention.* New York: Guilford Press.

Shapiro, E.S. 1992. Use of Gickling's model of curriculum-based assessment to improve reading in elementary age students. *School Psychology Review* 21:168–176.

ADDITIONAL SUGGESTED READING

Shinn, M.R., ed. 1989. *Curriculum-based measurement: Assessing special children.* New York: Guilford Press.

PSYCHOEDUCATIONAL MEASURES: COMPETENCY-BASED TRAINING

John M. Parrish

Purpose: to define competency-based training and describe, with examples, the characteristics of a competency-based training paradigm. A glossary of key definitions related to competency-based training is included at the end of this section.

DESCRIPTION OF COMPETENCY-BASED TRAINING

One of the most prevalent methods of instruction is simply to tell the student what to do. Then the instructor often assumes that the student has learned "the lesson." Such instruction is frequently insufficient when the student is a child with special needs. In recognition of this, many instructors will also offer a demonstration for the student of what to do. Although helpful, such demonstrations are also frequently inadequate.

In many instances, effective instruction requires a *competency-based* approach. Within such an approach, emphasis is placed on the acquisition (i.e., initial learning) and maintenance (i.e., continuation) of skills, in contrast to a focus on the provision of general information designed to improve attitudes or to increase the student's knowledge base.

The key features of a competency-based training model are:

1. identification and social validation of target skills
2. development of task analyses of such skills, with corresponding operational definitions and assessment instruments
3. collection of baseline data regarding a student's level of proficiency in targeted skill areas before training
4. specification of learner objectives
5. provision of systematic training through instruction, modeling, and/or training aids
6. completion of behavior rehearsals
7. repeated measurement of trainee performance during and subsequent to training in both simulated and criterion situations
8. when necessary, provision of remedial training consisting of additional instruction, role plays, and performance-based feedback

DESIGNING AND IMPLEMENTING A COMPETENCY-BASED CURRICULUM

Identification and Social Validation of Target Skills

At the onset of curriculum development and prior to actual provision of training, the trainer pinpoints target skills that must be acquired by the student. Requisite skills are determined typically through direct observation of competent performance, consultation with experts, and review of relevant literature.

Development of Task Analyses, Corresponding Operational Definitions, and Assessment Instruments

Every skill, however complex it may be, can be analyzed into and defined by component (i.e., elemental) steps that make up routine conduct of that skill. When the goal is to facilitate the acquisition of a new skill by a student, it is typically effective to develop a task analysis of the skill to be learned. A *task analysis* is a step-by-step de-

scription of what the student is and is not to do during the task. Each step is defined in terms of what the student is to say or do. Each step is therefore an action or set of actions that is observable and measurable. Once a provisional task analysis is developed, it is submitted to a panel of experts, experienced caregivers/educators, and, when applicable, skilled students, with a request that they evaluate both the relevance and the importance of each identified component of the planned curriculum. Revisions to the draft task analysis are then completed, based on the input and recommendations of these judges. This review by experts and consumers constitutes a critical aspect of determining the social as well as content validity of the task analysis. After a final task analysis becomes available, an *operational definition* is created for each step of the procedure, as illustrated immediately below. The definition details the scoring criteria used to determine whether each step is completed competently. The criteria should clearly state the limits of competent performance.

The following is an example of a task analysis for teaching a child to hold a pencil:

1. Position child's preferred hand such that child's little finger and side of palm are resting on sheet of paper. Child's hand is to be slightly cupped. Ensure small separation between child's thumb and index finger and between child's index and second fingers.
2. While guiding child's thumb and first two fingers of the nonpreferred hand, assist child to pick up pencil, just below eraser, allowing point of pencil to hang down.
3. Lay pencil into child's preferred hand with pencil point down and tape (colored or masking tape wrapped around pencil one inch above point) resting against first joint of child's second finger and shank of pencil laying across "V" formed by child's thumb and index finger.
4. Grasp pencil at tape with child's thumb and index finger, allowing pencil to rest against child's second finger. Provide

that minimal assistance necessary for child to hold pencil in this position.

5. Place child's nonpreferred hand at top of paper.
6. Guide point of pencil to paper.
7. Move pencil held by child down paper in order to make a mark.
8. Guide child to practice picking up pencil, holding it appropriately, and marking with pencil without cues or assistance.

A corresponding checklist of requisite steps is then developed, permitting the instructor to assess quickly whether each step is completed correctly in proper sequence by the student during structured skill rehearsals (see Table 7–18).

Collection of Baseline Data Prior to Training

Before training begins, the instructor uses the task analysis and corresponding assessment tool to determine those skills already mastered by the student. The competency-based trainer arranges a problem-solving vignette designed to require each of the identified elements of a target skill for satisfactory completion of a task. This *baseline assessment* is a brief series of direct observations of the student's performance of those skills selected for training. Usually, the trainer will offer the student at least three opportunities to demonstrate skills already mastered, while using the assessment instrument corresponding with the task analysis to score the child's performance. Baseline assessments will often reveal if and where further systematic training is required. In some instances, the child may demonstrate partial mastery even prior to training, thereby suggesting that some aspects of the curriculum merely require review or perhaps could be bypassed altogether. This should enable the trainer to pinpoint specific skill deficits and to tailor instruction accordingly.

The following is an example of a competency-based training paradigm baseline assessment for teaching a child to hold a pencil:

- Prerequisites
  1. Quiet place where trainer and child can be seated next to each other at a table
  2. Regular pencil with an eraser, with one-half-inch-wide tape around pencil one inch above pencil point
  3. Unlined piece of paper
- Baseline
  1. Have student sit at table with blank piece of paper and pencil on table in front of him or her.
  2. Say to student, "Write with the pencil." Do not provide any other cues or assistance.
  3. Observe student's performance to determine which steps of task analysis (specific steps are defined below) he or she does correctly.
  4. Record a "+" for each step the student completes correctly. Record a "–" for

---

Table 7–18 Checklist of Requisite Steps for Learning to Use a Pencil in a Competency-Based Training Paradigm

Steps	*Trial 1*	*Trial 2*	*Trial 3*
1. Place preferred hand on table.			
2. Pick up pencil using nonpreferred hand.			
3. Put pencil into preferred hand.			
4. Grasp pencil.			
5. Place nonpreferred hand on top of paper.			
6. Lower pencil point to paper.			
7. Mark paper.			
8. Pick up, hold, and mark with pencil without visual cues.			

Note: Scoring codes: C = correct; C:OOS = correct, but out of sequence; I = incorrect; N/A = not applicable; N/S = not scorable.

each step he or she omits, does incorrectly, or does out of sequence.

5. Repeat steps (1) through (4) at least three times until student's performance stabilizes.

6. Throughout each observation, do not provide consequences or assistance.

Specification of Learner Objectives

Following the baseline assessments, the trainer specifies *individualized training objectives* that address the student's particular needs. On the basis of these objectives, the trainer begins to provide systematic training through instruction, modeling through simulated or actual demonstration of needed skills, watching films when applicable, and so forth. The trainer focuses upon one skill component (i.e., one step of the task analysis) at a time in a predetermined sequence. The competency-based trainer defines individualized objectives for each learner.

The following are examples of a competency-based training paradigm learner objectives for holding a pencil:

- Learner 1: to learn to hold first a magic marker and then an oversized crayon before learning how to hold a pencil.
- Learner 2: to learn to hold a pencil independently and to attempt to write the first letter of his or her name with assistance.

Provision of Systematic Training

Often, component skills are introduced in exactly the sequence in which they are to be performed. On occasion, training actually begins with the last skill to be performed in a sequence, and training on each skill proceeds "backwards." Frequently, the trainer prescribes what is to be done (i.e., offers instruction) and then demonstrates (i.e., models) what is to be done.

The following is an example of a competency-based training paradigm systematic training sequence for learning to hold a pencil:

1. Demonstrate to child how to pick up pencil with nonpreferred hand and place it in preferred hand. At same time, say to child, "Do this...hold the pencil."

2. Lay pencil and paper on table in front of student and repeat, "Hold the pencil."

3. If student does not proceed to hold the pencil correctly, then teach student steps 1 through 4 of the task analysis. Demonstrate each step and manually guide student to perform the steps, if necessary. Fade assistance gradually until student completes each step independently when trainer says "Hold the pencil."

4. Model lowering point of pencil to paper and making a mark while saying "Do this...mark with the pencil."

5. Lay pencil and paper on table in front of student and repeat, "Mark with the pencil."

6. If the student does not use the pencil to make a mark, then model each step and provide that minimal physical guidance necessary for student to write with the pencil.

7. When student can pick up, hold, and make a mark with the pencil, fade the width of the tape from one-half inch to one-fourth inch to dark line or dotted line around pencil to one dot one inch above point of pencil to no visual cue.

8. Have student practice holding and writing with a pencil until the student does so without verbal or visual cues and without manual guidance.

9. Throughout training, provide praise (and, in select cases, consumable reinforcers) when the student correctly completes a step. Aim to ignore any delay or disruptive behavior by the student, and withhold praise and other reinforcers if the student otherwise misbehaves.

10. When the student picks up, holds, and marks with a pencil consistently for a week, fade use of praise and other reinforcers.

Some skill routines, such as those pertaining to self-administration of recommended medical procedures, are best learned through the use of *simulations*. Simulations may involve anatomically accurate dolls or may simply entail role plays involving the trainer and student. Use of simulations provides increased training opportunities, given that simulations are usually less time consuming, effortful, and anxiety provoking than practice in actual situations. The skillful trainer can often stage the simulation as if it were a game, perhaps better motivating the child to proceed with training. Use of simulations may serve to minimize the risk of introducing the student to dangerous or frightening situations before the child is adequately skilled to cope with them. In situations in which there is some risk associated with error, simulations afford the child with an opportunity to practice safely. In most instances, simulation training continues until the child meets a predetermined mastery criterion (e.g., 100% correct on all critical steps and 90% on all critical and relevant steps combined).

When the child demonstrates mastery in simulated situations, he or she is encouraged to participate in a highly similar training sequence centered upon practice in the actual situation. Such training usually includes additional instruction and modeling as a means of guiding the child to acquire requisite skills. For instance, when teaching a child to inject medication via a needle, the child is often taught to complete the same procedure learned with a doll with a soft cushion positioned on its plastic arm.

Completion of Skill Rehearsals

Once the child has demonstrated mastery under both simulated and actual training conditions, he or she is given several opportunities to practice learned skills. The trainer's primary role is

1. to arrange practice trials designed to require the child to encounter pivotal choice points requiring demonstration of recently taught skills in the correct sequence
2. to use the assessment checklist to observe carefully and score in regard to the satisfactory completion of each skill element

During practice sessions, scripts are often created to ensure that the simulation elicits practice of all critical skills. For example, if the curriculum included a focus upon teaching a parent to address a medical emergency such as choking, then the simulation would include a script by which the parent would demonstrate how to position the child for an effective intervention.

Repeated Measurement of Performance

Whether during a simulation or in an actual (i.e., criterion) situation, the competency-based trainer periodically administers what is termed a *probe*. A probe is typically conducted immediately following training and practice specific to each skill *element* (i.e., each component skill) or set of elements (i.e., a *skill domain*). During each probe, the student is asked to exhibit previously trained and untrained skills to determine the impact of training. The trainer scores the student's responses as correct or incorrect, just as during the baseline assessment and the training trials. But in the probe, unlike the training trials, the trainer provides no performance-based feedback or praise to the student.

Provision of Remedial Training

If the child fails to demonstrate mastery, then additional training is provided until the child exhibits competence during a probe. It is not uncommon for the child with special needs to require

1. additional instruction
2. use of *prompts* (which may be verbal directives, gestural hints, or minimal physical guidance)
3. modeling

4. behavior rehearsals (i.e., role plays and practice) and performance-based feedback

Training continues until a predetermined mastery criterion is achieved.

GLOSSARY

Baseline: direct observations of performance (e.g., skill level) prior to training.

Behavior rehearsal: practice of skill to be learned.

Competency-based training: a data-based, skills-focused instructional technology.

Criterion situation: the actual situation in which a target skill is to be performed.

Element: a component, or step, of a skill.

Modeling: demonstration of skill to be learned.

Operational definition: a description of an observable, measurable sequence of actions, stated in terms of what someone says or does.

Probe: an opportunity for a student to demonstrate learned skills without the assistance or performance-based feedback of the trainer.

Prompts: verbal hints or directives, gestural hints, or minimal physical guidance to assist a student's performance.

Remedial training: additional instruction, modeling, and practice predicated upon performance-based feedback.

Simulated situation: a contrived situation structured to be similar to the "real-world" situation so as to provide resources necessary to practice target skill repeatedly in "safe" context.

Skill domain: a set of skills relevant to completion of a task or procedure.

Target skill: a skill that has been selected for training.

Task analysis: the precise description of a skill through analysis and definition of each component step completed during routine performance of that skill.

SUGGESTED READINGS

Parrish, J. 1993. Training children. In *The care of children with long-term tracheostomies*, ed. K. Bleile, 249–266. San Diego: Singular Publishing Co.

Parrish, J., et al. 1986. Training respite care providers: A competency-based approach. In *Respite care provider training: Current practices and directions for research*, ed. C. Salisbury, 117–142. Baltimore: Paul H. Brookes.

PSYCHOEDUCATIONAL MEASURES: ECOLOGICAL ASSESSMENT

Peter W. Dowrick

Purpose: to provide a sample of methods for ecological assessment, which may be described as assessments of the life circumstances surrounding a child and her or his family at the time of designing services for them. The examples are based partly on those developed within the Mental Health Services Training Center in Anchorage, Alaska, for the Alaska Youth Initiative in 1989. The Alaska Youth Initiative has since become recognized as a nationally leading program for individualized, community-based, wraparound services for children and youth with severe emotional disturbances. It is thus a good model for the ecological assessment of a wide diversity of children experiencing severe and persistent disabilities.

It has become increasingly well recognized that full attention to the life circumstances in the development of programs of care deserves much more than polite reference. Appreciation of multiple circumstances bearing on a child's life is particularly important for children with disabilities. By definition, developmental disabilities require ongoing support across multiple life areas. If, for example, one cures a language disorder of a boy with autism in a clinic and sends him home, there is always the possibility that family or school circumstances will very much change—or even reverse—the outcome.

DEFINITIONS

An *ecological assessment* describes and quantifies the environment in terms of the resources and difficulties facing the child. It includes situations of living, school, social life, recreation, treatment (medical, psychosocial) agencies, and vocational training and legal situations where applicable. Such an assessment describes the *relationship* between the individual and his or her environment and is in contrast to frequently used "person-centered" assessments.

A *wraparound team* is an interdisciplinary, interagency group, including at least one family member, whose individual members are capable of and invested in consultation in the child's best interests. It usually includes

1. a parent, grandparent, or foster parent
2. a teacher and/or special educator or other school personnel
3. a social worker, psychologist, or psychiatrist
4. state or other local government agency personnel

It may also include medical and allied health people.

The *individual coordinator* is usually a professional in a health or human services agency with a mandated or contracted interest in the child. In some cases, he or she may be a family member or other person designated by the family. The coordinator's role is to see that the assessment is done appropriately and in reasonable time, to ensure that the relevant parties are consulted, and to convene meetings.

The *ecological assessor* is a person properly trained to carry out the assessments described in this chapter. It is usually a person with baccalaureate or master's level training in a human service area and with skills to interact with children, family members, and professionals in a range of disciplines. The training, not formally sanctioned by any certification, will include observational data gathering, interviewing, and report writing.

OVERVIEW OF THE ECOLOGICAL ASSESSMENT

In most cases where this approach is warranted, the child is of school, probably high school, age. Most often it is school personnel who identify the extent of the problem, and school failure, disruption, or dropout is one of the factors. Sometimes it is legal or medical personnel who seek additional resources. Occasionally, the family will approach a developmental center or university-affiliated program for help. Whoever identifies the need for intensive, individualized assistance can then get the system into action.

The first key meeting may take place in the school after hours or in some other setting slightly removed from the heart of circumstances. It will involve several key personnel with different perspectives and perhaps may not include a family member at this time. The next meeting should ensure the participation of the family and begin to clarify the team membership and their roles. Some talk will be focused at this time on who will pay for the assessment and the identified services. Some services may be obligatory for the school system to provide "a free and appropriate education" (see Chapter 8, section "Laws and Issues Concerning Education and Related Services"). Others may be covered by state welfare or health and social agencies, by private insurance, or out of pocket.

Once the wraparound team has been fully identified, the individual coordinator takes on the overall management of the situation. For the most part, the coordinator ensures that all perspectives are heard and that the assessment is suitably comprehensive. With so many people of different professional training lines of responsibility, the team may not always function smoothly, and the coordinator may spend quite some effort in diplomacy.

The ecological assessment usually takes between 20 and 40 hours of data gathering. Data are collected in different places and from different people; so the process may take two or three weeks. The whole team considers the findings and makes recommendations for services and supports. These recommendations may include simple adjustments to the environment, such as new sleeping arrangements for the family or a neighbor's assistance with transport. If possible, the individual coordinator provides continuing case management for the family.

PROCEDURES FOR CONDUCTING AN ECOLOGICAL ASSESSMENT

Activity Schema for Wraparound Services

1. A case manager, therapist, or family member convenes a wraparound team.
2. The team recommends an ecological assessment on the basis of serious complications to the child's development in at least three of the following areas: family or living situation; school or vocational training; social life or recreation; medical conditions or treatments; emotional and behavioral status; legal situations.
3. The team identifies an individual coordinator and the appropriate authority and funding or the means by which these supports can be obtained.
4. Likewise, the team identifies an ecological assessor and his or her support.
5. The originating case manager, therapist, or family member formalizes the contracts for the coordinator and the assessor.
6. The assessor carries out the ecological assessment.

7. The assessor presents the findings to the coordinator and the wraparound team.
8. The team makes recommendations for services and supports based on the assessment.

Wraparound Team Members

List the members of the team to be convened. Not all categories may apply in some cases.

1. parent or guardian
2. medical advisor (profession/agency)
3. psychological service (profession/agency)
4. social worker
5. educator (school/agency)
6. allied health professional (profession/agency)
7. child
8. other(s)
9. individual coordinator (name, phone, agency, address, authority, funding)
10. ecological assessor (name, phone, agency, address, authority, funding)

Scope of Ecological Assessment

Describe the areas of concern that apply:
- Primary
  1. family or living situation
  2. school or vocational training
  3. social life (friends) or recreation
  4. medical conditions or treatments
  5. emotional and behavioral status
  6. legal situation
- Secondary
  1. family or living situation
  2. school or vocational training
  3. social life (friends) or recreation
  4. medical conditions or treatments
  5. emotional and behavioral status
  6. legal situation

Specific Personal Contacts Required

List names and relationships.

Completion of Assessment

The wraparound team completes the Scope of Ecological Assessment for the assessor. The assessor then prepares firsthand observations of each of the areas of concern identified. Each identified area is described in one page or less of observations of *strengths and resources*, one page or less of *difficulties and impediments*, and one page or less of *recommendations*. Observations may be direct or via suitable informants, gathered firsthand by the assessor. Any forms or checklists used, as recommended in other chapters of this book, should be attached to the report.

Summary

The assessor, finally, will prepare a summary of findings to include the following:

1. child's name
2. birth date
3. dates of contract
4. contract with person/agency
5. dates of ecological assessment
6. number of hours of observations and interviews
7. number of people contacted and observed
8. a list of names (and relationship to the child) of primary observers and informants

---

SUGGESTED READINGS

Burchard, J.D., and R.T. Clarke. 1990. The role of individualized care in a service delivery system for children and adolescents with severely maladjusted behavior. *Journal of Mental Health Administration* 17, 87–98.

Caldwell, B., and R. Bradley. 1984. *Home observation for measurement of the environment.* New York: Dorsey Press.

Lutzker, J.R., et al. 1992. Project ecosystems: An ecobehavioral approach to families with children with developmental disabilities. *Journal of Developmental and Physical Disabilities* 4:1–13.

MacFarquhar, K.W., et al. 1993. Individualizing services for seriously emotionally disturbed youth: A nationwide review. *Administration and Policy in Mental Health* 20:165–174.

ADDITIONAL RESOURCES

For further information, contact:

1. Center for Human Development: UAP (University of Alaska, Anchorage), 2330 Nichols Street, Anchorage, AK 99508. Tel: (907) 272-8270; fax: (907) 274-4802.
2. Behavior Change Associates/Project Ecosystems, 29931 Rainbow Crest Drive, Agoura Hills, CA 91301.
3. National Clearinghouse on Family Support and Children's Mental Health, P.O. Box 751, Portland, OR 97207. Tel.: 800-628-1696, 503-725-4040; tdd: 503-725-4165; fax: 503-725-4180.

GUIDELINES FOR USE OF TESTS IN PEDIATRICS

Jerilynn Radcliffe and Edward M. Moss

Purpose: to describe the defining characteristics and uses of a variety of information-gathering methods commonly used by professionals for assessment of children. Special consideration is given to principles of test construction that must be considered in the selection, use, and interpretation of standardized or norm-referenced tests, as well as to ethical considerations for professionals involved in conducting and reporting assessment procedures.

Tests are helpful as one part of an assessment of a child's developmental, functional, learning, or cognitive needs. Tests may also be helpful in assessing behavioral issues such as anxiety, depression, or attentional problems. However, tests are not intended to be used in isolation from observation, interview, review of records, and other informal assessment pertinent to the referral (Sattler 1992; American Psychological Association 1992). Tests may be either *criterion referenced* (i.e., assessing the child's progress toward particular skills or goals) or *standardized or nomothetic* (i.e., comparing the child's performance against that of a normative group).

Testing must be used in conjunction with other types of assessment methods. These may include interviewing or obtaining histories from parents or care providers; making observations, which may range from informal observations of behavior in various settings to more structured observations of particular behaviors under study, as might be done through checklists or observational schemas; and considering the role of specific settings upon behavior. This latter approach, that of considering the effect of particular environments upon behavior, is known as *ecological assessment*. Children, in particular, are known to behave very differently across different settings such as home, care provider's environment, hospital, and school. Ecological assessment takes into account the degree of

behavioral variability shown across settings (see also the previous section, "Psychoeducational Measures: Ecological Assessment").

Regardless of the particular manner in which assessment is conducted, several steps are generally involved in the assessment process:

1. determining the reason for assessment
2. gathering relevant background information
3. selecting the appropriate tool or modality
4. administering the assessment tool or conducting the necessary investigation, such as interviewing or observing
5. scoring/interpreting/merging the results of the assessment with other sources of information
6. communicating/applying findings in relation to the purpose for assessment

CRITICAL FACTORS IN SELECTION OF TESTS

Since there are hundreds of measures available to evaluate various aspects of learning, behavior, or skill, professionals are challenged to select the most appropriate instrument(s) in relation to the referral question. Fortunately, several excellent references are available with up-to-date reviews of current tests. These references include *Tests in Print* and the *Mental Measurements Yearbook* (see the suggested readings at the end of this section).

Though not exhaustive, the following list reviews most of the important considerations in test selection.

Standardization

Standardized testing presupposes that the test will be individually administered under controlled circumstances similar to those under which the test was standardized. Typically, this requires a quiet, well-lit setting with minimal distraction, an examiner trained to administer tests following specific guidelines, a cooperative and well-motivated subject, and so forth. Standardized tests also allow us to compare an individual child's performance against a comparison group, called the *standardization sample*. This is the group of individuals chosen to represent "normal" test performance and variation. *The standardization sample must be reflective of the individual being tested to apply test scoring standards to that individual.* For example, to test a child in the United States, one must compare his or her performance with that of other children within the United States. Standardization samples of various tests vary in the number of variables taken into account in the standardization. Most tests include equal numbers of males and females and an equal distribution of ages across the age range of the test. Other variables that are important to include in a standardization sample are geographic distribution (area within the United States), urban/rural/suburban residence, level of parental education, level of parental occupation, and race/ethnicity. The percentages of children within each variable group should correspond to the percentages of the general population falling within each variable group at the time of the most recent census. The standardization group provides a kind of "melting-pot" standard of performance for children that takes into account important demographic factors proportionate to their representation within the overall population.

Reliability

Reliability refers to the degree to which a test consistently measures performance over time. Reliability is affected by the length of a test (i.e., the longer the test, the more reliable it is likely to be), the test–retest interval (i.e., the longer the interval, the less reliable the test is likely to be), guessing (i.e., the more guessing is present, the lower the reliability is likely to be), variation within the test setting (which leads to lower test

reliability), and intrinsic factors (i.e., motivation of the individual, willingness to comply with instructions, anxiety, state of health).

Reliability is described by a correlation coefficient ranging from 1.00 to .00. The closer a correlation coefficient approaches 1.00, the higher the reliability of the test. While a reliability coefficient of .80 or higher may be acceptable for screening instruments, a coefficient of .90 or higher is recommended when using a score to make important diagnostic or clinical decisions. Several different types of reliability may be studied and reported in the test manual, such as inter-rater, test–retest, split-half, and alternate-form. Different types of reliability are as follows:

1. *Inter-rater reliability* refers to the amount of variance in scores accounted for by judgments of different examiners. Training helps to reduce this type of error variance.

2. *Test–retest reliability* refers to the degree to which performance on a test is similar over a time period. The time interval may be as little as minutes apart for some tests or up to six weeks apart for other tests, depending on the nature of the task and how quickly skills are assumed to change over time.

3. *Split–half reliability* refers to the degree to which performance on a test, divided into two halves by alternate items, is consistent.

4. *Alternate-form reliability* refers to the extent that performance on two comparable forms of a test is consistent.

Validity

Validity refers to the degree to which a test measures what it purports to measure. A test must be reliable to be valid; however, a test may be reliable without necessarily being valid. To be valid, there must exist a high degree of relationship between performance on a particular test and performance on a particular criterion (such as a strong relationship between a score on a reading test and a child's ability to read a textbook at a certain level). *Tests are valid for specific purposes only.* As is the case with measures of reliability, factors affecting validity include individual variables (e.g., motivation, anxiety), factors relating to the criterion (e.g., the degree to which the criterion accurately reflects the construct under study), and intervening events and contingencies (e.g., acute states of illness or disturbance). Several types of validity exist:

1. *Content validity* refers to the degree to which the test items accurately represent the domain the test purports to measure.
2. *Criterion-related validity* refers to the relationship between test scores and the particular criterion of concern.
3. *Concurrent validity* is a measure of the extent to which test scores are related to those obtained from another currently available test.
4. *Predictive validity* indicates the relation between test scores and performance on a relevant criterion when there is a time interval between the test administration and performance on the criterion measure.
5. *Construct validity* indicates the extent to which a test measures a particular construct or trait.

Age Appropriateness

Although it should be obvious that children must be assessed with measures that were normed for their exact age, this is an important concept that must be stated explicitly. Although valuable *qualitative* information can sometimes be obtained through the use of tests that were normed on older or younger subjects, there are serious limitations to the predictive value of this procedure.

Cultural Bias

Despite recent improvements in test development, it is still the case that many tests have been normed exclusively on populations of Caucasian children from middle-class backgrounds. This raises concern about the applicability of such measures to children from other ethnic and socioeconomic backgrounds. It is not possible to devise a measure that is fair to all cultures, but efforts should be made to reduce cultural differentials.

There are several common forms of cultural bias within individual assessment. Frequently, children from minority groups either have an inadequate grasp of English or speak a nonstandard form of English. This is less problematic on nonverbal performance than verbal tests; thus most attempts to produce "culture-fair" tests have resulted in nonverbal formats. It is important to consider that children raised in other cultures may have been exposed to a variety of problem-solving strategies that are not readily assessed by paper-and-pencil testing. Children from impoverished socioeconomic backgrounds may have a decreased level of intellectual stimulation in the home environment. Finally, the child may find it difficult to establish rapport with an examiner who represents a different culture.

Practical Considerations

Other factors that influence the assessment are practical. The examiner must take into account the amount of time needed to administer, score, and interpret a particular measure versus the amount and quality of the information that measure will provide. A test requiring a great amount of time to administer must provide information that is important to the question under study. Similarly, a test requiring extensive training on the part of the examiner should also be one that provides important information.

Costs of tests and assessment measures may vary considerably. Again, costs of equipment need to be taken into account in terms of the nature of the information obtained from these. Another related expense is that of space and special equipment necessary for testing. Testing is normally conducted in an environment that is relatively free of distractions, is of sufficient size and dimensions, and contains equipment necessary to conduct the testing. Unless adequate space and equipment are available for testing, the results of the testing may be compromised to the point of providing no meaningful information.

APPROPRIATE/INAPPROPRIATE USES OF TESTS

Qualifications of Users

Those who use tests must do so only within the boundaries of their competence, based on their education, training, supervised experience, or appropriate professional experience. In emerging areas in which generally recognized standards for preparatory training do not yet exist, test users must nonetheless take reasonable steps to ensure the competence of their work and to protect patients, clients, students, research participants, and others from harm.

Ethical Considerations

The following summarizes ethical considerations for professionals involved in the assessment of children:

1. Tests should be performed only in the context of a defined professional relationship.
2. Assessments, recommendations, and reports should be based only on information and techniques sufficient to provide appropriate substantiation for their findings.
3. Psychologists and other users of psychological tests should use these tests in a manner and for purposes that are appropriate in light of the research on or evidence for the usefulness and proper application of the techniques.
4. Test results must be interpreted in light of the reliability, validity, and related stand-

ardization and outcome studies pertaining to the tests. Given these factors, limits to the certainty of the test results must be recognized.
5. Assessment decisions or recommendations should not be based on testing instruments, data, or test results that are outdated for the current purpose.
6. Unless the nature of the relationship is clearly explained to the person being assessed in advance and precludes providing an explanation of results, those who use tests must ensure that an explanation of the results is provided using language that is reasonably understandable to the person being assessed or to another legally authorized to act on behalf of the client, such as a parent or legal guardian.
7. Reasonable efforts must be made to maintain the integrity and security of tests and other assessment techniques, consistent with law, contractual obligations, and professional ethical codes.

Adaptation of Tests

In general, professionals who use tests are ethically responsible for identifying situations in which particular assessment techniques or norms may not be applicable. When factors such as individuals' gender, age, race, ethnicity, national origin, religion, sexual orientation, disability, language, or socioeconomic status differ from those in the normative group, the professional is obliged to decide whether administration or interpretations should be adjusted. When interpreting any assessment results, including computerized or automated interpretations, it is imperative to take into account the various test factors and characteristics of the person being assessed that might alter professionals' judgments or reduce the accuracy of interpretations. *Any significant reservations regarding the accuracy or limitations of interpretations must be stated clearly in the report or any feedback provided to the pa-*

tient, client, or others legally authorized to act on behalf of the patient.

Some of the more common reasons for adapting test administration with children who have developmental disabilities and special health needs are discussed in the following section.

Correction for Prematurity

When scoring tests for children born prematurely, it is standard practice to perform some correction in scores to take into account the degree of the child's prematurity. This should be done only when children are born at least four weeks before the estimated due date. Correction for prematurity is typically done until age two years, although some advocate discontinuing correction as early as 12 months of age (DenOuden et al. 1991). The most frequent practice is to give full correction for prematurity until the age of two years, with no further correction beyond that point. To give correction for prematurity, the test is scored using the estimated due date as the child's actual birth date. For example, a 10-month-old child born eight weeks early would be considered to be eight months of age for purposes of scoring on a developmental test such as the Gesell or the Bayley. The Revised Bayley provides explicit directions for giving this correction for prematurity (Bayley 1993). Scores obtained by using corrected age instead of gestational age must be described as such. This may be done through a statement such as "Full correction was made for the child's prematurity (child was born at 34 weeks' gestation)."

Adaptation for Severe Mobility Limitations

Severe mobility limitations cannot be ignored while conducting tests of function. Positioning of the child has been found to have a significant effect on scores for the Bayley Mental Scale (Miedaner and Finuf 1993), for example, and it is obvious that if a child has limitations in sitting or in performing the movements required by the testing tasks, these must be taken into account in the process of testing. The clinician must ascertain the child's ability to maintain an upright position while seated for the duration of the testing and to see, hear, and touch all relevant stimuli presented; the appropriateness of the chair in terms of size, support for the child's trunk, and support for the child's feet; the appropriateness of the table in terms of position for the child's reach or vision; and the appropriateness of the materials themselves (e.g., size, child's ability to grasp these, child's ability to maintain these within the visual field). Specific adaptations for children with severe mobility limitations must be done on an individual basis, preferably with consultation with therapists trained and experienced in work with children with mobility deficits. Good practice in conducting testing with children with physical impairments includes consultation with a physical or occupational therapist at the time of testing to adjust child's positioning, modify presentation of test items, or use adaptive equipment such as a chair with additional head and foot supports and a table positioned at the appropriate height and angle.

Adaptation for Sensory Impairment

Evaluation of children with sensory impairments is complicated by the relative lack of tests designed and developed for use with these populations. When possible, tests and measures designed for specific populations of individuals with sensory impairments should be used. This is important because it is well established that individuals with sensory impairments develop critical developmental skills somewhat differently from those without sensory impairments. For example, children with hearing impairment have been found to show significant delays not only in the development of speech (Quigley 1978) but also in the development of reading skills (Northern and Downs 1991). The use of tests referenced for children with hearing impairments allows for fairer comparisons to be made between the individual under study and the larger population of which that person is a member. Similarly, children with a visual impairment often present with delayed motor skill development (Batshaw and Perret 1992). Comparing a child with a significant visual impairment with normally sighted peers could result in an inappropriate diagnosis or an underestimate of a child's abilities.

Although some tests have been designed specifically for groups of individuals with sensory impairments, these may not be widely available. In addition, currently available measures have not been widely accepted as adequate to meet the needs of the populations (Gibbins 1989). In such a case, it is necessary to adapt tests or measures developed for individuals without sensory impairments to allow for some determination of functional skill levels. However, when a test is used with a member of a population for whom it was not intended, findings from such testing must be interpreted with a high degree of caution.

Adaptations that may be necessary to make are to exclude parts of tests that cannot be administered in light of the individual's perceptual impairment (e.g., visual items to a person with severe visual impairment, or spoken questions to a person with hearing impairment who does not lip-read) or to administer parts of tests in a format appropriate to the individual's sensory capabilities (e.g., providing instructions in sign language to a signing individual with hearing impairment). When adaptations are made to standard test administration procedure, these must be fully acknowledged in any reporting of results, and the results of the tests must be interpreted with extreme caution.

INTERPRETATION OF TESTS

Test scores must be interpreted only by those who are competent (i.e., trained and experienced) in doing so, or under the supervision of such an individual. Test scores must be interpreted in accordance with the stated purpose(s) of the test, in response to the particular referral question, and taking into account both the statistical properties of the tests and any factors, such as cultural differences, sensory or motor limitations, motivational and behavioral issues, or physical well-being issues, that might significantly influence the interpretation of the tests.

Scores from standardized tests are typically reported in *standard scores* (Figure 7–35). These are obtained by translating raw scores earned in performing tests into scores reflecting the percentage of the standardization sample that earned that particular score. Many standardized tests use 100 as a mean score. This means that a particular raw score that is translated into a standard score of 100 reflects the 50th percentile of raw score points obtained by the standardization group.

Tests of intelligence use a mean standard score of 100 with a standard deviation of either 15 or 16, depending on the test. *Standard deviation* refers to the degree of variability with a presumed normal range of variation. Scores within one standard deviation of the mean are expected to occur in 68 percent of cases under normal circumstances. Scores within two or more standard deviations from the mean are expected to occur much less frequently.

A single test score should never be regarded as a fixed point. Each score must be interpreted in light of the *standard error of measurement*. This refers to the degree that test scores for any one individual would be expected to vary, considering the reliability of the test. The standard error of measurement is the standard deviation of the distribution of the error scores. This forms the basis for forming the *confidence interval* surrounding the score obtained. This usually ranges from 68 percent to 99 percent. For example, in a 95 percent confidence interval, the chances are 95 out of 100 that an individual's true score falls within the score range indicated.

Scores are often described in reports in terms of their range. Scores falling within one standard deviation of the mean are described as *within normal limits*. For tests of intelligence, scores between about 90 to 110 are described as *average*. Beyond this, scores between about 80 and 90 are described as *low average*, between about 70 and 80 as *borderline*, between about 55 and 70 as *mildly deficient/delayed/retarded*, between about 40 and 55 as *moderately deficient/delayed/retarded*, between about 25 and 40 as *severely deficient/delayed/retarded*, and lower than about 25 as *profoundly deficient/delayed/ retarded*. The score ranges are approximate because they are determined by the number of standard deviation points of the test score's distance from the mean score, with some measures having standard deviations of 15 and others of 16 points. Scores above 110 are described as follows: 110 to 120, *bright average*; 120 to 130, *superior*; and 130 and above, *very superior*. These scores are illustrated in Figure 7–35.

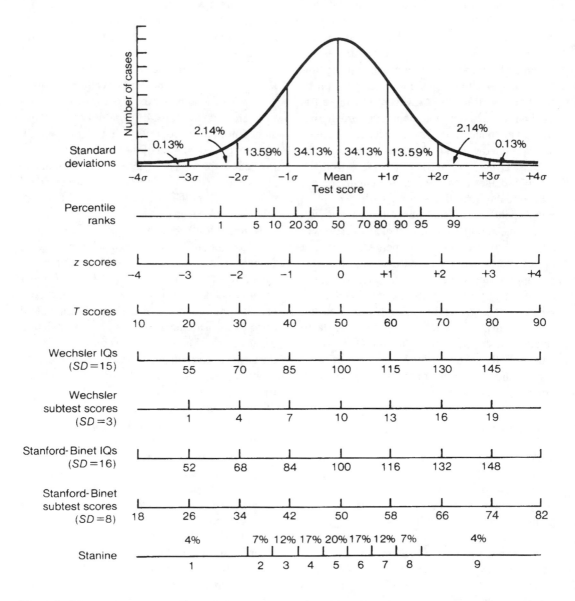

Figure 7–35 Relationship of Normal Curve to Various Types of Standard Scores. *Source:* From *Assessment of Children*, 3rd ed. (p. 17) by J.M. Sattler, San Diego, CA: J.M. Sattler, Publisher. Copyright © 1992 Jerome M. Sattler. Reprinted with permission.

REFERENCES

American Psychological Association. 1992. *Ethical principles of psychologists and code of conduct.* Washington, D.C.

Batshaw, M.L., and Y.M. Perret. 1992. *Children with disabilities: A medical primer.* 3rd ed. Baltimore: Paul H. Brookes.

Bayley, N. 1993. *Bayley Scales of Infant Development (Second Edition).* San Antonio, Tex.: The Psychological Corporation.

DenOuden, L., et al. 1991. Is it correct to correct? Developmental milestones in 555 "normal" preterm infants compared with term infants. *Journal of Pediatrics* 118:399–404.

Gibbins, S. 1989. The provision of school psychological assessment services for the hearing impaired: A national survey. *Volta Review*, Feb./Mar., 95–103.

Miedaner, J., and L. Finuf. 1993. Effects of adaptive positioning on psychological test scores for preschool children with cerebral palsy. *Pediatric Physical Therapy* 5:177–183.

Northern, J.L., and M.P. Downs. 1991. *Hearing in children..* 4th ed. Baltimore: Williams & Wilkins.

Quigley, S.P. 1978. Effects of hearing impairment on normal language development. In *Pediatric audiology*, ed. F.N. Martin. Englewood Cliffs, N.J.: Prentice Hall.

Sattler, J. 1992. *Assessment of children.* 3rd ed., rev. and updated. San Diego: Jerome Sattler, Publisher.

ADDITIONAL SUGGESTED READINGS

American Educational Research Association, American Psychological Association, and National Council on Measurement in Education. 1985. *Standards for educational and psychological testing.* Washington, D.C.: American Psychological Association.

Anastasi, A. 1982. *Psychological testing.* 5th ed. New York: Macmillan Publishing Co, Inc.

Bradley-Johnson, S. 1986. *Psychoeducational assessment of visually impaired and blind students: Infancy through high school.* Austin, Tex.: Pro-Ed.

Buros, O.K., ed. 1983. *The ninth mental measurements yearbook.* Lincoln, Neb.: Buros Institute on Mental Measurement.

King-Thomas, L., and B. Hacker. 1987. *A therapist's guide to pediatric assessment.* Boston: Little, Brown & Co.

Louick, D., and T. Boland. 1982. Psychologic tests: A guide for pediatricians. *Pediatric Annals* 11:470–489.

Lyman, H.B. 1991. *Test scores and what they mean.* 5th ed. Needham Heights, Mass.: Allyn & Bacon.

Mitchell, J.V., Jr. ed. 1983. *Tests in print III.* Lincoln, Neb.: University of Nebraska Press.

Zieziula, F.R. 1983. *Assessment of hearing impaired people: A guide for selecting psychological, educational, and vocational tests.* Washington, D.C.: Gallaudet College Press.

ANNOTATED INDEX OF SELECTED ASSESSMENT TOOLS

Lisa A. Kurtz, Mary F. Lazar, and Marleen Anne Baron

DEVELOPMENTAL TESTS INTENDED FOR NORMAL POPULATIONS*

Bayley II Scales of Infant Development

- Age Range: 1 to 42 months
- Testing Time: 45 to 90 minutes
- Intended Uses: To provide a comprehensive, diagnostic assessment of develop-

ment in infants and young children who are at risk for developmental delay and to assist in planning intervention

- Format: Individually administered, contains three subtests (mental scale, motor scale, and behavior rating scale)
- Standardization: Renormed on a stratified sample of 1,700 children (850 each gender) reflecting geographic and cultural diversity. Data are provided for the following groups: premature infants, HIV positive,

---

*Reviewed by Lisa A. Kurtz.

prenatal drug exposure, birth asphyxia, frequent otitis media, developmental delay, autistic, Down syndrome

- User Qualifications: Requires supervised training in administration, scoring, and interpretation by a qualified psychologist
- References: Bayley, N. 1993. *Bayley II Scales of Infant Development.* San Antonio, Tex.: The Psychological Corporation.

Denver II Developmental Screening Test

- Age Range: 1 month to 6 years
- Testing Time: Approximately 10 to 20 minutes
- Intended Uses: Designed to help health care providers detect early indications of developmental deviations in young children
- Format: Individually administered test measuring four domains of performance (language, fine motor/adaptive, personal social, gross motor) and supplemented by a brief behavioral scale. Measures based on a combination of parent report, observation, and direct elicitation of performance; each item scored on a pass/fail basis
- Standardization: 2,096 children living in Colorado; sample stratified by age, race, socioeconomic status, and urban vs. rural residence
- User Qualifications: Can be administered by professional or nonprofessional adults with limited training and supervision; because of the use of some subjective observations, some knowledge of child development is helpful; training videotape is available
- References: Frankenburg, W.K., et al. 1990. *The Denver II.* Denver: Denver Developmental Materials.
  Frankenburg, W.K., et al. 1992. The Denver II: A major revision and restandardization of the Denver Developmental Screening Test. *Pediatrics* 89, no. 1:91–97.

First Step

- Age Range: 2.9 to 6.2 years
- Testing Time: 15 minutes
- Intended Uses: Screening test for preschoolers designed to identify children at risk for developmental delay
- Format: Individually administered, play-based games designed to elicit measures in the following domains: cognition, communication, physical, social-emotional, and adaptive
- Standardization: Random, national sample of 1,400 children stratified for region, age, ethnicity, gender, community size, and parent's education. Scores are available as Z-scores, percentiles, or age equivalency
- User Qualifications: Educational, psychological, and medical personnel with knowledge of child development and testing principles
- References: Miller, L.J. 1992. *First Step manual.* San Antonio, Tex.: The Psychological Corporation.

Kent Infant Development Scale

- Age Range: 2 to 13 months
- Testing Time: 30 to 45 minutes
- Intended Uses: To assess overall developmental status of infants
- Format: Norm-referenced parent report measure based on observation. The scale consists of 252 items in five domains: cognitive, social, motor, self-help, and language. The scale was modified in 1987 by Morrow-Tlucak et al. to reduce the length and to simplify the language used
- Standardization: Original norms were based on 357 healthy infants, with 123 infants added to the database in 1982 and another 706 infants added in 1990
- User Qualifications: Caregivers with a high school education can complete the scale

- References: Reuter, J., and L. Bickett. 1985. *The Kent Development Scale*. Kent, Ohio: Kent Developmental Metrics.

  Long, T.M. 1992. The use of parent report measures to assess infant development. *Pediatric Physical Therapy* 4, no. 2:74–77.

  Morrow-Tlucak, et al. 1987. The Kent Infant Development Scale: Concurrent and predictive validity of a modified administration. *Psychological Report* 60:887–894.

Gesell Developmental Schedules, 1989 Revision

- Age Range: 0 to 36 months
- Testing Time: 10 to 30 minutes
- Intended Uses: Designed as a diagnostic developmental assessment to determine the integrity and functional maturity of the child's nervous system
- Format: Individually administered, combining information from parent history and a formal behavioral examination; yields developmental quotient in each of five domains (gross motor, fine motor, adaptive, language, personal social) as well as an overall developmental quotient derived through qualitative scoring procedures
- Standardization: 1980 revision based on sample of 927 infants residing in the Albany, New York, area who met the following criteria: delivery at term, within two weeks of expected date of confinement, birthweight of 2,500 grams or more, single birth, no developmental delay, and no abnormalities
- User Qualifications: Designed for use by physicians with thorough understanding of central nervous system development and pathophysiology; may be used by educational and other personnel with training and supervision to achieve inter-rater reliability
- References: Knobloch, H., et al. 1980. *Manual of developmental diagnosis*. Hagerstown, Md.: Harper & Row.

Test materials may be purchased from Developmental Evaluation Materials, Inc., P.O. Box 272391, Houston, TX 77277-2391. Tel.: (713) 529-2171.

Gesell Preschool Test

- Age Range: 2.6 to 6 years
- Testing Time: Approximately 40 minutes
- Intended Uses: Designed to help determine behavioral maturity as a factor in determining when to begin school and in what type of class setting
- Format: Individually administered behavioral assessment; measures developmental maturity as well as relative strengths and weaknesses in motor, adaptive, language, and personal social behavior
- Standardization: Restandardized on a cohort of 664 subjects (primarily Caucasian and upper middle class) residing in Connecticut
- User Qualifications: Not specified
- References: Haines, J., et al. 1980. *The Gesell Preschool Test manual*. Rosemont, N.J.: Modern Learning Press.

  Ames, L.B., et al. 1979. *The Gesell Institute's child from one to six: Evaluating the behavior of the preschool child*. New York: Harper & Row.

Miller Assessment for Preschoolers (MAP)

- Age Range: 2.9 to 5.8 years
- Testing Time: 30 minutes
- Intended Uses: Designed to screen normal children for evidence of mild to moderate developmental delay that might benefit from further evaluation; to identify children at risk for school-related problems
- Format: Individually administered test that yields scores (indices) in five areas of performance: foundations (sensory and motor maturity), coordination (gross, fine, and

oral motor), verbal (expressive and receptive language, auditory memory), nonverbal (visual perception, memory, and spatial organization), and complex tasks (combined sensory, motor, and cognitive tasks)

- Standardization: Random, national sample of 1,204 children stratified by age, sex, race, community size, and socioeconomic status

- User Qualifications: May be administered and scored by professionals with a wide range of backgrounds and experience with developmental or psychological assessment; a training videotape is available to help ensure adherence to standardized procedure; advanced training workshops are also available

- References: Miller, L.J. 1988. *Miller Assessment for Preschoolers manual.* Rev. ed. San Antonio, Tex.: The Psychological Corporation.

  Daniels, L.E., and S. Bressler. 1990. The Miller Assessment for Preschoolers: Clinical use with children with developmental delays. *American Journal of Occupational Therapy* 44, no. 1:48–53.

Mullen Scales of Early Learning (MSEL)

- Age Range: Infant MSEL, birth to 39 months

  Preschool MSEL, 24 to 69 months

- Testing Time: 15 to 35 minutes

- Intended Uses: To assess a child's learning style, strengths, and needs, using both visual and language skills at receptive and expressive levels. Useful in assessing early intellectual development and readiness for school, as well as in providing a baseline for a continuum of appropriate teaching methods

- Format: Individually administered, measuring skills in five domains: (1) gross motor base, (2) visual receptive organization, (3) visual expressive organization, (4) language receptive organization, and (5) language expressive organization

- Standardization: Infant MSEL sample included 1,231 children (0 to 38 months) stratified by age, gender, race, parental occupation, and urban/rural residence. Subjects were selected from over 100 sites representing all major geographic regions of the U.S.

- User Qualifications: Described as appropriate for use by a wide range of professionals working with young children

- References: Mullen, E.M. 1989. *Infant MSEL manual.* Cranston, R.I.: Total Child, Inc. (now available through American Guidance Service).

Vineland Adaptive Behavior Scales (VABS)

- Age Range: 0 to 19 years

- Testing Time: 20 to 90 minutes, depending on form used

- Intended Uses: To assess the social competence of individuals with and without disability by assessing adaptive behavior, which is defined as the ability to perform the daily activities required for personal and social sufficiency. The VABS can be used for three purposes: (1) to assist with the diagnosis of mental retardation and other disabilities; (2) to plan educational, habilitative, and treatment programs; and (3) as a research measure

- Format: Semistructured interview. The VABS consists of three forms: the Survey Form has 297 items, the Expanded Form has 577 items, and the Classroom Edition has 244 items. Each form measures adaptive behavior in four domains: communication, daily living skills, socialization, and motor skills. Spanish editions are available for the Survey and Expanded Forms

- Standardization: For the Survey and Expanded Forms, sample included 3,000 individuals ages birth to 18.11 years, randomly selected according to age, gender, community size, geographic region, parent's education, and race or ethnic group; supplemental norms are included for emotionally disturbed, physically disabled, and mentally retarded subjects. The Classroom Edition sample was also 300 individuals with similar stratification, but with ages 3.0 to 12.11 years

- User Qualifications: Administration and scoring by a psychologist, social worker, or other professional with a graduate degree and specific experience in individual assessment and test interpretation; a cassette training tape is available
- References: Sparrow, S.S., et al. 1984. *Vineland Adaptive Behavior Scales: Survey form manual, Interview Edition.* Circle Pines, Minn.: American Guidance Service.

  Campbell, I.A. 1985. Review of the Vineland Adaptive Behavior Scales. In *The ninth mental measurements yearbook*, ed. J.V. Mitchell. Lincoln, Nebr.: University of Nebraska Press.

DEVELOPMENTAL TESTS DESIGNED FOR CHILDREN WITH DISABILITIES*

Blind Learning Aptitude Test

- Age Range: 6 to 16 years
- Testing Time: 20 to 45 minutes
- Intended Uses: Designed to measure learning potential in students with serious vision impairments
- Format: Individually administered test consisting of 49 items using plastic sheets with figures in bas-relief; the student is asked to make selections based on tactile discrimination of the figures; knowledge of Braille is not required

---

*Reviewed by Lisa A. Kurtz.

- Standardization: Norm sample includes 961 visually impaired students from ages 6 through 21 (although norm tables only go to age 16). Students were drawn from 12 states that represent four regions of the country but do not correspond proportionately to census data. Most of the students were in residential programs
- User Qualifications: Not specified
- References: Newland, T.E. 1979. The Blind Learning Aptitude Test. *Journal of Vision Impairment and Blindness* 73:134-139.

Callier–Azusa Scale

- Age Range: 0 to 98 months
- Testing Time: Not specified
- Intended Uses: To provide developmental assessment linked with instructional objectives for deaf-blind children
- Format: Criterion-referenced, judgment-based observation scale that provides a general estimate of developmental age in the following areas: socialization, daily living skills, motor development, perceptual abilities, and language development
- Standardization: Not standardized
- User Qualifications: Not specified
- References: Stillman, R. 1974. *Callier–Azusa Scale (CAS): Assessment of deaf-blind children.* Reston, Va.: The Council for Exceptional Children.

  Diebold, L.T. 1978. Developmental scales versus observational measures for deaf-blind children. *Exceptional Children* 44:275–279.

Carolina Curriculum for Handicapped Infants and Infants at Risk

- Age Range: Children with disabilities who function within the 0- to 24-month developmental range
- Testing Time: Not specified

- Intended Uses: To provide assistance to early intervention personnel and other child caregivers in providing optimal curricular intervention to children with disabilities who function within the 0- to 24-month developmental range
- Format: Log of behavioral assessment sequences correlated with a curriculum based upon logical learning sequences. Activity suggestions include suggestions for incorporating learning principles into normal daily routines, as well as adaptations appropriate for specific disabilities (vision impaired, hearing impaired, motor impaired)
- Standardization: Not standardized; curriculum has been field tested in 22 intervention programs in North Carolina and 10 national sites from Alaska to Maryland
- User Qualifications: Not specified; considered an appropriate tool for use by a wide range of early intervention personnel
- References: Johnson-Martin, N., et al. 1991. *The Carolina curriculum for infants and toddlers with special needs.* 2nd ed. Baltimore: Paul H. Brookes.

Hawaii Early Learning Profile (HELP) and HELP for Special Preschoolers

- Age Range: 0 to 3 years (HELP)
  3 to 6 years (HELP for Special Preschoolers)
- Testing Time: Not specified
- Intended Uses: Designed for staff in early intervention programs for assessing the development of children using small, incremental steps and to correlate with suggestions for activities to teach developmental skills
- Format: Curriculum-based developmental assessment in checklist format for use with children on an individual basis. Assess skills in six areas of performance (cognitive, expressive language, gross motor, fine

motor, social-emotional, and self-help) based on direct observation of skill or interview with a parent or caregiver
- Standardization: Not standardized; developmental sequences are based on information from numerous developmental scales and standardized tests
- User Qualifications: Designed for reference by interdisciplinary personnel involved in the assessment and planning of comprehensive services for children in early intervention settings
- References: Furuno, S., et al. 1984. *Hawaii Early Learning Profile (HELP).* Palo Alto, Calif.: VORT Corporation.
  Santa Cruz County Office of Education. 1987. *HELP for Special Preschoolers.* Palo Alto, Calif.: VORT Corporation.
  Parks, S. 1992. *Inside HELP: Administration and reference manual for the Hawaii Early Learning Profile (HELP).* Palo Alto, Calif.: VORT Corporation.

Learning Accomplishment Profile, Revised Edition (LAP—R)

- Age Range: 36 to 72 months
- Testing Time: 2 to 2.5 hours
- Intended Uses: Designed to enable identification of developmental learning objectives and ongoing measures of progress for normal children as well as those with disabilities
- Format: Curriculum-based developmental assessment providing information about the following skill areas: gross motor, fine motor, prewriting, cognitive, language, self-help, and personal social
- Standardization: Not standardized. Criterion-referenced tool in which test items are drawn from several pediatric assessment tools; each item specifies the tool from which it originated
- User Qualifications: Not specified; any pediatric practitioner with experience in test-

ing should be able to use this tool. No training required
- References: Sanford, A.R, and J.G. Zelman. 1981. *Learning Accomplishment Profile, Revised Edition.* Winston-Salem, N.C.: Kaplan Press.

Reynell–Zinkin Scales: Developmental Scales for Young Visually Handicapped Children

- Age Range: 0 to 5 years
- Testing Time: Approximately 1 hour
- Intended Uses: To serve as an assessment tool for evaluation of the mental development of multihandicapped, visually impaired children; to provide guidelines to professionals as to the typical developmental progression of visually impaired children; and to help in determining appropriate instructional goals
- Format: Behavioral assessment scale based on a variety of sources of information, including parent report, direct observation, and administration of selected performance items. Behaviors are recorded on five scales, including social adaptation, sensorimotor understanding, exploration of environment, response to sound and verbal comprehension, and expressive language. Examiners must obtain test materials independently; because the test was developed in Great Britain, some instructions may be unclear to American examiners (e.g., "bricks" for "blocks")
- Standardization: Not standardized; age levels were determined based on a sample of 109 blind or partially sighted children
- User Qualifications: Designed for use by professionals who have a sound understanding of early intellectual development and its differences in visually impaired children
- References: Reynell, J. 1980. *Reynell–Zinkin Developmental Scales for Young Vi-*

sually Handicapped Children. Chicago: Stoelting Co.

Maxfield–Buccholz Social Maturity Scale for Blind Preschool Children

- Age Range: 0 to 6 years
- Testing Time: Not specified
- Intended Uses: To measure the personal and social development of blind children
- Format: Judgment-based interview format, adapted from the Vineland Social Maturity Scale. Measures skills in seven areas of performance: self-help general, self-help dressing, self-help eating, communication, socialization, locomotion, and occupation
- Standardization: Based on 605 ratings on 398 children who were considered "legally blind" since birth and who resided in New York City, New Jersey, Boston, Connecticut, Chicago, and Minneapolis
- User Qualifications: Experience and supervision with interviewing children and parents is suggested
- References: Maxfield, J., and B. Buccholz. 1957. *Maxfield–Buccholz Social Maturity Scale.* Louisville, Ky.: American Printing House for the Blind.

MOTOR PERFORMANCE TESTS*

Bruininks–Oseretsky Test of Motor Proficiency

- Age Range: 4.6 to 14.6 years
- Testing Time: 45 to 60 minutes; a short form of the full battery (14 items) may be used to obtain a general measure of motor proficiency and requires 15 to 20 minutes
- Intended Uses: To assess a range of motor performance areas in children with mild to

_____

*Reviewed by Lisa A. Kurtz.

moderate motor disability and to assist with educational placement

- Format: Includes eight subtests of fine motor and gross motor performance, including running speed and agility (one item), balance (eight items), bilateral coordination (eight items), strength (three items), upper limb coordination (nine items), response speed (one item), visual motor control (eight items), and upper limb speed and dexterity (eight items). Test requires sufficient space for an 18-yard running course
- Standardization: 765 subjects stratified by age, sex, race, community size, and geographic region
- User Qualifications: May be used by a variety of professionals with experience in standardized test administration
- References: Bruininks, R.H. 1978. *Bruininks–Oseretsky Test of Motor Proficiency examiner's manual.* Circle Pines, Minn.: American Guidance Service.

Jebsen Hand Function Test

- Age Range: Originally normed on adults; renormed on children from 6 to 19 years
- Testing Time: 10 to 15 minutes
- Intended Uses: Designed as a broad measure of hand function
- Format: Individually administered test consisting of seven timed subtests selected to be representative of various hand activities
- Standardization: Samples for pediatric norms included a minimum of 33 males and 33 females for each of five age categories attending randomly selected classrooms in an unspecified location
- User Qualifications: Not specified
- References: Jebsen, R.H., et al. 1969. An objective and standardized test of hand function. *Archives of Physical Medicine and Rehabilitation* 50:311–319.

Taylor, N., et al. 1973. Evaluation of hand function in children. *Archives of Physical Medicine and Rehabilitation* 54:129–135.

Movement Assessment of Infants (MAI)

- Age Range: 1 to 12 months
- Testing Time: 30 to 90 minutes
- Intended Uses: To identify motor dysfunction, establish a basis for early intervention, monitor intervention strategies, and aid in the research and teaching of infant motor development
- Format: Qualitative assessment of behaviors in the areas of muscle tone (10 items), primitive reflexes (14 items), automatic reactions (16 items), and volitional movements (25 items)
- Standardization: Not standardized; criteria drawn from commonly used developmental tests or the author's experiences
- User Qualifications: Not specified; specialized training is available
- References: Chandler, L.S., et al. 1980. *Movement assessment of infants.* Available from P.O. Box 4631, Rolling Bay, WA 98061.
  Harris, S.R., et al. 1984. Predictive validity of the Movement Assessment of Infants. *Journal of Developmental and Behavioral Pediatrics* 5:336–342.

Peabody Developmental Motor Scales

- Age Range: 0 to 83 months
- Testing Time: 45 to 60 minutes; may administer only the Fine Motor or the Gross Motor Scale (20 to 30 minutes for each scale)
- Intended Uses: To identify children with delayed or abnormal gross and fine motor skills, to measure performance over time and in response to intervention, and to aid in linking assessment to treatment
- Format: Individually administered test consisting of 170 items scored on a three-

point scale in the following areas of performance: gross motor (reflexes, balance, nonlocomotion, locomotion, receipt and propulsion of objects) and fine motor (grasping, hand use, eye–hand coordination, and manual dexterity). Accompanying activity cards are designed to assist in instructional programming

- Standardization: Sample of 617 children stratified by age, race, gender, and regional distribution
- User Qualifications: May be administered by a variety of persons experienced with children once procedures have been learned; agreement reliability with an experienced examiner (85 percent agreement of items administered) is recommended
- References: Folio, M.R., and R.R. Fewell. 1983. *Peabody Developmental Motor Scales.* Allen, Tex.: DLM Teaching Resources.

  Hinderer, K.A., et al. 1989. Clinical implications of the Peabody Developmental Motor Scales: A constructive review. *Physical and Occupational Therapy in Pediatrics* 9, no. 2:81–106.

Purdue Pegboard Test

- Age Range: Test originally designed for adults; norms have also been collected on children ages 5 to 19 years
- Testing Time: Approximately 10 to 15 minutes
- Intended Uses: To measure dexterity in fingertip activity; originally intended for use in selecting employees for industrial jobs but has other useful clinical applications
- Format: Performance test involving a series of peg and washer manipulations
- Standardization: Norms for children ages 5 through 15 are derived from 1,334 normal school children attending regular classes in Bergen County, New Jersey; norms for children 14 through 19 are derived from

176 volunteers from schools, a rural county fair, and a university in the seven-county Milwaukee area.

- User Qualifications: Not specified
- References: Tiffen, J. 1968. *Purdue Pegboard examiner manual.* Available from Lafayette Instrument Company, P.O. Box 5729, Lafayette, IN 47906.

  Gardner, R.A., and M. Broman. 1979. The Purdue Pegboard: Normative data on 1334 schoolchildren. *Journal of Clinical Child Psychology* 1:156–162.

  Mathiowetz, V., et al. 1986. The Purdue Pegboard: Norms for 14-to-19 year olds. *American Journal of Occupational Therapy* 40, no. 3:174–179.

Test of Motor Impairment

- Age Range: 5 to 12 years
- Testing Time: Approximately 20 minutes
- Intended Uses: Developed to serve as a quick, normative screening tool for identifying children in need of further motor evaluation or as a baseline for measuring the results of intervention. Designed to be used with children who have mild to moderate mental retardation, learning disabilities, or behavior difficulties
- Format: Individually administered test measuring the following categories of motor function: manual dexterity (speed, bilateral coordination, eye–hand coordination), static balance, dynamic balance (control during rapid and slow movements), and ball skills (catching and throwing). Additional qualitative measures identify aspects of motor performance and of attitudinal or temperamental behaviors that might influence scores
- Standardization: Standardized on two separate sets of children by two separate groups of investigators. The first sample included 442 children from 18 British primary schools, and the second included 480

reactivity in infants with regulatory disorders (e.g., difficult temperament), developmental delays, and those at risk for learning and sensory processing disorders (e.g., high-risk premature infants); to be used in conjunction with other developmental tests to provide an overall indicator of the child's developmental functioning

- Format: Criterion-referenced tool that measures skills in five domains of sensory processing and reactivity: reactivity to tactile deep pressure, adaptive motor functions, visual-tactile integration, ocular-motor control, and reactivity to vestibular stimulation
- Standardization: Not standardized; criterion validated for interobserver reliability, decision-consistency reliability, and test–retest reliability using samples of normal, regulatory-disordered, and developmentally delayed infants
- User Qualifications: Not specified
- References: DeGangi, G.A., and S.I. Greenspan. 1989. *Test of Sensory Functions in Infants.* Los Angeles: Western Psychological Services.

Test of Visual Perceptual Skills (Non-Motor; TVPS) and Test of Visual Perceptual Skills (Non-Motor)—Upper Level (TVPS—UL)

- Age Range: 4 to 12.11 years (TVPS)
  12 to 18 years (TVPS—UL)
- Testing Time: Variable; manual states 7 to 15 minutes, but experience suggests more time is usually needed
- Intended Uses: Both forms designed as diagnostic tools to provide a valid assessment of an individual's strengths and weaknesses in visual perceptual skills
- Format: Format is identical for both the TVPS and the TVPS—UL, but individual items in the TVPS—UL are more complex. Individually administered test requiring the

child to point or otherwise select from a multiple-choice field of pictures or geometric figures. Seven component areas of visual perception are assessed, including visual discrimination, visual memory, visual-spatial relationships, visual form constancy, visual sequential memory, visual figure-ground, and visual closure. Scores are derived for individual domains as well as for the total test

- Standardization: The TVPS was standardized on 962 normal children, all from the San Francisco Bay Area and all attending private or parochial schools, and fairly equally distributed across age and gender. The TVPS—UL was standardized on a group of 664 children, also residing in the San Francisco Bay Area
- User Qualifications: Advanced training or education is not required; appropriate for a range of professionals with familiarity with psychological or educational tests
- References: Gardner, M.F. 1988. *TVPS, Test of Visual-Perceptual Skills (Non-Motor) manual.* San Francisco: Health Publishing Company.

  Gardner, M.F. 1992. *TVPS—UL, Test of Visual-Perceptual Skills (Non-Motor) upper level manual.* Burlingame, Calif.: Psychological and Educational Publications, Inc.

TESTS OF FUNCTIONAL SKILL*

Klein–Bell Activities of Daily Living Scale

- Age Range: All ages
- Testing Time: Not specified
- Intended Uses: Designed to provide a universally applicable, reliable, and quantitative measure of independence in activities of daily living
- Format: Behavioral rating scale consisting of 170 items in six areas of function: dress-

---

*Reviewed by Lisa A. Kurtz.

ing, elimination, mobility, bathing/hygiene, eating, and emergency telephone communication. Component behaviors are observed and scored according to a three-point scale

- Standardization: Not standardized; criterion-referenced scale originally developed for an adult population and adapted for children
- User Qualifications: Not specified
- References: Law, M., and P. Usher. 1988. Validation of the Klein–Bell Activities of Daily Living Scale for children. *Canadian Journal of Occupational Therapy* 55, no. 2:63–67.

Pediatric Evaluation of Disability Inventory (PEDI)

- Age Range: 6 months to 7.5 years
- Testing Time: Variable; 20 to 30 minutes when scored by professionals who are familiar with the child; Approximately 45 minutes when scored based on parent interview
- Intended Uses: To provide a descriptive measure of function in children with a variety of disabilities, especially those with physical or combined physical and cognitive disabilities. May also be used to monitor change in function over time
- Format: Criterion-based assessment that measures both capability and performance of functional activities in three content domains: (1) self-care, (2) mobility, and (3) social function. Functional performance is measured by the level of caregiver assistance needed to accomplish tasks; a Modifications Scale provides a measure of environmental modifications and equipment used by the child in routine daily activities
- Standardization: 412 children and families in Massachusetts, Connecticut, and New York, stratified by age, gender, race and origin, level of parent education, commu-

nity size, and family marital and socioeconomic status

- User Qualifications: Should be administered by a professional with a background in pediatrics, experience with young children with disabilities, and an understanding of tests and measures. Procedures for specific training needed for test administration are included in the manual
- References: Haley, S.M., et al. 1992. *Pediatric Evaluation of Disability Inventory (PEDI) manual.* Available from the New England Medical Center Hospitals, Inc., and PEDI Research Group, 750 Washington Street, Boston, MA 02111-1901.

  Coster, W.J., and S.M. Haley. 1992. Conceptualization and measurement of disablement in infants and young children. *Infants and Young Children* 4, no. 4:11–12.

WeeFIM

- Age Range: 6 months to 7 years
- Testing Time: Not specified
- Intended Uses: Designed to serve as a basic indicator of the severity of disability in relation to the burden of care (type and amount of assistance) required for a child with disability to perform basic life activities effectively; designed to measure changes in function over time
- Format: The WeeFIM is a direct adaptation of the functional independence measure (FIM) used to measure functional independence in adults. It consists of 18 items organized in six domains: self-care, mobility, locomotion, sphincter control, communication, and social cognition. Each item is assessed on a seven-level ordinal scale that represents the range of independent function
- Standardization: Standardization of the WeeFIM is in process; several pilot studies have been conducted on normal and disabled populations; normative data have

been collected on 417 children from Buffalo, New York, with a goal of increasing the sample size to 1,500 and stratifying according to age, sex, race, and socioeconomic factors

- User Qualifications: Designed to be used by any professional discipline; training guides, videotape, and workshops are available

- References: *Guide for the Uniform Data Set for Medical Rehabilitation for Children (WeeFIM), version 4.0.* 1993. Available from the State University of New York at Buffalo, 232 Parker Hall, SUNY South Campus, 3435 Main Street, Buffalo, NY 14214-3007. Tel.: 716-829-2080.

  Msall, M.E., et al. 1993. Use of functional assessment on children with developmental disabilities. *Physical Medicine and Rehabilitation Clinics of North America* 4:517–527.

SPEECH/LANGUAGE TESTS*

Clinical Evaluation of Language Fundamentals (CELF—R)
CELF—Preschool

- Age Range: CELF—R, 5 to 18 years
  CELF—Preschool, 3 through 6.6 years

- Testing Time: CELF—R: Processing Subtests total, 46 minutes

  CELF—R: Production Subtests total, 30 minutes

  CELF—Preschool: Time is dependent on the child's cooperation but is generally 30 to 44 minutes.

- Format: Individually administered. Uses visual stimulus manuals for some subtests to elicit child's response

- Intended Uses: Designed to assist professionals in identifying the nature and degree

of language disabilities in school-aged children. It provides measures of selected specific language functions in the areas of phonology, syntax, semantics, memory, word finding, and retrieval

- Standardization: Six school systems in four different states with 50 examiners participated in the tryout of the revision. A total of 233 students were used in the study. Students were almost equally divided into four age groups of 7, 9, 11, and 15 years. Slightly more than half had language learning disabilities, and the rest were normally achieving age peers. Those reporting were reasonably balanced according to sex and race

- User Qualifications: Can be used by speech/language pathologists, special educators, psychologists, classroom teachers, and others proficient in identifying elementary and secondary school students with potential language disorders

- References: Semel, E.M., et al. 1980, 1987. *Clinical Evaluation of Language Fundamentals.* San Antonio, Tex.: The Psychological Corp.

  Semel, E.M., et al. 1989. *Clnical Evaluation of Language Fundamentals—Revised screening test.* San Antonio, Tex.: The Psychological Corp.

  Semel, E.M., et al. 1992. *Clinical Evaluation of Language Fundamentals—Preschool.* San Antonio, Tex.: The Psychological Corp.

Expressive One-Word Picture Vocabulary Test—Revised (EOWPVT—R), (1990 revision)
Expressive One-Word Picture Vocabulary Test—Upper Extension (EOWPVT—UE)

- Age Range: EOWPVT—R, 2 to 12 years
  EOWPVT—UE, 12 to 15.11 years

- Testing Time: Variable with age and vocabulary level; less than 20 minutes

---

*Reviewed by Marleen A. Baron.

- Intended Uses: To measure expressive single-word vocabulary and to provide a quick and valid estimate of a child's expressive language
- Format: Individually administered test. A book of black and white line drawings (one per page) is provided to elicit the child's response (verbal identification of the object). Standard scores and age levels are provided. A Spanish record form is available
- Standardization: This is a well-normed test, restandardized and renormed from the original EOWPVT. The EOWPVT—R was normed on 1,118 children whose primary language was English and who were enrolled in a variety of school settings. The original 110 items and an additional 33 new items were used. Otherwise, the test is unchanged
- User Qualifications: This test can be administered and scored quickly by teachers, principals, physicians, optometrists, speech/language pathologists, psychologists, counselors, and special educators
- References: Gardner, M.F. 1990. *Expressive One Word Vocabulary Test—Revised.* Novato, Calif.: Academic Therapy Publications.

  Gardner, M.F. 1983. *Expressive One Word Picture Vocabulary Test—Upper Extension.* Novato, Calif.: Academic Therapy Publications.

  Gardner, M.F. 1979. *Expressive One Word Picture Vocabulary Test.* Novato, Calif.: Academic Therapy Publications.

Goldman–Fristoe Test of Articulation

- Age Range: 2 through 16+ years
- Testing Time: 10 to 15 minutes for Sounds-in-Words subtest; varies for other subtests
- Intended Uses: To obtain an adequate and accurate sample of the subject's speech production under several conditions ranging from imitative to conversational speech. Consonants, vowels, and diphthongs are tested, comparing articulation in a simple response with those occurring in contextual speech
- Format: This test yields error scores and percentile ranks. The Sounds-in-Words subtest allows a rater to examine individual phonemes for errors. It contains 35 stimulus pictures intended to elicit 44 responses. The test form provides for recording either the presence of an error or the type of speech error produced
- Standardization: 37 children with articulation deficits between the ages of four and eight years were tested twice by eight speech pathologists. Six experienced judges determined median percentage of agreement on presence or absence of error for each sound at 92; median percentage of agreement on type of production was 88
- User Qualifications: May be used by a classroom teacher for use in referring a child for therapy or by a speech/language pathologist or student clinician with a minimum of training in phonetics and articulation
- References: Goldman, R., and M. Fristoe. 1986. *Goldman–Fristoe Test of Articulation.* Circle Pines, Minn.: American Guidance Service.

Peabody Picture Vocabulary Test, 1981 Revision (PPVT—R)

- Age Range: 2½ through 40 years
- Testing Time: Variable with age and vocabulary level, but typically requires only 10 to 20 minutes
- Intended Uses: To measure receptive vocabulary for Standard American English and to provide an estimate of the child's receptive verbal intelligence
- Format: The subject listens to a stimulus word, then identifies the word by pointing to one of four pictures. There are 3 practice and 150 test plates

- Standardization: The PPVT—R was standardized nationally on a carefully selected sample of 5,028 subjects (4,200 children and 828 adults). The sample closely approximated population data from the 1970 U.S. Bureau of the Census in terms of ethnic composition, family occupation, and socioeconomic level. Subjects ranged in age from 2.6 through 18.11 years, with an equal number of males and females tested in each age group

- User Qualifications: No formal course work in tests and measurements is necessary to administer the PPVT. However, interpretation of the test results is more complex, and formal training in behavioral measurement is strongly recommended. School teachers, psychologists, learning specialists, speech/language pathologists, physicians, and others in the helping professions should be able to administer and score the test accurately

- References: Dunn, L., and L. Dunn. 1981. *Peabody Picture Vocabulary Test.* Circle Pines, Minn.: American Guidance Service. Robertson, G., and J. Eisenberg. 1981. *Peabody Picture Vocabulary Test—Revised technical supplement.* Circle Pines Minn.: American Guidance Service.

Preschool Language Scale—3 (PLS)

- Age Range: 1 month through 6 years, 11 months

- Testing time: Birth to 11 months: 15 to 30 minutes

  12 months to 3 years, 11 months: 30 to 40 minutes

  4 years to 6 years, 11 months: 20 to 30 minutes

- Intended Uses: To assess the early stages of receptive and expressive language development and to evaluate maturational lags in language. There are three supplemental measures: the Articulation Screener, the Language Sample Checklist, and the Family Information and Suggestions Form

- Format: The test contains two standardized subscales measuring auditory comprehension and expressive communication and three supplemental measures (Articulation Screener, Language Sample Checklist, and Family Information and Suggestions Form). Language age equivalents, standard scores, and percentile ranks are available. A Spanish-language version is available

- Standardization: Normative data are based on a national sample of 1,200 children ages 2 weeks through 6 years, 11 months. Within each age group, 50 percent were female and 50 percent were male. A representative sample based on the 1980 U.S. Census of Population, 1986 update, was stratified on the basis of parent education level, geographic region, and race

- User Qualifications: Specific user qualifications are not stated in the manual. However, examiners should have a background in early childhood development

- References: Zimmerman, I.L., et al. 1991. *Preschool Language Scale—3.* The Psychological Corporation, San Diego, Calif.: The Harcourt Brace Jovanovich, Inc.

Sequenced Inventory of Communication Development (SICD)—Revised

- Age Range: 4 months through 48 months

- Testing Time: Ranges from 30 minutes (infants) to 75 minutes (ages 24 months and older)

- Intended Uses: To obtain a receptive communication age (RCA) and expressive communication age (ECA) for young children

- Format: Test items assess a variety of early communication skills, giving a broad perspective of the semantic, syntactic, and pragmatic processes of a child's expressive and receptive language systems. The combination of parental report (PR) items with behavioral items allows the tool to be used with children who are difficult to test. The use of manipulative materials helps to keep the attention of young children and allows the examiner to assess the pragmatic interactions of the child with people and objects. Assignment of age levels is limited to estimation of the child's level of development. Other editions of the SICD include a Cuban-Spanish edition and an Adapted SICD designed for use with severely disabled adolescents and adults whose language skills range from birth to four years or who are understood only by those closest to them

- Standardization: 252 children, 21 at each of 12 age levels ranging from 4 months to 48 months. Subjects were considered to be representative of the general population of Seattle, Washington. Children whose parents judged their language to be abnormal, who were living in a bilingual home, who displayed obvious physical or mental abnormalities, who had abnormal hearing, or who had ear pathologies within six weeks prior to testing were excluded from the sample
- User Qualifications: Speech/language pathologists, teachers in preschool programs, special education teachers, and psychologists
- References: Hedrick, D.L., et al. 1984. *Sequenced Inventory of Communication Development.* Seattle, Wash.: University of Washington Press.

Test of Language Competence—Expanded Edition (TLC—E)

- Age Range: 5 through 18.11 years
- Testing Time: Both levels of the TLC—E can be individually administered in less than 1 hour
- Intended Uses: To assess emerging metalinguistic abilities and linguistic strategy acquisition in children, adolescents, and young adults who have not acquired the expected levels of metalinguistic competence in semantics, syntax, and/or pragmatics. Since TLC—E is norm referenced,

it will help determine a student's need for language intervention based on a comparison to the performances of age-level peers

- Format: Each level of the TLC—E contains four subtests (Ambiguous Sentences, Listening Comprehension: Making Inferences, Oral Expression: Recreating Speech Acts, Figurative Language) designed to provide differential assessment and point out areas for follow-up assessment and language intervention. Level II contains a supplemental subtest for Remembering Word Pairs
- Standardization: Level 1 is standardized for children ages 5.0 to 9.11 years. Level 2 is standardized for preadolescents and adolescents, ages 9.0 to 18.11 years
- User Qualifications: Can be administered by speech/language pathologists, psychologists, and special educators
- References: Wiig, E.H., and W. Secord. 1989. *Test of Language Competence—Expanded Edition.* Harcourt Brace Jovanovich, Inc.: The Psychological Corporation.

Test of Adolescent and Adult Language (TOAL—3)

- Age Range: 12 through 25 years
- Testing Time: At least 2 hours for the entire test. Individual subtests can be administered in 10 to 20 minutes
- Intended Uses: To assess language proficiency in older adolescent populations and to identify individuals who perform significantly below their peers in language areas. Eight subtests assess receptive and expressive abilities for spoken and written language. It is appropriate for adolescents who can understand test directions, formulate the necessary answers, and can read or speak some English
- Format: The TOAL—3 contains subtests for listening, speaking, reading, writing, spoken language, written language, vo-

cabulary, grammar, and receptive and expressive language. It offers an extension of the norms from previous versions. The normative sample exceeded 3,000 persons in 22 states and three Canadian provinces representative of the U.S. population according to the 1990 U.S. census and was stratified by age
- User Qualifications: The TOAL can be administered by anyone who is reasonably competent in the administration of tests in education, language, and psychology
- References: Hammill, D., et al. 1994. *Test of Adolescent and Adult Language (TOAL—3)*. 3rd ed. Available from Services for Professional Educators, 5341 Industrial Oaks Boulevard, Austin, TX 78735.

Test of Early Language Development (TELD—2)

- Age Range: 2.0 to 7.11 years
- Testing Time: 20 minutes
- Intended Uses: To identify those children who are significantly below their peers in language development, to document progress in language, to serve as a measure for research in language, and to suggest instructional practices
- Format: The TELD—2 is an individually administered test that assesses various dimensions of receptive and expressive language, including form (syntax, morphology, and phonology) and content (the ability to decode and encode meaning). Performance is reported as standard scores, percentiles, and age-equivalent scores
- Standardization: The TELD—2 was standardized on 1,274 children representing 30 states, with the sample approximating the characteristics of the 1990 U.S. Bureau of the Census
- User Qualifications: Interpretation of results should be performed by someone who

is trained and experienced in normal language development and assessment
- References: Hresko, W.P., et al. 1991. *Test of Early Language Development (TELD—2)*. Austin, Tex.: PRO-ED.
  Hresko, W.P., et al. 1982. *Prueba del Desarrollo Inicial del Lenguaje*. Austin, Tex.: PRO-ED.

Test for Auditory Comprehension of Language TACL—R, 1985

- Age Range: 3 years and above
- Testing Time: Variable with age and auditory comprehension ability, but typically no longer than 20 minutes
- Intended Uses: To measure receptive/auditory comprehension of specific grammatical forms. The TACL—R measures knowledge of specific lexical and grammatical forms such as the meaning of common word classes and word relations, the meaning of grammatical morphemes, and the meaning of complex sentence constructions
- Format: Each stimulus consists of a word or sentence with a corresponding plate that has three black and white line drawings. One of the three pictures for each item illustrates the meaning of the word, morpheme, or syntactic structure being tested. The other pictures illustrate either two semantic or grammatical contrasts of the stimulus, or one contrast and one decoy
- Standardization: Norms for section scores and for the total score, based on 1,003 normal-language children ages 3 years through 9 years, 11 months, are available in percentile ranks, age-equivalent scores, and standard scores by age level and grade level
- User Qualifications: Specialists who are trained and experienced in the administration and interpretation of individual test measurements (speech/language patholo-

gists, psychologists, or equivalent qualified personnel)

- References: Woolfolk, E.C. 1985. *Test of Auditory Comprehension of Language—Revised.* Allen, Tex.: DLM and Teaching Resources.

  Anderson, J.D., et al. 1980. Test–retest reliability of the Test for Auditory Comprehension of Language when it is used with mentally retarded children. *Journal of Speech and Hearing Disorders* 45:195–200.

  Haynes, W., and M.B. McCallion. 1981. Language comprehension testing: The influence of three modes of test administration strategy and cognitive tempo on the performance of preschool children. *Language, Speech, and Hearing Services in Schools* 12: 74–81.

Test of Language Development—2 (TOLD—Primary and TOLD—Intermediate)

- Age Range: TOLD—Primary: 4.0 through 8.11 years

  TOLD—Intermediate: 8.6 through 12.11 years

- Testing Time: 30 minutes to 1 hour
- Intended Uses: To measure receptive and expressive language abilities, to identify children who are significantly below their peers in language proficiency, to provide a comparative index of a child's language strengths and weaknesses, to document progress in language as a consequence of special intervention programs, and to measure language in a research context
- Format: The TOLD assesses specific receptive and expressive language skills in the areas of syntax (grammatical structures), semantics (word meanings), and phonology (the sound system of language). There are seven subtests
- Standardization: The norms for the 1988 TOLD—2 Primary are based on the performance of 2,436 children residing in

29 states. The percentages of other characteristics are similar to those for the general population

- User Qualifications: Speech/language pathologists, psychologists, special and general educators
- References: Hammill, D.D., and P.L. Newcomer. 1988. *Test of Language Development—Intermediate.* Austin, Tex.: PRO-ED.

  Newcomer, P., and D.D. Hammill. 1982. *Test of Language Development—Primary.* Austin, Tex.: PRO-ED.

The Elementary Word—R Test

- Age Range: 7.0 through 11.11 years
- Testing Time: Approximately 30 minutes for the complete test
- Intended Uses: To assess an individual's expressive vocabulary and semantic abilities, including categorizing, defining, and verbal reasoning
- Format: The subject responds verbally to spoken questions by the examiner. Responses are scored 1 or 0 points based on appropriateness
- User Qualifications: The Word Test—R should be administered by a trained professional familiar with language disorders (e.g., speech/language pathologist, psychologist, teacher of the learning disabled, special education consultant)
- Standardization: Test norms have been established on children from 7 years, 0 months, through 11 years, 11 months. Over 2,300 subjects were included in the statistical studies. The item selection sample consisted of 805 subjects from 165 elementary schools. Subjects were randomly selected with consideration for race, sex, age, and school
- References: Huisingh, R., et al. 1990. *The Elementary Word-R Test.* East Moline, Ill.: Linguisystems, Inc.

INTELLIGENCE TESTS*

Detroit Test of Learning Aptitude—Third Edition (DTLA—3)

- Age Range: 6 through 17 years
- Testing Time: Not available
- Intended Uses: To measure intellectual capabilities of children via a multidimensional battery, assist in the identification of students who are deficient in general or specific aptitudes, and diagnose learning disabilities
- Format: Individually administered test consisting of 11 subtests from which 16 composite scores can be obtained, including an Overall Composite, Optimal Level Composite, Verbal and Nonverbal Composites, Attention-Enhanced Composite, Attention-Reduced Composite, Motor-Enhanced Composite, Motor-Reduced Composite, and 8 additional composite scores based on intelligence and cognitive-processing theories
- Standardization: Normed on a sample of 2,587 students. The sample corresponded to 1990 U.S. census data with regard to gender, geographic region, ethnicity, race, and urban/rural residence
- User Qualifications: Should be administered and interpreted by an individual with graduate-level training and experience in assessment
- References: Hammill, D.D. 1991. *Detroit Tests of Learning Aptitude*. 3rd ed. Austin, Tex.: PRO-ED.

Kaufman Assessment Battery for Children (K-ABC)

- Age Range: 2½ to 12½ years

---

*Reviewed by Mary F. Lazar, with contributions from Winifred Lloyds-Lender, Linda Gibson-Matthews, Edward M. Moss, and Jerilynn Radcliffe.

- Testing Time: 35 to 85 minutes
- Intended Uses: Designed to measure both intelligence and achievement through Mental Processing and Achievement Scales. Can be used in clinical and research settings, for psychological assessment, psychoeducational evaluation of exceptional children, educational planning, and neuropsychological assessment
- Format: Individually administered test consisting of 16 subtests—10 Mental Processing tests and 6 Achievement tests. Yields four Global Scales: Sequential Processing, Simultaneous Processing, Mental Processing Composite, and Achievement
- Standardization: Standardized on a sample of 2,000 children between the ages of 2½ and 12½ years of age. The population varied in race, ethnic group, and parental education
- User Qualifications: The examiner must be trained in the administration of intelligence tests and must be familiar with the K-ABC. The test should be interpreted by the same examiner who administered the test
- References: Kaufman, A.S., and N.L. Kaufman. 1983. *Kaufman Assessment Battery for Children*. Circle Pines, Minn.: American Guidance Service.

Kaufman Brief Intelligence Test (K-BIT)

- Age Range: 4 to 90 years
- Testing Time: 15 to 30 minutes
- Intended Uses: To be used as a brief measure of intelligence when trained professionals are unavailable to give a more comprehensive intelligence test. Examples include use as a screening device to identify high-risk children, screening for educational diagnosis, and periodic reevaluation of children who are recovering from neurologic deficit
- Format: Individually administered test with two subtests, Vocabulary (verbal measure requiring oral responses) and Ma-

trices (nonverbal measure using visual stimuli in a multiple-choice format). Yields Vocabulary, Matrices, and IQ Composite scores

- Standardization: Normed on a nationwide sample of 2,022 children and adults ages 4 to 90 years. Sample was based on 1990 census data with regard to gender, geographic region, socioeconomic status, and race/ethnic group
- User Qualifications: Can be administered by educational, psychological, vocational, and medical personnel. Interpretation should be performed by someone with formal graduate-level course work in psychology or special education programs or who has received structured in-service training, including one-on-one supervision, from a qualified professional
- References: Kaufman, A.S., and N.L. Kaufman. 1990. *Kaufman Brief Intelligence Test.* Circle Pines, Minn.: American Guidance Service.

  Naugle, R.I., et al. 1993. Validity of the Kaufman Brief Intelligence Test. *Psychological Assessment* 5:182–186.

Leiter International Performance Scale (LIP)

- Age Range: 2 years through adult
- Testing Time: Approximately 1 hour
- Intended Uses: To measure intelligence via a nonverbal format. Originally designed as a measure that could, by eliminating language, be more fairly applied across cultures, it has been most typically used to obtain IQs for those who are speech and language impaired or who lack functional communication skills. Most appropriate for use with individuals with cerebral palsy, or who are deaf, non-English-speaking, or culturally disadvantaged
- Format: Individually administered test that consists of a total of 54 subtests, 4 at each

year level from Year 2 through Year 16 and 6 at Year 18. Instructions and responses are provided within a nonverbal format, and timed items are at a minimum. Yields a mental age equivalent and an IQ score

- Standardization: Not clear from manual
- User Qualifications: Administration and interpretation should be performed by a trained professional (i.e., someone with a background of formal course work in assessment issues and procedures as well as direct supervised experience in test administration)
- References: Leiter, R.G. 1979. *Leiter International Performance Scale: Instruction manual.* Chicago: Stoelting Co.

  Levine, M.N. 1983. *Leiter International Performance Scale: A handbook.* Los Angeles: Western Psychological Services.

The McCarthy Scales of Children's Abilities

- Age Range: 2½ to 8½ years
- Testing Time: 45 to 50 minutes for children under 5 years and approximately an hour for children 5 years and older
- Intended Uses: To determine younger children's overall intellectual level and to assess their patterns of strengths and weaknesses in various cognitive and motor abilities. Designed for evaluation of normal children as well as those with learning disabilities and mental retardation
- Format: Individually administered; 18 tests grouped into six scales: Verbal, Perceptual-Performance, Quantitative, General Cognitive, Memory, and Motor
- Standardization: Normed on a sample of 1,032 "normal" children; sample corresponded to 1970 U.S. census data with regard to age, sex, race, geographic region, and father's occupational status
- User Qualifications: Could be administered by a supervised trained technician, but appropriate interpretation of results requires graduate-level training

- References: McCarthy, D. 1972. *Manual for the McCarthy Scales of Children's Abilities.* New York: The Psychological Corporation.

Stanford–Binet Intelligence Scale: Fourth Edition (SB—IV)

- Age Range: Ages 2 years to adult
- Testing Time: 60 to 90 minutes
- Intended Uses: To obtain a measure of cognitive abilities that provides both an overall level of cognitive development and the individual's pattern of cognitive abilities. Can be used to differentiate between students with mental retardation and those with specific learning disabilities, to evaluate a student's learning difficulties, to identify gifted students, and to study cognitive skill development across the life span
- Format: Individually administered; yields four area scores (Verbal Reasoning, Abstract/Visual Reasoning, Quantitative Reasoning, and Short-Term Memory) and an overall composite score
- Standardization: Normed on 5,013 individuals ranging in age from 5 years to 23 years, 11 months; sample corresponded to 1980 U.S. census data with regard to geographic region, community size, ethnicity, age, gender, and socioeconomic status
- User Qualifications: Should be administered and interpreted by an individual with graduate-level training and experience in assessment
- References: Thorndike, R.L., et al. 1986. *Guide for Administering and scoring, the Stanford–Binet Intelligence Scale.* 4th ed. Chicago: Riverside Publishing.

  Thorndike, R.L., et al. 1986. *Technical manual, Stanford–Binet Intelligence Scale.* 4th ed. Chicago: Riverside Publishing.

Wechsler Preschool and Primary Scale of Intelligence—Revised (WPPSI—R)

- Age Range: 3 years to 7 years, 3 months
- Testing Time: 75 to 90 minutes

- Intended Uses: To measure intellectual ability and to document change in performance over time. Can be used to diagnose exceptionality, including mental retardation and giftedness, and can be administered in educational, clinical, and research settings. It should not be administered to children with severe visual or auditory impairments or significant physical impairments
- Format: Individually administered test comprises two scales (Verbal and Performance) consisting of six subtests each. Yields Performance IQ, Verbal IQ, and Full Scale IQ scores
- Standardization: Normed on a sample of 1,700 children between the ages of 3 years and 7 years, 3 months. The sample was standardized based on 1986 census data with respect to geographic region of the U.S., ethnicity, and parental education and occupation
- User Qualifications: Can be administered by examiners experienced in administration of standardized, clinical instruments. Results should be interpreted by someone with appropriate graduate or professional training or with experience in psychological assessment
- References: Buckhalt, J.A. 1991. Test reviews: Wechsler Preschool and Primary Scale of Intelligence—Revised. *Journal of Psychoeducational Assessment* 9:271–279.

  Wechsler, D. 1989. *Wechsler Preschool and Primary Scale of Intelligence—Revised (WPPSI—R).* San Antonio, Tex.: The Psychological Corporation.

Wechsler Intelligence Scale for Children—Third Edition (WISC—III)

- Age Range: 6 years through 16 years, 11 months
- Testing Time: 90 minutes
- Intended Uses: To measure intellectual ability. Designed as a psychoeducational assessment for purposes of educational planning and placement, diagnosis of ex-

ceptionality in school-aged children, clinical and neuropsychological assessment, and research

- Format: Individually administered test comprises two scales (Verbal and Performance) consisting of a total of 12 subtests. Yields Verbal IQ, Performance IQ, Full Scale IQ, and four factors scores (Verbal Comprehension, Perceptual Organization, Freedom from Distractibility, and Processing Speed)
- Standardization: Normed on a sample of 2,200 children from age 6 years through 16 years, 11 months. The sample was standardized based on 1988 census data with regard to age, gender, race/ethnicity, geographic region, and parent education
- User Qualifications: Can be administered and scored by a trained technician under supervision, but test results should be interpreted by individuals with appropriate graduate or professional training in assessment
- References: Wechsler, D. 1991. *Wechsler Intelligence Scale for Children—Third Edition: Manual.* San Antonio, Tex.: The Psychological Corporation.

Woodcock–Johnson Psycho-Educational Battery—Revised (WJ—R)

- Age Range: 2 to 95 years
- Testing Time: 30 to 40 minutes for the Tests of Cognitive Ability; 50 to 60 minutes for the Tests of Achievement
- Intended Uses: To measure cognitive abilities, scholastic aptitudes, and achievement. Can be used in educational, clinical, and research settings to assess aptitude/achievement discrepancies, intracognitive discrepancies, and intra-achievement discrepancies. Can aid in diagnosis, program placement, individual program planning, and measuring growth over time
- Format: Individually administered battery using an easel format; includes the Woodcock–Johnson Tests of Cognitive Ability

(WJ—R COG) and the Woodcock–Johnson Tests of Achievement (WJ—R ACH). The WJ—R COG standard battery includes seven subtests that measure long-term retrieval, short-term memory, processing speed, auditory processing, visual processing, comprehension-knowledge, and fluid reasoning. The WJ—R ACH standard battery includes 12 subtests that measure reading, mathematics, written language, knowledge, and skills. Each of these two sections also includes a supplemental battery

- Standardization: Normed in the U.S. on a geographically and ethnically diverse sample of 6,359 subjects between the ages of 24 months and 95 years
- User Qualifications: Examiners must have formal training and supervision in test administration
- References: Woodcock, R.W., and N. Mather. 1989, 1990. Woodcock–Johnson Tests of Cognitive Ability—Standard and supplemental batteries: Examiner's manual. In *Woodcock–Johnson Psycho-Educational Battery—Revised*, ed. R.W. Woodcock and M.B. Johnson. Allen, Tex.: DLM Teaching Resources.

  Woodcock, R.W., and N. Mather. 1989, 1990. Woodcock-Johnson Tests of Achievement—Standard and Supplemental Batteries: Examiner's manual. In *Woodcock–Johnson Psycho-Educational Battery—Revised*, ed. R.W. Woodcock and M.B. Johnson, Allen, Tex.: DLM Teaching Resources.

BEHAVIOR AND ATTENTION TESTS*

ADHD Rating Scale

- Age Range: 6 to 12 years
- Testing Time: < 5 minutes
- Intended Uses: Designed to assess the 14

---

*Reviewed by Mary F. Lazar, with contributions from Jodie M. Ambrosino, James L. Karustis, Edward M. Moss, and Carla A. Stokes.

symptoms of ADHD from *DSM—III—R* diagnostic criteria. Can be used to supplement parent and teacher interviews of the diagnostic items in order to provide a more rigorous estimate of cutoff scores for more accurate diagnosis

- Format: Respondents (can be parents and/or teachers) are instructed to rate the severity of each of the 14 items from 0 to 3. T scores can be computed from normative data; three scores are calculated: Total, Inattention-Hyperactivity (Factor I), and Impulsivity-Hyperactivity (Factor II)
- Standardization: Normed on a sample of 55 urban, predominantly white lower middle class children (26 boys, 29 girls) enrolled in grades 1 through 6 across 45 public schools in Worcester, Massachusetts
- User Qualifications: Interpretation should be performed by clinicians with graduate-level experience and training in assessment and test interpretation.
- References: DuPaul, G.J. 1990. *The ADHD Rating Scale: Normative data, reliability, and validity.* Unpublished manuscript, University of Massachusetts Medical Center, Worcester, Mass.

  DuPaul, G.J. 1991. Parent and teacher ratings of ADHD symptoms: Psychometric properties in a community-based sample. *Journal of Clinical Child Psychology* 20:245–253.

Child Behavior Checklist (CBCL)

- Age Range: Two forms: 2 to 3 years and 4 to 18 years
- Testing Time: 10 to 20 minutes
- Intended Uses: Designed as an empirically based, standardized measure of behavior/emotional problems and competencies of children as seen by parents and parent surrogates. Can be used in outpatient and inpatient mental health services, schools, medical facilities, and court-related set-

tings. Can contribute to making diagnostic formulations, help guide decisions about the type and target of treatment interventions, and evaluate change as seen by the parents over time. Can also serve as a research tool in the study of the epidemiology, etiology, and treatment of problem behaviors

- Format: Parent responses yield eight syndrome scales scores (Withdrawn, Somatic Complaints, Anxious/Depressed, Social Problems, Thought Problems, Attention Problems, Delinquent Behavior, and Aggressive Behavior) and three competence scales (Activities, Social, and School). The eight scales can be further grouped into two broad-band factors (Internalizing and Externalizing)
- Standardization: Normed on a nationwide sample of 2,368 children. Separate norms are provided by sex and age
- User Qualifications: Because the CBCL can be self-administered and scored by computer, no special qualifications are needed for administration. Interpretation and use requires at least a master's degree and supervised clinical training with parents and children
- References: Achenbach, T.M. 1991. *Manual for the Child Behavior Checklist/4-18 and 1991 Profile.* Burlington, Vt.: Thomas M. Achenbach.

  Sattler, J.M. 1992. *Assessment of children.* 3rd ed. San Diego: Jerome M. Sattler, Publisher.

Conners' Parent Rating Scales (CPRS)

- Age Range: 3 to 17 years
- Testing Time: Not specified
- Intended Uses: To characterize the behaviors of a child and compare them to levels of appropriate normative groups. Three versions—93-item, 48-item, and 10-item—are available. Can be used as a rou-

tine screening device in a number of settings, including schools, outpatient clinics, inpatient settings, residential treatment centers, child protective services (including placement and referral decisions), special education and regular classrooms, juvenile detention centers, and private practice

- Format: Parent rates severity of child's symptoms on a four-point scale; the 93-item version yields eight factor scores: Conduct Disorder, Fearful-Anxious, Restless-Disorganized, Learning Problem-Immature, Psychosomatic, Obsessional, Antisocial, and Hyperactive-Immature. The 48-item version yields five factor scores: Conduct Problem, Learning Problem, Psychosomatic, Impulsive-Hyperactive, and Anxiety. The 10-item version yields a Hyperactivity Index

- Standardization: The 93-item did not account for child's age and gender. The 48-item version was normed on 578 children (same sample as the CTRS-28)

- User Qualifications: Can be used by professionals in psychology, education, medicine, social work, or allied fields who have an understanding of the basic principles and limitations of psychological assessment and test interpretation

- References: Conners, C.K. 1990. *Conners' Rating Scales manual.* Toronto, Ontario: Multi-Health Systems, Inc.

Conners' Teacher Rating Scales (CTRS)

- Age Range: 3 to 17 years
- Testing Time: Not specified
- Intended Uses: To characterize the behaviors of a child and compare them to levels of appropriate normative groups. Three versions—39-item, 28-item, and 10-item—are available. Can be used as a routine screening device in a number of settings, including schools, outpatient clinics,

inpatient settings, residential treatment centers, child protective services (including placement and referral decisions), special education and regular classrooms, juvenile detention centers, and private practice

- Format: Teacher rates severity of child's symptoms on a four-point scale; 39-item version yields six factor scores: Hyperactivity, Conduct Problem, Emotional Overindulgent, Anxious-Passive, Asocial, and Daydream-Attention Problem. The 28-item version yields three factor scores: Conduct Problem, Hyperactivity, and Inattentive-Passive. The 10-item version yields a Hyperactivity Index

- Standardization: The 39-item version was normed on 9,583 Canadian children. The 28-item version was normed on 578 children (same sample as the CPRS-48)

- User Qualifications: Can be used by professionals in psychology, education, medicine, social work, or allied fields who have an understanding of the basic principles and limitations of psychological assessment and test interpretation

- References: Conners, C.K. 1990. *Conners' Rating Scales manual.* Toronto, Ontario: Multi-Health Systems, Inc.

Gordon Diagnostic System (GDS)

- Age Range: 4 to 16 years
- Testing Time: Approximately 20 minutes
- Intended Uses: One of many commercially available types of continuous performance tests designed to assist with the evaluation of attention deficits by providing standardized data regarding a child's actual ability to (1) focus and sustain attention and (2) inhibit impulsive responding. Can be used to supplement information gained through subjective interviews and rating scales to aid diagnosis in educational, clinical, and research settings

Kaufman, A.S., and N.L. Kaufman. 1985. *Manual for the Kaufman Test of Educational Achievement, Brief Form.* Circle Pines, Minn.: American Guidance Service.

Peabody Individual Achievement Test— Revised (PIAT—R)

- Age Range: 5 years to 18 years, 11 months (kindergarten to Grade 12)
- Testing Time: 1 hour
- Intended Uses: To be used as a screening measure of achievement. Provides survey of individual's level of scholastic achievement and educational strengths and weaknesses for use in determining school placement and educational services and development of IEPs and use as a measure of effectiveness of educational interventions. Not designed for use as a diagnostic tool in specific content areas
- Format: Individually administered test comprises six subtests: General Information, Reading Recognition, Reading Comprehension, Mathematics, Spelling, and Written Expression. Yields two composite scores, Total Reading and Total Test (first five subtests) and optional Written Language composite (Written Expression and Spelling). Provides standard scores, percentile ranks, and grade and age equivalents
- Standardization: Normed on a national sample of 1,563 students stratified by four geographic regions, grade level, sex, race or ethnic group, and parental education
- User Qualifications: Can be administered and interpreted by psychological, educational, vocational, and medical professionals
- References: Markwardt, F.C., Jr. 1989. *Peabody Individual achievement Test—Revised.* Circle Pines, Minn.: American Guidance Service.

Wechsler Individual Achievement Test (WIAT)

- Age Range: 5 years to 19 years, 11 months (kindergarten to Grade 12)
- Testing time: 30 to 55 minutes
- Intended Uses: To assess achievement. Can be used along with the Wechsler scales to calculate ability–achievement discrepancies, to help identify areas of specific learning disabilities, and to assess academic progress in educational programs
- Format: Individually administered test comprises eight subtests requiring oral or written responses: Basic Reading, Reading Comprehension, Mathematics Reasoning, Numerical Operations, Listening Comprehension, Oral Expression, Spelling, and Written Expression. Yields a Total Composite score and Reading, Math, Language, and Writing Composites. Three of the subtests can be used as a brief screening instrument. Provides standard scores, percentile ranks, and grade and age equivalents for each subtest
- Standardization: Normed on a national sample of 4,252 children stratified by four geographic regions, age and grade level, gender, race or ethnic group, and parental education
- User Qualifications: Should be administered and interpreted by professionals involved in psychological and educational testing, with graduate-level training in the use of individually administered assessment instruments
- References: The Psychological Corporation. 1992. *Wechsler Individual Achievement Test manual.* San Antonio, Tex.

Wide Range Achievement Test—Third Edition (WRAT—III)

- Age Range: 5 to 75 years
- Testing Time: 15 to 30 minutes

- Intended Uses: Designed as a brief measure of achievement for assessing the development of reading, math and spelling skills. Used to identify reading, spelling, and arithmetic skills relative to age peers; to monitor the effectiveness of particular academic interventions; and, when used in conjunction with a measure of general intelligence, to screen for learning disabilities

- Format: Two alternate forms: each covers the entire age range and comprises three subtests, Reading, Spelling, and Arithmetic. The Spelling and Arithmetic subtests can be administered individually or in groups; the Reading subtest requires individual administration. Provides age-based standard scores, percentile ranks, and grade equivalents

- Standardization: Not available

- User Qualifications: May be administered by educational, psychological, vocational, and medical personnel. Interpretation should be performed by someone with appropriate training in psychometric theory and test interpretation

- References: Jastak, S., and G.S. Wilkinson. 1993. *The Wide Range Achievement Test.* 3rd ed. Wilmington, Del.: Jastak Associates, Inc.

Management and Treatment Approaches

cally focused contexts (e.g., in some early intervention programs, the special education teacher, speech/language pathologist, occupational therapist, and physical therapist are effectively transdisciplinary for many of their services); it is most economical for the provider but provides quality care in limited circumstances.

This section focuses on *interdisciplinary* strategies but is applicable to all forms of care in which multiple disciplines are involved.

CHARACTERISTICS OF SUCCESSFUL COLLABORATIONS

The following are characteristics of successful collaborations:

- *Comprehensive representation:* All "disciplines" with significant bearing on the situation, including family members and other community members, are represented.
- *Economic, balanced representation:* Interests are represented only to the extent that they are needed.
- *Stable, capable membership:* Participants are knowledgeable, have the authority to carry through any commitments, and maintain a long-term assignment to the collaboration. Sufficient resources are made available and equitable.
- *Shared responsibility:* Members participate equally in decisions, set mutual goals, and share the accountability and the rewards.
- *Equal access:* Information and opportunity to participate are available to all—there are no cliques or subgroups unless assigned by the group at large.
- *Open, positive attitudes:* Key individuals are flexible, trusting, pragmatic, and creative.
- *Frequent, full information:* Collaborators meet and communicate often. Acronyms and jargon are not used unless readily familiar to all.

- *Mutual understanding and respect:* Participants appreciate and learn from other perspectives, at the same time preserving and exercising their own expertise.
- *Frequent, equitable kudos:* Small gains are regularly celebrated, and contributions by all parties are acknowledged.

OUTCOMES TO BE ACHIEVED BY COLLABORATION

In about 1990, the state of Alaska officially adopted "Developmental Disabilities Service Principles" that have been widely endorsed by other state agencies in the United States. The list below is an adaptation based on other individualized services and additional focus on childhood considerations:

1. Services are the result of planning that is continually reworked and revised.
2. Services are built around what the child and family want and need.
3. Services promote opportunities that are age appropriate for the child.
4. The family has options of services from which to choose.
5. The family chooses the locality in which to live and attend school.
6. Families are provided supports and services necessary to succeed in their chosen environment.
7. Services are built from known best practices and are objectively evaluated.
8. Services are individually optimal and culturally appropriate.
9. Community participation and inclusion are maximized.

SOLUTION-ORIENTED COLLABORATIONS

Collaborations across disciplines and across departments or agencies are difficult. It is thus realistic to expect the occasional fumble and to work constantly to keep the team on task. Here are some characteristics of a self-managing collaboration:

- When problems arise, participants seek solutions rather than assigning blame.
- Participants act in a spirit of cooperation rather than competition.
- Responsibilities are assigned and accepted according to role.
- Individuals treat resistance as an obstacle to treatment, not as a personal affront.
- The more experienced the team member, the less he or she has to say on general issues.
- Opinions are aligned with facts, but collaborations are made with people.
- People show each other respect regardless of rank or title.
- Humor and enjoyment of the collaboration process are encouraged.

PLANNING THE PRESENT AND THE FUTURE

The collaborative team develops services to meet the child's and family's needs in the context of life span development. The plan always includes strategies and supports for the next major transition—educational, developmental, medical, or a change in locality or source of services. Collaborations on behalf of a child and family usually follow a sequence of activities:

1. clarification of general goals and roles for the team
2. identification of priorities for the child's development
3. specific assessments of the child's condition, including an *ecological assessment* (see Chapter 7 section "Psychoeducational Measures: Ecological Assessment"), by individual team members
4. team meetings and decisions to set up specific objectives, services, and supports
5. implementation of interventions

6. monitoring the effect of services—looping back, steps 3 above through 6, as necessary
7. outcome evaluation, recommendations for the next or alternative interventions, planning the next transition

TECHNIQUES FOR COLLABORATION

Listed below are general strategies of collaboration. Techniques for more specific situations are described in the following four subchapters.

- Identify team membership to include a parent plus educational and medical representation. Add others to the core as needed for key concerns.
- Reach a consensus on the membership and assign a team leader as someone who knows the child very well and has reasonable organizational skills.
- Establish ground rules such as meeting times and places and for conduct rules such as may be found in the next subchapter.
- Make information available in abundant and explicit ways concerning the child, the family, and all core team members.
- Identify other individuals as consultants or resources to be called upon as needed as the collaboration progresses.
- Establish enjoyable ways of managing the team process, such as fines of 10 cents for use of acronyms or unexplained technical language.
- Balance the distribution of chores (e.g., taking notes) and comparable commitment. But make it equally clear that professional contributions are on a basis of need and may not be equal.
- Respect people's time: have frequent meetings but make sure they are well organized and to the point, and expect some unavoidable absences.
- Offer personal respect: promote perspective taking, compliments, favors.

- Reward generously: thank people for their contributions, congratulate them on their successes, praise collaborative behavior (promptness, succinctness, complementarity, etc.), plan further collaborations and coauthorships.
- Reframe obstacles as opportunities: e.g., someone's interference in another's area may be recast as an expression of interest.
- Improve communication and problem solving through
  1. acknowledgments: greeting people by name, introducing newcomers
  2. conducive environment in terms of seating, lines of sight, etc.
  3. identification of concerns in advance—minimal surprises at meetings

4. identification of common problems
5. discussion of problems specific to individual disciplines
6. preannounced brainstorming, where "anything goes"
7. remaining focused on the best interests of the child

- Allow different roles within the team to vary with the situation. There is a time and place in which it is appropriate for participants
  1. to act together, share responsibility
  2. to act individually, perhaps go out on a limb
  3. to mediate among team members or other individuals

SUGGESTED READINGS

Davis, M., and A.M. Sanchez, eds. 1987. *Interdisciplinary collaboration between state mental health and higher education.* Boulder, Colo.: Western Interstate Commission for Higher Education.

Flynn, L.L., and H.C. Lewis, eds. 1994. *Early intervention curriculum compendium.* Denver: JFK Center for Developmental Disabilities, University-Affiliated Program of Colorado.

Klein, S.M., and S. Kontos. 1993. *Best practices in integration: Inservice training model.* Bloomington: Indiana University, University-Affiliated Program.

MacFarquhar, K.W., et al. 1993. Individualizing services for seriously emotionally disturbed youth: A nationwide review. *Administration and Policy in Mental Health* 20: 165–174.

Mariano, C. 1989. The case for interdisciplinary collaboration. *Nursing Outlook* 37: 285–288.

Singer, G.H.S., and L.K. Irvin, eds. 1989. *Support for caregiving families: Enabling positive adaptation to disability.* Baltimore: Paul H. Brookes.

ADDITIONAL RESOURCES

University-Affiliated Programs (UAPs) on Developmental Disabilities; these serve all states of the United States and specialize in collaborations—interdisciplinary and interagency. Further information may be obtained from the federal Administration on Developmental Disabilities (which funds UAPs), the American Association of UAPs, or a UAP near you (see Appendix A).

INTERAGENCY COLLABORATION

Lynn S. Paterna

Purpose: to describe the strategies and protocols to set up interagency collaborative teams with consumers, their families, service agencies, and community support to enable coordinated care and community integration.

Over the past 20 years, the goals of public services have been redefined as supporting the choice of each individual with disabilities to achieve a chosen lifestyle. In 1986, the Association for Persons with Severe Handicaps stated that to achieve integrated services, the related service personnel should collaborate with the family and important others to provide strategies and adaptations that increase participation in natural settings. These emerging support paradigms have presented challenges to agencies to coordinate services and cooperate with other agencies, the consumer, family, and community support to fulfill the child's needs and choices (Smull and Bellamy 1992). Interagency collaboration establishes a process to

- solve unique problems
- cooperate with other agencies to improve service
- explore resources and networks
- create better solutions by sharing different perspectives, knowledge, and ideas
- promote a caring atmosphere of support
- communicate effectively and resolve conflicts

THE COLLABORATIVE TEAM

Collaboration means "laboring together" in the spirit of willingness (Rainforth et al. 1992). The collaborative team is a group of individuals who share common beliefs and determination to reach mutual goals. Team members have varying areas of expertise and backgrounds. They allocate group tasks, responsibilities, and group leadership. No one person or agency dominates the group. All members are equal and practice collaborative skills to make decisions by consensus. This interactive process enables team members with diverse expertise and differing perspectives on and knowledge about the child to define problems and generate solutions that consider the wholeness of the child, not just fragments.

COLLABORATIVE TEAM MEMBERSHIP

Once the reasons to form a collaborative team are clarified, the decision of who will make up the team is made. Since the team evolves around the consumer's needs and problems, who belongs on the collaborative team is determined by the family members, who are primary members of the team. The other core team members are the important, trusted people in the child's life, such as community supporters, friends, service agencies, school personnel, and professionals. The members are invited to be on the team and must desire to "labor with others" for the sake of the child with disabilities. Additional short- or long-term support members may be invited to collaborate and consult when the team needs new resources and information or when the child's priorities change.

Members should be invited to participate in identifying additional core and support members:

1. Ask the child and family whom they want on the team.
2. List all agencies serving the child, and enlist the family's input on what agencies they prefer.
3. List all professionals such as psychologists, physicians, therapists, and school teachers who are involved with the child. Decide if they are appropriate members for the core team or if they should be invited for later consultation.

4. Invite core members, identified as above, to join team. The family members or designated other(s) can make this invitation.

The first core collaborative meeting should be held to build trust and clarify purpose. Trust is an important ingredient that binds the team together to cooperate and achieve decisions by consensus. Some methods of building trust are listed by Fox and Williams (1991):

- Take a few minutes and share something personal.
- Treat team members and their ideas with respect.
- Practice good listening and communication.
- Share team roles, responsibilities, blame, and success.
- Decide on issues by consensus.
- Support and assist one another.
- Resolve conflicts promptly and fairly.
- Encourage all to participate.
- Have fun together.

Discuss why a collaborative meeting is needed and what are the expectations of team members.

PROTOCOLS FOR EFFICIENT COLLABORATIVE TEAM MEETINGS

It is important to set meeting protocols for dealing with sensitive or controversial issues. The collaborative team meets frequently to review past efforts and plan for the future cooperatively. To have an atmosphere conducive to building trust, solving problems, and resolving conflicts, the team members must practice collaborative and communication skills so that all members are heard, all ideas are voiced, and all members work together for the good of the child and family.

Since all team members are equal, leadership and other roles are rotated to each member. At the beginning of the meeting, the members choose the following five positions:

1. *Facilitator:* facilitates the running of the meeting by setting the agenda from team suggestions and determining the amount of time for the agenda item to be discussed

2. *Timekeeper:* makes sure the agenda time is heeded and signals when time is running out

3. *Recorder:* records all pertinent information, task assignments, and decisions made at the meeting

4. *Encourager:* observes the team members' nonverbal cues and ensures that everyone participates

5. *Jargon buster:* makes sure the language is understandable and professional jargon is minimized

An agenda format sheet streamlines the meetings. It should be used at all meetings and filed in a notebook. Design the sheet around the time allotted for meetings and the number of agenda items normally discussed. Exhibit 8–1 shows an example. If someone is absent, he or she can review the minutes by looking in the notebook, or someone can be assigned to debrief or to pass on a copy of the minutes. Suggested meeting items that promote enthusiasm and accountability are

- celebrations of accomplishments and successes
- celebrations of failures (because they represent attempts and creativity)
- status reports of previous meeting task assignments
- future or ongoing agenda items

Knowing that consensus must be reached forces team members to be creative, open to ideas, and willing to discuss ideas. Arriving at consensus on tough issues and decisions is not an easy task. Allow all ideas and viewpoints to be put on the table, discuss ideas in context of what is best for child and family, and if there are different viewpoints and disagreements, discuss possible compromises.

At the conclusion of a meeting:

1. Summarize the meeting: decisions made, tasks assigned to whom.

Exhibit 8–1 Collaborative Team Meeting Agenda of Friends of Joey

Date: _____February 5, 1995_____
Facilitator: ___Bill_____
Recorder: ___Jane_____
Encourager: ___Dad_____
Timekeeper: ___Mrs. Smith_____
Attending the meeting:___Mary, Bill, Jane, Mrs. Smith, Mother, Dad, and Susan_____

Absent ___Nicole_____

Agenda Items	Time	Who
Task status report	5 minutes	Mary and Bill
Celebration of success	5 minutes	All—30 sec. each
Next week's target goals for behavior	10 minutes	All team members
Demonstration of teaching dressing skills	10 minutes	Jane
Review school progress and target skills	15 minutes	Mrs. Smith, teacher
Finalize next week's schedule of activities	10 minutes	All team members
Set next week's agenda and meeting place	5 minutes	All team members

Next Week Agenda Items	Time	Who
Introduce toilet-training procedures	15 minutes	Susan and Mother
Brainstorm community activities	10 minutes	All team members

Task Assignments	Due	Who
Plan toilet-training procedures for team	next week	Susan and Mother
Check with community pools for lessons	next week	Bill and Dad
Check children's play groups and activities	next week	Jane and Mary

Who will contact absent team members: ___Susan_____

Next Meeting:

Date: ___February 12, 1995___   Time ___4 P.M._____   Place: ___Joey's house___

2. Request future meeting agenda items. Items not discussed can be rolled forward to the next meeting.

3. Choose someone to debrief absent member(s).

4. If task assignments are shared between team members, nominate one as the "point person."

5. Set the date, time, and place of the next meeting.

Collaborative team skills should be periodically evaluated. Choose a scheduled time to evaluate the team meetings. The team can individually or collectively read over the checklist of collaborative team skills (see Exhibit 8–2). If the team sees deficiencies, discuss ways to improve and practice the skills.

Working together and allocating responsibility continues between the meetings. Sometimes task assignments are shared between agencies or other members of the team. Cooperation and

Exhibit 8–2 Collaborative Team Evaluation Checklist

Date _____

Check	Collaborative Skills
	Treat team members with respect
	Listen to others (maintain eye contact with the speaker, give nonverbal signs of acceptance and encouragement, and probe for information by asking questions, paraphrasing, and summarizing to check for understanding).
	Tell other team members something personal about yourself.
	Discuss your feelings openly and honestly.
	Offer support and assistance to others outside your job responsibilities.
	Distribute team roles and responsibilities among all team members.
	Share the blame if decisions go wrong or if plans are ineffective.
	Share success, recognition, and rewards if decisions are right and plans work.
	Decide by consensus building, not majority vote.
	Encourage all to participate in team planning, sharing ideas, and making decisions.
	Show respect and praise for each other's ideas.
	Criticize ideas, not people.
	During conflicts, practice six steps leading to resolution.
	Establish team goals and purpose of the team.
	HAVE FUN TOGETHER.

Date of the team's next collaborative skill review _____

communication continue by means of face-to-face interaction, telephone, fax machines, or electronic mail. If a member is having difficulty completing a task, he or she should seek assistance from other members.

How well the members listen and communicate with one another verbally and nonverbally is the key element in teamwork. Therefore successful collaborative strategies include

- Communication skills
  1. active listening
     (a) encouraging one another
     (b) clarifying what has been said
     (c) restating what has been said
     (d) reflecting basic feelings projected by speaker
     (e) summarizing the ideas and feelings expressed
     (f) acknowledging the value of others' issues, feelings, efforts, and actions
  2. observing nonverbal behavior
  3. conveying the message to be received
- Problem-solving skills
  1. recognizing there is a problem
  2. defining the problem
  3. thinking of many solutions (brainstorming)

(a) Take two to three minutes of individual thinking time and write ideas down.

(b) Use a round-robin format for each member to present ideas.

(c) Recorder writes ideas on the board, the overhead projector, or even flip charts.

(d) Encourage creative thinking and allow everything—even what seem to be silly ideas.

(e) Do not criticize or laugh at "off-the-wall" ideas because these generate creative solutions.

(f) After ideas seem to be exhausted, take two to three minutes to allow additional ones to be voiced.

(g) Discuss, reword, or combine similar ideas or create new ones from the existing list.

(h) Prioritize the list from most to least workable.

(i) Select the best ideas for action.

4. deciding what to do

5. trying a solution

6. evaluating the results and perhaps picking another solution

• Conflict resolution methods—ways to deal with controversy when the team members or agency representatives are at odds over an issue and meetings become uncomfortable (see Johnson and Johnson 1987)

1. Confront the opposition. Plan an airing of viewpoints when there is plenty of time. All opposing members or agency representatives take time to express fairly their own or their agency's views and feelings.

2. Remove the conflict from a win-lose struggle. Jointly define the conflict as a mutual problem to be solved. Steer away from labeling, accusing, or insulting the opposition.

3. Communicate positions and feelings throughout the negotiations. Use "I feel" statements such as "I feel defensive and am unable to express my true concerns when I do not agree with you." A positive statement might be "I agree with two of your points. I feel positive that we can come to some kind of an agreement. I appreciate that you gave me time to explain my view." If you are representing your agency, a positive statement might be "[Agency's name] can agree on two of the three points but cannot support the other because its mission does not endorse this type of action. Perhaps we could explore another way that the agency would accept. I'd be happy to discuss other options with my director."

4. Take the opponent's perspective. Listen intently to what is being presented. "What if I were in that position? What would I think or feel about this issue?" This perspective will increase your understanding of the issue and help to achieve a resolution.

5. Coordinate motivations to negotiate in good faith. Resolving conflict usually entails compromise, which increases or decreases cost and gains for each party. When it costs more to continue the conflict or when the parties gain more by reaching an agreement, there is higher motivation to continue negotiating.

6. Reach an agreement that is satisfactory to each party and have both parties agree to abide by it. The agreement should list both positions on the issues being adopted and include provisions for future meetings to check how well the agreement is working and how cooperation can be improved.

Case Study:

Linda was an 8-year-old child with mental retardation, autistic characteristics, and severe, continuous self-injurious behavior of hitting her face, her nose, and the kidney area of her back. She broke her nose twice in two months, and there was concern about possible kidney injury. She wore air splints 90 percent of her days and nights. Further, Linda's quality of life was poor. Her family felt strained and stressed. They had a new infant and a three year old who needed attention. Her mother found little time to sleep and her father had stressful demands at work. The family needed more relief to achieve a more tolerable situation.

Linda received a share-care grant for respite from her state Department of Mental Health and Developmental Disabilities (DMHDD), which was administered through the local ARC. The ARC employees wanted technical assistance to handle aberrant behaviors. Linda's school also needed technical assistance since Linda spent most of her day restrained in air splints and belted to a chair.

The Center for Human Development's University-Affiliated Program (CHD:UAP) had begun an intensive early intervention (IEI) program for children with autism. They had resources to provide technical assistance. Thus, in addition to the family, potential collaborating agencies included the local ARC, CHD:UAP, the school, school district administrators, and the state DMHDD.

The core team was chosen by Linda's parents with care providers:

1. mother and father
2. four ARC care and respite providers
3. ARC family services coordinator
4. CHD:UAP IEI team leader

The extended team, which would meet when necessary with the core team to coordinate treatment and teaching, consisted of

1. special education teacher
2. teacher's assistant
3. school district special education specialist
4. school occupational therapist
5. school physical therapist
6. school speech pathologist
7. school principal
8. CHD:UAP family training coordinator
9. CHD:UAP autism consultant

10. CHD:UAP IEI coordinator
11. state regional director of DMHDD

The first team meeting to build trust and understand purpose lasted two hours. The team planned a program to teach Linda new skills in language, social play, and daily living. They structured her day with teaching activities to take up time and build an active life. They also brainstormed ideas and used consensus to decide action plans.

To ensure efficient continued meetings, all members shared roles at meetings and divided up tasks; the agenda was set weekly to discuss celebrations of Linda's progress; the next week's schedule, lessons, and activities were planned; problems were discussed and solutions brainstormed; the status of task assignments was discussed; and active listening skills were encouraged. Finally, each month the team passed an evaluation around to check collaborative skills.

Between meetings, the IEI team leader set the week's meeting agenda and responded to needs of team members. All team members logged Linda's daily progress for everyone to read. The IEI team leader read logs and highlighted concerns for summary at collaborative meetings. Linda's parents contributed by keeping communication flowing among the team.

Conflict resolution was required when a conflict arose between Linda's special education teacher and Linda's team. A special meeting was called with the teacher and team for the purpose of resolving the conflict. The family and team received advice from the CHD:UAP IEI coordinator, who was experienced in resolving and handling conflicts. All feelings and views were fairly expressed. The family, in considering the teacher's views, realized that the teacher had a different philosophy from that of Linda's team: she wanted to implement her own ideas without consulting or collaborating with the family or team. The teacher felt she would lose her authority with decisions about Linda if she continued to negotiate a resolution. Therefore she was not motivated to work out the conflict or achieve a compromise.

The principal, school administration special education specialist, family, team members, and CHD:UAP consultant brainstormed ideas to negotiate a resolution. At last they decided that it would be better to place Linda in another class. There was another special education teacher who considered this an opportunity to collaborate with the team and to help Linda, whom she had previously had in her class. The other teacher was relieved and agreeable. Monthly meetings with the core team and school team were set to discuss Linda's progress, share ideas, and coordinate home and school teaching.

As a result of this collaboration, Linda's quality of life has continued to improve. Linda has learned to use a picture exchange system of communication. She can dress herself and is toi-

let trained. She eats by herself and helps with daily chores such as emptying the dishwasher and putting her dirty clothes in the hamper. She appropriately plays with her sisters and by herself for increasing periods of time. Although Linda continues to have challenges in her life, her self-injurious behavior appears only when she is sick and it is not as high in frequency as before. She participates in community activities such as play-by-play and swimming lessons. The best results of the interagency collaboration are for Linda that she has many friends and for the team members that the different agencies have learned from and enjoyed each other.

REFERENCES

Association for Persons with Severe Handicaps. 1986. *Position statement on the provision of related services.* Seattle.

Fox, T.J., and W. Williams. 1991. *Implementing the best practices for all students in their local school.* Burlington, Vt: Vermont Statewide Systems Support Project, Center for Developmental Disabilities, University-Affiliated Program.

Johnson, D.W., and R.T. Johnson. 1987. *Creative conflict.* Edina, Minn.: Interaction Books.

Rainforth, B., et al. 1992. *Collaborative teams for students with severe disabilities: Integrating therapy and educational services.* Baltimore: Paul H. Brookes.

Smull, M.W., and G.T. Bellamy. 1992. Community services for adults with disabilities: Policy challenges in the emerging support paradigm. In *Critical issues in the lives of people with severe disabilities*, ed. L.H. Meyer et al., 527–536. Baltimore: Paul H. Brookes.

CASE MANAGEMENT

Symme W. Trachtenberg and David F. Lewis

Purpose: to describe the concepts, uses, and tasks associated with case management as a system and as a service for children with developmental disabilities.

Case management may be defined as the collaborative provision of coordinated care by professionals from multiple disciplines, in one or more settings, over a stated period of time, to achieve specific outcomes. It is a process that serves to facilitate team consensus in the prioritization of assessment needs, problem identification, goal clarification, treatment planning, and resource allocation in the provision of intervention to the child and family. Outcomes that may be anticipated in the presence of effective case management include

- functional goal achievement
- caregiver proficiency in caring for the child

- coordinated interdisciplinary plan of services that is continuous, child and family centered, culturally sensitive, nonrestrictive, and effective

Many families of children with developmental disabilities benefit from a clinical process that helps to coordinate their care. Children with disabilities often have complex problems and may receive services from multiple medical, educational, and social service programs. Therefore an identified case manager who extends his or her services beyond the boundaries of a single agency is needed to coordinate the entire service network on behalf of a child and family (Rengo and Kunes 1995).

Case management needs to provide a continuum of care, intervening at key points and focusing on the allocation of resources and the

Exhibit 8–3 Sample Parent/Professional Worksheet

PLANNING FOR CHILD AND FAMILY NEEDS

PARENT/PROFESSIONAL WORKSHEET

Category	*Who/Where/How*
Advocacy	
Attendant/Nursing/Respite	
Case Management	
Developmental Needs	
Educational Services	
Equipment	
Financial/Health Insurance	
Housing/Placement	
Legal Guardianship	

Medical Supervision
  General
  Specific
  Dental
  Vision
  Hearing	

Psychosocial Needs	
Socialization/Recreation	
Therapeutic Modalities	
Physical Therapy	
Occupational Therapy	
Speech/Language Pathology	
Transportation	
Vocational Planning	
Other	

Name: _____   Date Completed: _____   By Whom:_____

sure the delivery of team care. The care manager functions in a clinical and administrative capacity. Team interaction, communication, and conflict resolution if necessary are essential to drive a productive case management process. Much of this communication takes place in conference settings with treatment plans organized and documented. As the team develops its skills, more communication can occur on an informal basis.

A child requiring complex rehabilitative treatment may have multiple professionals functioning in a case management role, including those assigned by the health provider, the insurance company, and the social service agencies. Working out mutually beneficial relationships among these agencies is essential in developing a comprehensive coordinated treatment plan to optimize the care and outcome effectively.

Responsibilities of the Case Manager

The primary responsibilities of a case manager in a clinic or hospital-based setting include:

- providing direction and consultation to the patient care team in prioritizing goals and resources and in implementing an integrated care plan
- communicating essential background information to team members, emphasizing the reason for current treatment as well as resource limitations
- coordinating the documentation of information essential to team decision making, including the family, referral source, insurance company, or managed-care provider
- objectively evaluating treatment plans in relation to both quality and cost-effectiveness
- focusing the team's efforts on the achievement of predetermined goals within a defined time frame and assisting in determining the necessary type, sequence, and intensity of resources needed to achieve outcomes

DETERMINING THE NEED FOR OUT-OF-HOME PLACEMENT*

Some parents find that even with increased supports and in-home services, they are no longer able to care for their child at home. Every effort should be made to assist a family in keeping their child at home, but professionals need to listen to parents who say that the care of their child is too much for them to handle.

A thorough evaluation of all the issues must take place. Such out-of-home placement may be foster care or community home care. The criteria listed below may help in determining the possible need for alternate placement:

- There is a history of abuse or neglect or inability to care for the child, as documented by the local children and youth agency, educational, or health care program.
- The family demonstrate a temporary inability to provide care in their home.
- The parents are unable to care for the child because of a serious medical condition and consequent care needs.
- The parents are unable to learn essential child care (e.g., to show consistency in knowledge and performance of critical therapeutic interventions).
- The parents are unable to adhere to safety precautions during therapy sessions or to demonstrate understanding of safety and emergency care.

The case manager, in collaboration with the child care team, needs to assess and ensure that

- The child will be cared for in a home environment that is safe and appropriately supervised.
- The child will have knowledgeable and competent caregiver(s).
- Essential communication occurs between the appropriate collateral agencies and

---

*Nina Szap Ditmar, MSW, contributed to this section.

funding sources to facilitate a new placement.

- A smooth transition between levels of care takes place as medically indicated.

In the event that the child has one case manager from the hospital and another from managed care, the managed-care case manager should receive periodic documentation of progress and be involved in the process of planning for the discharge. Every effort should be made to provide the least restrictive environment and the greatest opportunity for community integration.

CONCLUSION

The case management process is a collaborative effort that ensures the delivery of coordinated team care in support of an individual child's prioritized goals. The process provides direction to the care team in its efficient and effective provision of integrated services.

People who need ongoing case management services often have additional needs for social services. In particular, children with developmental disabilities and special health care needs require family-centered case management services that link families to all existing programs and entitlements.

As cost and quality concerns continue to grow, efficient and effective case management services will be in even greater demand. Strategic alliances and resources must be established to complement a successful case management program.

REFERENCES

Kernaghan, S. 1994. Case management certification: A SWA survey report. *Social Work Administration* 20, no. 3: 6–11.

Marcenko, M.O., and L.K. Smith. 1992. The impact of a family-centered case management approach. *Social Work in Health Care* 7, no. 1: 87–100.

Rengo, R., and C. Kunes. 1995. Outpatient case management: A role for social work. *Social Work Administration* 21, no. 1: 1, 3–6.

Rose, S. 1992. Empowering case management clients. *Aging International*, 19, no. 3: 1–2.

Zander, K. 1992. Critical pathways. In *Total quality management: The health care pioneers*, ed. M.M. Melum. Chicago: AH Publishing.

ADDITIONAL SUGGESTED READINGS

Feltes, M., et al. 1994. Case managers and physicians: communication and perceived problems. *Journal of the American Geriatric Society* 42, no. 1: 5–10.

Fox, H.B., et al. 1993. Health maintenance organizations and children with special health needs—a suitable match. *American Journal of Diseases of Children* 147: 546–552.

Fralic, M. 1992. The nurse case manager: Focus, selection, preparation, and measurement. *Journal of Nursing Administration* 22, no. 11: 13–15.

Kaufman, J. 1992. Case management services for children with special health needs. *Journal of Case Management* 1:53–56.

Keith, R.A. 1991. The comprehensive treatment team in rehabilitation. *Archives of Physical Medicine and Rehabilitation* 72:269–274.

Kirk, S.A., et al. 1993. Changes in health and job attitudes of case managers providing intensive services. *Hospital Community Psychiatry* 44, no. 2: 168–173.

Wadas, T.M. 1993. Case management and caring behavior. *Nursing Management* 24, no. 9: 40–42, 44–46.

Weil, M., and J.M. Karls. 1989. *Case management in human service practice.* San Francisco: Jossey-Bass Publishers, Inc.

Wolk, J.L., et al. 1994. The managerial nature of case management. *Social Work* 39, no. 2: 152–159.

RESOLVING CONFLICTS

Dana I. Klar

Purpose: to discuss conflict resolution and the management techniques that can be implemented to minimize conflict and the issues surrounding it.

Institutions by definition are components of integration that collectively bring together different tasks and work groups. It is this contrast that defines the organization and the way it functions. One of the most difficult challenges in the workplace is resolving conflict, and it takes skill to facilitate solutions and plan for improvement. Conflict resolution is an open process of debate and discussion that takes into account the collective group as a whole, emphasizing content rather than rank. It is a management tool that can be used to minimize problems and prevent them from escalating.

Conflict is inherent in every progressive organization and should not be viewed negatively. In most circumstances, conflict that is managed adroitly can have a beneficial effect on the involved participants. It is an open process that allows individuals to work through issues in a team-oriented way. If successfully initiated, conflict resolution can influence productivity and morale, minimize opportunities that can lead to confrontation, and transform conflicts into problem-solving exercises.

The remainder of this chapter draws on the discussion of conflict in Umiker (1994, 184–188).

Conflict takes place whenever change, empowerment, paradigm shifts, team building, or attempts at quality improvement occur. It forces people to take a second look at situations, and if handled properly it enhances interpersonal relationships.

The following are major sources of conflict:

- People do not know what is expected of them.
- Policies and rules are ambiguous, and some may think that they are only for other people.
- Communication is garbled.
- There are hierarchial conflicts: for example, someone with a PhD or MD degree resents taking orders from a young manager with an MBA.
- There are incompatibilities or disagreements based on differences of value systems, goals, temperaments, attitudes, or ethics.
- There are conflicts over funds, space, time, personnel, equipment, or staffing schedules.
- There is competition for power.
- There are operational or staffing changes.

The etiology is not always apparent. Often there is a covert issue beneath a less important overt factor. Other situations are murky because the etiology is complex.

The proactive goal is to prevent conflicts. When that is not possible, one should opt to keep small conflicts from escalating into big ones. Objectives include diffusing anger, venting feelings, and converting conflicts into problem-solving exercises.

There are five basic strategies for dealing with conflict. Each is appropriate for certain situations. The trick is to pick the right one.

- *Avoid:* This may be to deny that there is a problem, to escape physically, or to pass the buck. This strategy is appropriate when
  1. it is not your problem
  2. there is nothing you can do about it
  3. it is not important
  4. additional information is needed
  5. you or the other individual is emotionally upset
  6. the situation will probably ameliorate if you can wait it out
- *Fight:* This strategy is risky, and you may lose. Even if you win the skirmish, your

opponent may wait for another opportunity to retaliate, or he or she may become a saboteur. This strategy is appropriate when

1. quick action is needed (you do not convene a committee meeting when a fire breaks out)
2. there must be enforcement of rules, such as safety regulations
3. ethical or legal issues are involved

• *Surrender:* This is conceding or accommodating ("Okay, okay, I'll do it"). This strategy is appropriate when

1. you are wrong
2. it does not matter to you but is important to them
3. you have little or no chance to win
4. harmony and stability are important
5. giving in on a minor item means winning a more important one later

• *Compromise:* Compromise permits each party to get what it wants, so there is some satisfaction for both. Most union–management disputes are settled in this manner. This strategy is appropriate when

1. opposing goals are incompatible
2. a temporary settlement to complex issues is needed
3. time constraints call for an expedient solution

• *Collaborate:* Collaboration is working together to find solutions that satisfy both parties. This win-win approach is usually the best alternative, but it often requires a creative solution because the best answer is one that neither side originally considered. This strategy is especially appropriate when

1. the issue is too important to be settled any other way
2. commitment is sought via consensus
3. different perspectives are to be explored

What we call conflict resolution, others (attorneys, purchasing agents, union officials, and diplomats) call negotiating. Whatever it is called, planning is essential and, in the long run, time saving. The planning process consists of two steps: diagnosis (analysis) and strategy.

• Diagnose the situation by asking yourself the following questions:

1. What are likely to be the points of agreement and disagreement?
2. What do you want to accomplish?
3. What are your minimal acceptable resolutions?
4. What do you think the other person wants?
5. What are the strengths and weaknesses of your stance?
6. What false assumptions or incorrect perceptions might the other person have?

• Select a strategy from the previous list of five basic strategies. You may be able to avoid the confrontation, but this is usually a poor choice, and you always have the option of breaking off an encounter at any step of the way.

1. When you must face an aggressive person or situation, prepare yourself for the encounter, and then make your move. Do not procrastinate.
2. Be prepared, just as you would for a debate. Prepare the arguments you can make to maximize the value of positive aspects, to minimize the negatives, and to counter the other person's arguments.
3. Pick the best time and place. Do not meet when your self-esteem is low or when either of you is upset.

The three keys to assertive confrontations are

1. *Success imagery:* This consists of visualizing a successful confrontation. Picture your body language, hear your words and voice tone, and envision a successful outcome. Athletes and professional speakers have used this technique with great success for years.

2. *Self-talk:* This is simply converting negative thoughts to positive ones when we are talking to ourselves. All of us carry on inner dialogues with ourselves all day long. When we are in a passive mode, these internal conversations are negative and pessimistic; our minds conjure up statements such as "I could never say that" or "She'll just blow away." Let your positive affirmations take control. Say to yourself, "I will be in control." Avoid weak statements such as "I'm going to try to stand up to her next time."

3. *Rehearsals:* After you have selected your dialogue and appropriate body language, rehearse the anticipated encounter over and over. Do it front of a mirror. Verbalize out loud. Still better, get a friend or relative to role-play with you. Do not be satisfied until your performance is down pat.

For the confrontation itself, keep the following pointers in mind:

- Clarify the other person's viewpoint and your own. Do not proceed until these viewpoints and the desired outcomes are crystal clear.

- After outlining the problem, focus on areas of agreement (e.g., "Lynn, I think that we both want what is best for our patients, right?"). Regard the other person not as an enemy but as a partner in problem solving.

- Be an attentive listener, keying in on what the other person is saying. Do not be guilty of "mindscripting," which is switching your attention from what the other person is saying to what you want to say next. Be empathic. Respect the other person's feelings, but still feel free to respond in a manner of your choosing.

- Be assertive, not aggressive.
  1. Attack the problem, not the other person.
  2. Do not cause your opponent to lose face.
  3. Do not threaten or issue ultimatums.

- Do not be sarcastic or critical.

- Watch your body language. Maintain eye contact, sit or stand up straight, and appear relaxed. Do not fidget or squirm. Avoid threatening gestures such as finger pointing, fist making, crossing arms, placing hands on hips, or scowling. Smile when you agree; remain expressionless when you disagree.

- Control your voice. Keep its volume, pitch, and rate under control. Stop if you find it growing louder, faster, or high pitched.

- Let the person know that you hear and understand. Validate with something such as "As I understand it, Lynn, you're angry because _____, is that right?" Validating has two benefits: it clarifies the problem, and it lets the person know that what he or she is saying is important.

- Do not get stuck believing that your solution is the only good one. Seek a solution that satisfies both of you. Focus on the benefits of your argument to the other person. Often it pays to ask exactly what the person wants. An angry person may have to stop and think when faced with that, or you may find that he or she wants less than what you were prepared to offer.

- On the other hand, do not neglect to say what it is that you want. If you feel your heart pounding, face turning red, voice rising, and fists clenching, call a time-out. Say, "You're making me uncomfortable" or "I need a little time to collect my thoughts, Lynn." The person will usually back off or may even get derailed.

- To avoid retaliation, use the straw man technique. This is a way of expressing your opinion indirectly. It is most appropriate when dealing with a strongly opinionated individual. For example, instead of saying, "Dr. John, I think you are wrong," say, "Dr. John, how would you respond to a physician who claims that the therapy you ordered is outdated?"

- Be diplomatic and tentative when facing firm resistance. Use words such as *maybe*, *perhaps*, or *you may be right*.
- When cornered or upset, escape by pleading stress.
- Promise rewards ("If you…, then I'll…").
- End on a positive note.

At some point you may have to confront an angry person. People are most likely to express anger toward those who have less power. Sales representatives, service providers, spouses, chil-

dren, and pets take more than their share of abuse. Anger may be manifested by bitter sarcasm, accusations, crying, sulking, pouting, or walking away (often accompanied by door slamming and angry words). Yelling, threatening, and physical attacks are, of course, more frightening.

Some people are supersensitive. They may have explosive tempers or short fuses. These individuals take everything personally. Focus on your goal. Do not argue or lose your temper; just press your case. Say, "I know you're angry about this, but we must solve this problem."

REFERENCE

Umiker, W. 1994. *Management skills for the new health care supervisor*. 2nd ed. Gaithersburg, Md.: Aspen Publishers, Inc.

ADDITIONAL SUGGESTED READING

Metzger, N. 1988. *The health care supervisor's handbook*. Gaithersburg, Md.: Aspen Publishers, Inc.

Venigna, R.L. 1982. *The human side of health administration*. Englewood Cliffs, N.J.: Prentice Hall.

TRANSITION ISSUES

Peter W. Dowrick

Purpose: to summarize the circumstances of transition likely to be encountered by treatment teams and to provide information to assist transitions generically and in some specific, key situations.

Considerable literature has developed, reflecting strategies developed in recent years, partly because of initiatives supported by the U.S. Department of Education; this chapter provides a summary of transition issues related to age, location, changes in services, and other considerations.

Some transitions faced by a child are specifically related to the child's disability. Other transitions simply exacerbate the stress of providing and responding to treatment. But overall, transitions, more than any other factor, cause setbacks to development and loss of treatment gains.

Transition issues arise in a number of ways that affect children with developmental disabilities. These issues may be characterized under the following seven headings:

1. *Generic:* As noted above, significant impediments or even regressions are likely to occur at any transition. They are so likely to occur that service providers need to make special considerations at *all* transitions to minimize what are, in effect, losses to their previous work.

2. *Across services:* Associated with each child is a knowledge base to be transferred between providers; there is also potential "downtime" and difficulty of maintaining treatment gains when services change.

3. *Age related:* Additional impediments occur, as they do in the development of all children, at key stages, especially infant to toddler, toddler to preschool, preschool to school age, childhood to adolescence, puberty to teenage years, and teenage years to adulthood.

4. *Locality:* Families are far more likely to move now than they were 40 years ago. Some occupations, such as military and clergy, are more subject to transition than others, and some communities experience transitions at a higher rate (e.g., Alaska, where 70 percent of the population are Cheechakos, or newcomers, in the last 50 years, and the U.S. Northwest). Changes in service locality can also occur when the family does not move, especially when the child is discharged from the hospital or another circumstance takes place in which a change in *level* of service becomes appropriate.

5. *Into adulthood:* The most important age-related transition requires special mention. It is compounded by the complexity of changes in service—some of them mandated, such as aging out of legislated educational rights, and some of them advisable, such as moving from pediatric to adult health care. Individualized Transition Plans usually become part of the Individualized Education Program at age 14 and are mandated to begin at 16 years of age for "special education" students (see "The Individualized Education Program" later in this chapter).

6. *Cultural considerations:* All transitions have cultural implications at some level, even when they occur across suburbs or into a new classroom. Further considerations occur when providers and consumers have strongly differing ethnic, national, or linguistic backgrounds.

7. *Autism, anxiety disorders:* Some disabilities are associated with conditions that are especially threatened by transitional problems. In particular, pervasive developmental disorders (especially autism) and some anxiety disorders are differentially diagnosed, in part, by the difficulty in coping with change.

TECHNIQUES FOR IMPROVING TRANSITIONS

Listed below are a variety of techniques to improve the quality and the comfort of transitions. They are grouped according to the timing of the assistance (before, during, or after the transition), with subgroups under five headings that reflect the type of approach. These techniques are applicable to most routine circumstances of transition for children with developmental disabilities, drawn from the general literature as listed at the end of this chapter.

- Before: preparation for transition
  1. *Information:* Provide preparatory information to the child and family with respect to the organization, the activities, and the social milieu, especially in comparison with the present situation. Give only nonthreatening information. The question is often raised about when to give information about potential threats or noxious events. Parents indicate that the biggest stressor is in not knowing the future. The golden rule is to give challenging information only to the extent that the child has skills and resources to be comfortable with such a challenge.
  2. *Motivation:* Information on the benefits of the new situation and positive attitudes can be conveyed to motivate the transition. The most beneficial information is realistic examples of success by families in similar circumstances. It may become primarily important to look to the motivation of the parents. The extent to which they can genuinely anticipate the future will be key to supporting (or undermining) the motivation of the child.

3. *Support:* Arrange the awareness in the environment to be exited; arrange the anticipation in the new environment. Ensure support at the institutional, family, and peer levels. For example, take the child to the new situation for a first-hand appreciation and to meet potential cross-age peers who may become "buddies." Some schools hold workshops on transitions for parents.

4. *Skill development:* Teach specific skills for the new environment before they are called upon. Make a list of the "top five survival skills." Identify peer models, and arrange instruction and practice to achieve these top-priority skills. Involve the help of older children or adults who have "been there" (i.e., those who have successfully been through a similar transition).

5. *Participation:* Successful transitions often depend upon the extent to which the child and his or her family participates in and self-determines the preparation process. It is therefore important that the child and family develop ownership of the new destination and make choices about the processes and outcomes implied by the transition. Self-determination feeds back to the issue of motivation and thus influences the extent to which skill development and support can be effective.

• During: engaging in the transition

1. *Information:* Information becomes more meaningful once the new situation is fully encountered. Particulars of organization, expectations, and procedures can be provided in much more detail to the child and family who will be receptive to them. But it will be helpful to create systematic redundancies and to mete out new information.

2. *Motivation:* Confidence is under the greatest threat at this time. Self-efficacy is preserved and promoted by reminders

of the connection between specific actions and positive outcomes and information about physiological functioning.

3. *Support:* The key aspects at this time are quick access to support and the speed of responsiveness. Some transitions, such as changing schools, lend themselves to the techniques of assigning a peer or older child as a mentor. Awareness of staff and additional commitment by friends and family members can be arranged.

4. *Skill development:* This is better attended to prior to the transition. But sometimes it takes the urgency of a current situation to prime the receptiveness of the child or family members to skill training opportunities. Skills training that was previously unsuccessful or rejected can be offered at this time.

5. *Participation:* Offer choices wherever possible, but limit the range of choices. Create or express options that evoke similarities with the prior situation.

• After: succeeding in a new situation

1. *Information:* The child and family will lose their eagerness for new information after the settling in period, so increased repetition is useful. It is also important to be vigilant toward gaps in the information base grasped by the family. There comes a point when the providers and other members in the new community no longer treat the family as "new." At this point, information will be incompletely assembled but not as readily available.

2. *Motivation:* This will be sustained by the self-observation of success in the new environment. Therefore it is valuable to ensure that the family recognize their successes whenever these occur.

3. *Support:* Support can be faded after the transition, provided it is not done sud-

denly. Plans for "relapse prevention" can be put in place, acknowledging the likelihood that after a period of doing well, the family may need additional support again for a limited time. Often it is the parents or the siblings who need additional support after the transition.

4. *Skill development:* This is needed to cope with lapses of progress in the new situation. These include the recognition of vulnerabilities and practice in recovering from errors or asking for assistance. Videotapes can be provided of the family's successes in the mastery of health and behavior issues such as self-care or social interactions. These tapes can then be reviewed during difficult times to remind the family and to inform others of the skills and the capability of success in challenging situations.

5. *Participation:* Continue to give more and more ownership to the family for their decision making and control over their goals and the services they call upon to reach those goals.

VIDEO FUTURES

Some transitional situations require pulling out all the stops—that is, maximizing the five categories of approach noted above, especially in the "before" phase of intervention.

Futures planning generally refers to considering major aspects of children's (or adults') lives, with a particular future transition in mind, and balancing dreams with reality. The example given here focuses on the important transition from high school to adulthood. The future that is planned should incorporate enough detail so that objectives for the intervening years can be based upon it. Thus in *video futures* the plan is so specific that the projected future can be enacted by the individuals involved, recorded, and edited onto videotape. Whereas the example given below concerns teenagers with developmental disabilities anticipating adulthood, the same strate-

gies may be applied to other challenging transitions—such as the situation of a child with asthma or another chronic illness anticipating summer camp, a child with severe burns facing the return to school, or the family of a girl with mental retardation anticipating adolescent sexual development.

For a 16- or 17-year-old in special education, a picture would be built of what his or her life could look like soon after age 21 or 22, when adult life begins and the education system is no longer available for support. Lifestyle images would be sought in six domains:

1. living arrangements
2. relationship to family
3. social life
4. other recreation
5. employment
6. primary means of transport

Structured objectives and interview methods to assist development of the initial futures plan are available from many sources (e.g., Mount 1992). The process includes a series of meetings and activities involving the teenager, parents, teacher, and special educator, plus other family members, social worker, counselor, vocational agency personnel, and so on to the extent that they figure significantly in the teen's life.

The teen has the last say if the content of future scenarios is disputed (as it will be). Loose scripts are developed around each target domain. For example, what started out originally as "live independently" becomes the identification, say, of an apartment, with its associated costs and lifestyle and its implications for income, job, social life, household management, and so on. So a scene is planned with Ms. or Mr. T. (now the teen) in a real apartment, on the phone ordering a pizza, and Uncle Quon arriving at the door for dinner. The finished tape, covering important elements of all six domains, is six to ten minutes long. The tapes form a basis for intermediate objectives. They provide a motivation to engage in the educational activities and skills training necessary to meet these objectives. These tapes can be reviewed and referenced as progress is (or is not) made toward the long-term goals of the transition. They should be revised and remade each year.

The process of developing video futures tapes can be broken down as follows:

- "Discover" the consumer
  1. Identify who needs to be included.
  2. What is the knowledge base?
  3. Gain collaboration and participation.
- Assessment
  1. Agree on behavioral definitions.
  2. Establish individual and generic needs.
  3. Assess individual skills.
- Task analysis
  1. Select target behaviors.
  2. Establish components in/not in the repertoire.
- Planning video "capture"
  1. What is the desired outcome?
  2. How could that be shown?
  3. What can the individual do?
  4. What can the individual not do?
- Video recording
  1. Brainstorm what is needed.
  2. Suggest and demonstrate potential solutions.
  3. Provide cues and prompts.
  4. Give external support and opportunities to practice.
  5. Select camera angles and backgrounds.
  6. Video-record short scenes as planned.

- Editing
  1. Make copies and add timecode if necessary.
  2. Review "capture" recordings.
  3. Identify and document desired footage.
  4. Edit by copying, resequencing, and repeating selected segments.
  5. Check the edited version against skill components.
  6. Show desired behavior as a complete sequence.
- Viewing schedule
  1. Arrange viewing three times a week for two weeks.
  2. Write a schedule of planned dates for viewing.
  3. Document actual dates viewed and reactions.
- Evaluation
  1. Monitor behavior change.
  2. Determine plan for follow-up and follow-along.

The finished tape, six to ten minutes long, is then the property of the teenager. It is used to revise the Individual Education Plan. It is reviewed, primarily at the teenager's initiative, to motivate short-term objectives and to gain the cooperation of vocational trainers and other individuals who have an investment in the longer term opportunities. As noted, the technique can be adapted for a variety of other circumstances.

REFERENCE

Mount, B. 1992. *Personal futures planning: Promises and precautions.* New York: Graphic Futures.

ADDITIONAL SUGGESTED READINGS

Bandura, A. 1996. *Self-efficacy: The exercise of control.* New York: Freeman.

Blechman, E.A. 1992. Mentors for high-risk minority youth: From effective communication to bicultural competence. *Journal of Clinical Child Psychology* 21:160–169.

Brolin, D.E. 1989. *Life centered career education: A competency based approach.* 3rd ed. Reston, Va.: Council for Exceptional Children.

Chadsey-Rusch, J., et al. 1991. Transition from school to integrated communities. *Remedial and Special Education* 12, 23–33.

Cowen, E.L., et al. 1984. Risk and resource indicators and their relationship to young children's school adjustment. *American Journal of Community Psychology* 12:353–367.

Dowrick, P.W., et al. 1993. *Increasing skills necessary for self-determination through video-based personal futures planning.* U.S. Department of Education grant award (1993–1996) # H158K30024.

Eccles, J.S., et al. 1993. Development during adolescence: The impact of stage environment fit on young adolescents' experiences in schools and in families. *American Psychologist* 48:90–101.

Elias, M.J., and J.F. Clabby. 1989. *Social decision-making skills: A curriculum guide for the elementary grades.* Gaithersburg, Md.: Aspen Publishers, Inc.

Felner, R., and A. Adan. 1988. The school transitional environment project: An ecological intervention and evaluation. In *Fourteen ounces of prevention: A casebook for practitioners,* ed. R. Price et al., 111–122. Washington, D.C.: American Psychological Association.

Martin, J.E., et al. 1993. Transition policy: Infusing self-determination and self-advocacy into transition programs. *Career Development for Exceptional Individuals* 16:53–61.

Mellon, S., et al. 1993. Transition into adulthood: Stresses experienced by families of young people with severe disabilities. *Developmental Disabilities Bulletin* 21:34–45.

Moore, C. 1993. Letting go, moving on: A parent's thoughts. In *Housing, support and community: Choices and strategies for adults with disabilities,* ed. J. Racino et al., 190–204. Baltimore: Paul H. Brookes.

Reyes, O., et al. 1994. A longitudinal study of school adjustment in urban, minority adolescents: Effects of a high school transition program. *American Journal of Community Psychology* 22:341–369.

Rusch, F.R., ed. 1990. *Research in secondary special education and transitional employment.* Urbana: University of Illinois, Secondary Transition and Effectiveness Institute.

Tolan, P., and B. Cohler, eds. 1993. *Handbook of clinical research and practice with adolescents.* New York: John Wiley & Sons, Inc.

Tustin, R.D. 1995. The effects of advance notice of activity transitions on stereotypic behavior. *Journal of Applied Behavior Analysis* 28:91–92.

Ward, M. 1996. Promoting self-determination for individuals with disabilities: Content and process. In *Making our way: Building self-competence among children with disabilities,* ed. L.E. Powers. Baltimore: Paul H. Brookes.

Wehman, P., ed. 1992. *Life beyond the classroom: Transition strategies for young people with disabilities.* Baltimore: Paul H. Brookes.

Weymeyer, M.L. 1992. Self-determination and the education of students with mental retardation. *Education and Training in Mental Retardation* 27:302–314.

ADDITIONAL RESOURCES

University-Affiliated Programs all have transitions programs or access to experts on these issues. These and other supportive organizations can be identified in the Resource Directory in the back of this book. Some programs with specific national commitment to transition issues are listed below.

Office of Special Education Programs, Division of Educational Services, Secondary Transition Branch, U.S. Department of Education, 600 Independence Ave. SW, Switzer Bldg., Washington, DC 20202, Tel.: (202) 205-8109.

National Center for Youth with Disabilities, University of Minnesota, Box 721, 420 Delaware Street SE, Minneapolis, MN 55455, Tel.: (612) 626-4260.

Transition Research Institute, University of Illinois at Urbana-Champaign, 113 Children's Research Center, 51 Gerty Drive, Champaign, IL 61820. Provides workshops, site visits, and technical assistance to transition project developments, literature database, bibliographies, and other publications. Tel.: (217) 333-2325 v/tdd; fax: (217) 244-0851; e-mail: tritalk@uiucvmd.

PACER Center, 4825 Chicago Avenue South, Minneapolis, MN 55417. The Parent Advocacy Coalition for Educational Rights is founded on the concept of parents helping parents. Produces newsletter, workshops, special-topic guidelines. Tel.: (612) 827-2966 voice/tdd; fax: (612) 827-3065; e-mail: HN233@handsnet.org.

Community Transition Interagency Committees: Some school districts have these committees or equivalent, staffed by educators and other provider personnel. Inquire with your school district or regional University-Affiliated Program (see Appendix A).

Chapter 9

Early Intervention and Special Education

LAWS AND ISSUES CONCERNING EDUCATION AND RELATED SERVICES

Lee Kern, Beth A. Delaney, and Bridget A. Taylor

Purpose: to describe laws pertaining to education and related services for individuals with disabilities, to describe the Individuals with Disabilities Education Act (IDEA), to provide basic parameters of inclusive education, and to discuss procedural safeguards.

Social perceptions of individuals with disabilities have shifted dramatically in the last few centuries. Prior to the 1800s, children with disabilities were viewed as uneducable. Within the last century, although at an unfortunately slow pace, we have come to understand that individuals with disabilities can and should be productive and well-adjusted community members.

Several milestones contributed to the advancement of this important position. In the mid-19th century, the educational reform movement advocated training for the "disabled and disadvantaged." The efforts of leading educational reformers such as Horace Mann, Dorothea Dix, and Thomas Hopkins Galludet helped to establish the first schools for children with disabilities. Later, the civil rights movement forged the way for the right-to-education movement for "the disabled," based on the premise that separate is not equal. This movement helped to accelerate integration and inclusion of individuals with disabilities into society. In the last 20 years, laws have been enacted to ensure full educational opportunities for children with disabilities. These laws specify educational and related services to which children with disabilities are entitled. In addition, they delineate safeguards to protect the rights of children with disabilities and their families. The education-related laws are outlined below.

THE INDIVIDUALS WITH DISABILITIES EDUCATION ACT OF 1990 (IDEA)

The Individuals with Disabilities Education Act (Pub. L. 101-476) is a federal law that supports special education and related service programming for children and youth with disabilities. Enacted in 1975, it was originally titled the Education of All Handicapped Children Act (Pub. L. 94-142) and later the Education for the Handicapped Act (Pub. L. 99-457). It is due for reauthorization as this book goes to press.

Its initial purpose was to establish state grants for the education of children with disabilities. It has been amended several times since its inception. In its current form, it requires that a free and appropriate public education, including special education and related services, be available to children and youth with disabilities from birth to 21 years old.

Purposes

The several major purposes of IDEA are listed and described below:

1. To ensure that a free appropriate public education is available to all children with disabilities. This right specifically includes special education and related services. *Special education* is defined as specially designed instruction necessary to meet a child's or youth's unique needs. It can include classroom instruction, home instruction, or instruction in hospitals, institutions, or other settings. It can also include instruction in physical and vocational education. Related services are defined as transportation and developmental, corrective, and other supportive services that are required to assist a child with a disability to benefit from special education. Related services may include audiology, psychological services, physical therapy, occupational therapy, recreation, counseling, early identification and assessment, social work services, speech pathology, medical services for diagnosis or evaluation, school health services, and parent counseling and training.

2. To guarantee the rights of children and youth with disabilities and their parents. These rights include confidentiality, due process hearings, etc.

3. To assist states and localities financially in providing for the education of children and youth with disabilities through the use of federal funds.

4. To provide safeguards to assess and ensure the effectiveness of efforts to educate children with disabilities.

Children Served under IDEA

Children aged 3 to 21 with disabilities are eligible for services under IDEA. Infants and toddlers from birth through two years may be eligible for services under what is known as Part H (the Infants and Toddlers with Disabilities Program), established under the 1986 reauthorization (Pub. L. 99-457). Eligibility for the infants and toddlers applies in most states but depends on voluntary participation in Part H.

IDEA delineates 13 categories of disabilities under which children can qualify for special education and related services:

- *Autism:* According to IDEA, autism is defined as a developmental disability that significantly affects verbal and nonverbal communication and social interaction. Associated characteristics often include repetitive activities, stereotyped movements, resistance to change, and unusual responses to sensory stimuli.

- *Deaf-blindness:* Deaf-blindness involves a dual hearing and visual impairment. It must cause severe communication and other developmental and educational problems that cannot be accommodated in programs for children with only deafness or only blindness.

- *Deafness:* Deafness is defined as a hearing impairment so severe that the child's ability to process linguistic information, with or without amplification, is impaired to the extent of adversely affecting his or her educational performance.

- *Hearing impairment:* Children qualifying for this category have either permanent or fluctuating impairments in hearing that adversely affect educational performance. Children falling in this category are excluded under the definition of deafness.

- *Mental retardation:* Mental retardation is defined under the statute as significantly subaverage general intellectual functioning with associated deficits in adaptive behavior. Delays must be manifested during the developmental period.

- *Multiple disabilities:* Children with more than one impairment fall within this category. This may include mentally retarded-blind, mentally retarded-orthopedically impaired, and other combinations, but excludes deaf-blindness.
- *Orthopedic impairment:* Orthopedic impairments include impairments caused by congenital anomaly (e.g., clubfoot), impairments caused by disease (e.g., poliomyelitis, bone tuberculosis), and impairments from other causes (e.g., cerebral palsy, amputations). The child's educational performance must be adversely affected as a result of the impairment.
- *Other health impairment:* Contained in this category are individuals who have limited strength, vitality, or alertness due to chronic or acute health problems, such as a heart condition, tuberculosis, rheumatic fever, nephritis, asthma, sickle-cell anemia, hemophilia, epilepsy, lead poisoning, leukemia, or diabetes, that adversely affect educational performance.
- *Serious emotional disturbance:* To receive a label of serious emotional disturbance, a child must exhibit one or more of the following characteristics over a long period of time (exact duration may be specified by individual state regulations) and to a marked degree that adversely affects his or her educational performance:
  1. an inability to learn that cannot be explained by intellectual, sensory, or health factors
  2. an inability to build or maintain satisfactory interpersonal relationships with peers and teachers
  3. inappropriate types of behavior or feelings under normal circumstances
  4. a general pervasive mood of unhappiness or depression
  5. a tendency to develop physical symptoms or fears associated with personal or school problems

  This category does not include children who have what is considered less serious social maladjustment.

- *Specific learning disability:* A specific learning disability is defined as a disorder in one or more of the basic psychological processes involved in understanding or in using spoken or written language. It may manifest itself in an imperfect ability to listen, think, speak, read, write, spell, or to do mathematical calculations. The category also includes labels of perceptual disability, brain injury, minimal brain dysfunction, dyslexia, and developmental aphasia. The term does not apply to children who have learning problems that are primarily the result of visual, hearing, or motor disabilities, of mental retardation, of emotional disturbance, or of environmental, cultural, or economic disadvantage.
- *Speech or language impairment:* Speech or language impairments are communication disorders such as stuttering, impaired articulation, a language impairment, or a voice impairment that adversely affect a child's performance in school.
- *Traumatic brain injury:* Children with traumatic brain injury have received an injury to the brain caused by an external physical force. The injury has resulted in a disability that adversely affects their educational performance. This can include open head injuries (e.g., disability resulting from surgical procedures) or closed head injuries (e.g., trauma during a car accident). The injury must result in impairments in one or more of the following areas: cognition, language, memory, attention, reasoning, abstract thinking, judgment, problem solving, psychosocial behavior, physical functions, information processing, speech, and sensory, perceptual, and motor abilities. This category does not include children with brain damage caused by birth defects or other non external conditions.
- *Visual impairment, including blindness:* The category of visual impairment, including blindness, means an impairment in vision that, even with correction, adversely

affects a child's educational performance. This category includes both partial sight and blindness.

Eligibility

Individuals with disabilities are eligible for services under IDEA. To qualify, the following events must take place.

Initial Evaluation

Before a child can receive services, an initial or preplacement evaluation must be conducted. Parents or guardians who believe that their child has a disability may request an evaluation by calling or writing the director of special education in their area of residence. If school personnel agree that the child may have a disability, he or she must be evaluated. If the school district does not suspect a disability, it can refuse to conduct the evaluation. Then a written notice of refusal must be provided to the parent/guardian with a full explanation of the reasons for the refusal. In addition, a full explanation of the procedural safeguards available to parents/guardians under IDEA must be provided, including their right to challenge the refusal through an impartial due process hearing (described below).

If a teacher recommends evaluation, or if observations or test results indicate that a child may have a disability, the school can initiate an evaluation request. In this case, the parent or guardian must be notified in writing.

All written communication must be in a form the parents can understand (e.g., their native language). It must state the action that is proposed or refused; the reasons for the proposal or refusal; the evaluation procedures, tests, or records used to support the proposal or refusal; and an explanation of the rights of parents/guardians and alternative options if they disagree with the suggested actions. Regardless of who initiates the evaluation request, written consent must be provided by parents or guardians prior to conducting the evaluation.

The Evaluation Process

Specific regulations dictate the manner in which evaluations must be conducted. They must be conducted by a multidisciplinary team. This team must include at least one teacher or other specialist who is knowledgeable about the area of the child's suspected disability. Other individuals who are typically multidisciplinary team members are school psychologists, speech/language pathologists, occupational or physical therapists, adaptive education therapists, medical specialists, educational diagnosticians, and classroom teachers.

The law also states that no single procedure be used as the sole criterion for determining a child's appropriate educational program. Assessments must be conducted in all areas related to the suspected disability. Areas may include health, vision, hearing, social and emotional status, general intelligence, academic performance, communicative status, and motor abilities.

School districts must also ensure that tests are not racially or culturally discriminatory. For example, if a child is not fluent in spoken English, tests must be administered in a child's native language or through the child's primary mode of communication.

Summarizing the Evaluation Results

After assessments have been conducted, eligibility for special education services must be determined. Usually, an eligibility meeting is held to determine whether test results indicate that the child meets the definition of any of the categories of disability described above. The law does not require that parents attend this meeting. However, they must be informed of the outcome. The results of the evaluation are summarized in a written report.

Obtaining an Independent Educational Evaluation

If parents or guardians do not agree with the results of the evaluation conducted by the school, they have the right to obtain an independent educational evaluation. However, they may be required to cover the expense of this evaluation. In cases of disagreement, the school may automatically grant the request for an independent evaluation. Public funds would then cover the expense. However, school personnel may argue that the results of the evaluation were appropriate. In this case, a hearing is held.

Accessing Services

Once it is determined a child is eligible for services, IDEA mandates that an Individualized Educational Program (IEP) or an Individualized Family Services Plan (IFSP) be written. State regulations specify how quickly the IEP or IFSP must be written. Generally, around 20 school days are provided for its completion. The IEP and IFSP (described in detail in the next subchapter) are written documents establishing learning goals for a child and delineating the types of services the school district will provide. Parents or guardians must be provided the option of being included in the development of their child's IEP or IFSP and are entitled to receive a copy for their own records and to track their child's progress. Once the IEP or IFSP is approved by the parent or guardian, federal guidelines recommend implementation within 30 school days.

Delivery of Special Education and Related Services: Least Restrictive Environment

IDEA includes the doctrine of least restrictiveness. It is mandated that children with disabilities be educated with their nondisabled peers to the maximum extent possible. Under this doctrine, special education instruction must be provided in the regular education environment as much as possible. The law is clear that special classes, let alone separate schooling, are appropriate only when it has been established that satisfactory education in regular classes cannot be achieved, even with additional services.

Least restrictiveness applies to students in public and private facilities or other care facilities. This doctrine also requires that children be educated in the school they would attend if they did not have a disability. If some other arrangement is necessary, it must be documented in the child's IEP.

Review of the IEP

A child's IEP is typically effective for one year. After a year, it is reviewed and new goals are established. If parents or guardians are unhappy with their child's IEP, they can request a review at any time.

Reevaluation

Once a child has been placed in special education, every three years a "triennial reevaluation" must be conducted. This evaluation will determine continued eligibility. If circumstances warrant, reevaluations can occur more frequently. They may also be conducted any time at the request of the school or parent/guardian.

OTHER FEDERAL LAWS AFFECTING CHILDREN AND YOUTH WITH DISABILITIES

The Americans with Disabilities Act of 1990 (Pub. L. 101-336)

The Americans with Disabilities Act (ADA) is the most significant federal law ensuring the full civil rights of all individuals with disabilities. This act extends civil rights protections to individuals with disabilities similar to those provided on the basis of race, gender, national origin, and religion. The ADA guarantees equal opportunity in employment, public accommodation, transportation, state and local government services, and telecommunications.

The Developmental Disabilities Bill of Rights Act Amendments of 1987 (Pub. L. 100-146; reauthorized in 1990 and 1994)

Originally the Mental Retardation Facilities and Community Mental Health Centers Construction Act of 1963 (Pub. L. 88-162), this law now covers individuals with a severe and chronic disability that (1) is attributable to a mental or physical impairment or a combination of mental or physical impairments; (2) is manifested before age 22; (3) is likely to continue indefinitely; and (4) results in substantial functional limitations in three or more of the following areas of major life activities: self-care, receptive and expressive language, learning, mobility, self-direction, capacity for independent living, or economic sufficiency. The purpose of this act is to provide opportunities and assistance to enable individuals with disabilities to achieve their maximum potential through increased independence, productivity, and integration into the community.

This act authorizes grants to support the planning, coordination, and delivery of specialized services to persons with developmental disabilities. Specific entitlements under this act are grant programs to support the establishment and operation of state protection and advocacy systems, university-affiliated programs for people with developmental disabilities, and nationally significant programs to increase independence, productivity, and community integration of individuals with developmental disabilities. The act also mandates the establishment and operation of a federal interagency committee to plan for and coordinate activities related to persons with developmental disabilities.

The Rehabilitation Act of 1973, Section 504 (Pub. L. 93-112)

Section 504 of the Rehabilitation Act extends basic civil rights protections to individuals with disabilities. The legislation applies to all institutions, agencies, and organizations that receive federal financial assistance. The act states that individuals may not be excluded from, denied benefits of, or subjected to discrimination under any program or activity receiving federal financial assistance because of a disability. Under this act, institutions or organizations that engage in discriminatory practices may lose federal funding. Section 504 is increasingly used to secure support services for children with disabilities in school, even when these children do not meet criteria for special education under IDEA.

This act has been amended several times subsequent to 1973. For example, amendments of 1983 (Pub. L. 98-212) authorized demonstration projects to transition youth with disabilities from school to work.

The Technology-Related Assistance for Individuals with Disabilities Act of 1988 (Pub. L. 100-407)

The purpose of this act is to develop technology-related assistance programs and to extend assistive technology to individuals with disabilities and their families. Because a broad range of assistive devices may be included under this law, state programs are widely variable. Funding has been provided for state programs to develop model delivery systems, to conduct statewide needs assessments, to establish support groups, to initiate training and technical assistance programs, and so on.

The Handicapped Children's Protection Act of 1986 (Pub. L. 99-372)

Enacted in 1986, this law provides for reasonable attorneys' fees and costs incurred to parents or guardians who prevail in hearings where there is a dispute with a school system over their child's rights to free and appropriate special education and related services.

Temporary Child Care for Handicapped Children and Crisis Nurseries Act of 1986 (Pub. L. 99-401)

Part of the Children's Justice Act, this section (Title II) provides funding for temporary respite care for children with disabilities or chronic illness who are at risk of abuse or neglect. This law was amended by Pub. L. 101-127, the Children with Disabilities Temporary Care Reauthorization Act of 1989, to extend and expand services.

MAINSTREAMING AND INCLUSION IN EDUCATIONAL SETTINGS

The focus of much of the legislation described above is to ensure the rights of individuals with disabilities to function fully within their communities. The last ten years in particular have witnessed increased efforts to educate individuals with disabilities in regular education settings. These efforts have been viewed and approached in different ways:

- *Mainstreaming* refers to assigning a student with a disability to a regular education classroom for part of the school day. Typically, placement is in nonacademic classes (e.g., art, music). Placement into academic classes occurs only if the student's academic ability matches that of the students in the regular education class.

- An *inclusive* system of education, on the other hand, is based on the belief that all students, regardless of the presence of a disabling condition, should be educated within regular education settings with nondisabled peers of the same age and grade. Within such a system, students with disabilities receive their educational services in the general education classroom with appropriate in-class support.

- *Full inclusion* refers to the practice of educating children with disabilities in the setting where they would be placed if they did not have a disability. This means they receive all of their education in the same environment as their nondisabled peers. Necessary support or accommodations are provided such that the children remain in the general education setting throughout the entire school day.

- As written, the doctrine of the *least restrictive environment* (IDEA, Section 1412) does not delineate clearly the parameters of integration or inclusion. The legislation states that "each public agency shall insure: that to the maximum extent appropriate, handicapped children…are educated with children who are not handicapped" and that children should be segregated "only when the nature or severity of the handicap is such that education in regular classes with the use of supplementary aids and services cannot be achieved satisfactorily."

Nonetheless, it is often argued that the most integrated environment may not be the most appropriate. It is also argued that the effects on the education of other children should be considered. For these reasons, the extent of access and participation in integrated educational environments has been debated. Below is a discussion of the prominent issues regarding inclusion.

Benefits of Inclusion

There are currently many laws in place to protect individuals with disabilities against discrimination. The right to associate with others, including those without disabilities, is a personal liberty of individuals with disabilities and encompasses the concept of citizenry. It is believed that increased participation in society will increase the visibility of individuals with disabilities and, in doing so, will neutralize discriminatory attitudes and stigmatization. With increased acceptance, people with disabilities can participate fully in and contribute meaningfully to society. Below are arguments that have been forwarded by organizations such as TASH (The Association for Persons with Severe Handicaps) supporting fully inclusive educational settings for children with disabilities:

- Fully inclusive educational settings better prepare individuals with disabilities to function in integrated communities as adults. It is believed that inclusive education prepares students with disabilities for "real life" because regular education settings are more representative of society. More restrictive environments do not prepare students for less restrictive environments. For example, institutions do not prepare individuals for community living.

- Inclusive settings offer an enriched academic environment promoting improved learning. Poor academic outcomes of individuals educated primarily in special education settings have encouraged the inclusion movement. Data reflect poor outcomes on a number of measures, including grades, standardized test scores, high school graduation, and postsecondary employment.

- Inclusive environments provide opportunities for scholastic interactions and observational learning between individuals with disabilities and their nondisabled peers that are not available in special education settings.
- Inclusive settings promote socialization skills. Integrated settings allow students with disabilities to socialize with their nondisabled peers. It is believed that children with disabilities will learn age-appropriate social behavior by exposure to nondisabled peer models. Inclusive settings also enhance opportunities for friendships to develop between students with and without disabilities.
- Inclusive settings promote understanding and acceptance of differences by nondisabled peers. These settings minimize the deleterious effects of labeling and encourage the development and appreciation of individual differences and diversity.

Arguments against Inclusion

In spite of widespread support for the idea that individuals with disabilities should be educated with nondisabled peers, a number of researchers (e.g., Fuchs and Fuchs 1994; Lieberman 1992; Odom and McEvoy 1990) have set forth arguments against integrated placements. Below are the most common:

- Regular education classrooms are not able to meet the needs of students with special needs. Regular education teachers are often unprepared, unwilling, or lacking in the resources to make the curricular and instructional modifications necessary to meet a student's individualized needs.
- Placement in inclusive education is based on a value judgment rather than on the individual needs of the student. Some educators are quick to argue for inclusive education without fully evaluating the educational benefits for the child.

- Students with disabilities require a great deal of teacher time that will interfere with the progress of nondisabled classmates.
- Specialized services will not be provided within the context of the regular education setting, causing children with disabilities to fall further behind their nondisabled peers.

Strategies for Including Students in Regular Classes

To whatever extent inclusion practices are beneficial, there is general agreement that preparation and support are required to make education successful. Several strategies to promote successful inclusion are described below:

- Identify the individual support needs of the student. Children with disabilities will require various levels of support to benefit most fully from an integrated setting. This support may include an instructional aide who facilitates participation of the student in the regular education class or technological support such as computers, calculators, or speech output devices.
- Identify the type of instructional modifications needed for the student to learn within the integrated setting. Students with disabilities may have specific learning needs that will require regular education teachers to modify their instructional programs. Instructional modification can include providing small-group instruction, using preteaching strategies, giving immediate corrective feedback, or using summarization techniques. For students with visual impairments, instructional modifications may include using manipulatives, providing assignments orally, or using talking books or large-print materials.
- Adapt the curriculum to match the individual needs of the student. Because students with disabilities have unique needs, goals may need to be individualized for students with disabilities. Thus the regular education curriculum may need to be adapted to allow each child to participate

actively at his or her own level. For example, a goal for a student with a disability may be to learn to read "survival words," whereas a goal for his or her nondisabled peer may be to learn to read fourth-grade vocabulary.

- Encourage peer-mediated, cooperative learning activities. There is a growing body of research supporting the use of nondisabled peers to promote the social and learning behavior of students with disabilities. Further, including nondisabled peers in the teaching process encourages acceptance and facilitates social interactions.

- Identify environmental accommodations. Some children may require adaptations in the learning environment to participate successfully. For example, a child may need to sit at the front of the classroom to optimize attending, or a child may need to be seated next to a peer who can help when necessary.

- Prepare nondisabled students. "Attitude change" strategies have been successful in promoting acceptance and positive attitudes toward children with disabilities. For example, films, discussion groups, reading material, guest speakers, and role-play exercises can be useful.

- Use objective measures to assess the progress of students with disabilities in the integrated setting. Regular education report card procedures are usually not sufficient to document progress. Teachers should create ongoing assessment procedures to document the benefits (academic, social, and behavioral) of integrated education. Methods include curriculum-based measurement, informal testing, or competency-based testing (see Chapter 7).

PROCEDURAL SAFEGUARDS

Included in IDEA is a section entitled "Procedural Safeguards." Safeguards are laws designed to protect the rights of children with disabilities and their parents or guardians. They also provide families and schools with a mechanism for resolving disputes when there is disagreement. Specific procedural safeguards under IDEA are described below.

Confidentiality

Provisions under IDEA, as well as the Family Educational Rights and Privacy Act (Pub. L. 93-380), protect the confidentiality of all children's educational records. Safeguards apply to the following major areas:

- *Release of personally identifiable information:* Personally identifiable information includes the name of a child, parent, or family member; the address of a child; any personal identification number (e.g., social security number); and descriptions of personal characteristics that might cause the child to be recognized. Consent of the parent or guardian must be obtained before personally identifiable information can be released by school districts.

- *Access to a child's educational records:* Parents/guardians have the right to inspect or review their child's educational records. School districts or other agencies must respond to a request to access records within a reasonable amount of time, and in no case later than 45 days. Parents/guardians also have the right to reasonable explanations about their child's records. No one is permitted to view a child's school records without written permission of the parents or legal guardian.

- *Amendment of records:* Parents/guardians have the right to request that their child's records be amended. This applies when they believe that information is inaccurate or misleading, violates the child's right to privacy, or may be damaging to the child's future well-being.

Resolution of Disagreements

Occasionally parents or guardians disagree with a decision the school has made. In these cases, there are several procedures that can be followed. Depending on the situation, one or a combination of the following approaches may be most appropriate:

- *Discussion or conference with school staff:* Some disputes can be resolved during a discussion or conference. School staff typically involved include teachers, counselors, the principal, the director of special education, and sometimes the superintendent.

- *IEP review:* If parents or guardians believe their child is receiving inappropriate or insufficient services or is not making reasonable progress, they can request an IEP review at any time.

- *Negotiation or mediation:* Mediation is a process in which a neutral third person, such as an ombudsperson, tries to negotiate a solution or compromise. Although states may elect to utilize this process, the parents, guardians, or schools can refuse. In these cases, mediation cannot be used to delay or deny further action.

- *Due process hearing:* A due process hearing can be requested if parents/guardians do not agree with the identification, evaluation, educational placement, or any other facet of their child's education. A due process hearing involves arbitration based on requirements in IDEA by an impartial third party. This procedure is described in more detail below.

- *Complaint resolution:* If an individual or organization believes that the state or another participating agency has violated a requirement in IDEA, a complaint can be filed. The individual advancing the complaint must do so in writing to his or her state educational agency. The state educational agency is obligated to review all relevant information and make an independent determination of whether a requirement of IDEA has been violated. This process must be completed within 60 days of receipt of the written complaint. If the party filing the complaint disagrees with the state's decision, it can be appealed by requesting review by the U.S. Secretary of Education.

Due Process

In situations in which a parent or guardian disagrees with a decision related to his or her child's special education, a due process hearing can be requested. The due process hearing must be conducted by the state agency responsible for the child's education. The agency must hire an impartial third party to preside over the hearing. This hearing officer cannot be employed by the school district or have conflicting personal or professional interests. Prior to the hearing, parents/guardians must be informed of free or low-cost legal services if any are available in the area. The family's rights in achieving a satisfactory IEP are described in the next subchapter.

During the due process hearing, parents/guardians have the right to be accompanied by an attorney or other individual with specialized knowledge or training. They are entitled to present evidence and witnesses, require the attendance of appropriate individuals, and cross-examine. They can also prohibit evidence from being introduced that has not been disclosed to them at least five days before the hearing.

The hearing officer listens to the arguments presented by both parents/guardians and the school district. He or she then issues a decision based on the evidence and requirements of IDEA. Unless an extension is granted by the hearing officer, the decision must be provided to the parents or guardians in writing within 45 days of the initial request.

If one of the parties involved in the hearing disagrees with the decision, the state educational agency must conduct an impartial review of the hearing. The entire hearing record is examined, and, if necessary, additional information is sought. If the reviewing official requests, both parties can be asked to submit oral or written arguments. A final decision must be provided to both parties in writing within 30 days of the review request.

Additional Safeguards under IDEA

Additional safeguards of the rights of children and their parents/guardians are as follows:

- Parents/guardians have the right to receive prior written notice on matters regarding the identification, evaluation, or educational placement of their child.
- Parents/guardians have the right to give or refuse consent before a child is initially evaluated or placed in a special education program for the first time.
- Children have the right to remain in their present educational placement, unless the parent/guardian and the agency agree otherwise, while administrative or judicial proceedings are in progress.

- Parents/guardians have the right to reasonable attorney's fees from a court for actions or proceedings related to IDEA.

SUMMARY

As exemplified in this section, there is considerable legislation designed to ensure that children with disabilities receive a free and appropriate public education and to resolve disputes should they arise. By working closely and collaboratively, educators and parents/care providers can develop educational programs for exceptional children that are meaningful and productive. In doing so, they give children with disabilities the opportunity for experiences that will enhance independent functioning. Further, all individuals can become active, satisfied, and contributing members of society.

REFERENCES

Fuchs, D., and L.S. Fuchs. 1994. Inclusive schools movement and the radicalization of special education reform. *Exceptional Children* 60:294–309.

Lieberman, L.M. 1992. Preserving special education for those who need it. In *Controversial issues confronting*

special education, ed. W. Stainback and S. Stainback, 13–25. Boston: Allyn & Bacon, Inc.

Odom, S.L., and M.A. McEvoy. 1990. Mainstreaming at the preschool level: Potential barriers and tasks for the field. *Topics in Early Childhood Special Education* 10:48–61.

ADDITIONAL SUGGESTED READINGS

Anderson, W., et al. 1990. *Negotiating the special education maze: A guide for parents and teachers*. Rockville, Md.: Woodbine House.

Children's Defense Fund. 1989. *94-142 and 504: Numbers that add up to educational rights for children with disabilities*. Washington, D.C.

Gaylord-Ross, R., ed. 1989. *Integration strategies for students with handicaps*. Baltimore: Paul H. Brookes.

Kellegrew, D. 1995. Integrated school placements for children with disabilities. In *Teaching children with autism*, ed. R.L. Koegel and L.K. Koegel, 127–146. Baltimore: Paul H. Brookes.

Lipsky, K.D., and A. Gartner, eds. 1989. *Beyond separate education: Quality education for all*. Baltimore: Paul H. Brookes.

Nazario, T.A. 1988. *In defense of children: Understanding the rights, needs, and interests of the child, a resource book for parents and professionals*. New York: Charles Scribner's Sons.

National Center for Clinical Infant Programs. 1989. *Intent and spirit of P.L. 99-457: A sourcebook*. Washington, D.C.

Nisbet, J., ed. 1992. *Natural supports in school, at work, and in the community for people with severe disabilities*. Baltimore: Paul H. Brookes.

Sailor, W., et al. 1989. *The comprehensive local school: Regular education for all students with disabilities*. Baltimore: Paul H. Brookes.

Salend, S. 1990. *Effective mainstreaming*. New York: Macmillan Publishing Co., Inc.

Stainback, W., and S. Stainback, eds. *Educating all students in the mainstream of regular education*. Baltimore: Paul H. Brookes.

Tucker, B.P. and B.A. Goldstein. 1990. *Legal rights of persons with disabilities: An analysis of federal law*. Horsham, Pa.: LRP Publications.

ADDITIONAL RESOURCES

To obtain a copy of IDEA, contact the Superintendent of Documents, U.S. Government Printing Office, Washington, DC 20402, Tel.: (202) 783-3238.

To obtain a copy of your state's special education law, contact your state department of education's Office of Special Education.

To obtain information about the Americans with Disabilities Act, contact the U.S. Department of Justice, Civil Rights Division, Coordination and Review Section, P.O. Box 66118, Washington, DC 20035-6118, Tel.: (202) 514-0301, (202) 514-0381.

To obtain information about the Temporary Child Care for Handicapped Children and Crisis Nurseries Act, contact the Texas Respite Resource Network (TRRN), P.O. Box 7330, Station A, San Antonio, TX 78207-3198, Tel.: (512) 228-2794, or Access to Respite Care and Help (ARCH), Chapel Hill Training Project, 800 Easttowne Drive, Chapel Hill, NC 27514, Tel: (919) 490-5577.

To obtain information about Programs for Protection and Advocacy for Persons with Developmental Disabilities and Mental Illness, contact the National Association of Protection and Advocacy Systems (NAPAS), 900 Second Street, NE, Suite 211, Washington, DC 20002, Tel.: (202) 408-9514, (202) 408-9521.

To obtain information about inclusion, contact the following national organizations:

- Clearinghouse on the Handicapped, Office of Special Education and Rehabilitative Services, U.S. Department of Education, Switzer Building, Room 3131, Washington, DC 20202-2319, Tel.: (202) 732-1214.

- KIDS Project, Inc., 1720 Oregon Street, Berkeley, CA 94703, Tel.: (415) 548-4121.

- National Committee for Citizens in Education, 10840 Little Patuxent Parkway, Suite 301, Columbia, MD 21044-3199, Tel.: (301) 997-9300, (800) NETWORK.

- National Information Center for Children and Youth With Handicaps (NCHCY), P.O. Box 1492, Washington, DC 20013, Tel.: (800) 999-5599

- National Legal Resource Center for Child Advocacy, 1800 M Street, NW, Washington, DC 20036, Tel.: (202) 331-2250.

THE INDIVIDUALIZED EDUCATION PROGRAM

Lee Kern and Peter W. Dowrick

Purpose: to present an overview of the Individualized Education Program (IEP), to describe the content and development of the IEP, and to provide brief summaries of the Individualized Family Service Program (IFSP) and the Individualized Transition Plan (ITP).

In 1975, Congress passed Public Law 94-142, the Education for All Handicapped Children Act. It was amended most recently in 1990 as Public Law 101-476, the Individuals with Disabilities Education Act, and is due for reauthorization as this book goes to press. These laws were passed in an attempt to correct a number of known problems in the education of children with disabilities. The enactment of Public Law 94-142 significantly altered education by mandating a free and appropriate public education for all children with disabilities.

The legislation also provided mechanisms to accomplish appropriate, publicly supported education, as described in the preceding subchapter. One of these mechanisms is the Individualized Education Program (IEP). Each child receiving special education is required to have an IEP. The IEP is a document that specifies how schools will provide a meaningful education that is consistent with each child's needs and abilities.

There are strict guidelines for both the development and the documentation of the IEP. The guidelines are intended to serve as a means for holding schools accountable for providing an appropriate education and to enhance family-educator collaboration in developing a student's educational goals. The remainder of this section will describe the contents, development, and review of the IEP.

THE INDIVIDUALIZED EDUCATION PROGRAM (IEP)

The IEP is a written plan for students in special education. It lists skills the student already has and what he or she needs to learn. It also describes the type of assistance required for the student to accomplish his or her stated goals. Each student's IEP is reviewed annually to determine whether goals have been met. If special education is still indicated, the IEP is then rewritten to reflect appropriate goals for the next year. The student's parent or care provider participates in this meeting, in addition to a number of other individuals (see section below, "Development and Review").

Content

Public Law 101-476 requires that the following information be included in each student's IEP:

- A statement of the child's present level of educational performance
    1. *Reporting performance:* A student's current level of performance must be stated in the IEP. This statement reflects performance in academic areas (e.g., reading, math, communication) and nonacademic areas (e.g., daily living skills, mobility, prevocational-vocational skills). There should be a direct relationship between present levels of educational performance and other components of the IEP. For example, goals and objectives (described later) should be written to remediate areas of deficiency indicated under present level of performance.
    2. *Methods of assessment:* Because a major goal of assessment is to develop an appropriate educational curriculum, it is important that the reported level of performance be precise enough to assist in formulating specific educational objectives. Sometimes norm-referenced tests are used, but their usefulness is limited because scores are reported only in comparison to other students' performance. Criterion-referenced tests and adaptive behavior scales are generally more suitable because they report scores in terms of fixed criteria or the degree to which an individual functions independently. Informal assessments are also frequently used to report level of performance. For example, an informal assessment might consist of presenting flash cards of multiplication facts for the numbers 0 to 5 on three separate occasions and evaluating the student's percentage of correct responses.

- A statement of annual goals, including short-term instructional objectives
    1. *Annual goals:* The IEP must describe what the student should reasonably be expected to accomplish within a 12-month period. Annual goals should be tailored to the individual student's needs and must encompass the spectrum of short-term objectives in each specified area. For example, an annual goal might state, "Yen will engage independently in a leisure activity."
    2. *Short-term instructional objectives:* Short-term instructional objectives are intermediate steps between the student's current level of functioning and the annual objectives. They reflect how each annual goal will be accomplished. Objectives must be delineated in specific and measurable terms. For example, the following are short-term objectives to achieve Yen's annual goal of independently engaging in a leisure activity:
        (a) Yen will get the radio from the activity closet.
        (b) Yen will sit down in the leisure area.
        (c) Yen will place the headphones on his ears.

(d) Yen will turn the radio on.

(e) Yen will stop the activity when signaled that break is finished.

(f) Yen will turn the radio off.

(g) Yen will remove the headphones from his ears.

(h) Yen will place the radio in the activity closet.

- A statement of the specific special education and related services to be provided to the child, and the extent to which the child will be able to participate in regular educational programs

   1. *Special education services: Special education* refers to the special services that will be provided for the student. Traditionally, services have been provided in the form of special education programs. In some states, special education programs are organized categorically. Students are identified as having a specific type of disability and are placed in a program structured to serve only students with that type of disability. For example, a student whose difficulty in learning to read is identified as a learning disability may receive services in the Specific Learning Disabilities Program. A student labeled as emotionally or behaviorally disordered may receive services in the Emotionally Disabled Program. Other states have noncategorical programs. Students in these programs are generally placed in special education programs on the basis of the severity of their disability. For example, a program might be organized to serve students with mild, moderate, or severe disabilities. A student who is behind in mathematics might be identified as having a mild disability and placed in a resource class serving students with mild disabilities.

   2. *Related services:* Frequently students need additional services to benefit optimally from school. These are described as related services. Included are physical therapy, occupational therapy, speech pathology, audiology, psychological services, special transportation, special equipment, social services, and so on. The IEP must specify the type of related service the student is to receive and the individual responsible for providing the service.

   3. *Regular classroom inclusion:* In recent years, there has been a movement toward full inclusion. This means that all special services are provided within regular education contexts. Although full inclusion is increasingly being embraced as a right for students with disabilities, for the most part services are still being provided in settings other than the regular classroom environment. If this is the case, the amount of time the student is to participate in the regular educational program must be stated in the IEP. Modifications or adaptations that need to be made in the student's regular education program should be specified. For example, if a student with a visual impairment needs to use talking books, this must be stated in the IEP.

- Initiation and duration of services: the projected dates that services will begin and the duration for which those services will be provided (because the IEP is reviewed annually, the duration of services is typically one year)

- Appropriate objective criteria and evaluation procedures, with schedules for determining, on at least an annual basis, whether the short-term instructional objectives are being achieved

   1. *Conducting evaluations:* Although the law requires evaluation only once yearly to determine whether annual goals have been achieved, more frequent assessments by the individual providing the services are recommended. Assess-

ments must match the purpose of the assessment inquiry and use objective evaluation criteria. Sometimes assessments reflect individual skills that are determined by typically developing students. For example, Kevin's annual goal is to display language arts skills on a third-grade level. His short-term objective is to write one-paragraph creative stories with correct spelling, capitalization, and punctuation. An appropriate evaluation procedure and schedule would be to spell, capitalize, and punctuate weekly writing assignments with 80 percent accuracy. Other assessments reflect a comparison between the student's current adaptive skills and those he or she is likely to need in the future. For example, June's annual goal is to complete the self-care skill of tooth brushing. A short-term objective is to remove the cap from a toothpaste tube. An appropriate evaluation procedure might state, "June will independently unscrew and remove the cap from the toothpaste tube on nine of ten consecutive mornings."

2. *Evaluation procedures:* Short-term objectives reflect intermediate steps to achieve a larger goal. To evaluate whether students are making progress on short-term objectives, ongoing assessments need to be conducted. Three general methods can be used to measure performance:

   (a) *Task analytic assessment:* This procedure consists of measuring performance on each response in a chain of responses. For example, the first step in setting the table might be to remove the correct silverware from the drawer. Once the student is observed correctly performing this step a predetermined number of times, the next step is taught.

   (b) *Repeated trials:* This method provides the student with repeated opportunities to make a target response. For example, to measure progress on improving social interactions, a teacher may provide a student with ten opportunities throughout the day to respond to questions such as "How are you?" The teacher then records the number or percentage of appropriate responses.

   (c) *Time-based assessment:* This procedure is used to determine whether performance of a skill meets a normalized time criterion. For example, a student learning her multiplication facts might be given one minute to complete multiplication facts with multiplicands of 3. Time-based assessment can include measurement of rate, duration, or latency to responding.

Development and Review

When placement in special education is pending, an initial IEP meeting must be held. The purpose of this meeting is to determine what services the student needs and to develop an appropriate and meaningful educational program for the student. During this meeting, each participant shares relevant information about the student, such as the reasons for referral and the results of evaluations. The participants then draft the IEP.

Developing a student's IEP is intended to be a collaborative process. Therefore the law requires that specific individuals be present. The following is a list of those required to be present:

1. a representative of the public agency, other than the child's teacher, who is qualified to provide or supervise the provision of special education

2. the child's teacher

3. one or both of the child's parents
4. the child, if the participants and child determine it is appropriate
5. other individuals, at the discretion of the parent
6. other individuals, at the discretion of the agency

For students already receiving special education services, the school must hold an annual meeting to review placement and progress. During this meeting, the student's present level of performance is described. If special education is still indicated, annual goals and short-term objectives are formulated for the upcoming year.

THE INDIVIDUALIZED FAMILY SERVICE PLAN (IFSP)

Public Law 99-457, the Education of the Handicapped Act Amendments of 1986, Part H, mandated early intervention services for infants and toddlers. This legislation extended services provided in Public Law 94-142 to individuals with disabilities from birth to their third birthday. For these children, the Individualized Family Service Plan (IFSP) functions similarly to the IEP.

Content

The content of the IFSP is similar to the IEP. The following information must be contained in an IFSP:

- a statement of the infant's or toddler's present level of functioning
- a statement of the family's strengths and needs as related to the development of the family's infant or toddler
- a statement of the major anticipated outcomes for the child and the family and the criteria, procedures, and time lines that will be used to determine the degree to which progress is being made and whether revisions of the anticipated outcomes are necessary

- a description of the specific early intervention services necessary to meet the unique needs of the infant or toddler and the family
- the projected dates for initiation of services and the anticipated duration of the services
- the name of the case manager from the service most relevant to the child's and family's needs who is responsible for the implementation of the plan and coordination with other agencies and persons
- a plan for the transition of the toddler to preschool services

Development

Family Centered Approach

Because infants and toddlers are dependent on their families for survival and nurturance, early intervention services emphasize a family-centered approach. This approach encourages the recognition that infants and toddlers are part of a family system and that services must be provided within the context of the family. Specifically, the family is seen as the center of services, and intervention services are designed to be flexible, accessible, and responsive to family-identified needs. Family priorities shape the IFSP process and ultimately determine the IFSP outcomes.

Participants

Development of the IFSP is intended to be a collaborative effort between the family and professionals. Most often, this process is coordinated through the state social services agency. However, states differ. In some states, it is coordinated through a special education agency or an infant health agency. A team is formulated consisting of family members and professionals. Families are free to determine what members within their immediate and extended family they would like to have serve as members of this team. Because of the diverse and complex needs of infants and toddlers, a number of different agencies and disciplines are often involved, depending on the family's needs. Disciplines may include speech and language services, occupational therapy, physical therapy, and others. The team members work together to identify family concerns, resources, and priorities.

THE INDIVIDUALIZED TRANSITION PLAN (ITP)

Public Law 98-524, the Carl D. Perkins Act, requires transition planning and documentation for students enrolled in vocational education who are described as disadvantaged or disabled. The Individualized Transition Plan (ITP) was developed because IEPs failed to address the transitional needs of secondary students. The purpose of the ITP is to assist students in finding an appropriate job, to identify where students will be living, and to help students develop social and interpersonal networks after they complete high school.

Contents

Although legislation does not clearly stipulate the contents of the ITP, the following information is typically included:

- past and current services
- vocational goals and postsecondary goals
- future residential and employment options
- services needed to achieve desired transition outcomes
- the names of the service agencies to be involved
- specific objectives and time lines for completion of transitional goals

Development

The ITP must be developed by the time the student completes the eighth grade or by age 14. Because the ITP focuses on the individual's needs after he or she graduates from high school, it is student centered rather than family or school centered. That is, it reflects the student's interests and personal goals. The individual himself or herself typically participates in developing the ITP. In addition, it is recommended that both special and vocational educators be involved. The state is responsible for identifying a person to serve as primary reviewer. Generally, this is school personnel until the individual is 21 years old. After the individual turns 21, social services and vocational rehabilitation agencies become responsible.

GOAL SETTING

This section is adapted from Dowrick (in press, Chapter 3). The setting of specific, objective goals is indispensable to any intervention program for children with developmental disabilities. Nowhere is that more true than with individual educational programs and individual family service plans.

Types of Goals

There are different types of goals, depending on how short or long term they are and how directly they are related to the behavior change process. The goals to be focused on here are short term and very directly related to the educational or intervention process. But first a word of explanation on other goals:

- *Outcome goals:* These goals should be objectively verifiable but do not need to refer to a behavior. They are useful because it is easy to make them clearly indisputable, but they are insufficient unless backed up by other goals that do refer to behavior change.
  1. Example: "Cyola will lose 10 kg." This outcome goal may be clarified by adding "to be achieved in eight weeks and maintained at home for at least one month."
  2. Example: "Giles will return to school and participate fully." Very likely we would objectify the verbs (*return* and *participate*) and add a time frame.

- *Long-term goals:* As goals become more distant, they become more global, such as "experience no unnecessary medical complications" or "enjoy life as much as his peers." Such goals are useful for giving an overall sense of direction or for follow-up, but they are insufficient for an immediate plan of action.
- *Short-term goals:* These are sometimes called *objectives* to emphasize the distinction, but the terminology is arbitrary.

Criteria for Effective Goal Setting

The following are questions that can be used to determine behavioral goals for education or service planning:

- What behavior can be observed and recognized? For example: "Emmi will use sign language and vocalizations."
- In what circumstances will it be observed? For example: "after school at the recreation center, when Alfus asks Emmi questions about her day."
- What frequency will be looked for? For example: "at least one sign for each question and one vocalization for every three signs." Sometimes the sought-after frequency is zero—that is, a behavior such as aggression is targeted for reduction.
- What other dimensions will be necessary? For example: "more than 50% of the signs will be clear (so Alfus can understand them), and the vocalizations will be audible from six feet." A dimension useful in other circumstances is duration.
- By when and over what period will this change be evident? For example: "in the third week, three days in a row." This criterion gives a date for review, and by specifying a period of confirmation rather than a single episode, some assurance is established that the behavior change is robust.

Sometimes outcomes that are products (e.g., weight loss) are specified, even for short-term goals. Such goals can be justified when they are very closely tied to behavior. Weight (in Cyola's case) is inconsistently related to behavior in the short term, so it needs to be supplemented by behavioral goals (e.g., eating patterns, exercise). But number of drawings completed (for Giles) is more likely to reflect a developmentally useful behavior, so it could provide a suitable short-term goal.

The following is an example to illustrate all the criteria above:

> Emmi will use sign language and vocalize after school at the recreation center when Alfus asks her about her day; she will make at least one sign in response to each question; she will attempt vocalization at the rate of once for every three signs; half the signs will be clear to Alfus, and the vocalizations will be audible six feet away; these criteria will be met in the third week on three consecutive days.

What To Do with Goals

At preset points, review progress. This review can result in a more comprehensive intervention or educational program, a more selective intervention, or an entirely new direction.

Review the outcome goals. This evaluation can result in ending a program because it has been successful, continuing a promising program in progress, revising a struggling intervention, or redirecting the child from an unpromising situation to other services.

REFERENCE

Dowrick, P.W. In press. *Strategies of behavior change.* New York: John Wiley & Sons, Inc.

ADDITIONAL SUGGESTED READINGS

Anderson, W., et al. 1990. *Negotiating the special education maze: A guide for parents and teachers.* 2nd ed. Rockville, Md.: Woodbine House.

Arena, J. 1989. *How to write an I.E.P.* Novato, Calif.: Academic Therapy Publications.

Baker, B.L., and R.P. Brightman. 1984. Access of handicapped children to educational services. In *Children, mental health, and the law,* ed. N.D. Reppucci et al., 289–307. Beverly Hills, Calif.: Sage Publications, Inc.

Berger, E.H. 1981. *Parents as partners in education: The school and home working together.* St. Louis: C.V. Mosby Co.

Cutler, B.C. 1993. *You, your child, and "special" education: A guide to making the system work.* Baltimore: Paul H. Brookes.

Deno, S.L., et al. 1984. How to write effective data-based IEPs. *Teaching Exceptional Children* 16:99–104.

Des Jardins, C. 1993. *How to get services by being assertive.* Chicago: Family Resource Center on Disabilities.

Dunne, T., and C. O'Regan. 1990. Evaluating individual program plans. *Journal of Practical Approaches to Developmental Handicap* 14:15–19.

Dunst, C.J., et al. 1988. *Enabling and empowering families: Principles and guidelines for practice.* Cambridge, Mass.: Brookline.

Gajar, A., et al. 1993. *Secondary schools and beyond: Transition of individuals with mild disabilities.* New York: Charles E. Merrill Publishing Co.

Gearheart, B.R., et al. 1992. *The exceptional student in the regular classroom.* New York: Macmillan Publishing Co., Inc.

Halpern, A.S. 1985. A look at the foundations. *Exceptional Children* 51:479–486.

Horner, R.H., et al. 1990. Effects of case manager feedback on the quality of Individual Habilitation Plan objectives. *Mental Retardation* 28:227–231.

McAfee, J.K., and G.A. Vergason. 1979. Parent involvement in the process of special education: Establishing the new partnership. *Focus on Exceptional Children* 11:1–15.

Shea, T.M., and A.M. Bauer. 1994. *Learners with disabilities: A social systems perspective of special education.* Madison, Wis.: Brown & Benchmark.

Sigafoos, J., and P. DePaepe. 1994. Writing objectives to replace challenging behaviours with functional, age-appropriate alternatives. *Journal of Practical Approaches to Developmental Handicap* 18:24–28.

Turnbull, A.P., et al. 1986. *Developing and implementing individualized education programs.* Columbus, Ohio: Charles E. Merrill Publishing Co.

Wood, M. 1995. Parent-professional collaboration and the efficacy of the IEP process. In *Teaching children with autism,* ed. R.L. Koegel and L.K. Koegel. Baltimore: Paul H. Brookes.

ADDITIONAL RESOURCES

For publications and information about special education and listings of state and regional resources, see number for contacting the National Information Center for Children and Youth with Disabilities, P.O. Box 1492, Washington, DC 20013-1492, Tel.: (800) 695-0285, (202) 884-8200, (202) 884-8441 (fax).

Also, in the blue pages of phone book, contact the Board of Education for the number of the state department of education's Office of Special Education. The following are some possible contact agencies within the department (names may vary slightly by state):

- Programs for Children with Disabilities: Ages birth through two
- Programs for Children with Disabilities: Ages three through five
- State Vocational Rehabilitation Agency
- Office of State Coordinator of Vocational Education for Students with Disabilities
- State Mental Health Agency
- State Mental Health Representative for Children and Youth
- State Mental Retardation Program
- State Developmental Disabilities Planning Council
- Protection and Advocacy Agency
- Client Assistance Program
- Programs for Children with Special Health Care Needs
- State Agency for the Visually Impaired
- State Education Agency Rural Representative
- Disability Agencies, Listed by Specific Disability

SCHOOL-BASED VOCATIONAL TRAINING

Karen M. Ward

Purpose: to describe best practices in school-based vocational training programs and strategies to develop integrated vocational training.

The national unemployment rate is approximately 5 percent. However, the unemployment rate of youth with disabilities graduating from school is a staggering 44 percent for all students with disabilities and 85 percent for students with multiple handicaps (Wagner et al., 1992). School programs are being asked to assume more responsibility for vocational preparation and employment of students with substantial disabilities. Schools have relied on adult program entry criteria as the basis for educational goals. In recent years, many adult service providers have shifted their focus from employment preparation to providing supported employment. Thus schools are expected to provide employment as well as vocational preparation and to ensure that the supports needed to maintain employment are arranged (Sowers and Powers 1991). Adequate and appropriate vocational preparation of students with disabilities must provide systematic, longitudinal training in integrated vocational settings. As such, employment preparation has five primary functions:

1. matching student interests to potential jobs
2. assessing work and work-related skills
3. developing support for the individual's family
4. ensuring access to support services
5. training and job placement

BEST PRACTICES OF VOCATIONAL PROGRAMS

Several features are widely acknowledged as the most important in the design of effective vocational preparation of school-age students with disabilities:

- Jobs are identified to reflect those available in the local job market.
- Student preferences are reflected in the goals and objectives of the Individual Education Plan and the Individualized Transition Plan.
- Vocational goals include training in community survival skills.
- Vocational training occurs in real community jobs.
- Systematic instructional procedures are used to train students.
- Parents are involved in the vocational preparation of their children and actively participate in the development of goals for the IEP (Individualized Education Program) or ITP (Individualized Transition Plan).
- Cooperative relationships are developed with the adult service system agencies.
- Students are placed in paid employment before they graduate.
- Supports and other resources are identified and arranged upon graduation.
- School personnel follow up students in their adult environments to evaluate lifestyle opportunities.

PROGRAM DESIGN

Employment training programs should enable students to become as independent and productive as possible in the work setting. The amount of time devoted to vocational activities is related to age. As students get older, the amount of time spent in out-of-school vocational activity should increase from several hours per day to most or all of their day at a paid job:

- *Work experience and job sampling:* unpaid work in a variety of job types (ages 15–18)
- *Selection of a specific job alternative:* unpaid work in a specific occupational area (ages 17–19)
- *Job placement:* paid part-time or full-time employment (ages 19–21)

CREATING VOCATIONAL TRAINING AND EMPLOYMENT SITES

Employment training programs should be designed to ensure access to jobs that are consistent with both the capabilities and the vocational interests of individuals with severe handicaps. In addition, the training program must focus directly on employment opportunities available within the individual's local community (McDonnell et al. 1989.

Labor Market Survey

The first step in creating training and employment opportunities is to conduct a labor market survey. The goal is to identify jobs available in the local community as well as potential training sites.

The following is information to be included in the labor market survey:

- data about people
- data about jobs
- data about employers
- community demographics
- community economic conditions

The following are sources of information:

- state occupational information coordinating committees
- U.S. and state department of labor
- regional planning agencies
- state data center affiliated with the U.S. Bureau of the Census
- employment security offices
- state and local chamber of commerce

- newspaper want ads
- personal and business acquaintances
- telephone books
- volunteer organizations

Job Clusters

Information regarding labor market trends can be summarized into job clusters to identify the jobs most likely to be available to students upon graduation. Labor market surveys are community specific, and the number of occupational clusters available currently and projected for the future will vary from community to community. Typical job clusters are

- *Agriculture/horticulture:* jobs related to growing plant and animal products
- *Construction:* jobs related to building domestic, commercial, or public structures and/or systems such as roads, sewers, or communication networks
- *Distribution:* jobs related to handling, processing, storing, or selling goods and materials
- *Domestic and building services:* jobs related to the maintenance of private, public, or commercial building and grounds
- *Food services:* jobs related to preparation of food and beverages
- *Health and human services:* jobs related to support of individuals and families
- *Production/repair:* jobs related to the assembly or maintenance of consumer, commercial, or industrial goods
- *Office services:* jobs related to production, dissemination, or storage of correspondence and data
- *Communication:* jobs related to the transmission of private or public information

The *Dictionary of Occupational Titles* and a companion publication, *Selected Characteristics of Occupations Defined in the Dictionary of Occupational Titles*, are good resources regarding information on the data, people, and things functions of over 20,000 occupations.

Site Development

Following the identification of potential job clusters, the next task is to identify training sites. Since one of the primary functions of vocational preparation is to match students to jobs based on interest and skills, an array of employment opportunities must be available. Site development is very time intensive. We recommend that "training sites," not "job placement sites," be developed initially.

Sites should be identified in local businesses, using one or more of the following formats for each job cluster. Multiple site formats enable the program to accommodate different students on an ongoing basis.

- *Individual placement* is a one-person/one-job situation in a community business. Ongoing training and support is provided, as required for the student to meet the standards of the position and maintain performance. Training and support are faded over time as skills are developed. However, some level of support is continued throughout the duration of the placement. The individual placement is generally viewed as the least restrictive format.

- *Enclaves* provide a group placement alternative. A small group of students with disabilities (no more than eight) and a staff person work in close proximity. Enclaves are located within community businesses. They allow for continuous training and supervision that goes beyond the initial training period. Typically, enclaves are perceived as being for people with more severe disabilities who require very intensive support.

- *Work crews* are group placements that perform single-service tasks in multiple businesses. Services have typically been janitorial and groundskeeping. Crews consist of

not more than eight individuals and a staff member.

Marketing to Prospective Employers

Marketing strategies must be carefully developed to ensure that there is mutual benefit for the business and the program. An integrated, community-based vocational training program will not succeed without effective job development. Job development is selling a product to the employer: capable workers and support services of the school and/or adult service agency. School personnel must understand that employers are in business to make a profit. The employer wants and needs competent employees and cannot become involved with a program that directly or indirectly costs him or her money. Care must be taken not to overcommit or make promises that the program cannot honor. When contacting potential employers, school personnel must be able to describe what services will be provided in simple, jargon-free language.

General Strategies for Approaching Potential Employers

In approaching prospective employers, keep in mind the following pointers:

- Learn about the targeted businesses and their unique needs and problems. Many employers have not solved problems such as turnover, poor work quality, and the high cost of training.

- Use this information to address employers' concerns about hiring persons who experience disabilities, which include supervision, worker's compensation, poor productivity, coworker problems, strange and bizarre behavior, limited ability, and safety issues.

- Send a letter and/or brochure to businesses describing the program, types of service offered, and profile of the student(s)' knowledge, skills, and abilities.

- Arrange a personal interview by telephone. Expect rejection. Not all employers will want to talk, and some will avoid you. Do not give up after the first try. Keep in touch and try to develop a relationship.
- Meet with the employer. Be ready to explain in 20 to 30 minutes who you are, what you want, who you represent, what you can offer, and what is expected of the employer.
- Point out the benefits of working with your program. Typical benefits include solutions to one or more of the employer's problems, training support services offered by the school, employer incentives such as funding to pay wages, and a positive public image.
- Close the deal. School personnel must make it clear whether the site is a job-training placement in which students will rotate or a job placement in which the employer is hiring the student. Complete the agreements in writing.

Employer Incentives

The following are examples of employer incentives:

- *On-the-Job Training Funding:* available from ARC-United States, Job Training Partnership Act (JTPA), and the state office of vocational rehabilitation to defray the cost of training.
- *Department of Labor:* to promote community-based individualized education and training programs for the transition of students with disabilities from school to work, the U.S. Department of Labor has determined that wages do not have to be paid under certain conditions. All the following conditions must be met (U.S. Department of Education and U.S. Department of Labor 1992):
  1. Participants must be youth with physical and or mental disabilities for whom competitive employment at or above minimum wage is not immediately obtainable, and who due to their disability will require intensive ongoing support to perform in a work setting.
  2. Participation must be for vocational exploration, assessment, or training in a community-based placement worksite under the general supervision of public school personnel.
  3. Community-based placements must be clearly defined components of the student's Individualized Education Program (IEP).
  4. Documentation of the student's enrollment in a community-based placement program must be made available to the departments of Labor and Education.
  5. Activities of the students at the community-based placement site cannot result in an immediate advantage to the business, including displacement of employees.
  6. The student must be under continuous and direct supervision of representatives of the school or employees of the business; placement must be made according to the requirements of the student's IEP and not to meet the labor needs of the business; the periods of time spent by the student at any one site are limited by the IEP.
  7. As a general rule, each component will not exceed the following limitations during any one school year: vocational exploration (5 hours per job experienced), vocational assessment (90 hours per job experienced), vocational training (120 hours per job experienced).

JOB CARVING

Job carving is a method of defining a "piece" of a job for a person with a disability who may be unable to perform all the tasks typically associated with a traditional job description. The method involves matching the tasks with the available skills and motivations in a cost-effective way that satisfies the employer.

The following are examples of job carving (DiLeo and Langton 1993):

- Create a part-time mechanic helper by transferring the tasks of tool cleanup and storage from the mechanic/owner and grouping them with the tasks of tire storage and garage sweeping to increase productivity and profitability.

- Create a part-time clerical position by transferring the task of maintaining paper in printer in a large office from highly paid professionals and grouping it with the tasks of opening, sorting, and distributing mail to increase productivity.

- Develop a part-time assistant position at a bingo parlor with the tasks of preparing and packaging bingo cards to increase productivity and profitability of the owner.

JOB ANALYSIS

A *job analysis*, also referred to as a *job skills inventory*, identifies all the requirements of a job and the demands on the worker. It is used to match students with jobs, to plan logical, sequential training, and to select adaptive equipment and alternative strategies for job completion. The job analysis is not a screening process to block out students who lack job skills but a tool that increases staff knowledge about how to train someone for the job.

The best way to know a job is to do a job. A job analysis is a field-based process. Interview the employer or first-line supervisor to discuss the demands of the job, interview and observe a worker proficient at performing the job, and perform the job yourself for several days.

Factors to be included in a job analysis are

- personal appearance requirements
- behavior tolerances

- communication requirements, including requirements for providing personal information
- level of supervision provided
- task/routine changes
- time-telling requirements
- size and mobility requirements of the workspace
- physical job requirements, including standing, sitting, lifting, bending, carrying, and gross and fine motor skills
- endurance, strength, discrimination, and work speed requirements
- functional academic skill requirements, including reading, math, money, writing, and measurements
- environmental factors, including safety of the work area and cleanliness/orderliness of the work environment
- informal supports, including opportunities to interact/socialize with coworkers, management support, and organizational climate

STUDENT SKILL ASSESSMENT

Assessment information must be gathered from multiple sources that include interpreting formal evaluations (e.g., psychological, social/emotional, medical/psychiatric); interviewing students, family members, and former teachers; and informally observing students in various settings (e.g., with peers, with authority figures, in work groups).

Factors to be included on a student skill assessment are

- domestic/residential information, including relationships of people in the student's family, available family support, type of work that the parent/guardian feels is appropriate, typical routines of the student, friends and social groups, location of home in the community, services available near the home, and transportation availability

- educational information, including history and general performance in the educational program, community skills (e.g., use of money, use of transportation, use of restaurants and other community resources), and leisure skills
- previous vocational programming and work experience
- learning and performance characteristics
- preferences
- habits and idiosyncrasies
- physical health restrictions, including physical job requirements (e.g., sedentary, standing, navigating steps)
- behavioral challenges
- personal appearance
- communication skills
- level of independence
- tolerance/flexibility for changes in routine
- skills related to providing personal information
- time-telling skills
- mobility, including ability to orient self in space
- physical capacity, including bending, lifting, carrying, and fine and gross motor skills
- endurance
- functional academic skills
- discrimination skills
- work speed
- safety skills

JOB MATCHING

The process of correlating the student's interests, abilities and other characteristics (student skill assessment) to a potential job (job analysis) is called job matching. Training goals and objectives can be developed for the student on the basis of the discrepancy between skills identified in the job analysis and the student's ability to perform them. The student profile should be updated on a regular basis.

QUALITY ISSUES

At the final stage of training, when job placement is being considered, it is important to consider quality issues. Quality issues address elements that influence job satisfaction, future long-term success on the job, and quality of life for the student, including

- parental expectations for a job
- salary, including impact on federal benefits
- benefits
- location
- transportation
- work schedule
- integration of the work environment
- customer contact
- opportunity for advancement
- environmental stressors

SKILL TRAINING

The purpose of skill training is for the student to perform a job accurately without assistance.

Teacher Preparation

Teachers should prepare for skill training by developing three steps:

1. *The task design:* an appropriate method and sequence to complete the job efficiently. Good task designs minimize the number of different manipulations and discriminations to complete specific tasks.
2. *The task analysis:* an analysis that breaks a task into teachable steps and enables the teacher to maintain consistency during training and to establish an effective data collection tool (see Chapter 7, section "Psychoeducational Measures: Competency-Based Training").
3. *The work routine:* a macro task analysis that details the entire job or workday by its component parts. Work routines pro-

vide information that enables the teacher to develop a training schedule; identify low-frequency job events; define social demands, skills, and rules that must be trained; and plan fading and support activities. The work routine is used in conjunction with task analyses that are developed for individual tasks.

Job Modification and Restructuring

It is not uncommon for the teacher to identify ways in which a job could be organized and performed more effectively. Company employees and supervisors often do not have the time to assess a job systematically to determine the most efficient and/or organized way to perform it. Employers are often receptive to equipment modifications and additions that help individuals with disabilities to maintain employment:

- A disorganized supply closet may present training challenges that could be eliminated if supplies were organized in a predictable way. The teacher might help by organizing the supply closet so that cleaning supplies are kept in one place, mops and buckets in another place, etc.
- In a lumber mill, the foreman cut measuring sticks to determine various board lengths for a man who could not use a standard ruler.
- In an electronics plant, special fixtures were developed to assist a woman with poor dexterity to operate a drill.
- An employee's schedule may be changed to fit unique transportation needs.
- A 40-hour job may be divided into two 20-hour jobs for individuals who have limited endurance.

Training Phases

There are three phases of the training process: (1) orientation and assessment, (2) skill acquisition, and (3) fading and maintenance.

Orientation and Assessment

The teacher's primary focus during orientation and assessment is to introduce students to the people with whom they will be interacting and, in the process, to help everyone feel comfortable. He or she should concentrate on modeling what students need to do and how to perform job responsibilities efficiently. The teacher should anticipate that he or she will perform the majority of the work for the student during the orientation phase. He or she will be assisting the student to complete and understand the work routine. This means not only the activities and their sequence but the circumstances that the worker must recognize and respond to as cues (discriminative stimuli).

Baseline information should be collected on the student's performance. The teacher must determine what aspects of the job will require intensive skill training and what training strategies/adaptations will be used. Baseline data should also be collected on all related skills (e.g., transportation, eating, using vending machines, greeting coworkers).

Skill Acquisition

This phase begins when the student communicates that demonstrations are understood and are beginning to seem like overkill. Job skills should be taught systematically. Effective teaching strategies are:

- Provide lots of assistance.
- Provide a high level of reinforcement.
- Teach one step at a time.
- Teach how to do something and when.
- Gradually reduce assistance until the student is performing a step or a job independently.

Fading and Maintenance

The emphasis of the maintenance phase is on helping the student maintain performance in the presence of naturally occurring reinforcers available in the environment. Fading begins when the student has become independent on the steps of a task analysis or the tasks in a work routine.

In an enclave or group work setting, the student is expected to perform his or her job responsibilities independently without prompts or rewards from the teacher until the job is finished. Prompts should be directed toward strengthening the student's response to the natural cues in the environment. In an individual placement, the teacher will fade his or her presence from the job site. Initially, the teacher should fade proximity from the worker by moving to a different area of the worksite to do paperwork. As the student maintains performance, the teacher may reduce presence from the worksite in small increments and systematically increase the amount of time the student is alone.

The teacher should fade from the student only when

- the student performance is acceptable
- the student knows the teacher is fading
- the employer or host company is aware of and in agreement with the fading schedule
- the teacher can return to the site on short notice if the student requires more help

Supervisors and coworkers have important roles to play in the maintenance phase. Work supervisors should be involved in the initial training as much as possible so that the student and supervisor become accustomed to one another. The teacher can briefly describe the training process and encourage the supervisor to support the student. Praise for a job well done, presentation of paychecks, and social exchange are potential reinforcements that supervisors normally give all workers. Coworkers can be solicited to help individuals get through "tough spots." They can provide occasional work prompts and reinforcers while the teacher is still at the site and gradually increase interactions with the student as the teacher fades from the work area. The teacher should model ways to support the student and take the time to explain the student's disability and background, within the confines of confidentiality.

SELF-MANAGEMENT TECHNIQUES

Self-management techniques enable students to remain autonomous (i.e., work with as little supervision as possible) and independent after the teacher fades his or her assistance. They are used to provide prompts to get the task or job done, to help the student monitor work completion, and to provide reinforcement.

The following are examples of self-management techniques:

- Prompting
  1. pictures and checklists to remember task sequences
  2. Walkmans with recorded messages to remind the student about pace, quality, and what to attend to
  3. color coding to identify locations on shelf or bins (e.g., grocery shelves, linen closet)
- Monitoring
  1. checklists and charts to keep track of tasks that are done multiple times (e.g, vacuuming offices, making hamburgers)
  2. timers to maintain work pace
- Self-reinforcement
  1. short breaks initiated by the student when a task is completed ahead of schedule, if the supervisor approves
  2. charting of daily earnings until payday or saving of money each week for a special purchase

NONVOCATIONAL AND SOCIAL COMPETENCE SKILLS

Nonvocational skills and interpersonal competence are crucial to vocational success. A variety of studies has shown that people with severe disabilities often lose their jobs because of inadequate social and related skills. It is important that the vocational training program focus as much effort on teaching related nonvocational and social skills as on specific vocational tasks.

Some common reasons for job termination are

- maladaptive behaviors such as complaining, screaming, destroying property, interacting inappropriately with supervisors and coworkers, displaying stereotypical and self-abusive behavior, and being non-compliant
- stealing
- behaviors showing lack of social awareness or understanding of people and work settings (e.g., walking into meetings and talking about a TV show or inquiring into other people's affairs)
- excessive tardiness and poor attendance, or failure to notify an employer when unable to report to work
- poor communication and conversation ability

The following are recommended nonvocational standards of behavior:

- communicating basic needs
  1. involving thirst, hunger, sickness, pain, and toileting
  2. receptively by means of verbal expression, signs, or gestures
  3. expressively by means of verbal expression or gestures
- responding within half a minute to instructions requiring immediate compliance
- responding appropriately to safety signals given verbally through signs or through signals
- initiating contact with supervisors when
  1. cannot do the job
  2. runs out of materials
  3. finishes job
  4. feels too sick or tired to work
  5. needs drink, restroom
  6. makes a mistake
- reaching place of work by means of
  1. company-sponsored vehicle
  2. own arrangement
  3. public transit

- maintaining proper grooming by
  1. dressing appropriately after using the restroom
  2. cleaning self before coming to work
  3. cleaning self after using the restroom
  4. cleaning self after eating lunch
  5. eating food appropriately at lunch
  6. displaying proper table manners at lunch
- maintaining personal hygiene by
  1. shaving regularly
  2. keeping teeth clean
  3. keeping hair combed
  4. keeping nails clean
  5. using deodorant
- leaving job station inappropriately no more than one or two times per day
- displaying or engaging in major disruptive behavior no more than one or two times per week
- displaying or engaging in minor disruptive behavior no more than one or two times per week

FOLLOW-ALONG SUPPORT

An essential aspect of ensuring job success for students placed in a paid job situation is the provision of ongoing supports. The major concern of follow-along support is the early identification of problems so that they may be remediated to prevent the students from losing their jobs. Follow-along responsibilities are usually provided by school staff if students have not graduated, or by the adult service provider upon graduation. Some school programs negotiate transition agreements with adult service providers that shift responsibility for follow-along when the student has successfully mastered all aspects of the job.

Examples of follow-along activities are

- clarifying work schedules
- providing additional supervision
- making routine calls or visits to see how things are going

- mediating between the student and employer or coworkers regarding interpersonal relationships, response to supervision, and communication skills
- assisting in negotiating benefit and compensation issues
- providing information to employer about non-work-related issues that might affect job performance
- assisting in solving health and safety issues
- providing spot training or supervision of performance deficiencies observed during routine visits
- providing additional training to increase the student's ability to perform a broader range of job duties
- assisting coworkers to provide feedback, instructions, and friendships toward the student
- routinely soliciting feedback about the student's performance

ISSUES IN COMMUNITY TRAINING

Training students in community work settings poses several unique issues and constraints:

- *Complex demands on the teacher:* In enclaves, the training takes place in a group setting. At times, the teacher will have only one student in intensive training but will have to provide supervision to the other students. Shifting attention from one student to another increases the possibility of errors. Task analysis and work routines assist the teacher in maintaining consistency.
- *Concern about the image of the student's competence:* In community work settings, many eyes are on the students and the teacher. The teacher must be observed to communicate respect for the student but must train as unobtrusively as possible. When prosthetics are used, they should be as normalized as possible. For example, if a worker requires pictorial cues to perform the job, pictures should be wallet-size to fit in the student's pocket, rather than large posters on the wall.
- *Less control over the environment:* In community work settings, there are issues related to the social acceptability of certain instructional techniques such as physical guidance or behavior management procedures. Studies indicate that employers and other community members will accept only interventions that approximate those used in the normal workplace, such as clocking out and leaving work, and not interventions such as physical restraint. Further, some work environments are not conducive to rearranging the task sequence to increase student efficiency.
- *Increased risks to the student and the environment:* Businesses may have slippery floors, loading docks, power equipment, etc. Teachers must pay attention to these risks and develop strategies to protect the student. The work environment is also at risk. Students make mistakes that can be costly to the business, or they may behave in ways that offend customers and coworkers.
- *Strict employer requirements for quality and quantity of work, with little room for negotiation:* Teachers face major challenges when students perform slowly. Problems also occur related to quality. For example, janitorial tasks often have "clean enough" quality requirements. Students may scrub every sink even when wiping is enough. Food services have strict consistency requirements for food preparation and cleanliness of dishes and flatware. Failure to meet scheduling or quality requirements will result in termination of the placement and could jeopardize the program.

PARTNERSHIPS WITH ADULT SERVICE PROVIDERS

Cooperation and collaboration with the adult service system is critical to the long-term employment success of students following graduation. With the widespread adoption of the supported employment model, adult service providers have shifted their focus from employment preparation to creating employment opportunities for persons with substantial disabilities.

The following are benefits of partnerships:

- Partnerships with the adult service system (e.g., vocational rehabilitation, community providers, and the state office of developmental disabilities) can help leverage the limited resources available to develop meaningful paid employment for students upon graduation from high school.

- Adult providers typically have expertise in job development, knowledge of the local labor market, and suggestions about work-related skills. Some school districts develop contractual arrangements with adult providers for job development.

- Regular updates about students ready to graduate, including their skills and support needs, assist adult providers to serve them.

- Involving representatives of the adult service delivery system in the transition planning helps to ensure that needed supports and services are arranged upon graduation.

RESOURCE ALLOCATION

The staffing needs of a "best practices" vocational training program are different from those of a traditional, classroom-based program. A ratio of one adult to two to four students is recommended for community-based training. Since most classrooms are not staffed with this type of ratio, creative strategies are needed to accomplish vocational preparation of students with disabilities.

Some suggested strategies are

- *Cooperative or team teaching:* Sharing supervision of students increases flexibility. One teacher can be in the community with a few students and an aide or volunteer while the other teacher and/or aide remains at school with other students.

- *Support personnel:* Speech therapists and occupational and physical therapists implement IEP goals in the work setting, rather than in the classroom.

- *Volunteers:* Volunteers, recruited from parents, service organizations, universities, and nonhandicapped students, can be used to assist in teaching skills at the job site. Volunteers must be trained to use teaching procedures.

- *District policy:* If certified staff are required for direct supervision, aides and volunteers can be used to work with a small group of students while the teacher works nearby with another small group of students. The teacher can respond to emergencies.

REFERENCES

DiLeo, D., and D. Langton. 1993. *Get the marketing edge: A job developer's tool kit for people with disabilities.* St. Augustine, Fla.: Training Resource Network.

McDonnell, J., et al. 1989. Employment preparation for high school students with severe handicaps. *Mental Retardation* 27:396–405.

Sowers, J., and L. Powers. 1991. *Vocational preparation and employment of students with physical and multiple disabilities.* Baltimore: Paul H. Brookes.

U.S. Department of Education and U.S. Department of Labor. 1992. *Memorandum of understanding*, signed September 3, 1992. Washington, DC: U.S. Office of Special Education Programs (memo #92-20).

Wagner, M., et al. 1992. *What happens next? Trends in postschool outcomes for youth with disabilities: The second comprehensive report from the National Longitudinal Transition Study of Special Education Students.* Menlo Park, Calif.: SRI International.

ADDITIONAL SUGGESTED READINGS

Bellamy, G.T., et al. 1979. *Vocational habilitation of severely retarded adults: A direct service technology.* Baltimore: University Park Press.

Chadsey-Rusch, J. 1986. Identifying and teaching valued social behaviors. In *Competitive employment: Issues and strategies,* ed F.R. Rusch, 273–287. Baltimore: Paul H. Brookes.

Ettinger, J.M. 1992. *Improved career decision making in a changing world.* Garrett Park, Md.: Garrett Park Press.

Fadely, D.C. 1987. *Job coaching in supported work programs.* Menomonie: University of Wisconsin, Materials Development Center, Stout Vocational Rehabilitation Institute.

Fairweather, G.W., and E.O. Fergus. 1987. *Employment training specialist series: Job development.* Lansing: Michigan State University, Supported Employment Technical Assistance Project.

Falvey, M.A. 1986. *Community-based curriculum: Instructional strategies for students with severe handicaps.* Baltimore: Paul H. Brookes.

Griffin, C. 1991. *Job carving: A guide for job developers and employment specialists.* Greely: University of Northern Colorado.

Mank, D.M., et al. 1986. Four supported employment alternatives. In *Pathways to employment for adults with developmental disabilities,* ed. W.E. Kiernan and J.A. Stark, 139–153. Baltimore: Paul H. Brookes.

Noren, L., and A.J. Gantenbein. 1990. *Career planning and job development.* Vol. 3, *Tools of the trade.* Spring Lake Park, Minn.: Rise, Inc.

Rusch, F.R., and D.E. Mithaug. 1980. *Vocational training for mentally retarded adults: A behavior analytic approach.* Champaign, Ill.: Research Press.

Sale, P., et al. 1991. Quality indicators of successful vocational transition programs. *Journal of Vocational Rehabilitation* 1, no. 4:47–64.

Shafer, M.S. 1986. Utilizing co-workers as change agents. In *Competitive employment issues and strategies,* ed. F.R. Rusch, 215–224. Baltimore: Paul H. Brookes.

Specialized Training Program. 1987. Vocational training in community settings. Unpublished manuscript. Training workshop at ASETS, Inc., Anchorage, Alaska.

Ward, K.M., et al. 1993. Job coach follow-along activities: Analysis and recommendations. *Developmental Disabilities Bulletin* 21, no. 2:36–51.

Wehman, P., et al. 1988. *Transition from school to work: New challenges for youth with severe disabilities.* Baltimore: Paul H. Brookes.

ADDITIONAL RESOURCES

U.S. Department of Labor

Professional Organizations/Technical Assistance:

- Association for Persons in Supported Employment, 5001 W Broad St., Suite 34, Richmond, VA 23230, Tel.: (804) 282-3655.

- Supported Employment InfoLines, Training Resource Network, Inc., P.O. Box 439, St. Augustine, FL 32085-0439, Tel.: (904) 823-9800.

- Virginia Commonwealth University, Rehabilitation Research and Training Center on Supported Employment, 1314 W. Main St., P.O. Box 842011, Richmond, VA 23284-2011, Tel.: (804) 828-1851, TTD (804) 828-2494.

Chapter 10

Developmental Therapy Approaches

NEURODEVELOPMENTAL THERAPY

Lynette E. Byarm

Purpose: to provide an overview of the neurodevelopmental treatment (NDT) approach for management of children with neurologic impairment affecting motor control and to describe strategies for neurodevelopmental assessment along with suggested techniques and equipment used to manage abnormal muscle tone and facilitate desired movement patterns and functional skills.

The neurodevelopmental treatment or NDT approach was introduced in England in the 1940s by Berta Bobath, a physical therapist, and her husband, Dr. Karel Bobath. The approach was developed from their work with patients having central nervous system deficits resulting in abnormal patterns of movement. Although NDT is a dynamic approach that continues to evolve over time on the basis of increased understanding of the central nervous system, movement, and motor control, the basic theoretical principles have remained unchanged:

1. Damage to the central nervous system may result in abnormal muscle tone, atypical patterns of movement and posture, and limitations in various areas of function, including mobility, self-care, speech, feeding, and respiration.

2. Normal movement is dependent upon sensation. Sensory input is important for the learning, initiation, and direction of movement.

3. NDT is most effective given a team approach that includes the patient, family, therapists, and other caregivers, who collaborate to provide the child with therapeutic movement experiences throughout daily routines. Table 10–1 illustrates how members of the NDT team integrate the use of theory and specialized techniques to create a background of adequate postural tone and control for the development of functional skills.

Training in NDT occurs on several levels. Introductory courses are available that present a general overview of the NDT approach to a wide range of people, including health professionals, educators, and parents or caregivers. Certification courses approved by the Neuro-Develop-

Table 10–1 Members of the NDT Team

Team Member	Areas of Expertise
Physical therapist	Gross motor skill Mobility Gait
Occupational therapist	Fine motor skill Oral-motor function Activities of daily living Play Cognitive and perceptual development
Speech pathologist	Respiration Language Speech Oral-motor skill
Teacher	Use of handling and positioning principles to optimize the child's ability to learn and participate in the educational process
Physician	Early identification of abnormal development for referral and appropriate intervention
Parents and other caregivers	Providing consistency in management by helping to carry out handling and positioning principles into daily routines, including activities of daily living and sensorimotor play experiences

mental Treatment Association, Inc., are offered on a competitive basis and include an eight-week pediatric course, a three-week adult hemiplegia course, and a six-week course for special education teachers. These courses include both didactic instruction and intensive practical experience. Additional advanced-level courses are also available for individuals who have successfully completed basic certification.

NEURODEVELOPMENTAL ASSESSMENT

Neurodevelopmental treatment is based on a thorough understanding of the components of normal movement and the progression of normal and abnormal motor development. As a part of the assessment and treatment process, the therapist must be able to analyze the child's movement, identify missing components and compensatory strategies, and recognize the functional consequences of atypical patterns of movement. The therapist can then use the principles of normal development and movement to formulate functional goals and guide treatment. Assessment should include both subjective findings (information obtained from the child, parent or caregiver, medical record, teacher) and objective findings (information obtained from observation of the child's spontaneous movement and play, specific clinical assessments, and observation of the child's response to selected intervention techniques administered as trials during the assessment).

A suggested outline for neurodevelopmental assessment follows:

- Musculoskeletal evaluation
  1. active and passive range of motion
  2. orthopedic changes (e.g., scoliosis, lordosis, shape or diameter of rib cage, hip dislocation)

3. soft tissue mobility (include length, elasticity, and density of skin, muscle, tendons, fascia)

4. symmetry

- Neuromotor findings
  1. muscle tone (ability to generate appropriate levels of tone for functional movement or stability against gravity)
  2. ability to initiate, sustain, and terminate muscle activity as appropriate
  3. gradation of muscle activity (ability to generate sufficient muscle activity to allow smooth functioning, especially in midranges)
  4. coordination, timing, or sequencing of muscle activity (when and in what sequence to activate specific muscles)
  5. strength (ability to generate adequate power or muscle tension for function; note effect of alignment, length, or disuse atrophy)

- Reflexes and postural reactions
  1. presence of obligatory/abnormal activity as well as reliability and speed of response
     (a) righting reactions
     (b) protective reactions
     (c) equilibrium reactions

- Control of neuromotor status
  1. control of flexion and extension, weight shift, rotation (ability to control these motor components for smooth active movement)
  2. development of control against gravity (ability to assume, maintain, and transition between developmental positions)
     (a) prone, supine, side-lying
     (b) quadruped
     (c) sitting
     (d) kneeling, half-kneeling
     (e) standing
     (f) transitional movement

- Sensory/perceptual status
  1. influence of sensory information to initiate, guide, or adapt movement
     (a) visual
     (b) auditory
     (c) tactile
     (d) proprioceptive/kinesthetic
     (e) vestibular

- Respiratory status
  1. respiration and its effect on movement and function
     (a) pattern of breathing
     (b) support for sound production, vocalization
     (c) capacity for air exchange
     (d) endurance (aerobic capacity to support movement)

- Developmental function
  1. motor
     (a) gross motor
     (b) fine motor
     (c) oral motor
  2. cognitive
     (a) adaptive
     (b) language
  3. personal/social
     (a) self-care
     (b) play
     (c) social interaction

- Summary
  1. list of major strengths; these may be used as building blocks for treatment
  2. list of major problems that interfere with function (include core problems rather than symptoms: e.g., poor head control is a symptom; poor control of flexion and extension may be the core problem); problem lists should be prioritized to help guide and organize treatment

(d) decreased coordination, timing, sequencing

(e) asymmetry

2. treatment emphasis

(a) facilitating coactivation, or activation of muscles around a joint

(b) facilitating control in midranges

(c) facilitating controlled slow movement, predictable patterns

(d) emphasizing symmetry and midline orientation

(e) organizing movement

3. techniques to address fluctuating tone/increase control

(a) careful gradation of input to address fluctuations in tone

(b) placing and holding of extremity or posture against gravity

(c) intermittent compression or pressure applied through the joint surfaces, used in midrange for graded control to provide increased proprioceptive input

(d) sustained joint compression through well-aligned joints to encourage coactivation, control, and symmetry

(e) sustained deep pressure to quiet body through increased proprioceptive input

• Ataxia

1. common neuromotor findings

(a) tone often decreased, although fluctuations in tone are frequent

(b) able to initiate, sustain, and terminate movement with poor gradation and control

(c) intention tremors (tremulousness upon active movement)

(d) difficulty with balance and movement transitions; child may use flexion to lower center of gravity and resists shifting weight or rotating away from base of support

(e) proximal muscle shortening possible, secondary to holding for stability

(f) significant sensory and perceptual deficits

2. treatment emphasis

(a) promoting organization of sensory input and movement

(b) improving control of balance and increasing variety and quality of functional movement patterns

(c) working in small ranges to improve control

(d) emphasizing rotation and weight shift away from the base of support

3. techniques to address ataxia/improve coordination

(a) sustained joint compression to promote increased coactivation and improved holding and control of posture

(b) intermittent joint compression to provide increased sensory feedback during movement (use arrhythmical input to prevent accommodation to your rhythm)

(c) elongation of muscles to facilitate lateral and diagonal movement away from midline and extension out of flexed posture

(d) sustained, deep tactile input for increased sensory feedback

RECOMMENDATIONS FOR CAREGIVING AND ACTIVITIES OF DAILY LIVING

The NDT treatment approach is most effective when therapeutic strategies identified during direct therapy sessions are incorporated into the child's daily activities. Incorporation of these techniques should influence the child's muscle tone and motor control, resulting in increased ease in caregiving, and improved learning of functional skills. Techniques discussed in the previous section should be used as general guidelines for use during caregiving and daily living activities. Proper positioning and adaptive equipment should also be considered. Basic techniques are as follows:

- Increased tone

  1. Child should be approached in a calm, slow manner.

  2. If exaggerated extensor tone is a problem, avoid supine positions during caregiving. Lying prone over the caregiver's lap and side-lying are alternative positions that typically decrease strong extensor patterns (see Figure 10–1). If supine position must be used, encourage flexion by placing a pillow under the child's head, neck, shoulder girdle area, or pelvis.

  3. In general, try to incorporate flexion into caregiving activities by positioning head semiflexed forward, shoulders and arms forward toward midline, hips and lower extremities flexed and abducted (Figure 10–2).

  4. When moving, carrying, or dressing the child, try to incorporate rotation and dissociation of total patterns (Figures 10–3 through 10–5).

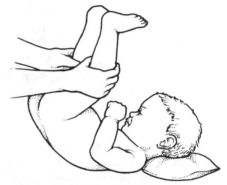

Figure 10–2 Positioning in Supine to Encourage Flexion in Child with Exaggerated Extensor Tone. *Source:* Copyright © 1996, Mark L. Batshaw, M.D.

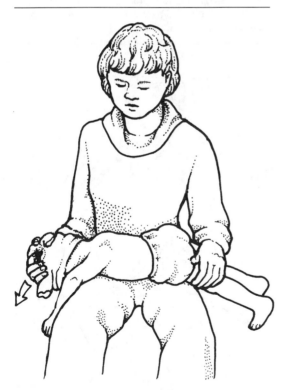

Figure 10–1 Prone Position to Decrease Strong Extensor Patterns. *Source:* Copyright © 1996, Mark L. Batshaw, M.D.

Figure 10–3 Use of Caregiver Body Position to Encourage Flexion in Sitting. *Source:* Copyright © 1996, Mark L. Batshaw, M.D.

- Decreased tone
  1. Approach the child with multisensory input to increase central nervous system arousal. Utilize tactile, proprioception, auditory, visual, and vestibular input.
  2. When possible, position the child upright against gravity (as in sitting) to encourage higher levels of tone through active trunk control (Figure 10–6). Lower positions such as supine tend to encourage the child to sink into the supporting surface and demonstrate low levels of tone and activity. Vary the amount of support according to the child's abilities.
  3. Encourage active participation by the child to assist in generating higher levels of tone.
- Asymmetry
  1. When dressing the child with asymmetrical involvement (as in hemiplegia), dress the involved side first.

Figure 10–4 Using Rotation through Trunk to Break Up Strong Pattern of Extensor Tone. *Source:* Copyright © 1996, Mark L. Batshaw, M.D.

Figure 10–5 Spreading Child's Legs Across Caregiver Hip to Decrease Tone. *Source:* Copyright © 1996, Mark L. Batshaw, M.D.

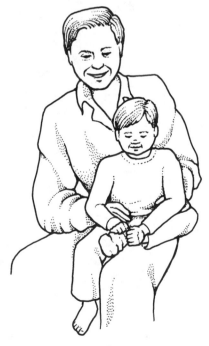

Figure 10–6 Use of Sitting Position to Increase Tone and Encourage Active Trunk Control. *Source:* Copyright © 1996, Mark L. Batshaw, M.D.

2. When possible, prepare the more involved side with general sensory stimulation or gentle stretching.

3. Child should be positioned well, with symmetry emphasized.

- Poor trunk control

1. Provide external trunk support to free the arms for increased function. Appropriate adaptive seating may be used, or the child may lie down or sit on the floor in the corner for truncal support (Figures 10–7 and 10–8).

- Increased movement

1. Provide external trunk support to inhibit excess movement. Adaptive seating or positioning on a solid, stable surface such as the floor may be helpful.

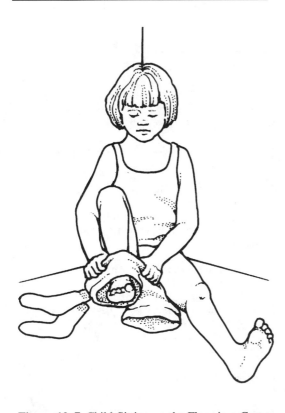

Figure 10–7 Child Sitting on the Floor in a Corner for Truncal Support. *Source:* Copyright © 1996, Mark L. Batshaw, M.D.

EQUIPMENT

Therapeutic equipment can provide the therapist with an extra pair of hands and thus assist in the development of the components of movement necessary for the acquisition of functional skills. Equipment may include movement and positioning devices such as balls, bolsters, and wedges; adaptive seating and positioning devices such as prone standers and customized chairs; and orthotics. This section will briefly discuss properties of specific positioning equipment typically used with handling techniques. Please refer to Chapter 15 for information regarding orthotics and Chapter 11, "Adaptive Positioning Devices" and "Wheelchair Selection and Maintenance" for information regarding adaptive seating and positioning.

Movable surfaces can facilitate automatic reactions, posture, and dynamic movement through space. Table 10–2 provides a comparison between two commonly used pieces of equipment to demonstrate how therapists may analyze the properties of equipment in relation to desired goals.

Static surfaces provide a stable base upon which movement can occur. Automatic reactions can be facilitated from a stable surface as the child initiates moving his or her center of gravity over the base of support. Table 10–3 offers a comparison of therapy benches and wedges.

Static surfaces and mobile surfaces can be used in combination when both mobility and a stable base are needed. For example, a bench placed over a ball will encourage weight shift over a stable surface.

EFFICACY AND ASSESSMENT OF TREATMENT

Neurodevelopmental treatment is a well-known and widely used approach to therapy for children with neuromotor deficits. Although the literature produces some evidence that this approach may produce effects in both the rate of acquisition of developmental motor skills and the quality of motor control, many studies may

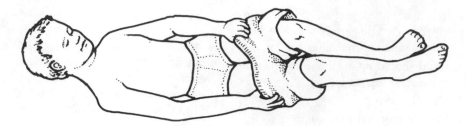

Figure 10–8 Child with Limited Trunk Control Lying Down to Dress. *Source:* Copyright © 1996, Mark L. Batshaw, M.D.

be criticized for their lack of scientific objectivity. Of particular concern is the fact that many motor assessment tools lack the sensitivity to detect subtle changes in the quality of movement that may be produced through therapy.

Therapists opting to use this approach must view ongoing assessment as a requirement of the total treatment process. Goal-directed treatment with careful monitoring and documentation of

goal attainment is necessary to measure the effectiveness of treatment. While standardized motor and developmental testing can be useful to measure skill acquisition as new motor components develop, subjective measures such as checklists and parent interviews can reveal important qualitative and behavioral changes. Important areas in which to measure change include increased ease in caregiving secondary to

Table 10–2 Comparison of Therapy Ball and Roll/Bolster

Therapy Ball	Therapy Roll/Bolster
Moves in multiple directions	Moves in only two directions
Facilitates postural reactions anteriorly, posteriorly, laterally, and diagonally	Facilitates postural reactions anteriorly, posteriorly, and laterally
Provides surface for mobile/dynamic weight bearing	Provides surface for dynamic and stable weight bearing
Provides vestibular, proprioceptive, tactile input with wide range in intensity	Provides proprioceptive input with less range in intensity
Can be used to increase range of motion, strength, and endurance	Can be used to increase range of motion, strength, and endurance
Can control degree to which gravity assists or resists movement by moving the ball	Can control degree to which gravity assists by altering the incline of the roll
May be difficult to control	Easier to control
Can adjust level of inflation to change intensity and type of postural adjustments	Generally fixed level of inflation
Base of support moves from under the child	Child generally moves over base of support (although therapist can move the roll under the child)

Table 10–3 Comparison of Therapy Benches and Wedges

Therapy Bench	*Therapy Wedge*
Stable surface for sitting, standing, climbing	Stable surface with incline for side-lying, sitting, standing, climbing
Horizontal work surface for fine motor skill	Inclined work surface for fine motor skill
Raises the child's center of gravity to increase work against gravity	Incline can alter the effect of gravity and encourage weight shift

changes in muscle tone; improved socio-emotional functioning secondary to increased ability for the child to be handled; and improved language, perceptual, or cognitive functioning secondary to increased opportunities for spontaneous and active movement.

SUGGESTED READINGS

Development

Alexander, R., et al. 1993. *Normal development of functional motor skills.* Tucson, Ariz.: Therapy Skill Builders.

Bly, L. 1994. *Motor skill acquisition in the first year: An illustrated guide to normal development.* Tucson, Ariz.: Therapy Skill Builders.

Theory

Bobath, B. 1971. *Abnormal postural reflex activity caused by brain lesions.* London: William Heinemann.

Bobath, B., and K. Bobath. 1978. *Motor development in the different types of cerebral palsy.* London: William Heinemann.

Treatment

Boehme, R. 1990. *Approach to treatment of the baby.* Tucson, Ariz.: Therapy Skill Builders.

Boehme, R. 1990. *Developing mid-range control and function in children with fluctuating muscle tone.* Tucson, Ariz.: Therapy Skill Builders.

Boehme, R. 1990. *The hypotonic child.* Tucson, Ariz.: Therapy Skill Builders.

Boehme, R. 1990. *Improving upper body control.* Tucson, Ariz.: Therapy Skill Builders

Hypes, B. 1991. *Facilitating development and sensorimotor function: Treatment with the ball.* Hugo, Minn.: PDP Press.

Langley, M.B., and L.J. Lombardino, eds. 1991. *Neurodevelopmental strategies for managing communication disorders with severe motor dysfunction.* Austin, Tex.: PRO-ED Inc.

Scherzer, A., and I. Tscharnuter. 1990. *Early diagnosis and treatment in cerebral palsy: A primer on infant developmental problems.* New York: Marcel Dekker Inc.

Family, Parents

Finnie, N. 1974. *Handling the young cerebral palsied child at home.* New York: E.P. Dutton.

Efficacy

Stern, F.M., and D. Gorga. 1988. Neurodevelopmental treatment (NDT): Therapeutic intervention and its efficacy. *Infants and Young Children* 1, no. 1: 22–32.

Royeen, C.B., and G.A. DeGangi. 1992. *Annotated bibliography of NDT peer-reviewed literature 1980–1990, inclusive.* Oak Park, Ill.: Neuro-Developmental Treatment Association, Inc.

SENSORY INTEGRATION THERAPY

Lisa A. Kurtz

Purpose: to provide an overview of the rationale and recommended applications of sensory integration therapy, to present guidelines for identifying children with probable sensory integration dysfunction along with a discussion of formal test procedures typically used to plan the therapy program, and to review general suggestions for helping children to cope with sensory processing difficulties.

Sensory integration may be defined as a normal developmental process involving the ability of the central nervous system to organize sensory feedback from the body and the environment to make successful adaptive responses. Sensory integrative dysfunction is inferred when (1) the child demonstrates impaired ability to plan and execute behaviors as necessary for effective motor, social, or conceptual learning, (2) the child shows evidence of sensory processing problems, especially involving the tactile, proprioceptive (body awareness), vestibular (gravity and movement awareness), and visual systems, and (3) these problems are not attributable to frank brain damage or to sensory receptive disorders, such as visual or hearing impairment. Sensory integrative dysfunction may be identified in children with a variety of developmental disabilities, including learning disabilities, attention-deficit disorders, pervasive developmental disorders, mental retardation, and cerebral palsy.

Sensory integration therapy is a specific methodology that advocates the controlled use of sensory input combined with the demand of an adaptive response; this is believed to enhance neural organization and promote more mature learning and behavior patterns (Ayres 1979). Not all children who show evidence of sensory integrative dysfunction are considered appropriate candidates for therapy using this methodology. For this reason, it is important to obtain a detailed assessment of the child's functional and sensory processing skills and to analyze the child's potential for improvement prior to initiating a course of therapy. Although sensory integration therapy is considered a controversial method, efficacy research suggests that it may be effective for some children (Cermak and Henderson 1989, 1990; Humphries et al. 1990). While inconclusive, studies have suggested the potential for increased language and reading development, improved organization of behavior, reduced self-abusive/self-stimulatory behaviors, improved quality of motor skills, and improved social and play interactions using these procedures.

The major theoretical principles underlying sensory integrative therapy are as follows:

1. Plasticity of the central nervous system allows for changes in neural organization through the provision of therapeutic experiences.

2. Sensory integration processes mature according to a predictable developmental sequence. Therapy attempts to recapitulate the normal sequence of neuromotor development through selected sensory and motor experiences.

3. Although the brain functions as a whole, higher level structures evolved from, and remain dependent upon, the lower structures. The goal of therapy is to enable subcortical brain structures to function more efficiently in order to enhance the brain's potential to function as an integrated whole.

4. The ability of a child to produce an appropriate adaptive behavioral response to sensory input is a reflection of sensory integration. Therapy that provides sensory input without demanding an adaptive response does not facilitate sensory integration.

5. Children have an inner drive to develop sensory integration through participation in sensorimotor activities; children with sensory integrative dysfunction often lack the motivation and self-confidence to attempt mastery of their environment.

CLASSIFICATION OF SENSORY INTEGRATIVE DYSFUNCTION

Sensory integrative dysfunction can be classified as follows:

- Vestibular/proprioceptive disorders
  1. postural/ocular movement disorder
     (a) poor prone extension
     (b) difficulty flexing neck from supine
     (c) hypotonicity, especially of extensor muscle groups
     (d) poor proximal joint stability
     (e) deficient postural adjustments/background movements
     (f) poor balance/equilibrium responses
     (g) attenuated (short-duration) post-rotary nystagmus
  2. gravitational insecurity
     (a) emotional/fear reaction out of proportion to threat/danger of postural challenge
     (b) fear reaction especially pronounced when feet are not in contact with floor
     (c) may be associated with aversion to movement
  3. bilateral integration and sequencing disorder
     (a) poor bilateral motor coordination
     (b) poor motor sequencing skills
     (c) tendency to avoid crossing the midline of the body
     (d) right/left confusion
     (e) poor performance of projected action sequences
- Somatosensory (tactile processing) disorders

  1. tactile defensiveness
     (a) avoidance of certain types of touch, such as scratchy/rough textures, certain food textures, "messy" play such as finger painting, or sports/games that involve body contact
     (b) aversion to non-noxious forms of touch; may complain, pull away, or rub skin after touch
     (c) negative behavioral reactions to non-noxious touch; may struggle when held/cuddled, act out or show behavioral disruptions when face washed or hair cut, be excessively fidgety
  2. poor tactile discrimination
     (a) impaired ability to discriminate shape, texture, location of stimulus with vision occluded
     (b) inefficiency in active exploration of environment through touch
     (c) poor body awareness
  3. developmental dyspraxia
     (a) clumsy, difficulty performing unfamiliar motor tasks, yet may perform certain rote, well-practiced motor schemes with ease and achieve early motor "milestones" at the expected age
     (b) poor tactile processing skills
     (c) inefficiency in functional motor skills, including ADLs, handwriting, playground skills
     (d) may have poor self-concept/self-esteem
     (e) may be manipulative, prefer "talking" to "doing"
     (f) may be disorganized, forgetful, easily frustrated
     (g) may have problems with sequencing
     (h) poor supine flexion
     (i) may have difficulty with constructional tasks (drawing, block de-

signs, puzzles), suggesting associated visual perception problem

- Disorders of hemispheric specialization
  1. left hemisphere dysfunction
     (a) better nonverbal than verbal intelligence
     (b) poor phonetic decoding of words
     (c) poor language skills relative to overall intelligence
     (d) poor ability to do complex math calculations, secondary to difficulty remembering details and the sequence of steps in a problem
     (e) poor motor sequencing skills; can affect handwriting fluency or ability to learn motor sequences such as shoe tying
     (f) poor communication skills may lead to behavior difficulties; child "acts out" as an alternative means of gaining social attention
     (g) may have excessive-duration postrotary nystagmus
     (h) problem is not believed to respond to therapy using sensory integrative procedures
  2. right hemisphere dysfunction
     (a) better verbal than nonverbal intelligence
     (b) difficulty organizing and synthesizing information; poor math concepts, time, money, measurement; fails to grasp the "main idea" in lessons
     (c) may have difficulty with early reading involving letter identification and sight word recognition, but good phonetic skills and decoding allow adequate compensation as child matures
     (d) may be talkative and use good vocabulary, grammar, and syntax but show problems with pragmatics (use of language that is contextually appropriate to social situations)

     (e) may miss inferences and nonverbal aspects of social communication
     (f) affect may be flat, depressed
     (g) difficulty with spatial perception and constructional tasks
     (h) may be clumsy in games or sports that require making judgments about movement of body or objects through space
     (i) may have poor haptic perception (stereognosis)
     (j) problem is not believed to respond to therapy using sensory integrative procedures unless accompanied by sensory processing disorders of a central nature

ASSESSMENT PROCEDURES

Components of a sensory integration assessment are as follows:

- Parent history/interview
  1. auditory/language
     (a) Does child over- or underreact to sudden or loud noises?
     (b) Does child have difficulty paying attention when there are other noises in the background?
     (c) Does child seem confused as to the location of sounds?
     (d) Does child seem to understand what is said to him or her?
     (e) Can child recognize common sounds, like a fire engine or washing machine, when not able to see the object making the noise?
     (f) Does child have difficulty saying words?
  2. visual
     (a) Does child make reversals when copying?
     (b) Does child hold head too close to books or tilt head at angle?

(c) Does child squint often, rub eyes, or get teary when performing visual work?

(d) Does child have difficulty seeing things that are very close or very far away?

(e) Does child have difficulty keeping his or her place when reading?

(f) Can child "find" a picture or object that is hidden against a visually distracting background?

3. tactile

(a) Does child dislike "messy" games, like finger painting?

(b) Does child especially dislike having face washed or hair brushed?

(c) Does child appear to be bothered by tags in clothing or certain fabrics or textures?

(d) Does child have strong avoidance of certain food textures?

(e) Does child startle when touched unexpectedly or dislike being held or cuddled?

(f) Does child "need" to touch everything in sight?

(g) Does child seem to feel pain more or less than others?

(h) Does child dislike standing in line or being bumped from behind?

(i) Does child pinch, scratch, bite, or otherwise hurt him/herself?

4. body awareness/movement

(a) Does child seem more or less fearful of heights or rapid movement than other children?

(b) Does child have good balance skills?

(c) Does child hold hands or other body parts in "odd" positions?

(d) Does child appear to be double-jointed?

(e) Does child seem stronger or weaker than other children?

5. motor skills

(a) Does child have normal coordination for managing small objects, such as buttons or beads?

(b) Did child "skip" certain milestones, such as crawling or cruising?

(c) Does child show confusion over which hand to use for different activities?

(d) Does child have unusual difficulty or frustration when learning new motor skills (pencil, tricycle, clothing fasteners)?

(e) Can child hold a pencil/crayon correctly?

(f) Can child throw/catch a ball?

(g) Does child avoid age-appropriate sports or playground activities?

• Developmental/learning profile (identifying measures of relative strengths/weaknesses)

1. cognitive

2. language

3. motor

4. personal-social

• Sensory processing skills (using standardized or clinical procedures)

1. visual perception

2. vestibular/proprioceptive

3. somatosensory

• Techniques for selected clinical observations related to sensory integration

1. evidence of hyperactivity/distractibility

(a) cannot sit still, fidgets

(b) engages in purposeless movement or object manipulation

(c) overfocuses on unimportant or irrelevant details

(d) overreacts to environmental stimuli

(e) consider Conner questionnaire or other standardized screening

2. evidence of tactile defensiveness

(a) avoids getting hands messy

(b) stiffens or struggles when held

(c) prefers to play alone

(d) dislikes being cuddled or hugged

(e) overly sensitive to clothing tags, haircuts, bath temperature

3. muscle tone

(a) palpate and check for hyper-mobility, especially in elbows, wrists, fingers; biceps/triceps group best for palpation

(b) check for right/left asymmetries

(c) elbow hyperextension greater than 5 degrees may be significant in children five years of age and older

4. quality of eye pursuits

(a) hold object 8 to 10 inches from eyes and move in slight arc to maintain distance and prevent combined vergent/tracking movements

(b) test quickly to avoid fatigue

(c) check horizontal, vertical, diagonal tracking, convergence, and rapid localization (saccades)

5. proximal stability/co-contraction

(a) child sits with hips/knees flexed to 90 degrees, shoulders flexed 45 degrees, elbows flexed 90 degrees; grasps examiner's thumbs and maintains position against varying resistance

(b) check for scapular stability (look for winging) in quadruped position

(c) poor indicator for child under six years

6. evidence of postural/gravitational inse-curity

(a) look for "guarding" or unusual fearfulness when positioned on un-stable therapy equipment (ball, equilibrium board, platform swing, etc.)

(b) fear may be especially pronounced when feet are not in contact with supporting surface, or when posi-tioned in supine

7. quality of postural background move-ments

(a) note the ease with which child spontaneously adjusts posture dur-ing visual motor tasks, especially crossing midline

(b) look for quality of postural adjust-ment during testing of equilibrium responses

8. quality of prone extension posture

(a) arms flexed at elbows, elbows about 4 inches away from body, legs held straight and hyperex-tended at hips

(b) easily assumes and maintains pos-ture for 15 to 20 seconds (upper body only for child under six years)

(c) must consider influence of underly-ing tone; low-tone child may as-sume position easily but fail to maintain

9. quality of supine flexion posture

(a) arms crossed over chest, ankles crossed, full flexion at neck, hips, and knees

(b) child under six years should assume easily and maintain briefly

(c) child age six and older maintains against slight resistance to forehead and knees

(d) child age eight and older should hold against resistance for 20 to 30 seconds

10. tactile discrimination skills

(a) check discrimination of textures, shapes, localization of light touch to fingers, graphesthesia (shape or letter drawn on back of hand); see Chapter 7, section "Sensory Screening: Sensibility Testing"

(b) look for hypersensitivity to touch, accuracy of responses, spontaneous manipulation of object when vision occluded, right/left difference

11. quality of motor planning

(a) rapid posture imitation, including asymmetrical and midline crossing

(b) oral motor imitation

(c) rapid alternating movements (e.g., forearm pronation/supination)

(d) opposition of thumb to fingers in sequence

(e) performance of motor sequences on verbal command (e.g., "Stand up, walk to the door, and knock three times")

(f) ease of experimentation when introduced to unfamiliar gross motor equipment

SUGGESTED TESTS FOR SENSORY INTEGRATION ASSESSMENT

The following tests may be helpful in sensory integration assessments. The first five tests are discussed in more detail in Chapter 7, the section "Annotated Index of Selected Assessment Tools."

1. Sensory Integration and Praxis Tests

2. Bruininks–Oseretsky Test of Motor Proficiency

3. Test of Sensory Functions in Infants

4. De Gangi–Berk Test of Sensory Integration

5. Miller Assessment for Preschoolers

6. Druker's Posture Imitation Test (Druker 1980)

7. MacQuarrie Test for Mechanical Ability (MacQuarrie 1953)

8. TIE: Touch Inventory for School Aged Children (Royeen and Fortune 1990)

9. TIP: Touch Inventory for Preschoolers (Royeen 1987)

See also Dunn 1981 and Jirgal and Bouma 1989.

TREATMENT CONSIDERATIONS

Sensory integration therapy is a specific treatment methodology that requires careful planning according to the individual child's sensory-processing profile and potential for improvement. Therapy should be conducted or supervised by an occupational or physical therapist with postgraduate training and experience in these methods. Although not intended as a substitute for a formal sensory integration therapy program, the following guidelines may be helpful for parents and other professionals to consider when working with a child who has sensory integration dysfunction.

Identify and Respect the Child's Sensory Preferences

Many children with sensory integration dysfunction show strong preferences for certain sensory experiences. They may insist on particular clothing textures or food types, crave fast movement, or touch and smell everything in sight. Sometimes children will become very upset if these cravings are prohibited. Remember that in general, children spontaneously seek the type of sensory information that their system "needs" in order to learn or to feel organized and "in control." Unless the child's preferences have serious social or behavioral consequences, it is best to respect the child's choices and to try to incorporate similar sensory feedback into learning tasks. For example, the child who "touches" everything may learn the alphabet more easily when given sandpaper letters or other manipulatives; the child who craves fast movement may enjoy learning new vocabulary words by jumping or hopping through an obstacle course following paths that lead to new words; the child who has poor balance and fear of movement experiences may concentrate better during reading comprehension if allowed to sit in a beanbag chair that cradles the body to give support.

Modify the Sensory Environment

Pay close attention to the child's responses to various sensory experiences. Some sensations will have the effect of increasing alertness and arousal, while other sensations will have a calming effect. We believe that when the child is paying attention appropriately and making successful adaptive responses, sensory inputs from the environment are having an organizing effect.

Similarly, when the child is not able to produce adaptive responses to a situation, sensory inputs may be producing a disorganizing effect. Modifying the environment so that disorganizing sensations are avoided and organizing sensations are promoted may help to improve attentional focus. Sometimes sensory activities (either calming or alerting) are used prior to a structured learning task to promote attentional focus. At other times, heightened sensory feedback is incorporated into a task to make learning more meaningful. Remember that children may respond differently to the same sensation. Also, an individual child's responses to a given sensation may vary over time depending on mood, fatigue, interest, motivation level, and so forth. Table 10–4 suggests sensory inputs that are typically arousing versus those that are typically calming.

Encourage Active Participation in Movement Challenges

Children with sensory integrative dysfunction may have problems with motor development, including clumsiness, difficulty learning new motor schemes, and a low frustration tolerance for physical activity. Most young children love to move, climb, and explore their environment. In normal development, children actively seek out sensorimotor play that challenges their motor

Table 10–4 Typical Sensory Responses

Sensation	Arousing Input	Calming Input
Touch	Light touch Tickling Soft touch Unexpected touch	Firm touch Hugging Stroking Massage
Movement	Fast movement Bouncing Jumping Spinning Rolling	Slow movement Rocking Swaying Moving against resistance (e.g., pushing, pulling, lifting weights)
Gravity	Head vertically aligned with body (sitting or standing)	Head supported, leaning forward or back
Sound	Loud or exciting music Loud noises Sudden noises Unexpected changes in pitch or tone	Soft or gentle music Quiet, rhythmic sounds
Vision	"Busy" or complicated decor Bright lights or colors Objects in motion	Few visual distractions Indirect, low-intensity light
Taste/foods	Salty, spicy, sour foods	Sweet or bland foods Crunchy or chewy textures Sucking through a straw
Temperature	Very cold or very hot	Warm, moderate temperature
Smell	Strong or noxious odors Unfamiliar odors	Familiar odors

development. As the child moves and explores, the body senses provide a dynamic source of feedback that tells the child whether the motoric goal was achieved. Accurate interpretation of this feedback allows the child to refine his or her approach to the task by making subtle adjustments in motor execution. Some children with sensory integrative dysfunction affecting motor planning are overly passive and avoid active games that challenge motor development. Others are willing to try but are unable to adjust their approach to a task and get "stuck" on repeating an unsuccessful motor scheme over and over again. Children should be encouraged to participate in a variety of movement activities that require thinking and planning as well as executing a motor response. Examples might include creative obstacle courses or "make-believe" play in which children imitate animal walks. Frequent, subtle changes in the demands of the task encourage the child to participate actively and to learn from the experience; this is a different kind of learning from simply practicing an exercise or rote skill. The following suggestions may help the child to plan movement more successfully:

1. Add resistance or increased tactile input to the activity to enhance body awareness; e.g., wear weighted cuffs, push a heavy cart through the obstacle course, use a vibrating pen to practice writing or drawing, or massage the body part that is having trouble "remembering" what it is supposed to do.

2. Teach the child to verbalize a motor plan, then to follow through with the plan; this often helps the child to pay better attention to what he or she is doing.

3. Take turns being "teacher" and allow the child to comment on your performance and suggest ways of improvement.

4. Encourage the child to "experiment" with his or her approach to a new task; e.g., say, "I wonder what would happen if you held your hand this way?" or "Is there a different way you could try?"

REFERENCES

Ayres, A.J. 1979. *Sensory integration and the child.* Los Angeles: Western Psychological Services.

Cermak, S.A., and A. Henderson. 1989. The efficacy of sensory integration procedures, part I. *Sensory Integration Quarterly* 17, no. 1:1–5.

Cermak, S.A., and A. Henderson. 1990. The efficacy of sensory integration therapy, part II. *Sensory Integration Quarterly* 18, no. 1.

Druker, R.H. 1980. Development of a posture imitation test for children ages 9 through 18. Unpublished master's thesis, University of Southern California, Los Angeles.

Dunn, W. 1981. *A guide to testing clinical observations in kindergartners.* Rockville Md.: American Occupational Therapy Association, Inc.

Humphries, T., et al. 1990. The efficacy of sensory integration therapy for children with learning disability. *Physical and Occupational Therapy in Pediatrics* 10, no. 1:1–17.

Jirgal, D., and K. Bouma. 1989. A sensory integration guide for children from birth to 3 years of age. *Sensory Integration Special Interest Section Newsletter* 12, no. 2:5.

MacQuarrie, T. 1953. *MacQuarrie Test for Mechanical Ability.* Monterey, Calif.: McGraw-Hill.

Royeen, C. (1987). TIP—Touch Inventory for Preschoolers: A pilot study. *Physical and Occupational Therapy in Pediatrics* 7, no. 1:29–40.

Royeen, C.B., and J.C. Fortune. 1990. TIE: Touch Inventory for School Aged Children. *American Journal of Occupational Therapy* 44:165–170.

ADDITIONAL SUGGESTED READINGS

Bissell, J., et al. 1988. *Sensory motor handbook: A guide for implementing and modifying activities in the classroom.* Torrance, Calif.: Sensory Integration International.

Clark, F., et al. 1989. Sensory integration and children with learning disabilities. In *Occupational therapy for chil-dren,* 2nd ed., ed. P.N. Pratt and A.S. Allen, 457–507. St. Louis: C.V. Mosby Co.

Fisher, A.G., et al. 1991. *Sensory integration: Theory and practice.* Philadelphia: F.A. Davis.

Mailloux, Z., ed. 1987. *Sensory integrative approaches in occupational therapy.* New York: Haworth Press.

Trott, M.A., et al. 1993. *Sensabilities: Understanding sensory integration.* Tucson, Ariz.: Therapy Skill Builders.

ADDITIONAL RESOURCES

Sensory Integration International, P.O. Box 9013, Torrance, CA 90508, Tel.: (310) 320-9986, fax (310) 320-9934.

Chapter 11

Mobility and Ambulation

LIFTING AND TRANSFER TECHNIQUES

Shirley A. Scull

Purpose: to describe methods used by a child to move from one position to another—for example, from a wheelchair to a bathtub.

Functional mobility in the environment must include the ability to move between various positions. Bed mobility includes the ability to roll from supine to and from prone, to move up toward the head or down toward the foot of the bed, and to move from supine to sitting over the edge. Children who use a wheelchair must learn to transfer from their chair to a variety of other seated positions, such as bed, toilet, tub, car, and perhaps school chair or sofa. Children who ambulate with assistive devices must also learn to transfer from sit to stand and back. More advanced transfer skills might include the ability to rise from the floor, for example, after a fall.

Some children are able to learn to transfer independently; while others are dependent and require a safe method for the caregiver to lift them. Dependent transfers done by lifting or pivoting the child must be safe for the caregiver as well as the child. The caregiver must not be placed at risk for back injury and should be instructed in proper body mechanics. Most parents will require a phase of supervised practice to achieve

safe technique. Mechanical devices may be needed if the weight of the child exceeds recommended limits or if the caregiver has a history of back complaints.

Independence in transfer may be a goal of rehabilitation training, and professionals should have a consistent method of scoring the child's performance. The degree of independence and the type of equipment required are usually specified on an ordinal scale. While some scales may vary, a typical scale might be:

1. *Independent:* Child performs all of the tasks that make up the activity safely and in a reasonable time frame. Assistive devices may be used but are noted.

2. *Verbal cues:* Child requires reminders to sequence the task properly.

3. *Close supervision:* Child performs task independently but requires someone to stand by for safety reasons.

4. *Minimal assistance:* Child performs more than 75 percent of the activity on his or her own, with minimal physical assistance from the caregiver. May also require set-up of equipment.

5. *Moderate assistance:* Child performs about 50 percent of the activity on his or her own, with moderate physical assistance from the caregiver.
6. *Maximal assistance:* Child performs only 25 percent of the activity on his or her own and requires lifting assistance from the caregiver.
7. *Dependent:* Child is unable to help caregiver with activity.

Often the proper prescription of adaptive equipment and accessories can assist in achieving the goal of independent transfers. For example, a wheelchair may have removable armrests to allow a side-sliding transfer, or brake extensions to allow a child with weakness to operate the locks.

The type of transfer chosen depends primarily on the portion of the body that is impaired. For example, children with weak lower extremities, as in paraplegia, use the upper body to maneuver. While the musculoskeletal exam is a leading factor in selecting the preferred transfer method, other impairments can also influence this decision, such as body build, cognition, or safety awareness.

GENERAL SAFETY PRECAUTIONS

The caregiver should observe the following safety precautions for transfers:

- All equipment involved in the transfer must be stable. Brakes should be applied if available. Braking alternatives include sandbags or manual stabilization.
- The area should be free of clutter. Wheelchair accessories such as footrests, armrests, or trunk supports should be removed.
- The caregiver and child should each wear nonskid shoes without heels.
- Choose a transfer method that has the potential to achieve eventual independence and makes optimal use of available motor skills.
- Explain and demonstrate the procedure to the child. Use a consistent method and set of verbal cues.

- Position the equipment so that the least amount of work must be done. Plan ahead so that you will not need to readjust the child's position once the transfer is complete.
- Stand in a position to protect from a fall. Sometimes a second person is needed to guard.
- Get help if necessary. Don't lift more weight than is safe for one person.
- Use proper body mechanics.
  1. Stand with feet spread apart, providing a stable base of support.
  2. Bend at the hips and knees while keeping the back straight.
  3. Keep the child's weight close to your body.
  4. Complete the lift phase before beginning to turn.
- Lift the child, using your hands on his or her trunk. A sturdy belt at the waist or a velcro gait belt may also be used as a handhold. Avoid lifting by applying a traction force to the shoulder joint: for example, by pulling on the arms.
- Transferring between objects that are the same height is easiest.
- Avoid skin breakdown, which can result from shearing forces placed on the buttocks when the body is dragged across a surface. The child should completely clear the surface.

TRANSFER METHODS FOR CHILDREN WITH SOME ACTIVE LOWER EXTREMITY CONTROL (AT LEAST UNILATERALLY)

The child will generally use the stronger side of the body to compensate for the weaker side. Transfer will be easier when moving toward the stronger side.

- Bed mobility
  1. moving up or down in bed
     (a) Child either actively positions legs in flexion or is assisted by caregiver, who stabilizes legs at the knees.
     (b) Ask child to bridge up (lift buttocks) and push toward head of bed or scoot toward foot of bed (Figure 11–1). Assistance may be given under buttocks if needed.
  2. moving side to side in bed
     (a) Bridge to move buttocks sideways, then adjust upper body alignment. Repeat.
  3. rolling
     (a) Move sideways in bed before beginning to roll.
     (b) Flex uphill hip and knee. May clasp hands together to provide additional momentum (Figure 11–2).
     (c) Push with leg and roll into side-lying position. Caregiver may place a hand on the pelvis and the shoulders if child requires help.
  4. coming from supine to sitting
     (a) Generally, the child will roll to a side-lying position first and prop on the elbow with the strongest arm downhill.

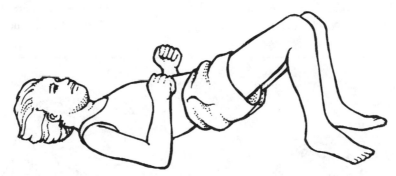

Figure 11–1 Child Bridging up To Move up or down a Bed. *Source:* Copyright © 1996, Mark L. Batshaw, M.D.

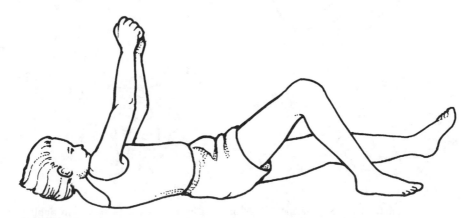

Figure 11–2 Position before Rolling for Child with Some Active Lower Extremity Control. *Source:* Copyright © 1996, Mark L. Batshaw, M.D.

(b) The legs are gradually lowered off the bed. The stronger limb may be hooked under a weaker one to achieve this (Figure 11–3).

(c) The upper extremity then pushes into extension until the child achieves sitting (Figure 11–4).

(d) Balance in sitting should be carefully guarded unless equilibrium reactions are intact.

- Transfers
  1. stand-pivot-sit transfer
     (a) If possible, park the wheelchair at a right angle to the transfer object so that only a quarter turn is required.
     (b) It will be easiest to lead with the stronger side.
     (c) Remove or swing away the footrests and abductor pommel, if used.

(d) Shift the child forward so he or she is sitting on the front of the wheelchair.

(e) Position the child's feet apart, with knees flexed, feet slightly behind knees. Lean child forward so nose is over toes (Figure 11–5).

(f) Child may assist by pushing up to standing, using hands on wheelchair armrest (Figure 11–6). Alternatively, the child may feel more secure by encircling arms around caregiver's trunk, or resting them on shoulders (Figure 11–7).

(g) Caregiver stands in front of child, placing one foot between child's feet and the other outside. By grasping the belt at the waist, caregiver helps child to standing. If

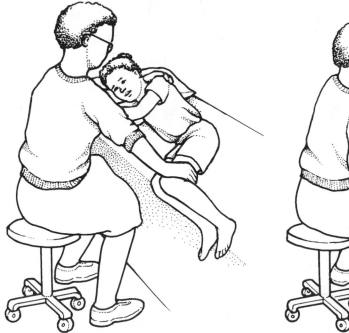

Figure 11–3 Transfer from Supine to Sitting for Child with Some Active Lower Extremity Control: Lowering Legs off Bed. *Source:* Copyright © 1996, Mark L. Batshaw, M.D.

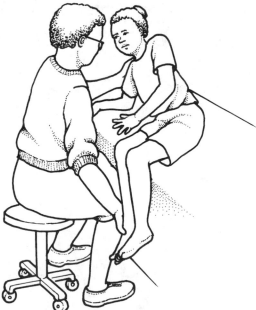

Figure 11–4 Transfer from Supine to Sitting for Child with Some Active Lower Extremity Control: Pushing Upper Extremity into Extension. *Source:* Copyright © 1996, Mark L. Batshaw, M.D.

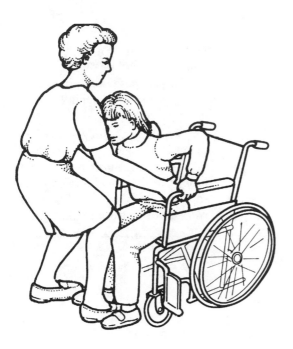

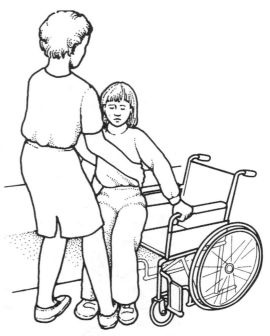

Figure 11–5 Transfer from Sitting to Standing for Child with Some Active Lower Extremity Control: Feet Apart, Leaning Forward. *Source:* Copyright © 1996, Mark L. Batshaw, M.D.

Figure 11–6 Transfer from Sitting to Standing for Child with Some Active Lower Extremity Control: Child Assists by Pushing Against Wheelchair Armrest. *Source:* Copyright © 1996, Mark L. Batshaw, M.D.

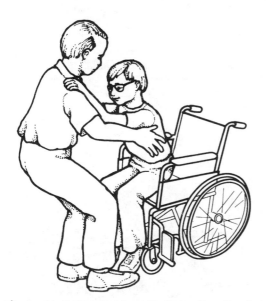

Figure 11–7 Transfer from Sitting to Standing for Child with Some Active Lower Extremity Control: Child Rests Hands on Caregiver's Shoulders. *Source:* Copyright © 1996, Mark L. Batshaw, M.D.

there is no belt, caregiver grasps and lifts from the buttocks. Caregiver's knees may be used against child's knees if weakness causes buckling.

(h) Pivot a quarter turn.

(i) Tell child to bend at hips and reach for transfer surface.

(j) While bending knees, slowly lower child to sitting.

TRANSFER METHODS FOR CHILDREN WITH BILATERAL LOWER EXTREMITY IMPAIRMENT

Children with bilateral lower extremity impairment must have strong upper extremities in order to maneuver. Flexibility of the hamstrings, which allows for a long-sitting posture, will be advantageous for bed mobility and ADLs.

- Bed mobility
  1. supine to sitting
     (a) From supine, push onto rear elbow prop (Figure 11–8).
     (b) Shift weight diagonally forward, extending one arm at a time to achieve long sitting (Figures 11–9 and 11–10). Alternatively, child may use a trapeze bar over the bed if he or she is unable to move independently from supine to sitting.

2. rolling
   (a) From supine, child will come to sitting as described above.
   (b) The legs are positioned prior to the roll by crossing the uphill leg over the opposite one.
   (c) The child with strong upper extremities and good sitting balance may rotate the upper body into a prone push-up and then lower to supine (Figure 11–11). The child with greater impairment may grasp

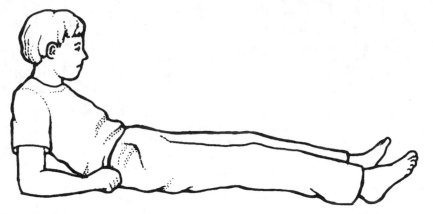

Figure 11–8 Supine to Sitting Transfer for Child with Bilateral Lower Extremity Impairment: Elbow Prop. *Source:* Copyright © 1996, Mark L. Batshaw, M.D.

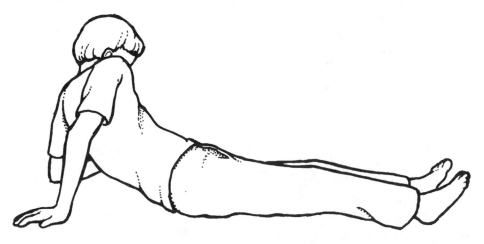

Figure 11–9 Supine to Sitting Transfer for Child with Bilateral Lower Extremity Impairment: Shifting Weight Diagonally Forward with Arm Extension. *Source:* Copyright © 1996, Mark L. Batshaw, M.D.

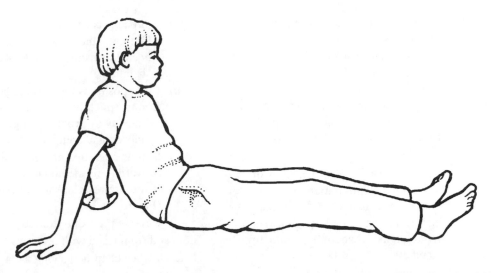

Figure 11–10 Supine to Sitting Transfer for Child with Bilateral Lower Extremity Impairment: Final Sitting Position. *Source:* Copyright © 1996, Mark L. Batshaw, M.D.

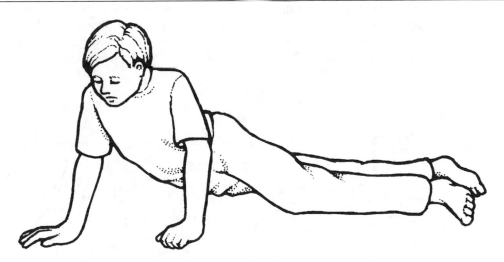

Figure 11–11 Rolling, for Child with Bilateral Lower Extremity Impairment: Upper Body Rotation to Push-up Position. *Source:* Copyright © 1996, Mark L. Batshaw, M.D.

the side of the mattress or railing and pull to complete a roll to side-lying position.

3. moving up or down in bed
   (a) Complete supine-to-sit maneuver, then reposition in bed by doing sitting push-up.

- Sliding transfers
  1. sideways without sliding board
     (a) Position wheelchair at a right angle to bed or other transfer surface.
     (b) Lock brakes. Remove armrest and hang on back push handle of chair.

(c) Child may either transfer in long sit or short sit. In long sit, legs are transferred to bed first. On return, leave them on bed until last.

(d) Child does sitting push-ups off seat frame (wheel or armrest sometimes used) until buttocks are safely positioned on next object (Figure 11–12).

(e) Caregiver can lift from a position of kneeling behind patient on bed. However, if balance is not good, caregiver may need to guard in front or ask a second person to stand by.

2. sideways with sliding board: same as sideways without sliding board, except child positions a smoothly sanded transfer board between the two surfaces to cover any gap (Figure 11–13). This may be helpful if there is a difference in height of the two objects.

3. forward/backward transfers
   (a) Child may find it easier to park the wheelchair facing the side of a bed or bathtub.
   (b) Child positions the legs on the surface to which he or she is moving, swings away front riggings, pulls up closer, and then locks chair.
   (c) Sitting push-ups are done sliding forward. This method must be used if the armrests are not removable (Figure 11–14).
   (d) Reverse procedure for return.

- Sit to and from stand with orthotics
  1. Lock wheelchair and swing away front riggings.
  2. Shift hips to front of chair, heels resting on the floor. May need to lock knee joint of one or both legs of hip-knee-ankle-foot orthosis (HKAFOs).
  3. Turn upper body halfway toward prone, and push up off armrests so that child

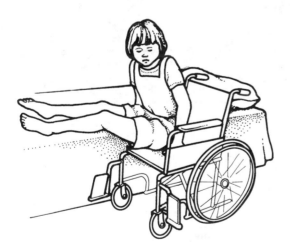

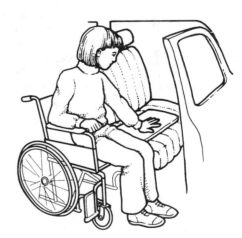

Figure 11–12 Sideways Sliding Transfer without Sliding Board. *Source:* Copyright © 1996, Mark L. Batshaw, M.D.

Figure 11–13 Sideways Sliding Transfer with Sliding Board. *Source:* Copyright © 1996, Mark L. Batshaw, M.D.

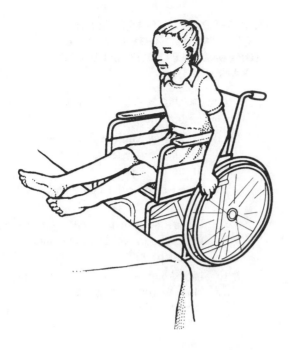

Figure 11–14 Forward/Backward Sliding Transfer. *Source:* Copyright © 1996, Mark L. Batshaw, M.D.

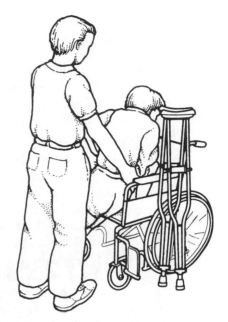

Figure 11–15 Transfer from Sit to Stand with Orthotics: Shifting Hips to Front of Chair, Turning Upper Body Halfway toward Prone. *Source:* Copyright © 1996, Mark L. Batshaw, M.D.

stands facing chair (Figures 11–15 and 11–16).

4. Hyperextend hips and lock if indicated.

5. Assistive device for walking should be available close by, such as back of wheelchair.

- Floor transfer
  1. getting down to the floor
     (a) Lock wheelchair. Flip up footrests, but do not swing them away.

     (b) Shift weight to front edge of chair.

     (c) Position legs so that knees are extended.

     (d) Grasping either seat frame or front rigging, gently lower self to floor (Figure 11–17).

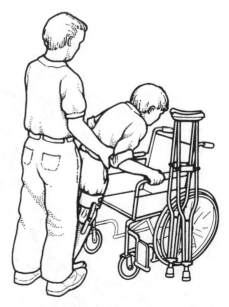

Figure 11–16 Transfer from Sit to Stand with Orthotics: Pushing off Armrests. *Source:* Copyright © 1996, Mark L. Batshaw, M.D.

(e) Training can be done on graduated stools until the full distance can be safely negotiated.

(f) If hamstring tightness precludes this position, some children can learn to move forward onto quadruped by reaching for the floor.

2. getting from the floor to the chair

(a) The child starts by long-sitting directly in front of the chair.

(b) If the child is tall enough to flex the elbows and position the hands on the seat, he or she can do sitting push-up into the chair.

(c) Alternatively, the child may approach the chair forwards and pull up to a kneeling position (Figure 11–18). Using the upper extremities, he or she drags hips into the chair, using a side-position strategy, and then turns the body to reposition into sitting (Figure 11–19).

TRANSFER METHODS FOR CHILDREN WITH TOTAL BODY INVOLVEMENT (DEPENDENT ON OTHERS FOR TRANSFER)

- Lifting transfers

1. One-person lift

(a) Lock wheelchair and remove armrest on the side from which you are lifting.

(b) Stand beside the chair and bend your knees.

(c) Place one arm under the child's knees and the other arm behind the child's back.

(d) Lift, keeping the child's body as close to you as possible. Complete the lift before turning (Figure 11–20).

2. Two-person lift

(a) Lock wheelchair parallel to the surface to which you are transferring.

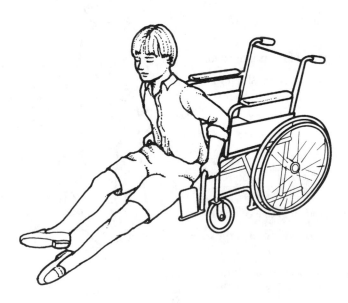

Figure 11–17 Transfer from Chair to Floor. *Source:* Copyright © 1996, Mark L. Batshaw, M.D.

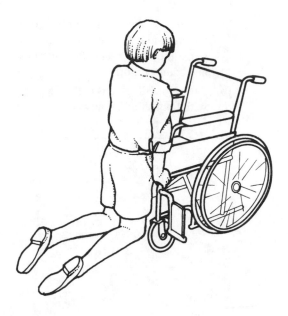

Figure 11–18 Transfer from Floor to Chair, Kneeling Approach. *Source:* Copyright © 1996, Mark L. Batshaw, M.D.

(b) Remove the footrests, and the armrest on one side.

(c) The taller caregiver stands at the head, and leads the transfer by verbal command (e.g., "Are you ready? One, two, three, lift").

(d) The child crosses arms on the chest, and the caregiver at the head reaches under the axillae and grasps the forearms.

(e) The second caregiver stands at the feet and, by bending at the hips, encircles the knees.

(f) The lifters assume a broad base of support and may place one knee on the surface to which the child is transferring, if it is low. Both per-

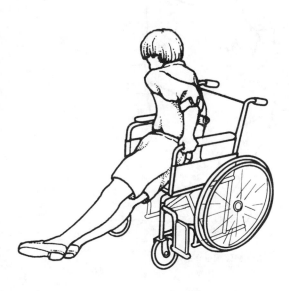

Figure 11–19 Transfer from Floor to Chair, Dragging Hips into Chair, Using Upper Extremities. *Source:* Copyright © 1996, Mark L. Batshaw, M.D.

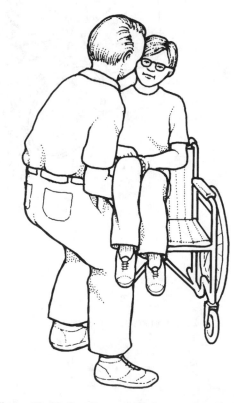

Figure 11–20 One-Person Lift. *Source:* Copyright © 1996, Mark L. Batshaw, M.D.

sons lift together, being sure to clear the wheel (Figure 11–21).

3. mechanical lift

(a) Position the sling under the child according to the manufacturer's directions. If the child is in bed, roll the child to side-lying position, and place the sling under the buttocks and trunk (Figure 11–22).

(b) Attach the lift chains to the support, with hooks facing outward.

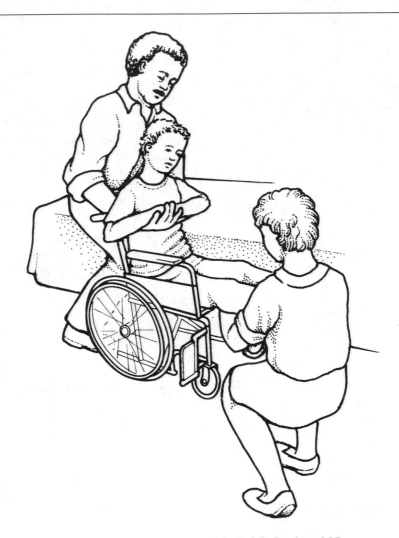

Figure 11–21 Two-Person Lift. *Source:* Copyright © 1996, Mark L. Batshaw, M.D.

(c) Position the wheelchair parallel to the bed, remove the armrest, and lock the brakes.

(d) Crank up the lift to clear the bed, and check the hooks again for security (Figure 11–23).

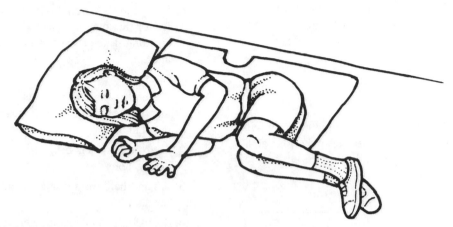

Figure 11–22 Initial Position for Mechanical Lift. *Source:* Copyright © 1996, Mark L. Batshaw, M.D.

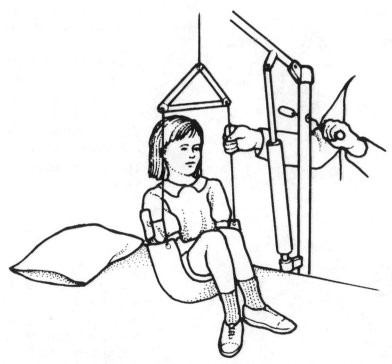

Figure 11–23 Lifting Child out of Bed by Mechanical Lift. *Source:* Copyright © 1996, Mark L. Batshaw, M.D.

(e) Move the lift so that the child is centered on the wheelchair. Lower into position, and detach the hooks (Figure 11–24).

(f) Reposition the child so hips are well back in the chair, and secure the seatbelt and other restraints.

SPECIAL TRANSFERS

• Toilet

1. Grab bars or a commode or potty with armrests and a seatbelt may offer additional support, allowing the child to relax and void.

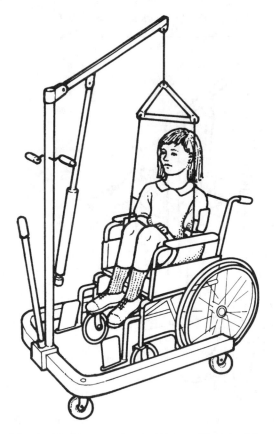

Figure 11–24 Lowering Child into Chair by Mechanical Lift. *Source:* Copyright © 1996, Mark L. Batshaw, M.D.

2. A stool may be useful to support the feet.

3. Transfer may be stand-pivot-sit or side transfer.

4. Pants can be lowered prior to the transfer, or this may be done while child is standing if he or she has sufficient balance.

• Bathtub

1. Generally one chair is outside the tub, and a second bath seat or bench is located in the tub.

2. Grab bars and a nonskid mat are helpful safety items.

3. A hand-held shower attachment will be needed.

4. Transfer methods include either a sideways or a forward slide.

5. The tub should be emptied and the child partially dried before transfer back to the outside chair, which is draped with a towel.

6. Hydraulic lifts are also available for assisting to lower and raise heavier children.

• Car

1. The safest location for a car seat is the middle of the back seat for a small child.

2. The front passenger seat is the easiest location for independent or assisted transfers.

3. The child may transfer sideways using a sliding board or may stand-pivot-sit. The front seat of the car should be moved as far back as possible and the seat back slightly reclined to allow maximum room to maneuver.

4. Refer to the section "Car Seat Safety" later in this chapter for further information on proper restraint. Full instruction should be given to the family about proper use of car seats as well as proper methods of folding and transporting the child's wheelchair.

SUGGESTED READINGS

Haley, S.M., et al. 1992. *Pediatric evaluation of disability inventory (PEDI) manual.* Boston: New England Medical Center Hospitals, Inc.

Jaeger, D.L. 1989. *Transferring and lifting children and adolescents: Home instruction sheets.* Tucson, Ariz.: Therapy Skill Builders.

Palmer, M.L., and J.E. Toms. 1986. *Manual for functional training.* Philadelphia: F.A. Davis Co.

State University of New York. 1993. *Guide for the Uniform Data Set for medical rehabilitation for children (WeeFIM).* Buffalo, N.Y.: Uniform Data System for Medical Rehabilitation, UB Foundation Activities, Inc.

ADAPTIVE POSITIONING DEVICES

Lesley Austin Geyer

Purpose: to discuss the appropriate selection and use of adaptive positioning devices for children with physical and neurological impairment affecting motor control.

An adaptive positioning device helps the child who lacks independent postural control by providing the external stability needed to maintain a position. A properly selected and fitted device

- promotes skeletal alignment
- helps to inhibit the effects of primitive reflexes
- improves the quality of muscle tone
- encourages normal movement and facilitates the ability to move normally and en-

gage in developmentally appropriate functional activity

- provides developmentally appropriate positioning

MAJOR CATEGORIES OF ADAPTIVE POSITIONING DEVICES

Sidelyers are firm devices that help the child maintain a position of lying on one side. These are beneficial for children who have muscle tone abnormalities and require some periods of floor or bed positioning (Figure 11–25).

Prone wedges are foam wedges that support the child and promote upper extremity weight

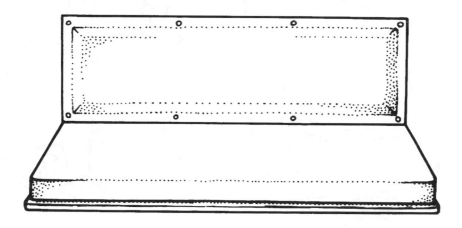

Figure 11–25 Sidelyer. *Source:* Copyright © 1996, Mark L. Batshaw, M.D.

SELECTION OF DEVICES

Table 11–2 compares positioning devices and gives guidelines for their use.

MATERIALS FOR FABRICATION OF CUSTOM DEVICES

Table 11–3 compares materials for fabrication of devices.

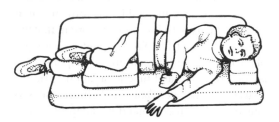

Figure 11–30 Child in Sidelyer. *Source:* Copyright © 1996, Mark L. Batshaw, M.D.

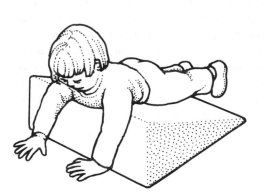

Figure 11–31 Child on Prone Wedge. *Source:* Copyright © 1996, Mark L. Batshaw, M.D.

Figure 11–32 Child in Corner Seat, Side View. *Source:* Copyright © 1996, Mark L. Batshaw, M.D.

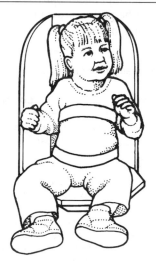

Figure 11–33 Child in Corner Seat with Three-Section Back. *Source:* Copyright © 1996, Mark L. Batshaw, M.D.

Table 11–2 Comparison of Positioning Devices

Illustration	Purpose	Special Contraindications	Minimum Measurements	Guidelines for Use
Sidelyer (Figure 11–30)	Improves balance between flexor and extensor muscle tone Encourages regard of hands and midline hand function Promotes extremity movement in a gravity-eliminated plane, allowing the child with muscle weakness to move independently	Subluxation of shoulder or hip joints, causing poor tolerance for bearing weight on the side of the body Poor circulation in the extremities on the weight-bearing side of the body	*Length* should be at least child's height plus 4″ *Height/Width:* select the larger of (1) largest body width (usually across the hips or shoulders) plus 3″, or (2) distance from behind the buttocks to the front of the knee when the hip is flexed to 90°, plus 4″. Additional length and height/width may be added to accommodate growth	Alternate lying on right and left sides of the body Pillow placed under the head promotes midline alignment and helps to relieve pressure on the lower arm Straps positioned snugly across the pelvis and chest help to maintain sidelying in the device and prevent arching or hyperextension
Prone wedge (Figure 11–31)	Promotes development of head control by facilitating head righting Reduces flexor posturing and encourages extension Promotes upper extremity weight bearing (on palms or on forearms, depending on height of wedge)	Insufficient strength in neck muscles to right head Insufficient scapular stability to prevent excessive scapular adduction during prone propping ≥90° of shoulder flexion Less than full or almost full hip extension	*Height† for forearm propping:* distance from the axilla to the elbow, minus 1/2″ *Height for propping on palms with elbows extended:* distance from the axilla to the palm (with full wrist extension) minus 1/2″ *Width:* distance from shoulder to shoulder, plus at least 4″ *Length* of the wedge should be the same as the distance from the axillae to the hips plus a few inches Additional length may be added to accommodate growth	The child who needs maximum trunk support is positioned so that the high end of the wedge is directly under the axillae. The child with better upper trunk control can be positioned so that the edge of the wedge is lower on the chest

continues

Table 11–2 Continued

Illustration	Purpose	Special Contraindications	Minimum Measurements	Guidelines for Use
Corner seat (Figures 11–32 and 11–33)	Provides upright positioning Promotes alert state Supports trunk in extension Promotes shoulder protraction and encourages hand use Promotes development of head and trunk control	Insufficient hip flexion (need at least 90°) to allow sitting with pelvis in neutral position Insufficient head control or sitting balance to tolerate full upright position Constructing seat with additional height, 3-section back, or reclining angle may compensate for limited head/trunk control	*Height:* distance from the floor to top of the shoulder/head (depending on need for head support) *Depth:* should be sufficiently large to support the lower extremities while the child is seated in a circle-sit position. *Width of back piece* (3-section back): distance between the medial border of one scapula to the medial border of the other scapula *Width of winged side pieces:* no less than the distance from the back of the seat to the elbow when the shoulder is held in 90° of flexion. Additional height, depth and width of winged sidepieces may be added to accommodate growth.	A strap is provided to go across the pelvis The child with poor trunk control may benefit from a chest harness strap to support the trunk
Adapted seat and seat insert (Figures 11–34 and 11–35)	Provides additional support for the child during upright positioning Promotes an alert state Provides proximal support needed to use arms functionally Promotes development of head and trunk control	Intolerance to upright positioning	See next section, "Wheelchair Selection and Maintenance," subsection "Measuring for a Wheelchair," sub-subsection "Sitting Measurements"	Head and trunk supports, shoulder protractors, and hip abductor or adductor pieces are added as needed A pelvic strap is provided; chest harness straps are added as needed

continues

Illustration	Purpose	Special Contraindications	Minimum Measurements	Guidelines for Use
Standing devices: prone, supine, and upright (Figures 11–36, 11–37, and 11–38)	Provides opportunity for lower extremity weight bearing Limits development of lower extremity flexion contractures Promotes biomechanical alignment of the femoral head in the acetabulum to foster proper hip joint formation Allows the child to interact with the environment from an upright position Promotes upper extremity movement Facilitates development of head and trunk control	Orthopedic conditions precluding weight bearing with the lower extremities Evidence of circulatory impairment to the lower extremities during positioning in the device Uncontrolled movement or rocking when in device	*Height* varies as needed to provide sufficient trunk support to allow an upright position. In prone and upright standing, a child with good trunk control will need less height than a child with less trunk control. In supine standing, full support to the top of the head is required *Width:* no less than the widest part of the trunk to be supported, plus at least 6″	Provide a tray for upper extremity support Feet should be strapped or blocked in place A strap or hip stabilizer block providing pressure across the buttocks maintains hip extension in prone standing In supine and upright standing, straps are placed across the front of the knees to maintain knee extension An additional strap around the midtrunk and/or lateral trunk support blocks assists in maintaining an upright trunk A hip abductor piece helps maintain neutral hip alignment for the child who tends to adduct the hips The angle of incline is adjusted according to the child's postural control and tolerance for upright positioning; the child often starts with the device in 45–60° of incline and gradually progresses to a more vertical position The child with a persistent positive support reaction causing an increase in spasticity in the lower extremities may need to be supported in some ankle dorsiflexion. The child with this problem should start in a more horizontal position and gradually move to a more inclined position

continues

Table 11-2 Continued

Illustration	Purpose	Special Contraindications	Minimum Measurements	Guidelines for Use
Trays (Figure 11–39)	Promotes upper extremity movement by minimizing the effects of gravity Provides play, feeding, or work surface Promotes forearm weight bearing (if positioned at elbow level) Can be inclined to promote upper trunk and neck extension for children with excess spinal flexion or weak spinal extensors	Head banging on tray Excessive banging or rubbing of the upper extremities on the tray	*Height* to support elbows and forearms with hands are at midline, usually 1 to 2″ below flexed elbow *Width* of the outer edge of the surface to be supporting the tray. If the tray is to be used on a wheelchair, ensure that the tray will fit through doorways *Depth* distance from the trunk to the tips of the fingers with the elbows fully extended	Fit close to the trunk so that materials placed on the tray do not fall between the tray and the body The tray should be securely attached to the device with which it is being used

Table 11–3 Comparison of Materials for Fabrication of Devices

Material	Tools and Supplies	Advantages	Disadvantages
Wood (usually plywood or pine)	Carpentry tools; cover with vinyl, paint, or varnish	Inexpensive; durable, adjustable (with proper tools and skill); can be easily obtained from a lumberyard	Heavy; requires moderate skill to cut/bond; can be messy; splinters unless well finished; not waterproof unless sealed; fasteners needed for bonding
Triple-thickness corrugated cardboard (1/2 to 3/4″ thick)	Cut with a saw or sharp knife; bond with dowels, glue; can use nuts, bolts, washers to attach adaptations; cover with paint (tape edges), vinyl, or contact paper	Lightweight; inexpensive; fast and easy to work with; can build in adjustability; can be easily obtained from a cardboard manufacturer	Not waterproof unless covered; limited durability; fasteners are needed to bond
Closed-cell construction foam (also known as Adaptafoam, Constructa Foam, Etha Foam)	Cut with knife or saw; bond with heat gun or glue; can cover with vinyl dip or contact paper	Fast, easy to work with and bond; relatively inexpensive; waterproof; can be easily cleaned; can be sculpted; very durable; lightweight; comes in varying densities and widths	Vinyl dip is messy and toxic (need ventilation); limited adjustability
Acrylic (Plexiglass TM)/Polycarbonate (Lexan TM)/Polyethylene (high-temperature plastics)	Cut with heavy carpentry tools; bond with carpentry materials or strong glue	Nice, finished appearance; extremely durable; waterproof; can be easily cleaned; skilled person can build in adjustability; can be easily obtained from hardware store or lumberyard	Heavy; expensive; heavy tools and much skill required for cutting; acrylics and polycarbonates tend to crack, and surfaces scratch and cloud easily

WHEELCHAIR SELECTION AND MAINTENANCE

Johanna E. Deitz-Curry

Purpose: to review the principles for selection, fitting, and maintenance of commercially available wheelchairs and other adapted seating or mobility systems that may be used by children with developmental disabilities.

A wheelchair that is properly fitted, carefully selected with respect to both the child's and family's needs, and functional within the child's personal environment can be an important component in the rehabilitation of a child with mobility limitations. Wheelchairs come in many shapes and sizes to meet the varied needs of users. The sophistication of current technology allows almost anyone to have a system individualized to meet his or her personal needs. However, it is sometimes difficult to secure adequate funding for costly systems. In addition, some users must live or function in environmental settings that allow limited use of certain mobility devices.

GENERAL PRINCIPLES FOR SELECTION OF SEATING SYSTEMS

A wheelchair or adaptive seating system can serve a multitude of purposes, depending on the individual characteristics of the child and his or her environment. A person in the seated position needs to be stable and secure to fulfill optimal functional potential. Most functional activities done in the seated position involve the use of the head (including eyes, ears, mouth, and internal structures) and/or the upper extremities (Bergen et al. 1990). Functional objectives for selection of a seating system may include any or all of the following:

- to provide a stable, secure base of support allowing for sitting with adequate postural support
- to increase the child's potential for participation in educational experiences

- to decrease the influence of abnormal muscle tone, pathologic reflexes, and poor motor control
- to prevent or minimize contractures and deformities
- to provide a means of mobility that affords the child a greater degree of social independence and environmental exploration
- to promote safe and easy access to cars, home, school, etc.
- to promote the progression of developmental skills
- to provide a greater awareness of body and orientation in space
- to promote health, hygiene, and safety
- to minimize caregiver stress

Wheelchairs also pose some potential limitations for users. Since a wheelchair is a static device, it cannot change as the client grows or has different needs. Alterations to size or function of an existing wheelchair require additional cost and "downtime" for the user. Further, wheelchairs have limiting social influences. A person sitting in a wheelchair is not at eye level for interaction or conversation with a person who is standing. And despite widespread efforts to promote public accessibility for people with disabilities, many architectural barriers continue to exist for wheelchair users. Transportation systems accommodating wheelchairs, particularly power wheelchairs, are limited. These are factors that need to be taken into consideration before embarking on the purchase of a wheelchair. Given the range of seating options that exist, therapists are challenged to identify the "best" system for a given child. Considerations that must assume high priority include

- identifying a system that provides the greatest level of functional independence and improves the user's quality of life

- providing a system that can be used in multiple contexts as needed by the user and family (e.g., for positioning, independent mobility, transportation)
- determining the minimal level of assistance needed and providing only the support that is needed
- striving to create a balance between aesthetic and functional considerations

THE IMPORTANCE OF TEAM COLLABORATION

Provision of an appropriate seating device for the child with a disability is a challenge that often surpasses the expertise of any one professional discipline. Table 11–4 provides an overview of the roles played by various professionals who influence the child who needs a wheelchair.

THE ASSESSMENT PROCESS

The list below provides a summary of areas that should be included in the initial assessment for seating, prior to taking specific measurements of the child:

- Neurodevelopmental
  1. Do abnormalities in muscle tone exist?
  2. Do primitive/pathologic reflexes compromise movement?
  3. Is the neurologic condition resolving, static, or progressive?
  4. What is the level of mastery of gross motor skills?
  5. What is the level of use of upper extremities?
  6. How does child communicate (receptive /expressive)?
  7. How does child interact socially?
  8. Are there behavioral concerns (impulsiveness, tantrums, combativeness, etc.)?
- Cognitive
  1. Does child understand/follow simple/ complex commands?
  2. Does child comprehend directions (right, left, up, down)?
  3. Is child aware of and interested in the environment?
  4. Can child exhibit self-control? Attend to safety issues?
- Musculoskeletal
  1. Are there limitations in range of motion (especially pelvis, hips, knees)?

Table 11–4 Team Approaches to Seating Decisions

Team Member	Role
Family and child	Provides input about the daily living situations in which the child will use the wheelchair
Physical/occupational therapist	Uses expertise in applied biomechanics, kinesiology, anatomy, and neuromuscular control to assess (1) the functional abilities of the child, (2) the positions that maximize function, and (3) the degree of support needed to facilitate postural alignment
Vendor	Provides information about the variety of products available to meet seating goals and the proper structural relationships of components
Orthopedist	Facilitates maximal function and comfort for the child in sitting through bracing or surgical management of contractures and deformities
Social worker	Advocates for the family to secure necessary funding to purchase and maintain the system
Pediatrician	Provides input as to the positional needs of the child in relation to feeding and other health concerns
Speech therapist	Addresses the impact of communication impairment on use of the system, particularly if there is a need for an augmentative communication system

2. What is the quality of strength and coordination?

3. Are the hips subluxed or dislocated?

4. Are there contractures or deformities (scoliosis/kyphosis, pelvic obliquity and/or rotation, knee flexion contractures, planovalgus feet)?

5. Are there asymmetries, leg-length discrepancies?

6. Does the child use braces or prosthetics?

- Skin integrity
  1. Are there any bony prominences that are particularly subject to pressure?
  2. Does the child bruise easily?
  3. Is there a history of skin breakdown or decubiti?

- Cardiopulmonary
  1. What is the level of energy/endurance?
  2. Are there any cardiac precautions?
  3. Can child maintain an upright posture without a change in blood pressure?
  4. What is the circulatory status (especially of the dependent lower extremities)?
  5. Does the child need breathing support?

- Sensory
  1. Does child have visual impairment (acuity or perception)?
  2. Are there any problems with hearing?
  3. Is sensation intact? If not, what is the distribution of the loss? How might it interfere with seating?
  4. Does the child have position sense, righting reactions?

- Family
  1. Does the child/family accept the need for a wheelchair? Do they accept its appearance?
  2. What are their expectations with regard to wheelchair use?
  3. Are there cultural or ethnic variables that need to be addressed?

4. What other concerns are raised by family (weight, size, ease of use, etc.)?

- Architectural/environmental
  1. Is the dwelling accessible for a wheelchair?
  2. Can the family make architectural modifications if needed to accommodate a particular wheelchair?
  3. Can the family's primary means of transportation accommodate a wheelchair?
  4. Is the school accessible? Will any adaptations need to be made in the classroom setting?
  5. Will the child be able to use the wheelchair for those community, social, or recreational activities that are important to the family?

- Financial
  1. What is the cost of the wheelchair? How does the family intend to pay?
  2. How much will medical insurance agree to pay? What are other potential sources of funding?
  3. What will it cost to maintain the chair?
  4. How long do you anticipate the child will be able to use the system before replacement/modification is needed?
  5. What are the hidden costs (tie-down system, home modifications, ramps, lifts, etc.)?

MEASURING FOR A WHEELCHAIR

Supine Measurements

Range-of-motion measurements taken from supine are needed for hip flexion and extension, hip abduction and adduction, knee flexion and extension, and popliteal angles. Limitations in these measurements due to spasticity, contractures, or skeletal deformities will affect the proper prescription for the seating system. Pelvic mobility also needs to be assessed in all three planes: anterior and posterior tilt, lateral tilt, and rotation.

Sitting Measurements

Sitting measurements, summarized in Table 11–5, are necessary for determining the proper dimensions of the wheelchair and placement of postural supports, if necessary. Measure the child while sitting on a firm surface, such as a treatment table or a straight-backed chair, with

- hips and knees flexed at 90 degrees
- pelvis in neutral position, corrected for tilt, obliquity, and rotation
- back extended, corrected for scoliosis and kyphosis
- head centered directly over the pelvis

- feet firmly planted on a supporting surface directly below the knees (Figure 11–40)

TYPES OF BASES FOR WHEELCHAIRS AND OTHER MOBILITY SYSTEMS

Transporter Chairs

Indications for Use

Because transporter chairs require an attendant to push the chair, equal consideration must be given to the caregiver's needs and to the positioning and seating needs of the child. Transporter chairs are appropriate for children who cannot access the wheels for independent mobil-

Table 11–5 Guidelines for Seating Measurements

Measurement	Technique	Special Considerations
Seat width	With braces on, the greater of width across hips or width across thighs plus 2 to 4″ to allow for growth	For lateral thigh guards on the seat, add 3″ For abduction pommel or medial thigh supports, add 3″
Seat depth (see Figure 11–40)	Measure from rear of buttocks to inside bend of each knee (in case of leg-length discrepancy), and subtract 1 to 1 1/2″	If using adjustable-depth hardware, add the amount of available adjustment to total depth (e.g., if child measures 12″, should be sitting at depth of 11″, and has 2″ of growth, order hardware with 13″ depth)
Back height (see Figure 11–40)	Measure from underside of buttocks to (1) axillae, (2) top of shoulders, and (3) top of head on both sides	Height should be to axillae for child who will self-propel chair and does not require anterior chest support Height should be to top of shoulders if child will require anterior chest support and headrest If using seat cushion, add 1/2 the thickness of the cushion to the measurement for height
Chest width	Measure across chest 1″ below axillae	Chest width is the minimal distance needed between lateral trunk supports
Chest depth	Measure the depth of chest at 1″ below axillae	Chest depth is the minimal length needed for lateral trunk support pads (if using planar pads) If using curved or contoured lateral trunk support pads, add at least 1″ to depth measurement
Footrest height (see Figure 11–40)	With the child wearing shoes and braces (if indicated), measure from the bottom of the thigh to the bottom of the heel with ankle at 90 degrees	If using seat cushion, subtract 1/2 the thickness of the cushion The footrest must clear at least 2″ above the floor surface If footrest angle is 90 degrees, the footrest must clear the height of the front caster

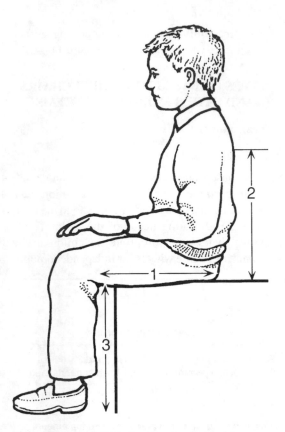

Figure 11–40 Child in Position for Sitting Measurements for Wheelchair: (1) Seat Depth, (2) Back Height, and (3) Footrest Height. *Source:* Copyright © 1996, Mark L. Batshaw, M.D.

ity or who lack the cognitive potential for maneuvering a power wheelchair. Generally, transporter chairs are for the very young (12 mo. to 3 yr.) child or the child with severe impairment who requires some type of adaptive positioning and transportation not available with commercial strollers.

Types

There are three general types of transporter chairs: (1) sling seat and back, (2) sturdy base with modular components, and (3) adaptive seating system on a manual wheelchair base.

Transporter chairs with *sling seats and backs* look and fold like umbrella strollers. These chairs are generally the least costly, ranging

from $500 up to and exceeding $1,200 depending upon the options chosen to supplement the base chair. These chairs offer no room for growth, cannot be used in vehicles, and do not provide support for postural abnormalities. Examples of this type of transporter chair include the Convaid Cruiser, Pogon buggy, and Mac-Claren stroller (Figure 11–41).

Another type of transporter chair has a *sturdy base and modular seating components*. These chairs resemble child strollers and may be a useful "first step" for parents who are not ready to accept the fact that their child needs a wheelchair with positioning components. Some models also offer systems for securing the chair in a vehicle so the chair can be easily transported. Others allow the modular seating system to be removed from the base for use as a car seat with the proper restraint system. Each state has its

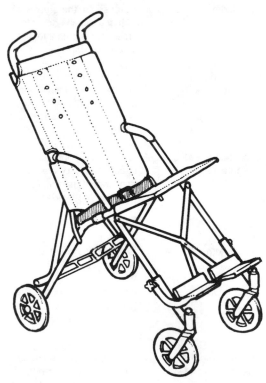

Figure 11–41 Transporter Chair with Sling Seat and Back. *Source:* Copyright © 1996, Mark L. Batshaw, M.D.

own regulations concerning what is considered acceptable as safe transport, and these should be consulted before a choice of system is made. These chairs are heavier than the folding chairs mentioned above. They often require some type of disassembly for transport. Their cost can be comparable to that of a manual wheelchair, ranging from $900 to $2,000 and more, depending on the system chosen and the various options added to the base chair. Examples of stroller-type transporter chairs are the Snug Seat, Kid Kart, Wizard, Safety Travel Chair, and Joey chair (Figure 11–42).

A third type of transporter chair is an *adaptive seating system in a manual wheelchair base*. These chairs usually have smaller wheels (usually 12 inches in diameter) than the regular manual wheelchair. They can be transported in a van or bus that has a tie-down unit for regular wheelchairs. The smaller wheels make the chair look more like a stroller than a wheelchair. The

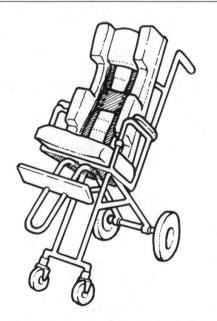

Figure 11–42 Transporter Chair with Sturdy Base and Modular Seating Components. *Source:* From *Children with Disabilities*, 3rd ed., (p. 458), by M.L. Batshaw and Y.M. Perret, Paul H. Brookes Publishing Co. Copyright © 1992 by Mark L. Batshaw. Reprinted with permission.

advantage of this type of chair is the potential for adjustments for growth using a grow kit to extend or widen the wheelchair frame. This chair can also be converted to large rear wheels if the child develops the potential for independent propulsion. Third-party payors generally cover wheelchairs more readily and easily than strollers. The disadvantage of these chairs is the weight. Often they weigh as much as or more than the stroller-type transport chairs. The cost can equal or exceed that of the stroller-type chair. Disassembly is required for transport in a regular car, and a car seat is necessary if the child cannot use the wheelchair as a support for sitting in a moving vehicle. This type of chair has various seating options with components from a multitude of manufacturers: Scott Therapeutic inserts, Freedom Design, Kozy Kraft and Quickie Convention insert systems by Quickie designs, Avanti seating systems by Action/Invacare, and others.

Manual Wheelchairs

Indications for Use

Manual wheelchairs are indicated for children who have the potential to propel the wheelchair by maneuvering the rear wheels. Using a manual wheelchair does not necessarily imply that the child lacks the potential to become a functional ambulator. Wheelchairs offer mobility for the child who is not able to walk independently or for the child who can crawl but finds this to be unacceptable. Wheelchairs allow the child to be at a similar height as peers, to participate in social and recreational activities, and to develop social independence.

Manual wheelchairs are also indicated for those individuals who need specialized seating support systems. The frame provides a base for the seating support systems, as well as means of mobility and transportation by a caregiver. Manual wheelchairs have a greater potential for growth than do transporter chairs. However, they are generally heavier and often require some strength, skill, and ingenuity to disassemble. They can be transported in a bus or van with a tie-down system. Most chairs are either partially or fully funded by third-party payors.

Types

Manual wheelchairs usually consist of a metal frame, large rear wheels, small front wheels, sling seat and sling back, some type of footrest, and push handles. Several varieties of manual wheelchairs are on the market, classified by weight, user, or functional attributes.

Lightweight, high-strength, manual wheelchairs usually weigh from 18 to 45 pounds and are the most commonly used everyday wheelchairs for active users (Figure 11–43). Many options are available to meet the individual's needs and preferences. Examples of lightweight manual chairs for the pediatric population are the Quickie Rx by WheelRing, Invacare Action Junior, and XL Pacer by Rally XL.

Ultralight weight (sport) manual wheelchairs are fabricated from lightweight materials, such as aluminum, which render frame weight less than 18 pounds. These wheelchairs were primarily used for racing but are now being marketed

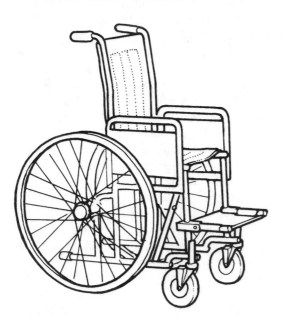

Figure 11–43 Lightweight Manual Wheelchair. *Source:* Copyright © 1996, Mark L. Batshaw, M.D.

for the everyday wheelchair user. On the whole, these chairs are more expensive than their lightweight counterparts. Ultralightweight manual wheelchairs require less energy to propel and are therefore ideal for the child who has good sitting balance but weakness or poor endurance in upper extremities. These chairs do not have many postural adaptation options available to them. Most have a fixed front end and limited footrest options. A majority of the ultralightweight chairs have a rigid frame and do not fold like conventional chairs. To disassemble for transport in a car, one removes the rear wheels and folds the back down onto the seat. The wheelchair frame is then shaped like a box for transport. Examples of ultralightweight manual wheelchairs for children are the Enduro Bantam, Action Rocket, and Quickie 2.

One-arm-drive manual wheelchairs are designed for individuals who have functional use of only one arm. Several propulsion designs are available. A double hand rim that has connections to both rear wheels is the conventional one-arm-drive system. Another variation is the pump system with a lever and ratchet. This is easier for the user to propel but more difficult for an attendant to use. One-arm-drive wheelchairs are generally not recommended for children who have cerebral palsy because the overflow of abnormal muscle tone to the unaffected extremity can deter proper control of the system.

Heavy-duty manual wheelchairs are usually manufactured from sturdy materials and weigh in excess of 40 pounds. They are rarely used with the pediatric population except when the user is exceptionally heavy or if the wheelchair will be subject to unusually heavy wear and tear, such as in an institutional setting. These wheelchairs require a significant force and energy to propel and are therefore less practical for everyday use by most users. An example of the heavy-duty wheelchair is the Vista by Everest and Jennings.

Tilt-in-Space Wheelchairs

Tilt-in-space wheelchairs have the ability to tilt back without changing the seat-to-back angle. These chairs are helpful for individuals who require a great deal of postural support, are incapable of weight shifts, have poor head control, or require management of muscle tone to inhibit extensor posturing. They are also useful for children who need to be tilted to manage feeding disorders. This option is available on lightweight wheelchair frames as well as on specialized strollers. It is also available on power wheelchairs with user controls to tilt the chair to any given angle. Examples of tilt-in-space wheelchairs are the Zippie TS from Quickie and the Invacare Action TS (Figure 11–44).

Power Wheelchairs

Indications for Use

Power mobility is indicated for children who lack the strength, control, or endurance to propel a manual wheelchair but have the cognitive ability to learn how to use the device safely. An example would be a child with spinal muscular atrophy who has severe muscle weakness along with intact cognitive abilities. In this case, a power chair is the only device that would allow for independent exploration of the environment needed to keep up with peers. Another example is a child who has sustained trauma or injury (closed head injury or spinal cord injury) or has lost independent mobility through a disease (Duchenne muscular dystrophy, Guillain–Barre, meningitis) and requires mobility to continue with daily living functions. A child who has the capability to propel a manual wheelchair but insufficient strength or endurance to use the chair functionally for daily living activities is also a candidate for power mobility. These children may also walk with assistive devices but this walking is classified as an exercise or household ambulation, and the child cannot functionally ambulate for distances. An example is a child with spastic diplegia cerebral palsy who can push the chair for short distances but is unable to use the chair independently for mobility in

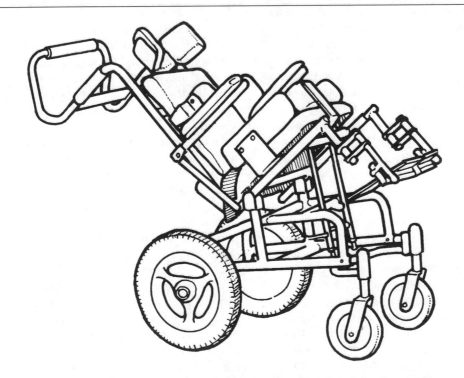

Figure 11–44 Tilt-in-Space Wheelchair. *Source:* Copyright © 1996, Mark L. Batshaw, M.D.

school, outdoors, or in recreational/social settings. At what age should power wheelchair mobility be considered? We know that two-year-old children without disabilities are able to run about, explore their environment, and interact with other children. The first two years of life are referred to as the sensorimotor period of development, and mobility provides the primary means by which the child can learn and explore, socialize, and develop independence and a healthy concept of self in relation to others. To promote overall development and not merely compensate for a neuromuscular disorder, power wheelchairs have been successfully used with children as early as two years of age. The keys to successful use are (1) relatively strong cognitive abilities and (2) motivation on the part of the child and family.

Characteristics

Power wheelchairs have either gel-cell or lead acid batteries that supply power to a motor. The power wheelchair comes in direct-drive or belt-driven systems. Batteries must be recharged on a regular basis. These chairs are quite heavy in order to accommodate the power mechanism and other adaptive devices that may be added to the wheelchair. The proliferation of technologic advances has presented the power wheelchair user with a greater selection of controls that can be easily accessed. The newer controls are capable of varied adjustments for various parameters such as speed, acceleration and deceleration, turning speed, and tremor dampening.

Controls: Proportional and Microswitch

There are two basic types of controls for power wheelchairs, proportional and microswitch. An example of a proportional control is a standard joystick mounted to the side of either armrest. The joystick, like the steering wheel and the gas pedal of a car, controls both the speed and the direction of movement and allows the wheelchair to move in proportion to the amount of force exerted on the joystick. The joystick can also be mounted at a different location, such as in the middle of the tray or at the

footrest, by a cable connection to the control box. The joystick can be positioned at the most functional location for the user. The microswitch type of control allows movement of the wheelchair to turn on or off, with no variations in speed at any particular setting. There are usually two or three settings with variations in speed for use in different environments: (1) high, for outdoor use; (2) low, for indoor use; and possibly (3) a third setting between high and low. There are various designs for switch control, such as four switches placed in a configuration with one switch for each direction (forward, backward, right, left) or a single switch to change the direction of the chair. A single-switch control system requires a high level of cognition and is generally used with the most severely physically involved individual who has very little motor control. Chapter 17, on assistive technology, describes other types of controls that might be adapted for use with a power wheelchair.

Designs

The standard design for a power wheelchair is a wheelchair frame with the motor mounted under the seat or behind the seat. Examples of this conventional design of power wheelchair specifically for the pediatric population are the Quickie P500 and the Invacare Jaguar (Figure 11–45).

Other designs include a pedestal base that houses the power mechanism with a seat atop the pedestal, such as those manufactured by the Fortress Scientific Company. This style of wheelchair is predominately used by the adult population but can accommodate seating and positioning systems for children as well. A third design can be disassembled to fit into a car or truck, but it is not easy to break the chair down into its component parts. The batteries weigh over 10 pounds each, and the chair frame exceeds 45 pounds. These chairs are available only for the older and larger child unless an insert system is added to give a smaller child postural support. Examples are the Everest & Jennings Commuter and the Quickie P110.

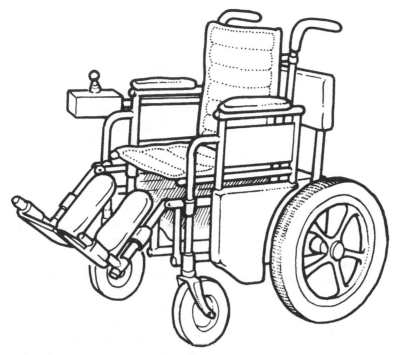

Figure 11–45 Power Wheelchair. *Source:* Copyright © 1996, Mark L. Batshaw, M.D.

Manual wheelchairs may be converted to power chairs by attaching a power pack. These chairs may also be disassembled to put into a car but are heavy. An additional disadvantage is that because the chair frame was not constructed to hold all the additional weight of the power units, the chair may sustain more breakdowns and require more frequent repairs. An example of this type of power add-on system is the Damaco system.

Special Considerations with Power Mobility for the Pediatric User

When considering a power wheelchair for the pediatric client, one must choose a chair that has the potential for growth of the frame and seating system. One should also be able to advance the power controls on the wheelchair as the child gains mastery over the controls.

An important factor to consider is how easily the power wheelchair system will interface with other assistive technology devices the child may require for independent function, such as augmentative communication or environmental control systems. Selection of compatible components may significantly reduce the overall cost of the assistive technology needed.

Scooters

Scooters are either three- or four-wheeled motor-driven carts, similar in concept to a golf cart. These devices do not look like wheelchairs and are not as expensive as regular power wheelchairs. They generally have a more narrow wheelbase than power wheelchairs, a feature that allows for easier maneuverability. Scooters have seats that are mounted on the power base and that can swivel to either side for easy access. They are mounted higher than power wheelchair seats and require the user to have control in standing as well as the strength and ability to transfer on and off the high seat. The scooter is driven by the steering mechanism, which is lo-

Table 11-7 Selection of Seats

Feature	Functional Considerations	tr/s	tr/m	lt	ult	one	hd	tlt	pwr	sco
Seat	Key points of control and ability are pelvis and hips; base of support for all functions									
Sling seat	Limits support to hips and may cause knees to press together	x		x	x	x	x	x	x	
Solid seat	Distributes pressure over broader area		x	x	x	x	x	x	x	x
Jackknife seat (seat-to-back angle less than 90 degrees)	Breaks up extensor tone through pelvis and lower extremities		x	x	x	x	x	x	x	
Antithrust seat	Built up in front with depression for buttocks and hips, assists in preventing forward thrusting of hips			x	x	x	x	x	x	
Split depth	Used for significant leg-length discrepancy			x	x	x	x	x	x	
Seat-to-back angle greater than 90 degrees	Promotes anterior pelvic tilt for individuals with slumped back		x	x	x	x	x	x	x	
Supports on Seat	Control upper leg, properly align pelvis to minimize the influence of abnormal tone, prevent contractures, promote stability									
Lapbelt or pelvic strap	Keeps hips back in seat; angle can control pelvic tilt	x	x	x	x	x	x	x	x	
Lateral guides (sides of hips)	Maintain pelvis in neutral position on seat		x	x	x	x	x	x	x	
Obliquity pads	On seating surface to compensate for pelvic obliquity			x	x	x	x	x	x	
Lateral thigh guides (adductor pads)	Used on outer portion of thigh to control abduction of the hips; must be used on solid seat		x	x	x	x	x	x	x	x
Medial thigh supports (abductor pommel)	Used on inside of thighs to control adduction of hips and prevent scissoring; can be removed for transfers; *not* to be used to prevent thrusting		x	x	x	x	x	x	x	

tr/s = transporter chair/sling; tr/m = transporter chair/modular; lt = lightweight manual wheelchair; ult = ultralightweight manual wheelchair; one = one-arm-drive manual wheelchair; hd = heavy-duty manual wheelchair; tlt = tilt-in-space wheelchair; pwr = power wheelchair; sco = scooter.

Table 11-8 Selection of Backs and Supports

Feature	Functional Considerations	tr/s	tr/m	lt	ult	one	hd	tlt	pwr	sco
Back										
Sling back	Key point of control to trunk; feels secure	X								
Solid back (attached to uprights)	Limited back support; contributes to kyphotic posture			X	X	X	X	X	X	X
	Supports pelvis and trunk; provides base to attach lateral trunk supports and headrest; when mounted to uprights with adjustable-depth hardware, allows for linear growth in child		X	X	X	X	X	X	X	
Solid back insert	Mounts in front of sling back; easier to use for folding chair; less support than attached solid back			X		X	X	X	X	
Contoured back	Provides more skin surface contact; assists to minimize shoulder retractions			X	X	X	X	X	X	X
Biangular back	Solid back that has a "break" at lumbar area to promote anterior pelvic tilt			X		X	X	X	X	
Reclining back	Seat and back angle opens up; for individuals with postural hypotention or who cannot sit upright		X	X			X	X	X	
Tilt in space	Seat and back angle unchanged, but chair tilts back from 90 degrees and forward up to 60 degrees		X	X		X	X	X	X	
Supports on Back	To control the trunk									
Lateral trunk supports	Mounted on solid back or on uprights of chair; control lateral trunk movement, maintain upright posture; planar or curved in a variety of sizes; mounted with stationary or swing-away hardware		X	X	X	X	X	X	X	
Anterior trunk supports	Control forward trunk flexion; can be incorporated into lateral trunk supports; can be vest-style or wide strap, or with straps over the shoulders	X	X	X		X	X	X	X	X
Shoulder pads	Prevent shoulder retraction (posterior mounting) or protraction (anterior mounting)		X	X		X	X	X	X	

tr/s = transporter chair/sling; tr/m = transporter chair/modular; lt = lightweight manual wheelchair; ult = ultralightweight manual wheelchair; one = one-arm-drive manual wheelchair; hd = heavy-duty manual wheelchair; tlt = tilt-in-space wheelchair; pwr = power wheelchair; sco = scooter.

REFERENCE

Bergen, A.F., et al. 1990. *Positioning for function: Wheelchairs and other assistive technologies.* Valhalla, N.Y.: Valhalla Rehabilitation Publications.

ADDITIONAL SUGGESTED READINGS

Butler, C., et al. 1984. Motorized wheelchair driving by disabled children. *Archives of Physical Medicine and Rehabilitation* 65, no. 2:95–97.

Chase, J., and D.M. Bailey. 1990. Evaluating the potential for powered mobility. *American Journal of Occupational Therapy* 44: 1125–1129.

Jaeger, D.L., et al. 1983. Pediatric chair prescription. *Clinical Management in Physical Therapy* 3, no. 1:28–31.

Jones, C.K. 1990. In search of power for the pediatric client. *Physical and Occupational Therapy in Pediatrics* 10, no. 2:47–68.

Letts, R.M., ed. 1991. *Principles of seating the disabled.* Boca Raton, Fla.: CRC Press.

Paquet, J.B. 1991. Wheelchair prescription. *Clinical Management* 11, no. 3:32–36.

Stout, J.D., et al. 1989. Safe transportation for children with disabilities. *American Journal of Occupational Therapy* 43, no. 1:31–36.

Trefler, E., ed. 1984. *Seating for children with cerebral palsy.* Memphis: University of Tennessee.

Trefler, E., et al. 1993. *Seating and mobility for persons with physical disabilities.* Tucson, Ariz.: Therapy Skill Builders.

York, J. 1989. Mobility methods selected for use in home and community environments. *Physical Therapy* 69: 736–747.

ADDITIONAL RESOURCES

The following is a list of manufacturers of wheelchairs and other adapted seating or mobility systems. See Appendix C for addresses and telephone numbers.

Wheelchairs

Atlantic Rehabilitation Inc.

Damaco

Electric Mobility

Everest and Jennings

Invacare

Kushall of America

Ortho-Kinetics Inc.

Permobil Inc.

Quickie Designs

Rehabco

Snug Seat

Stroller-Pack

Wheelchairs/Scooters

Amigo Mobility

Bruno Independent Living Aids Inc.

Seating Components

Adaptive Engineering Lab Inc.

Alimed Inc.

Canadian Posture and Seating Centre

Consumer Care Products Inc.

Creative Rehabilitation Equipment

Danmar Products Inc.

Dynamic Systems Inc.

Folio Products Inc.

Freedom Designs Inc.

Gunnell Inc.

J.A. Preston Corp.

Jay Medical Ltd.

LaBac Systems Inc.

Mobility Plus

Otto Bock Orthopedic Industry Inc.

Pin Dot Products

Quickie Designs/Safety Rehab

Rehabilitation Designs Inc.

Scott Designs

Snug Seat Inc.

Special Health Systems Ltd.

Wheel Ring, Inc.

AMBULATION AIDS

Shirley A. Scull

Purpose: to review medical equipment and training methods for teaching children to walk with assistive devices.

Recommendations for type of gait and assistive device selected depend on the child's weight-bearing precautions as well as consideration of other gross motor skills such as balance, strength, flexibility, or muscle tone. The gait achieved must be safe as well as energy efficient to be functional. A progression of skills is suggested, ultimately resulting in independent mobility in the community.

Ambulation with an assistive device may be only one portion of a total mobility plan for a child. Children may learn to walk with an assistive device but be limited to distances of 100 to 200 feet, requiring a manual or power wheelchair for mobility around the community (see also previous section, "Wheelchair Selection and Maintenance"). This category of skill is called *household ambulation.* To be functional in ambulation, the child must also be able to transfer from sitting to standing and back. If the child walks only in therapy and is not yet functional or independent, the skill is called *exercise ambulation. Community ambulation* is achieved when the child can walk on all surfaces, including rough terrain, stairs, ramps, and curbs, and have good endurance and speed for at least two city blocks.

Often orthotics, or braces, may be required to provide proper alignment or stability to the lower extremities. The quality of the gait cycle is assessed when planning orthotics, including alignment of the hip, knee, and ankle during stance, and clearance of the lower extremity during the swing phase. A molded ankle-foot orthosis (MAFO) may be prescribed to assist the child who toe-walks due to spasticity, with the goal of obtaining heel strike, a flat foot during stance, and clearance of the toe during swing phase. If the lower extremities are weak (with antigravity muscle strength of less than 3 out of 5), higher

bracing such as hip-knee-ankle-foot orthotics (HKAFOs) may be needed with joint locks that can provide stability. Further discussion of orthotics can be found in Chapter 15 under "Principles of Splint Design and Use."

The plan for ambulation should be based on a thorough assessment, generally completed by a physical therapist. Weight-bearing precautions, which may arise following surgeries or fractures, should be provided by the referring physician. The assessment should include musculoskeletal status, such as upper and lower extremity strength and flexibility, neuromuscular status (tone, balance, and coordination), gait evaluation, and endurance. Environmental accessibility needs of the child should be assessed: Are there stairs in the home or school? How long are the distances the child typically must travel each day? Are there any barriers to mobility?

On the basis of this assessment, the therapist can develop a plan that includes

- type of gait to be taught
- type of orthotic to be used
- type of assistive device
- safety concerns
- long- and short-term goals to progress the patient toward functional independence

GENERAL SAFETY PRINCIPLES

The following safety principles should be kept in mind during any ambulation training:

- Guard the child, using a sturdy belt around the waist. One hand grasps the gait belt from behind. The other hand is on the anterior shoulder.
- Stand on the more impaired side, using a broad base of support for balance. If the child is small, a rolling stool may be used instead to prevent the caregiver from straining his or her back while leaning over.

- Synchronize foot movements with the child.
- Keep your eyes directed at the child's waist.
- Always guard downhill when on stairs, curbs, or ramps.
- If the child starts to fall, lower the child safely to the floor rather than hurting either the child or yourself by attempting to reverse the momentum.
- For walking with crutches, teach the child to push down onto the hand pieces rather than taking weight through the axillae.
- Safety-check crutches periodically to be certain that all the screws are tight and that the rubber tips have adequate tread and are free of dirt and stones.

TYPES OF GAIT

Types of gait can be classified as follows:

- *Swing-to or swing-through:* The child advances the assistive device and, by pushing down with the arms, lifts the body and swings both legs simultaneously to the crutches (swing-to) or beyond the crutches (swing-through). Head position may be used to assist by teaching the child to extend the neck while swinging through. While learning this gait, the child may use a *drag-to* pattern if he or she does not clear the floor.
- *Four-point alternate:* The child walks using a reciprocal gait pattern, with the sequence of right crutch, left foot, left crutch, right foot. Children in hip spica casts can be taught to use a reciprocal gait pattern by using one crutch in front of the body and one behind. They require contact guard for safety.
- *Two-point alternate:* The child walks using a reciprocal gait pattern, but the opposite arm and leg are advanced simultaneously (e.g., right crutch and left-foot advance, left crutch and right-foot advance). Since only two points are on the ground at a time, this takes greater balance. Most children

learn a four-point alternate gait first and naturally progress to two-point alternate as they gain greater speed and confidence.

- *Three-point:* Two assistive devices and one limb make contact with the floor.
  1. *Non-weight-bearing:* The child with unilateral involvement walks by bearing weight on the uninvolved limb, advancing both crutches forward simultaneously, and then stepping through with the sound limb.
  2. *Partial weight-bearing:* The child stands on the uninvolved limb, advances both crutches simultaneously, touches the involved limb down, and then steps through while pushing down on the handpieces of the assistive device to relieve weight bearing. A heel-toe pattern is preferable to a toe-touch pattern, which promotes abnormal lower extremity alignment.

TYPES OF ASSISTIVE DEVICES

Walkers

A walker is a stable assistive device with four points in contact with the floor, especially useful if the child is young or has impaired balance. If it has four legs, it is termed a "pick-up" walker, since it is advanced by lifting it from the floor (Figure 11–47). More often in pediatrics, the front legs will be replaced with wheels, making it a "wheeled" walker, also called a *rollator* (Figure 11–48). Swivel wheels allow closer cornering on turns. Reciprocal walkers and hemiwalkers are also available.

Traditional walkers that patients push ahead of them are called *forward walkers*. For some children, such as those with cerebral palsy or spina bifida, a *reverse walker* may be chosen. The reverse walker trails behind the child and encourages a more erect stand (Figure 11–49).

Axillary Crutches

Standard crutches are available from tiny-tot sizes to adults. They are adjustable in one-inch

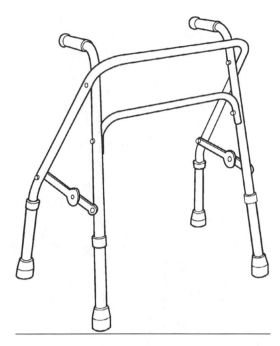

Figure 11–47 Pick-up Walker. *Source:* Copyright © 1996, Mark L. Batshaw, M.D.

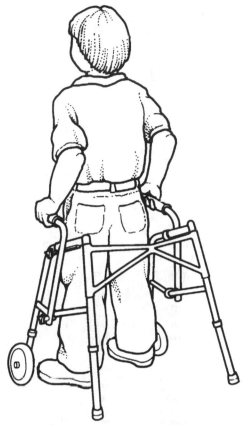

Figure 11–49 Reverse Walker. *Source:* Copyright © 1996, Mark L. Batshaw, M.D.

increments for correct length and hand position. When properly adjusted, the therapist should be able to place two fingers between the axilla and the crutch top so that no pressure will be applied to the brachial plexus. The elbow should be slightly flexed to about 20 degrees. Axillary crutches are placed under the armpits and pressed lightly into the ribs. Most of the pressure should be taken on the hands, not the arms (Figure 11–50).

Forearm Crutches (Loftstrand Crutches/ Canadian Crutches)

These crutches have a hand grip and a forearm cuff that encircles the arm just below the elbow. There is no risk of axillary pressure with these

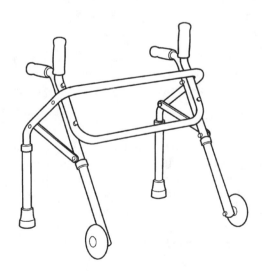

Figure 11–48 Rollater. *Source:* Copyright © 1996, Mark L. Batshaw, M.D.

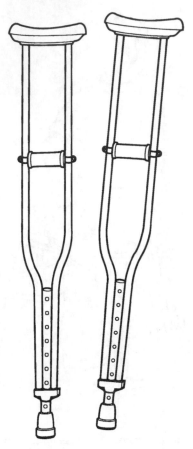

Figure 11–50 Axillary Crutches. *Source:* Copyright © 1996, Mark L. Batshaw, M.D.

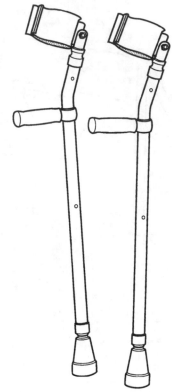

Figure 11–51 Forearm Crutches. *Source:* Copyright © 1996, Mark L. Batshaw, M.D.

devices, but they require good upper extremity strength and balance in order to use. They may have a front or side opening in the cuff for donning/doffing (Figure 11–51).

Quad Canes

A quad cane is a cane with a platform at the bottom that is supported by four legs (Figure 11–52). If the platform is small, the device is called a small-based quad cane. If the platform is large, the child will receive greater help with balance, and it is called a large-based quad cane. Children with unilateral involvement may use one cane in the hand opposite to their involvement. Children with bilateral involvement who can already walk

with a walker or other assistive device may be progressed to two quad canes if they continue to require the use of an assistive device for balance.

Single-Point Canes

A straight cane is called a single-point cane (Figure 11–53). It can be used if the child has unilateral impairment or if minimal support is needed, such as when attempting to walk on uneven ground. The top of the cane should be at the level of the greater trochanter. Some children must be reminded to use it in the hand opposite to their impaired limb.

Other Devices

Toys that can be pushed, such as doll strollers or riding toys with handles, can also be used as assistive devices.

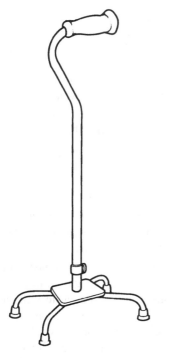

Figure 11–52 Quad Cane. *Source:* Copyright © 1996, Mark L. Batshaw, M.D.

Baby walkers must never be used as assistive devices. They have been banned by the American Academy of Pediatrics because of the multiple injuries attributed to them. Most children do not use an ambulation pattern in a baby walker; they often sit and push themselves backwards.

Platform attachments may be added to crutches or walkers if the patient is unable to bear weight through the wrist and elbow joints (Figure 11–54). This is indicated for children with juvenile rheumatoid arthritis.

Weight may be added to walkers or crutches if the patient moves the device too quickly or presents with involuntary motion, such as ataxia or athetosis.

AMBULATION TRAINING GUIDELINES

The following are special training guidelines for transfers with assistive devices (see also earlier section "Lifting and Transfer Techniques"):

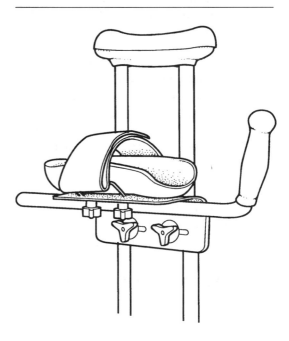

Figure 11–54 Crutch with Platform Attachment. *Source:* Copyright © 1996, Mark L. Batshaw, M.D.

Figure 11–53 Single-Point Cane. *Source:* Copyright © 1996, Mark L. Batshaw, M.D.

raised sill; levered door knob may be easier to operate than standard knob; automatic door with electric eye preferable for school entrances

5. building includes attached garage, oversized and with high ceiling to accommodate a raised-top van; canopied discharge area ideal for school buses

6. doorbell and mailbox placed at chair height

7. deck or level outdoor playing surface with fenced yard

- Building interiors
  1. one-story building preferable; if multilevel, bathroom and bedroom should be available on the first floor
  2. doorways at least 32 inches wide; low or no sills preferred
  3. hallways at least 42 inches wide
  4. low-pile carpeting or tile
  5. electrical switches and outlets placed at chair height
  6. large windows that can be easily opened with one hand; skylights may provide additional lighting for child with poor vision

- Kitchen accessibility
  1. front-control-operated range, preferably mounted into countertop
  2. tilted mirror over stove, allowing viewing into pots from seated position
  3. lowered wall oven
  4. side-by-side, frost-free refrigerator with water and ice dispenser in door
  5. front-loading appliances, including dishwasher, washer, and dryer
  6. lowered sink and counters with adequate leg room
  7. levered faucet handles

- Bathroom accessibility
  1. adequate turning radius for wheelchair;

ideal is 5 square feet clear, including handicapped stall in public restroom

2. either a pocket sliding door or a door that opens out

3. nonslip floors

4. toilet at wheelchair height (17–19 inches from floor) with sturdy grab bars that do not interfere with wheelchair access

5. roll-under sink and vanity top; sink with levered faucet handles

6. wheelchair height mirrors, shelves, cabinets, soap, and paper towel dispensers or dryers

7. tub chair or shower with fold-down or portable seat and hand-held shower head; if ample space exists, a roll-in shower without a lip may be possible

8. grab bars in tub or shower; nonskid mat or surface

- Bedroom accessibility
  1. open floor plan
  2. closets with sliding or bifold doors, lowered rods, and lowered adjustable-height shelves (shallow)
  3. accessible furniture with adequate clearance underneath for footrests; open shelves may be easier than drawers
  4. location close to accessible bathroom
  5. easy exit to outdoors from bedroom in case of fire
  6. intercom available if caregiver's bedroom is not within easy auditory monitoring

FUNCTIONAL SCHOOL ASSESSMENT CHECKLIST

Table 11–11 presents a screening checklist that may be used to screen for the child's ability to function successfully within the classroom environment.

Table 11–11 Functional School Assessment Checklist

Functional Area	I	S	V	P	D	N/A
Mobility						
Ambulates with/without assistive devices						
Straight, smooth surfaces						
Turn hallways						
Outdoor, rough surfaces						
Curbs						
Ascends/descends stairs						
Indoors						
School bus						
Maneuvers manual/power wheelchair						
Indoors, smooth surfaces						
Ramps						
Rough, uneven surfaces						
Curbs						
Maneuvers doors						
Interior						
Exterior						
Accesses playground equipment						
Participates in regular/adapted PE						
Keeps place in line						
Bathroom						
Indicates need to use toilet						
Opens door to bathroom stall						
Manages clothing fasteners						
Pulls pants down/up						
Transfers onto/off toilet/commode						
Directs waste in bowl without spillage						
Uses toilet paper						
Washes/dries hands						
Cafeteria						
Carries tray through line						
Sets up meal/drink; opens containers						
Self-feeds with/without adapted utensils (minimal spillage)						
Drinks from regular/adapted cup (minimal spillage)						
Chews/swallows food safely						
Uses straw						
Puts trash in receptacle						
Classroom skills						
Sits at regular desk						
Has adequate sitting balance for seatwork						
Has adequate posture for seatwork						
Picks up items dropped on floor						
Is mobile within classroom (can access various work areas)						
Obtains necessary materials for desk work (from desk, backpack, wheelchair bag, etc.)						
Organizes workspace effectively so materials are readily available						

continues

Table 11–11 Continues

Functional Area	I	S	V	P	D	N/A
Locates and keeps place on worksheets						
Copies assignments using pen/pencil/computer (legible, accurate, adequate speed)						
From near point						
From far point						
Operates tape recorder to record class notes						
Completes assignments in class						
Less than 25% of assigned work						
25–50%						
50–75%						
75% or more						
Uses pencil sharpener effectively						
Uses pencil eraser effectively						
Boots and uses PC for word processing/games						
Uses scissors/paste for crafts						
Uses ruler/stencil						
Uses stapler/hole punch						
Folds paper and places in envelope						
Organizes and places homework materials in backpack or bookbag						
Adequately attends to tasks in class						
5 minutes or less						
5–10 minutes						
Greater than 10 minutes						
Adequately recalls and follows instructions						
Dons/doffs sweater or coat						
Dons/doffs boots/shoes						
Dons/doffs mittens/hat						
Manages external clothing fasteners						

Note: I = independent (including adequate speed/endurance); S = supervision for safety required; V = supervision and verbal direction required; P = physical assistance required; D = dependent.

SUGGESTED READINGS

Cronburg, J.G., et al. 1993. *Readily achievable checklist: A survey for accessibility.* Boston: Adaptive Environments Center.

Johnson, P.M. 1988. *Creation of the barrier-free interior.* Millville, N.J.: A Positive Approach, Inc.

Kohlmeyer, K.M., and J.E. Lewin. 1993. *Environmental adaptation.* In *Willard and Spackman's occupational therapy,* 8th ed., ed. H.L. Hopkins and H.D. Smith, 320–324. Philadelphia: J.B. Lippincott Co.

ADDITIONAL RESOURCES

Adaptive Environments Center, 374 Congress Street, Suite 301, Boston, MA 02210, Tel.: (617) 695–1225 V/TDD.

Architectural & Transportation Barriers Compliance Board, 1331 F Street, NW, Suite 1000, Washington, DC 20004-1111, Tel.: (800) 872-2253, (202) 272-5434, fax (202) 272-5447.

Barrier-Free Design Center, Access Place Canada, College Park, 4444 Young Street, Toronto, Ontario M5B2H4, Tel.: (416) 977-5057 or (416) 977-5157, fax (416) 977-5264.

National Rehabilitation Hospital ADA Compliance Program, 102 Irving Street NW, Washington, DC 20010-

2949, Tel.: (202) 877-1932, TDD (202) 726-3996, fax (202) 723-0628.

National Easter Seal Society, 230 West Monroe Street, Suite 1800, Chicago, IL 60666, Tel.: (800) 221-6827, (312) 726-6200, fax (312) 726-1494.

Research Center for Accessible Housing, School of Design, North Carolina State University, Tel.: (800) 647-6777, fax (919) 515-3023.

Paralyzed Veterans of America, Tel.: (800) 424-8200, fax (202) 785-4452.

CAR SEAT SAFETY

Shirley A. Scull

Purpose: to outline the principles used to plan for proper car restraint for children with special needs.

Automobile accidents are the leading cause of death and injury among young children. According to the National Highway Traffic Safety Administration, using a child car seat correctly can significantly reduce the risk of death and injury from a crash (Kuhane 1986). The American Academy of Pediatrics distributes information regarding proper restraint of children, and most pediatricians provide anticipatory guidance regarding this topic (American Academy of Pediatrics 1991).

All 50 states and the District of Columbia require young children to be properly restrained in an approved child safety seat during transport. All drivers transporting children should be aware of local laws. Most hospitals will not discharge a newborn infant to home unless the family arrives with a proper car seat for transportation. Some service organizations have programs that provide loaner equipment to indigent families. It is important not only to purchase an approved seat but to ensure that it is used properly.

Infants and toddlers with special needs may be able to use standard commercial equipment, with family instruction on simple modifications. Older children who have neuromuscular problems such as poor head control, impaired sitting balance, or immobilization in casts may require special planning for safe transport. A health professional should be knowledgeable about the child's neuromuscular status as well as the safety principles involved with proper car restraint. Developmental centers and schools need to make a safe plan for transportation of children to and from their programs.

At present, the Federal Motor Vehicle Safety Standard 213 (FMVSS 213) defines design and performance standards of child restraint systems only for normal children weighing up to 50 pounds. No testing has successfully simulated children with disabilities, nor are special devices such as wheelchairs required to comply with federal standards.

GENERAL SAFETY PRINCIPLES

The following are general safety principles for child car seat use:

- Face the seat in the correct direction. Infants up to 20 pounds should ride in a reclined infant seat facing the rear of the vehicle. Infants over 20 pounds should ride face forward.

- The safest location in the car is the middle of the back seat. Do not use the front seat for rear-facing transport if it is installed with a passenger side airbag.

- The car seat must be appropriately secured in the car by correctly threading the seatbelt through the car seat frame or by anchoring with a tether. These straps are separate from the harness that secures the child in the seat.

- Be sure to read and follow the manufacturer's instructions.

- Be sure the harness is over the child's shoulders and adjusted to a snug fit.

- Dress the infant in clothing with legs so that the crotch strap can be properly positioned. If a blanket is used, holes may be cut to allow for the harness to fit properly.

REFERENCES

American Academy of Pediatrics. 1991. Safe transportation of premature infants. *Pediatrics* 87:120–122.

Kuhane, C.J. 1986. *An evaluation of child passenger safety: The effectiveness and benefits of safety seats* (DOT-HS-806-890). Washington, D.C.: National Highway Safety Administration.

ADDITIONAL SUGGESTED READINGS

American Academy of Pediatrics. 1986. Safety seat use for children with hip dislocation. *Pediatrics* 77:873–875.

American Academy of Pediatrics. 1993. Policy statement: Transporting children with special needs. *AAP Safe Ride News Insert*, Winter.

Bull, M.J., et al. 1989. Transporting children in body casts. *Journal of Pediatric Orthopedics* 9:280–284.

School bus safety: Tie downs and restraints. 1989. *Exceptional Parent* (Sept.):60–65.

Stout, J.D., et al. 1989. Safe transportation for children with disabilities. *American Journal of Occupational Therapy* 43:31–36.

Stroup, K.B., et al. 1987. Car seats for children with mechanically assisted ventilation. Pediatrics 80:290–292.

Stroup, K.B., et al. 1987. Safe transportation solutions for children with special needs. In *Proceedings of the 31st Annual Conference of the American Association for Automotive Medicine*, New Orleans, La.: American Association for Automotive Medicine, 297–308.

ADDITIONAL RESOURCES

Specific Equipment

(See Appendix C for addresses and telephone numbers.)

Special Car Seats

- Carrie car seats and bus seats (J.A. Preston Corporation)
- Columbia car seat (Columbia Medical Mfg. Corp.)
- Gorilla car seat (Snug Seat)
- Spelcast car seat for children in hip spica cast (Snug Seat)
- Snug seat with or without mobility base (Snug Seat)

Safety Vests

- E-Z-On Vest (E-Z-On Products, Inc., of Florida)

Wheelchairs

- Mulholland Positioning Systems
- Ortho-Kinetics Travel Chair

Wheelchair Tie-downs

- Q'Straint

Organizations

American Academy of Pediatrics, Safe Ride News, P.O. Box 927, Elk Grove Village, IL 60007, Tel.: (312) 228-5005.

Automotive Safety for Children Program, James Whitcomb Riley Hospital for Children, Indiana University School of Medicine, 702 Barnhill Drive, P-121, Indianapolis, IN 46223, Tel.: (317) 264-2977.

National Committee on School Transportation Safety for the Handicapped, 1250 Roth Drive, Lansing, MI 48910, Tel.: (517) 694-3957.

National Easter Seal Society, KARS/Special KARS, 70 East Lake Street, Chicago, IL 60601-5907, Tel.: 1 (800) 221-6827, ext. 171.

National Passenger Safety Association, 1705 DeSales St, NW, Suite 3000, Washington, DC 20036, Tel.: (202) 429-0515

Chapter 12

Feeding and Nutritional Concerns

THERAPEUTIC FEEDING

Peggy S. Eicher and MaryLouise E. Kerwin

Purpose: to discuss the many aspects of feeding disruptions, the underlying reasons, possible therapeutic interventions, and when they should be applied.

ETIOLOGY OF FEEDING PROBLEMS

Feeding is a learned skill that is influenced by multiple factors, including oral-pharyngeal competency, medical stability, developmental level, neuromotor control, and positive practice. If there is fluctuation, delay, or abnormality in any of these factors, a disruption may occur in feeding skills, resulting in a feeding problem. Thus children with developmental disability have a higher frequency of feeding problems.

For a child to eat successfully, the following prerequisites must exist:

- *Oral-pharyngeal competency:* To be a successful feeder, a child must control the progress of a bolus of food or liquid through the oral cavity and pharynx and into the esophagus without penetrating the airway. The swallowing mechanism is complex; it is controlled by voluntary and involuntary motor outputs and modulated by sensory and motor feedback from the mouth, pharynx, cerebral cortex, heart, lungs, and GI tract.

- *Medical stability:* feeding is especially vulnerable to instability in the primary organ systems that affect eating: the respiratory tract, gastrointestinal tract, and brain. Any medical problem that causes even temporary interruption or disruption to their function can result in a feeding problem.

- *Developmental readiness:* Oral-motor skill acquisition follows a developmental progression similar to that of other motor skills. To be successful, the child must function at a developmental level consistent with the skills required for the texture offered. For example, a child with global developmental function at six to seven

reflux episodes. A double-probe study with a distal and proximally placed sensor also indicates the height of each refluxate episode

3. Milk scan—nuclear medicine scan to look at emptying time of stomach, height and frequency of GER episodes, presence of aspiration with reflux

4. Heme test stools—if positive, may indicate esophagitis or ulcer

5. EGD (endoscopic gastroduodenoscopy)—direct examination (under sedation) of esophagus, stomach, and duodenum; biopsy performed

- Intestinal disorders:

   1. malabsorption: clinitest stools, hydrogen breath test, fecal fat, biopsy documentation

   2. constipation: see section "Elimination" later in this chapter

   3. diarrhea: see section "Elimination" later in this chapter

- Swallowing dysfunction

   1. modified barium swallow (MBS; see above)

   2. chest x-ray (for evidence of inflammation or infection associated with acute or chronic aspiration)

   3. salivagram—nuclear medicine study to look at aspiration of saliva from the oral cavity, minimal correlation with MBS

DEVELOPMENTAL READINESS AND MOTOR CONTROL

These two factors overlap in that they both focus on level of function, the expression of which is influenced by both developmental readiness and motor control. A neurodevelopmental examination should be performed to determine developmental levels (see Part I), tone, and function. Positioning for feeding (e.g., seating, handling) should also be noted. The child should have good breath support and head and neck aligned in neutral position.

ENVIRONMENTAL FACTORS

Variables in the environment can also influence a child's responses in the feeding situation. Because eating is a complex activity, *environment* is defined broadly.

By history, the examiner should ascertain the following:

1. time of meal in relation to GI meds, tube feedings

2. feeding environment: where does child eat, level of distraction (TV on, etc.), with family, meal pattern: time of meals

3. seating: does child sit or stand, what type of seating device, is it developmentally appropriate

4. feeding utensils: spoon size, cup, etc.

5. food presentation: type and texture of food, how presented (on one plate)

6. food preferences

7. eating response: acceptance/refusal; spitting out food; crying; letting food drool out; chewing food, then vomitting; long meal duration; gagging/coughing; throwing food/utensil: taking a long time to swallow; getting out of seat; falling asleep; problem with self-feeding

By feeding observation, the examiner may ascertain the following:

1. antecedents to negative mealtime behavior

2. consequences of positive and negative mealtime behaviors

3. pace of meal

4. size of bites

5. level of distraction

TREATMENT APPROACH

Treatment should focus on minimizing factors identified during the assessment as contributing to the feeding dysfunction and should then facilitate positive practice.

Oral-Pharyngeal Problems

Aspiration

An MBS is usually very helpful in elucidating the pathophysiology resulting in aspiration, as well as indicating compensatory maneuvers to avoid it. On MBS:

- If the child does not cover the airway quickly enough, thickening the liquid or food may be helpful.
- If the child does not trigger a swallow, cold stimulus or exercises that strengthen the posterior pharynx may help increase contraction.
- If the child aspirates residual after the swallow, the exercises or repeated swallow may help to decrease residual.

Lack of Swallowing

Swallowing is an involuntary action that must be triggered and can be modified from cortical and respiratory inputs. Therefore, if it is truly absent or so infrequent that it cannot be detected during an evaluation, one must rule out brainstem lesion (cranial nerve exam), decreased oral-pharyngeal sensation (oral-motor evaluation), respiratory decompensation (physical exam), and learned inhibition (medical and feeding histories).

In the absence of progressive neurologic disease, one would approach therapy trying to find a trigger stimulus to which the patient was sensitive either at baseline or after therapy to heighten response to sensation (e.g., thermal stimulation). Once a swallow can be triggered, the movements can be strengthened through various oral therapy techniques. Finally the swallowing act must be coordinated with oral transport before nutritive therapy can begin.

Lack of Sucking

The most common reason for lack of sucking is integration of the suckle reflex before functional bottle feeding is attained. In this case, the infant will have started with a few sucks from the bottle but will not maintain a coordinated rhythm for even an ounce. This occurs in the absence of progressive neurologic, respiratory, or gastrointestinal disease. In this situation, oral transport can be trained via a spoon; in our experience, these infants will not acquire competent bottle skills but rather will progress to liquids from a cup after they master spoon feeding.

A weak suck signals neurologic injury, hypotonia, or respiratory compromise. Once the underlying problem has been addressed, the oral facial musculature can be strengthened to be more effective. A weak or absent suck should never be treated solely by enlarging the nipple hole or plunger feeding.

Drooling

Drooling may result from poor handling of secretions or increased production of secretions. The former may be related to neurologic injury influencing oral-motor transport or swallowing frequency, hypotonia of the oral-facial musculature, respiratory compromise (e.g., acute wheezing), open-mouth posture (mouth breathing) secondary to enlarged tonsils or adenoids causing upper airway obstruction, or volitional inhibition, as with pharyngeal pain (e.g., pharyngitis). Once the underlying problem is addressed, oral-motor therapy can be used to enhance tone through the facial musculature, increase efficacy of oral-motor transport, or increase swallowing frequency.

Increased production of saliva in this population is most commonly associated with GER and will decrease with effective treatment of GER.

Gagging on Texture

Gagging on texture may be related to immature or pathologic oral-motor transport, hypersensitive gag on neurologic basis, increased gag response associated with GER, or learned refusal. If the gag is hypersensitive on a neurologic basis, it can be desensitized through oral-motor therapy.

If gagging results from an immature, centralized pattern of oral transport, lateralization can be facilitated by lateral placement of the spoon while feeding purees, coupled with tongue exer-

Finally, respiratory compromise may interfere with feeding. Therapies include

- adequate oxygenation for "work" of feeding
- using easiest texture for child to facilitate practice

Child Responses Interfering with Adequate Nutrition

The following feeding responses may interfere with adequate nutrition:

- *Total or partial food/liquid refusal:* Child accepts no food or does not eat enough to gain and grow (e.g., takes five bites and then stops). This is most commonly related to GER, but team also needs to rule out aspiration and constipation. Once medical problems are managed, the intervention should target acceptance. A program should be designed to increase systematically acceptance and/or volume of food consumed, using positive reinforcement and other effective behavioral procedures.

- *Overselectivity by food texture:* Child possesses requisite skills to munch/chew but accepts only puree food. Rule out gagging on texture and tactile sensitivity. After medical management, program should systematically introduce textures in hierarchical sequence from easiest (cheese curl) to hardest (meat), not advancing until oral-motor skills are well established and functional at the lower level.

- *Extreme food selectivity (variety or type):* Child consumes ten or fewer foods. Rule out allergies, then target acceptance as in total food refusal.

SUGGESTED READINGS

Babbitt, R.L., et al. 1994. Behavioral assessment and treatment of pediatric feeding disorders. *Journal of Developmental and Behavioral Pediatrics* 15:278–291.

Blasco, P., et al. 1991. *Consensus statement of the Consortium on Drooling.* Washington, D.C.: United Cerebral Palsy Associations, Inc.

Evans Morris, S., and M. Dunn Klein. 1987. *Pre-feeding skills: A comprehensive resource for feeding development.* Tucson, Ariz.: Therapy Skill Builders.

Fox, C.A. 1990. Implementing the modified barium swallow evaluation in children who have multiple disabilities. *Infants and Young Children* 32:67–77.

Geyer, L.A., and J. McGowan. 1995. Positioning children for videofluroscopic swallowing studies. *Infants and Young Children* 8, no. 2:58–64.

Iawata, B.A., et al. 1982. Pediatric feeding disorders: Behavioral analysis and treatment. In *Failure to thrive in infancy and early childhood,* ed. P.J. Accardo, 297–329. Baltimore: University Park Press.

Kramer, S.S., and P.M. Eicher. 1993. The evaluation of pediatric feeding abnormalities. *Dysphagia* 8:215–224.

Wolf, L.S., and R.P. Glass. 1992. *Feeding and swallowing disorders in infancy: Assessment and management.* Tucson, Ariz.: Therapy Skill Builders.

DIETS

Susan E. Levy

Purpose: to discuss the special considerations for evaluation and management of the nutritional needs of children with developmental disabilities.

Provision of adequate nutrition is crucial for children to achieve appropriate growth and to reach their developmental potential. Poor nutritional intake in the general pediatric population can lead to health problems related to nutrient deficiency, including failure to thrive (FTT), anemia, obesity, and rickets. Severe undernutrition affects human brain growth by decreasing the number of cells in the cerebrum and brainstem, with resultant overt delays in development. Subtle changes in development may be related to poor growth or nutritional intake, especially if growth deficits occur before six months of age.

Children with developmental disabilities or chronic illness are more vulnerable due to associated complications that may interfere with growth. Factors include

- oral-motor dysfunction limiting food intake and/or type of food texture
- GI problems: gastroesophageal reflux, malabsorption, constipation
- metabolic disorder with increased caloric needs and/or requirement of specialized diet (such as phenylketonuria)
- nutrient deficiencies such as iron or calcium, resulting in anemia or rickets
- growth deviations associated with specific syndromes or prenatal insult
- obesity due to excessive weight gain in relation to linear growth
- decreased or increased caloric requirements due to activity or concurrent medical condition
- nutrient–drug interactions

Additional factors that may affect the nutritional status of the child with developmental disability include practices of the family related to

- caregivers' socioeconomic status (e.g., access to appropriate quantity of food)
- influence of cultural or religious practices (e.g., dietary restrictions, clothing that restricts exposure to sun)
- age and educational level of parents (e.g., ability to understand and follow through on recommended interventions)
- family composition and support system
- housing and community resources

ASSESSMENT OF NUTRITIONAL STATUS

Assessment of nutritional status should include the following:

- *History*
  1. medical history (risk factors, including presence of chronic illness such as kidney disease, liver disease, gastrointestinal disease, anemia, neurologic disorders, genetic disorders)
  2. current dietary intake: food types, amount consumed, frequency of meals, fluid intake (type and amount)
  3. diet diary (record of three-day intake)
- *Clinical assessment*
  1. observation for evidence of illness, edema (swelling), overt undernutrition or obesity, dehydration, diminished muscle mass (see also Chapter 7, section "Assessment of Physical Well-Being," subsection "Growth and Nutrition").
  2. measurement of weight, height, and head circumference (see also Chapter 7, section "Assessment of Physical Well-being").
  3. special techniques used by nutritionists to assess quantitative data on body fat and muscle mass (and compare it to established norms):
     (a) measurement of skinfold thickness with specific calipers of triceps muscle and tip of scapula
     (b) midarm circumference
- *Growth charts*: all measurements should be graphed on the appropriate growth chart for the child's age and gender to determine how the child compares to other peers and to see if the measurements fall within the average range (e.g., between 5th and 95th percentile for age and gender)
  1. standard NCHS growth charts (see diagrams in Chapter 7)
     (a) girls: birth to 36 months, 2 to 18 years
     (b) boys: birth to 36 months, 2 to 18 years
  2. specialized growth curves are available, so that growth may be compared to ap-

propriate peers (see Additional Suggested Readings):

   (a) achondroplasia

   (b) Down syndrome

   (c) premature infants

- *Laboratory assessment:* blood tests may reveal evidence for anemia (abnormal hemoglobin, mean corpuscular volume [MCV], decreased iron stores, abnormal red blood cell size or shape), decreased serum protein, albumin or prealbumin, decreased creatinine, or electrolyte or mineral disturbances

NUTRITIONAL NEEDS

The following needs are estimates for healthy full-term infants. For a child who is ill or who has a developmental disability, the requirements will be greater.

- Breast feeding
  1. For adequate growth, the infant should receive six or more feedings per day.
  2. Mother's diet should include additional sources of energy, protein, minerals, vitamins, and fluid to produce adequate milk supply.
  3. Monitor infant's urine output (at least six wet diapers per 24 hours) and weight gain.
- Formula
  1. In the first four to six months of life, infant formula can serve as the sole source of nutrients; bottle feedings should be given every three to four hours.
  2. Caloric density varies; standard caloric density is 20 calories per ounce. By decreasing the water content, one can concentrate formula to provide up to 30 calories per ounce. As the concentration increases, so does the possibility of poor GI tolerance (e.g., diarrhea). Other methods are available to increase caloric density, including adding micro-lipids, MCT (medium-chain triglyceride) oil, or vegetable oil.
  3. Composition may vary according to type of protein, carbohydrate, fat, electrolyte, or iron content.
  4. Selection of type of formula depends on caloric needs, medical factors (e.g., need for a specialized formula due to metabolic disorder, allergies or intolerance to components).
  5. Several examples of formulas include
     - (a) standard: Carnation Good Start, Enfamil, Similac, SMA
     - (b) specialized: Isomil, Nutramigen, Pregestamil, ProSobee
     - (c) for additional listing, see Additional Suggested Readings
- Solid food
  1. Suggested time to introduce infants to solid food is at four to six months of age, usually starting single-ingredient foods to make certain the child does not have hypersensitivity to a component.
  2. Sequence usually includes starting with infant cereal and progressing to pureed fruits, vegetables, and meats (and combinations thereof).

Preterm infants have special needs for growth, including higher calories (105–130 kcal/kg/d), calcium and vitamin D supplementation, and iron supplementation at two months of age. Several commercial preterm formulas are available with caloric density of 24 calories per ounce. Infants weighing more than 2 kg at discharge often can be fed a standard formula, which may have to be concentrated to a higher caloric density.

Children with normal development of motor and oral-motor skills experience rapid transitions during the second year of life, related to improving motor skills in early childhood (increased mobility, chewing skills, increased independence in feeding). An important goal is maintaining a balanced diet, with snacks.

Adolescent nutrition is vulnerable because of additional needs due to stresses of puberty with associated increased growth rate, change in body composition, physical activity, hormonal changes, and onset of menses. Adolescents may also be at risk due to inconsistent intake or atypical food habits, with lower intake of calcium, vitamin A, vitamin C, and iron.

Older children with additional caloric or metabolic needs may not be able to take in appropriate nutrients in a regular diet or may be unable to eat by mouth and may require tube feedings. Some examples of specialized formulas are

- Ensure/ Ensure Plus
- Isocal
- Osmolite
- Pediasure
- Pediatric Vivonex
- Peptamen
- Sustacal

REQUIREMENTS FOR ENTERAL FEEDINGS

Energy

Caloric provisions must be adequate to meet caloric expenditure, as well as to support optimal growth of the child. There is no universally accepted method for determining the caloric requirements of children with developmental disabilities.

The *total energy expenditure* (TEE) of any individual will be affected by several variables, but children also have included in their TEE the energy needs associated with growth. For the child with a developmental disability, factors such as activity level (gross motor function, movement disorders), degree of muscle tone, and the impact of coexisting disease states must also be considered. These measurements may be obtained in conjunction with a nutritionist associated with a tertiary care center. The estimated energy requirements for infants is 90–120 kcal/kg/d. Caloric requirements for growth slowly fall from about 110 kcal/kg/d at one year, to about 50 kcal/kg/d at adulthood.

A more reliable method for assessment of caloric requirements or *resting energy expenditure* (REE) is to use a standard equation for predicting metabolic rate from body weight. For different age ranges, factors are added or subtracted from the weight, and then multiplied by another factor. This does not take into account height, activity level, or infection. Median weight for height and age should be used when calculating the REE of severely undernourished or obese children. These measurements may be available through a nutritionist associated with a tertiary care medical center.

Standards have been established for *recommended daily allowances* (RDAs) of protein, fat-soluble vitamins, water-soluble vitamins, and minerals (see Barness 1992, Appendix B–1). Protein requirements may vary; in situations of stress or injury, needs will be increased. Protein should supply 10 to 15 percent of the daily energy requirement. In the breast-fed infant, protein contributes 7 to 8 percent of calories consumed, and in the formula-fed infant 9 to 11 percent. Calcium, phosphorus, and magnesium are major constituents of mature bone that must be adequately provided by food for normal skeletal development.

PARENTERAL FEEDINGS

A population of children with gastrointestinal disorders (e.g., severe gastroesophageal reflux, Crohn's disease, short gut) or severe malnutrition will require parenteral feedings, also known as *total parenteral nutrition* (TPN) or *intravenous hyperalimentation* (HAL). Parenteral feeding may be administered by peripheral or central vein. When administered by peripheral vein (i.e., intravenous catheter in arm or leg), the concentration of glucose is lower (usually to 10 percent dextrose), as compared to 20 percent in central-vein administration. Central administration requires insertion of central catheter (e.g., Broviac or Hickman central-vein catheter) under sterile conditions.

Solutions are specially prepared by a pharmacist under sterile conditions and include a high percentage of glucose (up to 25 percent), amino acid solution (protein), minerals, vitamins, and trace elements. They may be administered in conjunction with a lipid solution (intralipids) to enhance calories further.

REFERENCE

Barness, L.A., ed. 1992. *Pediatric nutrition handbook.* 3rd ed. Chicago: American Academy of Pediatrics.

ADDITIONAL SUGGESTED READINGS

Bernbaum, J.C., and M. Hoffman-Williamson. 1991. *Primary care of the preterm infant.* St. Louis: Mosby Year-book.

Burton, B.T., and W.R. Foster. 1988. *Human nutrition: A textbook of nutrition in health and disease.* 4th ed. New York: McGraw-Hill Book Company

Food and Nutrition Board. 1989. *Recommended dietary allowances.* 10th ed. Washington, D.C.: National Academy of Sciences.

Walker, W.A., and J.B. Watkins, eds. 1985. *Nutrition in pediatrics.* Boston: Little, Brown & Co.

Suskind, R.M., ed. 1981. *Textbook of pediatric nutrition.* New York: Raven Press.

ELIMINATION

Susan E. Levy and Peggy S. Eicher

Purpose: to discuss the problematic processes of elimination, including diarrhea, constipation, enuresis, and encopresis.

Normal patterns of elimination or bowel movements are dependent upon a number of factors:

- *Age of the child* (developmental and chronologic): The pattern varies by age— for example, infants being fed breast milk or formula will have more frequent, seedy stools. Older children will have more solid, formed stools.
- *Diet*: Children who ingest a narrow range of diet with less fiber or fluid will have more difficulty passing stools.
- *Activity level*: Children who are less mobile and less active will probably be more constipated.
- *Neurologic state*: Children with neuromotor disorders such as cerebral palsy or spina bifida are at increased risk for constipation.
- *Other medical factors*: These include neurologic disorders, anatomical abnormalities, and gastrointestinal disorders.

DIARRHEA

Diarrhea is an increase in frequency, water content, or volume of stools compared to the normal pattern. Its causes include

- infection: viral or bacterial
- toxins: from food poisoning or with Clostridium difficile
- medication: side effects of antibiotics, laxative use
- allergic/immunologic: food allergy, immunologic disorder
- gastrointestinal disorders: malabsorption syndromes or enteropathy, short gut syndrome (anatomic abnormality or postsurgical treatment of necrotizing enterocolitis)

An examination should look for signs and symptoms of infection, fever, nature of stool output (e.g., blood, mucus), and state of hydration. Laboratory tests, where indicated, include stool gram stain, stool culture (viral and/or bacterial), electrolytes, CBC, creatinine, and BUN.

Treatment involves

- Investigating and treating the underlying neurologic, infectious, or anatomic cause
- Determining if dehydration is present: look for acute weight loss, skin turgor, moist mucous membranes, decreased urine output, level of consciousness. If dehydration is present, consider method of rehydration:
  1. oral rehydration (for mild to moderate dehydration)
     (a) clear liquids versus formula; a period of transient lactose intolerance may occur, necessitating soy-based, lactose-free formula.
     (b) oral rehydration solutions, with electrolytes included in glucose liquid
  2. intravenous rehydration (in the hospital) for more severe dehydration
- Modifying diet
  1. in infants there is controversy over continuing formula versus changing it (e.g., to soy based)
  2. in older children, institute "BRAT" diet (bananas, rice cereal, apple sauce, toast or tea), and advance as tolerated

CONSTIPATION

Constipation is decreased frequency of stools from usual pattern and pain or difficulty passing stools.

It may be functional/acquired, as in the case of anatomic abnormalities, a diet lacking fluid and/or fiber, or "voluntary" withholding (see section "Encopresis" below), or it may arise from disorders affecting the gastrointestinal tract, as in the case of diseases (e.g., Hirschsprung, metabolic disorders), drug effects, or neuromotor disorders (e.g., spina bifida, cerebral palsy, spinal cord injury).

Constipation may have an impact on other functions of the GI tract, with abdominal pain, emesis, decreased appetite, and feeding refusal. In general, it can be managed in the outpatient setting. Important historical factors include age of onset and duration of constipation, and presence of anatomic abnormalities (e.g., anal atresia), other symptoms or neurologic findings, and presence of fissures or bleeding. Functional constipation (unless complicated by fecal impaction, encopresis, or long-standing duration) can be handled in the outpatient setting.

If hypotonia is also present, constipation may arise from a disorder in thyroid function. If there is abnormal rectal tone, an imaging study may be necessary to evaluate for a mass, or myelomeningocele. If rectal tone is normal and rectal ampulla is empty, perform a barium enema to rule out Hirschsprung disease.

Treatment may consist of

- enemas to relieve fecal impaction
- bowel training to (re)institute a regular program
- high-fiber diet to add bulk to diet and increase movement through GI tract; increase fluids but limit milk, apple juice, and tea
- laxatives to soften stools and prevent stool withholding
  1. suppositories
  2. oral medicine: milk of magnesia; stool softeners (docusate); Dulcolax; mineral oil

ENURESIS

Enuresis is urinary incontinence beyond the age of four years if daytime or diurnal and beyond age of six years if nighttime or nocturnal. It may spring from diseases and structural abnormalities related to bladder dysfunction, abnormal sphincter control, anatomic anomalies of bladder or ureters or kidney disease. Its etiology is unclear, but contributing factors include familial predisposition, possible small bladder capacity, central nervous system factors (more common in children with developmental disabilities), history of decreased sleep arousal, and the contribution of stress.

History and physical exam are important to rule out medical factors, with emphasis on neurologic examination of the lower extremities, spine, and genitalia. Laboratory tests may include urinalysis and urine culture and other studies depending on physical findings (e.g., spine films); the suggestion of kidney disease might indicate renal ultrasound, voiding cystourethrom gram (VCUG), electrolytes, and creatinine. The spontaneous cure rate of nocturnal enuresis is 15 percent per year.

Treatment consists of

- motivational interventions and bladder-stretching exercises
- alarms—most successful treatment of nocturnal enuresis (70 to 80 percent successful), especially when used in conjunction with a behavioral modification program; alarm is attached to underwear or bedclothes and is set off when child urinates; parents wake child and bring him or her to bathroom: with time, the child will sleep through the night and remain dry
- Medications
  1. Imipramine—effective but 50 to 60 percent regression rate after discontinued
  2. DDAVP (desmopressin)—decreases the volume of urine; also has a high regression rate (40 to 60 percent), and is very expensive

ENCOPRESIS

Encopresis is the passage of formed or semiformed stools in a child's underwear (or other inappropriate places) occurring regularly (more than once a month) after four years of age. Some children have never been continent (primary or continuous) and others have completed toilet training and regress to incontinence. Causes are multifactorial:

- retention of stool—may be potentiated by constipation, congenital anorectal problems, medication side effects (contributing to constipation)
- psychosocial factors, including poor self-esteem, isolation, control issues

Constipation and/or retention of stool is usually the initiating factor. Retention of stool may be a result of pain on defecation due to large stool size or fissures. With retention the rectal wall stretches and decreases in contractile strength, with reabsorption of water, with resultant harder and larger feces. Painful defecation promotes toilet avoidance and more obstipation, with some passage of soft feces and mucus around impactions.

Evaluation involves

- *History*: including toilet training, current habits of toilet use, severity and frequency of incontinence, impact on child and family
- *Examination*: general examination, neurologic examination (including sensory and rectal tone), palpation of abdomen; abdominal x-ray to confirm stool retention

Treatment consists of

1. *Initial catharsis*: enema(s) plus Dulcolax suppository(ies) and/or tablet; establish regular schedule of bathroom use after meals.
2. *Maintenance regimen*: continue established schedule for bathroom use; mineral oil orally one to two times per day; high-roughage diet; oral laxative (initially)
3. *Follow-up*: duration of treatment can range six months to three years

SUGGESTED READINGS

Enuresis

Rappaport, L. 1993. The treatment of nocturnal enuresis: Where are we now? *Pediatrics* 92:465–466.

Wille, S. 1986. Comparison of desmopressin and enuresis alarms for nocturnal enuresis. Archives of Diseases in Children, 61:30–33.

Encopresis

Levine, M. 1992. Encopresis. In: *Developmental-behaviorial pediatrics*, ed. M. Levine et al. 389–397. Philadelphia: W.B. Saunders Co.

Nolan, T, and F. Oberklaid. 1993. New concepts in the managment of encopresis. *Pediatrics Review*, 14:447–451.

ADDITIONAL RESOURCES

Selected enuresis alarms are

- Nite Train'r Alarm, Koregon Enterprises, 9735 Southwest Sunshine Court, Beaverton, OR 97005, Tel.: (800) 544-4240.
- Nutone Medical Products, 2424 South 900 West, Salt Lake City, UT 84119, Tel.:(801) 973-4090.
- Sleep Dry Alarm System, Star Child Labs, P.O. Box 404, Aptos, CA 95001, Tel.: (800) 345-7243.
- Wet Stop Alarm, Placo Laboratories, 8030 Soquel Avenue, Santa Cruz, CA 95062, Tel.: (800) 346-4488.

Chapter 13

Medical and Nursing Issues

INFECTION CONTROL

Kathleen Ryan Kuntz

Purpose: to review general principles for controlling the spread of infections in pediatric settings. It is understood that specific infection control policies and procedures may vary according to the requirements of each facility.

Strict implementation of measures to control infection is an important responsibility of all persons involved in the care of children. Infection control practices are designed to ensure a safe and healthy environment for workers, as well as for patients and their families. The spread of infection requires three essential elements: (1) a *source* of infectious organisms, (2) a *means of transmission* for the organism, and (3) a *susceptible host*.

The *source* of an infectious agent may be the patient, family members, or staff members, including (1) individuals with active infection, (2) those who are in the incubation period of an infection, or (3) those who are carriers without active disease. Patients may also be infected with their own endogenous flora. Other potential sources of infection include objects in the environment that have been contaminated.

Infectious organisms may be *transmitted* by various routes, and some organisms may be transmitted by multiple routes. The four main routes of transmission are contact, vehicle, airborne, and vector borne. *Contact* may be (1) *direct contact* (physical transfer of pathogens from an infected host to a susceptible host through direct personal contact), (2) *indirect contact* (contact of a susceptible host with contaminated articles, such as toys or bed linens), or (3) *droplet contact* (contact of infectious droplets with the conjunctivae, nose, or mouth of a susceptible host, usually as a result of close proximity to an infected host while talking, coughing, or sneezing). *Vehicle* transmission is transmission through contaminated food or water, intravenous solutions, or blood or other body fluids. *Airborne* transmission occurs by dissemination of either droplet nuclei (residue from evaporated droplets that may remain suspended in air for a long time) or dust particles. Organisms transmitted in this manner are either inhaled by or deposited on a susceptible host. Finally, *vector borne* transmission occurs through an animate source (insect or animal).

The third element necessary for the establishment of an infection is a *susceptible host*. Resistance to infection varies markedly among individuals. Persons with diabetes mellitus, lymphomas, leukemias, other neoplasms, organ transplants, agranulocytosis, or uremia, and persons treated with certain antibiotics, corticosteroids, irradiation, or immunosuppressive agents may be particularly prone to infection. Age, chronic disease, coma, and trauma also influence susceptibility. When exposed to any given agent, some individuals may show an immune response, some may become asymptomatic carriers, and others may develop active disease.

CATEGORIES OF PRECAUTION

Although most organisms are transmitted by direct contact with an object soiled with an infectious droplet, some may be airborne and are inhaled (e.g., chickenpox), and others are transmitted only by direct contact with blood or specific body fluids (e.g., HIV, hepatitis B). For this reason, different types of precautions are recommended to protect yourself or others from exposure. The purpose and description of each type of precaution are provided in Table 13–1.

SPECIAL CONSIDERATIONS FOR UNIVERSAL PRECAUTIONS

Since an individual can be infected with a blood-borne pathogen and exhibit no symptoms, it is important for caregivers to prevent the possibility of transmission by treating all blood and potentially infectious materials as if they are infectious. The risks from exposure to these pathogens, such as the human immunodeficiency virus (HIV) and hepatitis B virus (HBV), are of concern to professionals serving children with chronic and developmental conditions. It is im-

portant to understand how these infections are transmitted and how to prevent exposure by practicing universal precautions at all times.

Prevalence of HIV has increased in women of child-bearing age, adolescents, and infants. An infant born to a woman with HIV may test positive for the infection for up to 18 months due to the maternally transferred antibodies. However, two-thirds to three-quarters are not infected.

HBV has been found to be common in populations where it is endemic (Alaskan Natives; Pacific Islanders; immigrants from HBV-endemic areas, particularly eastern Asia and Africa) and among residents of institutions for the developmentally disabled. The American Academy of Pediatrics (AAP) now recommends universal HBV immunization of all infants. Caregivers may also consider immunization if they are exposed to blood or blood products or if they care for individuals with developmental disabilities.

Although HIV and HBV are not as easily transmitted as other organisms, it is important to recognize the precise means of transmission and significance of exposure. The virus, to be spread from one person to another, must be in a potentially infectious body fluid, must have a route of entry to the uninfected person, and must be present in sufficient quantity (volume or repeated exposure). The Occupational Safety and Health Administration (OSHA 1992) identified blood-borne pathogens as those found in human blood, blood products or components, semen, and vaginal secretions, as well as body fluids such as cerebrospinal, synovial, pleural, pericardial, peritoneal, and amniotic fluids, saliva, and tissue where the integrity is compromised. Although HIV and HBV can be found in these various body fluids, transmission occurs with only a few. HIV is transmitted in blood, semen, vaginal and cervical secretions, and breast milk. HBV is also found in wound exudate and saliva. Saliva contains only small quantities of the virus and is not thought to pose high risk for transmission unless it is contaminated with blood (e.g., from a dental procedure).

Despite all that we have learned about human immunodeficiency virus (HIV) and acquired im-

Table 13–1 Purposes and Descriptions of Precaution Types

Precaution Type	Purpose	Common Organisms	Precautions
Universal precautions	Prevent spread of infection transmitted by contact with blood or blood-containing fluid	HIV, hepatitis B	Blood, including your own, should be considered infected and should not be contacted directly. Wear gloves for direct contact; mask/goggles/plastic-lined gown if splatter likely. Sanitize surfaces after contact with potentially infected fluids
Drainage and secretion	Prevent infection transmission by contact with wounds and secretions	Adenovirus, conjunctivitis, herpes simplex, impetigo, pediculosis, RSV, rubella, scabies, tracheitis, upper and lower respiratory infections	Wear gloves, with scrupulous hand washing after gloves removed. Gown to protect clothing if needed
Enteric	Prevent transmission by contact with infected stool	Enterovirus, giardiasis, hepatitis A, infant botulism, poliovirus, rotavirus, salmonella, shigella, viral diarrhea, viral meningitis	Wear gloves, with scrupulous hand washing after gloves removed. Gown to protect clothing if needed
Respiratory	Prevent transmission by large droplets	Epiglottis, measles, bacterial meningitis, mumps, pertussis	Wear gloves, with scrupulous hand washing after gloves removed. Gown to protect clothing if needed
Strict isolation	Prevent transmission of highly infectious organisms, both by air and by contact with secretions	Varicella, diphtheria, rabies	Isolation room with door closed, no contact with those who have no immunity
Protective isolation	Protect an individual who is highly susceptible to infection (due to decreased immunity or impaired resistance)	As individually indicated	As individually indicated
Pregnant woman precautions	Prevent transmission of infections that may be harmful to the fetus of a pregnant woman	Cytomegalovirus, rubella, varicella, parovirus	Wash hands before and after contact with individual. Pregnant women should have no contact

Source: Courtesy of Children's Hospital, Philadelphia, Pennsylvania.

mune deficiency syndrome (AIDS) over the past several years, many caretakers continue to be overly fearful that activities such as changing diapers, cleaning emesis or mucus, and providing therapies will place them at risk for exposure. Project CHAMP (Children's HIV and AIDS Model Program), at Children's National Medical Center, offers a method to assess the degree of risk that is encountered. Table 13–2 identifies factors that influence HIV transmission (body fluid, route of entry, and fluid dose or quantity) as they correlate with levels of risk (high, moderate, low, no proven risk, and no risk). Care providers can identify the level of risk in any situation they may encounter utilizing the procedure outlined in Exhibit 13–1.

GENERAL INFECTION CONTROL PRINCIPLES

Hand washing is the single most effective means of controlling the spread of infections. Always be aware of where your hands have been as you go on to a new activity. At a minimum, hands should be washed

1. at the start of a work shift
2. before and after each patient contact; when this is not practical (e.g., in a group treatment setting), consider using pop-up hand wipes as an alternative
3. after toilcting or diapering a patient
4. before and after your own meals and toileting
5. after handling materials or toys soiled by secretions
6. at the end of a work shift

The importance of careful hand washing cannot be overemphasized. The key steps in hand washing are:

1. Turn water on and wet hands.
2. Use soap or antimicrobial agent.
3. Lather hands well.
4. Apply friction, and be sure to clean all surfaces, between fingers, and under nails.
5. Rinse hands under running water.
6. Dry hands thoroughly with a clean towel or under air flow.

Table 13–2 HIV Risk Assessment Chart

| | Transmission Factors | | |
Level of Risk	*Body Fluid*	*Route of Entry*	*Fluid Dose*
High	Blood Semen	Infection Rectum, vagina, placenta	Large volume Repeated exposures

Moderate	Vaginal/cervical
	  secretions
		Break in skin, penis,
		  mouth
			Occasional exposures

Low	Breast milk	Newly inflicted wound Eyes, nose	Small volume One exposure
No proven risk	Saliva, tears, urine, vomit, nasal secretions		
No risk	Feces Sweat	Intact skin Clothing	No contact

Source: From *Caring in the Community with HIV: A Guide for Child Care Providers, Foster Families, Home Health Aides and Volunteers,* by Project CHAMP, Children's Hospital/Children's National Medical Center, M.C. Rathlev, M.R. Riley, and S.J. Jones. Copyright © 1992 by Children's Hospital/Child Welfare League of America. Reprinted with permission.

Exhibit 13–1 HIV Risk Assessment Procedure

Risk Assessment Procedure

Transmission risk factors have been organized on the preceding chart to show:

The type of factor, across the top of the chart:
- Body fluid
- Route of entry
- Dose

The risk associated with each individual factor, down the left side of the chart:
- High—consistently leads to infection with HIV
- Moderate—can lead to transmission but less consistently than high factors
- Low—not very efficient transmission factors
- No proven risk—largely theoretic risks
- No risk—cannot contribute to transmission

Human body fluids are organized according to how much HIV they can contain:
- Blood and semen: high risk—They contain a sufficient number of the cells for HIV to live.
- Vaginal and cervical secretions: moderate risk—They contain a lesser number of cells for HIV to live.
- Breast milk: low risk—Epidemiologically it has been implicated only in a few cases.
- Saliva, tears, urine, vomit, nasal secretions: no proven risk—Small amounts of the virus have been isolated from them; however, they do not contain enough cells for HIV to live.
- Feces and sweat: no risk—They do not contain even small amounts of the virus.

Routes of entry are organized according to how efficiently they lead to the bloodstream:
- Injection (by means of syringe or transfusion): high risk—This is the most efficient route to the bloodstream, followed by mucous membranes, such as rectal and vaginal tissues, which due to their fragility permit absorption by blood vessels.
- The penis and mouth: moderate risk—The outer skin and mucous membranes offer protection, but a break in the skin or mucous membranes allows ready access to a blood vessel.
- Newly inflicted wound, eyes, and nose: low risk—All provide protection through mechanisms of bleeding, tearing, and sneezing.

- Intact skin: no risk—The body's first line of defense against germs and an effective barrier between HIV and the bloodstream.

Dose is a factor more dependent on the other two:
- Large volume (of blood) or repeated exposures (frequent injections): high risk—This is equally effective in transmitting HIV.
- Occasional exposures: moderate risk—The incidence of heterosexual transmission to women is increasing dramatically.
- Small volume and one exposure: low risk—The incidence of transmission after accidental needlesticks by health care workers is 4 per 1,000.

Ask the following questions to determine transmission risk factors in any situation:
- To what body fluid is the uninfected person being exposed?
- How is the body fluid getting inside of his or her body?
- How often does this happen?
- Example: If a woman is having unprotected sexual intercourse with an infected man two to three times a week, she is being exposed to semen; the semen is getting into her body through her vagina; this is happening often.
  —Since all are high-risk factors, she is at high risk for becoming infected with HIV.
- Example: If a caregiver with open sores on her hands provides first aid for a child with HIV infection without gloves one time, she is being exposed to blood; the blood is getting into her body through open sores; this is one exposure.
  —Since one is a high-risk factor, one is a moderate risk factor, and one is a low-risk factor, she is at moderate risk for becoming infected with HIV.

If a transmission factor falls within the "no proven risk" or "no risk" category, then there is no need to proceed any further. While transmission may be theoretically possible, it has not happened based on "no proven risk" or "no risk" factors.

Source: Reprinted with permission from Project CHAMP, Children's Hospital/Children's National Medical Center, Washington, D.C.

---

7. Turn water off using towel; avoid contact with faucet after hands are clean.
8. Use hand cream as necessary to maintain the integrity of skin (prevent redness and dryness).

Other general measures that can help to prevent infection include:
1. Maintain adequate nutrition and rest.
2. Adopt good hygiene habits.
3. Restrict contact with infectious persons.

4. Avoid handling contaminated materials.

5. Keep dry and warm.

SANITIZATION OF TOYS AND EQUIPMENT

Working with children offers many unique challenges in control of infection. Infectious organisms can be present even when a child shows no symptoms, or only mild signs, of an infectious process. The risk of transmission increases when children play and mouth toys or cough and sneeze openly. Additional risks are present when children need help with toileting needs. By nature, children are inherently curious about their environment and are likely to touch anything and everything. Remember that it is not only your hands that you need to keep clean but also the child's hands and any objects or toys that have been manipulated by the child. When possible, avoid using toys that are difficult to sanitize, such as stuffed animals, or provide personal toys for each child. Store soiled linens and toys in closed containers until they can be cleaned. The following sequence is recommended for sanitization of mats, toys, or other objects with a nonporous surface:

1. Wear gloves.

2. Remove visible soiling with warm soapy water and rinse.

3. Soak or wipe down surface using disinfectant, such as a 1:10 solution of household bleach:water (one teaspoon bleach to one quart water). Allow to soak or remain wet for one minute.

4. Rinse.

5. Air-dry for 10 minutes.

6. Remove gloves and discard.

7. Wash hands.

REFERENCE

Occupational Safety and Health Administration. 1992. *Bloodborne pathogens and long-term care workers.* Washington, D.C.

ADDITIONAL SUGGESTED READINGS

American Academy of Pediatrics, Committee on Infectious Diseases. 1991. *Hepatitis B: Report of the Committee on Infectious Diseases.* Elk Grove Village, Ill.

Children's Hospital of Philadelphia. 1992. *Opinions about antimicrobials.* Philadelphia.

Jackson, M.M., and P. Lynch. 1991. An attempt to make an issue less murky: A comparison of four systems for infection precautions. *Infection Control and Hospital Epidemiology* 12:448–450.

Larson, E. 1989. Handwashing: It's essential—even when you use gloves. *American Journal of Nursing* 89:934–939.

Peter, G., et al., eds. 1994. *1994 Red Book: Report of the Committee on Infectious Diseases.* 23rd ed. Elk Grove Village, Ill.: American Academy of Pediatrics.

Rathlev, M.C. 1994. Universal precautions in early intervention and child care. *Infants and Young Children* 6, no. 3:54–64.

Rathlev, M.C., et al. 1992. *Caring in the community for children with HIV: A guide for child care providers, foster families, home health aides, and volunteers.* Washington, D.C.: Children's Hospital/Child Welfare League of America.

SAFETY

Kathleen Ryan Kuntz

Purpose: to review general considerations for prevention of accidents when caring for children with developmental disabilities or special health care needs.

Injury is the leading cause of death in children and adults to age 44 years and is responsible for more childhood deaths than all other causes combined (Centers for Disease Control 1990). Efforts to prevent injury can save thousands of lives and can prevent an even greater number of accidents. Efforts to instruct caregivers in safety principles are likely to be more effective if provided as specific suggestions rather than general advice.

Safety precautions are an important component of care for all children. The degree of precaution indicated is based on the individual child's motor ability, behavioral style, and cognitive awareness of potential hazards. While chronological age may be used to guide the level of precaution needed in a typically developing child, this is not usually true of children with disabilities. Instead, the necessary level of precaution must be based upon careful consideration of the individual child's maturity and mobility skills, combined with the degree of inquisitiveness, impulsivity, and judgment present in the individual child.

It is not sufficient to consider only the child's cognitive level of development when planning for safe child care practices. For instance, consider the challenge posed by a nine-year-old child who incurs a traumatic brain injury that results in a functional level of cognition at the 2½-year level with intact motor skills. This child may look like a nine year old and run as fast as a nine year old, causing an automobile driver who observes this child chasing a ball into the street to anticipate a different level of response than the child is capable of.

GENERAL SAFETY MEASURES

The following are some general safety measures that are necessary when caring for all children, including the child with developmental disabilities and special health care needs:

- Use a safety helmet whenever riding a bike or engaging in other high-risk activity.
- Keep hot liquids or appliances that generate heat out of reach of children.
- Maintain hot water settings at 120 degrees or lower.
- Avoid exposure to potentially noxious fumes, including cigarette smoke.
- Keep smoke detectors ready with fresh batteries, and review emergency evacuation procedures on a regular basis.
- Use a cool-mist humidifier instead of a steam vaporizer.
- Post the telephone number for emergency personnel by each phone (ambulance, physician, poison control center).
- Keep toxic substances and poisonous plants out of reach.
- Keep a supply of syrup of ipecac in the home.
- Make sure that all medications are clearly labeled, stored in childproof containers, and kept out of reach.
- Use nonskid mats in tubs and on noncarpeted stairs.
- Use rugs with non-skid backing.
- Install gates across staircases.
- Tie plastic bags in knots before discarding.
- Store objects smaller than 1 ¼ inches in diameter (e.g., button-size batteries) out of reach.

- Keep bathroom doors closed.
- Install fences with locked gates around pools; never leave children alone near pools or other bodies of water.
- Set electric garage doors to open automatically when contacting an object.
- Keep doors of major appliances closed at all times.
- Prepare foods in pieces that can be swallowed or managed easily.
- Maintain proper immunization against rabies for pets.
- Always use proper child restraint systems when transporting children in cars.
- Remember to wear sunscreen and drink plenty of fluids when outdoors in the sun.
- Make sure that children use only play equipment that is appropriate for their age, size, and skill.
- Use only Mylar balloons to avoid the risk of choking.

SPECIAL PRECAUTIONS

The following are special safety considerations for children with physical and medical problems:

- Be sure that babysitters or other "temporary" caregivers are fully aware of the child's special care needs and know whom to contact in the event of a problem.
- Use safety belts in high chairs and wheelchairs.

- Install grab bars for stairways and bathroom as necessary.
- Identify special restraint systems for safe travel in an automobile when the child has poor sitting balance or head control.
- Remember to engage the locks on wheelchairs or other mobility devices before initiating transfers.
- Remember that a child with difficulty ambulating may be at greater risk when walking on uneven terrain than when walking on a level floor.
- Children with limited visual acuity or visual perception difficulty may not recognize obstacles in their environment.
- Children with attentional difficulties (either overly distractible or overly perseverative) may not respond quickly to emergent situations, such as a door closing on the fingers.
- Be fully prepared for the potential of equipment problems in children with technologic dependence.
- Loss of sensation due to nerve damage may cause the child to be unaware of injury; for example, a child with spinal cord injury may be at risk for skin breakdown when sitting for long periods.
- Know your limits when attempting to lift or transfer a child with disabilities; use proper techniques when lifting.
- Be sure to plan ahead for special emergency and evacuation needs in the event of a natural disaster.

REFERENCE

Centers for Disease Control, Division of Injury Control, Center for Environmental Health and Injury Control. 1990. Childhood injuries in the United States. *American Journal of Diseases of Children* 144:627–646.

ADDITIONAL SUGGESTED READINGS

American Academy of Pediatrics. 1987. Car seats for children with mechanically assisted ventilation. *Pediatrics* 80:290–292.

American Academy of Pediatrics Committee on Injury and Poison Prevention and Committee on Fetus and Newborn. 1991. Safe transportation of premature infants. *Pediatrics* 87:120–122.

American Academy of Pediatrics Committee on Injury and Poison Prevention. 1993. Policy statement: Transporting children with special needs. *AAP Safe Ride News*, insert (Winter):1–4.

National Committee for Injury Prevention and Control. 1989. *Injury prevention: Meeting the challenge.* New York: Oxford University Press.

National Safe Kids Coalition. 1988. *Safe kids are no accident.* Washington, D.C.: Children's Hospital National Medical Center.

Richards, D.D. 1989. The challenge of transporting children with special needs. *AAP Safe Ride News* (Spring): 1–4.

Sewell, K.H., and S.K. Gaines. 1993. A developmental approach to childhood safety education. *Pediatric Nursing* 19:464–466.

Stout, J.D., et al. 1989. Safe transportation for children with disabilities. *American Journal of Occupational Therapy* 43, no. 1:31–36.

Valuzzi, J.L. 1995. Safety issues in community-based settings for children who are medically fragile: Program planning for natural disasters. *Infants and Young Children* 7, no. 4:62–76.

Zuckerman, B.S., and J.C. Duby. 1985. Developmental approach to injury prevention. *Pediatric Clinics of North America* 32:17–29.

ADDITIONAL RESOURCES

American Public Health Association and American Academy of Pediatrics. 1992. *Caring for our children: National health and safety performance standards: Guidelines for out-of-home child care programs.* Washington, D.C.

Richmond State School. 1992. *Wheelchair use and safety.* Wheelchair video series.

Safe Ride News, American Academy of Pediatrics, P.O. Box 927, Elk Grove Village, IL 60009-0927.

CARDIORESPIRATORY EMERGENCY MANAGEMENT

Kathleen Ryan Kuntz

Purpose: to provide an overview of principles and techniques for providing basic life support, including cardiopulmonary resuscitation, to infants and children in an emergency situation.

Most pediatric emergencies that require basic life support are the result of a respiratory arrest as caused by airway obstruction, apnea, illness, or injury. Typically, pediatric basic life support focuses attention on techniques for the infant (under one year) and the young child (one to eight years). It is important, however, to recognize that a large component of pediatric health care is directed toward children and young adults over eight years. These individuals require the techniques and procedures that the American Heart Association classifies as being for the "adult." The assessment of a child, regardless of age, remains the same. A comparison of techniques is provided.

BASIC LIFE SUPPORT

The sequence of basic life-support techniques is as follows:

- Determine unresponsiveness.
  1. Quickly assess the presence or extent of injury.
  2. Determine level of consciousness.
  3. Avoid movement of the child if a head or neck injury is suspected; keep the cervical spine completely immobilized.
  4. Initiate basic life support.
     (a) Up to eight years—Assess airway and continue basic life support for one minute before activating emergency medical system (EMS) yourself.
     (b) Over eight years—Activate EMS system yourself if alone, then re-

turn to assess the child and continue basic life support.

- Assess airway.
  1. Open airway, utilizing head tilt/chin lift method (if trauma suspected, avoid head tilt and open airway by jaw-thrust maneuver).
     (a) Under one year—Extend neck (do not hyperextend) to open airway (Figure 13–1).
     (b) One or more years—Hyperextend neck to open airway (Figure 13–2).
- Assess breathing.
  1. Position face near child's nose and mouth.
  2. Look at chest for rise and fall.
  3. Listen to hear breath in ear.
  4. Feel for breath against cheek; if child is not breathing, give two rescue breaths.

  (a) Under one year—Place mouth over child's nose and mouth (Figure 13–3).
  (b) One or more years—Pinch nose and place mouth over child's mouth (Figure 13–4).
- Assess circulation.
  1. Evaluate presence or absence of pulse (cardiac contractions), utilizing two fingers.
     (a) Under one year—at brachial artery (Figure 13–5).
     (b) One or more years—at carotid artery (Figure 13–6).
  2. If child has a pulse but continues not to breathe, administer rescue breathing.
     (a) Up to eight years—rate of 20 breaths/minute.
     (b) Over eight years—rate of 12 breaths/minute.

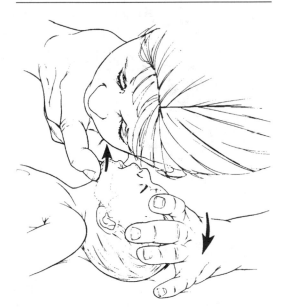

Figure 13–1 Assessing Airway of Infant (under One Year). *Source:* From "Guidelines for Cardiopulmonary Resuscitation and Emergency Cardiac Care," *Journal of the American Medical Association,* 286(16), pp. 2171–2302. Copyright © 1992 by the American Medical Association. Reprinted by permission.

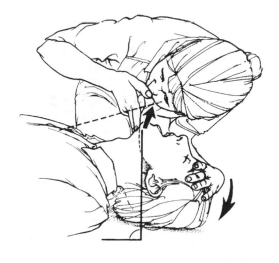

Figure 13–2 Assessing Airway of Child (One or More Years). *Source:* From "Guidelines for Cardiopulmonary Resuscitation and Emergency Cardiac Care," *Journal of the American Medical Association,* 286(16), pp. 2171–2302. Copyright © 1992 by the American Medical Association. Reprinted by permission.

Figure 13–3 Rescue Breaths to Infant (under One Year). *Source:* From "Guidelines for Cardiopulmonary Resuscitation and Emergency Cardiac Care," *Journal of the American Medical Association*, 286(16), pp. 2171–2302. Copyright © 1992 by the American Medical Association. Reprinted by permission.

Figure 13–5 Evaluating Pulse of Infant (under One Year). *Source:* From "Guidelines for Cardiopulmonary Resuscitation and Emergency Cardiac Care," *Journal of the American Medical Association*, 286(16), pp. 2171–2302. Copyright © 1992 by the American Medical Association. Reprinted by permission.

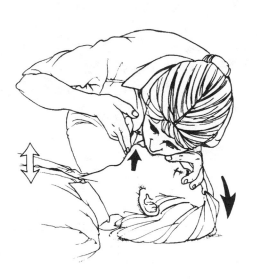

Figure 13–4 Rescue Breaths to Child (One or More Years). *Source:* From "Guidelines for Cardiopulmonary Resuscitation and Emergency Cardiac Care," *Journal of the American Medical Association*, 286(16), pp. 2171–2302. Copyright © 1992 by the American Medical Association. Reprinted by permission.

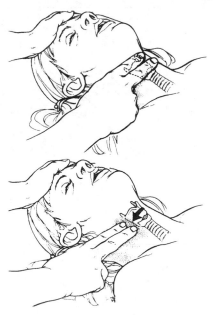

Figure 13–6 Evaluating Pulse of Child (One or More Years). *Source:* From "Guidelines for Cardiopulmonary Resuscitation and Emergency Cardiac Care," *Journal of the American Medical Association*, 286(16), pp. 2171–2302. Copyright © 1992 by the American Medical Association. Reprinted by permission.

3. If child has no pulse, initiate chest compressions with rescue breathing.

    (a) Under one year—rate of 100 compressions/minute with two fingers positioned one finger breadth below the nipple line (Figure 13–7).

    (b) One to eight years—rate of 100 compressions/minute with heel of one hand positioned one finger breadth above xiphoid process (Figure 13–8).

    (c) Over eight years—rate of 100 compressions/minute with heel of one hand and second hand on top, positioned one finger breadth above xiphoid process (Figure 13–9).

- Continue basic life support efforts for one full minute and reassess for return of pulse and/or respiration. If there is no spontaneous pulse and respiration, resume chest compressions and rescue breathing.

Table 13–3 summarizes cardiorespiratory emergency management measures.

FOREIGN-BODY AIRWAY OBSTRUCTION

The American Heart Association (1992) reported that more than 90 percent of deaths from foreign-body aspiration in the pediatric age group occur in children younger than five years of age; 65 percent of the victims are infants. If foreign-body aspiration is witnessed or strongly suspected, the rescuer should encourage the child to continue any spontaneous cough and breathing effort. If the cough becomes ineffective or if the child becomes unconscious, the rescuer should activate EMS as quickly as possible.

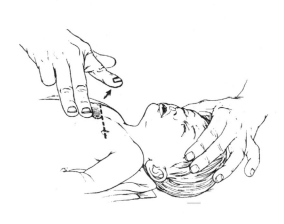

Figure 13–7 Cardiac Compressions to Infant (under One Year). *Source:* From "Guidelines for Cardiopulmonary Resuscitation and Emergency Cardiac Care," *Journal of the American Medical Association,* 286(16), pp. 2171–2302. Copyright © 1992 by the American Medical Association. Reprinted by permission.

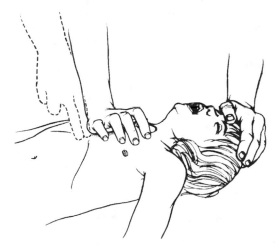

Figure 13–8 Cardiac Compressions to Child (One to Eight Years). *Source:* From "Guidelines for Cardiopulmonary Resuscitation and Emergency Cardiac Care," *Journal of the American Medical Association,* 286(16), pp. 2171–2302. Copyright © 1992 by the American Medical Association. Reprinted by permission.

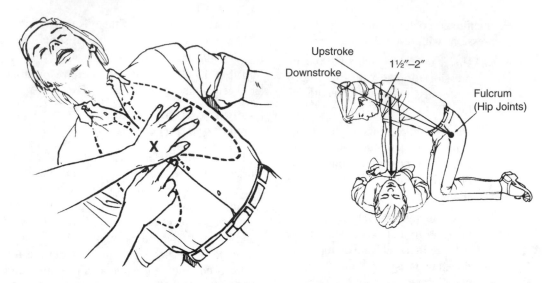

Figure 13–9 Cardiac Compressions to Child (over Eight Years). *Source:* From "Guidelines for Cardiopulmonary Resuscitation and Emergency Cardiac Care," *Journal of the American Medical Association*, 286(16), pp. 2171–2302. Copyright © 1992 by the American Medical Association. Reprinted by permission.

Table 13–3 Cardiorespiratory Emergency Management

Maneuver	Infant (<1 Yr.)	Child (1–8 Yr.)	Older Child (> 8 Yr.)
Airway	Head tilt/chin lift (if trauma present, use jaw thrust)	Head tilt/chin lift (if trauma present, use jaw thrust)	Head tilt/chin lift (if trauma present, use jaw thrust)
Breathing			
• Initial	2 breaths at 1–1½ sec./ breath	2 breaths at 1–1½ sec./ breath	2 breaths at 1–1½ sec./ breath
• Subsequent	20 breaths/min.	20 breaths/min.	12 breaths/min.
Circulation			
• Pulse check	Brachial/femoral	Carotid	Carotid
• Compression area	Lower third of sternum	Lower third of sternum	Lower third of sternum
• Compression width	2 fingers	Heel of one hand	Heel of two hands
• Depth	Approx. ½–1 in.	Approx. 1–1½ in.	Approx. 1½–2 in.
• Rate	At least 100/min.	100/min.	100/min.
• Compression–vent ratio	5:1 (pause for ventilation)	5:1 (pause for ventilation)	5:1 (pause for ventilation)
Foreign-body airway obstruction	Back blows/chest thrusts	Heimlich maneuver	Heimlich maneuver

Procedures for clearing foreign-body airway obstruction are as follows:

- Infant (under one year) (see Figure 13–10)
  1. Hold prone, resting on forearm, supporting head and neck.
  2. Deliver five back blows forcefully between shoulder blades with heel of hand.
  3. Place other hand on head and use forearm to support back, "sandwiching" infant between arms.
  4. Turn infant, supporting head and neck.
  5. Provide five downward chest thrusts in same location/position as chest compressions (lower third of sternum, one finger breadth below nipple line; depth of ½–1 in.; Figure 13–10).
  6. If infant is conscious, continue sequence of five back blows followed by five chest thrusts until obstruction relieved or until infant becomes unconscious.
  7. If infant becomes unconscious, place on firm surface and inspect mouth; remove foreign body if visualized.
  8. If foreign body is not retrieved, open airway and attempt rescue breathing.
  9. If airway remains obstructed, repeat sequence of back blows, chest thrusts, inspecting mouth, and attempting rescue breathing until successful.
  10. If at any time, the obstruction is relieved:
      (a) Deliver two breaths.
      (b) Assess pulse.
      (c) Initiate chest compressions if necessary.
- Child/young adult
  1. Stand behind child with arms directly under child's axillae, encircling child's chest (Figure 13–11).
  2. Place fist against child's abdomen in midline, slightly above navel (well below rib cage and tip of xiphoid process).

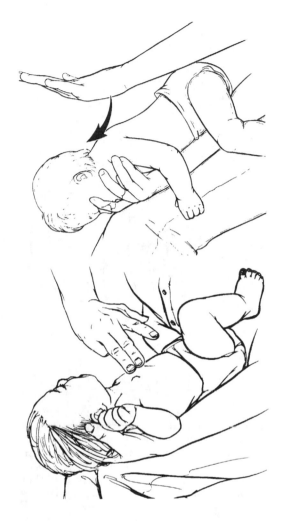

Figure 13–10 Clearing Foreign-Body Airway Obstruction for Infant (under One Year). *Source:* From "Guidelines for Cardiopulmonary Resuscitation and Emergency Cardiac Care," *Journal of the American Medical Association*, 286(16), pp. 2171–2302. Copyright © 1992 by the American Medical Association. Reprinted by permission.

  3. Grasp fist with other hand and deliver up to five upward thrusts, each being a separate and deliberate effort to relieve the obstruction.
  4. If obstruction persists, continue abdominal thrusts until foreign body is expelled or the victim becomes unconscious.

Figure 13–11 Clearing Foreign-Body Airway Obstruction for Child (One or More Years), Standing Abdominal Thrust. *Source:* From "Guidelines for Cardiopulmonary Resuscitation and Emergency Cardiac Care," *Journal of the American Medical Association*, 286(16), pp. 2171–2302. Copyright © 1992 by the American Medical Association. Reprinted by permission.

5. If child becomes unconscious, position on back, inspect mouth, remove foreign body if visualized.

   (a) Up to eight years—Do not place fingers in mouth unless object seen.

   (b) Over eight years—Rescuer can perform blind sweep with hooked finger in attempt to retrieve object, even if it is not seen.

6. If foreign body not retrieved, open airway and attempt rescue breathing.

7. If airway remains obstructed, deliver abdominal thrusts in the following manner:

(a) Kneel beside or astride the child's legs.

(b) Place heel of one hand on child's abdomen, slightly above the navel (well below rib cage and xiphoid process; Figure 13–12).

(c) Position other hand on top of first.

(d) Press both hands into abdomen with quick upward thrust. Each thrust is directed upward in midline. Deliver five thrusts, each being a separate and deliberate effort to relieve the obstruction.

(e) After five thrusts, inspect the mouth for object (performing sweep if over 8 years old), and attempt rescue breathing.

(f) If airway remains obstructed, repeat sequence of abdominal thrusts, inspection (sweep if over 8 years old), and attempt rescue breathing until successful.

Figure 13–12 Clearing Foreign-Body Airway Obstruction for Child (One or More Years), Kneeling Abdominal Thrust. *Source:* From "Guidelines for Cardiopulmonary Resuscitation and Emergency Cardiac Care," *Journal of the American Medical Association*, 286(16), pp. 2171–2302. Copyright © 1992 by the American Medical Association. Reprinted by permission.

8. If at any time, the obstruction is relieved:

    (a) Deliver two breaths.

    (b) Assess pulse.

    (c) Initiate chest compressions if necessary.

REFERENCE

American Heart Association. 1992. Guidelines for cardiopulmonary resuscitation and emergency cardiac care. *Journal of the American Medical Association* 268:2251–2261.

ADDITIONAL SUGGESTED READING

American Heart Association and American Academy of Pediatrics. 1988. *Textbook of pediatric basic life support.* Dallas.

THERAPY CONSIDERATIONS FOR THE MEDICALLY FRAGILE CHILD

Kathleen Ryan Kuntz

Purpose: to provide an overview of therapeutic interventions to the medically fragile child.

Medically fragile children are those children who require skilled nursing intervention with or without medical equipment to support vital functions (Patterson et al. 1992). These can include children with respiratory compromise, feeding difficulties, and neurologic conditions.

The condition that makes a child "medically fragile" often requires treatments and interventions that may need to be considered when planning a therapeutic regimen.

Table 13–4 highlights areas of need for medical support and considerations in providing therapeutic interventions. Areas addressed in greater detail in other sections are indicated by an asterisk.

Table 13–4 Areas of Need for Medical Support and Therapeutic Interventions for Medically Fragile Children

Area	Considerations	Intervention
Oxygen	Method of delivery	
	Nasal cannula	Ensure that delivery device is in place
	Face mask	
	Tracheostomy collar	
	Tolerance of activity	Observe for tolerance of activity
	May not tolerate dependent position (head lower than heart)	Signs of compromise
		Increased respiratory rate
	May not tolerate degree of activity	Increased work of breathing and use of accessory muscles
		Decreased oxygen to tissue; color becoming mottled or blue

continues

Table 13–4 continued

Area	Considerations	Intervention
Oxygen (continued)	Safety with oxygen-saturated environment Flammable Accessibility/security of tank	Avoid flame and spark-producing toys in area Ensure that cylinder is secure in holder to prevent tank's falling
	Supplemental administration Increasing concentration "Blow-by"	Requires MD prescription Delivered as 100% by face mask, holding mask up to face
Tracheostomy*	Tracheostomy tube patency Humidification device in place Suction available	Maintain humidity device to keep secretions thin If difficulty breathing, suction tracheostomy tube with pressure between 80 and 120 mm Hg If unable to clear a mucous plug by suction, tracheostomy tube should be changed
	Emergency tracheostomy equipment available Extra tracheostomy tube Endotracheal tube (half-size smaller) Scissors Suction catheters Suction unit Oxygen (if prescribed) Extra tape or collar to fasten	
Ventilator*	Tubing patency Condensation in tubing Can decrease pressures delivered Can precipitate aspiration Tubing disconnection Interrupts ventilation delivered	Maintain tubing position so that condensation can collect in trap; empty periodically Maintain connections
Ventriculoperitoneal shunt	Maintain adequate drainage of cerebrospinal fluid from ventricles Observe for signs of shunt malfunction/increased intracranial pressure (ICP) Nausea/vomiting Irritability High-pitched cry "Sunset" eyes Slurred speech Decreased level of consciousness Ataxia or decreased motor ability Seizure	Avoid direct pressure to site of reservoir on head (when palpated, feels like a bubble under the skin) Report information to parent/health care provider immediately
Intravenous catheter Peripheral	Maintain integrity of catheter insertion	Avoid direct pressure to insertion site and surrounding area Avoid tension on catheter or tubing that could cause it to dislodge or become disconnected. May cover area with Ace wrap or splint to guard

Table 13–4 continued

Area	Considerations	Intervention
Intravenous catheter (continued)		
Peripheral	Observe for signs of complications Swelling/redness to area Moisture, leaking, or bleeding at site	Avoid submersion in water or liquid
Central	Cuffed central venous catheter Maintain integrity of catheter insertion	Avoid direct pressure to insertion site and surrounding area Avoid submersion in water or liquid Avoid tension on catheter or tubing that could cause it to dislodge or become disconnected. May cover area with Ace wrap or dressing to guard
	Observe for signs of complications Moisture, leaking, or bleeding Catheter dislodged Catheter torn; potential air embolus	Clamp with padded hemostat above tear. Notify parent or a health care provider who may have been instructed in method of catheter repair
Seizure*	Know seizure history Type Precipitating activity Warning signs Frequency	Anticipate actions necessary Maintain protective measures required (i.e., helmet, medic-alert bracelet, padded chair or bed ralls)
	Protect from injury in event of a seizure	Stop potentially harmful activity If loses consciousness, ensure ability to breathe, and position to avoid aspiration If motor activity is involved, loosen any restraining devices/clothing Move potentially harmful objects out of range
	Observe and monitor seizure activity Duration Progression Area of involvement Characteristics of seizure Postictal state	Report information to parent/health care provider
	Recognize emergency situations	Activate emergency medical system
Enteral feeding* Nasogastric tube feedings	Maintain security of tube placement	Ensure that tubing placement is maintained, that tape is secure, and that tubing is secured to clothing to avoid tension
	Prevent disturbance in nutritional status	Avoid activity that could precipitate vomiting for at least 1 hr. after feeding Avoid activity placing child in a dependent position (head lower than stomach) while feeding is being administered (continuous feeding) and for at least 1 hr. after feeding

continued

Table 13–4 continued

Area	Considerations	Intervention

Enteral feeding*
(continued)
    Gastrostomy
    tube feedings
	Maintain security of tube placement	Ensure that tubing placement is maintained, that tape is secure, and that tubing is secured to clothing to avoid tension
		Avoid direct pressure to stoma during activities
		If tube becomes dislodged, use clean or sterile dressing to cover stoma and apply gentle pressure. Notify parent or health care provider, who may be instructed in inserting a new gastrostomy tube

	Prevent disturbance in nutritional status	

Indwelling
    urinary
    catheter*
	Maintain patency of catheter and drainage tube	Ensure that tube is secure to leg; avoid tension on tube
		Avoid kinking of tubing
		Maintain collection bag below level of bladder

	Maintain connection of catheter to collection bag	If disconnection occurs, swab connection carefully with alcohol before reconnection If spill or leak occurs, utilize universal precautions in cleaning
Infectious disease*	Know infectious process and route of transmission	Maintain precautions necessary to prevent spread of infection

	Know precautions required and protective equipment/procedures needed
	    Gown
	    Gloves
	    Goggles
	    Mask
	    Hand washing
	    Special solution to clean equipment/spills (i.e., 10% hypochlorite solution for blood or blood-contaminated material)
		Maintain environment that protects others from infection

Latex sensitivity	Sensitivity can build up over a period of time Allergic reaction can be exhibited acutely	Avoid exposure if sensitivity is known or suspected

	Observe and monitor for signs of sensitivity
	    Skin reaction (irritated) following contact with latex-containing object (up to 48 hr.)
	    Respiratory irritation when latex-containing substance is in the area	

	Know objects that contain latex protein (e.g., latex gloves, rubber catheters, band-aids), and how contact is established (direct contact, transfer from another, breathing in particles)	Utilize non–latex-containing items (e.g., vinyl gloves, cotton gauze with paper tape)

	Recognize emergency situations
	    Generalized skin reaction; color change (like sunburn)
	    Respiratory compromise
		Activate emergency medical system
		Parent or health care provider may be able to interrupt reaction with administration of epinephrine

*For more detailed information, see section on the topic in this chapter.

REFERENCE

Patterson, J.M., et al. 1992. Home care for medically fragile children: Impact on family health and wellbeing. *Developmental and Behavioral Pediatrics* 13:248–255.

ADDITIONAL SUGGESTED READINGS

Ehrhardt, B.S., and M. Graham. 1990. Pulse oxymetry: An easy way to check oxygen saturation. *Nursing* 20, no. 3:50–54.

Fritsch, D.E., and D.M. Fredrick. 1993. Exposing latex allergies. *Nursing* 23, no. 8:46–48.

Lenox, A.C. 1990. IV therapy: Reducing the risk of infection. *Nursing* 20, no. 3:60–61.

Messner, R.L., and M.L. Pinkerman. 1992. Preventing a peripheral IV infection. *Nursing* 22, no. 6:34–41.

Spearing, C., et al. 1990. Administering oxygen therapy: What you need to know. *Nursing* 20, no. 6:47–51.

Vessey, J.A., et al. 1993. Latex allergy: A threat to you and your patients? *Pediatric Nursing* 19:517–519.

Viall, C.D. 1990. Your complete guide to central venous catheters. *Nursing* 20, no. 2: 34–41.

Whitney, R.G. 1991. Comparing long-term central venous catheters. *Nursing* 21, no. 4:70–71.

MANAGEMENT OF PRESSURE SORES

Kathleen Ryan Kuntz

Purpose: to describe identification of skin abnormalities, staging degrees of bedsores, and treatment of bedsores and decubiti.

The development of pressure sores jeopardizes the health and well-being of the individual, increases the cost of treatment, and restricts the individual's normal activities. In many instances, the child will require hospitalization and rehabilitation. The emphasis of care for individuals at risk for the development of pressure sores is on assessment and prevention. To address this, it is important to have an understanding of the structure and function of the integumentary system (skin).

Skin serves to prevent the loss of body fluid and protect deeper tissues from infection, contact with irritating substances, or exposure to ultraviolet radiation. It also serves to regulate the body's temperature by providing the insulation of subcutaneous tissue, as well as a mechanism for cooling by evaporation of sweat from glands. The skin is also an important part of the sensory system, providing areas of reception of stimuli. In addition, skin plays an important role in the synthesis of vitamin D.

The structures of the skin are

- Layers
    1. *Epidermis*—a thin layer without blood vessels that is made up of an outer layer of dead cells and an inner layer where melanin and keratin are formed. This layer receives its nutritional supply from the dermis.
    2. *Dermis*—a layer well supplied with blood and sensory nerve endings. It is here that connective tissue, sebaceous glands, some sweat glands, and hair follicles are found.
    3. *Subcutaneous tissue*—a layer that contains fat, sweat glands, and the remainder of hair follicles.
- Skin appendages: hair, nails, sebaceous glands, sweat glands

Several factors associated with growth affect the function of skin. In children, most of these changes occur in the pubertal phase and involve the development of new areas of terminal hair and the enlargement of apocrine glands (in the axillae and genital areas). Children and young adults typically have healthy skin tissue that is well supplied with nutrition and has good turgor.

WOUND HEALING

When the structures of the skin are disturbed, a wound develops. The body's normal process of healing follows a certain pattern:

- *Tissue regeneration:* The body produces cells to replace those that are damaged with the same type. Only certain body tissues can regenerate.
- *Scar formation:* Tissue that cannot regenerate develops scar tissue.
- *Primary intention:* Wounds without tissue loss heal in this manner when the edges of the wound can be matched or approximated and there is minimal scarring (i.e., a surgical incision).
- *Secondary intention:* Wounds with tissue loss heal in this manner when the edges of the wound do not match up or approximate and scar formation depends on the amount of tissue loss. These wounds have a prolonged healing time and are at an increased risk for infection.

The stages of wound healing are

- Reaction
  1. inflammation
  2. vascular changes
- Regeneration (proliferation)
  1. epithelialization, or the reproduction of cells of the epidermis to cover the wound
  2. synthesis of collagen
  3. regeneration of capillaries
  4. formation of granulation tissue
     (a) translucent and red
     (b) fragile and bleeds easily
- Remodeling (maturation)
  1. collagen production stabilizes; fibers increase in strength

2. contraction of surrounding skin; reduction in size of wound

Aids to wound healing are

- Nutrition
  1. increased B-complex vitamins, fat-soluble vitamins (D, E, A), vitamin C, trace metals (iron, zinc, copper), and magnesium and calcium
  2. increased calories due to energy expended in the healing process
  3. increased protein to attain/maintain a positive nitrogen balance
- Oxygen—increases rate of collagen synthesis
- Prevention of trauma to healing tissue

Detriments to healing are

- Contamination of wound by bacteria
- Hypoxia to tissue
  1. vasoconstriction
  2. decreased O_2
  3. hypothermia
- Poor nutrition
- Radiation
- Metabolic disturbances (e.g., uremia, diabetes)
- Drugs
  1. chemotherapeutic agents
  2. corticosteroids
  3. anticoagulants

PRESSURE SORE FORMATION AND CLASSIFICATION

Pressure sores are the changes in the tissue that occur as a result of exerted pressure against the skin, usually over bony prominences (Figure 13–13). The pressure applied exceeds the normal capillary pressure (20–32 mm Hg), thereby decreasing blood supply to the area, preventing nutrients from reaching cells and removal of waste products, and causing cell death. Other factors that contribute to the development of

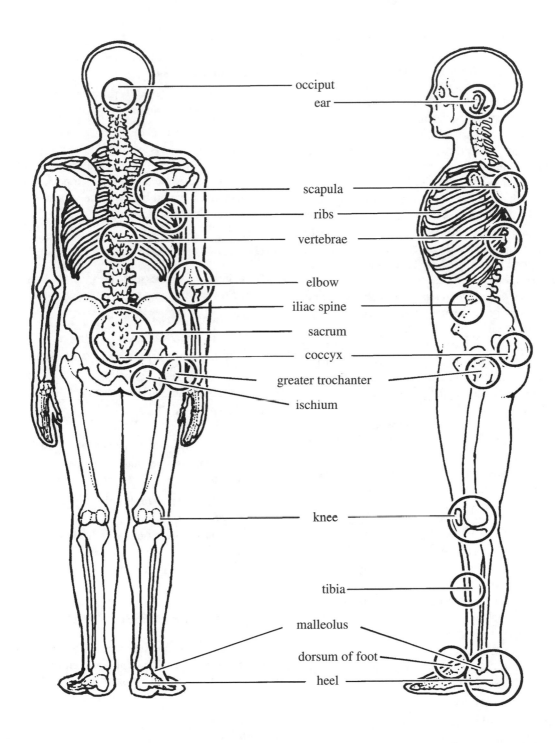

occiput
ear
scapula
ribs
vertebrae
elbow
iliac spine
sacrum
coccyx
greater trochanter
ischium
knee
tibia
malleolus
dorsum of foot
heel

Figure 13–13 Typical Pressure Sore Points. *Source:* From *Comprehensive Rehabilitation Nursing* (p. 245) by N. Martin, N.B. Holt, and D. Hicks, New York: McGraw-Hill. Copyright © 1981 by McGraw-Hill. Reprinted by permission.

pressure sores are shearing and excessive moisture.

The progression of tissue breakdown advances through stages of tissue ischemia, reactive hypothermia, and nonreactive hyperemia, producing an open pressure sore.

Tissue ischemia is localized blanching, or reduction of blood flow, producing altered sensation (numbness, cold).

Normal reactive hyperemia occurs after ischemia has persisted a few minutes to approximately two hours. Vasodilation occurs in response to repair cell damage. The skin appears pink or light red and will blanch when pressure is applied with fingertips. There is altered sensation (tingling, warmness to touch).

Nonreactive hyperemia occurs after ischemia has lasted longer than approximately two hours. Vasodilation becomes more pronounced. The skin appears pink to dark red and does not blanch when pressure is applied with fingertips. There is altered sensation (burning, aching, warmness to touch) and possible induration (localized edema).

An *open pressure sore* is broken skin surface, usually surrounded by edema and erythema. There is necrotic tissue and eschar (thick, hard crust or mass of dead tissue that is dark brown or black). The grading scale to determine extent of tissue damage is as follows:

- Grade I (Figure 13–14)
  1. intact epidermis
  2. erythema persists after pressure relief
  3. capillary refill time delayed, or skin does not blanch when pressure is applied
- Grade II (Figure 13–15)
  1. partial thickness
  2. limited to the epidermis and superficial dermis
  3. blistered, or skin loss
- Grade III (Figure 13–16)
  1. full thickness
  2. extends to the subcutaneous tissue
  3. loss of the epidermis and dermis

- Grade IV (Figure 13–17)
  1. extends through the subcutaneous tissue and fascia
  2. may extend slightly into the muscle, joint, and/or bone

Wounds may form pockets or tracts below the skin surface. A *fistula* is a tract between two epithelium-lined surfaces. A *sinus* is a tract that is open at one end. An *undermining* is a pocketed space that can develop between the subcutaneous tissue and the muscle.

PRESSURE SORE COMPLICATIONS

Complications of pressure sores can be complex and severe, including

- Infection
  1. to the open tissue
  2. to the bloodstream (can lead to septic shock and death)
  3. to the bone (can lead to a need for amputation)
- Negative nitrogen balance
  1. tissue breakdown exceeds rate of repair
  2. protein loss in wound drainage
- Anemia
  1. blood and protein loss in wound drainage
  2. negative effect on wound healing
- Pain
- Altered body image

TREATMENT OF PRESSURE SORES

The treatment of pressure sores is directed at two levels of involvement: prevention of wounds or impairment of skin integrity, and management of a wound once it occurs.

Prevention

The impairment of skin integrity can be prevented by the following measures:

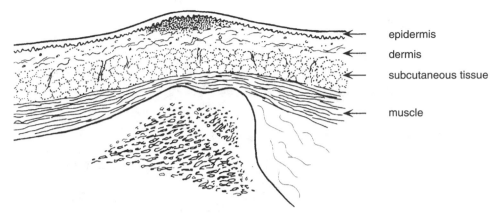

epidermis

dermis

subcutaneous tissue

muscle

Figure 13–14 Grade I Pressure Sore. *Source:* Copyright © 1996, Mark L. Batshaw, M.D.

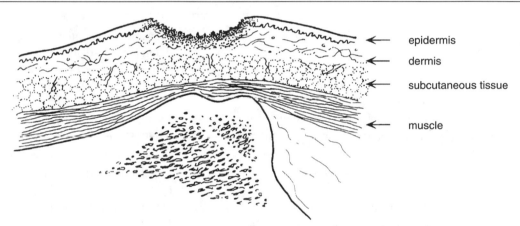

epidermis

dermis

subcutaneous tissue

muscle

Figure 13–15 Grade II Pressure Sore. *Source:* Copyright © 1996, Mark L. Batshaw, M.D.

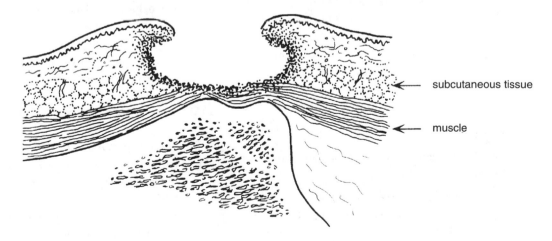

subcutaneous tissue

muscle

Figure 13–16 Grade III Pressure Sore. *Source:* Copyright © 1996, Mark L. Batshaw, M.D.

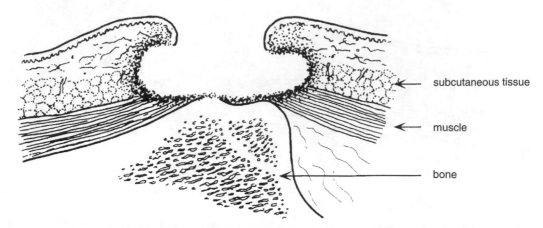

Figure 13–17 Grade IV Pressure Sore. *Source:* Copyright © 1996, Mark L. Batshaw, M.D.

- Perform a complete skin inspection with personal care at least each morning and evening.
- Check skin under pressure after turns, periods of sitting, application of splint/brace, tight-fitting clothing (should be avoided).
- Promote pressure relief by turning, weight shifting.
- Avoid shearing and friction or sliding of skin against surface.
- Maintain good body alignment/posture.
- Maintain/improve range of motion.
- Keep skin clean and dry.
- Avoid harsh soaps or preparations.
- Use skin softeners and protectors.
- Avoid use of heating pads or heat lamps.
- Use pressure-minimizing device (foam, fleece, cushion) and evaluate effectiveness.
- Promote nutritional status.

Management

Wound management involves the following measures:

- Treatment of impaired skin integrity
  1. Implement preventive skin care for normal skin.
  2. Carefully assess the wound.
     (a) Measure perimeter of shallow wound; depth of deeper wound to wound base; must be debrided (utilizing sterile cotton swab); can photograph with grid film.
     (b) Identify wound type and possible etiology.
     (c) Identify phase of wound healing.
     (d) Identify stage of pressure sore.
     (e) Classify wound, utilizing Three Color Concept® introduced by Marion Laboratories, Inc.
        (i) black—covered with thick necrotic tissue or eschar
        (ii) yellow—covered with a layer of yellow fibrous debris or viscous surface exudate
        (iii) red—all dead tissue has been removed and wound is ready to heal
  3. Monitor for signs/symptoms of infection.
  4. Provide wound care as prescribed.
     (a) Eliminate source of pressure as much as possible for healing to occur.
     (b) Debride, or remove necrotic tissue
        (i) surgical removal
        (ii) enzyme application

(iii) wet to dry dressing

(iv) transparent, moisture-permeable and vapor-permeable film (fosters body's own autolytic debridement)

(v) whirlpool/gentle irrigation therapy

- Increasing circulation to area of sore
  1. Position away from sore.
  2. Apply vibration/massage to healthy skin surrounding wound.
  3. Use hyperbaric oxygen therapy.
- Wound cleansing
  1. Use whirlpool therapy.
  2. Gently irrigate with normal saline solution.
- Use of absorption/cleansing agents
  1. These absorb exudate and adhere to loose debris.
  2. Remove from wound by irrigation with normal saline solution.
  3. Do not use in tracts or fistulas; difficult to remove all of product.
  4. Monitor electrolytes during therapy.
- Other topical treatments
  1. Products range from karaya, gelfoam, and sugar to antacid, gold leaf, and insulin.
  2. Some may work, perhaps only because they cause no harm and the wound is receiving regular cleansing.
  3. Substances to avoid include hexachlorophene, mercurochrome, alcohol, witch hazel, and tincture of benzoin (can be absorbed into system or cause vasoconstriction and damage to the skin).
- Wound packing
  1. This absorbs drainage and facilitates debridement; acts as a wick to absorb drainage away from base of wound; promotes healing from innermost aspect outward.
  2. Use proper technique.
     (a) Use gauze material of proper type and size.
     (b) Do not pack too tight; will cause pressure.
     (c) Do not pack too loose; will not absorb all of exudate.
- Damp dressings—dressing next to wound bed is removed while still damp (enhances growth of granulation tissue)
- Hydrocolloid dressings
  1. These maintain a moist environment; do not adhere directly to wound; form a protective paste or gel as they absorb exudate.
  2. Change every two to three days.
  3. Dressings are waterproof; patient can bathe and shower.
- Transparent dressings and moisture-permeable and vapor-permeable films
  1. These maintain a moist environment.
  2. Exudate collects under film and can be carefully aspirated.
  3. Change when film no longer adheres or when there is a need to inspect wound.
  4. Dressing/film acts as barrier to water and bacteria; patient can shower.
- Skin barriers
  1. These are pectin or gelatin wafers that protect skin and minimize maceration.
  2. Apply to intact or denuded skin.
  3. Use to protect skin from adhesives or drainage.
- Specialized bed or mattress
  1. Egg crate mattress.
  2. Air mattress overlay.
  3. Low-air-loss mattress overlay.
  4. Air-fluidized bed.
  5. Waterbed.

SUGGESTED READINGS

Brunner, L.S., and D.S. Suddarth. 1986. *The Lippincott manual of nursing practice*. 4th ed. Philadelphia: J.B. Lippincott Co.

Children's Seashore House. 1995. Decision tree for mattress overlay or specialty bed. *Nursing standards of care and practice*. Philadelphia.

Clanin, N. 1989. *Basic principles of skin and wound management*. Skokie, Ill.: Rehabilitation Nurses Foundation.

Colburn, L. 1990. Preventing pressure ulcers: How to recognize and care for patients at risk. *Nursing 90* 20, no. 12:60–63.

Constantian, M.B., and H.S. Jackson. 1980. Biology and care of the pressure ulcer wound. In *Pressure ulcers: Principles and techniques of management*, ed. M.B. Constantian. Boston: Little, Brown & Co.

Cuzzell, J.Z. 1988. Wound care forum: The new RYB color code. *American Journal of Nursing* 18:1342–1346.

Garvin, G. 1990. Wound healing in pediatrics. *Nursing Clinics of North America* 25:181–192.

Krasner, D., ed. 1990. *Chronic wound care: A clinical source book for healthcare professionals*. King of Prussia, Pa.: Health Management Publications.

Krasner, D. 1992. The 12 commandments of wound care. *Nursing* 22, no. 12:34–41.

Maklebust, J. 1987. Pressure ulcers: Etiology and prevention. *Nursing Clinics of North America* 22:359–377.

Martin, N., et al. 1981. *Comprehensive rehabilitation nursing*. New York: McGraw-Hill Publishing Co.

McCourt, A., ed. 1993. *The specialty practice of rehabilitation nursing: A core curriculum*. 3rd ed. Skokie, Ill.: Rehabilitation Nurses Foundation.

Stotts, N.A. 1990. Seeing red and yellow and black: The three-color concept of wound care. *Nursing* 20, no. 2:59–61.

Willey, T. 1992. Use a decision tree to choose wound dressings. *American Journal of Nursing* 92, no. 2:43–46.

PERCUSSION AND POSTURAL DRAINAGE

Kathleen Ryan Kuntz

Purpose: to review the indications for performing chest percussion and postural drainage as well as the specific techniques involved in the intervention.

Mucus is a filmy, liquid substance that offers lubrication and protection to internal areas of the body, including the lungs and bronchioles. Mucous membranes serve to humidify inspired air and trap dust and dirt. When an infection or other irritation is present, the body produces thicker mucus. When this thickened mucus blocks the airways, breathing becomes more difficult. Percussion and vibration assist in loosening this mucus in the airways. When combined with postural drainage, aided by gravity, the mucus moves into the larger airway, where it can be coughed or suctioned out.

INDICATIONS FOR PERCUSSION/ POSTURAL DRAINAGE

Percussion and postural drainage may be needed when the child with congestion wakes up from sleep, since lying reclined and shallow breathing allow mucus to accumulate in the airways. If the child requires respiratory treatments (metered-dose inhalants or nebulized treatments) that may assist in loosening the secretions, these should be administered prior to percussion and postural drainage to maximize the effect of the procedure. It is also important to perform this procedure well in advance of feedings or meals, since the movement of secretions may stimulate coughing, which could cause emesis if the stomach is full.

PROCEDURES

Performing percussion and postural drainage takes approximately 20 to 30 minutes. There are eight main segments of the lung targeted and three positional changes. Each segment is percussed for approximately one minute. To create the percussion, the hand is held cupped, with fingers close together (see Figure 13–18). Commercial percussors can be utilized to achieve this effect as well. The motion taken is to strike the child on the chest with the oval of your cupped hand. When this is done correctly, a "popping" sound will be heard and the strike will not hurt the child, in contrast to the "slapping" sound and reddened skin that would result if the hand were flat. The child should wear a light T-shirt or have a light blanket across the chest during percussion.

Vibration is an alternative if percussion is not tolerated. Vibration is achieved by placing a flat hand firmly on the chest wall over the appropriate segment (see Figure 13–19). With the arm extended, tense and relax the muscles of the forearm in rapid succession to create a shaking motion. A commercial vibrator or a padded electric toothbrush (for neonates) can be utilized as well.

Postural drainage can be achieved in several ways. Having the child sit up on your lap, or in bed, facilitates access to the upper segments. If the child can be positioned against a firm surface (e.g., pillow or bed), there is a greater effect of the vibration when the chest wall is percussed. Lower segments can be drained with the child lying in a dependent position in your lap or in bed. If the child cannot tolerate being in a dependent position (head below heart), positioning side to side will still effect the drainage of secretions toward the larger airway for expectoration.

One general approach to effective percussion and postural drainage is the sequence shown in Table 13–5.

Following this process, the child should be encouraged or stimulated to breathe deeply or cough. This can be achieved in several ways, including eliciting a laugh in the infant, having the toddler blow bubbles, having the young child pretend to take a deep breath and blow out candles, or having the older child play a game of "air hockey" in which he or she tries to blow a rolled piece of paper across the table to score a goal.

Figure 13–18 Cupped Hand for Percussion. *Source:* Copyright © 1996, Mark L. Batshaw, M.D.

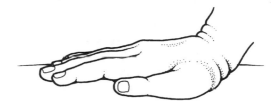

Figure 13–19 Flat Hand for Vibration. *Source:* Copyright © 1996, Mark L. Batshaw, M.D.

Table 13–5 Sequence of Percussion and Postural Drainage

Child's Position	Segment Percussed	Movement over Area
Sitting up (Figures 13–20 and 13–21) 	Anterior, upper left lobe Anterior, upper right lobe Posterior, upper left lobe Posterior, upper right lobe	Moving hand over clavicle and shoulder as each side percussed

continues

Table 13–5 Continued

Child's Position	Segment Percussed	Movement over Area
Lying supine with head lowered (dependent) (Figure 13–22) 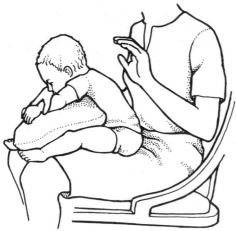	Anterior, lower left lobe Anterior, lower right lobe	Moving hand to midaxillary level on each side, with special attention to area of right middle lobe
Lying prone with head lowered (dependent) (Figure 13–23)	Posterior, lower left lobe Posterior, lower right lobe	Moving hand to midaxillary level on each side, with special attention to area of right middle lobe
Lying on right side on flat surface (alternative to dependent)	Anterior, lower left lobe Posterior, lower left lobe	Moving hand to midaxillary level on each side, with special attention to area of right middle lobe
Lying on left side on flat surface (alternative to dependent)	Anterior, lower right lobe Posterior, lower right lobe	Moving hand to midaxillary level on each side, with special attention to area of right middle lobe

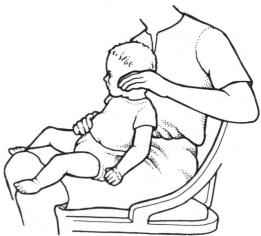

Figure 13–20 Percussion and Postural Drainage, Sitting Position, Posterior Upper Lobes. *Source:* Copyright © 1996, Mark L. Batshaw, M.D.

Figure 13–21 Percussion and Postural Drainage, Sitting Position, Anterior Upper Lobes. *Source:* Copyright © 1996, Mark L. Batshaw, M.D.

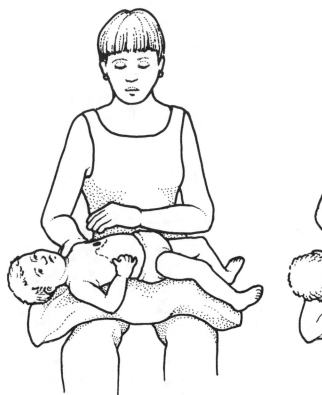

Figure 13–22 Percussion and Postural Drainage, Supine Position. *Source:* Copyright © 1996, Mark L. Batshaw, M.D.

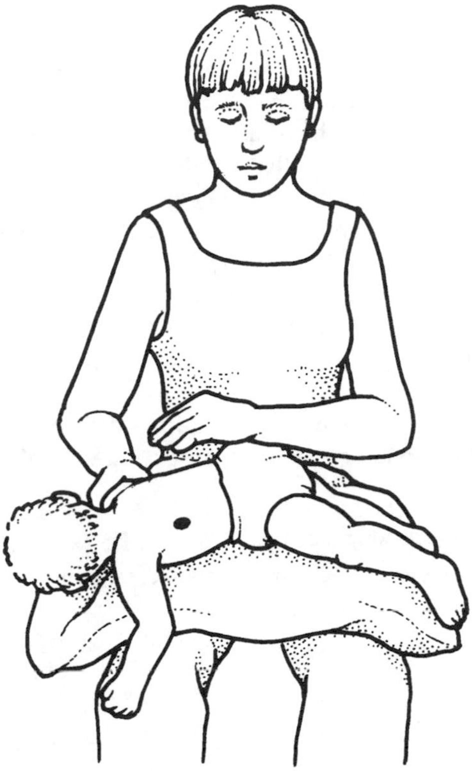

Figure 13–23 Percussion and Postural Drainage, Prone Position. *Source:* Copyright © 1996, Mark L. Batshaw, M.D.

SUGGESTED READINGS

Children's Seashore House. 1991. *Patient/family education resource manual*. Philadelphia.

Cystic Fibrosis Foundation. 1992. *Consumer fact sheet: An introduction to chest physical therapy*. Bethesda, Md.

Wong, D., and L. Whaley. 1990. *Clinical manual of pediatric nursing*. Philadelphia: C.V. Mosby Co.

CARDIORESPIRATORY MONITORS

Kathleen Ryan Kuntz

Purpose: to describe the uses and indications for cardiorespiratory monitors.

The use of a cardiorespiratory monitor is an asset when caring for children at risk for cardiac or respiratory distress. There are many different makes and models with countless features for monitors in the hospital and at home. Essentially, however, all cardiorespiratory monitors have a similar purpose and function, and we will describe some of the general principles.

MONITORING MECHANISMS

The mechanism by which the monitor measures breathing is *impedance pneumography*. This means that the measurement of respiratory rate is detected by the monitor through electrodes as there is a change in chest wall movement. This movement causes a shift in air and tissue between the electrodes that register the respiratory rate. The heart rate is measured by electrocardiogram (ECG) signals. This is a small electrical signal emitted from the heart each time it beats.

To be effective as a monitoring device, the cardiorespiratory monitor must be used in the proper

- electrode placement
- integrity of electrodes/contact to skin
- connection to monitor
- accuracy of settings
- power supply
- safety

Electrode Placement

There are two types of electrodes: adhesive electrodes (two or three used); (see Figures 13–24 and 13–25) and the electrode belt (two large pads used); (see Figure 13–26).

To apply electrodes, identify the level on the chest where expansion is greatest on inspiration. Place electrodes at this level, halfway between the nipple and midaxillary line on the right and left. A third electrode may be used on the lower chest.

Integrity of Electrodes/Contact to Skin

The skin should be clean and dry with no lotion or oils. The adhesive electrode should have fresh conductive gel. The pad electrode should be clear of dirt and show no cracking; the belt should be snug but should not restrict chest expansion.

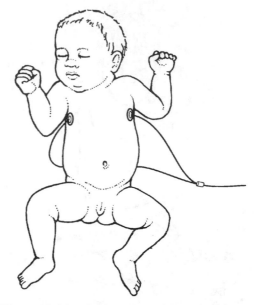

Figure 13–24 Adhesive Electrodes (Two-Electrode Set-up). *Source:* Copyright © 1996, Mark L. Batshaw, M.D.

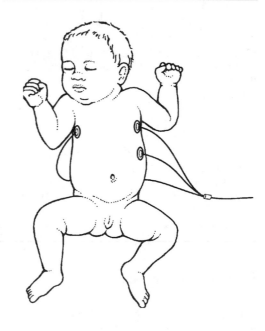

Figure 13–25 Adhesive Electrodes (Three-Electrode Set-up). *Source:* Copyright © 1996, Mark L. Batshaw, M.D.

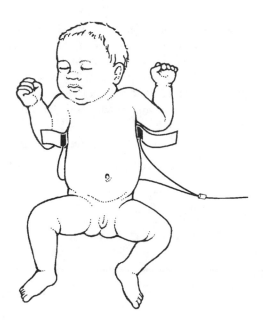

Figure 13–26 Electrode Belt Set-up. *Source:* Copyright © 1996, Mark L. Batshaw, M.D.

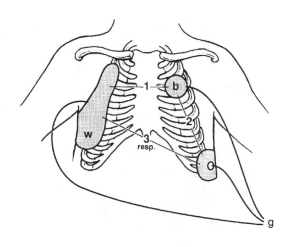

Figure 13–27 Color Coding of Lead Wires Attached to Electrodes. w = white, b = black, g = green (may also be red). *Source:* Copyright © 1996, Mark L. Batshaw, M.D.

Connection to Monitor

Lead wires should attach to electrodes utilizing color coding, with white on the right chest, black on the left chest, and green or red (if used) on the lower left or right chest (see Figure 13–27).

Settings

Settings should be according to physician prescription. *Heart rate* should have a high limit and a low limit; the monitor will alarm if these parameters are violated. *Respiratory rate* should be set to indicate delay; the monitor will alarm if the time period between breaths exceeds the setting.

Power Supply

Hospital models should include a hospital-grade plug, an emergency generator access outlet, and an internal battery to signal loss of power. *Home models* should use household AC current. They should have an internal battery to signal loss of power and an alternate DC battery (this may be internal or may require external connection).

Safety

Observe the following precautions:

- Verify accuracy of measurement by comparing the reading from the monitor to a palpated or auscultated heart rate and respiratory rate.
- Always run lead wires away from face for safety and comfort.
- Protect all electrical devices from exposure to water and excessive moisture.
- With any sign of malfunction, have monitor replaced.

SUMMARY

A cardiorespiratory monitor is usually required whenever the child is not directly supervised. Depending on the condition of the child, a physician may determine that it is necessary only when the child is asleep. Caution must be maintained not to develop a false sense of total security. The occasional false alarm does not indicate that each alarm is false. The caregiver should respond to *every* alarm. The immediate response to an alarming monitor should be to check first the condition of the child and then the accuracy of the monitor. A machine can be only as effective as we make it. Measurements that are not verified can lead to increased frequency of false alarms due to improper application or situations in which changes in the child's condition will not be detected.

SUGGESTED READINGS

Children's Seashore House. 1991. *Patient/family education resource manual.* Philadelphia.

Edentech. 1990. *Assurance heart and respiration monitor instruction manual.* Eden Prairie, Minn.

Elder, A.N. 1991. Setting up and using a cardiac monitor. *Nursing* 21, no. 3:58–63.

Wong, D., and L. Whaley. 1990. *Clinical manual of pediatric nursing.* Philadelphia: C.V. Mosby Co.

CARE OF TRACHEOSTOMY SITES

Kathleen Ryan Kuntz

Purpose: to describe the techniques for caring for a child with a tracheostomy, including necessary supplies and emergency procedures.

When a child has a tracheostomy, the air inspired no longer passes through the nose and mouth and therefore is no longer naturally warmed, moistened, and filtered before entering the lungs. To provide these mechanisms, it is necessary for the child with a tracheostomy to have a device to filter and humidify the air breathed in. In addition, it is important to emphasize systemic hydration to maintain thin secretions. Environmental factors that pose an increased risk to this child include smoke, aerosol sprays, powder, dust, and animal dander.

EMERGENCY SUPPLIES AND EQUIPMENT

When caring for a child with a tracheostomy, it is necessary to maintain certain emergency equipment with the child at all times. This includes

- spare tracheostomy tube (same size)
- endotracheal tube or tracheostomy tube (half-size smaller)
- portable suction
- suction catheters
- twill tape or tracheostomy collar
- scissors (blunt end)
- hemostat
- self-inflating resuscitation bag
- oxygen (if child is oxygen dependent)

SPECIFIC PROCEDURES

The care of the child with a tracheostomy entails ensuring that the artificial airway remains patent and securely in place, that the child remains free from infection and experiences no respiratory compromise, and that the skin is protected from breakdown with exposure to secretions. The necessary procedures include

- suctioning
- tracheostomy site care
- twill tape or collar change
- tracheostomy tube change
- cardiorespiratory emergency management

Suctioning the Tracheostomy Tube

Indications for suctioning are

- "noisy" respirations
- inability to cough and clear secretions
- restlessness
- difficulty breathing
- difficulty eating (particularly bottle feeding)
- color change (pale)
- increased work of breathing

The procedure (clean technique used with long-term tracheostomy, maintaining sterility of catheter) is as follows:

- Gather supplies and equipment.
  1. suction machine
  2. suction catheters
  3. sterile water
  4. small cup
  5. clean gloves (if indicated; may not be necessary after discharge to home)
- Wash hands before beginning procedure.
- Don gloves (if indicated).
- Prepare suction and maintain appropriate setting (80–120 mm Hg).
- Prepare suction catheter, maintaining sterility.
- Identify correct length of catheter to be passed into tracheostomy tube (1 cm beyond tip); (see Figure 13–28).
- Suction tracheostomy tube, utilizing intermittent suction pressure (thumb on and off opening).
- Rotate catheter as removed, maintaining suction for only a few seconds.

Tracheostomy Site Care

Tracheostomy site care should be performed daily, and additionally when there are excess secretions or soiling.

The procedure is as follows:

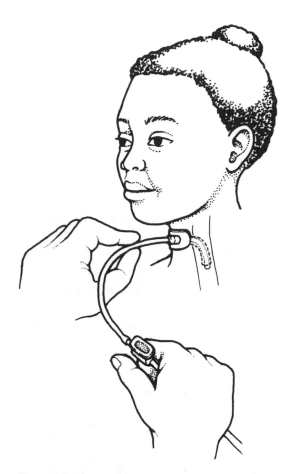

Figure 13–28 Identifying Correct Length of Catheter To Be Passed into Tracheostomy Tube. *Source:* Copyright © 1996, Mark L. Batshaw, M.D.

- Gather supplies and equipment.
  1. dressings
  2. sterile water
  3. small cup
  4. cotton-tip applicators or gauze squares
  5. hydrogen peroxide (half-strength if drainage or crusting present)
  6. barrier cream or petroleum jelly
  7. pipe cleaners (if tracheostomy tube has inner cannula)
- Wash hands before beginning procedure.
- Remove dressing from beneath flanges.

- Inspect skin at stoma, under flanges, and under string/collar.
- Cleanse stoma and neck, utilizing clean water and cotton-tip applicator or saturated gauze square, with motion beginning at stoma and moving away.
- Identify signs of need to utilize half-strength hydrogen peroxide to clean stoma (crusting, drainage).
- Assess skin for signs of irritation/ infection (redness, swelling, drainage).
- Apply a thin layer of barrier cream or Vaseline to intact skin to protect from irritation of secretions or rubbing of dressing.
- Replace dressing under flanges.
- Verify tightness of strings/collar (one finger breadth); (see Figure 13–29).
- Remove inner cannula (if present) and clean with pipe cleaners in sterile water.

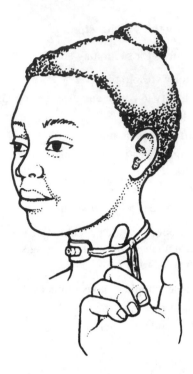

Figure 13–29 Verifying Tightness of Twill Tape. *Source:* Copyright © 1996, Mark L. Batshaw, M.D.

Tape or Collar Change

Tape or collar change should be performed weekly or with tracheostomy tube change; it should also be performed when tape or collar is soiled, wet, or loose. The procedure is as follows:

- Gather supplies and equipment.
    1. twill tape or collar
    2. scissors
    3. hemostat
    4. adhesive-backed foam (if indicated with twill tape)
- Wash hands before beginning procedure.
- Attach clean tape/collar to flanges, drawing through from back to front.
- Fasten clean tape/collar at appropriate length (so only one finger can slip behind).
    1. *Tape*—so that knot is in different location each time to protect the skin; cover with adhesive backed foam if indicated (see Figure 13–30)

Figure 13–30 Twill Tape with Foam Fastened at Appropriate Length. *Source:* Copyright © 1996, Mark L. Batshaw, M.D.

2. *Collar*—trimming collar so Velcro fastens firmly (see Figure 13–31)

- Remove soiled tape/collar.

Tracheostomy Tube Change

The tracheostomy tube should be changed weekly; it should also be changed when secretions cannot be adequately removed, when there are flange breaks, or when decannulation occurs. The procedure (clean technique used with long-term tracheostomy, maintaining sterility of tracheostomy tube) is as follows:

- A second person should participate.
- Gather supplies and equipment.
  1. tracheostomy tube
  2. scissors
  3. dressing
  4. twill tape or collar
  5. hemostat
  6. sterile water
  7. small cup
  8. clean gloves (if indicated)
  9. adhesive-backed foam (if indicated with twill tape)
  10. oxygen with resuscitation bag (to administer supplemental oxygen and/or ventilation, if indicated)
- Wash hands before beginning procedure.
- Attach tape/collar to tracheostomy tube, maintaining sterility.
- Lubricate end of tracheostomy tube with sterile water, maintaining sterility.
- Position child with airway visible and accessible (roll under shoulders); (see Figure 13–32).

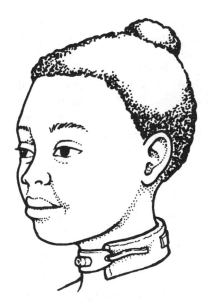

Figure 13–31 Collar Fastened at Appropriate Length. *Source:* Copyright © 1996, Mark L. Batshaw, M.D.

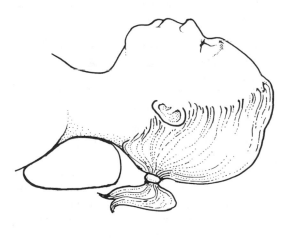

Figure 13–32 Child Positioned So That Airway Is Open, Visible, and Accessible. *Source:* Copyright © 1996, Mark L. Batshaw, M.D.

- Administer supplemental oxygen and/or ventilation prior to tracheostomy change if needed for child to tolerate the procedure (as prescribed).
- Assistant holds child and removes old tracheostomy tube on count of three, grasping flanges.
- Insert new tracheostomy tube, grasping

flanges, guiding along airway (downward motion).
- Ascertain breath sounds in right and left lung fields with stethoscope.
- Fasten tape/collar at appropriate length.
- Insert dressings under flanges.
- Verify tightness of strings/collar (one finger breadth).

SUGGESTED READINGS

Children's Seashore House. 1991. *Patient/family education resource manual.* Philadelphia.

Jennings, P. 1988. Nursing and home aspects of the care of a child with a tracheostomy. *Journal of Laryngology and Otology,* suppl. 17:25–27.

Kennelly, C. 1990. Tracheostomy care: Parents as learners. *Maternal-Child Nursing* 2:264–267.

Runton, N. 1992. Suctioning artificial airways in children: Appropriate technique. *Pediatric Nursing* 18, no. 2:115–118.

Wong, D., and L. Whaley. 1990. *Clinical manual of pediatric nursing.* Philadelphia: C.V. Mosby Co.

GASTROSTOMY CARE

Kathleen Ryan Kuntz

Purpose: to describe care of the child with a gastrostomy tube, including types of tubes, techniques for skin and stoma care, changing the tube, and administration of tube feeding.

There are many reasons for surgically placing a gastrostomy feeding tube in a child. In all cases, the child is not receiving adequate calories to promote growth and development. This can be related to poor oromotor control, increased respiratory effort and energy expended in work of breathing, or gastroesophogeal reflux, among other reasons. The gastrostomy tube is generally not a short-term intervention but in many cases is not viewed as a *permanent* means for nutrition. For this reason, feedings given via gastrostomy tube should be provided in conjunction with usual feeding activities.

For instance, the infant should be held close and offered a pacifier as the feeding is administered (the position that would be assumed if bottle feeding); (see Figure 13–33). A toddler

should sit in a high chair and be offered foods to taste, finger-feed, or play with. A young child should be permitted to receive his or her feeding while at the table with the family for a meal. In this way, the child associates these activities with the feeling of having hunger satisfied. When the gastrostomy tube is no longer needed, the feeding activity is naturally continued.

The care of the child with a gastrostomy tube entails ensuring that the tube remains patent and securely in place, that the child tolerates the feeding, and that the skin is protected from breakdown with exposure to gastric contents. The necessary procedures include

- gastrostomy site care
- verifying gastrostomy tube placement/residuals
- gastrostomy tube feeding administration
- gastrostomy tube change

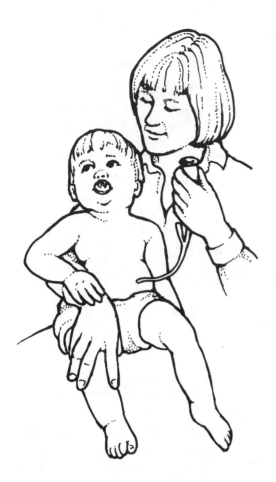

Figure 13–33 Feeding an Infant with a Gastrostomy Tube. *Source:* Copyright © 1996, Mark L. Batshaw, M.D.

GASTROSTOMY SITE CARE

Securing the Gastrostomy Tube

A *Foley catheter or Mushroom/Malecot tube* should be taped in place to the anchor by bridge taping or a Hollister device (Figure 13–34). Place a piece of cloth tape around the tube to make a tab; safety-pin the tab to the underside of the child's clothing out of the child's reach. For an *MIC tube*, slide the Secure-Lock Ring close to the abdomen to maintain placement. For a *button tube*, no additional measures to secure are necessary.

Care to Skin

The gastrostomy site should be cleaned daily with soap and water during routine washing. Clean open or draining areas with half-strength peroxide and sterile water; rinse them with sterile water and allow them to air-dry. Avoid pressure or tension on the tube to prevent skin breakdown. Notify a physician if the area is draining. The child may require a larger sized tube if gastric contents are leaking. Split dressing may be applied around the tube to absorb drainage.

VERIFYING PLACEMENT AND RESIDUAL VOLUME

Placement and residual volume should be verified before each feeding and when child is irritable or complains of "fullness." The procedure is as follows:

- Foley, Mushroom/Malecot, or MIC tube
  1. Attach catheter-tip syringe without plunger to gastrostomy tube, holding above level of stomach.
  2. Unclasp tube.
  3. Stomach contents may return.
     (a) If positive, allow stomach contents to return by gravity.
     (b) If negative, clamp tube, insert plunger into syringe, attach to gastrostomy tube, unclasp tube, and withdraw contents with syringe.
- Button tube
  1. Attach specialized "venting" tube to button with leur-lock syringe, holding above level of stomach.
  2. Stomach contents may return.
     (a) If positive, allow stomach contents to return by gravity.
     (b) If negative, clamp tube, insert plunger into syringe, attach to gastrostomy tube, unclasp tube, and withdraw contents with syringe.

If residual is greater than half the volume of feeding, additional feedings should be delayed.

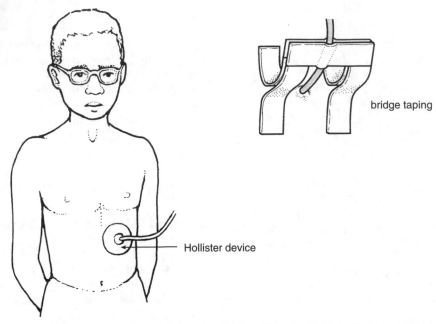

bridge taping

Hollister device

Figure 13–34 Securing the Foley Catheter or Mushroom/Malecot Tube by Hollister Device or Bridge Taping. *Source:* Copyright © 1996, Mark L. Batshaw, M.D.

GASTROSTOMY TUBE FEEDING ADMINISTRATION

Gastrostomy tube feeding is performed as prescribed or at usual mealtime. The procedure is as follows:

- Gather supplies/equipment.
  1. correct amount of formula or blenderized diet
  2. equipment for feeding delivery
     (a) for Foley, Mushroom/Malecot, or MIC Tube, a 50-cc or 60-cc catheter-tip syringe or enteral feeding bag (Figures 13–35 and 13–36)
     (b) for a button tube, a specialized extension tube and a 50-cc or 60-cc leur-lock syringe or enteral feeding bag
- Position child correctly.
  1. head of bed elevated to 45-degree angle or upright in chair
  2. prone or on right side, with the head of the bed raised at least 45 degrees

- Administer feeding.
  1. Prepare feeding at room temperature.
  2. Pour feeding into syringe or feeding bag (fill syringe only half to three-quarters full at a time).
  3. Prime tubing to purge air and fill tubing with feeding.
  4. Verify placement of gastrostomy tube.
  5. Connect feeding to gastrostomy tube.
  6. Adjust rate of administration, using clamp.
  7. Administer feeding over a minimum of 30 minutes or longer.
  8. When feeding is completed, add a small amount of water to the syringe or feeding bag to flush formula through (do not allow air to enter tubing between feeding and flush).
  9. Disconnect tube from delivery set and secure gastrostomy tube to child's clothing.
  10. Rinse delivery set thoroughly with warm water after each feeding. If the

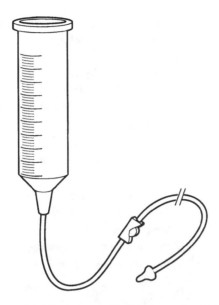

Figure 13–35 Catheter-Tip Syringe for Foley, Mushroom/Malecot, or MIC Tube. *Source:* Copyright © 1996, Mark L. Batshaw, M.D.

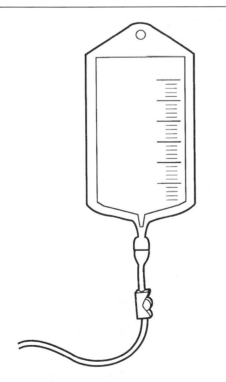

Figure 13–36 Enteral Feeding Bag for Foley, Mushroom/Malecot, or MIC Tube. *Source:* Copyright © 1996, Mark L. Batshaw, M.D.

child receives a continuous feeding, rinse the bag out every eight hours.

11. Change delivery set every 24 hours in the hospital or every three days in the home.

- Monitor tolerance of feeding.

1. Maintain upright or sitting position, or prone or right side with head elevated.

2. Monitor for signs that child may not tolerate the feeding (vomiting, gagging, diarrhea, abdominal distention).

- Identify safety factors/issues in caring for a child receiving gastrostomy tube feedings.

1. If vomiting or gagging occurs, stop the feeding and turn the child on his or her side. When child is calmed down, try to finish the feeding (unless vomiting/gagging is related to virus).

2. If abdominal cramping or diarrhea occurs or if vomiting and gagging persist, stop the feeding and notify the physician.

GASTROSTOMY TUBE INSERTION (FOLEY, MIC)

The gastrostomy tube must be inserted whenever it comes out or every month when the tube is replaced. A Mushroom or Malecot tube is replaced by a Foley or MIC tube once the site is well healed; the button tube is replaced with a button by the physician or trained health care professional. The button tube can remain in place six months or longer.

The procedure is as follows:
- Gather supplies.

1. gastrostomy tube of appropriate type and size

2. water-soluble lubricant

3. 10-cc leur-lock-tip syringes (2)

4. 10 cc water

5. 60-cc catheter-tip syringe

6. gloves (as indicated; may not be used in the home)

7. securing device utilized for child (i.e., Hollister device)

8. clean 4 × 4 gauze pads

9. normal saline

- Open package and verify integrity of balloon by injecting volume of water required for tube.
  1. Foley (2–3 cc)
  2. MIC, low-volume (2–3 cc)
  3. MIC, standard-volume (7–10 cc)
- Completely deflate balloon, leaving syringe attached.
- Lubricate end of tube with water-soluble lubricant.
- Return to sterile package until ready to insert.
- Remove old gastrostomy tube.
  1. Wipe area around tube so that it is clean and dry (utilize soap and water unless area is open).
  2. Attach leur-lock syringe to adapter and withdraw water (*do not cut port to remove*).
  3. Remove tube (may need to exert a gentle pull; if resistance is met, *stop and notify MD*).
  4. Cover site with gauze, reinsert new tube as soon as possible.
- Insert new gastrostomy tube, utilizing the following technique:
  1. Wash hands thoroughly.
  2. Put on gloves.
  3. Gently insert new tube in stoma vertically for ¼ to ½ inch (dependent on size of child), then direct toward umbilicus.
  4. Exert gentle push until balloon is inside of stomach.
  5. Inflate balloon with water (*do not use air*); (see Figure 13–37).
- Verify correct placement of tube, utilizing three methods. If any of these checks is not successful, withdraw tube, cover opening with a 4 × 4 gauze damp with normal saline, and *notify MD*.
  1. Exert gentle pull on tube a few centimeters (if it is in place, there will be resistance against the stomach wall).

2. Utilizing a catheter-tip syringe, gently aspirate stomach contents (replace all stomach fluid).

3. Disconnect syringe from tube, remove plunger, replace syringe barrel, and funnel 10–20 cc water into the tube (should flow freely).

- Secure tube.
  1. Foley catheter or Mushroom/Malecot tube
     (a) Tape tube in place to anchor, using bridge taping or Hollister device
     (b) Place piece of cloth tape around tube to make a tab; safety-pin tab to underside of clothing out of child's reach.
  2. MIC tube
     (a) Slide Secure-Lock Ring close to abdomen to maintain placement.

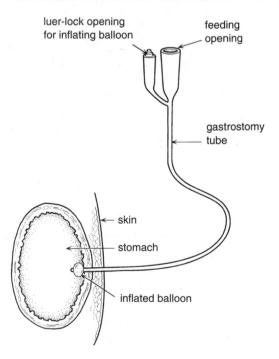

Figure 13–37 Gastrostomy Tube Inserted in Stomach, with Balloon Inflated. *Source:* Copyright © 1996, Mark L. Batshaw, M.D.

SUGGESTED READINGS

Bockus, S. 1993. When your patient needs tube feedings: Making the right decisions. *Nursing* 23, no. 7:34–42.

Eisenberg, P. 1994. A nurse's guide to tube feeding. *RN* 57, no. 10:62–69.

Haas-Beckert, B., and M. Heyman. 1993. Comparison of two skin level gastrostomy tubes for infants and children. *Pediatric Nursing* 19:351–354.

Huddleston, K.C., and A.R. Ferraro. 1991. Preparing families of children with gastrostomies. *Pediatric Nursing* 17:153–158.

Webber-Jones, J., et al. 1992. How to declog a feeding tube. *Nursing* 22, no. 4:63–64.

NASOGASTRIC TUBES/FEEDING PUMPS

Kathleen Ryan Kuntz

Purpose: to describe indications for nasogastric (NG) tube feedings, techniques for placement and care of an NG, and use of a feeding pump to administer tube feedings.

Tube feedings are sometimes required to provide nutrition when a child is unable to take food by mouth completely or in adequate amounts for growth. This could be related to poor oral-motor control, increased respiratory effort and energy expended in work of breathing, anomalies of the throat or esophagus, or unconsciousness. Nasogastric tube feedings are often utilized if the intervention is viewed as short term or as an interim means for nutrition.

Though not intended as a long-term treatment plan, many times a nasogastric tube is required for an extended period until an oral feeding regimen can be established. Feedings given via nasogastric tube should be provided in conjunction with usual feeding activities in order to foster the child's development. As discussed with gastrostomy tube feedings, the infant should be held close (as if bottle feeding) and offered a pacifier to satisfy oral needs. The toddler should sit in a high chair during the feeding; a young child should sit at a table with others during a meal whenever possible. This promotes the socialization and feeding behaviors normally associated with eating. When tube feedings are no longer required, the feeding activity naturally continues.

Nasogastric tube feedings are similar in many ways to gastrostomy tube feedings in delivery technique but hold a greater risk of displacement and complication. The natural position of the tube in the back of the throat may cause an uncomfortable feeling or irritation, making an oral feeding program difficult. Because of this, the use of a silastic tube, with its soft, flexible construction, is often preferred to a plastic tube. This type of tube is also designed to remain in place for a longer period of time (one month vs. three to five days), thereby minimizing the invasive procedure of tube placement. The nasogastric tube may contribute to episodes of regurgitation or reflux because it passes into the stomach, maintaining a continuous opening even as the sphincter tightens as the stomach fills. Displacement of the tube during insertion, with activity, or with coughing/vomiting episodes could pose a risk for aspiration of formula.

Nasogastric tube feedings are frequently delivered utilizing a feeding pump. The feeding pump ensures an even flow of formula to the stomach, preventing episodes of regurgitation and vomiting. Feeding pumps can be utilized with gastrostomy tube feeding as well when a formula is being administered.

The care of the child with a nasogastric tube entails ensuring that the tube is patent and in the correct placement, that the child tolerates the feeding, that the skin at the nares and face is protected from irritation of the tube and securing adhesive, and that precautions are maintained to prevent the risk of aspiration. The necessary procedures include

- insertion site care
- verification of tube placement/residual
- nasogastric tube feeding administration
- nasogastric tube change

NASOGASTRIC TUBE INSERTION SITE CARE

Securing the Nasogastric Tube

Procedures for securing the tube are as follows:

1. Mark tube at distance that should be at nostril.
2. Position tube to the side of the face, directing it toward the top of the ear.
3. Utilize a protective skin barrier on the cheek.
4. Tape tube in place, securing adhesive to the skin barrier (Figure 13–38).

Care to the Skin

Clean the area daily and as needed to keep secretions from soiling the tube. Keep the area of tape and protective skin barrier dry to maintain security. Monitor the skin at the nostril closely for signs of redness or irritation. If irritation is noted, the tube should be removed and replaced in the other side. Nares should be alternated with each tube insertion.

VERIFYING PLACEMENT AND RESIDUAL VOLUME

Placement and residual volume should be verified before each feeding or administration of medication, when child is irritable or complains of "fullness," and at least every four hours with continuous feeding.

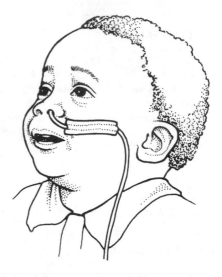

Figure 13–38 Secured Nasogastric Tube. *Source:* Copyright © 1996, Mark L. Batshaw, M.D.

There are two procedures for verification: aspiration and auscultation. *Both* procedures should be used before administration of feeding or medication.

The *aspiration* technique involves attaching a leur-lock syringe to the end of the tube with the plunger depressed and pulling back to obtain stomach contents. If the residual formula returns, measure the amount and allow it to return to the stomach by gravity. If the residual volume is greater than half the amount of the feeding, additional feedings should be delayed. If gastric secretions are obtained, test their pH utilizing a testing strip (gastric pH = 4–6). If no aspirate is obtained, move on to the second test and then try again. This may occur if the end of the tube is not low enough in the stomach or if the opening of the tube is against the stomach wall.

The *auscultation* technique involves drawing 5 cc of air into a leur-lock syringe and inserting it into the tube. Place the diaphragm of a stethoscope over the stomach at the epigastric area. Inject air into the tube utilizing a "puffing" motion on plunger while listening for an associated "whoosh" sound. Repeat process until placement can be positively identified, being careful not to distend the stomach with excessive air.

NASOGASTRIC TUBE FEEDING ADMINISTRATION

Frequency of feeding should be as prescribed by the health care professional. The procedure is as follows:

- Gather supplies.
  1. correct amount of formula
  2. equipment for feeding delivery
  3. 50-cc or 60-cc leur-lock syringe with extension set (with roller clamp) or enteral feeding bag (Figures 13–39 and 13–40)
- Position child correctly.
  1. head of bed elevated to 45-degree angle or upright in chair
  2. prone or on right side with the head of the bed raised at least 45 degrees
- Administer feeding.
  1. Prepare feeding at room temperature.
  2. Pour feeding into syringe or feeding bag (fill syringe only half to three-quarters full at a time).

3. Prime tubing to purge air and fill tubing with feeding.
4. Verify placement of nasogastric tube.
5. Connect feeding to nasogastric tube.
6. Adjust rate of administration, using clamp.
7. Administer feeding over a minimum of 30 minutes or longer.
8. When feeding is completed, add a small amount of water to the syringe or feeding bag to flush formula through (do not allow air to enter tubing between feeding and flush).
9. Disconnect tube from delivery set and cap nasogastric tube. Coil length of excess tube and secure to child's clothing with tape.
10. Rinse delivery set thoroughly with warm water after each feeding. If the child receives a continuous feeding, rinse the bag out every eight hours.
11. Change delivery set every 24 hours in the hospital or every three days in the home.

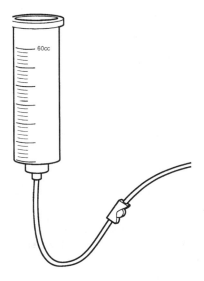

Figure 13–39 50-cc or 60-cc Leur-Lock Syringe with Extension Set for Nasogastric Tube Feeding. *Source:* Copyright © 1996, Mark L. Batshaw, M.D.

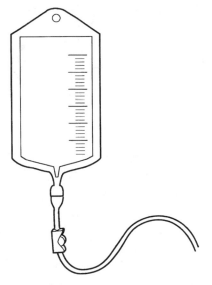

Figure 13–40 1000-cc Enteral Feeding Bag for Nasogastric Tube Feeding. *Source:* Copyright © 1996, Mark L. Batshaw, M.D.

- Set up feeding pump. (Note that there are variations in the type and design of feeding pumps available.)
    1. Utilize feeding bag for use with feeding pump.
    2. Add formula to bag and prime tubing.
    3. Insert drip chamber of feeding bag into slot on pump, being sure chamber is clear of droplets at the level that the electric eye monitors drops.
    4. Stretch the silastic portion of the tube around the roller and hook small disk onto slot (Figure 13–41).
    5. Connect feeding bag to end of nasogastric tube.
    6. Set desired infusion rate on the pump in cc/hr.
    7. Set pump to "run."
- Monitor tolerance of feeding.
    1. Maintain upright or sitting position, or prone or right side with head elevated.
    2. Monitor for signs that child may not tolerate the feeding (vomiting, gagging, diarrhea, abdominal distention).

- Identify safety factors/issues in caring for a child receiving nasogastric tube feedings.
    1. If vomiting or gagging occurs, stop the feeding and turn the child on his or her side. When he or she is calmed down, try to finish the feeding (unless symptoms are related to virus). It is necessary to verify placement after such an episode, as vomiting and gagging can cause the tube to move out of position.
    2. If abdominal cramping or diarrhea occurs or if vomiting and gagging persist, stop the feeding and notify the physician.

NASOGASTRIC TUBE INSERTION

The procedures for tube insertion are as follows:

- Gather supplies.
    1. feeding tube of correct size
    2. water-soluble lubricating jelly
    3. protective skin barrier (e.g., Duoderm)
    4. tape to secure tube

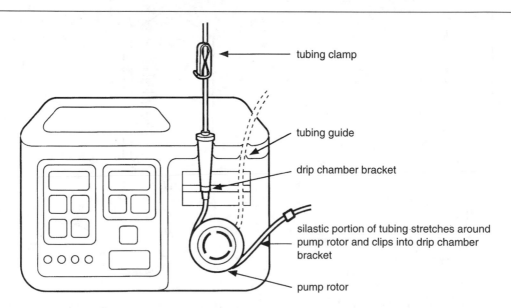

tubing clamp

tubing guide

drip chamber bracket

silastic portion of tubing stretches around pump rotor and clips into drip chamber bracket

pump rotor

Figure 13–41 Feeding Pump and Attached Feeding Bag. *Source:* Copyright © 1996, Mark L. Batshaw, M.D.

5. pen to mark tube

6. stethoscope and syringe for checking placement

- Measure and mark tube.

    1. Hold NG tube with uppermost hold at the end of the tube at the tip of the nose.

    2. Measure tube from nose to ear lobe to halfway between substernal notch and umbilicus (Figure 13–42).

    3. Mark this point with pen.

- Prepare tube.

    1. Plastic tubes need no preparation.

    2. Silastic tubes may require the use of a

wire guide. If the infant or child can suck on a pacifier or take sips of water through a straw during the procedure, the wire guide may not be needed. Placing the tube on ice for five minutes prior to insertion may also make it stiff enough to insert without the wire guide.

3. Lubricate tip of tube with water-soluble jelly.

- Insert tube.

    1. Insert tube gently into right or left nostril.

    2. Direct tube along flow of nostril.

    3. When tube reaches nasopharynx, have patient tilt head forward and encourage to swallow sips of water or suck on pacifier.

    4. Continue to push gently until pen marker is at nose.

- Identify safety factors.

    1. If resistance is met or if gag is stimulated, withdraw tube slightly until action subsides, then reinsert.

    2. Check that the tube is not coiling in patient's mouth.

    3. Persistent resistance, choking, or color changes are reasons for withdrawing tube immediately.

    4. Secure tube in place.

    5. If stylet used with silicone tube, remove and store in a clean package (can be used to reinsert).

CARE OF TUBE

Irrigate an unused tube with 5 cc water each day to ensure patency.

Plastic tubes should be changed every three to five days. *Silicone tubes* should be changed every month. If the tube becomes dislodged, the same tube can be reinserted within the one-month period if there is no damage to it. The nostrum should be altered to avoid skin irritation.

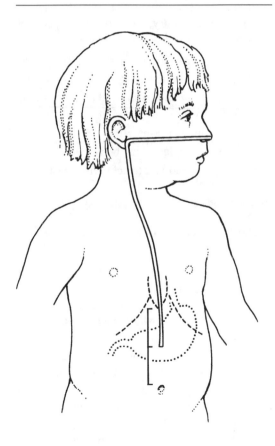

Figure 13–42 Measuring Nasogastric Tube Length. *Source:* Copyright © 1996, Mark L. Batshaw, M.D.

SUGGESTED READINGS

Bockus, S. 1993. When your patient needs tube feedings: Making the right decisions. *Nursing* 23, no. 7:34–42.

Camp, D., et al. 1990. How to insert and remove nasogastric tubes. *Nursing* 20, no. 9:59–63.

Children's Seashore House. 1991. *Patient/family education resource manual*. Philadelphia.

Eisenberg, P. 1994. A nurse's guide to tube feeding. *RN* 57, no. 10:62–69.

Webber-Jones, J., et al. 1992. How to declog a feeding tube. *Nursing* 22, no. 4:63–64.

Wong, D., and L. Whaley. 1990. *Clinical manual of pediatric nursing*. Philadelphia: C.V. Mosby Co.

CAST CARE

Kathleen Ryan Kuntz

Purpose: to describe techniques used to apply a cast, the medical risk factors that must be monitored, and skin and circulation care.

A cast is utilized to keep a part of the body immobile, most often so that an injury or surgical area can heal. Casts are made from different types of material, usually plaster or a synthetic with a fluid applied to provide rigidity. Children with developmental disabilities may have casts in place for a variety of reasons, including fracture, immobilization post orthopedic surgery, or as a means of influencing abnormal muscle tone (see Chapter 15, the section "Serial and Inhibitive Casting").

Before casting material is applied, the skin is protected with a stretch cloth and cotton padding. The casting material is then applied over this protective layer. When first applied, the cast will feel warm for approximately 10 to 15 minutes. Then it will appear cool and damp. A plaster cast will remain damp for several hours, whereas a cast made of a synthetic material will dry within 30 minutes.

During the drying period, it is important to avoid any pressure areas that may cause indentation of the material and pressure to the skin underneath. If it is necessary to touch the cast while it is drying, it is important to use the palms of the hands, not the fingers. Changing position of the part of the body that is casted will facilitate the drying process. Heated dryers or lights pose the risk of burns and *should not be used*. A fan can be used to facilitate circulation of air in the room.

Once the cast is dry, the important aspects of care to the child and the cast include

- skin and circulation assessment
- skin care around the edges of the cast
- maintaining circulation and mobility to the extremity
- maintaining cast integrity
- dietary considerations (body cast)
- lifting and moving the child in a cast

SKIN AND CIRCULATION ASSESSMENT

Skin and circulation should be assessed as follows:

1. Monitor for redness or irritation to skin at cast edges.

2. Observe for any odor emitted from beneath the cast, which may indicate an infection.

3. Observe for any drainage seeping through the cast, which may indicate an injury.

4. Monitor skin temperature below the level of the cast, which may indicate interrupted circulation.

5. Monitor pulse and/or capillary refill below the level of the cast (capillary refill should be less than three seconds upon blanching).

6. Monitor for sensation below the level of the cast (or sign of numbness or tingling).

7. Monitor for movement to extremity with cast.

8. Observe for excessive swelling to area of cast.

SKIN CARE

To petal rough cast edges:

1. Cut two- to three-inch strips of one-half-inch-wide adhesive tape or moleskin, with one end having curved edges (to prevent peeling).

2. Tape flat end of tape to inside of cast, bringing it over the edge.

3. Secure the curved end of tape to the outside of the cast.

4. Apply each subsequent strip so that it overlaps the previous one slightly (Figure 13–43).

5. Repeat until open edge of cast is covered (Figure 13–44).

Lotions should not be applied to skin at cast edges; this may soften skin and increase the risk of breakdown.

If child complains of itching of skin under the cast:

• *Do not* put anything inside of cast to scratch skin.

• Rub skin around cast edges.

• Rub opposite arm or leg.

• Blow *cool* air from hair dryer into cast.

MAINTAINING CIRCULATION AND MOBILITY

To maintain circulation and mobility:

• Elevate casted extremity above level of heart when possible to prevent swelling (Figure 13–45).

1. Rest cast on pillows or blankets.

2. Provide a sling for an arm cast.

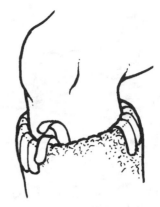

Figure 13–43 Petaling Rough Cast Edges. *Source:* Copyright © 1996, Mark L. Batshaw, M.D.

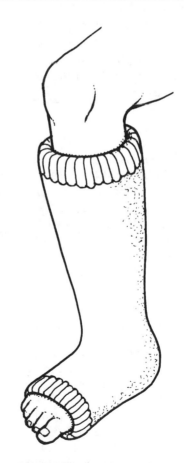

Figure 13–44 Finished Petaled Cast. *Source:* Copyright © 1996, Mark L. Batshaw, M.D.

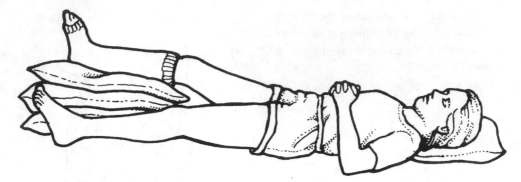

Figure 13–45 Elevating Casted Extremity above Level of Heart To Prevent Swelling. *Source:* Copyright © 1996, Mark L. Batshaw, M.D.

- Perform activities/games that encourage range of motion of extremity joints above and below the level of the cast.
- Utilize crutches/cane as prescribed to ambulate (with a weight-bearing cast).
- Utilize wheeled cart or scooter board for independent mobility (with long leg cast(s) or body cast).

MAINTAINING HYGIENE

For a *body cast*, sponge bathing is required. Plastic should be taped to the cast edge at the perineal area. A disposable diaper should be tucked into the cast. For *long leg casts*, sponge bathing is required. The patient with a lower leg or arm cast should bathe with the cast kept out of water and shower with the cast completely covered by plastic covering or a waterpoof cast cover.

MAINTAINING CAST INTEGRITY

If the cast gets wet, the plaster may soften and need to be replaced by a health care provider. A synthetic cast, however, may be thoroughly dried with a fan or hair dryer on the *cool* setting.

If the cast cracks or breaks, it will require reinforcement or replacement by a health care provider. *Do not* move the child in a body cast by grasping the bar between the child's legs (this is only for maintaining the position of the legs).

If the petaling becomes soiled, it can be removed and replaced.

DIETARY CONSIDERATIONS (BODY CAST)

Prevent constipation related to decreased mobility by encouraging consumption of fruits, vegetables, beans, whole grains, and fluids. Prevent excessive weight gain with inactivity by discouraging frequent snacking and the consumption of sugared drinks, candy, and "empty" calories.

LIFTING/MOVING

For protection of the joint:

- Support of the casted extremity is necessary when lifting to prevent excessive strain on joint.
- The patient, while casted, should avoid activities that naturally have extremity hanging (e.g., horseback riding).
- The cast should be supported (e.g., in a sling) whenever suspended.

Some caretaker considerations are:

- Be aware of additional weight of cast when lifting or moving child.
- Bring child close before lifting or when providing care to avoid strain on back.

- Bend knees and utilize legs when lifting child (do not bend over at the waist).
- Consider if two people are needed to lift child safely.

- Consider weight of cast in play activities to prevent injury to another part of the body or to another child.

SUGGESTED READINGS

Children's Seashore House. 1991. *Patient/family education resource manual.* Philadelphia.

Wong, D., and L. Whaley. *Clinical manual of pediatric nursing.* Philadelphia: C.V. Mosby Co.

VENTILATORS

Kathleen Ryan Kuntz

Purpose: to describe reasons an infant or child may require assisted mechanical ventilation, types of ventilatory support commonly used, use of the ventilator, and criteria for weaning from ventilatory support.

Infants and children may require assisted mechanical ventilation for several reasons, including

- respiratory failure or insufficiency, which can result from an immature or impaired respiratory system
- apnea, or periods of not breathing, which can result from impaired oral-motor function or structures of the upper respiratory system
- poor oxygenation, which can result from impairment of the neuromuscular system that supports the respiratory effort

Infants and children who required such ventilatory support were historically maintained in the hospital until this support was no longer necessary. The advent of home care for these technology-assisted children came in the mid-1980s. Home care has become a viable option not only for the premature infant with this need but also for older children with degenerative neuromuscular disorders. Providing care in the home allows the child to obtain services and live in an environment that will optimally promote growth and development.

MANAGEMENT OF CHILDREN ON VENTILATORS

Two types of ventilators are commonly utilized to support infants and children with respiratory insufficiency or failure. These are *negative pressure* and *positive pressure*. Positive-pressure ventilators can be *volume preset* or *pressure preset*.

Negative-Pressure Ventilation

The negative-pressure ventilator may be indicated for children who have poor oxygenation due to neuromuscular impairment. These children become easily fatigued, rather than having acute respiratory distress. This type of ventilatory support requires the external application of a device around the chest that may appear to be like a shell or a frame covered by an airtight poncho. The device is connected to a machine that creates a negative pressure (suction) around the chest wall, causing it to expand and the child to draw in a breath. When the pressure is released, the natural relaxation of the chest causes the expiration.

Children who receive this type of ventilation use the device when in bed napping or sleeping at night. When they are out of the device, there is no special treatment required in the child's care. Respiratory status is evaluated primarily by the level of activity tolerance.

Positive-Pressure Ventilation

The positive-pressure ventilator may be indicated for infants and children who have an immature respiratory system or an impairment to the upper respiratory structures. Positive-pressure ventilation is usually administered via an endotracheal tube (passing through the mouth and upper airway to a point below the vocal cord) or, in cases of long-term ventilation, via a tracheostomy tube (passing through a stoma in the neck into the trachea below the vocal cord). Positive-pressure ventilation can be delivered by presetting the pressure or the volume delivered.

Pressure Preset

The pressure-preset ventilator delivers a certain amount of pressure at a predetermined rate. The amount of air (tidal volume) given with each breath varies. This is required in cases in which the lungs have a decreased compliance. Such is the case with bronchopulmonary dysplasia (BPD) or other restrictive lung disease. The lungs are stiffer than usual and require a higher pressure forcing the lungs to inflate.

Volume Preset

The volume-preset ventilator delivers a certain volume of air at a predetermined rate. The amount of pressure required with each breath varies. This is indicated when the child requires a certain volume of air and can withstand a higher pressure if necessary. Children with BPD may develop a pneumothorax and have poor blood return to the heart with excessive pressure. A child with an impaired neuromuscular system contributing to decreased oxygenation is a better candidate for volume-preset ventilation.

Modes of Positive-Pressure Ventilation

The following are modes of positive-pressure ventilation:

1. *Assisted:* With every breath initiated by the child, a ventilator breath is triggered so the child receives a full breath. This may be used when the child has spontaneous respirations but inhales an inadequate amount of air with each breath.

2. *Controlled:* The ventilator delivers a breath at a set rate. This may be used when the child has few or no spontaneous respirations.

3. *Intermittent mandatory ventilation (IMV):* Periodic controlled breaths are interspersed with the child's own spontaneous respirations. This is used to ease the work of breathing and allow for conservation of energy and strengthening of respiratory muscles.

4. *Synchronized intermittent mandatory ventilation (SIMV):* Periodic controlled breaths allow the child to breath independently, while the ventilator breath is synchronized with the child's effort.

Ventilator Requirements

With mechanical ventilation, breaths delivered are set considering the child's need for respiratory support. The factors included are

1. *Tidal volume (V_t):* The amount of air exchange with each breath.

2. *Peak inspiratory pressure (PIP):* The amount of pressure within the lungs at the point of maximal inspiration (greatest force).

3. *Positive end expiratory pressure (PEEP):* The amount of pressure within the lungs at the end of expiration (residual pressure).

4. *Continuous positive airway pressure (CPAP):* The amount of pressure continu-

ally within the lungs. CPAP is sometimes used interchangeably with PEEP, though PEEP refers to pressure administered by mechanical ventilation; while CPAP does not require mechanical ventilation.

5. *Inspiration to expiration ratio (I:E ratio):* The amount of time allowed for the inspiratory versus the expiratory phase of each breath.

6. *Fraction of inspired oxygen (O$_2$):* The percentage of oxygen concentration of inspired air.

Ventilator Alarms

Table 13–6 offers information regarding ventilator alarms and causes. This may be of assistance to troubleshoot alarms when caring for the child that is ventilator assisted. In *all* cases, when a ventilator alarm sounds, the first action is to assess the child's status to ensure stability before attending to the machine. If the child's status, in question or the cause of alarm or problem with the ventilator cannot be *immediately* detected, the child should receive bag-valve-mask ventilation set at pressures congruent with the ventilatory support required (settings on the ventilator).

WEANING FROM VENTILATORY SUPPORT

Weaning from ventilatory support can be a very long process for children with bronchopulmonary dysplasia, impairment to respiratory structures, or neuromuscular disease that is nondegenerative. Positive indicators that decreases in ventilatory support may be tolerated include weight gain, growth, and continued improvement of pulmonary function. Factors to be considered when weaning are

1. *Nutrition/anthropometric measurements:* Is the child making gains in growth percentiles? The nutritional requirements of the child are based on specific energy needs. The ventilator-assisted child should consistently show progress with weight, length, and head circumference. Nutritional intake may be as high as 120 calories per kilogram per day, or two to three times the basal caloric requirements. Improved lung compliance and chest wall strength correlate with increasing age and body size.

2. *Developmental milestones:* Is the child increasing his or her abilities to perform gross motor, fine motor, and other play activities? Continuing achievement of developmental milestones indicates that nutritional and ventilatory support are adequate to meet present and future needs.

3. *Ventilatory requirements:* Is the child requiring less ventilatory support such as suctioning, chest percussion and postural drainage, and/or manual ventilation with O$_2$ to maintain good breath sounds? Are the secretions white and thin compared to thick and yellow-green due to infection? Chest percussion and postural drainage three to four times each day should adequately mobilize secretions and maintain clear breath sounds. The child should not require supplemental O$_2$ during periods of increased physical activity.

4. *Physical assessment:* Does the child look comfortable breathing during activities of daily living (ADLs), at play, and at rest? Vital signs within normal limits for the child are a good indicator of physical stability. The ability to recognize physical signs of respiratory distress—retractions, color change, and change in respiratory rate—is important.

5. *Infection:* Is the child infection free? Laboratory values demonstrating normal white blood cell count and sputum tests showing absence of tracheitis are positive signals for weaning. Nutritional and ventilatory requirements typically increase during periods of infection.

Table 13–6 Ventilator Alarms

Condition	Cause	Action
Low pressure alarm	Disconnection	Manually ventilate until reconnected
	Leak in circuit	Manually ventilate until tubing is replaced or reconnected
	Condensation in alarm system	Remove water from alarm tubing Repair/replace alarm system
High pressure alarm	Water in ventilation circuit	Manually ventilate Remove water from tubing
	Kink in ventilator tubing	Check patency of airway and ventilator tubing
	Increased secretions	Manually ventilate Suction airway Check patency of airway
	Suspected obstruction of artificial airway	Manually ventilate Attempt suction Change tracheostomy tube
	Coughing	Identify methods to relieve coughing
Humidifier problems	Empty humidifier or water supply system	Check tubing for condensation Check/replace water supply
	System malfunction	Ensure that ventilation is not interrupted Check temperature indicator, warmth of tubing, probe connections Replace heater unit
	Water accumulation in circuit	Empty system
Oxygen analyzer	Alarm limits set improperly	Check that limits are set at ±3% of required FiO_2
	Change in FiO_2 without change in limits	Check for required FiO_2 as prescribed Check calibration of O_2 analyzer
	Analyzer malfunctions	Repair/replace analyzer

SUGGESTED READINGS

Baum, G., and E. Wolinsky. 1980. *Textbook of pulmonary diseases.* 3rd ed. Boston: Little, Brown & Co.

Children's Hospital of Philadelphia. 1989. Positive pressure ventilation, 4:1:a. In *Nursing policy and procedure manual.* Philadelphia.

Children's Seashore House. 1991. Nursing orientation to the care of the ventilator-assisted child. In *Nursing orientation resource manual.* Philadelphia.

Children's Seashore House. 1994. Positive/negative pressure ventilation. In *Nursing procedure manual.* Philadelphia.

Dougherty, J.M. 1990. Negative pressure devices in pediatric practice. *Pediatric Nursing* 16:135–138.

Ferland, P.A. 1991. Are you ready for ventilator patients? *Nursing* 21, no. 1:42–47.

Kettrick, R. 1991. Chronic respiratory failure in children. In *Hospital management in pediatric critical care review series, part III*, ed. F. Gioa and T. Yeh, 91–99. Fullerton, Calif.: Society of Critical Care Medicine.

Office of Technology Assessment. 1988. *Technology-dependent children: Hospital versus home care.* OTA-M-H-38. Washington, D.C.: Government Printing Office.

BLADDER CATHETERIZATION

Kathleen Ryan Kuntz

Purpose: to review the indications for chronic bladder catheterization, in particular the technique of clean intermittent catheterization (CIC), and to discuss potential complications and caregiver considerations.

Clean intermittent catheterization may be necessary with certain conditions such as spina bifida or spinal cord injury. The nerves that control bladder function are located in the spinal column. When a nerve is injured or interrupted, the reflexes necessary for bladder control are impaired, reacting either too strongly or not strongly enough, and the child is considered to have a neurogenic bladder.

The problems identified are:

- The bladder fills, but not to capacity; reflexes signal that make the bladder contract and eliminate the urine, causing frequent incontinence.
- The bladder fills and becomes distended. The reflexes do not coordinate a signal to the brain that the bladder is full, and urine "dribbles" from the bladder, causing frequent incontinence and contributing to urine's becoming stagnant in the bladder, so that infection may result.
- The bladder fills, and reflexes signal a need to empty the bladder, but the bladder does not empty fully, leaving urine to become stagnant, so that infection may result.
- The reflexes of the bladder are not coordinated and act out of synchrony with each other, causing urine to flow back into the ureter, which can cause kidney damage.

CIC promotes regular emptying of the bladder to prevent the complications associated with neurogenic bladder. Factors to consider when caring for the child requiring CIC include

- dietary considerations
- signs/symptoms of infection or other complications
- steps in catheterization
- caregiver considerations
- equipment management

DIETARY CONSIDERATIONS

Constipation contributes to increased effort to have a bowel movement, which can cause the bladder to release urine. Encourage fruits, vegetables, beans, whole grains, and fluids.

Sporadic drinking of large amounts of fluid contributes to variations in the amount of urine in the bladder. Large amounts of fluid before bedtime contribute to incontinence during the night.

SIGNS/SYMPTOMS OF COMPLICATIONS

The color, clarity, and odor of urine may all signal complications. Indications for treatment are

1. concentrated urine
2. strong odor
3. visible blood in urine

4. burning/pressure sensation

5. flank pain

Note that the child with interruption of spinal nerves may not have the sensory feedback of burning/pressure sensation or flank pain.

STEPS IN CLEAN INTERMITTENT CATHETERIZATION

The steps of the CIC procedure are as follows:
- Prepare a clean work area.
- Gather supplies and equipment.
  1. catheter
  2. gloves (if indicated)
  3. water-soluble lubricant
  4. povidone wipes
  5. soap/water/washcloth
  6. collection receptacle
- Wash hands before beginning procedure.
- Prepare equipment, opening packages, maintaining cleanliness.
- Lubricate end of catheter with water-soluble lubricant, maintaining cleanliness of catheter tip.

- Position for accessibility of urinary meatus (opening).
- Don clean gloves. (Note: gloves may not be necessary for self-catheterization while maintaining one clean hand.)
- Cleanse perineal area with soap and water.
- Discard soiled gloves.
- Wash hands prior to catheterization.
- Don clean gloves.
- Cleanse area of urinary meatus with povidone, using hand identified as "dirty," maintaining one hand as "clean."
- Identify location of urinary meatus.
- Direct open end of catheter into receptacle.
- Insert catheter length to reach bladder until urine flows (Figures 13–46 and 13–47).

CAREGIVER CONSIDERATIONS

The caregiver should be aware of the intimate nature of the procedure and the need to consider the child's feelings. He or she should plan a space and time for procedure that offers privacy and discuss the procedure discreetly so as not to embarrass the child.

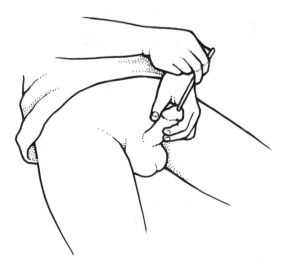

Figure 13–46 Inserting Urinary Catheter—Male Patient. *Source:* Copyright © 1996, Mark L. Batshaw, M.D.

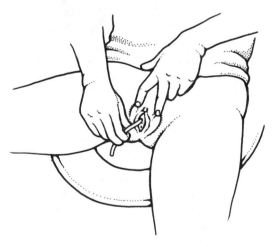

Figure 13–47 Inserting Urinary Catheter—Female Patient. *Source:* Copyright © 1996, Mark L. Batshaw, M.D.

Further, the caregiver should consider the child's developmental stage and when to initiate teaching of self-catheterization. This should be when the child

- understands the need for the procedure
- can describe the procedure, equipment, and supplies
- can identify important aspects of a "clean" procedure
- can initiate as a "helper" in the procedure

EQUIPMENT MANAGEMENT

Clean catheters for reuse (at home):
1. Place catheters in warm, soapy water.
2. Rinse catheters well with warm, clear water.
3. Pat dry with clean cloth.
4. Place in clean container to air-dry thoroughly.
5. Store clean, dry catheters in clean, covered container until use.

SUGGESTED READINGS

Segal, E.S., et al. 1995. The determinants of successful self-catheterization programs in children with myelomeningocele. *Journal of Pediatric Nursing* 10, no. 2:82–88.

Wong, D., and L. Whaley. 1990. *Clinical manual of pediatric nursing.* Philadelphia: C.V. Mosby Co.

SEIZURES

Kathleen Ryan Kuntz

Purpose: to address the management and treatment of children that may exhibit seizure activity or have a chronic seizure disorder.

Children with developmental disabilities frequently are at risk for the development of a seizure disorder for reasons that coincide with the nature of the disability. Causes of seizure activity include possible metabolic/electrolyte disturbance, central nervous system injury, infection, trauma, tumor, and vascular disturbance. Seizures may also be of unknown origin. A premature infant with perinatal asphyxia may experience seizures in the neonatal period and have an abnormal EEG. A child with a neural tube defect requiring a ventriculoperitoneal shunt may be at risk for seizures due to increased intracranial pressure.

By definition, a *seizure* is an episodic, involuntary alteration in consciousness, motor activity, behavior, sensation, or autonomic function. It is a *symptom* of an underlying process. *Epilepsy* is defined as recurrent seizures that are unrelated to

febrile episodes. *Status epilepticus* is a prolonged or recurrent state of seizure activity lasting over 30 minutes, during which period the child does not regain consciousness. The latter is treated as a medical emergency.

INTRODUCTION TO MANAGEMENT OF SEIZURES

The primary treatment regimen for seizure activity includes the administration of anticonvulsant agents (see section "Medications," subsection "Anticonvulsants" later in this chapter) and maintaining safety precautions to protect the child from injury or harm in the event of a seizure. Since an effect of anticonvulsant therapy is sedation of the central nervous system, the goal is to strike a balance at which there is "reasonable control" of the seizure activity and a level of functional ability. For example, the anticonvulsant therapy would sedate the central nervous system to a point that the child would remain seizure free, or have only periodic seizures, and still remain alert enough to participate in learning activities in school.

Table 13–7 identifies types of seizures, their characteristics, and the primary anticonvulsant therapy.

MANAGEMENT OF AN ACUTE EPISODE

A key to the treatment of an acute seizure episode is obtaining a comprehensive history that includes the following:

- Description of the event
  1. time of occurrence
  2. duration of episode
  3. setting of event
  4. precipitating activity
- History of illness, fever or infection, trauma, medications taken, exposure to toxins
- Physical examination
  1. vital signs
  2. level of consciousness
  3. general findings (e.g., alterations in cardiovascular system)

Table 13–7 Characteristics and Treatment of Seizures

Type of Seizure	Characteristics	Treatment
Partial		
Simple partial seizure (formerly called a *focal motor* or *focal sensory seizure*)	Stereotyped, sudden sensation or movement—the same sudden sensation or movement during every seizure (i.e., sudden feeling of pain, perception of a foul odor, or feeling of nausea). Does not affect consciousness	Carbamazepine Phenobarbital Valproic acid Phenytoin Clonazepam
Complex partial seizure (formerly called a *psychomotor seizure* or *temporal lobe epilepsy*)	Unusual stereotyped behaviors, such as staring, fumbling with clothes, lip smacking, and automatic hand movements, accompanied by a change in or loss of consciousness	
Partial with secondary generalization	May initiate as a partial seizure and progress to include a generalized response	
Generalized		
Atonic (formerly called *drop attacks*)	A sudden loss of muscle tone, usually resulting in a fall. In most cases this also includes a loss of consciousness	Carbamazepine Phenobarbital Valproic acid Phenytoin
Myoclonic	Generalized jerking of extremities, lasting less than five seconds, usually with a brief period of unconsciousness that can go unnoticed. May occur in clusters	
Absence (formerly called *petit mal*)	Loss of consciousness, usually lasting less than 15 seconds, with no other visible change. May involve eye blinking or lip smacking	Ethosuximide Valproic acid Clonazepam
Generalized tonic-clonic (formerly called *grand mal*)	Tonic phase involves generalized stiffening of muscles usually lasting less than one minute. This is followed by a clonic phase of rapid jerking. The individual is unconscious during both phases and will not remember it afterward	Carbamazepine Phenobarbital Valproic acid Phenytoin

4. neurological findings (e.g., asymmetry, paralysis, behavioral change)

- Diagnostic studies

  1. serum studies

     (a) electrolytes

     (b) magnesium (Mg)

     (c) blood urea nitrogen (BUN)

     (d) creatinine clearance (Cr)

     (e) glucose

     (f) toxicology screen

  2. additional studies

     (a) electroencephalogram (EEG)

     (b) electrocardiogram (EKG)

     (c) magnetic resonance imaging (MRI)

     (d) computerized topography (CT) scan

     (e) lumbar puncture (LP)

MANAGEMENT OF CHRONIC SEIZURE CONDITIONS

It is necessary to be prepared for the possibility of a seizure when an individual is known to have a seizure disorder. Knowledge about the child's seizure history will help to anticipate the effects most likely to be encountered in the event of a seizure. The following list identifies safety considerations and actions to protect the child.

- Monitor the child closely, especially during activities that could be dangerous if a seizure occurred (e.g., swimming, bicycle riding).

- Know the child's seizure history.

  1. type of seizure, or if more than one type

  2. frequency

  3. when was last seizure

  4. any current illness, fever, or infection

  5. precipitating activities that can trigger a seizure

  6. warning signs or aura (sensory signal of an impending seizure, such as a smell or sensation)

- Know the child's medication history.

  1. what medication is taken to control the seizures

  2. when it is to be taken

  3. whether the medication has any adverse reactions

  4. whether there are any allergic reactions to any medications

  5. what other medications are taken

- Ensure that anticonvulsant medications are administered as prescribed and taken at time intervals to maintain therapeutic blood levels.

- Maintain use of protective device if required (e.g., helmet, medic-alert bracelet, padded chair or bed rails).

- Protect from injury.

  1. Stop potentially harmful activity.

  2. If loss of consciousness, ensure ability to breathe and position to avoid aspiration (have suction and oxygen available if generalized tonic-clonic seizures).

  3. If motor activity is involved, loosen restraining devices or clothing (take out of wheelchair).

  4. Move potentially harmful objects out of range.

- Observe and monitor seizure.

  1. duration

  2. progression

  3. area(s) of involvement

  4. characteristics of seizure

     (a) aura

     (b) loss of consciousness

     (c) incontinence of urine or stool

     (d) motor activity

     (e) postictal state (after seizure)

- Recognize emergency situations.

  1. aspiration if vomited or excessive salivation

  2. decreased oxygen to tissue; color changes

3. respiratory arrest (if seizure with apnea is prolonged)
4. status epilepticus
   (a) secure airway
   (b) correct metabolic disturbance

(c) administer anticonvulsant(s)
   (i) Lorezepam or diazepam
   (ii) Phenytoin
   (iii) Phenobarbital

SUGGESTED READINGS

Brunquell, P.J. 1994. Listening to epilepsy. *Infants and Young Children* 7, no. 1:24–33.

Callanan, M. 1988. Epilepsy: Putting the patient back in control. *RN* 51, no. 2:48–55.

Friedman, D. 1988. Taking the scare out of caring for seizure patients. *Nursing* 18, no. 2:52–59.

O'Brien, K. 1991. Managing the seizure patient. *Nursing* 21, no. 1:63–65.

Penny, J., ed. 1986. *Epilepsy: Diagnosis, management, quality of life.* New York: Raven Press.

MEDICATIONS

Mark L. Batshaw, Nathan J. Blum, Cynthia Borda, Anna-Maria DaCosta, Sonia V. George, Audrey E. Mars, H. Lynn Starr, and Paul P. Wang

Purpose: to describe effects, benefits, and risks of medications commonly used to treat children with developmental disabilities. Some of these alleviate maladies experienced by all children, such as fevers and infections. Others treat disorders specifically associated with developmental disabilities, such as antiepileptic drugs for seizure control and antispasticity medications to improve muscle tone.

Due to the nature of their medical problems, children with developmental disabilities may require a complex medication regimen, often including drugs in several of the following categories: antiepileptic, antispasticity, and antireflux medications; antibiotics; medications to influence mood and behavior; skin preparations; and medications to improve respiration. Caregivers knowledgeable about the common side effects and potential interactions of the various medications are in a position to alert the physician to possible improvements in the medication regimen. Table 13–8 lists drugs by use category, and Table 13–9 lists drugs alpha-betically by trade name with corresponding generic name; Table 13–10 lists drugs alphabetically by generic name, with effects, dosages, side effects, and contraindications.

ANTIEPILEPTIC DRUGS

An individual is considered to have a seizure disorder (also called epilepsy) if he or she has had repeated seizures and an abnormal electroencephalogram. In the general population, the incidence of epilepsy is 6 percent (Aicardi 1986); however, among individuals with developmental disabilities, particularly severe mental retardation and cerebral palsy, the incidence approaches 25 percent (Wallace 1990). Among individuals with epilepsy and normal intelligence, the incidence of learning disabilities is increased, possibly as a consequence of the medication (Aldenkamp et al. 1990).

Seizures are transient physiological disturbances caused by abnormal, excessive electrical discharge of nerve cells in the brain. Seizures may manifest as a change in level of conscious-

Table 13–8 Medications According to Use (Trade Names in Parentheses)

Antiepileptic	Antispasticity	Antireflux	Antibiotic	Mood	Skin	Respiratory
ACTH (Corticotropin)	Alprazolam (Xanax)	Cimetidine (Tagamet)	Acyclovir (Zovirax)	*CNS Stimulants* Adderall	Benzoyl peroxide (Clearasil, Oxy, Fostex, Desquam X)	Albuterol (Ventolin, Proventil)
Carbamazepine (Tegretol)	Baclofen, intrathecal	Cisapride (Propulsid)	Amoxicillin (Amoxil)	Clonidine hydrochloride (Catapres)	Calcium undecylenate 10% (Caldesene powder)	Beclomethasone (Beclovent, Vanceril)
Clonazepam (Klonopin)	Baclofen, oral (Lioresal)	Famotidine (Pepcid)	Amoxicillin + clavulanic acid (Augmentin)	Dextroamphetamine sulfate (Dexedrine)	Cetyl alcohol (Cetaphil)	Cromolyn (Intal)
Ethosuximide (Zarontin)	Clonazepam (Klonopin)	Magnesium hydroxide + aluminum hydroxide (Maalox)	Cefixime (Suprax)	Methylphenidate hydrochloride (Ritalin)	Chloroxine 2% (Capitrol)	Flunisolide (Aerobid)
Felbamate (Felbatol)	Dantrolene sodium (Dantrium)	Metoclopramide (Reglan)	Cefuroxime (Ceftin)	Nortriptyline (Pamelor)	Clindamycin (Cleocin-T)	Ipratropium bromide (Atrovent)
Gabapentin (Neurontin)	Diazepam (Valium)	Ranitidine (Zantac)	Cephalexin (Keflex)	Pemoline (Cylert)	Clotrimazole 1% (Lotrimin, Mycelex)	Metaproterenol (Alupent, Metaprel)
Lamotrigine (Lamictal)			Cephradine (Velosef)	Sertraline (Zoloft)	Colloidal oatmeal (Aveeno)	Prednisone and methyl-prednisolone (Solu-Medrol, Medrol)
Phenobarbital (Luminal)			Clarithromycin (Biaxin)	*Antidepressants* Amitriptyline hydrochloride (Elavil)	Crotamiton (Eurax)	Salmeterol (Serevent)
Phenytoin (Dilantin)			Cloxacillin (Tegopen)	Desipramine hydrochloride (Norpramin)	Erythromycin, 2% (T-Stat)	Terbutaline (Brethine, Azmacort)
Primidone (Mysoline)			Dicloxacillin (Pathocil)	Fluoxetine (Prozac)	Griseofulvin (Fulvicin)	Theophylline (Theo-Dur, Slo-Bid, Uniphyl, Aerolate)
Valproic acid (Depakene, Depakote)			Erythromycin (various brands)	Imipramine (Janimine, Tofranil)	Hydrocortisone (Caldecort Cort-Dome, Hytone)	Triamcinolone (Azmacort)
			Nystatin (Mycostatin)	*Antipsychotics* Chlorpromazine hydrochloride (Thorazine)	Hydrocortisone + Polymyxin B + Neomycin (Cortisporin)	
			Penicillin (Pen Vee K)	Haloperidol (Haldol)	Lanolin oil (Balmex)	
			Sulfisoxazole (Gantrisin)	Thioridazine (Mellaril)	Lanolin (A & D ointment)	
			Trimethoprim + sulfamethoxazole (Bactrim, Septra)	Thiothixene (Navane)	Lindane (Kwell)	
					Miconazole 2% (Monistat)	
					Mineral oil (Lubriderm, Nivea)	
					Mineral oil (Alpha Keri)	
					Mupirocin, 2% (Bactroban)	
					Nystatin (Mycostatin)	
					Permethrin 5% (Elimite)	
					Permethrin 1% (Nix)	
					Petrolatum (Eucerin)	
					Retinoic acid derivative (Accutane)	
					Selenium sulfide 2.5% (Selsun Blue)	
					Tetracycline (Sumycin)	
					Tolnaftate (Tinactin)	
					Triamcinolone (Kenalog, Aristocort)	
					Zinc oxide (Caldesene ointment)	

Table 13–9 Medication Trade Names

Trade Name	Generic Name	Trade Name	Generic Name
A&D ointment	Lanolin, petrolatum, vitamin A and D, mineral oils	Elavil	Amitriptyline hydrochloride
		Elimite	Permethrin (5%)
Accutane	Retinoic acid derivative	Eucerin	Petrolatum, mineral oil and wax, alcohol
Adderall	Adderall		
Aerobid	Flunisolide	Eurax	Crotamiton
Aerolate	Theophylline	Felbatol	Felbamate
Alpha Keri	Mineral oil	Fostex	Benzoyl peroxide (2.5–10%)
Alupent	Metaproterenol	Fulvicin	Griseofulvin
Amoxil	Amoxicillin	Gantrisin	Sulfisoxazole
Aquachloral	Chloral hydrate	Haldol	Haloperidol
Aristocort	Triamcinolone	Hytone	Hydrocortisone
Atarax	Hydroxyzine	Intal	Cromolyn
Atrovent	Ipratropium bromide	Janimine	Imipramine
Augmentin	Amoxicillin + clavulanic acid	Keflex	Cephalexin
Aveeno	Colloidal oatmeal	Kenalog	Triamcinolone
Azmacort	Triamcinolone	Klonopin	Clonazepam
Azmacort inhaler	Terbutaline	Kwell	Lindane
		Lamictal	Lamotrigine
Bactrim	Trimethoprim (TMP) + sulfamethoxazole	Lioresal	Baclofen
		Lotrimin	Clotrimazole
Bactroban	Mupirocin (2%)	Lubriderm	Mineral oil, petrolatum, lanolin
Balmex	Lanolin oil	Luminal	Phenobarbital
Beclovent	Beclomethasone	Maalox	Magnesium hydroxide and aluminum hydroxide
Benadryl	Diphenhydramine		
Biaxin	Clarithromycin	Medrol	Methylprednisolone
BOTOX	Botulinum A toxin	Mellaril	Thioridazine
Brethine PO	Terbutaline	Metaprel	Metaproterenol
Buspar	Buspirone	Monistat	Miconazole (2%)
Caldecort Cort-Dome	Hydrocortisone	Mycelex	Clotrimazole
		Mycostatin	Nystatin
Caldesene powder	Calcium undecylenate (10%)	Mysoline	Primidone
		Navane	Thiothixene
Caldesene ointment	Zinc oxide, cod liver oil, lanolin, petrolatum	Nerve Blocks and Motor Point Blocks	Phenol Injections
Capitrol	Chloroxine (2%)		
Catapres	Clonidine hydrochloride	Neurontin	Gabapentin
Ceftin	Cefuroxime	Nivea	Mineral oil, petrolatum, lanolin
Cetaphil	Cetyl alcohol, prophylene glycol, stearyl alcohol (oil-free)	Nix	Permethrin (1%)
		Noctec	Chloral hydrate
Clearasil	Benzoyl peroxide (2.5–10%)	Norpramin	Desipramine hydrochloride
Cleocin-T	Clindamycin	Oxy	Benzoyl peroxide (2.5–10%)
Corticotropin	ACTH	Pamelor	Nortriptyline
Cortisporin	Hydrocortisone polymyxin-B and neomycin	Pathocil	Dicloxacillin
		Pen Vee K	Penicillin
Cylert	Pemoline	Pepcid	Famotidine
Dantrium	Dantrolene sodium	Prednisone	Prednisone
Depakene	Valproic acid	Propulsid	Cisapride
Depakote	Valproic acid	Proventil	Albuterol
Desquam X	Benzoyl peroxide (2.5–10%)	Prozac	Fluoxetine
Dexedrine	Dextroamphetamine	Reglan	Metoclopramide
Dilantin	Phenytoin		
Duoderm	Duoderm		

continues

Table 13–9 continued

Trade Name	Generic Name	Trade Name	Generic Name
Ritalin	Methylphenidate	Tinactin	Tolnaftate
Selsun Blue	Selenium sulfide (2.5%)	Tofranil	Imipramine
Septra	Trimethoprim (TMP + sulfamethoxazole)	Trexan	Naltrexone
		Uniphyl	Theophylline
Serevent	Salmeterol	Valium	Diazepam
Slo-Bid	Theophylline	Vanceril	Beclomethasone
Solu-Medrol	Methylprednisolone	Velosef	Cephradine
Sumycin	Tetracycline	Ventolin	Albuterol
Suprax	Cefixime	Vistaril	Hydroxyzine
T-Stat	Erythromycin (2%)	Xanax	Alprazolam
Tagamet	Cimetidine	Zantac	Ranitidine
Tegopen	Cloxacillin	Zarontin	Ethosuximide
Tegretol	Carbamazepine	Zoloft	Sertraline hydrochloride
Theo-Dur	Theophylline	Zovirax	Acyclovir
Thorazine	Chlorpromazine		

ness or behavior and/or abnormal movements and/or abnormal sensory experiences. The various types of seizures have been recently reclassified, improving descriptive accuracy. The classification of a seizure disorder allows one to ascertain which medication is likely to be the most effective (see Table 13–11). Within each seizure type, the medications listed are, in general, equally effective. For example, carbamazepine, phenobarbital, phenytoin, and valproic acid are all effective in treating tonic-clonic seizures. Thus the reason for choosing a medication is often based on side effects, cost, and the doctor's experience. Antiepileptic drugs generally work by inactivating calcium channels that normally permit depolarization of the neuron (e.g., phenytoin), by inhibiting the release of excitatory neurochemicals (e.g., felbamate), or by enhancing the inhibitory neurochemical GABA (e.g., valproic acid). The hoped-for result is to prevent the initiation of a seizure or to contain its spread.

In managing seizures, the physician usually begins using one medication and slowly raises the dosage until there is control of seizures, maximum dosage has been exceeded, or side effects become too difficult to manage. In children with resistant seizures, the use of two drugs may be necessary; use of more than two drugs is

rarely indicated. The most common cause of poorly controlled seizures is noncompliance. Once the condition is stabilized, drug levels in the blood are measured about twice a year to ensure that they are in the therapeutic range; blood tests for liver function or other studies may be taken at the same time. Drug levels will be obtained more frequently when the medication dosage is being altered. Effectiveness of drug therapy is dependent on the family's compliance in giving/taking the medication regularly. If the child has been seizure free for two years and has an improved EEG pattern, an attempt of stopping the medication is usually made.

ANTISPASTICITY MEDICATIONS

Pharmacologic treatment is often a component in the management of spasticity; however, it is rarely the initial treatment modality and should not be used without accompanying rehabilitation therapies. Although drug treatment of spasticity has been investigated for many years, firm conclusions regarding efficacy, particularly in children with spasticity of cerebral origin, remain elusive because most research has been done in adults with acquired brain lesions, spinal cord injuries, or multiple sclerosis. No medica-

Table 13–10 Drug Dosage, Usage, and Side Effects (Trade Names in Parentheses)

Medication	Category	Effect/Usage	Typical Application	Side Effects/Contraindications
ACTH (Corticotropin)	Antiepileptic	Infantile spasms and Lennox–Gastaut seizures	Injection; many regimens exist; 20–40 U/d IM; generally used for weeks to months; taper slowly	Glucose in urine, high blood pressure, cataracts, brittle bones
Acyclovir (Zovirax)	Antiviral agent	Used primarily in children who are immunocompromised to treat or protect against herpes simplex and varicella (chicken pox)	Tablets, capsules, liquid: depends on clinical situation	Renal impairment
Adderall	CNS stimulant	ADHD, obesity, narcolepsy	Tablets. For ADHD: not recommended for children <3 yo 3–5 yo: 2.5 mg/d initially with increase of 2.5 mg/wk to optimal response ≥6 yo: 5 mg/d or twice a day initially; increase by 5 mg/wk until optimal response. Dose q4–6h	Insomnia, loss of appetite, emotional liability, addictive potential, arrhythmias
Albuterol (Ventolin, Proventil)	Respiratory	Bronchodilator used for treatment of acute asthmatic attacks and for the chronic treatment of patients with persistent symptoms	Oral: 2–6 yo: 0.1–0.2 mg/kg/dose 3 times a day; max 12 mg/d 6–12 yo: 2 mg/dose 3–4 times a day; max 24 mg/d Adult: 2–4 mg/dose 3–4 times a day; max 32 mg/d Syrup: 2 mg/5 ml Tablets: 2 mg, 4 mg Inhaler (90 mcg/spray): <12 yo: 1–2 puffs q6h ≥12 yo: 1–2 puffs q4–6h Nebulizer (0.5 mg/dl): 0.01–0.05 ml/kg q4–6h. Patients may need more frequent doses during acute attacks	Tachycardia, palpitations, tremor, nervousness, hyperactivity, insomnia, gastrointestinal distress, and increased appetite. Paradoxical bronchospasm can occur and should result in discontinuation of the medication
Alprazolam (Xanax)	Anxiolytic	Anxiety, aggression, panic attacks	Tablets: Titrate starting at minimal dose—.125 mg three times a day. Safety and efficacy in children <18 yo are not known	Drowsiness, insomnia, decreased salivation. Contraindications: sensitivity to benzodiazepines

continues

Table 13–10 continued

Medication	Category	Effect/Usage	Typical Application	Side Effects/Contraindications
Amitriptyline hydrochloride (Elavil)	Antidepressant	ADHD, depression	Tablets: 1mg/kg/d 3 times a day up to 1.5 mg/kg/d 3 times a day. Not recommended in children <12 yo	Sedation, dry mouth, blurred vision, very rare sudden death from cardiac arrhythmia. *Contraindications:* with guanethidine, MAO inhibitors
Amoxicillin (Amoxil)	Antibiotic	First-line drug for otitis media	Tablets, capsules, chewables, liquid: 40 mg/kg/d given 3 times a day	Diarrhea, rash
Amoxicillin + clavulanic acid (Augmentin)	Antibiotic	Otitis media	Tablets, chewables, liquid: 40 mg/kg/d (amoxicillin) given 3 times a day	Diarrhea (worse than amoxicillin alone), rash
Baclofen (Lioresal)	Antispasticity	Effective in spasticity of cerebral or spinal origin	Tablets: begin at 5 mg by mouth 2–3 times a day. Increase by 5 mg every 4–7 days to a maximum of 30–80 mg/d	Common: drowsiness, muscle weakness. Others: nausea, dizziness, paresthesias. Abrupt withdrawal can cause hallucinations and seizures
Beclomethasone (Beclovent, Vanceril)	Respiratory	Inhibition of airway inflammation in patients with chronic asthma symptoms	Inhaler (42 mcg/spray): 6–12 yo: 1–2 puffs 3–4 times a day. Adults: 2 puffs 3–4 times a day	Cough, sneezing, dry mouth, headache. Rinse mouth after using to prevent *Candida* infection
Benzoyl peroxide (2.5–10%) (Clearasil, Oxy, Fostex, Desquam X)	Skin cleansers (acne prep)	Acne	Lotion/cream/gel: apply to cleansed, dry areas of skin 1–2 times daily	Skin irritation, peeling
Buspirone (Buspar)	Anxiolytic	ADHD, anxiety, aggression	Tablets: Safety and efficacy in children <18 yo are not known	Chest pain, tinnitus, sore throat, nasal congestion. *Contraindications:* severe depression, with MAO inhibitors
Calcium undecylenate (10%) (Caldesene powder)	Skin diaper rash	Diaper rash	Ointment/powder: apply 3–4 times a day after bath or changing	Irritation or allergic reaction

continues

Table 13–10 continued

Medication	Category	Effect/Usage	Typical Application	Side Effects/Contraindications
Carbamazepine (Tegretol)	Antiepileptic	Generalized tonic-clonic, complex partial, simple partial	Tablets, suspension: dosage 5–20 mg/kg/d 2–4 doses/day Blood level: 4–14 mcg/ml	Ataxia, double vision, drowsiness, slurred speech, dizziness, tremor, headache, nausea, abnormalities in liver function, low white blood count
Cefixime (Suprax)	Antibiotic	Severe infection	Tablets, liquid: 8 mg/kg/d given once a day	Diarrhea; gastrointestinal upset
Cefuroxime (Ceftin)	Antibiotic	Second-line drug for otitis media	Tablets and liquid: 20–30 mg/kg/d twice a day	Allergic reactions
Cephalexin (Keflex)	Antibiotic	Useful against staph infections	Tablets, capsules, liquid: 25–50 mg/kg/d 4 times a day	Upset stomach
Cephradine (Velosef)	Antibiotic	Useful against staph infections	Capsules, liquid: 25–50 mg/kg/d 4 times a day	Upset stomach
Cetyl alcohol, propylene glycol, stearyl alcohol (oil-free) (Cetaphil)	Skin emollient	Dry skin	Cleansing solutions: use as a cleanser with or without water	Allergic reaction
Chloral hydrate (Aquachloral [supp.], Noctec)	Sedative	Sedation	Capsules, suppositories, syrup: 25–50 mg/kg/dose q8h orally or rectally to a maximum dose of 2 g	Mucous membrane and gastrointestinal irritation, paradoxical excitement, hypotension. *Avoid* in hepatic or renal impairment, furosemide or anticoagulant use, cardiac disease
Chloroxine (2%) (Capitrol)	Skin scalp prep	Antidandruff	Shampoo: massage into wet scalp, wait 3 min., rinse, repeat, and rinse thoroughly. Use twice weekly	Local skin irritation
Chlorpromazine (Thorazine)	Antipsychotic	Psychosis, anxiety, aggression, severe hyperactivity in mental retardation	Tablets, suppositories, syrup, injection IM, IV, and oral dosage is 1.5–6 mg/kg/d divided into 3–4 doses per day, to a maximum of 40 mg in children less than 5 yo or 75 mg in children 5–12 yo	Drowsiness, tardive dyskinesia, ECG changes, agranulocytosis, rash, hyperpigmentation of skin
Cimetidine (Tagamet)	Gastrointestinal	Gastroesophageal reflux, gastric/duodenal ulcers, inhibits gastric acid secretion	Liquid, tablets: 10–40 mg/kg/d given 4 times daily	Rare side effects: include diarrhea, headache, decreased white blood count, hepatotoxicity

continues

Table 13–10 continued

Medication	Category	Effect/Usage	Typical Application	Side Effects/Contraindications
Cisapride (Propulsid)	Gastrointestinal	Antireflux; increases gastric emptying	Tablets, liquid (special preparation): 0.7–1.0 mg/kg/d given 3 times daily	Abdominal pain, diarrhea
Clarithromycin (Biaxin)	Antibiotic	Used against staph, strep, and mycoplasma ("walking pneumonia"). Newer drug with wider spectrum than that of erythromycin and more convenient dosing	Tablets, suspension: 15 mg/kg/d divided into 2 times a day for 10 days	Stomach upset, but better tolerated than erythromycin
Clindamycin (Cleocin-T)	Skin antibiotic	Acne	Solution/gel/ointment: apply thin film twice daily	Diarrhea, colitis, irritated eyes
Clonazepam (Klonopin)	Antiepileptic	Lennox–Gastaut, absence, atonic, myoclonic, infantile spasms, and partial seizures	Tablet: dosage 0.01–0.2 mg/kg/d. Usual maintenance dose is 0.1–0.2 mg/kg/d in two divided doses Blood level is not helpful	Sedation, hyperactivity, confusion, depression; needs to be withdrawn slowly. Tolerance to anticonvulsant activity may develop
Clonidine hydrochloride (Catapres)	CNS stimulant	Hypertension, hyperactivity	Tablets: .005–.025mg/kg/d given 4 times a day; increase every 5–7 days as needed	Dry mouth, sedation, low blood pressure, headache, nausea. *Avoid* in renal disease
Clotrimazole (Lotrimin, Mycelex)	Skin antifungal	Antifungal, ringworm	Cream/lotion/solution: apply 2 times a day	Peeling, itching, skin irritation
Cloxacillin (Tegopen)	Antibiotic	Useful against staph infections (e.g., impetigo)	Capsules, liquid: 50–100 mg/kg/d given 4 times a day	Allergic reactions, diarrhea
Colloidal oatmeal (Aveeno)	Skin emollient	Dry skin, itching	Oil/cleansing bar/cream/lotion: add to bath or apply as needed	Allergic reaction
Cromolyn (Intal)	Respiratory	Prevention of broncho-spasm in patients with asthma	*Nebulizer* (20 mg/ampule): 20 mg 3–4 times a day *Inhaler* (800 mcg/spray): 2 puffs 3–4 times a day	Dosage should be decreased in patients with impaired hepatic or renal function
Crotamiton (Eurax)	Skin scalp prep	Scabicidal	Cream/lotion: massage into entire body from chin down; reapply after 24 hr.; bathe after 48 hr.	Skin irritation

continues

Table 13–10 continued

Medication	Category	Effect/Usage	Typical Application	Side Effects/Contraindications
Fluoxetine (Prozac)	Antidepressant	Depression, self-injurious behavior, ADHD, Tourette syndrome	Capsules, liquid: safety and efficacy in children have not been established. In adults, begin at 20 mg/d in morning, to a maximum of 80 mg/24 h	Anxiety, agitation, sleep disruption, decreased appetite, seizures. *Avoid* concurrent use of MAO inhibitor
Gabapentin (Neurontin)	Antiepileptic	Adjunctive therapy in partial and secondarily generalized seizures	Capsules: dosage: 20–30 mg/kg/d. Safety and effectiveness in children <12 yo have not been established	Sedation, dizziness, ataxia, fatigue
Griseofulvin (Fulvicin)	Skin antifungal	Antifungal, ringworm	Tablets/capsules/oral liquid: 11 mg/kg/d (microsize) or 7 mg/kg/d (ultramicrosize)	Skin rash, nausea, headache
Haloperidol (Haldol)	Antipsychotic	Self-injurious behavior, tics, severe agitation, psychosis, hyperkinesia	Tablets, liquid: 0.01–0.13 mg/kg/d for agitation, 0.05–0.15 mg/kg/d divided into 2–3 doses per day for psychosis, and 0.05–0.075 mg/kg/d divided into 2–3 doses per day for Tourette syndrome	Extrapyramidal symptoms, neuromalignant syndrome. Lowers seizure threshold in epilepsy, *caution* in cardiac disease
Hydrocortisone (Caldecort Cort-Dome, Hytone)	Skin steroid	Eczema, dermatitis, poison ivy	Cream/ointment/powder: apply a thin film 2–4 times daily	Skin irritation, dryness, rash
Hydrocortisone polymyxin-B and neomycin (Cortisporin)	Skin steroid	Steroid-responsive skin conditions with secondary infection	Cream/ointment: apply sparingly and massage into skin 2–3 times daily	Local irritation, kidney/ear toxicity (if neomycin is absorbed in large amounts)
Hydroxyzine (Atarax, Vistaril)	Antihistamine	Antihistamine, sedation	Capsules, tablets, liquid: 2mg/kg/d q6–8h	Sedation, anticholinergic effects, insomnia, dizziness, euphoria. *Contraindications:* gastrointestinal or urinary tract obstruction, concurrent use of MAO inhibitor
Imipramine (Tofranil, Janimine)	Antidepressant	Depression, enuresis, ADHD	Tablets, capsules: initial dose is 1.5 mg/kg/d divided into 3 doses per day, to a maximum of 5 mg/kg/d; therapeutic blood level for depression is 150–225 ng/ml	Dry mouth, drowsiness, constipation, ECG changes, increased blood pressure. *Contraindications:* cardiac conduction defects, urinary retention, concurrent use of MAO inhibitors, thyroid meds

continues

Table 13–10 continued

Medication	Category	Effect/Usage	Typical Application	Side Effects/Contraindications
Ipratropium bromide (Atrovent)	Respiratory	Use generally limited to acute asthma attacks that are not responding to beta-agonists and anti-inflammatory medications	Inhaler (18 mcg/puff): 2 puffs 4 times a day; max 12 puffs/day Not approved for children <12 yo	Palpitations, nervousness, dizziness, headache, rash, blurred vision, gastrointestinal distress, cough, dry mouth. In some patients, it may exacerbate asthma symptoms
Ketogenic diet (Schwartz et al. 1989)	Antiepileptic	Infantile spasms, Lennox–Gastaut seizures, mixed-type seizure disorder	Diet is high in fats and low in carbohydrates; resulting ketosis can reduce seizure activity in about half the children treated; antiepileptic drugs may be reduced or eliminated	Supplemental vitamins and minerals must be provided; height and weight gain is controlled, so diet is rarely used for more than 2 yr.
Lamotrigine (Lamictal)	Antiepileptic	Adjunctive therapy in partial and secondarily generalized seizures. May be effective in primary generalized seizures	Tablets: safety and efficacy in children <12 yo has not been established. Usual dose 5–15 mg/kg/d (1–5 mg/kgd if coadministered with valproate)	Sedation, dizziness, rash
Lanolin oil (Balmex)	Skin emollient	Dry skin	Lotion: apply as needed	Irritation or allergic reaction
Lanolin, petrolatum, vitamin A and D, mineral oils (A&D ointment)	Skin diaper rash	Diaper rash	Ointment: apply thin film at each diaper change	Allergic reaction
Lindane (Kwell)	Skin scalp prep	Scabicidal and lice	Cream/lotion/shampoo: apply thin layer and massage into body from neck down; wash off after 8–12 hr.	*Contraindication:* patients with seizure disorders and premature neonates
Magnesium hydroxide and aluminum hydroxide (Maalox)	Gastrointestinal; antacid	Heartburn; also helps treat constipation, which can contribute to GER	Liquid: 1–2 tsp. with meals and at bedtime	Minimal

continues

Table 13-10 continued

Medication	Category	Effect/Usage	Typical Application	Side Effects/Contraindications
Metaproterenol (Alupent, Metaprel)	Respiratory	Bronchodilator is used for treatment of acute asthmatic attacks and for the chronic treatment of patients with persistent symptoms	*Oral:* <2 yo: 0.4 mg/kg/dose q6–8h; infants should receive dose q8–12h 2–6 yo: 1.0–2.6 mg/kg/dose q6–8h 6–9 yo: 10 mg/dose q6–8h >9 yo: 20 mg/dose q6–8h Syrup: 10 mg/5 ml Tablets: 10 mg; 20 mg *Inhaler* (0.65 mg/spray): >12 yo: 2–3 puffs q3–4h; max 12/day *Nebulizer* (5 mg/dl): 6–12 yo: 0.1–0.2 ml q4–6h >12 yo: 0.3 ml q4–6h	Tachycardia, palpitations, hypertension, tremor, nervousness, hyperactivity, insomnia, headache, and gastrointestinal upset. Paradoxical bronchospasm can occur and should result in discontinuation of the medication
Methylphenidate (Ritalin)	CNS stimulant	ADHD	Tablets: initially 0.6 mg/kg/d, given twice a day, with increase to 1–2 mg/kg/d divided into 2–3 doses per day	Appetite suppression, insomnia, arrhythmias, hypo- or hypertension, abdominal pain. *Contraindications:* hypertension, concurrent use of vasopressors or MAO inhibitors, glaucoma
Methylprednisolone (Solu-Medrol, Medrol)	Respiratory	Reduction of airway inflammation during acute asthma attacks	1 mg/kg/dose IV q6h 1 mg/kg/dose PO twice a day for 3–5 days Tablets: 2 mg, 4 mg, 8 mg, 16 mg, 24 mg, 32 mg	Side effects usually mild with short-term use. *Contraindicated* in tuberculous, fungal, varicella, or herpes infection
Metoclopramide (Reglan)	Gastrointestinal	Antireflux; increases gastric emptying	Tablets, liquid: 0.1–0.5 mg/kg/d, given 4 times a day	Acute dystonic reactions; drowsiness
Miconazole (2%) (Monistat)	Skin antifungal	Antifungal, candidal yeast infections	Cream: apply 2 times a day for 2–4 wk.	Skin irritation, peeling
Mineral oil (Alpha Keri)	Skin emollient	Dry skin	Soap/oil/spray: add to bath or rub into wet skin as needed; rinse	Allergic reaction
Mineral oil, petrolatum, lanolin (Nivea, Lubriderm)	Skin emollient	Dry skin	Cream/moisturizing lotion/bath oil; apply as needed	Allergic reaction
Mupirocin (2%) (Bactroban)	Skin antibiotic	Impetigo, skin ulcers, burns	Ointment: apply sparingly 3 times a day; may cover with gauze	Burning, itching, pain at site of application

continues

Table 13–10 continued

Medication	Category	Effect/Usage	Typical Application	Side Effects/Contraindications
Naltrexone (Trexan)	Opiate antagonist	Self-injurious behavior	Tablets; injectable: safety and efficacy in children <18 yo have not been established	None in opioid-free individuals. *Contraindications:* acute hepatitis or liver failure
Nortriptyline (Pamelor)	Antidepressant	Depression	Maintenance: 50 mg daily in adults Capsules, syrup: not recommended for children <12 yo Adolescent: 10 mg 3 times a day, 20 mg bedtime	Dry mouth, drowsiness, constipation, ECG changes, increased blood pressure, mania; sudden death from cardiac arrhythmia has been reported with overdose. *Contraindications:* cardiac conduction defects, urinary retention, concurrent use of MAO inhibitors, thyroid meds
Nystatin (Mycostatin)	Skin antifungal, antibiotic	Yeast/thrush antifungal; *Candida* infections of the mouth and gastrointestinal tract (e.g., thrush)	Cream/ointment/powder: apply twice daily Oral suspension: 0.5–1 ml to each side of mouth 4 times a day Liquid: up to 5 cc "swish and swallow"	Diarrhea (oral form), redness, skin irritation, gastrointestinal upset
Pemoline (Cylert)	CNS stimulant	ADHD	Tablets: not recommended for children <6 yo Initial: 37.5 mg/d in morning; increase weekly to desired dose; max 112.5 mg/d	Insomnia, anorexia, abdominal discomfort, hepatotoxicity/history of renal failure
Penicillin (Pen Vee K)	Antibiotic	Drug of choice for strep throat, which also can be treated by a single IM injection of Bicillin	Tablets, liquid: 25–50 mg/kg/d given 4 times a day for 7 days	Allergic reactions, diarrhea
Permethrin (1%) (Nix)	Skin scalp prep	Head lice	Cream rinses (with comb): apply to washed and towel dried hair and scalp. Allow it to remain for 10 min., then rinse. Remove nits with fine toothed comb	Burning, stinging, itching, rash, redness (avoid eyes)
Permethrin (5%) (Elimite)	Skin scalp prep	Scabies	Cream: massage into scalp and body, then wash off after 8–14 hr	Burning, stinging, itching, rash, redness (avoid eyes)

continues

Table 13–10 continued

Medication	Category	Effect/Usage	Typical Application	Side Effects/Contraindications
Petrolatum, mineral oil and wax, alcohol (Eucerin)	Skin emollient	Dry skin, itching	Cream/lotion/facial lotion with sunscreen/cleansing bar/lotion: apply as needed	Allergic reaction
Phenobarbital (Luminal)	Antiepileptic	Generalized tonic-clonic and simple partial and secondarily generalized seizures	Tablets, capsules, elixir: pediatric dose is 2–5 mg/kg/d; adolescents, 1–2 mg/kg/d Blood level: 10–40 mcg/mL	Paradoxical hyperactivity, sedation and learning difficulties in older children; 50% of children under 10 yo have behavioral difficulties. Others: rash, irritability, unsteady gait
Phenytoin (Dilantin)	Antiepileptic	Generalized tonic-clonic and complex partial seizures	Tablets, capsules, suspension: maintenance dosage: 4–8 mg/kg/d; blood level is 10–20 mcg/mL	Swelling of gums, excessive hairiness, rash, coarsening of facial features; may have adverse effects on learning and behavior. Risk of birth defects if taken during pregnancy. Nystagmus and unsteady gait with toxic levels
Prednisone	Respiratory	Reduction of airway inflammation during acute asthma attacks	Tablets: 1 mg/kg/dose twice a day for 3–5 days Liquid: 1 mg/ml (taste limits usefulness)	Side effects usually mild with short-term use. *Contraindicated* in tuberculous, fungal, varicella, or herpes infection
Primidone (Mysoline)	Antiepileptic	Generalized tonic-clonic and complex partial seizures	Tablets, suspension: pediatric dose is 10–25 mg/kg in divided doses; adolescents, 125– 250 mg 3 times a day Therapeutic blood level of primodone 5–12 mcg/mL; also metabolized to phenobarbital 20–40 mcg/ml	Drowsiness, dizziness, nausea, vomiting, and personality change (see also side effects of phenobarbital)
Ranitidine (Zantac)	Gastrointestinal	H2-blocker; decreases stomach acidity, used for GER	Tablets, liquid: 2–4 mg/kg/d given twice a day	Headache, gastrointestinal upset, rare hepatoxicity
Retinoic acid derivative (Accutane)	Skin cleansers (acne prep)	Severe acne in adolescents (or adults)	Capsules: 0.5–2 mg/kg/d given in 2 doses for 15–20 wk.	Rash, gastrointestinal upset, skin irritation, CBC changes, eye irritation, elevated blood sugar, musculoskeletal pain

continues

Table 13–10 continued

Medication	Category	Effect/Usage	Typical Application	Side Effects/Contraindications
Salmeterol (Serevent)	Respiratory	Long-acting beta-agonist for patients with chronic asthmatic symptoms; should not be used for acute attacks	Inhaler (21 mcg/spray): 2 puffs q12h Not approved for children under 12 yo	Tachycardia, palpitations, nasopharyngitis, cough, tremor, headache, and gastrointestinal distress. Paradoxical bronchoconstriction may occur and should result in discontinuation of the medication
Selenium sulfide (2.5%) (Selsun Blue)	Skin scalp prep	Scalp conditions (dandruff or seborrhea)	Lotion/shampoo: apply to wet scalp, wait 3 min., rinse, repeat. Use twice daily for 2 wk., then as needed	Irritation, dry or oily scalp
Sertraline hydrochloride (Zoloft)	Antidepressant	Depression	Adult initial dose 50 mg/d, to a max of 200 mg/d. Safety and efficacy not established in children	Anxiety, agitation, sleep disruption, decreased appetite, seizures. *Avoid* concurrent use of MAO inhibitor
Sulfisoxazole (Gantrisin)	Antibiotic	Otitis media prophylaxis	Tablets, liquid: 120–150 mg/kg/d divided 4–6 times a day	Bone marrow suppression, allergic reactions
Terbutaline (Brethine PO; Azmacort inhaler)	Respiratory	Bronchodilator used for treatment of acute asthmatic attacks and for the chronic treatment of patients with persistent symptoms	*Oral* <12 yo: 0.05 mg/kg/dose q8h, max 0.15 mg/kg/dose 12–15 yo: 2.5 mg/dose q8h; max 7.5 mg Adults: 2.5–5 mg/dose q6–8h; max 15 mg Tablets: 2.5 mg, 5 mg *Inhaler* (0.20 mg/spray): >12 yo: 2 puffs (60 sec. apart) q4–6h *Subcutaneous* >12 yo: 0.25 mg/dose, max 0.5 mg over 4 hr. Ampules 1 mg/ml	Tachycardia, palpitations, hypertension, tremor, nervousness, hyperactivity, insomnia, headache, and gastrointestinal distress. Paradoxical bronchoconstriction may occur and should result in discontinuation of the medication
Tetracycline (Sumycin)	Antibiotic	Acne	Tablets/capsules/suspension: 25–50 mg/kg/d (2–4 times a day, then 1–2 times a day of a lower dose). Do not give to children <8 yo	Gastrointestinal upset, kidney/liver toxicity, decreased blood cell counts

continues

Table 13–10 continued

Medication	Category	Effect/Usage	Typical Application	Side Effects/Contraindications
Theophylline (Theo-Dur, Slo-Bid, Uniphyl, Aerolate)	Respiratory	Bronchodilator that may be used in conjunction with other treatments for acute or chronic asthma	Oral theophylline dose: *Age:* 6 wk. to 6 mo.: 10 mg/kg/d; 6 mo.–1 yr: 12–18 mg/kg/d; 1–9 yr: 20–24 mg/kg/d; 9–12 yr: 20 mg/kg/d; 12–16 yr: 18 mg/kg/d; Max adult dose: 900 mg/d; Dosing is different for smokers	Nausea, vomiting, and epigastric pain especially common at high blood levels. *Contraindicated* in patients with uncontrolled arrhythmias or hyperthyroidism
Thioridazine (Mellaril)	Antipsychotic	Self-injurious behavior, psychosis	Not recommended for children <2 yo; 2–12 yo: 0.5–3 mg/kg/d; >12 yo: mild disorders: 10 mg 2–3 times daily; Severe disorders: 25 mg 2–3 times daily	Drowsiness, extrapyramidal reactions, ECG changes, arrhythmias, pigmentary retinopathy, autonomic symptoms
Thiothixene (Navane)	Antipsychotic	Self-injurious behavior, psychosis	Tablets, syrup, suspension: not recommended for children <12 yo; Usual dosage: 2 mg 3 times a day; increase to 15 mg/d if needed	Tardive dyskinesia, neuroleptic malignant syndrome, tachycardia, hypotension, drowsiness, agranulocytosis/blood dyscrasia
Tolnaftate (Tinactin)	Skin antifungal	Antifungal, ringworm	Cream/liquid/powder/aerosol: apply 1–2 drops of solution or small amount of cream or powder 2 times a day for 2–6 wk.	Nontoxic
Triamcinolone (Kenalog, Aristocort [skin]; Azmacort [respiratory])	Skin steroid, respiratory	Eczema, dermatitis, poison ivy; inhibition of airway inflammation in patients with chronic asthma symptoms	Powder/cream/ointment/lotion: apply a thin film 2–4 times daily; Inhaler (100 mcg/spray): 6–12 yo: 1–2 puffs 3–4 times a day; Adult: 2 puffs 3–4 times a day	Skin irritation, rash, dryness; cough, hoarseness, dry mouth, increased wheezing. Rinse mouth after use to prevent *Candida* infection
Trimethoprim (TMP) + sulfamethoxazole (Bactrim, Septra)	Antibiotic	Convenient dosing for otitis media and for urinary tract infections	Tablets, liquid: 8–10 mg/kg/d TMP given twice a day	Bone marrow suppression, allergic reactions

continues

Table 13–10 continued

Medication	Category	Effect/Usage	Typical Application	Side Effects/Contraindications
Valproic acid (Depakene, Depakote)	Antiepileptic	Myoclonic, simple absence, generalized tonic-clonic seizures, mixed seizure disorders, Lennox–Gastaut, infantile spasms	Capsules, syrup, sprinkles: dosage 15–60 mg/kg/d. Therapeutic blood level 50–100 mcg/mL	Hair loss, weight loss or gain, abdominal distress, static tremor, low platelet count. Risk of birth defects if taken during pregnancy. Major adverse reaction is fatal liver necrosis (risk is 1:800 in children with developmental disabilities less than 2 yo on more than one anticonvulsant drug)
Zinc oxide, cod liver oil, lanolin, petrolatum (Caldesene ointment)	Skin diaper rash	Diaper rash	Ointment: apply 3–4 times/day after diaper change or bath	Allergic reaction

Note: The purpose of this table is to indicate the usual dose of medication for a particular condition in a particular situation. It should not be used to prescribe medication.

Table 13–11 Seizure Types

Seizure Type	Typical Age of Onset	Symptoms	Duration	Anticonvulsant Medications	Outcome
Generalized* Tonic-clonic (previously called *grand mal*)	6 mo. to adulthood	Aura often precedes seizure; loss of consciousness and tone; followed by tonic-clonic movements; lethargy on recovery	Tonic—rigid; 30–60 sec. Clonic—rhythmic jerking of body; 30 sec. to 5 min. May occur multiple times per day or <1/yr.	Carbamazepine; phenobarbital; phenytoin; valproate	Usually readily controlled by antiepileptic drug; seizure may represent an isolated disorder or part of a developmental disability. Medications can be stopped if seizure-free 2 yr. Status epilepticus—prolonged seizure (>1/2 hr.) can be life threatening or cause brain damage
Absence (previously called *petit mal*)	4–15 yr.	Sudden arrest of activity with vacant stare; may be accompanied by fluttering or drooping of the eyelids. Muscle tone remains fairly normal, so child does not fall, may have brief arm jerking	Lasts less than 10 sec. and may occur hundreds of times a day	Ethosuximide is the antiepileptic drug of choice; for pure absence, valproate, clonazepam	With use of antiepileptic drugs (AED), 80% of these seizures go into remission; no relation to other developmental disabilities

continues

Table 13–11 continued

Seizure Type	Typical Age of Onset	Symptoms	Duration	Anticonvulsant Medications	Outcome
Atonic (also known as *akinetic*)	3–10 yr.	Sudden loss of muscle tone; person may fall to the ground (drop attack); may only stumble or have head nodding	Attacks are brief	Valproate; clonazepam	Prognosis is variable and depends on the underlying etiology, age of onset, and association with other seizure types
Lennox–Gastaut syndrome	Often occurs in children who previously had infantile spasms	Seizures are of a mixed type that includes generalized tonic-clonic, atypical absence, myoclonic, and atonic seizures	Frequent and often severe	Valproic acid, clonazepam, ACTH; ketogenic diet may also be successful	Seizures are difficult to control with medications, associated with mental retardation in >80% of cases
Myoclonic West syndrome (infantile spasms— type of myoclonic seizure)	Before the first year	Spasms may occur as flexor or extensor movement; some children have both; West syndrome—Triad of Infantile Spasms, arrest of psychomotor development, and hypsarrhythmia (highly variable and dynamic EEG pattern)	Occurs in clusters, frequent	ACTH, valproic acid, clonazepam, ketogenic diet	Early treatment with ACTH usually stops the spasms; even with treatment, over two-thirds of children have mental retardation, often associated with underlying disorders; better prognosis in ideopathic cases

continues

Table 13–11 continued

Seizure Type	Typical Age of Onset	Symptoms	Duration	Anticonvulsant Medications	Outcome
Partial**					
Simple partial (e.g., focal-motor, also called Jacksonian march)	4–12 yr.	Depends on which area of the brain is the focus of the seizure: *Aura*—visual changes or alterations of sensations *Focal-sensory*—produces a variety of sensations such as feeling of numbness, flashing lights, unpleasant odor, buzzing or humming sounds *Focal-motor*—typically starts in one limb and then moves upward slowly to involve other parts of the body	Depends on type of seizure	Carbamazepine, phenytoin, primidone, clonazepam	About 75% of affected children can be found to have structural brain lesions, most of congenital origin; approximately 70% of simple partial seizures can be controlled with AED; Benign Rolandic epilepsy has excellent prognosis
Complex partial (previously known as psychomotor or temporal lobe)	6 yr. to adult (occasionally occurs in infancy)	About half of individuals have an aura; most seizures originate in the temporal lobe; typically the person has an episode of staring, automatic behavior such as facial grimacing or fumbling; may have stiffening of one or both upper extremities or loss of body tone	30 sec. to 5 min.; occurs infrequently, rarely more than a few times a day	Carbamazepine, phenytoin, primidone, clonazepam	Most children respond to AED; spontaneous remission occurs in about 20% of cases; with intractable epilepsy, focal resective surgery should be considered

Note: For each classification of seizures, the antiepileptic drugs are not significantly different in their efficacy. Treatment will be guided by experience of the physician and observed side effects.

*involve the entire cortex; are associated with sudden loss of consciousness; may begin as generalized seizures or arise from partial seizure activity that then becomes generalized

**limited to one hemisphere of the brain; divided into simple and complex, depending on whether there is loss of consciousness

tion has been uniformly successful in the treatment of spasticity. Medications currently available include those that act systemically (e.g., benzodiazepines, oral baclofen, dantrolene sodium) and those that act locally (intrathecal baclofen, botulinum toxin, and phenol injections).

Systemically Acting Medications

Benzodiazepines have been shown to have positive effects in spasticity of spinal and cerebral origin. They have been used extensively in patients with spasticity of spinal cord origin and have been shown to be effective in decreasing global spasticity scores, particularly in those with incomplete spinal cord lesions (Whyte and Robinson 1990). Benzodiazepines act within the central nervous system by enhancing inhibitory neurons in the spinal cord and at the supraspinal level by means of the inhibitory neurotransmitter GABA (gamma amino butyric acid). Diazepam (Valium) has been used most frequently, but others include clonazepam (Klonopin) and alprazolam (Xanax). Diazepam has also been studied in children with cerebral palsy. Improvements were found on subjective clinical evaluations; however, it is unclear whether the improvements were based on behavioral changes rather than on actual measures of spasticity (Whyte and Robinson 1990).

Baclofen, oral (Lioresal) (Alonso and Mancall 1991; Aisen et al. 1992) works primarily at the spinal cord level to decrease the release of excitatory neurotransmitters. It has been most effective in decreasing spasticity caused by spinal cord injury or demyelinating disease (e.g., multiple sclerosis). Studies in children with cerebral palsy are few. Its side effects are similar to benzodiazepines but also include stomach upset.

Dantrolene sodium (Dantrium) (Whyte and Robinson 1990) prevents the release of calcium, which is required for muscle contraction. It is equally effective for central and spinal spasticity in adults; little is known about its effects in children. Side effects include sedation, weakness, and hepatotoxicity.

Locally Acting Medications

Intrathecal baclofen has been shown to decrease tone and spasms in patients with spinal cord injury and multiple sclerosis (Abel and Smith 1994). It is being studied in children with cerebral palsy and has demonstrated significant decrease in tone in both upper and lower extremities as well as improvements in activities of daily living (Albright et al. 1993). It is currently approved for use in spasticity secondary to spinal cord injury and multiple sclerosis; it is under investigation for use in cerebral palsy.

Botulinum A toxin (BOTOX) is a potent neuromuscular blocking agent that can be injected directly into muscle to produce a dose-dependent and reversible weakness or paralysis. Botulinum toxin injections have been shown to be effective in selectively decreasing spasticity and strength in "target" muscles in patients with cerebral palsy (Das and Park 1989) and multiple sclerosis (Borg-Stein et al. 1993), although studies thus far have been limited. It is currently approved for treatment of strabismus, blepharospasm, facial spasms, and a variety of facial dystonias.

Phenol (or other caustic agent) injections (nerve blocks and motor point blocks); (Glenn 1990) act to impair conduction along a nerve through chemical neurolysis (destruction of a portion of the nerve). The duration of effect is extremely variable, lasting from several months to a few years. Nerve blocks are used to overcome spasticity in a group of muscles controlled by one nerve (which contains both motor and sensory fibers). Motor point blocks involve selective blockage of a specific motor nerve within a particular target muscle.

ANTIREFLUX MEDICATIONS

Gastroesophageal reflux (GER) is a condition in which the stomach contents back up into the esophagus, causing discomfort or aspiration (see also Chapter 12, the section "Therapeutic Feeding"). Although many healthy infants have some degree of GER (which results in "spitting up" or "wet burps"), they quickly clear the stomach contents out of their esophagus, and they do not have any other symptoms. However, GER is almost always abnormal when it occurs in older children and in children with developmental disabilities. Its most common symptom is heartburn, which can be severe. The esophagus can become inflamed and may even develop strictures as a result of GER. The inflammation, in turn, may make swallowing painful and uncoordinated. This can significantly interfere with food intake. GER also can result in retching, vomiting, and aspiration of stomach contents into the lungs. In infants, GER may present as apnea or seizure-like episodes. GER is often diagnosed by using a "pH probe," which is passed down the esophagus to record acidity levels over the course of a day, or by a "milk scan," in which the patient is fed radiolabeled milk and the passage of the milk through the GI tract is monitored over one to two hours.

GER can arise when there are abnormalities of the esophagus, of the stomach, or of the lower esophageal sphincter, which is the normal barrier between the stomach and the esophagus. For example, if the stomach empties into the duodenum too slowly, the likelihood of GER is increased. Increasing acidity of the stomach contents not only increases the irritation to the esophagus when GER occurs but also decreases the tone of the lower esophageal sphincter, making GER more likely to occur. Increased abdominal pressure from abnormal posture and muscle tone also can increase the likelihood of GER. Some children have volume-sensitive reflux, in which GER occurs with overdistention of the stomach. Constipation may also contribute to GER.

Mild cases of GER in infants often can be controlled by thickening the feeds (by adding rice cereal to the formula, for example) and by making sure that the infant is properly positioned during and after feeds. Pharmacologic therapy has two general strategies: (1) promoting stomach emptying, thus decreasing stomach distention; and (2) decreasing stomach acidity, thereby tightening the lower esophageal sphinc-

ter and decreasing the irritation from any GER that does occur. In severe cases of GER, a surgical procedure (called *fundoplication*) can be performed to tighten the sphincter.

ANTIBIOTIC MEDICATIONS

Antibiotics are the drugs most commonly prescribed for children. When infections are caused by bacteria, antibiotics may shorten the duration of the illness, decrease its severity, and help avoid complications. However, many common infections, including colds and a large fraction of ear infections, are caused by viruses, for which antibiotics are ineffective. These viral infections generally resolve spontaneously and require treatment only for accompanying fever and discomfort. A very small fraction of childhood infections are caused by fungi and respond to special antifungal agents. In the healthy child, the only commonly encountered fungal infections affect the skin, hair, and oral mucosa (e.g., thrush and some diaper rashes).

The indiscriminate use of antibiotics can lead to the development of antibiotic-resistant bacteria and is unjustifiably costly. Therefore antibiotics must be judiciously prescribed and carefully chosen. For major infections such as sepsis, meningitis, and infections of bone and joints, cultures of blood, spinal fluid, or other infected specimens should be obtained. The bacteria that are cultured can be tested for their sensitivity to different antibiotics. The patient is then treated with an antibiotic that is shown to be effective against that particular bacterium. For most outpatient infections, and when obtaining cultures is not feasible, broad-spectrum antibiotics are chosen empirically to cover all the bacteria that commonly cause these infections. If such infections are caused by unusual bacteria or common bacteria that are resistant to the antibiotic that is chosen, a second antibiotic may need to be prescribed.

For most infections, antibiotics are given in oral form for a specified length of time (often seven to ten days). Even when the symptoms of the infection clear before the course of treatment is completed, the antibiotic should be continued to ensure eradication of the infectious organism and to prevent a disease recurrence. In some cases, a single long-acting intramuscular injection may be substituted for a multiday course of oral antibiotics. Oral antibiotics also may be prescribed for long-term use as prophylaxis for recurrent urinary tract or middle ear infections.

Like all drugs, antibiotics can cause undesirable side effects. Stomach upset and diarrhea are probably the most common side effects. Depending on their severity, the antibiotic causing those GI symptoms may be stopped. Allergic reactions may take the form of hives, other rashes, or even severe difficulty breathing. The offending antibiotic should always be discontinued in the case of allergic reactions. Any antibiotic that is used chronically may cause overgrowth of nonsensitive bacteria and fungi, causing diarrhea, diaper-area rashes, intestinal inflammation, and other symptoms.

MEDICATIONS TO INFLUENCE MOOD AND BEHAVIOR

Medications are commonly used in children with developmental disabilities to influence mood and to modify disruptive behaviors such as hyperactivity, aggression, and/or self-injury. These drugs work by blocking or enhancing neurochemicals found in regions of the brain that affect behavior. Because these neurochemicals are commonly found in other areas of the brain as well, altering their levels may cause unanticipated behavioral or cognitive side effects.

The six basic categories of psychotropic drugs used in children with developmental disabilities are central nervous system (CNS) stimulants, antidepressants, antipsychotics, opiate antagonists, anxiolytics, and sedatives.

CNS Stimulants

Stimulants have been used as the first choice for management of behaviors found in children with attention-deficit disorders. Although the mode of action is not completely understood, stimulant medications are felt to increase norepinephrine and dopamine levels and activate the brainstem arousal system. Clonidine has a different mechanism of action than stimulant medications but is also used in the management of attention deficit disorder. Clonidine, an alpha-adrenergic agonist, actually decreases norepinephrine release in the brain.

Antidepressants

In addition to their use in the treatment of children and adolescents with depression, antidepressants have also been found to be effective in treating attention-deficit disorders that present with anxiety or depression. These medications also have been successfully used in children for whom stimulant medications are not effective or who have developed side effects. Antidepressants increase dopamine, norepinephrine, and/or serotonin availability.

Antipsychotics

In addition to their use in the management of psychosis, antipsychotics have been used to reduce hyperactivity, tics, aggression, self-injurious behaviors, and anxiety in children and adults with mental retardation and severe hyperkinesia. These medications block the effects of the neurotransmitter dopamine and increase its turnover rate.

Opiate Antagonists

Opiate antagonists are most commonly used to prevent and reverse the effects of opioids. Low doses, however, have been used in the management of self-injurious behaviors.

Anxiolytics

Most commonly used for the management of anxiety and convulsions, anxiolytics may be used to decrease aggression and muscle tone. They act by altering the release of serotonin in the brain.

Sedatives

Chloral hydrate is the most commonly used sedative. It has been used for sedation in short procedures and to treat sleeplessness in children for less than two weeks.

Antihistamines

Although antihistamines are most commonly used to treat allergic reactions, they have also been used to induce sleep in children. They act by competing with histamine for cell receptor sites.

SKIN PREPARATIONS

Children with physical disabilities and limited mobility are at increased risk for developing skin conditions (i.e., skin ulcers), which may lead to further functional impairment if they are not adequately treated. Adaptive equipment (including wheelchairs, splints, and orthoses) is often a necessary part of treatment for many of these children. However, the friction or direct pressure applied to the skin may produce contact rashes, abrasions, or breakdown of adjacent or underlying skin layers. A number of different skin rashes may also be the external manifestation of systemic viral or bacterial infections in these children. Alternatively, allergic reactions or insect stings/bites may produce either localized or generalized skin rashes in affected patients. Health care providers and therapists for children with disabilities must be aware of the need to include routine proper skin care techniques and treatment for each patient.

Pressure Sores/Decubitus Ulcers (See Also the Section "Management of Pressure Sores" Earlier in This Chapter)

Skin ulcers usually occur as a result of poor patient nutrition and limited activity, along with direct pressure on the skin from internal bony prominences (e.g., backbone or hips). Skin tissue layers begin to break down over time, and this often leaves the affected patient with deep sores that can be quite difficult to treat. These ulcers may take weeks to months to heal completely. Children who are bedridden or confined to wheelchairs (e.g., with cerebral palsy, spina bifida, or muscular dystrophy) are particularly prone to develop these sores and require close monitoring. Careful and complete skin surveillance should be performed daily on all patients who are at risk for this type of skin breakdown. Additional preventive measures include maintaining adequate nutrition and skin hygiene in these children. Good nutrition is especially important because it allows a protective barrier of supportive tissue to grow. Frequent changes in positioning and soft surfaces (e.g., foam/egg crate mattresses or sheepskin padding) are recommended to relieve prolonged pressure to susceptible areas of the body.

Treatment measures are as follows:

- Wet-to-dry dressings should be applied to skin sores that are discovered.
- Allow dressings (sterile gauze soaked in a normal saline solution) to dry on the sores, then replace them with new wet dressings after 10 to 15 minutes. This technique aids in the removal of infected or dead tissue. This should be repeated three to four times per day.
- Following the wet soaks, an occlusive ointment should be applied along with a protective clean and dry dressing (e.g., Duoderm sterile dressing with hydroactive granules, paste or gel formula).
- In uncomplicated cases, antibiotics may not be a necessary part of treatment.
- Skin grafting may be required in extremely deep and/or large ulcers.

Allergic Skin Rashes/Eczema

Allergic skin rashes include hives, which usually respond to oral antihistamines (e.g., Benadryl). Eczema is another type of skin irritation that is felt to be related to allergic reactions. It may appear after contact with a specific product (e.g., soaps/cosmetics) or environmental allergen (e.g., house dust/animal dander). The skin develops an inflammatory response, with itchy, scaly, and dry patches in different regions of the body. Elbows, behind knees, and the back of the neck may be especially affected and irritated during flare-ups of this condition.

Treatment often involves the use of steroid creams and creams to prevent water loss from skin. In addition, the following measures should be taken:

- Restrict/limit bathing (particularly lengthy baths). Maintain cool bathing water and pat the skin dry. Apply emollient immediately after bathing.
- Avoid harsh soaps or other topical irritants (including some synthetic fibers in clothing).
- Humidify the room during the winter season.
- Avoid sweat stimuli (e.g., extremely hot weather conditions or overdressing).
- Avoid allergens in the environment (e.g., dust/pollen).
- Wear vinyl gloves (with a cotton lining) or long sleeves when contact with irritants is unavoidable (e.g., walking where poison ivy might be found).

RESPIRATORY MEDICATIONS

Respiratory medications are divided into two categories: anti-inflammatory agents and bronchodilators. Most patients with an acute asthma attack or chronic reactive airway symptoms will be treated with at least one anti-inflammatory medication and one bronchodilator.

Inhaled Anti-Inflammatory Agents

Airway inflammation is believed to be the primary process associated with bronchial hyperreactivity in patients with asthma. Thus inhaled

anti-inflammatory drugs have a major role in the prophylactic treatment of patients with reactive airway disease (i.e., asthma). The inhaled anti-inflammatory agents can be further subdivided into two groups: cromolyn (Intal) and glucocorticoids (such as flunisolide [Aerobid], beclomethasone [Beclovent, Vanceril], and triamcinolone [Azmacort]). Cromolyn inhibits mast cell degranulation following exposure to an allergen and thereby prevents bronchospasm. The glucocorticoids inhibit the development of airway inflammation and thus bronchial hyperreactivity. They have limited systemic absorption and thus decrease but do not entirely eliminate the risks of systemic side effects. They are used in patients with increasing symptoms despite treatment with cromolyn or in patients with chronic symptoms.

Systemic Anti-Inflammatory Agents

Oral or intravenous glucocorticoids are potent anti-inflammatory medications that are used to reduce airway inflammation during acute asthma attacks that do not respond to bronchodilators alone. They may also be used in patients with severe disease and persistent symptoms despite the use of bronchodilators and inhaled glucocorticoids. In these cases they should be used at the minimum dose possible and preferably on alternating days. These include prednisone and methylprednisolone (Solu-Medrol, Medrol).

Bronchodilators

Bronchodilators relax the smooth muscle in the bronchial walls and thereby decrease bronchial constriction. They are used in the treatment of acute asthma attacks and may be an adjunct to anti-inflammatory agents in the treatment of patients with persistent symptoms. Bronchodilators can be divided into two categories: beta-adrenergic agonists and anticholinergics. *Beta-adrenergic agonists* provide rapid relief of bronchospasm and may be used prior to exercise to prevent exercise-induced bronchospasm.

They are generally short-acting medications, although a new medication not yet approved for use in children under 12, salmeterol (Serevent), may extend the duration of action to 10 to 12 hours. However, salmeterol should not be used for acute asthma attacks. Others include albuterol (Ventolin, Proventil), metaproterenol (Alupent, Metaprel), and terbutaline (Brethine,

Azmacort). *Anticholinergic medications* (ipratropium bromide [Atrovent] and theophylline [Theo-Dur, Slo-Bid, Uniphyl, Aerolate]) result in bronchial dilation by inhibiting the vagal reflex on bronchial smooth muscle. Use is generally limited to acute asthmatic exacerbations that are not responding to beta-adrenergic agonists and anti-inflammatory medications.

REFERENCES

Abel, N., and R.A. Smith. 1994. Intrathecal baclofen for treatment of intractable spinal spasticity. *Archives of Physical Medicine and Rehabilitation* 75:54–58.

Aicardi, J. 1986. *Epilepsy in children.* New York: Raven Press.

Aisen, M.L., et al. 1992. Clinical and pharmacokinetic aspects of high dose oral baclofen therapy. *Journal of the American Paraplegia Society* 15:211–216.

Albright, A.L., et al. 1993. Continuous intrathecal baclofen infusion for spasticity of cerebral origin. *Journal of the American Medical Association* 270:2475–2477.

Aldencamp, A.P., et al. 1990. Neuropsychological aspects of learning disabilities in epilepsy. *Epilepsia* 31(supp.4):59–520.

Alonso, R.J., and E.L. Mancall. 1991. The clinical management of spasticity. *Seminars in Neurology* 11:215–218.

Borg-Stein, J., et al. 1993. Botulinum toxin for the treatment of spasticity in multiple sclerosis. *American Journal of Physical Medicine and Rehabilitation* 72:364–368.

Das, T.K., and D.M. Park. 1989. Botulinum toxin in treating spasticity. *British Journal of Clinical Practice* 43:401–403.

Glenn, M.B. 1990. Nerve blocks. In *The practical management of spasticity in children and adults*, ed. M.B. Glenn and J. Whyte, 227–258. Philadelphia: Lea & Febiger.

Schwartz, R.H., et al. 1989. Ketogenic diets in the treatment of epilepsy: Short-term clinical effects. *Developmental Medicine and Child Neurology* 31:145–151.

Wallace, S.J. 1990. Risk of seizures (Annotation). *Developmental Medicine and Child Neurology* 32:645–649.

Whyte, J., and K.M. Robinson. 1990. Pharmacologic management. In *The practical management of spasticity in children and adults*, ed. M.B. Glenn and J. Whyte, 201–226. Philadelphia: Lea & Febiger.

ADDITIONAL SUGGESTED READINGS

Batshaw, M. 1991. *Your child has a disability.* Boston: Little, Brown & Co.

Batshaw, M., ed. 1993. The child with developmental disabilities. *Pediatric Clinics of North America* 40, no. 3. Special issue.

Batshaw, M., and Y. Perret, eds. 1992. *Children with disabilities: A medical primer.* 3rd ed. Baltimore: Paul H. Brookes.

Davidoff, R.A. 1985. Antispasticity drugs: Mechanisms of action. *Annals of Neurology* 17, no. 2:107–116.

Fenichel, G. 1993. *Clinical pediatric neurology: A signs and symptoms approach.* Philadelphia: W.B. Saunders.

Katz, R.T. 1988. Management of spasticity. *American Journal of Physical Medicine and Rehabilitation* 67, no. 3:108–116.

Lapierre, Y., et al. 1987. Treatment of spasticity with tizanidine in multiple sclerosis. *Canadian Journal of Neurological Science* 14:513–517.

Medical Economics Data Production Company. 1994. *Physicians' desk reference.* 48th ed. Montvale, N.J.

Mercugliano, M. 1993. Psychopharmacology in children with developmental disabilities. *Pediatric Clinics of North America* 40:593–616.

National Institutes of Health. 1991. Clinical use of botulinum toxin: Consensus conference. *Connecticut Medicine* 55:471–477.

Pellock, J., ed. 1989. Seizure disorders. *Pediatric Clinics of North America* 36, no. 2. Special issue.

Prescribing reference for pediatricians. 1994. Vol. 5, no. 1. New York: Prescribing Reference, Inc.

Snow, B.J., et al. 1990. Treatment of spasticity with botulinum toxin: A double-blind study. *Annals of Neurology* 28:512–515.

BOWEL AND BLADDER FUNCTION IN NEUROMUSCULAR DISORDERS

Stephanie R. Ried

Purpose: to review the types of neurogenic bladder associated with specific neurologic disorders; associated complications of bladder dysfunction and their available treatment options, and the causes of poor bowel motility and dysfunction and their available treatment options.

Depending upon the level of neurologic impairment or damage, a different clinical picture of bowel and bladder dysfunction will be present, with associated complications. Table 13–12 provides an overview of dysfunction commonly associated with disorders of the nervous system.

TYPES OF NEUROGENIC BLADDERS

An *upper motor neuron* or *spastic bladder* usually implies a lesion in the spinal cord or brainstem. Bladder function is characterized by reflex or uninhibited contractions of the bladder detrusor muscle. This results in wetting (or incontinence) with or without voluntary control, depending on the extent of the lesion.

A *lower motor neuron* or *atonic bladder* implies an injury to the nerve roots or peripheral nerves supplying the bladder. This leads to the inability to void either reflexively or voluntarily. With sphincter involvement or decreased urethral resistance, incontinence may be associated with any increase in abdominal pressure, such as coughing or laughing.

A *mixed lesion* results in bladder function with some characteristics of both the upper and lower motor neuron bladder, depending on the degree of involvement of the spinal cord and nerve roots.

POTENTIAL COMPLICATIONS OF BLADDER DYSFUNCTION

Potential complications of bladder dysfunction are as follows:

- *Detrusor sphincter dyssynergy (DSD)* is an incoordination between bladder contractions and bladder outlet opening that can result in increased pressure being transmitted through the upper tracts (ureters) to the kidneys. Over time, elevated pressure increases the risk of renal damage.

- *Urinary tract infection* may be caused by large amounts of residual urine sitting in the bladder when emptying is incomplete. This increases the risk of urinary tract infection, which, if transmitted to the upper tracts, increases the risk of scarring and permanent renal damage.

- *Decreased bladder storage capacity* may result from uncontrolled hyperactivity of the detrusor (usually in a spastic bladder), with concomitant thickening of the bladder wall.

- *Skin breakdown* may occur due to incontinence and persistent perineal moisture.

SPECIFIC TECHNIQUES AND PROCEDURES FOR BLADDER MANAGEMENT

Bladder management is based on the specific neurologic lesion and the consequent functional impairment.

Assessment

Assessment is by urodynamic studies and/or renal ultrasound. *Urodynamic studies* are the best way to characterize bladder function. They assess the presence of reflexic bladder contractions during bladder filling, the pressure generated within the bladder during these contractions, and whether the bladder sphincter is open or closed during contractions. *Renal ultrasound* is a noninvasive means of routine monitoring of

Table 13–12 Examples of Bowel and Bladder Dysfunction Associated with Nervous System Disorders

Disorder	Level of Injury	Bladder Dysfunction	Bowel Dysfunction
Myelomeningocele	Spinal cord: injury affects the neural elements involved in innervation to the bladder and sphincter muscles	Spastic, flaccid, or mixed	Absent anocutaneous reflex most commonly; lack of continence
Spinal cord injury	Spinal cord: trauma or ischemia of spinal cord	Spastic bladder; management with intermittent catheterization with or without medication unless there is increased bladder tone or pressure (surgery such as vesicostomy may be necessary)	Anocutaneous reflex usually present; lack of continence
Cerebral palsy	Brain: disorder of movement and posture due to nonprogressive lesion or injury	Incontinence often secondary to defects in cognition, communication, mobility; incidence of spastic bladder and detrussor sphincter dyssynergy higher than previously recognized	Normal anorectal function; difficulties due to constipation associated with musculoskeletal abnormalities and diet
Duchenne muscular dystrophy	Myopathy: fatty infiltrates, atrophy and focal necrosis of myofibers have been reported in bladder smooth muscle and colon specimens	End-stage: bladder dysfunction secondary to urinary retention associated with poor contractility	Constipation related to progressive immobility and muscle weakness

the upper urinary tract (to look for dilation, blockage, etc.).

Toilet Training

Attempts at continence are usually initiated in the preschool years at between three and five years of age, depending upon the developmental level and maturation of the child. Toileting should be considered a social skill rather than a medical procedure. Bladder training instructions and education should always be developmentally appropriate and consistent with the child's attention span. Whenever possible, children should be taught to perform or direct their own intermittent bladder catheterization (see below). This is usually possible in the child who is developmentally at the five- or six-year-old level.

Procedures

Intermittent bladder catheterization is recommended for children who cannot sufficiently empty the bladder at low voiding pressures. The goal of catheterization is to provide safe bladder emptying between dry intervals. Generally, children who are at the five-year-old developmental level can be taught self-catheterization (see the section "Bladder Catheterization" earlier in this chapter).

Medications can be used to modulate bladder function. The bladder detrusor has cholinergic receptors. Anticholinergic medications may be used to decrease uninhibited contractions and improve bladder storage capacity. These medications also decrease the risk of elevated pressures in the system if detrusor sphincter dyssynergy is present. Conversely, bladder contractions and thus emptying may be augmented by cholinergic agonists. Further, the proximal urethra and bladder outlet are supplied by alpha-adrenergics, which serve to tighten the bladder outlet. This allows alpha-adrenergic agonists to be used to improve urine storage when proximal urethral resistance is inadequate and to facilitate continence between catheterizations.

Surgical procedures such as augmentation cystoplasty (revision of ureters or urethra) or vesicostomy (surgical connection of bladder to opening in skin or stoma) may be necessary to protect renal function when medication fails to decrease detrusor tone and/or storage capacity is inadequate.

BOWEL DYSFUNCTION

Contributing factors to poor gastrointestinal motility and/or bowel incontinence include

- Immobilization
- Diet low in fiber or poor fluid intake
- Constipation (see Chapter 12)
- Abdominal wall weakness
- Neuromuscular abnormalities
  1. spasticity or extensor spasms (e.g., in upper motor disorders such as cerebral palsy or acquired brain injury)
  2. disruption of the nerve supply to the bowel (e.g., in lesions involving the spinal cord such as spina bifida or in spinal cord injury)
  3. severe skeletal deformity

Successful bowel management enhances the potential of the child to achieve satisfactory adult independence and social acceptability. Problems with bowel management may represent a significant source of emotional turmoil for both the child and his or her family.

TECHNIQUES AND PROCEDURES FOR BOWEL MANAGEMENT

The goal of a bowel program is to have the bowel empty regularly and adequately. General approaches include promoting mobility, increasing dietary fiber and fluid intake, spasticity management, and appropriate positioning in the nonambulatory child (a flexed, supported position may facilitate improved bowel function).

Bowel training should start during the preschool years. It should include selection of a private, relaxed time either in the morning or 30 minutes after a meal to take advantage of the gastrocolic reflex. Offering the child a book or another distraction may make this training less stressful. Routine and consistency are critical to a successful bowel program that results in social continence by allowing regular rectal emptying at predictable times. Many of the problems of bowel control are due to overloading of the bowel and incomplete emptying, with loss, over time, of rectal motility and sensation.

For a bowel program to work, it must be compatible with the daily demands on the child and his or her family, both at home and in the community. Also, the success of a bowel program is influenced by the presence or absence of the anocutaneous reflex (anal wink), which is a reflex contraction of the anal sphincter. When this reflex is absent, the anal sphincter has less tone, and the ability both to expel and to retain feces is impaired. In addition, there may be constant passage of stool or "smearing," which is increased with movement, coughing, or laughing. Presence of the anal wink usually indicates a better prognosis for continence, as stool is usually retained by the sphincter tone.

If there are difficulties in evacuation, a high-fiber diet will help by making the stool bulky. Older children can learn to push down actively to aid in evacuation, whereas manual evacuation may be necessary in the younger child. Digital stimulation or a bisacodyl (Dulcolax) suppository can used in conjunction with the natural gastrocolic reflex. The child is placed on the toilet or commode approximately 30 minutes following a meal on a regular schedule (daily or every other day) to promote emptying of the rectal vault. The suppository stimulates relaxation of the anal sphincter and reflex contraction of the rectum, which facilitates bowel evacuation.

In addition, adjuncts to the bowel program may include oral stool softeners such as docusate sodium (Colace) and mild laxatives such as senna preparations (Senekot). Biofeedback has also been introduced as a method for teaching voluntary muscle activity in response to the sensation of rectal distension.

SUGGESTED READINGS

Agnarsson, U., et al. 1993. Anorectal function of children with neurological problems with cerebral palsy. *Developmental Medicine and Child Neurology* 35:903–908.

Bauer, S.B. 1987. Neurogenic bladder dysfunction. *Pediatric Clinics of North America* 34:1121–1132.

Decter, R.M., et al. 1987. Neurogenic bladder: Urodynamic assessment of children with cerebral palsy. *Journal of Urology* 138:1110–1112.

Huvos, A.G., and W. Pruzanski. 1967. Smooth muscle involvement in primary muscle disease: ii. Progressive muscular dystrophy. *Archives of Pathology* 83:234–240.

Korman, S.H., et al. 1991. Orocaecal transit time in Duchenne muscular dystrophy. *Archives of Disease in Childhood* 66:143–144.

McCarthy, G.T. 1990. Management of the neuropathic bowel. In *Clinics in Developmental Medicine* No. 111, *Neuropathic Bladder in Childhood*, ed. M. Borzyskowski and A.R. Murdy, 72–80. Philadelphia: J.B. Lippincott Co.

McNeal, D.M., et al. 1983. Symptomatic neurogenic bladder in a cerebral-palsied population. *Developmental Medicine and Child Neurology* 25:612–616.

Molnar, G.E., ed. 1992. *Pediatric rehabilitation*. 2nd ed. Baltimore: Williams & Wilkins.

Nowak, T.V., et al. 1982. Gastrointestinal manifestations of the muscular dystrophies. *Gastroenterology* 82:800–810.

Reid, C.J.D., and M. Borzyskowski. 1993. Lower urinary tract dysfunction in cerebral palsy. *Archives of Diseases in Childhood* 68:730–742.

vonWendt, L., et al. 1990. Development of bowel and bladder control in the mentally retarded. *Developmental Medicine and Child Neurology* 32:515–518.

Weber, J., et al. 1985. Effect of brain-stem lesion on colonic and anorectal motility: Study of three patients. *Digestive Diseases and Sciences* 30:419–425.

PAIN MANAGEMENT

Mary L. Osborne and David E. Cohen

Purpose: to outline approaches that incorporate pharmacological and behavioral management aimed at relieving pain.

The goal of pain management is the maximum relief of pain and suffering. Effective pain control involves tailoring a regimen that combines medication, the development of coping skills, and problem solving on ways to function as normally as possible.

The presence of pain can limit a child's function and development. Effective management needs to consider the physiological and psychological basis of the pain as it affects the functioning of the whole child. Treatment is then based on accurate diagnosis and the careful integration of pharmacological, psychological, and physical interventions.

Communicating "pain" is difficult for the verbal adult. The accurate assessment, diagnosis, and treatment of pain may be further complicated when the patient is a child with limited cognitive and language skills. For the child with developmental disabilities, tailoring of this process is key and requires knowledge of the child's medical status and developmental functioning. To minimize the deleterious effects of both undetected and undertreated pain, the treating professional must be attentive to the particular child's expression of pain and discomfort. Similarly, effects of treatment interventions must be viewed with the same degree of attention to avoid unwanted and sometimes dangerous interactions of the treatment and problems associated with the developmental or physical disability.

PAIN ASSESSMENT

Careful assessment, conceptualization of the pain in relation to the patient, development of a multimodal intervention, and evaluation of the interventions form the basis of pain management (Figure 13–48). Children often present special dilemmas in each of these areas. Adult patients

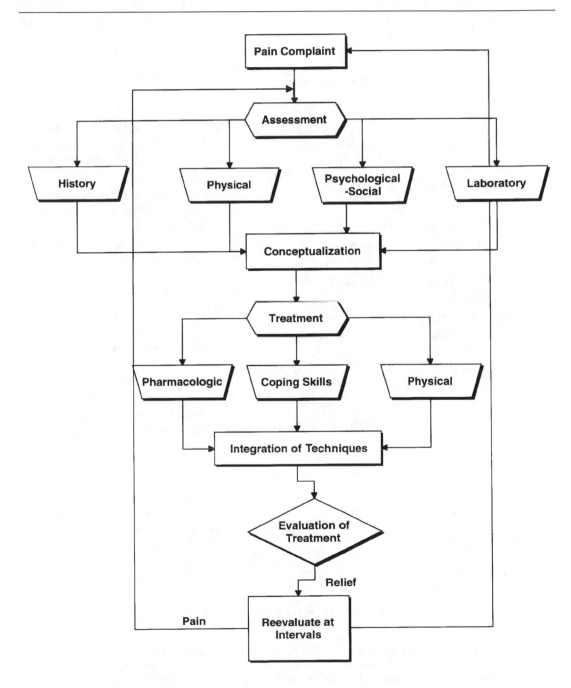

Figure 13–48 Pain Management Flowchart. *Source:* Copyright © 1996, Mark L. Batshaw, M.D.

verbally complain about a pain; they can usually characterize its nature in terms of its quality, temporal characteristics, location, and precipitating and ameliorating factors. Similarly, they report the success and failures of interventions and understand a complex treatment plan. Children, however, may be unable to provide this key information verbally or to comprehend intricate management plans. For the child with developmental disabilities, these problems may be further complicated by the presence of the disability.

The assessment of pain in children should consider their cognitive-developmental levels as well as developmental disability, as follows:

- Sensorimotor child (0–2 years)
  1. Understanding of pain
     (a) Pain is experienced.
  2. Implications for pain assessment
     (a) Use observational scales.
     (b) Observe child in activities of daily life.
     (c) Observe physiological parameters that change with distress, like heart rate and blood pressure.
- Preoperational child (2–7 years)
  1. Understanding of pain
     (a) Child is unable to sequence events accurately; the pain of an injection will never end.
     (b) Co-occurrence is often perceived as causality; the child may inaccurately associate a serendipitous event with causal factors (e.g., hot packs signal intravenous cannulations).
     (c) Beware of multiple meanings of words because of their literalness and concreteness—injecting intravenous dye may promote radiographic examinations but not life.
  2. Implications for pain assessment
     (a) Assessment tools should not require ordering or sequencing.
     (b) Use happy–sad scales (Bieri et al. 1990); child only needs to attend to one aspect of the stimulus (Figure 13–49).
     (c) Use poker chip scales; children choose from none to four chips to indicate "pieces of hurt." The child needs only to understand that more means more hurt (World Health Organization 1986).
- Concrete operational child (7–11 years)
  1. Understanding of pain
     (a) Child is able to sequence events; the pain of an injection is temporary.
     (b) Avoid abstract explanations (e.g., say that eating healthy foods will make the child's body stronger so that it heals faster rather than that good nutrition will make your pain better).

Note: The child is asked to pick the picture that most represents how he or she feels. A score of 1 to 7 is given to the answer, with 1 being the face on the left and 7 the face on the far right.

Figure 13–49 Happy–Sad Scale. *Source:* From "The Faces of Pain Scale for the Self-Assessment of the Severity of Pain Experienced by Children: Development, Initial Validation, and Preliminary Investigation for Ratio Properties" by D. Bieri et al., 1990, *Pain* 41, p. 144. Copyright © Elsevier Science. Reprinted by permission.

(c) Causal relationships that do not involve abstractions are understood (e.g., following surgery there will be pain until the incision heals).

2. Implications for pain assessment

(a) Use visual analogue scale: children indicate their pain by marking the line appropriately (Figure 13–50).

(b) Have child verbally rank pain on a scale of 1 to 10.

• Formal operational child (11 years or older)

1. Understanding of pain

(a) Abstract explanations are usually understood.

2. Implications for pain assessment

(a) Give verbal interview that examines intensity, location, meaning (Savedra et al. 1993; Figure 13–51).

Careful physical examination that attends to the complaint as well as to the effects of the child's physical disabilities is crucial. Likewise, appropriate laboratory investigations (e.g., identifying occult blood in the stool or low hemoglobin) may identify problems not visible though painful, such as esophagitis or ulcers in the child with reflux. Attempting to understand how the child and his or her family cope with the problem is also key, providing additional information about the nature of the problem for the health professional.

PHARMACOLOGIC TREATMENT OF PAIN (also see previous Section "Medications")

Treatment needs to be based on a working conceptualization of the problem as presented upon assessment. Treatment specific to the type or types of pain that the child may be experiencing is key. The child may have pain with neuropathic or somatic components, as well as inappropriate or poor coping skills. Integrating pharmacological, physical, and psychological techniques in a multimodal treatment plan enhances the success of a pain management plan.

Different types of pain benefit by different interventions. *Nociceptive pain* (pain after injury or inflammation) differs from *neuropathic pain* (pain associated with nerve injury or involvement) in character and treatment. Nociceptive pain is given varied descriptions; it improves with time. Neuropathic pain is described as burning, lancinating, or "pins and needles" pain, and the affected area is sensitive to light touch. Pain is persistent and often intensifies, and it can be present even in the absence of injury or after recovery from injury.

Treatment of Nociceptive Pain

With nociceptive pain, treatment usually is adjusted to the intensity of the pain, with weak analgesics used for mild pain and more potent analgesics for more severe pain. A stepwise approach beginning with less invasive and milder

No Pain   **Worst Possible Pain**

Note: Patients are asked to mark the position on the line where their pain is. The distance from an end is the pain rating.

Figure 13–50 Visual Analogue Pain Scale.

Point to or circle as many of these words as you can that describe your pain.

1 annoying bad horrible miserable terrible uncomfortable	5 blistering burning hot	10 awful deadly dying killing	15 off and on once in a while sneaks up sometimes steady
2 aching hurting like an ache like a hurt sore	6 cramping crushing like a pinch pinching pressure	11 crying frightening screaming terrifying	if you like, you may add other words: _____ _____ _____
3 beating hitting pounding punching throbbing	7 itching like a scratch like a sting scratching stinging	12 dizzy sickening suffocating	
4 biting cutting like a pin like a sharp knife pin like sharp stabbing	8 shocking shooting splitting	13 never goes away uncontrollable	
	9 numb stiff swollen tight	14 always comes and goes comes on all of a sudden constant continuous forever	

Note: The numbers of words selected in each of four categories are examined: *sensory* words, found in groups 2 through 9 ($n = 37$); *affective* words, found in groups 10 through 12 ($n = 11$); *evaluative* words, found in groups 1 and 13 ($n = 8$); *temporal* words, found in groups 14 and 15 ($n = 11$).

Figure 13–51 Portion of the Adolescent Pediatric Pain Tool. *Source:* From *Adolescent Pediatric Pain Tool*, 1993, M.C. Savedra, M.D. Tesler, and W.L. Holzemer, Ward University of California, School of Nursing, San Francisco, California. Adapted by permission.

forms of treatment is usually indicated, adjusting the starting point to the severity and nature of the initial pain complaint.

Pharmacologic treatment involves proceeding stepwise up an "analgesic ladder" (World Health Organization 1986):

- Nonopioid analgesic (acetaminophen or a nonsteroidal anti-inflammatory drug [NSAID])

- Weak opioid (e.g., codeine, oxycodone), with or without nonopioid analgesic and/or adjuvant, or a low-dose potent opioid

- Strong opioid (e.g., morphine, hydromorphone, methadone) with or without nonopioid analgesic and/or adjuvant

Nonsteroidal anti-inflammatory medications should be used with caution in patients with preexisting renal disease, platelet dysfunction, or rapidly changing hemodynamics.

The choice of opioid should depend on the duration and acuity of pain, available routes of administration, and the experience of the prescriber and patient caretakers. Short-acting analgesics, like fentanyl, are more useful for procedural pain than for pain of prolonged duration.

Enteral administration is preferred unless the child's gastrointestinal tract is dysfunctional or the pain complaint is so acute that slow enteral absorption is unacceptable. Intravenous delivery ensures a more rapid action and predictable absorption. Avoid intramuscular delivery because the pain and anxiety caused by the injection deter the child's pain complaint. Alternative opioid delivery routes should be reserved for specific indications and by those with special expertise. Patient-controlled analgesia provides significant control for the child; it is usually best used by cognitively normal children older than seven years. Epidural injection of medication requires an anesthesiologist's expertise; intense analgesia can be obtained with delivery of the opioid to spinal cord receptors. Rectal administration of opioids provides consistent action in a specific patient but has large population variations. Transdermal delivery of fentanyl provides constant opioid levels for long periods but should not be used in opioid-naive patients or in patients with pain problems lasting several days or less.

Avoid *prn* (as-needed) administration whenever possible for pain that is more than just an infrequent, intermittent complaint. Providing "around-the-clock medication" prevents wide swings in pain. Allowing patients to refuse medications rather than expecting them to ask for an analgesic —ordering "q4h, patient may refuse" rather than "q4h *prn*"—is more efficacious and provides greater patient control and access to pain medication.

Use one or two opioid analgesics for the majority of patients. Efficacy and side effects are usually similar for most opioids, though patients may have individual variation. Switches between opioids should be done at about 80 percent of equipotent doses to minimize the effect of incomplete cross-tolerance (see Table 13–13). Safety is increased as experience with a medication increases.

Respiratory depression, nausea and vomiting, pruritis, and dysphoria are the most common side effects of opioid analgesics. Abnormal mental status, pharyngeal dysfunction, and pulmonary compromise often require more careful evaluation and use of opioid analgesics. Frequent reevaluation of a patient's status while receiving analgesics increases the safety of the intervention.

Adjuvants include medications that specifically address specific issues like sleep, anxiety, and depression. Medications such as anticon-

Table 13–13 Commonly Used Opioids

Opioid	Parenteral Dose	Oral Dose
Morphine	10 mg	20-30 mg
Hydromophone	7.5 mg	1.5 mg
Meperidine	300 mg	100 mg
Codeine	130 mg	75 mg
Methadone	10 mg	20 mg
Fentanyl	0.1 mg	NA
Oxycodone	NA	30 mg

Source: Reprinted from *Acute Pain Management: Operative or Medical Procedures and Trauma,* Agency for Health Care Policy and Research, Washington, D.C., U.S. Department of Health and Human Services. 1992.

vulsants and antidepressants also address pain problems that have a neuropathic component.

Treatment of Neuropathic Pain

The management of neuropathic pain is frustrating, often necessitating a trial-and-error approach and careful titration of medications that have often poorly tolerated side effects. Because the total amelioration of neuropathic pain is often not feasible, clearly defined functional goals developed from an interdisciplinary approach to care are key to the management of neuropathic pain.

Unfortunately, scientific studies demonstrating the efficacy of medications in the treatment of pediatric neuropathic pain are lacking. Current practice is extrapolation from adult practice and needs to be considered in light of developmental and pharmacological differences between children and adults.

Psychotropic Medications

Tricyclic antidepressants, usually at low doses, often have a positive effect on adult patients with neuropathic pain. Even when pain is not affected, the soporific effect of medications, like amitriptyline, may be beneficial to these children, who often have sleep disturbances. Cardiac toxicity, especially rhythm disturbances, needs to be continually evaluated with the use of these medications. Cardiac evaluation is indicated in patients with a history of cardiac symptoms or use of a cardiotoxic medication as well as physical symptoms.

Anticonvulsants

The anticonvulsants carbamazepine and phenytoin are often useful in lancinating pain. The side effects and toxicity require careful monitoring.

Opioids

Neuropathic pain is often opioid "resistant" at low doses. Increased doses may have an ameliorative effect in some children. Side effects and other aspects of care need to be followed carefully. Long-term use has to be integrated into the comprehensive program.

Local Anesthetics

Local anesthetics are rarely useful in neuropathic pain. Side effects and minimal efficacy are usually limiting factors.

NONPHARMACOLOGICAL APPROACHES TO PAIN MANAGEMENT

The goal of nonpharmacological approaches to pain management is to provide the child with an experience of mastery and to facilitate coping skills, adjusted for appropriate developmental expectations.

- Sensorimotor period
  1. comfort measures: physical contact (e.g., holding, rocking)
  2. massage
- Preoperational period
  1. comfort measures: physical contact, light touch
  2. massage
  3. diaphragmatic breathing (a.k.a. belly breathing)
  4. progressive muscle relaxation (be as concrete as possible—for example, when targeting the muscles of the face state, "Make believe that you just bit into a lemon"; demonstrate muscle tension with an elastic band)
  5. guided imagery—talk through a relaxing scene
  6. distraction—divert child's attention from pain or painful stimulus
  7. blow bubbles
  8. watch a favorite video
  9. play a video game
  10. engage in a self-identified preferred activity
  11. counting

- Concrete operational period
  1. comfort measures: physical contact, light touch
  2. massage
  3. diaphragmatic breathing (a.k.a. belly breathing)
  4. progressive muscle relaxation
  5. rehearsal or hospital play (what will happen, what it feels like, why it is needed)
  6. imagery—focus child's attention to a pleasant situation

  7. child can begin to direct situation
- Formal operational period
  1. comfort measures: physical contact, light touch
  2. massage
  3. diaphragmatic breathing
  4. progressive muscle relaxation
  5. imagery
  6. hypnosis/relaxation techniques
  7. education

REFERENCES

Bieri, D., et al. 1990. The Faces Pain Scale for the self-assessment of the severity of pain experienced by children: Development, initial validation, and preliminary investigation for ratio properties. *Pain* 41:139–150.

Savedra, M.C., et al. 1993. Assessment of postoperative pain in children and adolescents using the Adolescent Pediatric Pain Tool. *Nursing Research* 42:5–9.

World Health Organization. 1986. *Cancer pain relief.* Geneva.

ADDITIONAL SUGGESTED READING

Agency for Health Care Policy and Research. 1992. *Acute pain management: Operative or medical procedures and trauma.* Washington, D.C.: U.S. Department of Health and Human Services.

ORTHOPEDIC INTERVENTION

John P. Dormans

Purpose: to describe the range of musculoskeletal abnormalities seen in children with developmental disabilities and the specialized techniques used by orthopedists for evaluation and treatment.

Chronic musculoskeletal abnormalities may occur more frequently in children with developmental disabilities, as they may be more commonly associated with a number of disorders that may cause disability. Causes of musculoskeletal abnormalities include neurologic disorders, congenital defects, brain or spinal cord injury, and vascular accidents of the brain or spinal cord (see Exhibit 13–2). In addition, children with disabilities may be at increased risk for acute orthopedic abnormalities such as fracture or dislocation due to tonal abnormalities, immobilization, or abnormal or unsteady gait.

Purposes for evaluation and/or treatment may include

- Identification and treatment of deformities (e.g., contractures, limb discrepancy) to avoid further effects
- Medical impact (e.g., progressive scoliosis leading to decreased lung capacity; hip dislocation in child with spastic cerebral

Exhibit 13–2 Common Disorders Associated with Musculoskeletal Abnormalities

1. Central nervous system
   - cerebral palsy
   - traumatic brain injury
2. Peripheral nerve
   - peroneal muscular atrophy (Charcot–Marie–Tooth)
   - other hereditary and motor-sensory neuropathies
3. Muscle
   - myopathies
   - muscular dystrophies
   - metabolic disorders

4. Spinal cord
   - spinal cord tumors
   - spina bifida
   - spinal cord injury
   - tethered cord
   - spinal muscular atrophy
   - polio
   - arthrogryposis
   - spinal cerebellar degeneration
   - Friedreich's ataxia

palsy, leading to pain and difficulty with perineal hygiene)
- Impact on function
  1. limits in participation in activities of daily living (ADLs) or self-care (with loss of independence)
  2. ambulation/mobility/transfers
  3. pain (limiting full activities)
  4. limits in full use of upper extremities (for play or other developmental activities)
  5. employment

EVALUATION TECHNIQUES (see also Chapter 7, Section "Procedures for Musculoskeletal Assessment")

The following should be assessed to determine whether orthopedic interventions are necessary:

- General appearance and physical examination to classify abnormalities
  1. identification of syndrome (e.g., missing limbs, short limbs)
  2. identification of deformities or contractures
- Developmental progress (see Chapter 7's listing of ambulatory and postural milestones)
  1. gross motor milestones

  2. posture: standing/sitting
  3. equilibrium reactions
- Gait
  1. observational gait analysis: classification into categories of ambulators
     (a) community
     (b) household
     (c) exercise
     (d) nonambulatory
  2. formal measurement
- Range of motion
  1. measurement of angles at joints; identify short muscles, fixed deformity
  2. stages of contracture
     (a) dynamic shortening
     (b) fixed shortening
     (c) fixed shortening with joint damage
- Recognition of short muscles
  1. short psoas
     (a) fixed flexion of the hip
     (b) increased lumbar lordosis (prominent buttocks)
     (c) reduced straight leg raising (due to contralateral hip flexion contracture)
     (d) Staheli (best, child prone), Thomas test (Figure 13–52)
  2. short adductors (< 30 degrees short)
     (a) scissored gait (bilateral, walking child)

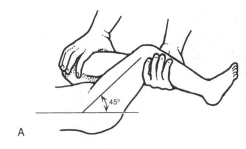

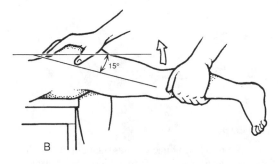

Note: A) Thomas test with 45-degree hip flexion contracture of right hip. B) Staheli test done in prone position. Fifteen degree hip flexion contracture of left hip.

Figure 13–52 Examination for Hip Flexion Contracture. *Source:* From "Orthopaedic Management of Children with Cerebral Palsy" by J.P. Dormans, 1993, *Pediatric Clinics of North America* 40, pp. 645–658. Copyright © 1993 by W.B. Saunders. Reprinted with permission.

(b) apparent leg-length discrepancy (unilateral, walking child)

(c) Trendelenburg limp (occurs with hip subluxation, weak abductors, or coxa vara)

(d) decreased hip abduction (Figure 13–53)

(e) progressive hip subluxation/dislocation

3. short hamstrings

(a) reduced straight leg raising

(b) hip extension contracture

(c) fixed flexion contracture of the knee (late—capsule and cruciate ligaments)

(d) lumbar kyphosis

(e) short stride length

(f) knee flexion during stance (crouch gait)

(g) "false equinus" (flexed knee lifts heel off the ground)

(h) internal femoral torsion (if medial > lateral)

(i) inability to touch toes

(j) reduced popliteal angle (Figure 13–54; most accurate at 90 degrees hip flexion)

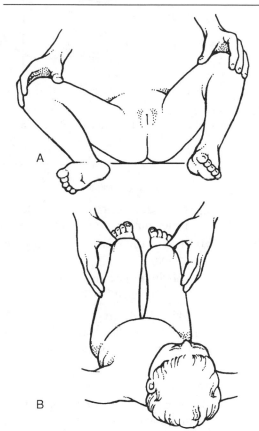

Note: A) Decreased abduction of the left hip. B) Right femoral shortening.

Figure 13–53 Examination for Adduction Contracture and Femoral Shortening. *Source:* From "Orthopaedic Management of Children with Cerebral Palsy" by J.P. Dormans, 1993, *Pediatric Clinics of North America* 40, pp. 645–658. Copyright © 1993 by W.B. Saunders. Reprinted with permission.

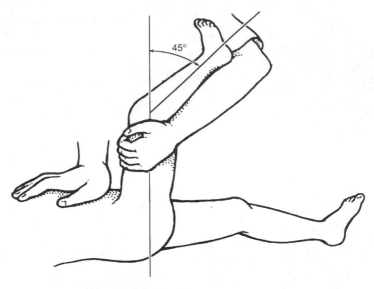

Note: This patient has a popliteal angle of 45 degrees from full extension.

Figure 13–54 Examination for Hamstrings Contracture. *Source:* From "Orthopaedic Management of Children with Cerebral Palsy" by J.P. Dormans, 1993, *Pediatric Clinics of North America* 40, pp. 645–658. Copyright © 1993 by W.B. Saunders. Reprinted with permission.

---

4. short quadriceps
   (a) stiff-legged gait (decreased knee flexion during swing phase of gait)
   (b) Ely test (iliopsoas fires with knee flexion)
   (c) inability to flex knee when hip extended (Figure 13–55)
   (d) high patella
5. short tendo Achilles and calf muscles (gastrocnemius and soleus muscles)
   (a) ankle equinus (Figure 13–56)
   (b) tiptoe gait
   (c) severe flatfoot ("stretching out" at midfoot joints)
   (d) recurvatum of the knee (linkage concept)

MANAGEMENT TECHNIQUES

A multidisciplinary approach to orthopedic interventions is the most effective, given the multiple factors interfering with functional skills in children with disabilities. Factors influencing walking abilities are

1. *Weight:* children with obesity may have delayed ambulation; children underweight may have decreased muscle mass and/or weakness
2. *Motivation:* may be related to cognitive skills
3. *Cognition*
4. *Neurologic picture:* spasticity and deformity will influence walking ability, particularly if there is asymmetry

It is necessary to know the natural history of the condition. For example, cerebral palsy is a "static encephalopathy"; a spastic type may be more amenable to orthopedic intervention. Children with extrapyramidal CP may be less amenable to surgical intervention, as they may be depending upon rigid tone to accomplish transfers. On the other hand, Duchenne muscular dystrophy is a disorder of progressive weakness, with a changing picture over time.

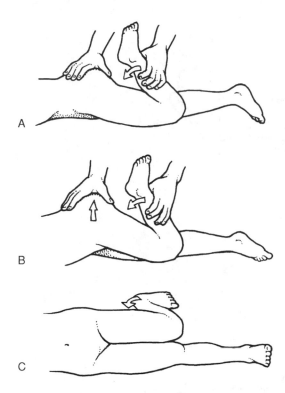

Note: A) and B) Ely's test. The buttocks rise from the examination table with knee flexion, suggesting a contracted rectus femoris, but this may be due to reflex contracture of the iliopsaos muscle. C) The side-lying knee flexion test is a better indicator of rectus contracture.

Figure 13–55 Examination for Rectus Femoris Contracture. *Source:* From "Orthopaedic Management of Children with Cerebral Palsy" by J.P. Dormans, 1993, *Pediatric Clinics of North America* 40, pp. 645–658. Copyright © 1993 by W.B. Saunders. Reprinted with permission.

Priorities of health professionals and educators may differ from those of parents. Issues that may be more important for parents include communication, ability to participate independently in activities of daily living, and mobility. Parents frequently rank ambulation as a first priority.

Modalities of intervention for muscle tone abnormalities are

- *Physical/occupational therapy:* helpful early, particularly for maintaining range of motion, promotion of transitional skills (especially for children under ten years of age)
- *Braces* (used to be very popular, now mostly molded ankle-foot orthosis [MAFO]; little place for bracing the knee; may be used to allow the normal developmental sequence to proceed; see also Chapter 15, section "Principles of Splint Design and Use")
  1. parapodium
  2. HKAFO (hip-knee-ankle-foot orthosis)
  3. reciprocation HKAFO—hip flexor power is harnessed by a gearbox to produce hip extension on the opposite side
  4. KAFO (knee-ankle-foot orthosis)
  5. AFO (ankle-foot orthosis)
  6. FO (foot orthosis)
- *Casting* (also see Chapter 15, section "Serial and Inhibitive Casting")
  1. inhibitive—only small children with no fixed deformities
  2. corrective—for example, for dynamic equinus or mild fixed equinus; more success with casting in younger patients; may be combined with motor point blocks
- *Surgery* (see below)
  1. should have a goal (prevention of dislocation, functional improvement, cosmetic improvement)
  2. should be done early (preschool child), when structural changes develop
  3. should correct all significant deformities at one time when appropriate
  4. should encourage early return to function

SPECIFIC DEFORMITIES

Orthopedic interventions for specific deformities are as follows:

- Scoliosis
  1. High failure rate with orthotic management for neuromuscular scoliosis,

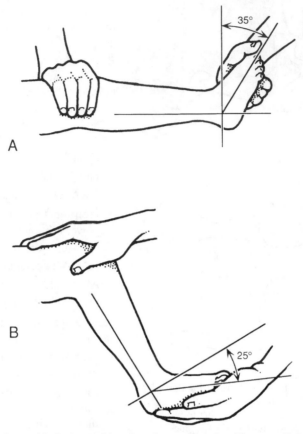

Note: This test may be done with the knee either flexed or extended to "factor out" the gastrocnemius (crosses both knee and ankle joints) and the soleus muscle (crosses the ankle joint only).

Figure 13–56 Examination for Heel Cord (Tendo Achilles) Contracture. *Source:* From "Orthopaedic Management of Children with Cerebral Palsy" by J.P. Dormans, 1993, *Pediatric Clinics of North America* 40, pp. 645–658. Copyright © 1993 by W.B. Saunders. Reprinted with permission.

though bracing may improve sitting. Spinal fusion improves sitting, transfers, feeding, nursing care, and transportation. Indications for fusion are

(a) >45 degrees curvature in immature patient

(b) >60 degrees curvature in mature patient

(c) however, fusion is done earlier in patients with Duchenne muscular dystrophy

The procedure, for most types of neuromuscular scoliosis, involves Luque "unit" rod instrumentation and fusion from the upper thoracic spine to the pelvis and anterior disc excision and grafting for "stiff" curves (>60 degrees on bending films). For children with higher level spina bifida, spinal deformity is more common. Bracing is difficult due to anesthetic skin. However, bracing may be used for a child who is too young for surgery. In children with rapidly progressing spinal curvature, first rule out hydromyelia or tethering lesions.

• Kyphosis—kyphectomy and fusion needed when kyphosis interferes with sitting

- Hip problems—nonambulatory patients
  1. Spastic hip subluxation/dislocation (hip-at-risk has hip abduction of <25 degrees; Shenton's line broken on x-ray; cerebral palsy usually)
     (a) adductor tenotomy
     (b) consider psoas and hamstring release—at same time if needed
     (c) Petrie casts for three to four weeks, followed by abduction pillow with knee immobilizers and MAFOs following
  2. Hip flexion-abduction contracture (spina bifida and polio)
     (a) prevent early splinting
     (b) if contracture is established, perform soft tissue release (Ober Yount fasciotomy)
     (c) more severe hip flexion contracture (>40 degrees) may require additional surgery
  3. Hip subluxation (e.g., in children with cerebral palsy)
     (a) if migration percentage is 50 percent or less, do soft tissue releases (Rang, 1990)
     (b) if migration percentage is 50 percent or more, do proximal femoral varus derotation osteotomy
     (c) Dega procedure or posterior-superior shelf procedure may be needed in older children if significant acetabular deformity
  4. Hip dislocation (particularly in children experiencing unremitting pain, interference with perineal hygiene, and concerns about pelvic obliquity)
     (a) femoral varus shortening osteotomy, pelvic osteotomy (open reduction if needed) may be helpful if condition is not long-standing and there is no femoral head deformity
     (b) salvage procedures for painful dislocation in older patient

     (i) Shantz valgus osteotomy—may be helpful
     (ii) femoral head and neck excision—not good prognosis
     (iii) excision plus interposition—better prognosis
     (iv) fusion—good prognosis
     (v) total hip arthroplasty—advocated in selected cases
     (vi) no treatment is an option if pain is minimal
  5. Hip subluxation/dislocation in spina bifida—correct deformity and balance muscle forces
     (a) newborn to 18 months—consider abduction splinting
     (b) varus derotation osteotomy of the proximal femur (want 90- to 100-degree neck/shaft angle)
     (c) muscle transfer procedures
        (i) external oblique abdominous transfer (Lindseth 1990)
        (ii) iliopsoas transfer (Sharrard or Mustard procedures)

- Hip problems—ambulatory patients
  1. Hip adduction contracture causing scissoring (e.g., in children with spastic hemiplegia cerebral palsy)
     (a) adductor transfer—attractive concept
     (b) adductor release—easier with same results
        (i) release attachment of gracilis, adductor brevis, and adductor longus
        (ii) obturator neurectomy may lead to abduction contracture
  2. Hip flexion contracture
     (a) psoas release—for nonwalkers (with adductor release)
     (b) Psoas recession (i.e., suture into hip joint capsule)

REFERENCES

Lindseth, R.E. 1990. Myelomeningocoele. In *Pediatric orthopaedics*, ed. R.T. Morrissy, 507–538. Philadelphia: J.B. Lippincott Co.

Rang, M. 1990. Cerebral palsy. In *Pediatric orthopaedics*, ed. R.T. Morrissy, 465–506. Philadelphia: J.B. Lippincott Co.

ADDITIONAL SUGGESTED READINGS

Asher, M., and J. Olson. 1983. Factors affecting ambulatory status of patients with spina bifida custica. *Journal of Bone and Joint Surgery* 65A:350.

Dormans, J.P. 1993. Orthopaedic management of the child with cerebral palsy. *Pediatric Clinics of North America* 40:645–657.

Drennan, J.C. 1990. Neuromuscular disorders. In *Pediatric orthopaedics*, ed. R.T. Morrissy, 381–463. Philadelphia: J.B. Lippincott Co.

Hoffer, M.M., and J. Perry. 1973. Functional ambulation in patients with myelomeningocele. *Journal of Bone and Joint Surgery* 55A:137.

Lonstein, J.E., and B.A. Akbarnia. 1983. Operative treatment of spinal deformities in patients with cerebral palsy or mental retardation. *Journal of Bone and Joint Surgery* 65A:43.

Menelaus, M.B. 1980. *The orthopaedic management of spina bifida custica.* Edinburgh: Churchill-Livingstone.

Perry, J., and M.M. Hoffer. 1977. Preoperative and postoperative dynamic EMG as an aid in planning tendon transfers in children with cerebral palsy. *Journal of Bone and Joint Surgery* 59A:531.

NEUROSURGICAL INTERVENTION

Ann-Christine Duhaime

Purpose: to discuss the role of neurosurgical intervention on the management of children with spasticity associated with cerebral palsy, focusing on selective dorsal rhizotomy.

Dorsal (sensory root) rhizotomy has been known to be an effective treatment for spasticity since the last century, but the accompanying sensory loss made the procedure impractical. In the 1970s, selective dorsal rhizotomy, a modification in which lumbosacral sensory roots were divided into rootlets that were selectively sectioned or spared based on intraoperative electrophysiologic findings, was reported as a means to reduce lower extremity spasticity without disabling sensory loss. The procedure is now commonly performed and has been found to be an effective means to decrease spasticity, increase range of motion, and improve selective functions in certain patients. Success of the operation is largely dependent on careful selection of patients and intensive postoperative therapy, as will be described below. A program approach involving neurosurgery, physical therapy, and orthopedics is best equipped to evaluate candidates for selective dorsal rhizotomy. Selection criteria and postoperative care may vary among centers, and the following discussion reflects the practice of the team at Children's Seashore House and the Children's Hospital of Philadelphia.

SCREENING CANDIDATES

The following factors should be assessed to screen candidates for selective dorsal rhizotomy:

- History
    1. Etiology of patient's spasticity (prematures are generally the most favorable candidates)

2. Other medical problems—specifically rule out other treatable causes of spasticity (e.g., hydrocephalus) or those with poor prognosis (e.g., progressive degenerative disease, or choreoathetoid cerebral palsy)

3. Course of spasticity

   (a) Are range of motion and tone increasing in spite of adequate physical therapy?

   (b) Is the child improving or worsening with respect to tone and function?

4. Other treatments for spasticity

   (a) Has the child had tendon-lengthening procedures or nerve blocks that may lead to overcorrection if combined with decreased tone from rhizotomy?

   (b) Has medication been tried?

5. Has physical therapy alone been tried with adequate frequency and appropriate techniques?

- Physical examination

  1. Tone—high resting, variable, low?

  2. Hyperreflexia

  3. Clonus, Hoffman's sign, clasp-knife reflex

  4. Does spasticity affect function?

  5. Balance, coordination, sensation

  6. Strength, with squat-to-stand testing

  7. Gait analysis/videotaping

- Ideal candidate

  1. *Ambulatory*—"pure" spastic diplegia affecting multiple muscle groups; good balance, strength; high resting tone and scissoring interfering with ambulation; no prior orthopedic surgery; able to cooperate with therapy; younger child

  2. *Nonambulatory*—tone interferes with sitting balance, mobility; adequate strength; cooperative; age three to five years

- Contraindications

  1. Progressive neurologic disease

  2. Other treatable etiology of spasticity

  3. Severe athetosis or dystonia

  4. Weakness for which spasticity provides functional compensation (e.g., for stand-pivot-sit); includes some children with extrapyramidal cerebral palsy

SURGICAL TECHNIQUE

After anesthesia is given, a narrow L_2 to L_5 laminectomy or, in some cases, a one- or two-level laminectomy is performed at the level of the conus medullaris. Intraoperative stimulation of rootlets of L_2 through S_1 or S_2, EMG recording, and visualization of leg movement are used to select the more abnormal roots to be sectioned. After watertight dural closure, an epidural catheter is placed for postoperative analgesic administration (morphine).

COMPLICATIONS

Complications are uncommon, but include cerebrospinal fluid leak, infection, weakness or sensory loss, and bladder dysfunction.

REHABILITATION

Rehabilitation includes intensive therapy (at least twice daily for three to six weeks), with therapeutic goals including improvement in range of motion, strength and endurance, sitting balance, and ambulation.

COMPARISON WITH OTHER TREATMENTS OF SPASTICITY

Advantages of selective dorsal rhizotomy are:
1. Effects are permanent.
2. Mobilization can begin soon after the operation.

3. Postoperative pain is readily controlled

4. The single procedure can affect all major muscle groups of lower extremities, with some reports of improvement in upper extremity function also.

Disadvantages are:

1. The procedure is irreversible.

2. It requires an inpatient rehabilitation stay for maximal effectiveness.

3. The patient may still need some orthopedic procedures to "fine-tune" joints (e.g., heel cord release).

SUGGESTED READINGS

Abbott, R., et al. 1993. Selective dorsal rhizotomy: Outcome and complications in treating spastic cerebral palsy. *Neurosurgery* 33:851–857.

Boscarino, L.P., et al. 1993. Effects of selective dorsal rhizo-tomy on gait in children with cerebral palsy. *Journal of Pediatric Orthopedics* 13:174–179.

Fasano, V.A., et al. 1978. Sirtoca: Treatment of spasticity in cerebral palsy. *Child's Brain* 4:289–305.

Chapter 14

Functional Skills Training

ACTIVITIES OF DAILY LIVING

Lesley A. Geyer, Sandra J. Okino, and Lisa A. Kurtz

Purpose: to discuss the appropriate selection and use of adaptive aids to promote independence in routine activities of daily living, such as eating, dressing, toileting, grooming, and tool use.

Adaptive equipment may be of great value in promoting independence in activities of daily living (ADLs) for the child with developmental disabilities or in easing the burden of care provided by parents or other caregivers. Numerous options exist, including the purchase of commercially available devices, the design and fabrication of custom-made devices, or the modification of everyday tools and equipment. The following considerations are essential to the selection of an appropriate device and to ensuring its successful use:

- The child must have acquired developmental readiness to perform the targeted ADL and must possess sufficient cognitive and physical ability to learn how to use the device.

- The child, along with significant caregivers, must demonstrate motivation to increase independence in the targeted ADL and must demonstrate acceptance that special devices are indicated.

- Use of the device must not pose any risk to the child's personal safety.

- The device must be cosmetically acceptable to the child and significant family members.

- Time and energy expenditure required to use the device must be considered reasonable by the child and significant family members.

- Sufficient resources must be available for fabricating or purchasing the selected device.

To determine the most appropriate technique or device for promoting independence or ease of skill in ADLs, one must first identify the reason for the child's inability to complete the task effectively. Commonly encountered problems that may limit performance may include

- limitations in movement or postural control
- inability to use one side of the body
- vision impairment
- cognitive impairment

LIMITATIONS IN MOVEMENT AND POSTURAL CONTROL

Limitations in movement and postural control may be caused by such factors as muscle weakness, incoordination, muscle shortening, or fixed contractures and may affect the child's performance in ADLs through impairment of

- reach
- grasp
- ability to assume sitting or standing position
- general strength or endurance
- motor coordination
- ability to use two hands together

Limitations in Reach

General principles of adaptation for reaching are:

- Compensate for limited movement by using devices with extended or elongated handles.
- Reduce or eliminate the need to reach.

The following are examples of devices and techniques of adaptation:

- For dressing
  1. *Dressing stick*—a stick with a hook at its end(s) that enables the child to pull upper body clothing around the back or to pull lower body clothing over the feet and legs (Figure 14–1).
  2. *Long shoehorn*—assists the child in donning and removing shoes, without the need to reach hands to feet (Figure 14–2).
  3. *Elastic shoelaces*—allows the child to slip in and out of shoes without having to reach down to tie/untie.
  4. *Sock-donning aids*—the sock is placed over a fabric or plastic frame, the foot is inserted, and cord handles are used to pull the sock over the foot. However, for total independence, the child must have sufficient hand function to assemble the sock and aid prior to use (Figure 14–3).
- For grooming/hygiene
  1. *Comb/brush with extended handle*—compensates for limited shoulder motion and eliminates the need to reach over the head (Figure 14–4).
  2. *Long-handled sponge*—allows the child with limited reach to wash back and lower extremities when bathing (Figure 14–5).
- For toileting
  1. *Toilet aid or wiping tongs*—used to hold toilet tissue in place while extending reach to perineal region (Figure 14–6).
- For feeding
  1. *Electric self-feeder*—enables a child to self-feed when lacking shoulder and elbow movement needed to move the utensil from plate to mouth; operated by a chin switch or remote hand/foot control (Figure 14–7).

Figure 14–1 Dressing Stick. *Source:* Copyright © 1996, Mark L. Batshaw, M.D.

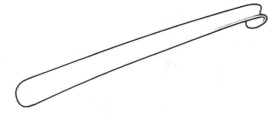

Figure 14–2 Long Shoehorn. *Source:* Copyright © 1996, Mark L. Batshaw, M.D.

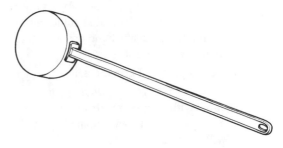

Figure 14–5 Long-Handled Sponge. *Source:* Copyright © 1996, Mark L. Batshaw, M.D.

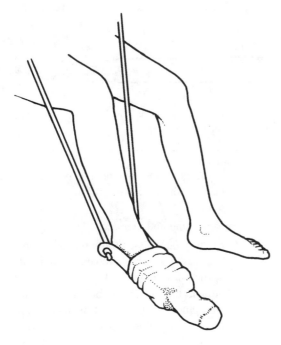

Figure 14–3 Sock-Donning Aid. *Source:* Copyright © 1996, Mark L. Batshaw, M.D.

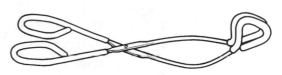

Figure 14–6 Toilet Aid or Wiping Tongs. *Source:* Copyright © 1996, Mark L. Batshaw, M.D.

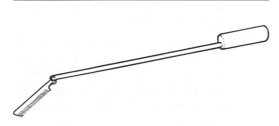

Figure 14–4 Comb with Extended Handle. *Source:* Copyright © 1996, Mark L. Batshaw, M.D.

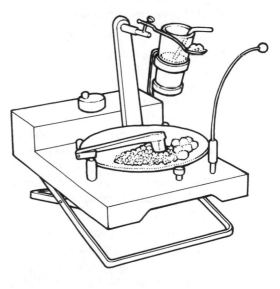

Figure 14–7 Electric Self-Feeder. *Source:* Copyright © 1996, Mark L. Batshaw, M.D.

2. *Mechanical self-feeder*—activated through single motion of shoulder internal rotation, causing hand or forearm to hit a dowel control.

- For school material management
    1. *Elevated/tilted desk surface*—allows child with limited reach to write, turn book pages, and manage other materials with less effort.
    2. *Backpack/wheelchair bag*—allows child to carry needed materials without having to reach into classroom closets/shelves.

Limitations in Grasp

General principles of adaptation for grasp are:

- Use loop handles or cuffs that hold devices around the child's palm or finger and eliminate the need for grasp.
- Use devices with built-up (large-diameter) handles to compensate for inability to grasp tightly when finger flexion is limited.
- Select devices that eliminate the need to use the hands.
- Use orthotic devices to position the wrist and hand better for functional grasp.

The following are examples of devices and techniques of adaptation:

- For dressing
    1. *Zipper pull*—child places finger in loop or ring attached to the zipper tab, then pulls the zipper (Figure 14–8). Zipper pull hooks are also available on handles (for the child with gross grasp) or attached to bendable cuffs that contour around the palm (for child with no functional grasp).
    2. *Velcro closures*—substituted for buttons, snaps, or other fasteners.
    3. *Button aid*—handle with metal loop at one end (Figure 14–9). Child holds handle (using gross grasp or palmar cuff), then hooks the loop through the

Figure 14–8 Zipper Pull. *Source:* Copyright © 1996, Mark L. Batshaw, M.D.

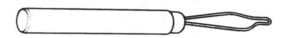

Figure 14–9 Button Aid. *Source:* Copyright © 1996, Mark L. Batshaw, M.D.

buttonhole and around the button; by pulling, button moves through the buttonhole.

- For grooming and hygiene
    1. *Built-up handles*—toothbrushes, combs, hairbrushes can be purchased with built-up handles (Figure 14–10). Or regular utensil handles may be enlarged by wrapping a washcloth around handle and securing it with adhesive tape or fitting handle with commercially available cylindrical foam padding.
    2. *Universal cuff*—attaches around the child's palm and has a "pocket" to insert the handle of a toothbrush or other utensil (Figure 14–11).
    3. *Cloth or sponge bath mitt*—placed over the child's hand and secured around the wrist, this eliminates the need to hold a washcloth (Figure 14–12). Some models have pocket to hold a bar of soap.
- For toileting
    1. *Wiping tongs*—used to grasp toilet paper, some models are designed to re-

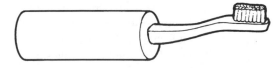

Figure 14–10 Toothbrush with Built-up Handle. *Source:* Copyright © 1996, Mark L. Batshaw, M.D.

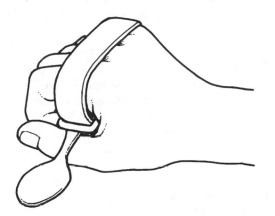

Figure 14–11 Universal Cuff. *Source:* Copyright © 1996, Mark L. Batshaw, M.D.

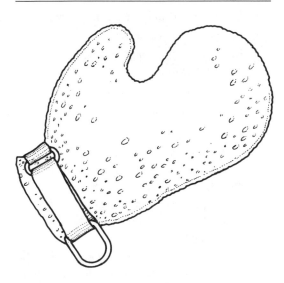

Figure 14–12 Sponge Bath Mitt. *Source:* Copyright © 1996, Mark L. Batshaw, M.D.

lease the paper when pressed against the commode bowl. Or toilet tissue may be wrapped around the child's hand to eliminate the need for grasp.

- For feeding
    1. *Wrist cock-up splint*—promotes slight wrist flexion, placing the hand in the optimal position for grasping a utensil (see Chapter 15, section "Principles of Splint Design and Use").

- For school material management
    1. *Pen/pencil grips*—many varieties are available, from those that provide a slightly enlarged circumference of the shaft to those that passively affix the pencil to the child's hand.
    2. *Computers/word processors/cassette recorders*—reduce or eliminate the need for manual writing of classroom notes or assignments (see Chapter 17).
    3. *Automatic page turner*—holds a book and turns pages when activated by a pressure-sensitive switch.

Limitations in Assuming Sitting or Standing

General principles for adaptation for sitting and standing are:

- Provide external support so that the child can assume and maintain the position.
- Use techniques and equipment that allow for completion of the task while eliminating the need for sitting or standing.

The following are examples of devices and techniques of adaptation:

- For dressing
    1. *Dressing in supine or side-lying position*—may be easier for the child who has poor sitting balance. Rolling side to side and bridging (lifting hips off weight-bearing surface) is used to get lower body clothing over hips (see Chapter 11, section "Lifting and Transfer Techniques").

2. *Dressing while seated (chair or wheelchair)*—a chair with armrests may be necessary to provide additional support for the child with poor sitting balance. The child pulls clothing over the hips by alternately shifting weight from side to side (allowing child to pull clothing over one free hip, then the other) or by using elbows and forearms on chair arm rests to slightly bridge the hips while pulling clothes over hips.

- For grooming and hygiene
  1. *Tub or shower seat*—allows the child to bathe or be bathed while seated (Figure 14–13). Some models allow child to be in a reclined position when sitting balance is poor. A hand-held shower helps the child to control the flow of water when showering in a shower seat.
  2. *Grab bars*—assist the child in performing a standing transfer to the shower bench.

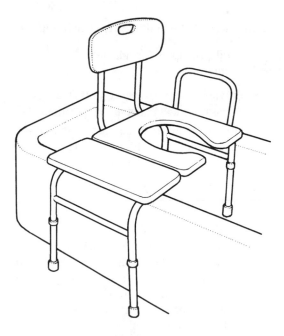

Figure 14–13 Tub or Shower Seat. *Source:* Copyright © 1996, Mark L. Batshaw, M.D.

3. *Transfer board*—may be used to assist in a sliding transfer from wheelchair to tub or shower (see Chapter 11, section "Lifting and Transfer Techniques").
- For toileting
  1. *Toilet safety frames or rails*—assist in transferring to the toilet, and may provide some support for the child with poor sitting balance.
  2. *High-back toilet supports and commodes*—provide support for sitting balance.
- For school material management
  1. *Height-adjustable desk*—to accommodate child who must remain in wheelchair during school day. Adaptations may include tilting top or cutout section to provide increased support to arms when working at desk.

Limitations in General Strength or Endurance

General principles of adaptation for strength and endurance limitations are:

- Use lightweight devices.
- Use powered equipment if necessary.
- Use gravity to assist motion.
- Reduce or eliminate the need to move against gravity.

The following are examples of devices and techniques of adaptation:

- For dressing
  1. *Dressing in supine or side-lying position*—allows for dressing with the demand of gravity eliminated.
  2. *Loose-fitting, front-opening clothing*—requires less effort to don/doff.
- For grooming/hygiene
  1. *Elevated toilet seat*—helpful for the child who has difficulty assuming standing from a low sitting position secondary to lower extremity weakness.

- For feeding
  1. *Plastic utensils and cups*—are light-weight and easier to manipulate for the child with weak upper extremities.
  2. *Elevated table or tray*—decreases the distance required to move against gravity when moving hand to mouth.
  3. *Ball-bearing feeder*—supports arms against gravity, allowing child to scoop food and bring spoon to mouth using minimal active arm movement.
- For school materials management
  1. *Buddy system*—identify classmate to serve as "helper" for carrying books from one class to another, carrying lunchroom tray.

Limitations in Motor Coordination

General principles of adaptation for limitations in motor coordination are:

- Use weighted devices and friction surfaces to increase accuracy of movement.
- Use adaptive positioning devices to stabilize proximal body parts (head, trunk, hips, shoulders).
- Teach child to stabilize upper extremities by holding them close to the body, or by weight bearing on a table surface or tray.

The following are examples of devices and techniques of adaptation:

- For dressing
  1. *Weighted button hooks/zipper pulls*—improve control.
  2. *Velcro closures*.
- For grooming/hygiene
  1. *Soap on a rope*—prevents dropping a slippery bar of soap; can be handmade by using awl or pointed knife to cut hole in center of soap.
  2. *Rubber suction bath mat*—helps to facilitate safe tub transfers.

- For feeding
  1. *Covered cup with sipping spout or straw*—helps to prevent spillage (Figure 14–14). Child can be taught to use both hands and to keep elbows against sides of trunk to improve stability for drinking.
  2. *Nonslip mat*—commercially available mat may be placed under plate or bowl to stabilize when scooping or stabbing food; a wet towel or cloth placed under the plate will also work.
  3. *Scoop dish and weighted spoon*—allows increased control as child uses the raised side of a dish to scoop food onto a spoon (Figure 14–15).

Figure 14–14 Covered Cup with Sipping Spout. *Source:* Copyright © 1996, Mark L. Batshaw, M.D.

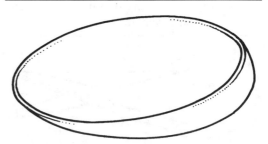

Figure 14–15 Scoop Dish. *Source:* Copyright © 1996, Mark L. Batshaw, M.D.

- For school material management
    1. *Weighted cuff*—worn on arm or wrist, cuff may provide greater stability when writing.
    2. *Loop scissors*—allow cutting by simple grasp motion; easier to control than conventional scissors (Figure 14–16).
    3. *Typewriter/word processor with raised keyguard*—allows greater control on hitting correct keys; may be used with mouth stick or head stick (see Chapter 17).

INABILITY TO USE ONE SIDE OF THE BODY

The general principle of adaptation for hemiplegia is:

- Compensate by substituting the uninvolved extremity (using one-handed techniques).

The following are examples of devices and techniques of adaptation:

- For dressing
    1. The *involved extremity* is dressed first and undressed last.
    2. *Slip-on garments* for lower extremity dressing, *loosely fitted garments*, and *front closures* are recommended.
    3. Donning front-opening shirt
        (a) Place shirt on child's lap with inside up, collar toward stomach, shirttails draped over legs.
        (b) Open sleeve on involved side, place involved hand in the opening, and pull over elbow.

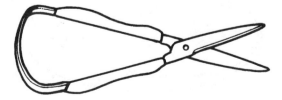

Figure 14–16 Loop Scissors. *Source:* Copyright © 1996, Mark L. Batshaw, M.D.

(c) Place uninvolved extremity into its sleeve and raise to shake sleeve over the elbow.

(d) Grasp shirttails, and gather shirt hem to collar. With uninvolved hand, raise shirt over head and adjust by leaning forward, working the shirt over shoulders, pulling down by tails.

(e) Button shirt from bottom to top to help alignment; cuff button of uninvolved arm can be prebuttoned with elastic thread so hand can slip through.

4. Removing front-opening shirt
    (a) Unbutton shirt.
    (b) Grasp collar with uninvolved hand, or gather in back, collar to hem.
    (c) Lean forward and pull shirt over head.
    (d) Remove sleeve from uninvolved arm, then from involved arm.

5. Donning pants
    (a) From sitting position, cross involved leg over uninvolved leg, which is positioned directly in front of midline of body.
    (b) Slip pants over involved leg until the foot is completely through the opening.
    (c) Uncross legs and slip pants over uninvolved leg.
    (d) If safe, child can stand to pull pants over hips, and can place the involved hand in the pocket, slip a finger into a belt loop, or use prefastened suspenders to prevent pants from dropping.

6. Removing pants
    (a) Unfasten pants and pull down as far as possible from seated position.
    (b) Stand, allowing gravity to drop pants. If unable to stand, the child can lean back in the chair, push down with uninvolved leg to el-

evate hips, then work pants down past hips.

(c) Seated, cross involved leg over uninvolved leg, remove pants from involved leg.

(d) Uncross legs, remove pants from uninvolved leg.

- For grooming/hygiene
  1. *Suction brush*—secures to flat surface to allow one-handed nail care (Figure 14–17).
  2. Wash the uninvolved arm by placing a soapy washcloth across the knees, then rubbing the arm back and forth.
- For feeding
  1. *Rocker knife*—a knife with a sharp curved blade, stabilizing the food to be cut as the knife rocks back and forth (Figure 14–18).
  2. *Scoop dish/food guard*—used for foods that are difficult to pick up.
- For school materials management
  1. Use clipboards, paperweights, or tape to stabilize paper when writing.
  2. Use push pens or other writing tools without caps.

VISUAL IMPAIRMENT (see also Chapter 7, section "Vision Assessment," and the next section in this chapter, "Low-Vision Management")

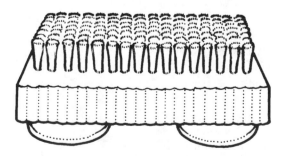

Figure 14–17 Suction Brush. *Source:* Copyright © 1996, Mark L. Batshaw, M.D.

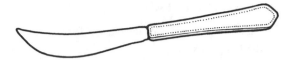

Figure 14–18 Rocker Knife. *Source:* Copyright © 1996, Mark L. Batshaw, M.D.

The general principle of adaptation to visual impairment is:

- Use other senses and memory to compensate for lack of visual input.

The following are examples of devices and techniques of adaptation:

- For dressing
  1. Organize closets and storage places so that items are always in the same place and can be found.
  2. Use tags or fasteners to identify the directionality of clothes.
  3. Use embroidered French knots to "code" the color of clothes.
  4. Store color-coordinated outfits together.
- For grooming/hygiene
  1. Use braille labels, odor, or location to identify objects in their storage areas.
- For feeding
  1. *Sectioned plate*—keeps food separated and aids in location.
  2. *Cup with lid*—prevents spilling, especially when used in combination with nonslip mat.
  3. *Clock method*—child is taught to locate food on plate by groups—for example, meat at 12 o'clock, potatoes at 6 o'clock, etc.
  4. Practice estimating the size of bites by estimating weight of the loaded utensil.
  5. Place a finger near the top of a cup to gauge the quantity for pouring liquids.
- For school materials management—see the next section in this chapter, "Low-Vision Management."

COGNITIVE IMPAIRMENT

General principles of adaptation for cognitive impairment are:

- Use patience, repetition, and routine in teaching
- Use behavior modification techniques
- Use predictable, organized structure to conduct teaching sessions
- Teach by *reverse chaining* method:
  1. Analyze task to determine sequence of discrete steps leading to completion (see Chapter 7, section "Psychoeducational Measures: Competency-Based Training").
  2. Assist child with each step, asking child to perform only the last step independently.
  3. When child can consistently perform last step, ask child to perform last two steps independently, and so forth until child has learned entire sequence.

The following are examples of devices and techniques of adaptation:

- For dressing
  1. Coding clothes for right/left may aid directionality.
  2. Place clothes in the correct order to don in order to help the child recall the sequence.
  3. Use pictures to aid in recall of steps or routines.
- For feeding—plan frequent meals with smaller portions to help child with decreased attention to complete a meal and experience success
- For school materials management—use schedules or journals to help orient the child with confusion or limited memory skills

---

SUGGESTED READINGS

Christansen, C., ed. 1994. *Ways of living: Self-care strategies for special needs.* Rockville, Md.: American Occupational Therapy Association, Inc.

Coley, I.L. and S.A. Procter. 1989. Self-maintenance activities. In *Occupational therapy for children*, 2nd ed., ed. P. Pratt and A. Allen, 260–294. St. Louis: C.V. Mosby Co.

ADDITIONAL RESOURCES

Databases

ABLEDATA, National Rehabilitation Information Center (NARIC), 8455 Colesville Road, Suite 935, Silver Spring, MD 20910-3319, Tel.: (301) 588-9284, (800) 346-2742. A public database containing information on commercially available rehabilitation products including personal care and educational aids.

Accent on Information, Inc., P.O. Box 700, Bloomington, IL 61702, Tel.: (309) 378-2961.

Suppliers of Commercial Adaptive Devices (refer to Appendix C for addresses/phone numbers)

Achievement Products, Inc.

Adaptive Design Shop

Adrian's Closet

Alimed, Inc.

Best Priced Products, Inc.

Columbia Medical Manufacturing, Inc.

Cleo, Inc.

Convaid Products, Inc.

Crestwood Company

Fred Sammons, Inc.

Guardian Products

J.A. Preston Corporation

Kaye Products, Inc.

North Coast Medical

Special Clothes

J.A. Preston Corporation

Susquehanna Rehab Products

North Coast Medical, Inc.

AdaptABILITY

LOW-VISION MANAGEMENT

Lisa A. Kurtz

Purpose: to discuss the common developmental and behavioral sequelae of vision impairment in children, to introduce methods for assessing functional use of residual vision in partially sighted children, and to present strategies for encouraging children to make the most effective use of residual vision, along with general principles for teaching children to compensate for vision loss.

Vision is a sense that develops throughout early childhood; it must be *used* to develop to its fullest potential. Most children with visual impairment have some remaining vision that may provide cues necessary for effective interaction with the environment. Functional vision intervention begins with a detailed assessment of the child's responses to visual stimuli within an environmental context and offers a carefully designed program of visual stimulation that encourages the child to orient and respond meaningfully to visual cues.

GENERAL CONSIDERATIONS FOR FUNCTIONAL VISION ASSESSMENT

The child should always receive assessment and medical management from an ophthalmologist prior to initiating a program of functional intervention (see also section Chapter 7, the section "Sensory Screening: Vision"). The following represent characteristics commonly found in children with vision impairment:

- Physical signs and symptoms of vision impairment
  1. redness, tearing, discharge of eyes
  2. abnormal size, shape, or position of eyes
  3. asymmetry
  4. child reports pain, headaches, blurred or double vision

- Common behavioral characteristics of congenital or acquired vision impairment
  1. odd or repetitive self-stimulatory behaviors
     (a) eye poking, squinting, frequent blinking
     (b) spinning or twirling objects close to face
     (c) staring at hands or flicking fingers in front of eyes
  2. asymmetrical head or trunk posture present only during periods of sustained visual attention
  3. limited eye contact or decreased visual regard of toys
  4. mobility concerns
     (a) difficulty negotiating obstacles
     (b) disregard or neglect of one side of the environment
     (c) over/undershooting of targets during reach
     (d) fearful negotiating of curbs or steps
- Common developmental characteristics of young children with visual impairment
  1. normal development of postural skills but delayed initiation of movement and/or environmental exploration (reaching, crawling, walking)
  2. delayed acquisition of facial expressions of emotion
  3. preference for supine over prone; crawling with head flexed (five-point crawl) to protect face
  4. tactile defensiveness, resisting manual exploration of toys or environment
  5. delayed use of hands for play at midline of body
  6. failure to demonstrate developmental progression of visual-motor skills consistent with cognitive potential (see Table 14–1)

Table 14–1 Visual Development Sequences

Age	Typical Sequences
0–1 month	Corneal reflex to touch
	Pupils react to light
	Reflexive eye closing to bright light
	Fixates on face and may imitate
	Cries real tears
	May use monocular fixation
	Visually prefers horizontal and vertical edges, larger sizes, simple black and white patterns
	Fixation best when in quiet alert state, lasts only a few seconds
2–3 months	Horizontal tracking slightly past midline
	Beginning vertical tracking
	Nystagmus present during vestibular stimulation
	Enjoys lights and bright colors
	Hand regard using asymmetric tonic neck reflex (ATNR)
	Shifts eyes toward sound source
	Defensive blink to threat
	Beginning convergence
4–6 months	Rapidly shifts gaze from hand to object and from object to object
	Has color perception
	Full horizontal and vertical tracking, starting circular
	Convergence consistently present
	Demonstrates preference for novel patterns
	Begins visually guided reaching
	Begins visual memory and object permanence; looks for dropped toy
	Discriminates different facial expressions
7–11 months	Beginning depth perception
	Enjoys exploring tiny objects
	Interested in shapes
	Follows with eyes and not with head; uses saccadic eye movements
12–18 months	Binocular vision developed
	Acuity 20/200
	Discriminates simple geometric forms
	Marks and scribbles with crayon
	Interested in pictures in books

SUGGESTED PROCEDURES FOR ASSESSMENT OF FUNCTIONAL VISION

Before a functional vision assessment is conducted, there should be a medical assessment by an ophthalmologist. Such an assessment should cover

1. etiology/diagnosis/prognosis of visual impairment
2. estimate of residual visual acuity, light sensitivity, visual fields
3. eye range of motion
4. recommended medical management, including surgery or corrective lenses
5. potential side effects of medication that may influence vision
6. necessary precautions or activity restrictions

The following are some common terms used in medical vision assessment:

- *Accommodation:* The process of focusing in which the lens changes curvature to adjust for distance of the visual target

- *Acuity:* The clearness or sharpness of vision
- *Amblyopia:* Dimness of vision without any apparent disease of the eye
- *Cataract:* An opacity of the crystalline lens of the eye; causes loss of visual acuity
- *Convergence:* Turning the two eyes inward to look at a near object and retain a single image
- *Diplopia:* Double vision
- *Esophoria:* Tendency of the eye to turn inward (toward the nose)
- *Esotropia:* Constant turning in of the eye
- *Exophoria:* Tendency of the eye to turn outward (away from the nose)
- *Exotropia:* Constant turning out of the eye
- *Field of vision:* The total area that can be seen when gazing steadily at a target in the direct line of vision
- *Hemianopsia:* Blindness of one-half the visual field of one or both eyes
- *Hyperopia:* Farsightedness; difficulty seeing near objects
- *Legal blindness:* Central visual acuity of 20/200 or less in the better eye after correction, or visual acuity greater than 20/200 when there is a field loss in which the widest angle of the field subtends an angle distance of no greater than 20 degrees
- *Nystagmus:* An involuntary, rapid movement of the eyeball in any direction
- *Oculomotor:* Pertaining to movements of the eye as controlled by the six extraocular muscles
- *Peripheral vision:* Ability to perceive presence, motion, or color of object when outside of the direct line of vision
- *Ptosis:* Paralysis of the eyelid, causing it to droop
- *Pupillary reactions:* Contraction or dilation of the pupil in response to changes in light or changes in the distance of the object viewed

- *Myopia:* Nearsightedness; difficulty seeing far objects
- *O.D.:* Oculus dexter; right eye
- *O.S.:* Oculus sinister; left eye
- *O.U.:* Oculus uterque; both eyes
- *Saccade:* A rapid eye movement from one point in space to another to allow a shift in gaze; a series of saccades results in scanning a moving target
- *Strabismus:* Muscle imbalance that causes the two eyes to have difficulty simultaneously directing gaze at the same object

Functional vision assessment must be conducted by a professional with advanced training/experience in this area (typically a vision specialist, special educator, occupational therapist, or optometrist). It predicts how residual vision will affect function in daily routines. It also describes optimal environmental conditions for encouraging adaptive use of residual vision:

1. optimal lighting/contrast conditions
2. optimal size/shape/color of stimulus items
3. optimal positioning/object placement to encourage visual attention
4. optimal teaching methods for encouraging use of vision (e.g., pairing visual stimulus with touch, sound, or smell)

SUGGESTED TECHNIQUES FOR MANAGEMENT OF LOW VISION

The following techniques should be used in the management of low vision:

- Adapting the environment for safety and consistency
  1. Infant/toddler (prior to crawling or walking)
     (a) Warn the infant by saying his or her name before touching or picking up to prevent alarm.
     (b) Touch the hand and make noise before placing an object (prevents the

"good fairy" syndrome—believing that objects come from and disappear into nowhere).

(c) Aim for as much consistency in routine as possible: e.g., do not use nicknames until child knows full name, use same brand bottles, diapers, etc.

(d) Conduct teaching in areas where background noise is kept to a minimum; this helps the child to focus on the more important sound cues.

(e) Place sound toys in crib near infant so that accidental movement will cause noise.

(f) Teach cause and effect by helping infant to activate noise: e.g., tie rattles around wrist, use overhead frame to suspend rattles, place limbs on crinkly paper bags or squeaky toys to encourage movement.

(g) When infant is awake, do not allow long periods of inactivity in crib or playpen; caregiver can carry and talk to the child while completing household routines.

2. Crawling or ambulatory child

(a) Organize and simplify the arrangement of household or classroom furniture; consistently return objects to their proper place; keep drawers and cabinet doors closed.

(b) Pad or remove obstacles at eye level.

(c) Remove area rugs or secure with tape or backing.

(d) Ensure adequate lighting arrangements for any area the child will be expected to negotiate.

(e) Place bright strips of tape on steps, doorknobs, light switches, or any other environmental targets.

(f) Place decals on picture windows or sliding doors to prevent accidents.

(g) Attach strip of sandpaper on stair rail to warn when approaching the bottom.

• Stimulating use of residual vision

1. Use creative selection of materials and toys with high visual appeal:

(a) flashlights with colored filters, flicker lights, blinking Christmas ornaments

(b) neon or silver-colored toys

(c) objects that pair vision with another sensory input

(i) bright "smelly" stickers

(ii) orange or lemon instead of rubber ball

(iii) puppets with bells attached

(iv) Leggs eggs with beans inside

(v) moving or vibrating toys

(vi) toys with interesting textures

(d) "glow in the dark" objects

(e) fluorescent objects (use black light)

(f) consistent use of familiar objects (e.g., bottle) that have been adapted to be more visually stimulating

(g) high-contrast food items: e.g., silver cake decorations, brightly colored cereals

2. Be prepared to use trial and error to make an object more visible by enhancing the image.

(a) Use larger item, or move closer to item to accommodate for decreased acuity.

(b) Use smaller item, or move farther away to accommodate to limited visual field.

(c) Change contrast between object/background.

(d) Change color of item.

(e) Illuminate item (place on light table; use flashlight; certain items can be lit from within using penlight).

(f) Dim or enhance lighting, taking care to avoid shadows or glare.

- Mobility and orientation principles (ambulatory child)

  1. Child with serious visual limitations should receive formal instruction.

  2. Practice counting the number of steps it takes to get from one area to another; learn to feel for objects that can serve as fixed reference points.

  3. Teach self-protection in walking.

     (a) In "free space," extend arm parallel to floor with elbow flexed slightly less than 90 degrees and fingers extended.

     (b) Use "trailing" technique to follow wall—hand closest to wall is extended at hip level so back of fingers can touch the wall.

     (c) To locate a dropped object, localize by sound, then stoop with hand held to protect head and locate object with broad sweep of hand.

  4. Orient child to an unfamiliar room by drawing on the child's back or using a cardboard box to represent the room.

  5. When walking with the child, offer your arm, but do not push or pull the child.

  6. When showing child to a chair, place the child's hand on the back of the chair and allow child to sit independently.

- Teaching compensatory strategies for daily skills (see also previous section, "Activities of Daily Living")

  1. Use hand-over-hand instruction to teach the child the "feel" of daily living skills; consider standing behind the child to initiate hand-over-hand training.

  2. Facilitate toilet training through use of a consistent schedule and route to the bathroom and by establishing an association between wet clothes and going to the toilet.

  3. Teach "clock" system for locating food on plate (meat at 12 o'clock, vegetables at 6 o'clock, etc.); can use bread or roll as "pusher" to keep from spilling over edge of plate.

  4. To pour liquids, place finger over lip of container and fill until liquid reaches finger.

  5. Use cardboard guide for writing signature.

  6. For partially sighted student, use an easel to present visual materials in an upright orientation; this helps to reduce fatigue from bending close to work.

  7. Teach organization of personal items in closets, bathroom, kitchen, etc., so child can learn to recognize object by location.

  8. Embroider French knots on clothing to "code" by color, or hang matching items on the same hanger.

  9. Teach money management by tactile recognition of coins; fold paper money so that each denomination is different.

  10. Obtain adaptive aids to increase independence in self-care and recreation: e.g., elbow-length oven mitt to prevent burn when reaching into oven, marking kits for canned goods, recessed or braille board games.

  11. Use nonslip trays to hold materials for manipulative or cooking activities to help prevent spilling.

  12. Aggressively teach good grooming, posture, and understanding of "style" in clothes to help with social acceptance by peers.

SUGGESTED READINGS

Barraga, N.C., and J.N. Erin. 1992. *Visual handicaps and learning.* 3rd ed. Austin, Tex.: PRO-ED.

Bouska, M.J., et al. 1990. Disorders of the visual perception system. In *Neurological rehabilitation*, 2nd ed., ed. D. Umphred, 552–585, St. Louis: C.V. Mosby Co.

Chapman, E.K., and J.M. Stone. 1988. *The visually handicapped child in your classroom.* London: Cassell Educational Ltd.

Dietz, S.J., and K.A. Ferrel. 1993. Early services for young children with visual impairment: From diagnosis to comprehensive services. *Infants and Young Children* 6, no. 1:68–76.

Greenblatt, S.L. 1991. *Providing services for people with vision loss: A multidisciplinary perspective.* Lexington, Mass.: Resources for Rehabilitation.

Jose, R.T., et al. 1980. Evaluating and stimulating vision in the multiply impaired. *Journal of Vision Impairment and Blindness* 74, no. 1:2–8.

Scholl, G., ed. 1986. *Foundations of education for blind and visually handicapped children and youth: Theory and practice.* New York: American Foundation for the Blind.

Scott, E.P., et al. 1985. *Can't your child see?* 2nd ed. Austin, Tex.: PRO-ED.

Smith, A.J., and K.S. Cote. 1982. *Look at me: A resource manual for the development of residual vision in multiply impaired children.* Philadelphia: Pennsylvania College of Optometry Press.

Younger, V., and J. Sardegna. 1992. One *way or another: A guide to independence for the visually impaired and their families.* Available from Sardegna Productions, 710 Almondwood Way, San Jose, CA 95120.

Zambone, A.M. 1989. Serving the young child with visual impairments: An overview of disability impact and intervention needs. *Infants and Young Children* 2, no. 2:11–23.

ADDITIONAL RESOURCES (refer to Appendix C for addresses/phone numbers)

Sources of Information, Referrals, and Supplies

American Foundation for the Blind

American Printing House for the Blind

Bernell Corporation

Blind Children's Center

Lighthouse Low Vision Products

National Association for the Visually Handicapped

National Association of Visually Impaired

National Association for Parents of the Visually Handicapped

National Center for Vision and Child Development

National Federation of the Blind

National Library Service for Blind & Physically Handicapped

NOIR Medical Technologies

Vis-Aids, Inc.

Suggested Tests of Functional Vision

Barraga, N.C., and J. Morris. 1980. *Program To Develop Efficiency in Visual Function.* Available from the American Printing House for the Blind.

Langley, M.B. 1980. Functional Vision Inventory for the Multiple and Severely Handicapped. Available from the Stoelting Company.

STYCAR Vision Test (Screening Test for Young Children and Retardates). Available from NFER Publishing Company, Ltd.

Chapter 15

Orthotics

PRINCIPLES OF SPLINT DESIGN AND USE

Doré Blanchet and Sandra M. McGee

Purpose: to discuss the basic principles for selection and use of splints and orthoses used in pediatric rehabilitation; to present examples of common splint designs for the upper extremities, trunk, and lower extremities, along with a description of their function and indications for their use; to discuss methods for fabricating splints using low-temperature thermoplastics, including a comparative analysis of the working properties of available materials; and to offer precautions and instructions for wear and care of splints.

Splints are useful and often necessary adjuncts to the treatment of many pediatric disabilities. Splints may be either *static* (immobile) or *dynamic* (made with movable parts, and often providing variable resistance to motion). They may be used for a variety of purposes, including

- to support or immobilize a body part, allowing healing to occur
- to provide joint stability by preventing undesired movement
- to prevent or correct deformity by maintaining or increasing range of motion

- to allow assisted motion for weakened extremities
- to provide a base of support for the attachment of toys or self-help devices

Distinction is sometimes made between orthoses (made by a certified orthotist) and splints (made by a therapist). Although there is some variability among facilities, upper extremity splints are most commonly made by occupational therapists, whereas lower extremity splints are made by physical therapists. In pediatrics, orthoses, often using high-temperature thermoplastics, are more often recommended for the lower extremities than for upper extremities. Several factors need to be considered when choosing between a therapist-made splint and an orthosis for the lower extremities, including

- *Age:* Young children with rapidly growing feet may be better served by having therapist-made splints, which are less expensive to make than orthoses. Most insurance companies will pay for only one orthosis per year.

- *Developmental level:* A child who is not yet standing and walking will put less stress on the splint than one who has achieved those milestones.
- *Size:* Larger children often require the durability of polypropylene, which is much stronger than the low-temperature thermoplastics commonly used by therapists.
- *Duration of need:* Children who will require an orthosis for more than six months should have it fabricated by an orthotist.
- *Evaluation:* One of the benefits of therapist-made splints is the ease and speed with which they can be made. This allows the therapist to fabricate a trial splint at low cost, assess its appropriateness for the patient, and make alternative designs as indicated by the assessment.

ASSESSMENT AND DESIGN OF SPLINTS

Splints and orthoses must be custom designed to meet the particular needs of the patient. A thorough understanding of anatomy (including surface landmarks) and biomechanical principles of the part to be splinted must be attained prior to splinting. Although basic patterns can be used as a starting point for developing a custom-made device, no two finished splints look exactly the same, and the therapist must be highly creative, flexible, and objective to achieve optimal results. Suggested components of assessment that should be conducted prior to selection of splint design are

- For upper extremity splints
  1. history
     (a) diagnosis, relevant medical history and prognosis
     (b) child/parent concerns and goals
     (c) hand dominance
     (d) functional limitations influenced by hand use
  2. hand evaluation/screening
     (a) active and passive range of motion
     (b) strength
        (i) manual muscle test
        (ii) standardized grip and pinch strength
     (c) sensibility
        (i) *light touch*—localization of touch by cotton ball
        (ii) *deep pressure*—localization of touch by eraser end of pencil, applied hard enough to blanch skin
        (iii) *pain and temperature*—discrimination of sharp vs. dull end of safety pin for older child; use temperature discrimination (vials filled with hot and cold water) for younger child who is fearful of the pin
     (d) edema, measured either by circumferential tape measures at landmarks or using volumeter (water displacement)
     (e) functional assessment of dexterity, preferably using standardized measures, e.g.:
        (i) Purdue Pegboard Test
        (ii) Jebsen Hand Function Test for Children
        (iii) Minnesota Rate of Manipulation Test
- For lower extremity splints
  1. history
     (a) diagnosis, relevant medical history and prognosis
     (b) child/parent concerns and goals
  2. lower extremity evaluation/screening
     (a) active and passive range of motion
     (b) strength
     (c) sensation
     (d) gait analysis

UPPER EXTREMITY SPLINTS

Table 15–1 presents a description of selected upper extremity splints that may be considered as an adjunct to treatment for children with developmental disabilities.

Table 15-1 Examples of Upper Extremity Splints

Type of Splint	Purpose/Goal	Position	Wear Schedule	Other Considerations
Resting hand splint (Figure 15–1)	Maintains the spastic or flaccid hand in a functional position to prevent deformity	Wrist 0–30° extension; MPs 60–70° flexion; IPs neutral; thumb in opposition/abduction	For nonfunctional hand, wear 2 hr. on/2 hr. off during day and continually during sleep; for functional hand, wear continually during sleep or when not using hand	Volar placement is most common, but dorsal placement may be helpful for spasticity
Wrist cock-up splint (Figure 15–2)	Provides support to wrist and hand arches while allowing finger movement	Wrist 0–30° extension	As needed for function	
Ball abduction splint (Figure 15–3)	Decreases spasticity through reflex-inhibiting pattern of thumb and finger abduction	Wrist 0–30° extension; MPs 45° of flexion; IPs slight flexion; fingers and thumb abducted	If tolerated, wear at night for prolonged stretch; can also be used intermittently during the day as tolerated	Difficult splint for one person to make on a very spastic hand
Soft thumb loop (Figure 15–4)	Decreases thumb flexion and adduction in the spastic hand through use of a reflex-inhibiting pattern; allows use of hand for function	Thumb abduction and opposition; line of pull of thumb strap goes across thumb web space	During functional activity	Use Neoprene, Neoplush, or strapping material
Short or long opponens (Figure 15–5)	Supports weak thumb in abducted and opposed position to allow function	Wrist 0–30° extension (for long opponens); thumb abducted and opposed, with IP left free for function	During functional activity	
C bar (Figure 15–6)	Supports weak thumb at web space to enhance opposition	Thumb abducted and opposed; should not impede digit function	During functional activity	See soft thumb loop for less rigid alternative

continued

Table 15–1 continued

Type of Splint	Purpose/Goal	Position	Wear Schedule	Other Considerations
Wrist cock-up with C bar (Figure 15–7)	In the presence of weakness, holds wrist and thumb in functional position and assists with utensil placement or support for improved function	Wrist 0–30° extension, thumb in opposition. If needed, can support index MP in slight flexion to assist with pinch	During functional activity	Use extra thermoplastic material to attach additional supports for pencil or other tools
Dynamic wrist extension splint (Figure 15–8)	Provides assistance for weak muscles or provide dynamic traction to increase joint ROM or tissue mobility	Traction must be given at a 90° angle to the joint being mobilized	For function as needed to assist with wrist extension; for dynamic mobilization, increase wear time to tolerance; gentle traction for prolonged period (8 hr.) is most beneficial	Outrigger is often made of wire, and traction is provided via a rubber band; fabrication requires considerable expense; may be difficult for child to put on correctly; needs constant monitoring for adjustments in fit and mount of pull as ROM increases
Static elbow extension splint (Figure 15–9)	Prevents elbow movement (e.g., to allow healing or to prevent self-abuse)	Elbow in 0–40° flexion (or follow MD prescription for wound healing); when used for behavioral problems, can serially increase range of flexion as behavioral control improves	In accordance with MD prescription (for wound healing) or with behavioral program	Use Ace wrap during fabrication to achieve smooth fit. May substitute Ace wrap for straps to prevent child from removing. Check skin frequently if left on for prolonged periods

Note: MP, metacarpophalangeal joint; IP, interphalangeal joint.

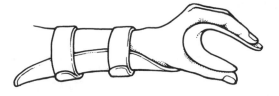

Figure 15–1 Resting Hand Splint. *Source:* Copyright © 1996, Mark L. Batshaw, M.D.

Figure 15–2 Wrist Cock-up Splint. *Source:* Copyright © 1996, Mark L. Batshaw, M.D.

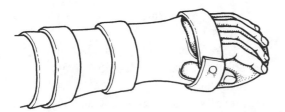

Figure 15–3 Ball Abduction Splint. *Source:* Copyright © 1996, Mark L. Batshaw, M.D.

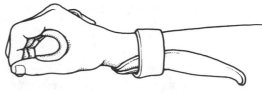

Figure 15–7 Wrist Cock-up with C Bar. *Source:* Copyright © 1996, Mark L. Batshaw, M.D.

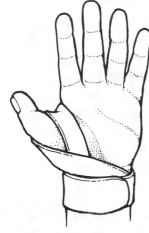

Figure 15–4 Soft Thumb Loop. *Source:* Copyright © 1996, Mark L. Batshaw, M.D.

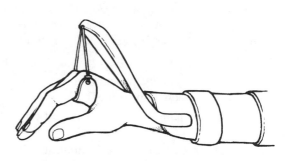

Figure 15–8 Dynamic Wrist Extension Splint. *Source:* Copyright © 1996, Mark L. Batshaw, M.D.

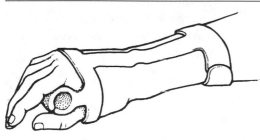

Figure 15–5 Opponens Splint. *Source:* Copyright © 1996, Mark L. Batshaw, M.D.

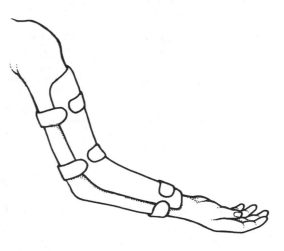

Figure 15–9 Static Elbow Extension Splint. *Source:* Copyright © 1996, Mark L. Batshaw, M.D.

Figure 15–6 C Bar. *Source:* Copyright © 1996, Mark L. Batshaw, M.D.

TRUNK AND LOWER EXTREMITY SPLINTS AND ORTHOTICS

All orthoses are identified by the joints that they control, from proximal to distal. The first letter of each joint (or body part in the case of the foot) is used to form an eponym for the orthosis. For example, an orthosis that extends from the calf to the toes is an ankle-foot orthosis or AFO.

With the exception of the solid ankle AFO, joints must be built into any orthosis that surrounds an anatomical joint. This section cannot begin to delineate all the different artificial joints available, but the various joints fall into three basic types:

1. joints that allow free action in one plane but limit motion in another
2. joints that limit allowable range of motion
3. joints that assist or resist motion in one direction

Tables 15–2 through 15–5 describe the types of orthoses by joints controlled, function of the orthoses, and indications for their use.

PRINCIPLES AND TECHNIQUES FOR FABRICATION

Some design considerations for orthotics fabrication are:

- Avoid pressure areas by increasing the area of force.
  1. Make splint trough wider or longer.
  2. Roll/round the edges to increase strength.
- Increase mechanical advantage—splint should extend two-thirds of the length of the area to be splinted to the next joint (e.g., wrist splint extends two-thirds up the forearm toward the elbow).
- Eliminate friction and provide contour.
  1. Use wide straps.
  2. Select material with appropriate conformity properties.
  3. Maintain hand arches.
- Avoid pressure over bony areas.
  1. Attend carefully to malleoli, ulnar styloid, elbow, etc.
  2. Pad only as necessary.
- Immobilize involved joint (if possible), leaving free those joints that are distal and proximal to the immobilized joint.
- Appreciate cosmesis.
  1. Attend to child's preference for color of splint materials.
  2. Decorate with stickers or drawings to increase acceptance and cooperation in wearing.

Table 15–2 Examples of Foot Orthoses (FOs)

Type	Function	Indications
Heel cup (UCBL; Figure 15–10)	To provide medial/lateral ankle stability	Foot muscle weakness Ligamentous laxity
Supramalleolar orthosis (SMO; Figure 15–11)	To provide medial/lateral ankle stability	Severe pronation or supination of the foot

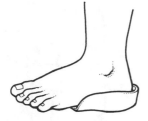

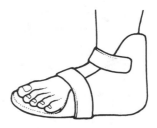

Figure 15–10 Heel Cup (UCBL). *Source:* Copyright © 1996, Mark L. Batshaw, M.D.

Figure 15–11 Supramalleolar Orthosis (SMO). *Source:* Copyright © 1996, Mark L. Batshaw, M.D.

Table 15–3 Examples of Ankle-Foot Orthoses (AFOs)

Type	Functions	Indications
AFOs	To provide ankle stability To maintain ankle range of motion To improve gait pattern and reduce energy expenditure during gait	Leg and ankle weakness Ankle muscle imbalance Foot/ankle joint instability Abnormal tone (spastic or flaccid)
Plastic solid ankle (Figure 15–12)	To maintain ankle range of motion To prevent motion during gait	Pain with movement (e.g., juvenile rheumatoid arthritis [RA]) Severe spasticity Paralysis of the foot and ankle Immediately after achilles tendon lengthening to prevent over-stretching
Plastic articulating ankle (Figure 15–13)	To provide ankle stability To allow selected motion during gait	Mild/moderate spasticity Weak dorsiflexors or foot drop
Plastic anticrouch (floor reaction; Figure 15–14)	To prevent excessive dorsiflexion in stance To reduce weight-bearing forces on the ankle (if patellar weight-bearing)	Weak quadriceps Overstretched heel cord Mild knee flexion contracture
Plastic leaf spring (Figure 15–15)	To provide a dorsiflexion assist	Weak or absent dorsiflexors
Single or double metal upright AFO	Functions like any of the plastic othoses but does not provide support for the foot	Edema Insensate foot

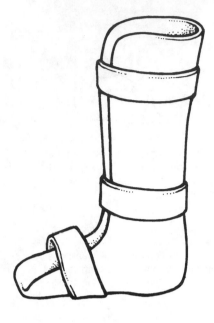

Figure 15–12 Plastic Solid Ankle. *Source:* Copyright © 1996, Mark L. Batshaw, M.D.

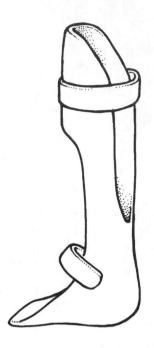

Figure 15–14 Plastic Anticrouch (Floor Reaction). *Source:* Copyright © 1996, Mark L. Batshaw, M.D.

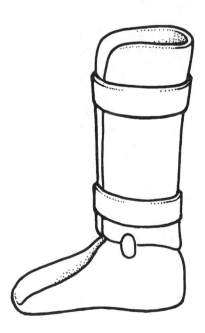

Figure 15–13 Plastic Articulating Ankle. *Source:* Copyright © 1996, Mark L. Batshaw, M.D.

Figure 15–15 Plastic Leaf Spring. *Source:* Copyright © 1996, Mark L. Batshaw, M.D.

Table 15–4 Examples of Knee-Ankle Orthoses (KAFOs) and Hip-Knee-Ankle Foot Orthoses (HKAFOs)

Type	Functions	Indications
Knee-ankle-foot orthosis (Figure 15–16) 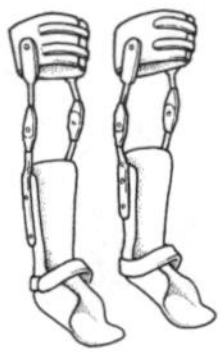 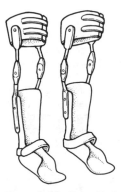	To provide joint stability (knee and ankle) To prevent deformity related to joint instability or weakness To assist in standing and/or walking To correct deformities (to a lesser extent)	Thigh and lower leg weakness or paresis (e.g., paraplegia, spina bifida) Muscular dystrophy Knee instability Knee contractures Postsurgically to maintain range of motion
Hip-knee-ankle-foot orthosis	Same as for KAFOs, with the addition of providing hip stability	Lower extremity (including hip) weakness or paralysis
KAFO with pelvic band	To control hip internal or external rotation Hip joints may be locked or unlocked	Low thoracic or high lumbar paresis
Reciprocating gait orthosis (RGO; Figure 15–17) 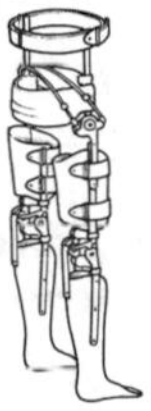 	To allow a reciprocal gait pattern in children with weak or absent hip flexors	Low thoracic or high lumbar paresis or paralysis (spinal cord injury or spina bifida)
Parapodium (Figure 15–18) 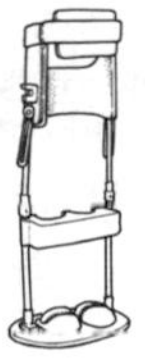	To provide lower extremity weight bearing in an erect position to increase bone density	Severe trunk and lower extremity hypotonia Lower extremity paresis in the young child (e.g., spina bifida)

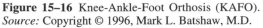

Figure 15–16 Knee-Ankle-Foot Orthosis (KAFO). *Source:* Copyright © 1996, Mark L. Batshaw, M.D.

Figure 15–17 Reciprocating Gait Orthosis (RGO). *Source:* Copyright © 1996, Mark L. Batshaw, M.D.

Figure 15–18 Parapodium. *Source:* Copyright © 1996, Mark L. Batshaw, M.D.

Table 15–5 Examples of Spinal Orthoses

Type	Functions	Indications
Soft thoracolumbosacral orthosis (TLSO)	To stabilize the thoracic spine to facilitate sitting and prevent collapse	Hypotonic trunk Paretic trunk (young patient)
Rigid TLSO Boston brace (prefabricated; Figure 15–19)	To stop progression of scoliosis To correct scoliosis To support an unstable spine To limit spinal motion	Idiopathic thoracolumbar or lumbar scoliosis (20–40°) Neuromuscular diseases Postoperatively to immobilize (e.g., postlaminectomy)
Custom-molded TLSO		
Cervicothoracolumbosacral orthosis (CTLSO) Milwaukee brace	To correct scoliosis or stop progression	Idiopathic juvenile or adolescent scoliosis Kyphosis
Cervical orthosis (CO) Philadelphia collar (Figure 15–20)	To stabilize the cervical spine To limit C-spine motion To effect mechanical unloading	Unstable neck fractures Instability or subluxation due to rheumatoid disease, tumor removal, etc.
Halo vest or Minerva jacket		

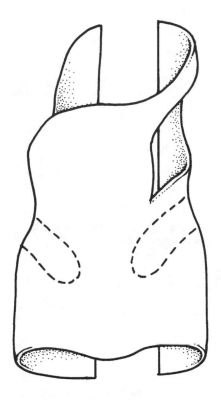

Figure 15–19 Rigid Thoracolumbosacral Orthosis (TLSO; Boston Brace). *Source:* Copyright © 1996, Mark L. Batshaw, M.D.

Figure 15–20 Cervical Orthosis (CO; Philadelphia Collar). *Source:* Copyright © 1996, Mark L. Batshaw, M.D.

PROPERTIES OF THERMOPLASTIC MATERIALS

A variety of thermoplastic materials are available for fabrication of splints and temporary orthoses. Table 15–6 presents an overview of the qualities and characteristics of commonly used materials.

Table 15–6 Properties of Selected Thermoplastic Materials

Material	Working Properties	Advantages	Disadvantages
Aquaplast: Sticky and nonsticky ⅛, 1/16, 1/32″ thick Many colors Smooth or perforated	Molds at 160–180° Cools in 2–4 min. Transparent when heated Apply lotion to skin prior to application Shrinks with cooling Elastic memory	Good molding to hand Transparency allows skin inspection Colors No fingerprints OK to reheat Good for small splints	Edges difficult to smooth Dry heat = very sticky
Ezeform: Smooth or perforated ⅛″ thick White	Molds at 170° Cools in 4–6 min.	Self-bonding Easy to handle No excessive stretch No fingerprints Good strength and rigidity	Limited drape and contour

continues

Table 15–6 continued

Material	Working Properties	Advantages	Disadvantages
Orthoplast: Smooth or perforated White	Molds at 160–180° Cools in 8–10 min. Some shrinkage when cooling	Same as for Ezeform	Limited drape and contour Susceptible to yellowing
Polyform*: ⅛″ thick White, pink, blue Smooth or perforated	Molds at 160° Cools in 3–5 min. Bonds with splint cement	Excellent contour and drape Good for small splints Edges smooth easily	Fingerprints Overheating causes increased stretching
Polyflex II: ⅛″ thick White, pink, blue Smooth or perforated	Molds at 160° Cools in 3–5 min. Bonds with solvent	Good contour and drape Edges smooth easily Good for small or large splints	Same as for Polyform

*Also available in superthin Polylite form for small, lightweight splints.

EXAMPLES OF SPLINT FABRICATION TECHNIQUE

Required supplies for splinting are

- splint unit or nonstick fry pan for heating water
- plastic net to prevent splint material from sticking to the bottom of the pan
- tongs to remove splint material from water
- thermoplastic splint material
- scissors
- Velcro
  1. self-adhesive hook for anchor
  2. nonadhesive loop for straps
  3. one- and 2-inch widths most common
- paper and pen for drawing pattern for upper extremity splints
- utility knife for cutting splint material
- stockinette for lower extremity splints
- towel to dry heated material

Optional supplies are
- heat gun
- moleskin or foam to line/pad finished splint

- Ace wrap to hold/conform splint to extremity
- icepack for rapid cooling of splint

Resting Hand Splint

To make a resting hand splint, follow these instructions:
- Making the pattern
  1. Place child's hand on paper.
  2. Mark landmarks (wrist crease, midpoint of thumb web space, second and third digit web spaces).
  3. Trace child's hand and forearm according to Figures 15–21 and 15–22.
- Cutting the material
  1. Heat water to the appropriate temperature for the selected thermoplastic material.
  2. Cut out paper pattern and place on a piece of thermoplastic material that is slightly larger than the pattern; trace around the pattern, using light marks with a pen or pencil.
  3. Place material into water; remove when soft and place on towel to dry.

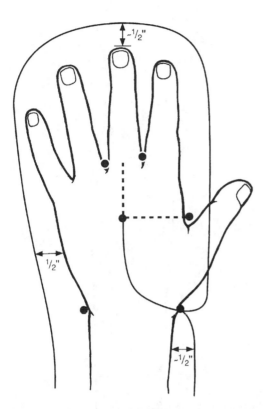

Figure 15–21 Making the Pattern for a Resting Hand Splint: Tracing the Hand and Forearm. *Source:* Copyright © 1996, Mark L. Batshaw, M.D.

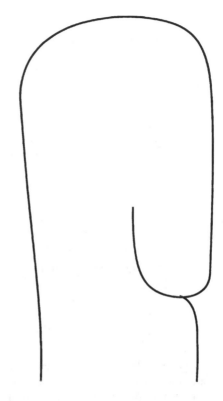

Figure 15–22 Making the Pattern for a Resting Hand Splint: The Finished Tracing. *Source:* Copyright © 1996, Mark L. Batshaw, M.D.

4. Cut, using long strokes with scissors to avoid rough edges; return to water to keep pliable until ready to mold.

• Molding the splint

1. If possible, have child position forearm upright, resting on the elbow with wrist in extension.

2. Remove splint material; dry and cool slightly to avoid burns.

3. Place splint over volar surface of forearm so that thumb piece is flush with the thumb web space and fingertips are proximal to edge of the hand piece.

4. Secure the forearm piece, using Ace wrap that is snug but not tight.

5. Position the hand piece to achieve the following measurements as possible; wrist 30-degree extension, thumb abducted and opposed, fingers flexed 70 degrees at the IPs.

6. Hold in place or Ace-wrap the hand until the material cools and becomes rigid.

7. Remove the Ace wrap and splint, maintaining the position. Run under cool water if incompletely rigid.

• Adding straps

1. Select width of strap based on size of splint. Cut seven one-inch lengths of self-adhesive Velcro hook and slightly round the corners.

2. Place bilaterally on the underside of the splint at the base of the forearm, wrist, and just distal to the MPs. Place the seventh piece below the proximal phalanx

of the thumb. Carefully heating the adhesive with the heat gun may help to improve adhesion.

3. Cut lengths of loop and slightly round the corners to prevent fraying. Place straps across base of forearm, across wrist, and across the proximal hand phalanges. Place a final strap across the proximal metacarpal of the thumb (Figure 15–23).

Solid Ankle MAFO (Molded Ankle-Foot Orthosis)

To make a solid ankle MAFO, follow these instructions:

- Cutting the material
    1. Measure the limb to determine the size of the splint material as follows: from the calf at the level of the fibular head, around the calcaneus, to the tip of the great toe for the length; circumferentially around the instep for the width (Figure 15–24).
    2. Mark the measurements on the thermoplastic material; deeply score the material along the lines with a utility knife and then bend the material back on itself along the score lines until it pops a seam; tear or cut the material apart.

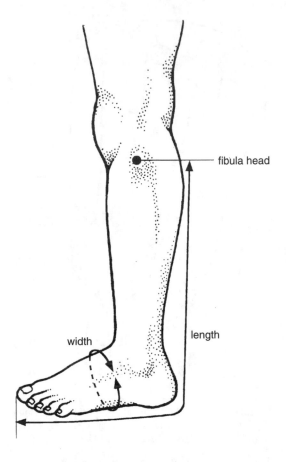

Figure 15–24 Determining the Size of the Splint Material for a Solid Ankle MAFO. *Source:* Copyright © 1996, Mark L. Batshaw, M.D.

- Padding and positioning
    1. Pad bony prominences to relieve pressure; typically padding is over the lateral malleolus, medial malleolus, and navicular; adhesive-backed plastazote or other dense foam can be applied directly to the skin (Figures 15–25 and 15–26).
    2. Replace the child's sock and add a layer of snug-fitting cotton stockinette.
    3. Position the child prone with pelvis neutral, hips extended, and knee flexed for optimal visualization of all planes of the foot; if this position cannot be

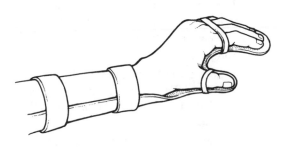

Figure 15–23 Adding Straps to a Resting Hand Splint. *Source:* Copyright © 1996, Mark L. Batshaw, M.D.

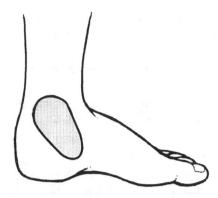

Figure 15–25 Padding of Medial Malleolus for Solid Ankle MAFO. *Source:* Copyright © 1996, Mark L. Batshaw, M.D.

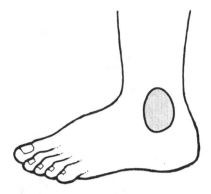

Figure 15–26 Padding of Lateral Malleolus for Solid Ankle MAFO. *Source:* Copyright © 1996, Mark L. Batshaw, M.D.

achieved or tolerated for at least 10 minutes, sitting with hips and knees at 90 degrees is an alternative—mirrors behind and on either side of the foot will improve visual access.

- Molding the splint
  1. When the splinting material is soft, remove it from the water and blot both sides dry with a towel.
  2. Draping the material over your forearm will prevent it from sticking to itself and will also allow you to determine when it is cool enough to place on the child's leg.
  3. Drape the splinting material over the child's leg and foot and pinch the edges together on the anterior surface, being careful to avoid wrinkles; wrapping the material with the foot plantarflexed and then quickly dorsiflexing the foot to the desired angle helps to prevent wrinkles at the ankle joint.
  4. Using the palmar surface of the hand and fingers (except the fingertips), mold the desired contours of the foot, beginning at the calcaneus.
  5. Mark the trim lines, using a wax pencil or washable crayon, as the splint sets.

  6. When the material is opaque, pop the seam, cut the stockinette up the front, and remove the splint.
- Finishing the splint
  1. Cut the splint along the trim lines.
  2. Smooth the edges; an easy method is to heat the edges either with a heat gun or by dipping the edges of the splint back into the splint pan to soften and then smooth them with your thumb.
  3. Flare the proximal border by heating it and gently working it into a flare while the material hardens.
  4. Replace the pads in the splint and cover with moleskin to keep them in place.
  5. Apply the straps; at the least, you will need one strap proximally and one strap across the ankle; a figure-eight strap is often used at the ankle (Figure 15–27).
  6. Post the heel to gain frontal plan stability and to minimize rocking if necessary.

PRECAUTIONS AND SPECIAL CONSIDERATIONS

The following precautions for splint use should be noted:

- Frequent inspection is required for extremities with edema or impaired sensation.
- Avoid pressure over bony prominences or nerves.
- All splints require ongoing assessment to ensure that they fit properly and are meeting the goals of therapy.
- Discontinue splint if
  1. Skin appears red or discolored for more than 15 minutes following removal.
  2. Splint causes an increase in pain or edema.
  3. Splint fit is altered due to edema, growth, or breakage of the splint.

SPLINT WEAR AND CARE

Keep splints away from sources of heat that could change the contour (e.g., in a warm car or on a sunny windowsill). Wash the splint in cool, soapy water. Wash straps by hand and line-dry. A stockinette may be worn if excessive perspiration occurs.

Figure 15–27 Applying Figure Eight Strap to Solid Ankle MAFO. *Source:* Copyright © 1996, Mark L. Batshaw, M.D.

SUGGESTED READINGS

Anderson, L.J., and L.M. Anderson. 1988. Hand splinting for infants in the intensive care and special care nurseries. *American Journal of Occupational Therapy* 42:395.

Barr, N. 1978. *The hand: Principles and techniques of simple splint making in rehabilitation.* Boston: Butterworth Publishing.

Bora, F. 1986. *The pediatric upper extremity: Diagnosis and management.* Philadelphia: W.B. Saunders.

Cusick, B. 1990. *Progressive casting and splinting for lower extremity deformities in children with neuromotor dysfunction.* Tucson, Ariz.: Therapy Skill Builders.

Fess, E. 1987. *Hand splinting: Principles and methods.* 2nd ed. St. Louis: C.V. Mosby Co.

Gardner, R.A., and M. Broman. 1979. The Purdue Pegboard: Normative data on 1334 school children. *Journal of Clinical and Child Psychology* 1:156–162.

Hunter, J., et al. 1990. *Rehabilitation of the hand.* St. Louis: C.V. Mosby Co.

Jebsen, R.H., et al. 1969. An objective and standardized test of hand function. *Archives of Physical Medicine and Rehabilitation* 50:311–319.

Malick, M. 1972. *Manual on static splinting.* Pittsburgh, Pa.: Harmaville Rehabilitation Center.

Malick, M. 1978. *Manual on dynamic splinting with thermoplastic materials.* Pittsburgh, Pa.: Harmaville Rehabilitation Center.

Mathoiwetz, F., et al. 1986. The Purdue Pegboard: Norms for 14-to-19 year olds. *American Journal of Occupational Therapy* 40:174–179.

Melvin, J. 1982. *Rheumatic diseases: Occupational therapy and rehabilitation.* Philadelphia: F.A. Davis Co.

Redfern, J., ed. 1980. *Orthotics etcetera.* 2nd ed. Baltimore: Williams & Wilkins.

Redfern, J., ed. 1987. *Orthotics.* Philadelphia: Hanley & Belfus.

Taylor, N., et al. 1973. Evaluation of hand function in children. *Archives of Physical Medicine and Rehabilitation* 54:129–135.

Tiffin, J. 1968. *Purdue Pegboard examiner manual.* Chicago: Science Research Associates.

Trombly, C.A. 1989. *Occupational therapy for physical dysfunction.* 3rd ed. Baltimore: Williams & Wilkins.

SERIAL AND INHIBITIVE CASTING

Sandra M. McGee and Lesley A. Geyer

Purpose: to discuss the appropriate selection and use of serial and inhibitive casts to manage hypertonia and muscle and soft tissue contractures in the upper and lower extremities.

Inhibitive casting can be effective in temporarily reducing muscle tone in hypertonic muscle groups; however, the long-term effects are less apparent. The concept behind inhibitive casting is that the casted limb position inhibits the influence of abnormal postural and tonic reflex patterns. In addition, for the lower extremity, casting provides positional stability in stance, as well as a more normal proprioceptive sense of standing posture.

Serial corrective casting of muscles and soft tissue in a lengthened state can be effective in increasing joint range of motion and functional movement. Casts are applied, removed, and then reapplied successively to gain extensibility in the soft tissues surrounding the casted joint. The increased range of motion at the joint is gradual enough to allow for cellular physiologic changes to occur, so that the soft tissues actually grow by the addition of sarcomeres.

SPECIAL CONSIDERATIONS

Casting is used to manage muscle and soft tissue contracture resulting from

- persistent hypertonus
- muscle imbalance due to paralysis
- prolonged immobilization following traumatic injury
- motion limitation caused by joint disease (arthritis, hemophilia, etc.)

A cast should not be applied when there is

- a skin problem that requires skin to be left exposed (open wound or sore)
- progressive edema

- heterotopic ossification, or formation of bone in an abnormal location; symptoms of this condition include inflammatory changes (redness, pain, warmth, swelling, and possible fever) and decreasing joint range of motion in the involved area or joint
- static hypoextensibility in cerebral palsy due to trophic regulation (muscle growth does not keep pace with bone growth) rather than due to persistent hypertonus; casting a child with this condition is not harmful, but it is not beneficial in increasing joint range of motion
- an unhealed fracture
- need for easy accessibility of the limb(s) to administer medication; monitor vital signs, etc.
- allergic reaction to casting materials
- joint contracture in children with cerebral palsy that is not associated with persistent hypertonus or an imbalance of muscle activity around the joint; in these children, the hypoextensibility of the muscles is due to a defect in trophic regulation, so that muscle growth does not keep up with bone growth; casting a joint with this type of contracture is not harmful but will not result in increased range of motion

Other factors to be considered are

- child's medical stability
- child/family's acceptance of casting
- effect of temporary loss of functional use of the extremity
- child/caregiver's ability to monitor the casted extremity, seek medical attention if problems occur, and be compliant with follow-up
- effect of casting on treatment provided by other disciplines (aquatic therapy, gait training, etc.)

COMPARISON OF CASTING MATERIALS

Table 15–7 lists advantages and disadvantages of different casting materials.

Table 15–7 Comparison of Casting Materials

Material	Advantages	Disadvantages
Cast Padding		
Cotton	Tears well Is thinner, gives better fitting cast	Absorbs and holds moisture
Synthetic	Does not absorb and hold moisture	Does not tear as easily Thicker, gives greater opportunity for cast slippage
Casting Tape		
Plaster	Allows for long working time Molds nicely into body contours Can be removed by soaking extremity in one gallon water to one cup of vinegar Additional tape can be added and will adhere to hardened cast	Messy to work with Dries slowly (can take up to 48 hours to reach maximum load-bearing capacity depending on humidity in the environment) Not as strong as fiberglass, is heavier Cracks easily, weakens when finished cast gets wet Finishing materials don't adhere well Must be removed for x-rays
Fiberglass	Is strong and durable yet lightweight. Is less messy to work with (must wear gloves, as resin is tacky until dry) Dries quickly (approximately 1 hour to reach maximum load-bearing capacity) Finished cast does not weaken if it becomes wet. Finishing materials adhere well Is x-ray translucent	Is tacky until dry Does not mold to body contours as well as plaster Material hardens quickly, allowing less time to work Additional tape will not adhere to hardened cast

PROCEDURES FOR APPLYING/ REMOVING/FINISHING CASTS

To apply a cast:

1. Carefully check the skin for any areas of breakdown. Do not cast over open sores. If a pressure area is noted upon removal of a cast but the skin is intact, that area may be protected by foam padding or other skin protecting material before re-casting.

2. Position the patient to achieve optimum range and view of the area to be casted. For upper extremity casting, sitting or side-lying position may be used. For ankles, prone or sitting is the preferred position. Protect work surface and patient with sheet.

3. Cover the extremity with close-fitting stockinette, and specifically pad bony prominences and ends of area to be casted with two extra layers of padding. (Additional padding with self-adhesive foam may also be beneficial over bony prominences.) Wrap extremity with cast padding twice, overlapping by half a layer each wrap. Extra padding may be added along the future cast cut lines.

4. Activate plaster or fiberglass in water according to package directions. Apply cast by wrapping material in diagonal fashion around limb, overlapping by one-half to

two-thirds of a layer each wrap. Mold closely, but do not pull material tightly. The cast should be sufficiently tight so that two fingers can be snugly inserted into either end of the cast. A cast that is too tight can cause tissue constriction; a cast that is too loose will tend to slip. Once wrapping is completed, hold the extremity at the desired position until the material is set. For the initial cast, do not force excessive range, but cast at comfortable "resting" angle.

5. Leave the cast on for five to ten days, unless emergency removal is indicated (see section below).

6. Remove the cast (as per procedures below). Carefully check skin for any signs of pressure. Gently mobilize joint(s) and recast.

7. Repeat the procedure until the desired range of motion has been achieved (do not try to stretch too fast; it can take several weeks). Once the desired range is reached, apply a final holding cast for five to ten days (bivalving may be sufficient if tone is not too high).

8. If the desired reduction in muscle tone or increase in joint range of motion has not been obtained after the application of seven casts, casting should be discontinued (but may be resumed at a later date). Discontinuation is also recommended if the static positioning of the cast seems to increase stiffness of the joint or if range of motion does not increase by more than 5 degrees with a single cast.

To remove a cast:

1. Position the child so that the cast is supported and cut line is easily accessible. Cover the supporting surface with a sheet or towel. Provide earplugs or foam earphones (for noise reduction) and goggles (for eye protection) for the patient and yourself.

2. Before cutting, check to be sure the cast cutter blade is sharp and securely fastened.

3. Mark cut lines. Maintain a firm grasp on the cast and cut into the cast. The proper method is to cut into the cast, lift the saw up, and cut into the cast again slightly further down. (Do not drag the saw *along* the cast: due to friction caused by the resistance of the material against the blade, heat will develop on the blade and may burn the skin.) To avoid burns, the saw should be turned off occasionally to allow the blade to cool.

4. Once both sides of the cast have been cut, use a cast spreader bar to separate the halves. Cut the cast padding with surgical scissors and remove the cast.

To finish a bivalved cast:

1. Padding and stockinette may be removed and replaced.

2. Tape is used to finish the edges of the bivalved cast.

3. Velcro straps may be applied or Ace wrap may be used, and the finished cast may be worn intermittently as a splint to maintain the range of motion that has been gained.

If any of the following occur, the cast should be removed as soon as possible:

1. any change in the cast (cracking, softening, stains bleeding through)

2. bad odor from the extremity

3. distal extremity becoming cold or swollen or turns bluish

4. child complaining of numbness or tingling in the casted extremity

5. change in skin around the edges of the cast (redness or breakdown that is not relieved with additional padding)

TYPES OF CASTS

The types of casts are as follows:

- *Full arm cast:* This cast is indicated for individuals with contractures in the elbow and wrist joints, as well as for those with supination or pronation limitations. It may

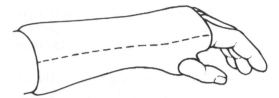

Figure 15–36 Wrist/Metacarpophalangeal Cast with Thumb IP Joint Free. *Source:* Copyright © 1996, Mark L. Batshaw, M.D.

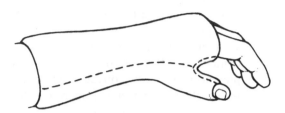

Figure 15–37 Wrist/Metacarpophalangeal Cast with Thumb Enclosed. *Source:* Copyright © 1996, Mark L. Batshaw, M.D.

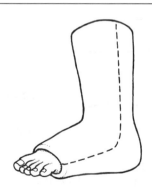

Figure 15–38 Ankle Cast with Markings for Bivalve. *Source:* Copyright © 1996, Mark L. Batshaw, M.D.

tures. For severe contractures (>40 degrees), wedge casting may be considered (Figure 15–39).

- *Dropout knee cylinder cast:* This cast is used with individuals with knee flexion contractures without hypertonicity. It is most often used with children with juvenile arthritis or hemophilia when total immobility would increase stiffness. If one cuts out the anterior tibial portion of the cast, the child can continue to work on active knee extension while further flexion is blocked. Cutting out the anterior femoral portion of the cast allows the weight of the cast on the distal portion of the leg to assist with hamstring stretching in the prone position. This should not be used when there is tibial subluxation (Figures 15–40 and 15–41).

- *Wedge casting:* Wedging is used with cylindrical elbow or knee casts when multiple casts will be needed to achieve the desired range of motion. The initial fiberglass cast is applied in the usual manner but with additional padding over the joint. Instead of removing the cast, however, in seven to ten days, the cast is cut approximately three-fourths of the circumference at the joint line (Figure 15–42). Pressure is applied on each side of the cut line to separate the cast and increase the joint range of motion. Two small wooden blocks are placed in the opening created in the cast as far apart as possible (Figure 15–43). The wedged area is then cast over to maintain integrity of the

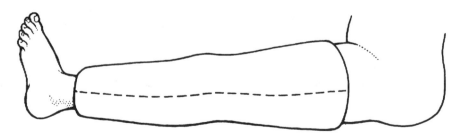

Figure 15–39 Cylinder Knee Cast with Markings for Bivalve. *Source:* Copyright © 1996, Mark L. Batshaw, M.D.

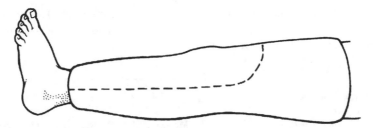

Figure 15–40 Dropout Knee Cylinder with Dropout of Tibial Portion. *Source:* Copyright © 1996, Mark L. Batshaw, M.D.

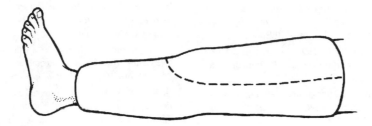

Figure 15–41 Dropout Knee Cylinder with Dropout of Femoral Portion. *Source:* Copyright © 1996, Mark L. Batshaw, M.D.

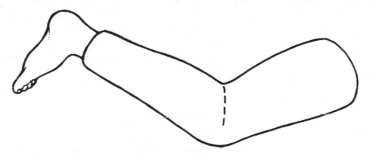

Figure 15–42 Wedge Cast: Cut Lines Three-Quarters of the Way around Cast. *Source:* Copyright © 1996, Mark L. Batshaw, M.D.

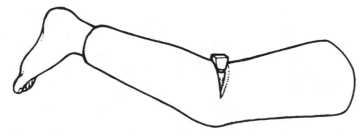

Figure 15–43 Wedge Cast: Open Wedge around Cast with Medial and Lateral Blocks. *Source:* Copyright © 1996, Mark L. Batshaw, M.D.

cast. Wedging can be done once, and then the entire cast must be removed and reapplied. This new cast can then be wedged the following week. This process decreases the time and expense incurred with serial casting.

SUGGESTED READINGS

Boehme, R. 1988. *Improving upper body control.* Tucson, Ariz.: Therapy Skill Builders.

Booth, B.J., et al. 1983. Serial casting for the management of spasticity in the head injured adult. *Physical Therapy* 63:1960–1966.

Cusick, B.D. 1990. *Progressive casting and splinting for lower extremity deformities in children with neuromotor dysfunction.* Tucson, Ariz.: Therapy Skill Builders.

Glenn, M.B., and J. Whyte, eds. 1990. *The practical management of spasticity in children and adults.* Philadelphia: Lea & Febiger.

Hill, J. 1994. The effects of casting on upper extremity motor disorders after brain injury. *American Journal of Occupational Therapy* 48:219–224.

King, T.I. 1982. Plaster splinting as a means of reducing elbow flexor spasticity: A case study. *American Journal of Occupational Therapy* 36:671–673.

Law, M., et al. 1991. Neurodevelopmental therapy and upper-extremity inhibitive casting for children with cerebral palsy. *Developmental Medicine and Child Neurology* 33:379–387.

Massagli, T.L. 1991. Spasticity and its management in children. *Physical Medicine and Rehabilitation Clinics of North America* 2:867–885.

Occupational Therapy Division, University of Michigan Hospitals, Department of Physical Medicine and Rehabilitation, producer. 1986. *Inhibitory casting of the upper extremities for occupational therapists.* Rockville, Md.: American Occupational Therapy Association. Film.

Smith, L.H., and S.R. Harris. 1985. Upper extremity inhibitive casting for a child with cerebral palsy. *Physical and Occupational Therapy in Pediatrics* 5, no. 1:71–78.

Tali, A.C., et al. 1990. Effect of serial casting for the prevention of equinus in patients with acute head injury. *Archives of Physical Medicine Rehabilitation* 71:310–312, 387.

Watt, J., et al. 1986. A prospective study of inhibitive casting as an adjunct to physiotherapy for cerebral-palsied children. *Developmental Medicine and Child Neurology* 28:480–488.

Yasukawa, A. 1990. Upper extremity casting: Adjunct treatment for a child with cerebral palsy hemiplegia. *American Journal of Occupational Therapy* 44:840–884.

ADDITIONAL RESOURCES

Suppliers of Cast Material (Refer to Appendix C for addresses/phone numbers.)

Smith & Nephew Rolyan Inc.

North Coast Medical, Inc.

Fred Sammons, Inc.

Johnson & Johnson

3M Health Care

Carapace, Inc.

Stryker Instruments (cast cutting supplies only)

Chapter 16

Communication Skills

SPEECH AND LANGUAGE STIMULATION ACTIVITIES

Marleen Anne Baron

Purpose: to present a sample of developmentally appropriate speech and language stimulation activities for the child with delayed and/or impaired communication skills.

Children with early speech and language delays may be at risk for later and more significant developmental disabilities affecting school performance. Therefore attention to communication delays and impairments is important for a child's overall cognitive and social growth and well-being. Though direct intervention is often appropriate, it is necessary to remember that communication is an interactive process and that learning occurs naturally throughout the child's day. Optimal language learning will occur if families, teachers, and other significant caregivers can be integral members of the therapy process. It is important for professionals to teach these adults how to provide appropriate speech and language stimulation techniques.

Children with suspected developmental delays can benefit from increased language stimulation techniques. Though many families and caregivers intuitively know how to encourage language growth, specific strategies can further facilitate vocabulary acquisition, comprehension, and analytic thinking. Some children with serious developmental delays are abandoned without the expectation that they can benefit from intervention. There is also the population of children with serious physical or neurological disabilities who have normal or near-normal cognitive abilities, yet are treated as if intellectually limited. It is important to recognize and understand each child's physical, mental, and developmental status when implementing language stimulation strategies. It is also important to remember that although adults can maximize a child's learning, cognitive-linguistic performance cannot exceed an individual's intellectual abilities.

The following are general guidelines for early speech/language development activities:

1. Try to attach a pleasurable feeling to speech. For many children, attempting to

communicate has become associated with failure.

2. Reward the child's attempts to speak. Smile and respond warmly, even if you do not understand every word.

3. Do not interrupt the child's speech attempts.

4. Give the child your full attention whenever possible.

5. Use a moderate rate of speech; do not speak too rapidly.

6. Do not use "baby talk"; speak simply, clearly, and slowly.

7. Do not talk about the child's communication difficulties in front of him or her.

8. Speak to the child as much as possible. Verbal stimulation is of great importance, even if the child does not respond and has no language.

9. Use developmentally appropriate materials and toys during language stimulation activities. (Suggested activities and materials by developmental sequence can be found in Chapter 19.)

10. Remember that hesitations, such as sound or word repetitions, in a young child's speech attempts are often normal and not always indicative of stuttering.

11. Remember: parents are the models children copy. Almost everything parents say will be heard and interpreted in some way by their child.

12. Eye contact is an important part of the communication process. Try to look at the child whenever he or she speaks to you.

13. Parents, teachers, and other health professionals should seek professional guidance whenever they are concerned about a child's speech and language skills.

The following are specific techniques for stimulating language:

1. *Self-talk:* The adult uses a short sentence to describe what he or she is doing while the child watches. This technique is most appropriate for children 12 to 24 months of age.

2. *Parallel talk:* The adult uses a short phrase or sentence as he or she observes the child at play and describes what the child is doing, hearing, or seeing.

3. *Expansion:* The adult expands the child's immature utterance into a more sophisticated form in a natural, noncorrective way. The adult can then add an additional piece of information in a second phrase or short sentence.

4. *Indirect language stimulation:* The adult provides labels for familiar objects, people, and actions without requiring the child to say anything.

5. *Direct language stimulation:* The adult asks questions that require a response from the child. The questions should be formulated to avoid a yes/no response.

6. *Reading:* Reading a picture or storybook daily, even from six months of age, is a pleasurable interactive activity. It also enhances a child's listening and vocabulary skills. As the child matures, increasing the child's participation in reading stories is fun and stimulating.

7. *Imitation and modeling:* If the child incorrectly says a sound or phrase, the adult correctly repeats the utterance without forcing the child to say the words correctly.

The following list suggests language stimulation activities for children at different age levels. These activities apply to children who are developing typically except in the areas of speech and language. For children who have developmental delay, it is appropriate to select activities from the age range in which the child is functioning.

• Birth to six months

1. Talk in a soothing voice.

2. Cuddle and hold the baby closely.

3. Talk often to the baby during daily activities.

4. Imitate the baby's vocalizations.

5. Look at the baby as much as possible. Infants enjoy visually scanning adults' faces.

6. Provide visual and auditory stimulation in the form of mobiles, music, and bright toys and pictures.

7. Be animated. Use gestures and facial expressions.

8. Provide the baby with a variety of safe and interesting toys.

9. Label objects and people in the home environment.

10. Sing softly and often.

- 6 to 12 months

1. Use short phrases and sentences. Repeat these over and over, giving the baby time to respond.

2. Talk throughout the day, describing activities in the environment.

3. Use gestures and animated facial expressions when speaking.

4. Read daily. Picture books and magazines are an excellent source of vocabulary expansion.

5. Do not pressure the baby into repeating sounds and words.

6. Do not correct the child's speech attempts; instead, repeat the word correctly.

7. Allow the baby uninterrupted time to play with his or her vocalizations.

8. Imitate the baby's movements and utterances.

9. Encourage imitation and turn-taking games. Use nursery rhymes and finger-plays, such as patty-cake, peekaboo, Eency Weency Spider.

10. Don't pressure the baby to perform. Encourage and reward early attempts at communication.

- 12 to 18 months

1. Speak simply and clearly, in a way that the child can understand.

2. Describe out loud what you are doing, seeing, hearing, and feeling.

3. Describe out loud what the child is hearing, seeing, feeling, and doing.

4. Read to the child daily. Parents can make this part of the bedtime routine.

5. Allow the child to watch children's television programs such as *Sesame Street*. Parents and child can watch these educational programs together; specific episodes and segments can be a springboard for further language discussion and expansion.

6. Continue to provide large, safe toys of bright colors and varied textures. Demonstrate how objects and toys work by taking them apart and putting them back together again. Talk about the activity as you do it.

7. Encourage listening skills. Talk about sounds that objects and things make; provide music and tapes.

- 18 months to two years

1. Continue reading books with large colorful pictures. Allow the child to "fill in" some words as he or she becomes familiar with the text.

2. Use parallel and self-talk throughout the day.

3. Repeat words over and over.

4. Do not correct the child's speech, but provide correct models. Be a patient listener whenever the child is speaking.

5. As the child begins to use single words and short phrases, use expansion techniques.

6. Take the child on excursions. Talk about your experiences at the supermarket, doctor's office, playground, zoo, and bank.

7. Listening to stories, records, and tapes will increase attention and listening skills.

8. Encourage creative play. Use pots and pans to make drums and have a parade.

Make a house with blankets and pillows.

9. Begin to ask questions that require a simple one-word answer (e.g., "Do you want a cookie or cracker?").

10. Play games that involve following simple directions.

- Two years to three years

1. Continue reading time. Engage the child in this activity. Talk about the story; ask questions. Discuss the book. Talk *with* the child and not *to* him or her.

2. Expand the use of nursery rhymes, songs, and rhyming games.

3. Provide play activities with other children to develop peer interactions.

4. Continue parallel and self-talk. Use expansions whenever possible.

5. Praise the child's speech efforts. Model correct productions, but do not force accurate imitations.

6. Be a patient listener, even if you do not understand what the child is saying.

- Three to four years

1. Continue to use expansion techniques. Try to develop what the child says by adding new words, grammar, and concepts.

2. Converse with the child. Do not underestimate what a child knows by this age.

3. Ask questions that will stimulate language associations, similarities, and differences.

4. Talk about daily events and activities.

5. Talk about shapes, colors, and numbers.

6. Provide peer socialization experiences.

7. Remember that the child will be able to understand more than he or she is able to express.

- Four to five years

1. Talk to the child in much the same way you would speak to an adult, but simplify complex sentence constructions.

2. Continue to provide daily language experiences. Children of this age enjoy being part of household and classroom routines, and these routines provide numerous opportunities for vocabulary and concept expansion: for example, measuring ingredients and performing the sequential steps in cooking, sorting foods by category, and sorting clothes by colors.

3. To expand vocabulary and conceptual skills, work on descriptive words, verbal analogies, and similarities and differences. Children of this age enjoy classification and categorization of activities.

4. Reinforce and encourage the child's creativity and flair for drama. Provide opportunities for "dress-up" and pretend play.

5. Children at this age begin to comprehend time sequences. Talk about events in the past and future. Refer to the time of day and how long the child must wait for a specific event to occur.

6. As the child's attention and listening skills mature, read longer stories. Discuss the stories; have the child devise his or her own story.

7. Play tabletop games to encourage turn taking and comprehension of rules. These games also provide numerous opportunities for vocabulary and concept acquisition.

8. To improve dialogue and conversational skills, play act, create and complete stories, design commercials, and engage in imaginary monologues and dialogues. Role-playing activities, such as store clerk and customer, are helpful.

9. Children of this age frequently show an increased interest in numbers and letters. Activities that stimulate these skills should be presented in a nondemanding and nonthreatening format,

as maturity and reading readiness are very different for each child.

- Five to six years

    1. Children of this age are competent conversationalists, although they may exhibit mild and inconsistent grammatical and articulation errors. Speak to the child as you would to another adult, but remember that the child's comprehension is greater than his or her verbal abilities.

    2. Encourage the child to ask questions and express his or her feelings.

    3. Allow the child to obtain books of his or her choice. Children should have the opportunity to make frequent trips to the library.

    4. Provide opportunities for the child to learn songs, nursery rhymes, and stories by memory.

    5. To improve problem-solving and verbal reasoning skills, help the child to recognize, discuss, and correct absurdities heard in oral material and to understand verbal humor.

    6. To improve inferential thinking skills, help the child solve riddles and play guessing games.

    7. Parent-teacher collaboration and cooperation are essential to ensure a child's success in school.

SUGGESTED READINGS

Barach, C. 1983. *Help me say it: A parent's guide to speech problems.* New York: Harper & Row.

Brooks, M., and D. Engmann-Hartung. 1976. *Your child's speech and language: Guidelines for parents.* Austin, Tex.: PRO-ED.

Hatten, J.T., and P.W. Hatten. 1975. *Natural language: A clinician-guided program for parents of language-delayed children.* Tucson, Ariz.: Communication Skill Builders, Inc.

Reidlich, C.E., and M.E. Herzfeld. 1983. *0–3 years: An early language curriculum.* Moline Ill.: Linguisystems, Inc.

Schneider, M.J. 1979. *A guide to communication development in pre-school children: Birth–5 years.* Danville, Ill.: Interstate Printers and Publishers, Inc.

U.S. Children's Bureau. *Your child from 1 to 6.* Publication No. 30. Washington, D.C.: Government Printing Office.

ADDITIONAL RESOURCE

American Speech-Language-Hearing Association, 10801 Rockville Pike, Rockville, MD 20852, Tel.: (301) 897-5700.

ALTERNATIVE COMMUNICATION SYSTEMS

Laura Fus-Rowe

Purpose: to discuss the social context of communication and the importance of facilitating interactions between children with language disabilities and their communication partners and to describe low-technology forms of alternative communication (specifically sign language, picture communication boards, object communication, and the Picture-Exchange Communication System) that address the needs of those children who have significant developmental delays and are nonverbal.

Many speech/language pathologists and developmental psychologists (e.g., Bruner 1975) have suggested that there exist inseparable bonds among communication, social interactions, and learning. A child's first use of communication, promoting joint and shared interactions with a caregiver, has a social basis. Communication continues to occupy the key role in socialization and learning throughout a child's development (Dowrick 1986). Social interaction and communication are in a reciprocal relationship: a child acquires a form of communication through his or her interactions with people in the environment and uses communication to interact socially. Thus the ability to partake in social interactions must be considered when determining and establishing a child's form of communication.

Consideration of the social context of communication is especially important for children with developmental disabilities. Communication is the means by which a child can interact with others in his or her society. If a child has disabilities, especially those beyond a speech impairment, identifying a means by which he or she can interact with the environment is essential in attaining educational and social goals. A child with disabilities may be set apart from peers due to his or her special needs; inclusion of the social aspects of communication will improve interactions in this facet of the child's life.

There are four possible social purposes of an interaction: expression of needs and wants, information transfer, social closeness, and social etiquette (Light 1988):

1. *Expression of wants and needs*—to regulate the behavior of another as a means to fulfill needs and wants. The focus of interaction is to attain desired objects or to influence the behavior of others.

2. *Information transfer*—to share information. The focus of the interaction is to attain information.

3. *Social closeness*—to establish, maintain, or develop personal relationships. The focus of interaction is to form interpersonal relationships.

4. *Social etiquette*—to conform to social conventions of politeness. The focus of interaction is to use social convention.

The nonverbal child requires a communication system that will provide a means to express each of these purposes in order to interact with the environment. The selection, development, and use of an alternative communication system must also take into account other aspects of a child, such as cognition, motoric abilities, and communication partners.

CASE STUDY

Anna was an 18-month-old child who was nonverbal secondary to a tracheostomy. Developmental testing revealed deficits in expressive language and gross motor skills; however, her receptive language and cognitive skills were age appropriate. Because of the large gap between her expressive and receptive language skills, Anna was limited in her interactions with others. She could smile, blink playfully, participate in gestural games (e.g., peekaboo, patty-cake), and use simple gestures (e.g., wave hi and bye, blow kiss). But Anna began to use a gesture consistently that no one understood (two hands tapping her cheek), and it became apparent that Anna was having difficulty interacting socially with her environment because of her expressive language limitations. She was beginning to show frustration in her inability to be understood, and it was necessary to investigate an alternative form of communication for her.

In determining which alternative form of communication would be most beneficial for Anna, special consideration was given to her social skills, as she was a child who thrived on social interactions. Sign language was chosen for Anna on the basis of her abilities and needs. She was able to fulfill the social purposes of interactions through the use of signs: attainment of a desired object, influencing the behavior of another, sharing information, and actively participating in interactions to establish relationships. Cognitively, Anna's receptive language skills enabled her to understand the relationship between a sign and its meaning. Motorically, Anna's skills were adequate to produce manual signs. Anna also had a limited number of communication partners who needed to learn her signs.

Anna was very successful with sign language and was able to participate in, as well as initiate, social interactions. She quickly learned conventional signs and even taught her communication partners some of her original signs—two hands tapping her cheek translated to "I want a kiss." Anna was no longer frustrated by social interactions simply because she was nonvocal subsequent to her tracheostomy.

TECHNIQUES

Four types of alternative communication systems—sign language, a picture communication board, object communication, and the Picture-Exchange Communication System (PECS)—are described in terms of how they meet the social goals of communication, as well as their selection criteria and procedures for use. It is important to encourage and reinforce any vocalizations or attempts at communication.

Sign Language

Sign language is a system of communication through the use of designated hand gestures. It fulfills four social goals:

1. sharing information with another person about feelings and desires
2. using a conventional or designated sign to attain the item or activity desired
3. promoting the establishment, maintenance, and development of personal relationships
4. attaining attention of communication partner before initiating request

Selection criteria are

1. cognitive ability at nine-month level or greater
2. sufficient manual dexterity to produce signs
3. availability of at least one communication partner who knows the signs

Procedures for using sign language are as follows:

1. Select vocabulary appropriate for the individual child's setting. A child who is in an acute care hospital would need different signs than a child who is home with his or her parents.
2. Select vocabulary based on a child's cognitive level. A child functioning at the two-year level may need only one sign, "drink," for juice, milk, and water, whereas a child at the three-year level may need three separate signs.
3. Select vocabulary based on a child's motoric abilities. A child with use of only one hand has to have bimanual signs amended. Also, a child with poor manual dexterity may be limited to open-hand signs. Dunn (1982) described a methodology for analyzing the motoric difficulty of various signs along with therapeutic strategies for promoting motor skills prerequisite to using sign language.
4. Train the child to use the signs within all aspects of his or her day. The child should spontaneously use the sign at the appropriate time: for example, sign "eat" when it is time to sit at dinner.
5. If the child does not spontaneously sign, provide a verbal prompt: for example, "If you are hungry for dinner, sign 'eat.'"
6. If the child does not sign after the prompt, provide a model: for example, "Sign 'eat'" (modeling the sign).
7. If the child does not sign after the model, provide the child with physical assistance to form the sign.
8. Reinforce the use of signs by providing what has been requested and praising the use of signs, regardless of the level of prompting required.

Picture Communication Board

The picture communication board is a form of communication using a series of pictures on a board to represent a child's feelings and desires. It fulfills four social goals:

1. sharing information with another person about feelings and desires
2. indicating desire by pointing to a specific picture or series of pictures on the communication board
3. promoting the establishment, maintenance, and development of personal relationships
4. attaining the attention of communication partner before initiating requests

Selection criteria are

1. cognitive ability to associate pictures or symbols with meaning
2. motoric ability to point to the picture, using a finger, hand, or prosthetic device (e.g., head stick)
3. visual ability to see and differentiate pictures
4. continual availability of communication board (may be difficult for an ambulatory child)
5. communication partner who knows the subsequent response for each picture

Procedures for using the communication board are as follows:

1. Choose a vocabulary that can be represented in pictures and will enable the child to request desired items or activities.
2. Determine the level of abstraction for the pictures (e.g., Polaroid photos, color pictures, black and white pictures, drawings of the items, Bliss symbols). Photographs are the least abstract form of picture, and Bliss symbols are the most abstract. Selection of the type of picture will depend on the child's ability to associate the picture with the subsequent result (e.g., understanding that pointing to the picture of a cup will lead to a drink of water).
3. Train the child to use the pictures to request the item or activity during all aspects of his or her day. The child should

spontaneously point to a picture at the appropriate time (e.g., point to the cup when thirsty).
4. If the child does not spontaneously indicate the picture, ask him or her to point to the picture.
5. If the child does not indicate the picture after the verbal prompt, model pointing to the picture and the subsequent response.
6. If the child does not indicate the picture after the model, provide physical assistance to point to picture.
7. Reinforce the use of the picture communication board by providing the appropriate response and praising use of the board, regardless of the level of prompting required.

Object Communication

Object communication is the use of objects, actual size or miniatures, to indicate a child's desire for an item or activity. It fulfills four social goals:

1. sharing information with another person regarding desire for an item or activity
2. indicating desires by pointing to or picking up an object that is among other objects
3. promoting the establishment, maintenance, and development of personal relationships
4. attaining attention of communication partner to initiate requests, unless object can be handed to partner without need for prior attention

Selection criteria are

1. cognitive ability to associate object with activity (e.g., spoon $\rightarrow$ eating, audio cassette $\rightarrow$ listen to music); objects are more salient than pictures

2. motoric ability to point to an object or pick up an object
3. visual ability to see objects or ability to identify objects by touch
4. objects' ready availability to the child; this may be difficult if the child is ambulatory
5. communication partner who knows the subsequent response when an object is indicated

Children with autism who do not respond well to social interactions may use this system since prior attention is not necessary if the child can bring the object to the communication partner.

The procedures for using object communication are as follows:

1. Choose a vocabulary that can be represented by objects and will enable the child to request desired items or activities.
2. Choose objects based on the level of association that the child will be able to comprehend (e.g., small plastic cup vs. tippy cup with juice to represent a drink of juice).
3. Train the child to use the objects to request the item or activity during all aspects of his or her day. The child should spontaneously indicate the object at the appropriate time (e.g., pick up the cup when thirsty).
4. If the child does not spontaneously indicate the object, provide a verbal prompt to point to or pick up the object.
5. If the child does not indicate the object after the verbal prompt, provide modeling to point to or pick up the object, and the subsequent response.
6. If the child does not indicate the object after the model, provide physical assistance to point to or pick up the object.
7. Reinforce the use of object communication by providing the appropriate response and praising the use of objects, regardless of the level of prompting required.

Picture-Exchange Communication System (Bondy and Frost 1994)

In the Picture-Exchange Communication System, the child *gives* a picture of a desired item to a communication partner in exchange for a desired item or activity. The system fulfills four social goals:

1. sharing information with another person about feelings and desires
2. indicating desired item by giving appropriate picture to communication partner
3. promoting the establishment, maintenance, and development of personal relationships
4. initiating communication for a specific outcome within a social context

Selection criteria are

1. cognitive ability to associate pictures/symbols with meaning
2. motoric ability to pick up picture and physically hand it to the communication partner
3. visual ability to see and differentiate pictures
4. availability of the individual pictures (not permanently placed on a board); this may be difficult for an active child
5. communication partner who knows subsequent response when a picture is handed over

Children with autism who do not socially interact except to obtain a desired outcome would benefit from this method.

Procedures for using the Picture-Exchange Communication System are as follows:

1. Place an assortment of objects on a table and observe what the child consistently picks up and either plays with or eats, if edible.
2. Choose pictures of each of the objects; the level of abstraction of the pictures will depend on the child's ability to associate the picture with the object or activity.

3. Train the association between an object and the picture one at a time. A trainer and a communication partner should work together.

4. Place the picture of the object between the child and the actual object on the table. As the child reaches for the object, physically guide him or her to pick up the picture and place it in the open hand of the communication partner. No verbal prompting should be used.

5. After the child hands the partner the picture, the partner hands the child the object and says, "Oh, you want the (object)? Here is the (object)!"

6. Continue training the picture/object relationships one at a time, giving the child the object each time the picture is handed to the communication partner, regardless of the amount of physical guidance required. The physical guidance should be gradually faded out.

7. For more complete directions and advanced levels of this communication system, please see the Picture-Exchange Communication System (Bondy and Frost, 1994).

REFERENCES

Bondy, A.S., and L.A. Frost. 1994. The Picture-Exchange Communication System. *Focus on Autistic Behavior* 9:1–19.

Bruner, J.S. 1975. From communication to language: A psychological perspective. *Cognition* 3:255–287.

Dowrick, P.W. 1986. *Social survival for children*. New York: Brunner/Mazel.

Dunn, M.L. 1982. *Pre-sign language motor skills*. Tucson Ariz.: Communication Skill Builders.

Light, J. 1988. Interaction involving individuals using augmentative and alternative communication systems: State of the art and future directions. *Augmentative and Alternative Communication* 4:66–82.

ADDITIONAL SUGGESTED READINGS

Bleile, K. 1993. *The care of children with long-term tracheostomies*. San Diego: Singular Publishing Group, Inc.

Simon, B., and J. McGowan. 1989. Tracheostomy in young children: Implications for assessment and treatment of communication and feeding disorders. *Infants and Young Children* 1:1–9.

ADDITIONAL RESOURCES

Autistic Society of America, 8601 Georgia Avenue, Suite 503, Silver Spring, MD 20910, Tel.: (301) 565-0433.

Association for the Care of Children's Health, 7910 Woodmont Avenue, Suite 300, Bethesda, MD 20814. Offers free listing of publications concerning children with special needs.

National Self-Help Clearinghouse, 25 W. 43rd Street, New York, NY 10036. Refers people to support groups nationwide.

Picture-Exchange Communication System Training Protocol, Andrew S. Bondy, PhD, Director, Delaware Autistic Program, 144 Brennan Drive, Newark, DE 19713.

United Cerebral Palsy Association of America, Suite 1112, 1522 K Street, N.W., Washington, DC 20005, Tel.: (800) 872-5827.

AMPLIFICATION

Carol A. Knightly

Purpose: to examine the process of selecting, fitting, and utilizing amplification in a pediatric population; to discuss preselection considerations and verification procedures geared to the professional; and to present a fitting and troubleshooting guide to be shared with parents and caregivers.

The selection and use of amplification for pediatric patients, particularly children with developmental disabilities, differs significantly from the procedures used in adult fittings. Adults are capable of providing feedback regarding difficult communication situations and their adjustment to and benefit from amplification. Indeed, sclf-assessment questionnaires are frequently used to assist in the fitting process. The fitting process with a child is significant in two ways. First, the selection of hearing aids for a child is an ongoing process that extends far beyond the identification of a hearing loss and the initial fitting. Second, the electroacoustic parameters of the system are subject to change as new information regarding the hearing loss and verification of fit is obtained (Ross and Tomassetti 1980).

GUIDELINES FOR PROFESSIONALS

The following are preselection considerations for obtaining amplification devices:

* Obtain an accurate quantification of the hearing loss, but do not delay fitting as a result. It is important to document the existence of a hearing loss, but the exact configuration of the loss may take several assessments. In this case, it is prudent to fit the patient with an extremely flexible hearing aid, one with potentiometers to control frequency response and gain, not just maximum output.
* Decide if the child is a candidate for a hearing aid or aids. Candidacy for amplification, particularly in a school-age child, is dependent on more than the degree of hearing loss alone. It is important to obtain information about the child regarding speech and language skills, developmental delays, listening environments, and school performance.

* Be familiar with the acoustical spectrum of normal speech patterns and understand what impact the hearing loss has on the recognition of speech.

* Choose an amplification system with electroacoustic properties that will meet the needs of the child for auditory and language learning based on the requirements indicated above. Use a prescriptive method that considers the possibly limited information obtained from a child, such as the desired sensation level (DSL) approach, to select the system (Seewald 1992).

* Consider whether to fit monaurally or binaurally. As a rule with children, if there is a hearing loss in both ears, a binaural fitting is recommended. Consideration should be given to a monaural fitting only if chronic drainage from the middle ear or structural abnormality of the outer ear would prevent a useful fitting. If there is no measurable hearing sensitivity in a given ear, a fitting of that ear should still be considered until information is available that would suggest detrimental consequences from a fitting (Johnson 1987).

* Consider the type of hearing aid: behind-the-ear (BTE), in-the-ear (ITE), or body aid.
  1. BTE hearings aids, because of their casing size, can accommodate more potentiometers and circuitry, allowing for more flexibility, especially important if audiometric information is incomplete

or if the possibility of progressive hearing loss exists. In addition, BTE hearing aids are capable of direct audio input, which allows coupling of the hearing aid to assistive listening devices, such as an FM auditory trainer, particularly important in the classroom (Figure 16–1).

2. The advantage of ITE hearing aids is primarily cosmetic. In young children, cosmetic considerations are rarely the concern of the patient and most often initiate with the caregivers. The microphone on an ITE hearing aid may take advantage of the function of the pinna in directing sound to the microphone. As the child grows, however, an ITE hearing aid will need to be recased. This is covered by the manufacturer's initial warranty but can be costly once the warranty expires (Figure 16–2).

3. Body hearing aids are less frequently used currently than in the past. It may be possible to achieve more gain with a body aid before encountering acoustical feedback because of the distance between the microphone and the receiver, but feedback is less likely now with the softer earmold materials available for

BTE hearing aids. A body hearing aid may also reduce the risk of feedback in the extremely hypotonic child whose BTE hearing aid may constantly be positioned against a bed or head support. It may be less expensive to fit a child with one body aid with a "Y" cord to two receivers than to fit two BTE hearing aids, but it does not allow for independent adjustments if there are differences in hearing sensitivity between the ears.

• Strong consideration should be given to fitting the child with an FM auditory train-

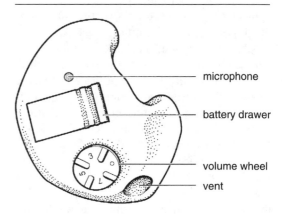

Figure 16–2 ITE Hearing Aid. *Source:* Copyright © 1996, Mark L. Batshaw, M.D.

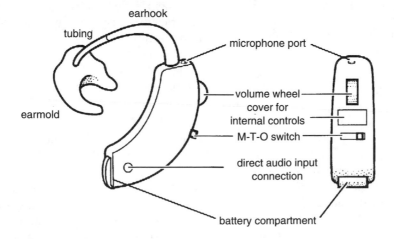

Figure 16–1 BTE Hearing Aid. *Source:* Copyright © 1996, Mark L. Batshaw, M.D.

ing system, either in conjunction with hearing aids or as the primary amplification system. The purpose of an FM system is to provide improved quality of auditory information to the child. Since hearing aids amplify every sound equally loudly, it is likely that the important speech signal will be degraded by the presence of background noise. With an FM system, the speaker wears a lapel microphone, and the speaker's voice is sent directly to the child's ears via FM radio signals. Since the microphone is only six to eight inches from the speaker's mouth, it is as if the speaker is only six to eight inches from the listener's ear.

- Choose an earmold material and style that will be comfortable for the child, provide an appropriate acoustic seal for very pliable auricles, and enhance the choice of electroacoustic properties of the hearing aid. Materials such as vinyl or silicone or some of the newer soft materials recently patented by earmold laboratories are recommended, especially if the hearing aid is a high-gain instrument. If possible, use a horn effect to enhance the higher frequencies, which are the most important for speech recognition.
- Determine which additional features in a hearing aid might be required by the child. At the least, every hearing aid selected for a child should come equipped with tamper-resistant battery compartments and volume wheel covers and with direct audio input capability. Pediatric earhooks, directional microphones, and an additional means of anchoring the hearing aid to the ear (e.g., "Huggie Aids") should be considered.

To verify selection of the amplification device:

1. Verify the appropriateness of the selection, preferably using real-ear measurements as an initial step. Remember to measure not only gain and frequency response but also saturation output.

2. Monitor the speech and language development of the child by gathering anecdotal reports and objective measures from caregivers and teachers.
3. Perform regular and periodic hearing aid checks (minimally at six-month intervals) to monitor the child's use of amplification.

GUIDELINES FOR PARENTS AND CAREGIVERS

The remainder of this section will focus on information that should be conveyed to the caregivers and family of the child. As the family enters the process of selection and fitting of appropriate amplification for their child, they will come into contact with a number of professionals:

- The *otolaryngologist* is the physician who specializes in the treatment of ear disorders that might result in reversible, or temporary, hearing loss. A child under the age of 18 years must receive medical clearance prior to being fitted with hearing aids.
- The *audiologist* is responsible for assessing hearing sensitivity, evaluating amplification systems, and initiating or coordinating (re)habilitative strategies.
- Purchase of hearing aids and repair of the aids is made through the audiologist or *hearing instrument dispenser*. In some cases, the dispenser is also able to evaluate amplification systems for the child.
- The *speech/language pathologist* and the *teacher of children with hearing impairments* can provide speech, language, and hearing therapy and can guide the family in their efforts to stimulate language acquisition in the child.

It is important to ascertain that each of these professionals is comfortable and familiar with the needs of children. The otolaryngologist should be familiar with the etiologies and treatment of disorders predominant in children that result in hearing loss. The audiologist should be aware of normal infant auditory behavior and developmental milestones. He or she should also be comfortable working with the various dispositions of children. Taking earmold impressions or real-ear measurements can be exceptionally challenging. The dispenser should also be comfortable working with children, and the services provided should be geared to the needs of the population. For example, if a child's hearing aid requires repair service, a loaner hearing aid should be made available to the child.

Throughout the evaluation process, the family must be counseled regarding realistic expectations from amplification. The family should understand that hearing aids only make sounds louder; they do not make speech clearer, nor do they selectively amplify speech over other ambient noise. Other sounds in the room with the child will be amplified just as much as the speech. As noted above, the signal-to-noise ratio can be improved through the use of an FM auditory training system.

The family should be aware from the start that a hearing aid does not restore normal hearing sensitivity. Many people with hearing loss have auditory systems that distort incoming speech sounds. It can be compared to a radio not tuned properly to a station; the sound is loud enough, it is just not clear. It is for this reason that a child identified with hearing loss must be enrolled in a language stimulation program immediately to ensure that the child makes the most of his or her amplification system. Information on language stimulation programs and activities can be found elsewhere in this book.

The family should receive an orientation to the functioning and parts of a hearing aid, as well as to maintenance and troubleshooting.

FUNCTIONING OF A HEARING AID

The microphone of a hearing aid receives sound waves and changes them into analogous low-voltage electrical energy. The signal from the microphone is directed to one or more amplifiers that increase the voltage of the signal. From there, the signal is sent to the receiver, which converts the electrical signal back into sound energy and delivers it to the ear. A battery supplies the power for a hearing aid.

The following are the parts of a hearing aid:

1. *Case:* Made of plastic, the case houses and protects the parts of the hearing aid.

2. *Microphone:* The microphone is usually located behind a screened opening near the top of the case.

3. *O-T-M switch:* This switch controls the "mode" of the hearing aid (Off-Telecoil-Microphone). Under normal use, the aid would be set in the "M" position. The "T" position is for use on compatible telephones, or when using certain assistive listening devices. In some cases, there is no "O" position; the aid is then turned off by opening the battery drawer or rotating the volume wheel to the lowest level to activate the integral on/off switch. There may be other markings on this switch, depending on the features of the particular hearing aid.

4. *Volume control:* This dial controls the loudness of the sound delivered to the ear. The divisions on the dials are arbitrary. For children, it is recommended that the dial be kept at the setting determined during the hearing aid evaluation. To prevent the child from changing the volume control, it is possible to obtain a cover for the dial.

5. *Battery drawer:* Usually, there is a "+" on the battery drawer, indicating correct placement of the battery. In some cases, the drawer will not close if the battery is inserted improperly. Because a hearing aid battery can be fatal if swallowed, a battery drawer should be made "tamperproof."

6. *Earhook:* This is the part of the hearing aid that connects to the tubing of the earmold and channels the sound from the receiver.

7. *Internal controls:* These controls are usually housed behind a hinged or sliding door on the case of the hearing aid. They are set to meet the amplification needs of the child on the basis of the results of the hearing aid evaluation and should not be changed unless new measurements are made to verify the appropriateness of the changes.
8. *Earmold:* The earmold is custom made by taking an impression of the child's ear. It is the final step in channeling the amplified sound into the ear canal and may be altered to allow for additional shaping of the signal to meet the child's amplification needs. The earmold should fit snugly to prevent sound from escaping from the ear and causing the whistling known as feedback. New earmolds will need to be made as the child outgrows the old ones. The frequency of remakes will depend on the age and growth patterns of the child. In addition, for children the earmolds should be made of a soft material such as vinyl or silicone, both for comfort and for the ability to create a better seal in the ear.

General rules for hearing aid use are:

1. Do not allow the hearing aid to get wet. Likewise, do not place it near extreme heat, as on a radiator or in the glove compartment of a car.
2. When the aid is not being worn, keep it in a safe place away from children and pets. Dogs appear to be especially attracted to hearing aids.
3. Always keep a spare pack of batteries on hand.
4. Do not drop the hearing aid. If you are replacing a battery or performing a listening check, do it over a soft area, such as carpeting or a bed.

A child will benefit from amplification system only if it is kept in good working order every day. The family should be supplied with a "hearing aid care kit." It should include the following:

1. *Battery tester:* The tester is used to ensure that the battery is still supplying correct voltage.
2. *Hearing aid stethoscope:* The family should be instructed to listen to the hearing aid to become familiar with normal function.
3. *Silica gel:* This is provided for hearing aids in various packagings to remove moisture from the aid.
4. *Earmold blower:* This is used to blow moisture out of the earmold or the tubing.

Care of the earmold requires the following measures:

1. Routinely examine the mold, including the tubing, for cracks or tears. Make sure the tubing is securely attached to the mold. Look at the fit of the mold in the child's ears. If irritation is present from pressure on the ear, or if gaps appear between the mold and the ear, it may be necessary to have the molds remade.
2. Ensure that the opening of the mold to the ear canal is free of wax. If wax is in the earmold opening, remove it gently with a pipe cleaner.
3. The earmold can be washed with warm, soapy water. Dishwashing liquid works well. Alcohol should not be used, as it can erode the earmold material. Remove the mold and tubing from the earhook by grasping onto the tubing. Wash the mold and dry it thoroughly with a soft towel. Use the air blower to remove any remaining moisture from the tubing and canal portion of the earmold. If possible, allow the earmold to dry overnight before reattaching it to the hearing aid.

Care of the hearing aid requires the following measures:

1. Batteries come in different sizes and voltages, as well as different compositions (e.g., zinc air, silver oxide). Make sure to replace the batteries with the correct type.

The life of the battery will depend on the power of the hearing aid (i.e., a high-gain hearing aid requires more current) and how frequently the aid is used. Generally, a battery should last between two and three weeks with daily use. The battery should be removed each night from the hearing aid. Even if the aid is "off," the battery will continue to drain as long as it is touching the battery contacts. Remember to store the battery in a safe place to prevent accidental swallowing. Check the battery each morning with the battery tester. Always keep spare batteries handy, especially at school. Insert the battery correctly into the battery drawer and close it completely.

2. Perform a listening check of the hearing aid each morning. Remove the earmold and tubing from the earhook. Turn the hearing aid on ("M") and, with the volume wheel in the minimum setting, attach the aid to the stethoscope. Rotate the volume wheel and listen for a relatively linear increase in the volume. Make sure there is no static or intermittent operation during rotation of the wheel. Turn off the aid and remove it from the stethoscope.

3. Reattach the earmold, set the volume wheel at the correct setting, and, with the aid still turned off, insert it into the child's ear. Once the hearing aid is seated properly in the child's ear, turn it on.

The following are suggestions for troubleshooting the hearing aid:

1. *Feedback:* Feedback is the squealing noise that a hearing aid makes if the amplified sound that comes from the receiver is allowed to enter the microphone again. It is expected under some conditions. For instance, feedback will occur if the hearing aid is turned on and held with the hands cupped around it. In addition, particularly with high-gain instruments, feedback will occur if a child places his or her aided ear against a caregiver's chest or on the floor or bed. Feedback should not occur during regular use of a hearing aid. If necessary, adjust the fit of the earmold. If feedback continues, remove the aid from the child's ear and, with the aid turned on, place a finger over the ear canal opening in the earmold. If feedback stops, the mold may be too small, and a new one should be made. If feedback does not stop, the problem may be a cracked case or tubing. In either situation, the audiologist or the dispenser should be contacted.

2. *"Dead" hearing aid:* If there is no sound coming from the hearing aid, first check to see if the battery is working and inserted properly. Also check the canal opening of the earmold to make sure it is not plugged with wax. Make sure the earmold tubing is not crimped or filled with condensation. If condensation is noted, remove the earmold tubing from the earhook, and dry the tubing with the earmold blower.

3. *Static coming from the aid:* Place the hearing aid in a container with silica gel overnight.

4. *Intermittent operation:* Check the earhook and earmold tubing for condensation. If condensation is noted in the earhook, place the hearing aid in a container with silica gel. If it is seen in the earmold tubing, detach the tubing from the earhook and use the earmold blower to dry out the tubing.

5. *Muffled sound:* Check the microphone screen to make sure that it has not become occluded with debris. Remove any debris with a soft brush, such as an artist's brush. Examine the mold and tubing for water droplets or wax. Remove the mold and tubing from the earhook and wash the mold to remove wax, or blow the mold dry with the earmold blower.

6. *Weak volume:* Check the battery with a battery tester. Check the mold and tubing for wax or condensation. Ensure that the mold is positioned properly in the ear. Examine the tubing with the aid in the ear for crimping.

7. *Buzzing:* Make sure that the switch of the aid is set to "M." The "T" setting will produce this sound if there is no appropriate input, such as a signal from the electromagnetic field of a telephone receiver. In some cases, a dying battery will result in a "motorboating" sound. Check the voltage of the battery.

If the above suggestions for troubleshooting do not resolve the problem with the hearing aid, contact the audiologist or hearing instrument dispenser immediately.

Remember that it is important with children to have warranty coverage for loss, damage, and service. In general, most new hearing aids come with a one-year manufacturer's warranty for some or all of the above. There may be additional cost associated with replacement of the aid during the warranty period or for shipping and handling while under the policy. Read the insurance policy that comes with the hearing aid carefully. If necessary, it is possible to supplement the manufacturer's policy through the purchase of additional coverage at a modest cost. In addition, it may be possible to insure the aid through an existing homeowner's policy.

REFERENCES

Johnson, E.W. 1987. Binaural amplification—naturally! *Hearing Instruments* 38, no. 12:20–23.

Ross, M., and C. Tomassetti. 1980. Hearing aid selection for preverbal hearing-impaired children. In *Amplification for the hearing-impaired*, ed. M.C. Pollack, 213–253. New York: Grune & Stratton.

Seewald, R.C. 1992. The desired sensation level method for fitting children: Version 3.0. *Hearing Journal* 45, no. 4:36–41.

ADDITIONAL SUGGESTED READINGS

Northern, J.L., and M.P. Downs. 1991. *Hearing in children.* 4th ed. Baltimore: Williams & Wilkins.

Northern, J.L., et al. 1990. Pediatric considerations in selection and fitting hearing aids. In *Handbook of hearing aid amplification* Vol. 2, ed. R.E. Sandlin, 113–132. Boston: College Hill Press.

Schwartz, S. 1987. *Choices in deafness: A parents' guide.* Rockville, Md.: Woodbine House, Inc.

ADDITIONAL RESOURCES

Academy of Dispensing Audiologists (ADA), 3008 Millwood Ave., Columbia, SC 29205, Tel.: (803) 252-5646.

Academy of Rehabilitative Audiology, P.O. Box 26532, Minneapolis, MN 55426, Tel.: (612) 920-6098.

Alexander Graham Bell Association for the Deaf, 3417 Volta Place NW, Washington, DC 20007, Tel.: (202) 337-5220 (V/TTY). Brochures, books for auditory/oral deaf community.

American Academy of Audiology, 1735 N. Lynn St., Suite 950, Arlington, VA 22209, Tel.: (800) 222-2336. Information regarding audiology services, hearing loss, and amplification.

American Society for Deaf Children, 814 Thayer Ave., Silver Spring, MD 20910, Tel.: (800) 942-2732. Referrals to support groups. Supports American Sign Language.

American Speech/Language/Hearing Association, 10801 Rockville Pike, Rockville, MD 20852, Tel.: (800) 638-8255 (V/TDD). Referrals and brochures for speech/language and hearing services.

Auditory-Verbal International, 2121 Eisenhower Ave., Suite 420, Alexandria, VA 22314, Tel.: (703) 739-1049 (V), (703) 739-0874 (TDD).

Beginnings for Parents of Hearing-Impaired Children, Tel.: (800) 541-4327. Support and information for parents.

HEAR NOW, 9745 E. Hampton, Suite 300, Denver, CO 80231, Tel.: (800) 648-HEAR. Free hearing aids and cochlear implants for children of parents who cannot afford them and who do not qualify for public assistance.

John Tracy Clinic, 806 W. Adams Blvd., Los Angeles, CA 90007, Tel.: (800) 522-4582. Free correspondence course for parents of hearing-impaired children.

Midwest Hearing Industries, Inc., 4510 West 77th Street, Suite 201, Minneapolis, MN 55435, Tel.: (612) 835-5242. Hearing aid insurance.

Miracle-Ear Children's Foundation, Tel.: (800) 234-5422 (V), ext. 751 (TDD). Free hearing aids for children of parents who cannot afford them and who do not qualify for public assistance.

National Cued Speech Association, P.O. Box 3145, Raleigh, NC 27622, Tel.: (919) 828-1218 (V/TDD).

Self Help for Hard of Hearing People, Inc., 7800 Wisconsin Ave., Bethesda, MD 20814, Tel.: (301) 657-2248 (V), (301) 657-2249 (TDD). Consumer organization.

Sound Assurance, P.O. Box 10088, Birmingham, AL 35202, Tel.: (800) 277-9051. Hearing aid insurance program administered by St. Paul Fire and Marine Insurance Company.

Chapter 17

Assistive Technology

Mary Lisa Wright and Amy S. Goldman

Purpose: to define assistive technology and describe the range of applications available for children with developmental disabilities; to review issues related to the acquisition and procurement of assistive devices and services; and to discuss basic principles underlying the selection of appropriate assistive technology strategies, equipment, and intervention techniques.

The success of assistive technology in helping individuals with disabilities achieve greater independence, inclusion, productivity, and quality of life requires the following principles to be understood and carried out by professionals who seek to evaluate, recommend, and implement assistive technology:

- The goal of assistive technology is to improve function in the most effective, efficient, and satisfying way.
- Assistive technology is not a luxury. For children with disabilities, technology may be the only intervention that can enable the child to participate in important daily activities.
- Assistive technology is not limited to expensive or complicated pieces of equipment. Many common devices found in lo-

cal retail stores may serve to assist the function of persons with developmental disabilities, used in the same way for which they are designed for the general public. For example, replacing a typical shower head with a hand-held shower massage unit may increase bathing independence for a person with limited reach.

- For users who require high-technology devices, back-up devices should be identified and provided for those times when the device is "down" (e.g., for repairs or recharging of batteries), when the environment threatens the mechanical integrity of the device (e.g., when used outdoors in wet conditions), or when the use of the device is inappropriate or inadvisable (e.g., when bathing or toileting).
- Appropriate provision of assistive technology requires services to support the use of recommended devices, which in some cases may be more costly than the device itself. Without support services, the device is at risk for not meeting the expectations for which it was designed and may be underutilized or abandoned as a result.

- The consumer knows best when it comes to the specific challenges encountered within his or her environment and should therefore be included in the assessment of needs and subsequent plan for intervention. Consumers should be empowered with sufficient knowledge to make informed choices where there are options for types of equipment, aesthetic variations, or approaches to use.
- There is no one device that will answer all the communication, mobility, or independent living needs for an individual user. Typically, assistive technology applications involve the identification of multiple components that collectively provide solutions to enhance function in a variety of environments, for a variety of tasks, and when the user is in a variety of positions.

Categories of assistive technology may include

- *Assistive technology to enhance activities of daily living*: Devices and adaptations to improve participation or increase independence in activities such as eating, dressing, meal preparation, laundry, or bathing. These devices may range from simple Velcro closures or built-up handles on utensils to more technologically complex devices such as electronic feeders. (Also see Chapter 14, the section "Activities of Daily Living.")
- *Assistive listening devices:* Devices used to amplify signals, especially speech, including hearing aids or personal listening devices. (Also see Chapter 16, the section "Amplification.")
- *Augmentative and alternative communication devices:* Devices that supplement or replace natural speech, ranging from language boards to computers with speech synthesizers and specialized software. (Also see Chapter 16, the section "Alternative Communication Systems.")
- *Communication devices:* Equipment and services related to face-to-face communication, telecommunication, and writing.

- *Environmental controls:* Electronic or computerized systems with switch controls that enable persons without mobility or sufficient dexterity to control household appliances and devices such as television or lights.
- *Home modification:* Adaptations to the home to permit access or independent mobility, ensure safety, and increase independence or interaction. This may include provision of stair glides, ramps, grab bars, intercom systems, automatic door locks, and changes to fixture or counter heights. For persons with sensory impairments, this may also include appliances that substitute one type of signal for another, such as doorbells that activate a flashing light or smoke detectors that vibrate. (Also see Chapter 11, the section "Environmental Accessibility.")
- *Leisure/recreation modification:* Specialized equipment or adaptations to permit participation in a variety of leisure and recreational pursuits, such as knitting machines, page turners, hand-powered bikes or adapted tricycles, sports chairs, and drawing software for the computer. (Also see Chapter 19.)
- *Learning aids:* Devices that facilitate learning or execution of multistep tasks or other skills, including computers with specialized software, hand-held spell checkers, electronic datebooks, and calculators.
- *Manual mobility:* Four-wheeled chairs used for personal mobility that may or may not afford independent movement, depending on the user's physical capacity to propel the chair manually. Custom applications may be selected around the individual needs of the user, such as a one-arm-drive control for a user with hemiplegia.
- *Mobility aid:* Any device or modification to a device that is used to increase personal mobility, such as a walker or cane. (Also see Chapter 11, the section "Ambulation Aids.")

- *Power mobility:* Three- or four-wheeled battery-powered vehicles or chairs allowing independent personal mobility in any combination of movements in space, including general locomotion, tilting the angles of seating in space, or moving to a standing position and back. (Also see Chapter 11, the section "Wheelchair Selection and Maintenance.")
- *Seating and positioning:* Modifications or adaptations to wheelchairs or other positioning systems that
  1. support trunk stability and head support in an upright posture, as required for performance of functional activities
  2. reduce pressure on weight-bearing surfaces to prevent skin breakdown
  3. allow the placement of controls or other equipment to increase independence (also see Chapter 11, the section "Adaptive Positioning Devices")
- *Vehicle modifications:* Devices or adaptations to vehicles required for driver control or passenger safety, such as tie-downs, wheelchair lifts, hand controls, and driving aids.
- *Vision aids:* Devices that assist persons with limited vision by increasing contrast, enlarging images, or substituting tactile or auditory cues for visual information. Examples include braille text or labels, magnifiers, enlarged-print books, and tape-recorded materials.

DETERMINING SUGGESTED APPLICATIONS

It is helpful to categorize the many possible applications of assistive technology according to the skills they support (such as communication, mobility, cognition, environmental mastery, recreation, and activities of daily living) rather than by type of device (such as power chairs, environmental control units, or augmentative communication devices).

Communication

Consider all forms of communication that require intervention:

- face-to-face conversation, including gestures and nonverbal elements, in one-on-one and group conversations
- writing
- telephone communication

Consider a range of applications, including both augmentative and alternative communication strategies (AAC). *AAC* refers to all methods for communication that supplement available speech, including the use of special symbols, aids, or strategies. It may be used as a replacement for or alternative to speech, and may be used either temporarily or permanently. It may be "aided" (ranging from low-tech language boards to high-tech systems with voice output and print capability) or "unaided" (using signs or gestures). It may help to facilitate the development of language comprehension as well as the development and quality of the speech itself.

Mobility

Consider all the aspects of mobility that may need to be addressed:

- presence and quality of developmental motor skills (rolling, crawling, standing, walking, jumping, running)
- potential for independent exploration of the environment
- potential for efficient and independent locomotion
- need for physical access and physical proximity to objects and people (inclusion)

Consider a range of application from simple mobility aids to power options:

- *Mobility aids* can include adaptations to a device or to a vehicle for safe independent access or control, including platforms, grip handles, hand controls, wheelchair tie-downs, and lifts.

- *Manual devices* include two- or four-wheeled equipment such as walkers or wheelchairs that are pushed or propelled by a child's upper and/or lower extremities. Device features need to be matched to a child's physical abilities.
- *Power options* include three- or four-wheeled devices that are powered through a battery and operated by an input device such as a joystick or switches. Power options offer a range of choices in terms of access and control, such as speed dampening or use with other devices such as an environmental control unit (ECU).

Learning

All aspects of the learning experiences to be introduced must be considered before assistive applications are introduced:

- *sensory processing demands* involving visual, auditory, and tactile perception and/or interpretation
- *sensorimotor requirements* that may influence motor planning and control
- *cognitive aspects*, including level of information processing, sequencing, and memory required of the task

Consider a range of devices from "generic" aids to computer systems:

- *"generic" learning devices* such as hand-held spell checkers, calculators, or electronic datebooks that can serve as memory or sequencing aids
- *devices or modified techniques*, such as raised markers on keys to cue finger placement on keyboard for the user with a visual impairment, or speakers with headphones and volume control to enhance auditory feedback for a user with auditory deficits, that enhance or can substitute for visual, auditory, or tactile deficits
- *computer systems* with software packages and various input modes that can address

multiple sensory, motor, and cognitive aspects

Environmental Mastery

Environmental mastery requires a range of abilities that must be fully understood before selecting technology options:

- the ability to access, move within, and explore one's environment freely
- the ability to control features of the environment such as lighting or climate control
- the ability to use objects or appliances that occupy the space, such as the television, computer, or telephone

The multidimensional nature of environment requires that applications for technology be varied and include

- *Modifications to physical space* permitting access into and within natural environments such as work, home, or school. These modifications range from furniture arrangement or height adaptations to structural changes such as installation of ramps, elevators, and automatic doors.
- *Adaptive devices*, or products that allow for independent control of both features and objects within the environment. These devices can range from generic products such as battery-operated scissors or electric staplers to products specially adapted for users with disabilities, including reachers, one-handed knives, and extension handles.
- *Environmental control systems* that involve an activation method (switch, voice, etc.) and a control unit that picks up the activation signal and sends it to targeted appliances or devices. These systems can be customized for a user's physical and sensory capabilities.

Recreation

Appreciate the value of play before introducing assistive technology into recreational/leisure pursuits. Play skills move along a developmental continuum throughout the life span; play is as important to the adult as it is to the child. Children learn many important skills and attitudes through play. Early play can lead to leisure or recreational pursuits that will follow a child into adulthood. As children mature, their play/recreational interests expand to include organized team sports, individualized athletic competition, or more complex strategy games that are contingent upon prerequisite physical, mental, or psychological abilities.

Assistive technology applications, ranging from simple adaptation to toys to complex computerized systems or sports equipment, may allow alternate forms of play or may help to enhance play experiences for children with disabilities:

- Many off-the-shelf toys can be chosen or adapted for a child with special needs (e.g., larger sized knobs, or electronic features).
- Specially adapted toys and switches can be purchased when off-the-shelf toys are not appropriate or do not meet a child's needs.
- Computer systems with various input/output modes and software packages provide alternate forms of play (e.g., drawing programs or board games).
- Specialized equipment such as sports wheelchairs, adapted skis, and adapted boats allow for participation in team sports, athletic competition, or a variety of leisure pursuits.

Activities of Daily Living

Consider all aspects of daily living that need to be addressed before recommending assistive technology:

- *personal hygiene*, including bathing, hair care, tooth brushing, and other activities
- *dressing*, including the donning and doffing of orthotics
- *feeding*, including meal set-up, oral-motor skills needed for managing and swallowing food safely, and use of utensils to self feed

- *household management*, including laundry, meal planning and preparation, and cleaning activities

Applications of assistive technology can both facilitate skill acquisition and promote independence with ADLs through a variety of options, including

- process modifications that offer training in specialized or customized techniques to promote the development of needed skills
- site modifications or environmental adaptations such as closet rearrangement or installing grab bars to increase access
- use of adapted devices such as plate guards, dressing sticks, and transfer benches to promote independence
- use of sophisticated devices with various input/output options

PROCESS OF ACQUISITION

There are many steps to acquiring appropriate assistive technology devices and services for children with disabilities, starting with a team that has a vision of the child's achieving the highest level of independence possible and an awareness of assistive technology devices and services available to accomplish this purpose. Funding sources must be identified, and legislative provisions or entitlements regarding assistive technology must be understood. Thus the process of acquisition involves a comprehensive assistive technology evaluation, a competent team, identification of funding sources, and an understanding of legislative provision or entitlements pertaining to technology.

Assistive Technology Evaluation

Evaluation is a formalized process of assessing the needs of the child and matching them with the features of assistive technology devices or systems. There is no one best approach or evaluation method that can be applied to every situation, but the following characteristics may guide the process:

1. An evaluation identifies or defines a problem that may be "solvable" through assistive technology.
2. A needs assessment is developed, encompassing personal preferences and daily routines as well as the environmental and situational demands that occur throughout that child's day.
3. Desirable features to be included in an assistive technology device or system are identified.
4. The selection of specific devices is recommended.
5. Provisions are made for hands-on experience with the device prior to purchase.
6. A formal report documents assessment findings and finalizes recommendations for needed assistive devices and services. These recommendations should include a service plan that addresses maintenance issues, back-up systems, upgrades, and the need for ongoing assessment to ensure acquisition and implementation.
7. Outcomes are monitored to measure the utilization and appropriateness of the employed assistive technology.

Team Competencies

Teams are identified and roles specified by the many professionals who may be involved, including the occupational therapist, physical therapist, and speech/language pathologist. While assistive technology is considered within the scope of practice for a variety of professionals, not all practitioners will have the requisite knowledge or skills to function effectively in this specialized area of practice:

- Team members need to have expertise in the range and scope of technology, including hands-on experience with a wide variety of devices, knowledge of what is cur-

rently on the market, and experience with the process from acquisition to implementation.

- The team needs to be interdisciplinary in its approach. To ensure effective collaboration, there must be mutual respect, understanding of areas where skills may overlap, and willingness to release a role to another skilled professional. Team collaboration should begin with the evaluation process and continue throughout intervention.

- A team must be consumer responsive and respectful of the child and parents as integral team members.

Legislation and Funding

Making technology happen requires a thorough knowledge of entitlements and provisions that pertain to assistive technology (see also Chapter 9, the section "Laws and Issues Concerning Education and Related Services"):

- The Technology-Related Assistance for Individuals with Disability Act of 1988 (Tech Act) defines assistive technology devices and services.

- The Americans with Disabilities Act of 1990 provides mandates for assistive technology as the "acquisition or modification of equipment or devices" and requires reasonable accommodations that support the provision of devices and services to both children and adults with disabilities.

- 1994 Amendments to the Tech Act articulate findings supporting the importance of assistive technology in the lives of people with disabilities in allowing greater control over their lives, increased participation in activities across all environments, greater interaction with nondisabled individuals, and opened options that are taken for granted by the nondisabled population.

- IDEA provides for the provision of assistive technology devices as required for a free and appropriate public education for children with disabilities. If the educational necessity of assistive devices is identified in an evaluation report and embedded in IEP goals, the school has a legal responsibility to ensure that technology is provided.

Identification of all possible funding sources is also a way of ensuring that assistive technology happens. Although funding sources vary from state to state, some generic sources include

- private commercial insurance policies with riders for durable medical equipment
- medical assistance, although restrictive fee schedules, long authorization processes, limits to the amount of equipment provided over a period of time, and willingness to pay only for equipment deemed medically necessary may limit the availability of funds
- service organizations, foundations, or clubs such as Kiwanis, Rotary, United Cerebral Palsy Association, Sunshine Foundation, and Variety Club
- private contributions, donations, or fund-raising efforts
- community-based services such as Family Driven Support funds, fund-raising events, church groups, and local businesses

ACCESS

Access in the context of assistive technology implies the ability of a user to control or operate a device. This section will provide an overview of general principles underlying access, along with a discussion of input modes, software modifications or processing modes, and output modes.

General Principles Underlying Access

Access is not device specific. A technology system may need to include a number of devices to meet a child's multiple needs.

Access is influenced by a child's seating and positioning system. Proper positioning can en-

hance voluntary movement, inhibit involuntary movement, minimize fatigue, and help the user to activate devices independently. It may be necessary to address positioning issues before evaluating access potential.

Determining a method of access is often based on an assessment process that is dynamic, is nonsequential, and includes an element of trial and error. There is never one best solution for access. Many children with disabilities require several different access options that are contingent on the type of tasks, the environment, the time of day, or fatigue factors.

Access can be broadly categorized into three methods:

1. *Direct selection* involves an input method in which the user is able to choose all available options. These input methods could include physically touching keys to type, directing a beam to select letters, or using the voice to speak words that are reproduced on the computer screen.

2. *Scanning* involves a selection set of items that can be scanned by a user. In *automatic scanning*, a user selects an item as it is highlighted; in *inverse scanning*, the user makes a selection by interrupting the cursor at a particular item; in *step scanning*, the user moves the cursor through one item at a time and then stops it at an item to make a selection. Common input methods include switches or joystick.

3. *Coded selection* uses symbols, letters, icons, or numbers to represent words. One type of coded access is Morse code, which can be used with a switch input method to make selections by sending a series of dots and dashes.

Remember that access solutions do not always require a complicated system or the latest technology.

Input Modes

Input is a general term that describes what the user needs to do in order to achieve a result or produce output from a system. It includes both how a user accesses a system and what type of information must be entered by the user. Input modes may be categorized as follows:

- *Unaided modes:* Modes of access that do not require aids or devices are called *unaided.* For example, some children with juvenile rheumatoid arthritis (JRA) may have handwriting difficulty and use a computer to augment their writing skills. In most cases they can access a standard keyboard without modification.
- *Physical extension devices:* This input mode encompasses a variety of devices that allow the user to enter information into a system by means of physically extending their reach. Devices can include
    1. head stick (Figure 17–1)
    2. mouth stick (Figure 17–2)
    3. chin stick (Figure 17–3)
    4. hand stick (Figure 17–4)
- *Adapted keyboards:* This is an input mode that allows access to a computer keyboard through physical adaptations to the workstation or standard keyboard, including
    1. *Keyguard:* a hard transparent or colored

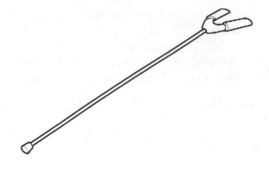

Figure 17–2 Mouth Stick. *Source:* Copyright © 1996, Mark L. Batshaw, M.D.

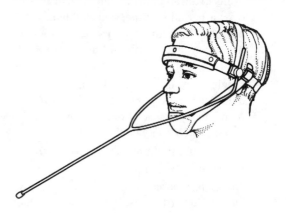

Figure 17–3 Chin Stick. *Source:* Copyright © 1996, Mark L. Batshaw, M.D.

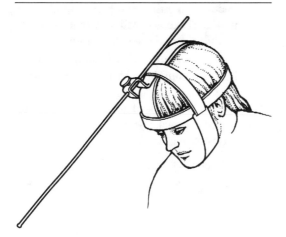

Figure 17–1 Head Stick. *Source:* Copyright © 1996, Mark L. Batshaw, M.D.

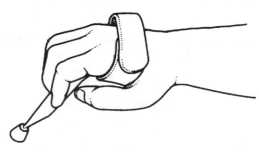

Figure 17–4 Hand Stick. *Source:* Copyright © 1996, Mark L. Batshaw, M.D.

surface with holes that line up with the keys and attaches to the keyboard with Velcro (Figure 17–5). This device will help the user who can select individual keys but is not always accurate and either misses a key or hits the wrong key.

2. *Wrist support:* a system that attaches to the end of a keyboard or computer table to provide stability to the wrist joint (Figure 17–6). Wrist supports can improve speed and key punch accuracy because with support the hand and digit movements can be isolated and controlled. Also wrist support can prevent repetitive injuries such as carpal tunnel syndrome.

3. *Adjustable keyboard:* keyboard that pulls apart and can be angled to reconfigure the location of keys (Figure 17–7).

4. *Mobile arm supports:* can be mounted onto table top or positioning device to support the weight of the arm, allowing a user with limited strength to use larger muscle groups to move the forearm or hand across the keyboard (Figure 17–8).

• *Assisted keyboards:* software modifications that allow the user to access a standard keyboard by changing the number or nature of keystrokes to perform a given function.

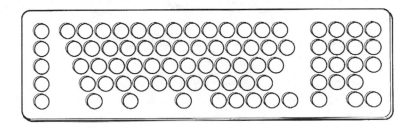

Figure 17–5 Keyguard. *Source:* Copyright © 1996, Mark L. Batshaw, M.D.

Figure 17–6 Wrist Support. *Source:* Copyright © 1996, Mark L. Batshaw, M.D.

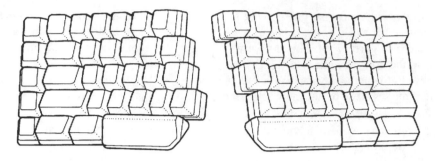

Figure 17–7 Adjustable Keyboard. *Source:* Copyright © 1996, Mark L. Batshaw, M.D.

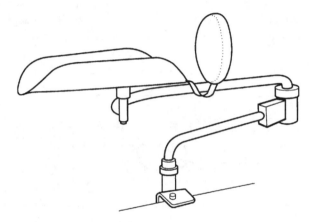

Figure 17–8 Mobile Arm Support. *Source:* Copyright © 1996, Mark L. Batshaw, M.D.

- *Mice and trackballs:* input devices that offer an alternative way to communicate with a computer; options include
  1. A *standard mouse*, which has a small ball mounted on the underside of the device that moves a marker on the screen. A button allows the user to click on features and make selections (Figure 17–9). There are also child-size mice designed to fit smaller sized hands.
  2. A *head-controlled mouse* that operates by using head position relative to a fixed reference point. As the head moves away from the reference point, the cursor is moved around the screen (Figure 17–10).

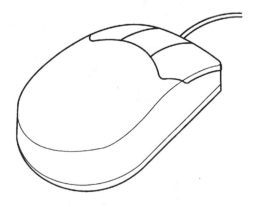

Figure 17–9 Standard Mouse. *Source:* Copyright © 1996, Mark L. Batshaw, M.D.

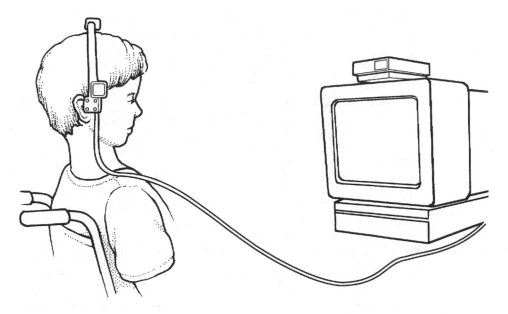

Figure 17–10 Head-Controlled Mouse. *Source:* Copyright © 1996, Mark L. Batshaw, M.D.

3. A *trackball* that functions like an upside-down mouse; these come in a variety of sizes, shapes, and weights (Figure 17–11).

4. A *mouse emulator,* which uses the arrow keys on the standard keyboard or overlays on a membrane keyboard with software to emulate mouse function (Figure 17–12).

• *Switches:* an input mode that interfaces with many devices such as ECUs, computers, and power mobility, augmentative, and alternative devices. A wide variety of switches can be selected according to user preferences and capabilities. Switches may be categorized according to the number of functions, the type of feedback they provide, and the type of activation required.

1. *Function modes* include single switches that provide one function (e.g., jelly bean switch by AbleNet), dual switches that provide two functions (e.g., rocker plate switch by Enabling Devices), and multiple switches that provide multiple

functions (e.g., Star, Wafer, Penta, and Joystick with pad by Tash).

2. *Types of feedback* include tactile, auditory, visual, and proprioceptive signals to indicate to the user that the device has been activated.

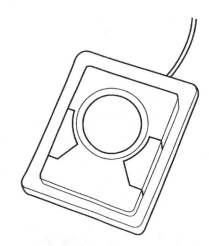

Figure 17–11 Trackball. *Source:* Copyright © 1996, Mark L. Batshaw, M.D.

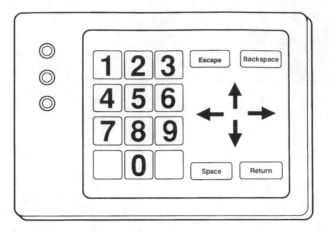

Figure 17–12 Mouse Emulator. *Source:* Copyright © 1996, Mark L. Batshaw, M.D.

3. *Activation types* include

   (a) physical contact or force: e.g., touching or pushing a button to activate the device (Figure 17–13)

   (b) air pressure, such as pneumatic switches, which allow the user to sip or puff into a switch to activate the device (Figure 17–14)

   (c) motion, such as mercury switches

mounted on a body part, which activate the device through sensing a change in position (Figure 17–15)

   (d) sound sensitive, such as microphone switches, which activate a device through voice sounds (Figure 17–16)

   (e) light sensitive, such as photoelectric or photosensitive (sensor)

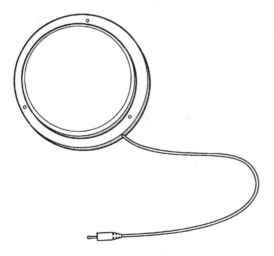

Figure 17–13 Switch Activated by Physical Contact or Force. *Source:* Copyright © 1996, Mark L. Batshaw, M.D.

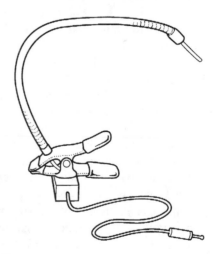

Figure 17–14 Switch Activated by Air Pressure (Pneumatic Switch). *Source:* Copyright © 1996, Mark L. Batshaw, M.D.

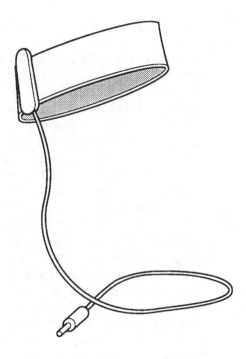

Figure 17–15 Switch Activated by Motion (Mercury Switch). *Source:* Copyright © 1996, Mark L. Batshaw, M.D.

switches, which activate the device when the light beam is interrupted by movement of a body part, or optical pointers that can be mounted to a body part and activate a device through direction of a light beam to a sensor (Figure 17–17)

(f) muscle tension, such as electromyographic switches, which detect small changes in muscle activation (Figure 17–18)

(g) energy sensitive, such as electric magnetic switches, which are activated by electrical charges

It should be noted that technology for activation is constantly changing and that this list is a broad generalization of activation types. Activation can be contingent on the access mode, types of devices, and the assistive technology system.

- *Alternate keyboards:* provide an input mode when a user is unable to activate a standard keyboard. They are usually mem-

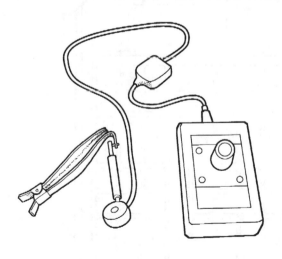

Figure 17–16 Switch Activated by Sound (Microphone Switch). *Source:* Copyright © 1996, Mark L. Batshaw, M.D.

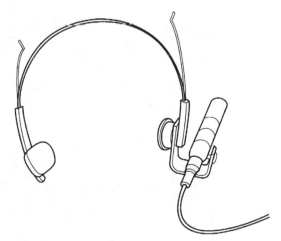

Figure 17–17 Switch Activated by Light (Optical Pointer). *Source:* Copyright © 1996, Mark L. Batshaw, M.D.

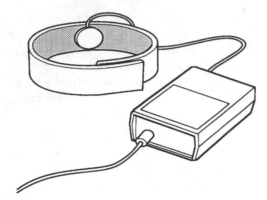

Figure 17–18 Switch Activated by Muscle Tension (Electromyographic Switch). *Source:* Copyright © 1996, Mark L. Batshaw, M.D.

brane keyboards with overlays that take the place of actual keys. Many can be customized in terms of key location, key function, feedback, and visual representation. The boards come in a variety of types and sizes, including

1. *Enlarged keyboards* such as the Unicorn board or Key Largo by Don Johnston products. Enlarged keyboards provide the user with a larger access and are helpful if the user needs to use a whole hand rather than a single digit for activation (Figure 17–19).

2. *Downsized or mini keyboards* such as the Tash Mini board or Magic Wand. These are recommended for the user who has better fine motor control but poor control of larger muscle groups. They also require little force to activate if strength is an issue (Figure 17–20).

3. *Touch window systems.* The touch window allows a user to touch and activate whatever is displayed on the computer screen; this system often succeeds for users who require a direct cause-and-effect input mode secondary to issues related to cognition, visual attention, motor planning, and visual-motor skills (Figure 17–21).

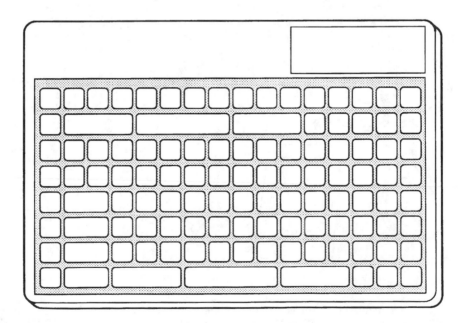

Figure 17–19 Enlarged Keyboard. *Source:* Copyright © 1996, Mark L. Batshaw, M.D.

Figure 17–20 Mini Keyboard. *Source:* Copyright © 1996, Mark L. Batshaw, M.D.

Figure 17–21 Touch Window System. *Source:* Copyright © 1996, Mark L. Batshaw, M.D.

4. *Bar code systems* such as Intellikeys by Intellitools. Intellitools with bar-coded overlays are easy to set up and make the computer "user friendly" for the novice programmer. The system functions as an enlarged keyboard but has special features such as response rate (the speed that a key has to be depressed before the board accepts it) and required lift option (requires a user to lift finger from keyboard between key punches). These special features are solutions for the individual who presses unwanted keys while reaching for a specific key (Figure 17–22).

5. *Electronic communication devices.* Devices such as the Dynavox, Light Talker, Touch Talker, and the Liberator can all be used as alternate keyboards. They require a special cable from the manufacturer of the device and the KE:NX system from Don Johnston Inc. Thus users of an electronic communication device can use the same system of access for the computer as they do for communication (Figure 17–23).

- *Keyboard emulators* (virtual). Emulation of the keyboard or mouse functions is done with a video image of the keyboard generated on the monitor and various input devices. Without a physical board, this system performs standard keyboard functions with scanning, direct, or coded selection options, using input devices such as a mouse, switch, or touch window.

- *Chordic keyboards*, which facilitate one-handed access through a series of buttons that when used in various "chord" combinations can represent messages.

- *Voice input systems*, such as Dragon Dictate or Voice Navigator systems, which involve speaking into a microphone.

- *Braille keyboards*, such as Braille Mate by Telesensory Inc.

- *Scanning devices:* optical character recognition units or optical-to-tactile converters that work with a hand-held camera or optical pointer that scans text or graphic material and transmits it to the computer and other devices so it can be read, transmitted, or translated into an alternate form for a user with sensory impairments.

- *Tongue touch keypad* that consists of nine switches that are molded into a dental acrylic and fit against the user's hard palate. The user then uses the tip of his or her tongue to activate a switch and transmit a radio fre-

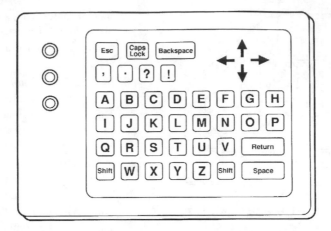

Figure 17–22 Bar Code System. *Source:* Copyright © 1996, Mark L. Batshaw, M.D.

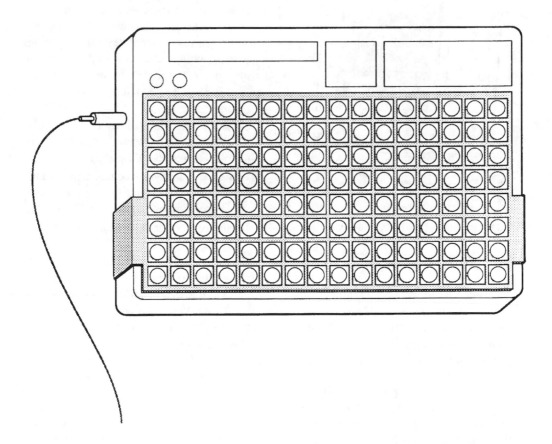

Figure 17–23 Electronic Communication Device. *Source:* Copyright © 1996, Mark L. Batshaw, M.D.

quency signal to a processor that in turn sends an infrared signal to the computer.

Processing Modes

These modes are usually software programs that interface input and output device modes that require some method of translating information to the computer or assistive device. Some may require a hardware device that provides plug or pin sites and cables for the hook-up of input or output devices. These software programs and hardware devices not only provide an interface but also allow for customization or modification based on user needs. This could be simple software customization, such as a slow speed of scan for a user with a motor impairment who uses switch access. An example of more complicated system to meet the needs of a low-vision user would be a software program that provides auditory output and enlarged text to facilitate reading and hearing what is displayed on the screen in conjunction with an alternate keyboard with large letters for modified access.

Output Modes

In simple terms, *output* refers to production of information to be received by the user and how that information is presented. Output modes are varied and can be customized to meet a user's needs:

- *Printers:* producing visual or tactile output that is copied onto paper. They are somewhat varied in terms of print quality and color. Inkjet and laser printers produce the highest quality of text or graphics. Printers can be black and white or color. There are also braille printers that work with a translation program that converts text characters to braille cell dot patterns.

- *Visual output:* producing a visual display through light indicators or screens. They can be customized for the user in terms of color or size. There are also variations in graphic quality depending on resolution (e.g., dot matrix).

1. *Light indicators:* usually are light-emitting diode (LED) display in a variety of colors used to give information about the functioning of the device (e.g., indicating that the device is on or off or that the battery is low). They are common to ECUs, power chairs, visual display monitors, and TDDs (telephone devices for the deaf).

2. *Monitors:* Types of displays include LEDs, liquid crystal displays (LCDs), and electroluminescent (light-emitting material or gas). Monitors can also vary in quality of resolution and may be color or black and white displays.

3. *Magnification aids:* ranging from simple aids such as hand-held magnifiers to electronic systems such as closed-circuit television (CCTV), including a camera, video display, and an information processor. Computer software can produce larger size images or text.

- *Auditory output:* ranging from simple indicators that provide auditory cues to indicate that a system is on and functioning, to speech synthesis ("reading" text or material produced on screen). Examples of such devices include screen readers that use an optical character recognition unit to scan printed text and reproduce it in an auditory form. There are also electronic augmentative devices that produce speech output to augment or replace expressive language skills. Many computer software programs provide auditory output, and some allow for the programming of speech output that can simulate an electronic communication device. It should be noted that there is a range of quality, speed, and tone with speech synthesis, and these characteristics need be considered when choosing "voice" for communication or rate of speed for auditory recognition.

- *Tactile output:* There are two types of ways to represent graphic or text in a tactile output mode:

1. Braille as a computer output method can use a refreshable braille display, which uses vibrating pins that push through a membrane covering or hard copy produced by a printer.
2. Tactile facsimile uses a small camera that scans graphic images, computer output, and printed text and transmits it into a tactile input similar to refreshable braille display with vibrating pins that reproduce letter, number, or graphic images.

INTERVENTION

The following strategies apply to virtually any intervention in which assistive technology is a component:

- A team approach is just as important to effective intervention as it is to appropriate evaluation. Team members may include the parent(s), the child (as appropriate), other significant interaction partners in multiple environments (e.g., teachers and other educational personnel), and therapist(s). At times, it may be appropriate to include peers to assist in such tasks as selecting vocabulary or recording for digitized voice-output communication.

- Evaluation performed within an ecological context should result in intervention that may be implemented across physical and social contexts, in all settings of relevance to the user, and with consideration to multiple task variables. To the fullest extent possible, assistive technology must be integrated into environments experienced by the child's nondisabled age peers, including shopping malls, playgrounds, and classrooms.

- Assistive technology interventions tend to be extraordinarily labor intensive, especially when first established. In addition to the time needed for direct intervention with the child, sufficient therapist time must be allocated for the creation, customization, adjustment, and ongoing modification of equipment and to provide parent and staff consultation and training.

- Program plans (Individualized Education Plans, Individualized Family Service Plans) should reflect the need for technology to follow the child in all environments, including taking technology home when it may support educational goals. Program plans should also clearly specify the amount of therapist time needed to implement the plan, as well as the specific roles and responsibilities expected of team members.

- It is important to develop a specific plan for ongoing monitoring of assistive technology interventions. Follow-up evaluations establish the efficacy of current interventions, provide an opportunity to consider the changing needs of the child and family, and ensure that new team members have an opportunity to enter into collaborative management of assistive technology needs.

ADDITIONAL RESOURCES

See Appendix C, the Section "Organizations and Associations." In addition, each state has an office funded under the Technology-Related Assistance for Individuals with Disabilities Act of 1988. Current information is available from RESNA Technical Assistance Project, Suite 1540, 1700 N. Moore Street, Arlington, VA 22209-1903, Tel.: (703) 524-6686, Fax (703) 524-6630, TTY (703) 524-6639. The listing is also updated each year in *Exceptional Parent*.

SUGGESTED READINGS

Baumgart, D., et al. 1990. *Augmentative and alternative communication systems for persons with moderate and severe disabilities.* Baltimore: Paul H. Brookes.

Bergen, A., et al. 1990. *Positioning for function.* Valhalla: Valhalla Rehabilitation.

Beukelman, D.R., and P. Mirenda. 1993. *Augmentative and alternative communication: Management of severe communication disorders in children and adults.* Baltimore: Paul H. Brookes.

Blackstone, S.W., ed. 1986. *Augmentative communication: An introduction.* Rockville, Md.: American Speech-Language-Hearing Association.

Blackstone, S.W. 1990. Assistive technology in the classroom: Issues and guidelines. *Augmentative Communication News* 3, no. 6:1.

Blackstone, S.W., et al., eds. 1988. *Augmentative communication: Implementation strategies.* Rockville, Md.: American Speech-Language-Hearing Association.

Church, G., and S. Glennan. 1992. *The handbook of assistive technology.* San Diego: Singular Press.

Cook, A., and S.M. Hussey. 1995. *Assistive technologies: Principles and practice.* St. Louis: C.V. Mosby Co.

Goldman, A. 1993. Speaking aids: Augmentative and alternative communication. *Advance for Rehabilitation Directors* (Sept./Oct.):39–41.

Hulme, J.B., et al. 1987. Behavioral and postural changes observed with the use of adaptive seating by clients with multiple handicaps. *Physical Therapy* 67:1060–1067.

Hulme, J.B., et al. 1988. The influence of adaptive seating devices on vocalization. *Developmental Medicine and Child Neurology* 30 suppl., no. 57:35.

Hulme, J.B., et al. 1987. Effects of adaptive seating devices on eating and drinking of children with multiple handicaps. *American Journal of Occupational Therapy* 41:81–89.

Jaffe, K. 1987. *Childhood powered mobility: Developmental, technical and clinical perspectives.* Washington, D.C.: RESNA.

Landers, A.L. 1994. The ABLEDATA database of assistive technology. *Exceptional Parent* 24, no. 3:56.

Lett, R.M. 1991. *Principles of seating the disabled.* Boston: CRC.

Mann, W.C., and J.P. Lane. 1991. *Assistive technology for persons with disabilities: The role of the occupational therapist.* Rockville, Md.: American Occupational Therapy Association.

Miedaner, J., and L. Finuf. 1993. Effects of adaptive positioning on psychological test scores for preschool children with cerebral palsy. *Pediatric Physical Therapy* 5, no. 4:177–182.

Neely, R.A., and P.A. Neely. 1993. The relationship between powered mobility and early learning in young children with physical disabilities. *Infant Toddler Intervention* 3, no. 2:85–91.

Petty, L. 1994. Powered mobility for your child? *Exceptional Parent* 24, no. 3:33–35.

Quist, R.W., and D.M. Blischak. 1992. Assistive communication devices: Call for specifications. *Augmentative and Alternative Communication* 8:312–317.

Rainforth, B., et al. 1992. *Collaborative teams for students with severe disabilities: Integrating therapy and educational services.* Baltimore: Paul H. Brookes.

Reichle, J., et al. 1991. *Implementing augmentative and alternative communication: Strategies for learners with severe disabilities.* Baltimore: Paul H. Brookes.

RESNA. 1994. *Proceedings of the RESNA '94 Annual Conference.* Arlington, Va.: RESNA Press.

RESNA Technical Assistance Project. 1992. *Assistive technology and the Individualized Education Program.* Available from RESNA TA Project, 1101 Connecticut Avenue, NW, Suite 700, Washington, DC 20036.

Sullivan, M.W., and M. Lewis. 1993. Contingency, means-end skills, and the use of technology in infant intervention. *Infants and Young Children* 5, no. 4:58–77.

Tretler, E., et al. 1994. *Seating and mobility for persons with physical disabilities.* Tucson, Ariz.: Therapy Skill Builders.

Wheeled mobility selection: A guide for parents. 1994. *Exceptional Parent* 24, no. 3:23–30.

Chapter 18

Psychosocial Management

COLLABORATION WITH PARENT AND CHILD

Symme W. Trachtenberg and Nancy Hale Sills

Purpose: to discuss the importance of the role of parents in the assessment and intervention for children with developmental disabilities, the process of identifying family strengths and needs, the differences between parent and professional perspectives, communication regarding the child's diagnosis and prognosis, and how to obtain services and resources for families.

The parent should be considered an active participant and a valuable resource within the team process in the provision of services. Parents are the primary advocates, providers of care, and observers of their child with a disability. As such, they should be approached and listened to with respect and recognition of their strengths and adaptability. Professionals have a responsibility to approach each family in a way that is open to discovering its unique situations, background, diversity, abilities, and needs. Every effort should be made to ensure interactive dialogue and an understanding of the family's goals for their child.

The professional and the family together can participate in the assessment and development of an intervention plan. The professional brings knowledge of the field, expertise, and training. The parent brings knowledge of the child's abilities and personality and the experience and understanding of the child over time and within the family and community. Thus the parent and professional are in a partnership. The professional's involvement with the child is episodic and time limited. The involvement and responsibility of the parent is ongoing and continuous.

To practice effectively in the field of child development and developmental disabilities, it is necessary to view the child within the context of the family. The age of the child, the birth order, and the ages and developmental phases of other family members are all part of the picture.

Where family members are in their own life experience and their own development will determine how they react and cope with a diagnosis of disability. Parents with a strong support system prior to the birth and the diagnosis may handle the flood of emotions better than parents with fewer resources. The youngest child in a family with many siblings may have multiple caregivers available to provide parental assis-

526

tance. A family with illness in a significant family member may be less able to manage all the demands. A teenage mother who dropped out of high school and who has little familial support may be unable to take on the training needed to take home a child dependent on technology.

A parent whose brother or sister had a developmental disability during childhood has a different life experience from a young couple with no previous personal experience with disability or chronic illness. These individuals will interact in very different ways with their professional caregivers. They will react differently to the diagnosis and in the ways they plan and follow through with intervention. Parents' receptiveness to recommended intervention depends on when the professional enters their lives—at diagnosis, several years after diagnosis, or after many years of failed school or treatment programs. The success or failure of forming a working relationship depends on how professionals approach a parent, what their personal experiences and professional training have been, what history the parents bring to the task, and how this information is used.

IDENTIFYING FAMILY STRENGTHS AND NEEDS

A psychosocial family assessment should be part of the evaluation of any child who has a developmental disability (see Chapter 5, the sections "Psychology" and "Social Work," and Chapter 7, the section "Psychoeducational Measures: Ecological Assessment"). This assessment should include the family's strengths as well as their ability to participate actively in the evaluation, discussion, and treatment of their child.

A family that is likely to function well will have

- support systems—emotional support, assistance, extended family, friends, religious community
- financial stability—insurance coverage, income to cover bills and living expenses

- adequate housing—space, safety, comfort, accessibility
- demonstrated ability to understand and articulate the child's diagnosis, medical issues, and functional problems/abilities
- ability to cope with and adapt to the child's diagnosis, problems, and skills
- ability to advocate for the needs of the child
- limited family stress outside of child's disability

Not all families have these resources and strengths. Even those fortunate families that do have resources may experience difficulty managing the stress of the child's diagnosis or prognosis, the demands of the daily care requirements, or ongoing professional follow-up. Some families who experience problems in one or more of these areas still show remarkable strength and resilience regarding their child with a disability.

IDENTIFYING FAMILY VALUES— DIFFERENCES BETWEEN PARENT AND PROFESSIONAL

Differences in perspectives, beliefs, and values exist between professionals and parents, both from their roles and from their differences as individuals. Table 18–1 presents some of these differences. The differences in parents' and professionals' roles can affect the interaction, communication, and understanding between them, as well as the success of recommendations, interventions, and follow-through for the child with a developmental disability.

Consider the following items related to cultural background and life experience, and the impact of potential differences between parents and professional:

- *Ethnicity*—Where is the family from? What ethnic group do they identify with?
- *Cultural practices*—What are the beliefs about child rearing? Who are the primary caregivers? What are the patterns of com-

Table 18–1 Differences between Parents and Professionals That Affect Perspectives on Child's Care

Professionals	Parents
Deal with a large number of children with similar diagnoses (similar diagnostic categories; experience with a broad range of children)	Care for one unique, loved child
Particular area of concern focuses typically on child's problems; specialization; unidimensional	Relationship to whole child; parents serve many roles in child's life
Typically trained in "cure" or "fix" model—focus is on the child patient's illness or imperfection	Focus is on overall daily care and nurture of the child within the family unit
Hospital-based training may overlook home setting	Hospital is an unnatural, hostile environment
See child and family in circumscribed, time-limited, and time-specific visits; snapshot of child's life	24-hour exposure; long haul
Authoritarian tradition; control through knowledge and skill; paternalistic tradition emphasizes power	Look to partnership with professionals who are "consultants"; prefer joint decision-making power; will bear ultimate consequences of decision
Have chosen their roles	Have not chosen to have a child who is anything other than healthy and whole

Source: From *Building the Healing Partnership: Parents, Professionals and Children with Chronic Illnesses and Disabilities* by P.T. Leff & E.H. Walizer, 1992, Cambridge, MA: Brookline Books, Inc. Copyright 1992 by Patricia T. Leff and Elaine H. Walizer. Reprinted by permission.

munication with people outside the family or outside the culture? Who are the authority figures (elders, parents, doctors, teachers, sons, government)?

- *Religious beliefs and practices*—Is faith and/or a religious community a central part of their lives? How do these beliefs and practices affect daily life and the child?

- *Language*—What is the primary language spoken at home? Is English easily used and understood by significant family members? Is an interpreter needed?

- *Education*—What are family members' levels of schooling, ability to read, learning styles, facility with understanding and retaining new information, attitudes toward value of learning?

These elements all affect the family's approach to their child, their child's developmental disability, and the service providers. Ultimately, culture affects a family's ability and willingness to be active participants in planning intervention for the child.

The following are issues that may serve as a basis for exploring and understanding a family's perceptions and attitudes:

- Family's perception of the child's disability
  1. Are there cultural or religious factors that would shape family perceptions?
  2. To what/where/whom does the family assign responsibility for their child's disability?
  3. How does the family view the role of fate in their lives?
  4. How does the family view their role in intervening with their child? Do they feel they can make a difference, or do they consider it hopeless?
- Family's perception of health and healing
  1. What is the family's approach to medical needs?
     (a) Do they rely solely on Western medical services?
     (b) Do they rely solely on holistic approaches?

    (c) Do they utilize a combination of these approaches?

2. Who is primary medical provider or conveyer of medical information? Family member? Elders? Friends? Folk healer? Family doctor? Medical specialists?

3. Do all family members agree on approaches to medical needs?

- Family's perception of help seeking and intervention

1. From whom does the family seek help—family or outside agencies/individuals?

2. Does the family seek help directly or indirectly?

3. What are the general feelings of the family when seeking assistance—ashamed, angry, demanding assistance as a right, viewing it as unnecessary?

4. With which community systems do they interact (educational/medical/social)?

5. How are these interactions made (face to face, telephone, letter)?

6. Which family member interacts with other systems?

7. Does that family member feel comfortable when interacting with other systems?*

Professionals and parents are capable of radical differences in their views of the world, the child with the disability, and personal backgrounds and experiences. The professional must guard against making assumptions about the child and family and be willing to explore and respect the diversity that exists. She or he should recognize family strengths, individuality, and different methods of coping and managing.

---

*From Wayman, K.I., Lynch, E.W., & Hanson, M.J. (1990). Home-based early childhood services: Cultural sensitivity in a family systems approach. *Topics in Early Childhood Special Education*, *10*, 65–66. Copyright © 1990 by PRO-ED, Inc. Adapted by permission.

COMMUNICATION REGARDING THE CHILD'S DIAGNOSIS AND PROGNOSIS

Active communication is the key to any positive working relationship between parents and professionals. Areas of discussion include a child's strengths, problem areas, diagnosis, recommendations, predictions, and progress. The process should be interactive and open. Table 18–2 illustrates principles to consider in building positive communication.

These principles apply to any communication between parent and professional, whether it is one to one or in a team setting. The following pointers may also be useful:

- A conversation that begins in the hallway may need to become a scheduled "sit-down" conference.

- Define what characteristics make some families challenging for you to work with.

- Note the impact of your mood on particular interactions and discussions.

- Recognize your own family values and experiences and how they differ from those of others.

- Do not avoid contact with parents because they make you uncomfortable.

- Planned and structured interactions may make the relationship more comfortable and productive.

- Ask for assistance from a colleague or supervisor.

- Remember that strengths and abilities are just as important as deficits and problem areas.

INTERVENTION: OBTAINING SERVICES AND RESOURCES

For families to find and utilize resources that potentially will benefit them and their child, the professional must assess what is really needed. Not all psychosocial services are equal. For example, counseling includes a variety of ap-

Table 18–2 Guidelines for Positive Communication

Principle	Ideal	What To Avoid	Rationale
Physical space	Meeting place should be private, quiet, comfortable	Place should be free of distractions (e.g., peripheral noises or activity)	Privacy equals confidentiality, undivided attention, and caring
	Parent and professional should sit and talk on same physical plane	Professional should not stand while the parent sits	Difference in physical plane can be felt as difference in power, ability to speak candidly, importance
	Space should be free of physical barriers	Avoid desks or other pieces of furniture between participants	Physical barriers can be barriers to open communication
Time	Make sure there is opportunity for information to be given and discussed, questions to be asked, etc.	Parent/professional discussions should not be rushed. Primary participants need to allow enough time to spend with the family	A hurried atmosphere stifles questions and discussion
	If there is not ample time, acknowledge and schedule another time to meet		Parent may perceive professional as "too busy" to care about child
Participants	Key people in the child's intervention team should be present together to talk with the parents	Do not include staff who are not directly involved with the child	Too many people and too much information discussed at one time are potentially overwhelming
	Encourage both parents to attend or to consider inviting a significant family member or friend	Be careful not to exclude one parent on a regular basis (e.g., to be always talking with the mother because the father works every day)	Both parents should actively receive information and make decisions. Differing perspectives need to be reconciled and understood
			One parent with a group of staff may feel uncomfortable. Another family member can be a support and a "second set of ears"
Language	Use person-centered language: e.g., "Your child has a developmental delay"	Refrain from referring to "a Down syndrome child" or "a spina bifida" (for a child that has spina bifida)	Child is a child first and a child *with* a disability second
	Use language that is understandable to all participants, adding explanation or descriptions when possible	Do not use technical or medical terms that may be unfamiliar to the family	Using language that matches a parent's education and experience fosters a willingness to ask questions and thus better understanding and cooperation
	Ask if the information makes sense, if the parents understand. Explain in a new way if necessary		Offering to repeat an explanation tells parents that you care about them and their understanding of child's situation

continues

Table 18–2 continued

Principle	Ideal	What To Avoid	Rationale
Answers/ information	Answer questions to the best of your ability and experience	Do not give information that you are not sure of	Neither parents nor professionals have all the answers. Most people have more respect for one who is able to say, "I don't know"
	Know the limits of the situation and your own knowledge and ability to give the answer to a question	Do not be afraid to say "I don't know"	
	Refer to another professional for a further opinion or additional information	Do not withhold options or information that might further the parents' understanding	Referral to another professional communicates a willingness to learn new information along with the parents
Listening/ parent input	Validate parents' comments, questions, fears, concerns	Do not ignore or belittle parents' thoughts and feelings	Parents need to know that their input is important. Questions and comments build a combined understanding and a stronger working relationship
	Listen in a nonjudgmental way		
	Take time to be sure that you understand what a parent is trying to say		Active involvement helps the parent feel more invested in the intervention plan
Challenging emotions	Be honest with parents, and share as much information with them as possible, even if it is "bad news"	Do not avoid bringing up issues and information that you think might be upsetting to the family	Honesty and sensitivity will foster a closer relationship
			Parents may have unspoken thoughts and questions and feel relieved to talk about them
Sadness	Acknowledge that an issue is difficult to discuss	Do not ignore tears	Sadness is a normal reaction to difficult news and is a coping strategy. It may be key in understanding how parents are feeling
	Be prepared for an expression of sadness (tears), and encourage the parent to share what is triggering this emotion		
Anger	If a parent becomes loud or angry, remain calm and continue talking at a normal, or lower volume	Do not take a parent's anger or frustration personally	It is unproductive to argue with a parent. Responding in a challenging way will escalate the situation
	If you feel anger toward the parent, it may be necessary to conclude the interaction and resume at another time	Never raise your voice or express anger at a parent	Parents' anger and frustration may represent a struggle to cope with powerful emotions regarding their child
	Processing your feeling of anger with a colleague will help you plan how to reapproach the parent		

proaches. These range from information sharing (diagnostic and treatment information) to supportive counseling, psychotherapy, and crisis intervention (identification of abuse, neglect, and suicidality).

When resources are recommended, the child and family should be given a choice. Table 18–3 offers suggestions for referrals.

Exhibit 18–1 shows a useful psychosocial needs assessment worksheet to assist in the decision of a psychosocial referral for a particular child/family. The child and family members may need the same or different types of interventions.

Families benefit from being offered multiple resource options. Working with parents and children to find appropriate resources can empower them to learn and use self-advocacy. Skills related to the sequence of seeking services, making phone calls, writing letters, and accessing the agency/city/state hierarchy can be of much use to parents. (See Appendix A, especially the protection and advocacy agencies, and Appendix B.)

Professionals, in their work with parents and children, have the responsibility to

- offer local resources and information, such as a directory, with instructions on how to use it
- inform about legal rights and advocacy services
- be persistent and creative in seeking new referral options
- monitor the delivery of services offered
- help families understand the limitations and frustrations in acquiring services
- inform about differences among services and funding from state to state and county to county
- empower families to realize their rights to choose or refuse services

Professionals should be knowledgeable about support and peer groups. These groups may or may not have professional backing. They usually focus on a situational category. They are mostly developed around specific needs at a

Table 18–3 Criteria for Referrals

Problem	Suggestions
Decreased social/emotional supports	Counseling, support group, respite care, diagnosis-specific national organization/local chapter, religion
Financial problems	Information on entitlement—Supplemental Security Income, WIC, Medical Assistance
Housing problems	Social service agency, problem solving on other living arrangements
Substance abuse	Substance abuse program offering detox; counseling; support group
Noncompliance—not showing up for appointments; may be due to family/life problems that interfere with the parents' perceived priorities, financial issues, parental burnout, or lack of understanding about the value of the evaluation/intervention	Agency social work department, social service agency, children and youth agency if child is in danger (neglected/abused)
Increased sorrow, grieving (e.g., due to family illness, chronic sorrow, mental health problem)	Counseling, psychotherapy, time to find ways to cope (see section "Prevention of Burnout in Parents and Professionals" later in this chapter); dependent on presenting issue; see Exhibit 18–1's grid of therapeutic modalities

Exhibit 18–1 Psychosocial Needs Assessment Worksheet

Person's Name: _____

Date: _____

Age: _____　　Ethnic Origin: _____

Religion: _____

Language: _____

Description of Family Constellation: _____

Significant Medical Issues: _____

Therapeutic Modalities		
	Child	*Family*
Behavior modification		
Cognitive-behavioral therapy		
Expressive arts therapy		
Family therapy		
Information		
Medication		
Other individual/group therapy/ counseling		
Psychotherapy		
Relaxation techniques		
Spiritual guidance/counseling		
Supportive counseling		
Support/peer group		
Other		

given time (e.g., teens who are hospitalized with spinal cord injuries) or as part of a program (e.g., an "Early Intervention Program Parent Support Group"). Support groups can help to reduce isolation and often offer a new approach to a problem. Professionals can help parents and children find an appropriate support group or assist in getting one started.

Current social policy emphasizes preventive measures such as family counseling, education, and homemaker services aimed at maintaining children with special needs in their own homes. Even with appropriate support, home care may remain difficult because of the child's physical problems or situations within the family (e.g., homelessness, health of parents). At times, it may be necessary to consider out-of-home placement (see Chapter 8, section "Case Management").

CONCLUSION

The parents and other family members contribute integrally to the child's experiences and deserve full membership on the child's assessment and intervention team. Parents are of primary importance in the care and progress of the child: whether their influence is positive or negative, the impact must be addressed and the parents must be included in any intervention discussion. A successful working partnership is built on open communication, mutual under- standing, and respect. The family members and professionals can work together to determine what information, supports, and services are needed for the family to make informed deci- sions and to participate actively in the care of their child.

SUGGESTED READINGS

Gartner, A.L., et al. 1991. *Supporting families with a child with a disability.* Baltimore: Paul H. Brookes.

Leff, P.T., and E.H. Walizer. 1992. *Building the healing partnership: Parents, professionals, and children with chronic illnesses and disabilities.* Cambridge, Mass.: Brookline Books.

Lynch, E.W., and M.J. Hanson. 1992. *Developing cross-cul- tural competence: A guide for working with young chil- dren and their families.* Baltimore: Paul H. Brookes.

Mulick, J.A., and S.M. Pueschel, eds. 1983. *Parent-profes- sional partnerships in developmental disability services.* Cambridge, Mass.: Academic Guild Publishers.

Seligman, M., et al. 1989. *Ordinary families/special chil- dren: A systems approach to childhood disability.* New York: Guilford Press.

Singer, G.H.S., and L.K. Irvin, eds. 1989. *Support for caregiving families: Enabling positive adaptation to dis- ability.* Baltimore: Paul H. Brookes.

Turnbull, A., ed. 1978. *Parents speak out: Views from the other side of the two-way mirror.* Columbus, Ohio: Charles E. Merrill Publishing Co.

Wayman, K.I., et al. 1990. Home-based early childhood serv- ices: Cultural sensitivity in a family systems approach. *Topics in Early Childhood Special Education* 10:65–66.

FOSTERING INDEPENDENCE AND SELF-ESTEEM

Valerie Wolf Shopp

Purpose: to describe assessments, interven- tions, and resources to build independence and self-esteem and to describe the process of social skill development in the contexts of family and school as a major contribution to the child's learning to act independently and feelings of self-confidence and worth.

Advances in medical technology have re- duced mortality rates for many childhood dis- eases. Extended life with a chronic illness or physical disability significantly affects the child's cognitive, emotional, and social develop- ment. The roles that family, social support net- works, and the health care system play in the child's adjustment require careful consideration.

Defining the impact of chronic illness or devel- opmental delay on young, school-age children is a complex biopsychosocial task. Historically, children with special needs have been associated with limitations and failure. For individuals with disabilities, physical and financial independence has been difficult. There have been vast changes in the past 20 years. Parents and professionals now determine together, with positive expecta- tions, the support and development of each child.

Independence can be defined as choosing how to live one's own life within one's inherent abili- ties and means and consistent with one's per- sonal values and preferences. On the basis of this definition, guiding values of independence are consent, choice, and self-direction. An important part of independence is social competence. Developing social competence and independence will foster self-esteem (Dowrick 1986).

Social skills are

- interpersonal and interrelated
- purposeful and self-controlled
- learnable

Aspects of social skills and independence to consider in developing individual goals and training programs include

- attributes of the skill
- situations that the skills serve
- personal processes involved

The purpose of independence training is to develop appropriate skills that will equip the child to deal with interactions common to everyday living.

ASSESSMENT AND GOAL IDENTIFICATION FOR INDEPENDENCE, SOCIAL SKILLS TRAINING, AND SELF-ESTEEM

Independence

Various tools can be used to gain a thorough understanding of a child's level of independence. The Parent Education Network publication *Transition: Preparation for Adult Living* (1993) offers excellent checklists on

- Living arrangements
  1. self-care—toileting, hygiene
  2. dressing
  3. eating
  4. cooking
  5. home chores
  6. medical/personal safety
  7. community/travel mobility
  8. independent living
- Work
  1. work-related skills
  2. social skills relating to work

- Community experiences
  1. group/community/school activities
  2. individual leisure activities
  3. individual activities
  4. higher education or training
- Adult services: Vocational resources, entitlements—Social Security, public assistance, etc.

These checklists target specific strengths and needs related to transition. They are designed to help parents ask the right questions of educators and other agency personnel.

Social Skills

Consider the social skills listed in Table 18–4. They are conversation and interpersonal skills that build on each other. That is, each skill depends to some extent on the ability to incorporate skills earlier in the list. Thus the table can be used as a checklist for a quick assessment of a child's independence and self-confidence mastered through effective interpersonal interactions.

Other tools can be useful in assessing a child's strengths and deficits in order to choose target skills for social skills training. Dowrick's *Communication Analysis: Verbal and Nonverbal Skills* and Dowrick and Hood's *Social Survival Situation Analysis Inventories* (Dowrick 1986) are useful instruments. The following assessment tools are also available (Baker and Brightman 1989):

- *Play Skills Checklist*
- *Self-Care Assessment*
- *Home-Care Assessment*
- *Self-Help Skills Inventory*
- *Time Skills Assessment*
- *Sight Word Assessment*
- *Behavior Chart*

Still other assessment tools are

- parent interview
- child interview

Table 18–4 Social Skills

Social Conversation		
Basic	*Intermediate*	*Advanced*
Greeting	Sharing minimum information	Sharing personal details, feelings, values
Introducing self	Introducing others	Expressing self spontaneously
Asking other's name	Asking details about another	Respecting others' contributions
Asking permission	Commenting on others' ideas	Directing conversation to others
Saying thank you	Giving and accepting compliments	Giving and accepting criticism
Asking for help	Giving and accepting help	Giving and accepting apologies
Answering questions	Taking turns talking	

Interpersonal Behaviors		
Basic	*Intermediate*	*Advanced*
Joining together in play	Joining a new group	Joining a variety of groups
Following rules established by others	Generating and implementing rules with others	Monitoring other group members in adherence of rules
Sharing objects, taking turns in a game	Sharing experiences and ideas	Eliciting experiences and ideas of others
Managing teasing	Managing exclusion from a group	Managing various forms of ostracism
Recognizing feelings	Understanding feelings	Responding with empathy
Recognizing strengths	Rewarding self through concrete means	Rewarding self through positive self-statements
		Dealing with winning, losing, and peer pressure

- behavior rating scales
  1. *Child Behavior Checklist* (Achenbach 1991)
  2. *Functional Disability Inventory,* Parent Version (Walker and Green 1991)
  3. *Health Resources Inventory* (Gesten 1976)
- behavioral observation in the home, school, or hospital setting
- sociometric assessments

Assessment has a dual purpose: to enable evaluation of an intervention and to guide the intervention itself. The assessment goals are to

- limit the number of skills to be taught
- identify those skills most crucial to survival or enhancement

- identify the skills most reasonably amenable to change

To identify those skills from which the child will derive most benefit, a checklist should be developed with two scales: ability and benefit. Once specific goals for social competence have been identified, the methods to teach the skills must be defined.

Self-Esteem

Several instruments are available that may provide information regarding a child's self-esteem:

- The *Social Skills Rating System* (SSRS; Gresham and Elliot 1990): This assessment uses multiple rates of children's prosocial behaviors and their problem behaviors.

Teacher, parent, and student rating forms are available for evaluating children between the ages of 3 and 18. The *SSRS* is nationally standardized and has separate norms for boys and girls.

* *The Self-Perception Profile for Children: Revision of the Perceived Competence Scale for Children* (Harter 1985) and the *Self-Perception Profile for Adolescents* (Harter 1988) are both available from the University of Denver.

A simple checklist can be used to establish in a general way whether a child has a healthy self-image. The following questions should be answered, by or on behalf of the child, with "yes" or "no," according to how he or she feels "most of the time":

1. Do you accept constructive criticism?
2. Are you at ease meeting new people?
3. Are you honest and open about your feelings?
4. Do you value your closest relationships?
5. Are you able to laugh at and learn from your mistakes?
6. Do you notice and accept changes in yourself as they occur?
7. Do you look forward to and tackle new challenges?
8. Are you confident about your physical appearance?
9. Do you give yourself credit when credit is due?
10. Are you happy for others when they succeed?

Questions answered affirmatively represent strengths, to be acknowledged and built upon. Questions answered negatively suggest areas to target for specific support to self-esteem.

STRATEGIES TO DEVELOP INDEPENDENCE

In general, the keys to strategies for developing independence are (1) establishing appropriate expectations/goals for and with the child and (2) determining realistically what roles parents and educators can play in implementing a plan to teach independence.

Steps to Teaching Independence

Steps to teaching independence are:

* Target a skill.
  1. What skills are you now doing *for* your child?
  2. Which skills does your child want to learn?
  3. Which skills is your child ready to learn?
  4. Which skills do you want to teach?
  5. Target one skill to teach at a time.
* Establish steps.
  1. Analyze the skill into small, manageable steps.
  2. Make a list of these steps.
  3. Teach gradually.
* Identify rewards that will support the skill development until the child becomes independent and self-confident. Then teach the next skill.

Case Study

Brian was a nine-year-old with cerebral palsy, spastic quadriplegia, and moderate mental retardation. His problems with high muscle tone, contractures, and lack of adequate hip strength led to an inability to walk. Brian had difficulty being independent in the use of his manual wheelchair because of upper extremity weakness and lack of coordination. Brian's mother consulted with the physical therapist and the occupational therapist at school on the potential of a power wheelchair. Assessments of Brian's cognitive abilities, visual motor skills, fine motor and manual dexterity, and positioning indicated that he would probably be successful in learning to use a power wheelchair. Brian's mother, teacher, and therapists talked with him about what would be involved in his learning this skill. Brian expressed a strong interest and high level of motivation to learn.

Brian's mother and school staff (teacher, PT, and OT) wrote specific goals related to power wheelchair mobility into Brian's Individual Education Plan (IEP). These goals included activities to help learn directionality and visual scanning, practicing the use of a joystick, and improving Brian's position in the wheelchair to maintain his head in a midline position. It was determined which of the new skills could be practiced at home. Over the course of the school year, Brian progressed in mastering these skills and used a loaner power wheelchair to begin practicing mobility. After daily repetitions of practicing in the power wheelchair, Brian was able to be independent, requiring only occasional verbal cues to slow down or to negotiate a difficult space.

The impact that Brian's mastery of power mobility had on his self-esteem was evident from anecdotal reports. Brian appeared to get great enjoyment and satisfaction from using his power wheelchair. He typically held his head high with a grin on his face when using the chair. He would "show off" by going fast and would spin the chair around slightly when stopping as if to say "ta da!" When Brian became a teenager and was hospitalized, a nurse attempted to take over the joystick on the chair to get Brian to come to his room for medicine and was met with much anger and frustration. Attempting to get Brian's compliance in this way was like picking up a typically developing Brian and carrying him to his room (which the nurse would never think of doing). The nurse was able to see how her intervention was an affront to Brian's sense of autonomy and control. When Brian's chair needed repairs, there was a definite change noted in his mood as Brian became more limited in his ability to enjoy social interactions and independence.

STRATEGIES TO DEVELOP SELF-ESTEEM

Components important in the development of self-esteem include

- *Limit setting:* Self-esteem increases when children are provided with appropriate structure and freedom within the structure.
- *Acceptance:* Unconditional parental love and acceptance of the child are correlated with self-esteem. Acceptance by school personnel can greatly supplement the family situation.
- *Success:* Children with high self-esteem lead active and productive lives outside their families.
- *Values:* Adults who teach children definite values and a clear idea of what they regard as appropriate behavior will encourage children to have confidence in themselves.
- *Peer relationships:* Being an active member of a peer group provides valuable opportunities for self-evaluation and the development of social skills.
- *Security and protection:* Children need to know that their community is a good, safe place. Children need a sense of belonging to a family or group and need to know that parents and other adults will help them when they are faced with strange or frightening situations.
- *Independence:* Children need encouragement to try new things and need to be offered confidence in their abilities to do things for and by themselves.

A child with a disability has the same need as other children for nurturing of a sense of dignity and self-worth. This nurturance and development of self-esteem is a lifelong process. Fostering a child's confidence and feelings of self-esteem can be achieved by emphasizing the attainment of goals that are important to the child. In adolescence, having a secure, strong sense of self and an appreciation for one's unique strengths and positive qualities is especially important. The adolescent urge for "sameness" among peers creates tremendous conflict for the teen with a disability, whose developmental task is also to accept his or her "difference." Teens with disabilities need a great deal of support as they struggle with issues of peer relationships and socialization, sexuality, establishing their own level of independence and autonomy, planning for future education, vocational training, job opportunities, and independent living.

INDEPENDENCE AND ACCESS

People with a disability cannot be independent unless they have access to the same opportunities in life as individuals who do not have a disability. Access poses fundamental problems of equality (see also Chapter 11, the section "Environmental Accessibility"). There are several important areas of environmental access, including transportation, education, employment, public accommodations, telecommunications, accessible housing, residential alternatives, and attendant care. Each area is reviewed briefly below.

Transportation

Access to people with disabilities is being furthered by developments in the following areas:

1. *Public transportation:* The Americans with Disabilities Act (ADA) is designed to ensure that all types of public transportation will be accessible to people with disabilities. As of August 26, 1990, public bus and rail systems cannot buy new vehicles unless they are accessible.
2. *Automobile transportation:* Increasingly, automobile manufacturers are offering modification packages that are more readily installed. The "big three" U.S. auto makers (Chrysler, Ford, and General Motors) are considering a variety of special needs and alternative control systems.

3. *Airplane transportation:* The Air Carrier Access Act of 1986 states in general that airlines may not discriminate against people with disabilities. In 1990, more specific regulations gave guidance to airlines and people with disabilities. Airlines cannot require a passenger with a disability to travel with an attendant. Passengers with folding wheelchairs must be permitted to store them on board in the coat closet. If problems are encountered while traveling, ask for the complaint resolution official.

Transportation questions can be directed to the U.S. Department of Transportation, Office of the Assistant General Counsel for Regulation and Enforcement, 400 7th St. SW, Washington, DC 20590, Tel.: (202) 366-9305; (202) 755-7687 (tdd).

Education

For information on access to education, see Chapter 9.

Employment

As of July 1994, companies with 15 or more employees have been subject to specific laws concerning the employment of qualified individuals with disabilities. An employer cannot refuse to hire, train, or promote simply on the basis of a disability. Employers are required to make "reasonable accommodation" to permit the job to be done properly, unless it would cause them "undue hardship." Reasonable accommodation might include making the workplace accessible to wheelchairs, modifying office equipment, or providing an interpreter.

Public Accommodations

Every business that is open to the public must allow people with disabilities to use its facilities on an equal basis with others unless this would impose an unreasonable cost.

Telecommunications

All telecommunications companies were required to make their services accessible to individuals with speech or hearing impairments by July 26, 1993. People who use a telecommunication device for the deaf (TDD) must be able to communicate via telephone with people who do not have a TDD. People with disabilities will not be charged any more to use telecommunications systems than people without disabilities.

Accessible Housing

By law, public housing projects must create a certain percentage of accessible units. Resources include the local public housing authority, which should be contacted for information on availability and eligibility guidelines; the local government office for persons with disabilities; and local chapters of organizations that advocate for individuals with disabilities, such as United Cerebral Palsy.

Attendant Care

Personal care assistance consists primarily of help with activities of daily living (e.g., dressing, grooming, toileting, and bathing) and household responsibilities (e.g., cleaning, meal preparation, and shopping) to adults with disabilities. Attendant care enables access to community residential environments rather than requiring institutions or excessive dependence on families. However, attendant care can become diminished by the complexity of funding criteria and service restrictions.

REFERENCES

Achenbach, T.M. 1991. *Manual for the Child Behavior Checklist/4-18 and 1991 Profile.* Burlington, Vt.: University of Vermont, Department of Psychiatry.

Baker, B.L., and A.J. Brightman. 1989. *Steps to independence: A skills training guide for parents and teachers of children with special needs.* Baltimore: Paul H. Brookes.

Dowrick, P.W. 1986. *Social survival for children.* New York: Brunner/Mazel Publishers.

Gesten, E.L. 1976. Health resources inventory: Development of a measure of the personal and social competence of primary grade children. *Journal of Consulting and Clinical Psychology* 44:775–786.

Gresham, F.M., and S.N. Elliot. 1990. *Social Skills Rating System.* Circle Pines, Minn.: American Guidance Service.

Harter, S. 1985. *Manual for the Self-Perception Profile for Children.* Denver, Colo.: University of Denver.

Harter, S. 1988. *Manual for the Self-Perception Profile for Adolescents.* Denver, Colo.: University of Denver.

Parent Education Network. 1993. *Transition: Preparation for adult living.* York, Pa.

Walker, L.S., & J.W. Green. 1991. The functional disability inventory: Measuring a neglected dimension of child health status. *Pediatric Psychology* 16:39–58.

ADDITIONAL SUGGESTED READINGS

Batshaw, M.L. 1991. *Your child has a disability: A complete sourcebook of daily and medical care.* Boston: Little, Brown & Co.

Blum, R.W., et al. 1985. Developing independence. *Journal of Adolescent Health Care* 6, no. 2:120–124.

Clark, H.B., et al. 1989. A social skills development model: Coping strategies for children with chronic illness. *Children's Health Care* 18, no. 1:19–27.

Eisenberg, M.G., et al. 1984. *Chronic illness and disability through the life span: Effects on self and family.* New York: Springer Publishing Co., Inc.

Goldfarb, A., et al. 1986. *Meeting the challenge of disability or chronic illness: A family guide.* Baltimore: Paul H. Brookes.

Hostler, S.L., et al. 1989. Adolescent Autonomy Project: Transition skills for adolescents with physical disability. *Children's Health Care* 18, no. 1:12–18.

Kreegsman, K.H., et al. 1992. *Taking charge: Teenagers talk about life and physical disabilities.* Rockville, Md.: Woodbine House.

Resnick, M.D., et al. 1985. Social maturation. *Journal of Adolescent Health Care* 6, no. 2:102–107.

Thomas, C.E. 1986. *Raising a handicapped child.* New York: William Morrow.

Turnbull, A.P., and H.R. Turnbull. 1985. Developing independence. *Journal of Adolescent Health Care* 6, no. 2:108–119.

ADDITIONAL RESOURCES

The Adolescent Autonomy Program, Kluge Children's Rehabilitation Center, 2270 Ivy Road, Charlottesville, VA 22903, Tel.: (804) 924-2345 or (800) 627-8596, tdd (804) 982-HEAR, provides exercises to build social skills, such as assertiveness training and peer group activities, during a teen's hospitalization. An Adolescent Apartment enables independence from staff and younger children and provides an environment to practice independent living skills such as chore delegation, cooking, and cleaning.

The Adolescent Employment Readiness Center (AERC), Children's Hospital National Medical Center, 111 Michigan Avenue NW, Room 1301, Washington, DC 20010, Tel.: (202) 745-3203, offers individual help for teens with chronic illness and physical disabilities to prepare for employment and plan for their future. The AERC staff provides educational workshops and is available to speak to groups about employment issues concerning youth with health concerns. This program is sponsored by the Maternal and Child Health Bureau and a variety of private foundations.

After High School...? Building on Today for Tomorrow (Chicago Family Resource Center on Disabilities, 1993) is a 20-page manual providing step-by-step information for designing and implementing a community-based, family-centered, transition planning program. Transition-related legislation, listings of regional and national transition resources, forms, and other materials are included in the appendixes. Write to the Family Resource Center on Disabilities, 20 E. Jackson, #900, Chicago, IL 60604.

Canine Companions for Independence (CCI), 1215 Sebastopol Rd., Santa Rosa, CA 95407, Tel.: (707) 528-0830, provides trained service, hearing, and social dogs with supportive services to ensure the success of the working team. Service dogs perform tasks such as turning on/off light switches, pulling a wheelchair, and retrieving items. Hearing dogs alert people with hearing impairments to crucial sounds such as telephone, smoke alarm, or baby's cry. Social dogs are provided for children with disabilities for any situation in which the supervision of a third party is required.

The National Rehabilitation Information Center (NARIC), 8455 Colesville Rd., Silver Spring, MD 20910, Tel.: (800) 346-2742, voice/tdd (301) 588-9284, fax (301) 587-1967, offers a periodical called *Guide to Disability and Rehabilitation* and a book entitled *Providing Information for an Independent Life* (1991). It also provides information about periodicals on administration, advocacy, counseling, health care, independent living, special education, specific disabilities, technology, vocational training, and employment.

The National Center for Youth with Disabilities (NCYD), Box 721-UMHC, Harvard St. at East River Rd., Minneapolis, MN 55455; Tel.: (800) 333-6293 or (800) 612-2825, is an information and resource center focusing on adolescents with chronic illnesses or disabilities and the issues associated with making the transition to adult life. Staff can answer questions about training, education, and other transition issues; make referrals to other resources; and search the NCYD database.

The National Easter Seal Society, 70 East Lake St., Chicago, IL 60601, Tel.: (312) 726-6200, is a nonprofit organization dedicated to increasing the independence of people with disabilities through research and services. Local affiliates offer therapies, counseling, and vocational assistance and advocate on behalf of people with disabilities.

The North Carolina Assistive Technology Project, 1110 Navaho Drive, Suite 101, Raleigh, NC 27609, Tel.: (919) 850-2787 or (800) 852-0042, engages in activities including technical assistance, an information and referral service, awareness and training, expansion projects, consumer groups, statewide networks, systems change, and a newsletter.

Partners for Youth with Disabilities, Inc., Massachusetts Office on Disability, One Ashburn Place, Room 1305, Boston, MA 02108, Tel.: (617) 727-7440 or (800) 322-2020, is a regional, private, not-for-profit organization for youth with physical, sensory, and learning disabilities. The program assists young people to reach their full potential for personal development by arranging one-to-one mentoring relationships between youth with disabilities and adults with similar disabilities. The organization sponsors training, activities, events, and a newsletter.

CHILD ABUSE AND NEGLECT

Karen M. Hudson and Angelo P. Giardino

Purpose: to discuss a variety of issues related to child maltreatment, with particular attention to its relationship to children with disabilities; to offer guidelines for the identification of maltreatment in children with and without disabilities; to describe evaluation techniques, along with case examples; and to offer pointers to manage child abuse and child neglect cases.

Child abuse and child neglect are serious problems affecting the health and well-being of large numbers of children. Of all children maltreated each year, the majority are victimized by their caregivers. There is a growing recognition that children with disabilities may be at increased risk for abuse and neglect. Child maltreatment is a complex problem whose resolution requires a cooperative effort among medicine, social work, law enforcement, the judiciary, mental health, and other related fields working together for the child and family (Krugman 1991). Accordingly, the potentially abused or neglected child is best served by a coordinated and comprehensive interdisciplinary effort.

The following are some child abuse facts:

- Annually over 1 million children in the United States are abused (U.S. Dept. of Health and Human Services 1994).
- Over 1,000 children are known to die each year from injuries sustained: that is, approximately three children a day die as a result of abuse or neglect (McCurdy and Daro 1993).
- Child abuse and neglect occur in families of all racial and ethnic backgrounds, socioeconomic levels, and types of family configurations.
- In the majority of cases, the maltreatment is not an isolated act but a reflection of a pattern of ongoing victimization (Gelles 1987).

- All 50 states have laws against child abuse and neglect. Health care providers are regularly included as mandated reporters in these statutes.
- Disabilities including serious emotional disturbance, learning disability, speech or language delay or impairment, and varying levels of physical impairment are believed to contribute to a higher risk for abuse or neglect.
- The number of new cases of maltreatment in a given period of time among children with disabilities is approximately 1.7 times higher than the incidence among children without disabilities (U.S. Dept. of Health and Human Services 1995).
- Abuse and neglect are known to contribute to, or directly cause, a wide range of disabilities.
- Data from 1992 indicate that 2,936,000 reports of abuse were made to child protective services throughout the United States (U.S. Dept. of Health and Human Services 1994). This statistic represents a 50 percent increase in reports since 1985 (Figure 18–1).
- After investigation and correcting for duplicate reports, 1,160,400 were "substantiated" (i.e., determined to have occurred by child protective services investigations) in 1992. Approximately 43 percent of these children were neglected, 24 percent were physically abused, 19 percent were sexually abused, 7 percent were emotionally abused, and 7 percent were in unclearly defined categories.

DEFINITIONS

The National Center on Child Abuse and Neglect (NCCAN) defines the abused or neglected

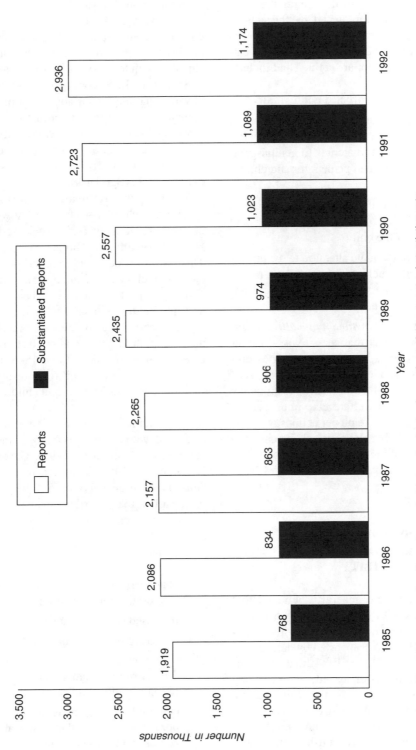

Child Abuse and Neglect
National Estimates

Reports

Substantiated Reports

Year

Number in Thousands

Note: Figures for substantiated reports are derived on the basis of an estimated 40 percent substantiation rate.

Figure 18–1 Reports and Estimated Substantiated Reports of Child Abuse and Neglect in the United States, 1985–1992. *Source:* From *Child Health USA '93,* U.S. Department of Health and Human Services, Pub. No. HRSA-MCH-94-1, 1994.

child as one whose physical or emotional well-being is harmed or threatened by the acts or omissions of his or her caregivers (U.S. Dept. of Health and Human Services 1988). Several categories of maltreatment are defined and include

- *Physical abuse:* inflicted bodily injury
- *Sexual abuse:* involvement of the child in sexual activities ranging from viewing sexually explicit materials to genital-genital contact between perpetrator and child
- *Emotional abuse:* psychologic harm inflicted on the child by the perpetrator's constant criticism, belittling, insulting, and rejection of the child
- *Neglect:* inadequate attention to the child's basic needs, such as protection from physical harm, supervision, nurturing, and opportunities for education
- *Out-of-home or institutional maltreatment:* abuse or neglect that occurs when institutions, agencies, or persons (such as employees of residential facilities or any staff providing out-of-home care) responsible for the child's welfare take improper actions or fail to take proper actions, with the end result being the physical, sexual, and/or emotional victimization of the child, including the inadequate provision of basic needs

CHILD ABUSE AND NEGLECT: CONSIDERATIONS FOR THE CHILD WITH A DISABILITY

Professionals have generally believed that children with disabilities are at a high risk of abuse when compared to children without disabilities. This belief is supported by data and by explanations (e.g., Helfer 1987) that maltreatment arises from a complex interaction among (1) the child's caregiver, (2) the child's needs, and (3) the caregiving environment. Thus a stressed parent caring for a behaviorally demanding child in a relatively unsupportive environment would pose a high-risk situation, whereas a similar child being cared for by a parent with excellent coping skills and several supportive family members would be viewed as a situation with less risk for victimization.

Sexual abuse is conceptually distinct from physical and emotional abuse and neglect. Explanatory models revolve around an abuse of power and control over the child, which culminates in the sexual exploitation of a dependent child's trust by a perpetrator who has authority over the child (Sgroi 1982).

Recently, NCCAN undertook a study examining 1,834 children who were known to have been abused during a six-week period (U.S. Dept. of Health and Human Services, 1995). This study was designed to report on (1) the incidence of child abuse among children with disabilities, (2) relationships between child abuse and the children's disability, and (3) the incidence of children who developed disabilities as a result of child abuse and neglect. Their findings are summarized in Table 18–5, indicating that children with disabilities are at a higher risk for abuse and neglect than children without disabilities.

Other studies of abused children report high rates of developmental disabilities among these children (Sullivan et al. 1991). Garbarino and Brookhouser (1987) identified five sets of circumstances, as an elaboration of the points identified earlier, that contribute to an increased risk for maltreatment. These categories are applicable to children with disabilities and their families and include

- characteristics that make a child unacceptable or difficult to care for
- increased caregiver stress
- caregiver vulnerabilities and lack of coping strategies
- a deteriorating pattern of interaction between caregiver and child
- cultural beliefs, such as reliance upon corporal punishment, that foster attitudes or actions conducive to abuse

Table 18–5 Incidence of Maltreatment of Children with vs. without Disabilities, Reported by National Council on Child Abuse and Neglect, 1995

Type of Maltreatment	Incidence for All Children (per 1,000)	Incidence for All Children with Disabilities (per 1,000)	Incidence for All Children without Disabilities (per 1,000)	Ratio of Incidence for All Children with Disabilities to Incidence for All Children without Disabilities
Any maltreatment	22.6	35.5	21.3	1.67
Physical abuse	4.9	9.4	4.5	2.09
Sexual abuse	2.1	3.5	2.0	1.75
Emotional abuse	3.0	3.5	2.9	1.21
Physical neglect	8.1	12.3	7.7	1.60

Source: From *A Report on the Maltreatment of Children with Disabilities*, U.S. Department of Health and Human Services, James Bell Associates, Inc., No. 105-89-16300, Westat, Inc., 1995.

EVALUATION TECHNIQUES

The comprehensive interdisciplinary evaluation of any allegation of abuse or neglect includes the following (see Giardino et al. in press).

Complete History

The history-taking process in the case of an injured child, in addition to a general medical history, should include details about the abusive event, the child's injuries, and the circumstances surrounding the child's supervision immediately before and after the injury was discovered. Details include

- date and time of injury
- place where injury occurred
- who was watching the child
- whether anyone saw the injury occur
- what events preceded the injury
- how the child reacted to the injury
- how the caregiver responded after the injury was discovered

The history is modified for the various subcategories of abuse. For example, in emotional abuse, the history would focus more on the pattern of meeting the child's emotional needs. In cases of sexual abuse, questions about nonspecific behavioral changes in the child such as

fearfulness, change in school performance, and increased moodiness are more pertinent because many cases do not present with physical findings. In cases of neglect, questions can focus more on how care is provided to the child, what the caregiver's expectations are of the child, and who primarily supervises the child.

Histories are most concerning if they are implausible in view of the child's developmental ability, if they change over time, if they ascribe blame to the child or a younger sibling, or if they contradict other caregivers. For example, claiming that a nonambulatory child ran and fell and thus sustained a femur fracture is implausible and suggestive of abuse. Histories that fail to provide a reasonable explanation for a delay in seeking care are also concerning.

The Physical Examination

Injuries

If specific injuries are present, these areas are best left until last because they are most likely to lead to pain or discomfort. The child can be reassured of health during the examination if no injuries are found. If injuries are found, the child can be reassured that the health care provider will help in the child's recovery. Diagrams and forms have proved helpful for a number of child abuse teams and may serve as an efficient organizing tool (see Exhibits 18–2 and 18–3).

Exhibit 18–2 Preprinted Diagram That May Prove Helpful in Documenting Injuries Suggestive of Child Abuse or Neglect

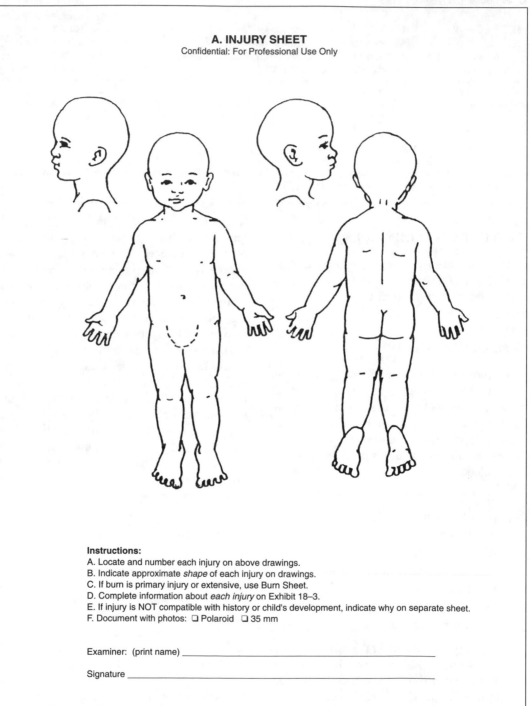

A. INJURY SHEET
Confidential: For Professional Use Only

Instructions:
A. Locate and number each injury on above drawings.
B. Indicate approximate *shape* of each injury on drawings.
C. If burn is primary injury or extensive, use Burn Sheet.
D. Complete information about *each injury* on Exhibit 18–3.
E. If injury is NOT compatible with history or child's development, indicate why on separate sheet.
F. Document with photos: ❑ Polaroid ❑ 35 mm

Examiner: (print name) _____

Signature _____

Source: Courtesy of Charles Felzen Johnson, MD, Children's Hospital, Columbus, Ohio.

Exhibit 18–3 Preprinted Form That May Prove Helpful in Documenting Injuries Suggestive of Child Abuse or Neglect

For Professional Use Only

Child's Name _____

Medical Record Number _____

Complete in Black Ink.

B. INJURY SHEET   PATIENT IDENTIFICATION

INJURY NUMBER	TYPE OF INJURY	SIZE	SHAPE	OBJECT	COLOR	OBSERVED AGE OF INJURY	STATED AGE OF INJURY	EXPLANATION BY: a) mother; b) father; c) child; d) other	IS INJURY COMPATIBLE WITH HISTORY? Yes	No*	Unsure

*If not compatible, why? (Comment by injury number.)

Source: Courtesy of Charles Felzen Johnson, MD, Children's Hospital, Columbus, Ohio.

Sexual Abuse

Specific attention must be given to the anogenital examination. However, the health care provider should be aware, contrary to popular belief, that the majority of sexual abuse cases in prepubertal children do not have specific physical findings (Giardino et al. 1992). In sexual abuse, the child's disclosure remains the most important part of the evaluation process. Children or young adults with disabilities may be physically or psychologically unable to report an experience of sexual abuse or to report the details of an abusive event. However, they may display symptoms that should alert caregivers (see Exhibit 18–4).

The Laboratory and Diagnostic Assessment

The laboratory and diagnostic assessment can be a valuable adjunct in the evaluation of potential child maltreatment. However, the laboratory must be used judiciously, and consultation with child abuse experts may be helpful prior to ordering large batteries of tests. The following are some general guidelines to laboratory and diagnostic testing:

- Skeletal examinations are indicated in all potentially maltreated children under two years of age but are rarely helpful in children over five years of age. Between the ages of two and five years, the clinical situation determines if a skeletal survey is required (American Academy of Pediatrics 1991).
- Blood screenings are not automatically indicated in bruised children; rather, clinical history should guide the ordering of such tests.
- Toxicology screens are useful if poisoning is suspected. However, a great deal of variability exists among laboratories. Urine *and* blood samples are needed for accurate assessment (Wiley 1991).
- Screening for sexually transmitted diseases and the forensic collection of evidence are

part of the sexual abuse evaluation. Consultation with pediatricians familiar with these topics will assist in the accurate collection of these specimens.

Psychosocial Assessment

A complete psychosocial assessment should include at least the following:

- the strengths and weaknesses of the child and the child's caregiving environment (see Table 18–6)
- an evaluation of the child's home and caregiving environment for risk factors associated with abuse
- prior injuries to the child or siblings
- active or former caregiver substance abuse
- history of family violence
- unemployment and financial pressures
- inadequate, overcrowded, or nonexistent housing
- availability of family and community support systems
- caregiver coping strategies
- caregiver's acceptance of responsibility and request for help

Meticulous Documentation

Careful documentation of all evaluation results and caregiver-patient interaction is essential. Specific details related to the history, physical examination, laboratory and diagnostic information, and psychosocial assessments are required. Information should be clear and objective in all notations, and the medical record should be free of any subjective comments.

Importance of Accurate Diagnosis

Missing a diagnosis of maltreatment is serious because a child then remains at risk for further victimization. An incorrect diagnosis, however, is equally damaging because family and child are subjected to a potentially intrusive social and

Exhibit 18–4 Indicators of Abuse and Neglect

- Physical abuse
  1. bruises
     (a) unexplained
     (b) multiple, of differing ages
     (c) forming regular patterns (e.g., shape of an object or hand)
     (d) in uncommonly bruised areas (e.g., chest, groin, abdomen)
  2. burns
     (a) unexplained
     (b) circular cigarette burns, especially on soles, palms
     (c) immersion burns, especially with signs of restraint
     (d) forming regular patterns (e.g., shape of an iron or other household item)
     (e) delay in treatment
  3. fractures or dislocations
     (a) unexplained
     (b) multiple, in different stages of healing
     (c) fractures in nonambulatory infant
- Sexual abuse
  1. nonspecific behavioral indicators
     (a) fearfulness/phobias
     (b) compulsive masturbation
     (c) sexualized play
     (d) excessive distractibility
     (e) nightmares
     (f) difficulty in separating
     (g) aggression

     (h) change in behavior
     (i) suicide attempts
  2. physical indicators
     (a) pain, swelling, or itching in genital area
     (b) bruises, bleeding, or lacerations in external genitalia or in anal areas
     (c) vaginal/penile discharge
     (d) sexually transmitted diseases
     (e) pregnancy
- Physical neglect
  1. physical indicators
     (a) significantly underweight, poor growth pattern ("failure to thrive" [FTT])
     (b) consistent lack of supervision, especially in dangerous activities or for long periods
     (c) inadequate attention to routine health care
     (d) abandonment
- Emotional neglect
  1. nonspecific physical indicators
     (a) speech and language delay or dysfunction, such as stuttering
     (b) physical developmental delay
     (c) hyperactive or disruptive behavior
  2. nonspecific social/emotional indicators
     (a) quiet, withdrawn, passive
     (b) loud, aggressive, hyperactive
     (c) poor self-esteem
     (d) criminal activity
     (e) truancy

Source: American Medical Association 1992; Fleisher and Ludwig 1988.

legal investigation (Kirschner and Stein 1985). Therefore the health care provider is obliged to consider any medical or behavioral condition that may mimic the findings uncovered during the evaluation. It may be necessary to make part of the assessment using a communication board or sign language interpreter. It is also important to have interviewers that are comfortable in various interview modalities.

Some children, more usually with mental retardation, may have self-injurious behaviors that result in bruising for which families or institutions may be charged. Children may suffer bruising from sitting in ill-fitting wheelchairs or other assistive devices. Children who have

bowel and bladder dysfunction may have perineal chafing that could raise the concern of genital injury. A formal differential diagnosis in these circumstances is highly complex. But careful evaluations will uncover the non-abuse-related reasons for the findings and lead to appropriate health care intervention.

On the extreme end of the spectrum of abuse, there may be caregivers who receive secondary gains by causing or amplifying illness or injury in a child (Sullivan et al. 1990). Health care providers can be deceived by the caregiver's history and perform potentially harmful procedures in search of an elusive diagnosis. Such cases can be extremely difficult to identify.

Table 18–6 Family Dysfunction Model

Family Task	Dysfunctional Inadequacy	Dysfunctional Excess
Supplying Physical Needs		
Protection	Failure to protect Child abuse	Overprotection and overanxiety
Food	Underfeeding Failure to thrive	Overfeeding, obesity
Housing	Homelessness	Multiple residences "Yo-yo"/vagabond children
Health care	Medical neglect	Excessive medical care Munchausen syndrome by proxy
Providing Developmental Behavioral and Emotional Needs		
Stimulation (developmental, cognitive)	Understimulation Neglect	Overstimulation "Hothousing" Parental perfectionism Overindulgence, "spoiled child"
Guidance (approval, discipline)	Inadequate approval Overcriticism Psychological abuse	Overindulgence, "spoiled child"
Affection (acceptance, intimacy)	Inadequate affection Emotional neglect Rejection Hostility	Sexual abuse Incest
Socialization		
Intrafamilial relationships	Attenuated family relationships Distanced parents	Parenting enmeshment Overinvolved relationships
Extrafamilial (community, relationship)	Boundaryless families Deficiency in training in extrafamilial relationships	Insular families Excessive restriction from extrafamilial relationships

Source: From *Developmental-Behavioral Pediatrics*, 2nd ed., (p. 148) by M.D. Levine, W.B. Carey, and A.C. Crocker, Philadelphia, Pa.: W.B. Saunders. Copyright © 1992 by W.B. Saunders. Reprinted by permission.

PEOPLE OBLIGATED TO REPORT SUSPECTED CHILD ABUSE

All health care providers who come into contact with children whom they suspect, on the basis of their professional training, to be abused or neglected are obligated to report their suspicions to child protective services and/or the police. Families should always be notified by the professional of the filing of this report. State laws grant immunity from civil or criminal liability to providers who file such mandated reports in good faith. This does not mean that a disgruntled caregiver is prevented from bringing suit against the health care provider, but if litigation occurs,

the provider may claim such immunity if he or she was acting in good faith to comply with the legal mandates governing child abuse in that jurisdiction. It is imperative that all health care providers learn what the specific reporting requirements are in the area in which they practice.

CASE STUDY 1: SUSPICIOUS INJURY RELATED TO CORPORAL PUNISHMENT IN A CHILD WITH OSTEOGENESIS IMPERFECTA

Nelica was an 11-year-old African American girl with a diagnosis of osteogenesis imperfecta

(OI). Previously, she had sustained a left femur fracture that was healed in a malunion requiring surgical intervention in the future. She had been immobilized in a long leg cast with a pelvic extension. She was admitted to the hospital for inpatient rehabilitation

1. to maximize her physical functioning
2. to increase strength and range of motion in bilateral lower extremities
3. to increase strength in her upper extremities
4. to increase functional status from weight bearing to ambulation
5. to coordinate outpatient services with physical therapy and community support services

Nelica lived with her single mother (Ms. H.) and two siblings and had little or no involvement with her father. Her mother was employed part time as a receptionist. In most respects, Nelica was developing typically but was in a special education classroom because she required some assistance for her motoric functioning.

During the hospitalization, Ms. H. revealed that she would spank Nelica when necessary "to keep her in line." As she further explained, she did not want to treat Nelica differently because of her special needs. She wanted all her children to be treated fairly and equally. The team became alarmed at the risk for further fractures. Ms. H. resisted discussion. She stated that this form of punishment was typical in her culture and that she knew this kept Nelica compliant and would make her a better person.

The team talked with the mother about the need to file a suspected child abuse report with the county. Counseling was offered to Ms. H. on alternative methods of discipline. The team encouraged the mother's efforts to normalize Nelica's life experiences but reinforced the danger of physical punishment. A home evaluation by the county child protection agency resulted in in-home services designed to monitor family functioning and provide support.

CASE STUDY 2: EXCESSIVE FEEDING IN A PATIENT WITH CEREBRAL PALSY

Ana was a three-year-old weighing approximately 70 pounds who was initially seen in our Cerebral Palsy Program for evaluation. Previous extensive evaluation could not identify a cause for her obesity. Ana was diagnosed with cerebral palsy with spastic quadriparesis affecting her left side more than the right, developmental delay, and bilateral plantar flexion contractures. She did little more than stay in one position and was unable to sit up, roll, or reach. The goals of admission were weight reduction and intensive physical rehabilitation with the possibility of orthopedic surgery.

Ana was the second child of a young couple who had ongoing marital difficulties. Ana's older brother Jarod was six years old. Ana's mother (Mrs. B.) was a homemaker and complained of low self-esteem. Ana's father struggled to keep a full-time job. He also struggled to remain connected to his family and meet their emotional needs.

Mrs. B. had difficulty complying with diet restrictions, and Mr. B. did not participate in hospitalization. At discharge, Ana had lost about ten pounds. She was sitting up, reaching, and rolling over.

The team made a referral for supportive services through a local community agency. Ana returned to her early intervention program and continued to be followed in the Cerebral Palsy Out-Patient Program. She regained the weight that was taken off during the hospitalization. The team was obliged to report suspected child neglect. Given Ana's rapid growth, there was concern that her weight could cause cardiac problems, leading to possible fatal consequences.

POINTERS FOR MANAGEMENT OF CHILD ABUSE AND NEGLECT CASES

The following are suggestions for managing cases of child abuse and neglect:

- Identify a team of professionals in your institution who have experience with child abuse cases and can serve as consultants.
- Post reminders and use other prompts for the vigilant identification of children who have been abused and neglected.
- Gather a library of information regarding abuse and neglect.
- Provide adequate medical care for the injuries.
- Provide appropriate psychosocial intervention for the child.
- Provide appropriate psychosocial intervention for the parent, guardian, or caregiver.
- Follow legal obligations of filing a verbal and/or written report of suspected child abuse to the appropriate child welfare or adult protective agencies.
- Refer clients over 18 years old with mental retardation to an adult protective agency.
- Contact the police in the event of serious injury that is life threatening.
- Remain objective in all work with the parents or caregivers.
- Identify a team representative to be the liaison with community agencies.
- Develop ongoing team support.
- Work with other community agencies to develop plans to keep the child safe.
- Make referrals for ongoing counseling of the patient if necessary upon discharge.
- Arrange follow-up for the child and family to return to your facility.

CONCLUSION

Children with developmental disabilities are often at high risk for maltreatment. Child abuse intervention must begin with an understanding of the existence of the problem and include prevention services. Many prevention programs and curricula do not mention children with disabilities. Health care providers need to be vigilant in identification of symptoms that could lead to a suspicion of abuse. Professionals working with children with disabilities must be trained and their skills constantly upgraded in the detection of abuse, intervention, treatment, and follow-up services. Adequate services require medical intervention, special education, appropriate communication, and mental health interventions for this special population.

REFERENCES

American Academy of Pediatrics, Section on Radiology. 1991. Diagnostic imaging of child abuse. *Pediatrics* 87, no. 2:262–264.

American Medical Association. 1992. *Diagnostic and treatment guidelines on child physical abuse and neglect.* Chicago.

Fleisher, G.F., and S. Ludwig. 1988. *Textbook of pediatric emergency medicine.* 2nd ed. Baltimore: Williams & Wilkins.

Garbarino, J., and P. Brookhouser, eds. 1987. *Special children, special risks: The maltreatment of children with disabilities.* New York: Aldine.

Gelles, R.J. 1987. *Family violence.* 2nd ed. Newbury Park, Calif.: Sage Publications, Inc.

Giardino, A.P., et al. In press. *A practical guide to the evaluation of physical abuse and neglect.* Newbury Park, Calif.: Sage Publications, Inc.

Giardino, A.P., et al. 1992. *A practical guide to the evaluation of sexual abuse in the prepubertal child.* Newbury Park, Calif.: Sage Publications, Inc.

Helfer, R.E. 1987. The developmental basis of child abuse and neglect: An epidemiological approach. In *The battered child*, 4th ed., ed. R.E. Helfer and R.S. Kempe, 60–80. Chicago: University of Chicago Press.

Kirschner, R.H., and R.J. Stein. 1985. The mistaken diagnosis of child abuse. *American Journal of Diseases in Childhood* 139:873–875.

Krugman, R.D. 1991. Closing remarks. In *Child sexual abuse: The Twenty-Second Ross Roundtable on Critical Approaches to Common Pediatric Problems*, ed. R.D. Krugman and J.M. Leventhal, 100–101. Columbus, Ohio: Ross Laboratories.

McCurdy, K., and D. Daro. 1993. *Current trends in child abuse reporting and fatalities: The results of the 1992 An-*

nual Fifty State Survey. Chicago: National Committee To Prevent Child Abuse.

Sgroi, S.M., ed. 1982. *Handbook of clinical intervention in child sexual abuse*. Lexington, Mass.: Lexington Books.

Sullivan, C.A., et al. 1990. Munchausen syndrome by proxy: A portent for problems? *Clinical Pediatrics* 30, no. 2:112–116.

Sullivan, P.M., et al. 1991. Patterns of physical and sexual abuse of communicatively handicapped children. *Annals of Otology, Rhinology, and Laryngology* 100:188–194.

U.S. Dept. of Health and Human Services. 1988. *National study of the incidence and severity of child abuse and ne-glect*. DHHS Pub. No. OHDS 81-30329. Washington, D.C.: National Center for Child Abuse and Neglect.

U.S. Dept. of Health and Human Services. 1994. *Child health USA '93*. DHHS Pub. No. HRSA-MCH-94-1. Washington, D.C.

U.S. Dept. of Health and Human Services. 1995. *A report on the maltreatment of children with disabilities*. James Bell Associates, Inc., No. 105-89-16300. Washington, D.C.: Westat, Inc.

Wiley, J.F. 1991. Difficult diagnoses in toxicology: Poisons not detected by comprehensive drug screen. *Pediatric Clinics of North America* 38:725–737.

ADDITIONAL SUGGESTED READINGS

Baladerian, N.J. 1991. *Interviewing skills to use with abuse victims who have developmental disabilities*. Available from Disability, Abuse and Personal Rights Project, Spectrum Institute, P.O. Box "T," Culver City, CA 90230.

Benedict, M.I., et al. 1990. Reported maltreatment in children with multiple disabilities. *Child Abuse and Neglect* 14:207–217.

Brookhouser, P., et al. 1991. Patterns of physical and sexual abuse of communicatively handicapped children. *Annals of Otology, Rhinology, and Laryngology* 100:188–194.

Cohern, S., and R.D. Warren. 1990. The intersection of disability and child abuse in England and the United States. *Child Welfare* 69:253–262.

Crossmaker, M. 1986. *Empowerment: A systems approach to preventing assaults against people with mental retardation and/or developmental disabilities*. Columbus, Ohio: National Assault Prevention Center.

Elvik, S.L., et al. 1990. Sexual abuse in the developmentally disabled: Dilemmas of diagnosis. *Child Abuse and Neglect* 14:497–502.

Garfinkel, L., and C. Gorka. 1988. *Pacer Center's description of children with disabilities: A silent statistic in child abuse literature*. Minneapolis: Pacer Center.

Jones, D., and L. Garfinkel. 1993. Defining the unknown: Therapy for children with disabilities who have been sexually abused. *Journal of Child Sexual Abuse* 2:127–129.

Jones, D., and S.A. Martinson, eds. 1990. *Let's prevent abuse: A prevention handbook for early childhood profes-sionals and families with young children, with special emphasis on the needs of children with disabilities*. Available from Pacer Center, Inc., 4826 Chicago Avenue South, Minneapolis, MN 55417-1055.

Kienberger, P., and L. Diamond. 1985. The handicapped child and child abuse. *Child Abuse and Neglect* 9:341–347.

Kline, D. 1987. *The disabled child and child abuse*. Chicago: National Committee To Prevent Child Abuse.

Lanyado, M. 1991. Putting theory into practice: Struggling with perversion and chaos in the analytic process. *Journal of Child Psychotherapy* 17, no. 1:25–40.

Ludwig, S., and A. Rostain. 1992. Family function and dysfunction. In *Developmental behavioral problems*, ed. M.D. Levine, 147–159. Philadelphia: W.B. Saunders Co.

Mayer, P., and S. Brenner. 1989. Abuse of children with disabilities. *Children's Legal Rights Journal* 10:16–20.

Morgan, S.R. 1987. *Abuse and neglect of handicapped children*. Boston: Little, Brown & Co.

Valentine, D.P. 1990. Double jeopardy: Child maltreatment and mental retardation. *Child and Adolescent Social Work Journal* 7:487–499.

White, R., et al. 1987. Physical disabilities as risk factors for child maltreatment: A selected review. *American Journal of Orthopsychiatry* 57:93–101.

Zirpoli, T.J., et al. 1987. Characteristics of persons with mental retardation who have been abused by caregivers. *Journal of Special Education* 21:31–41.

ADDITIONAL RESOURCES

National Committee To Prevent Child Abuse, P.O. Box 2866, Chicago, IL 60690, Tel.: (312) 663-3520. Information available on parenting and child abuse prevention.

National Council on Child Abuse and Family Violence, 1155 Connecticut Ave. NW, Suite 400, Washington, DC

20036, Tel.: (800) 222-2000 for child abuse information, (800) 221-2681 for Family Service America.

Covenant House Nineline, 346 West 17th Street, New York, NY 10011, Tel.: (800) 999-9999. A national toll-free hotline for young people and parents requiring crisis intervention and referrals throughout the country.

American Academy of Pediatrics, 141 NW Point Blvd., P.O. Box 927, Elk Grove Village, IL 60009-0927, Tel.: (800) 433-9016.

American Humane Association, 63 Inverness Dr. East, Englewood, CO 80112-5117, Tel.: (303) 792-9900, fax: (303) 792-5333.

American Professional Society on the Abuse of Children (APSAC), 407 S. Dearborn Ave., Suite 1300, Chicago, IL 60605, Tel.: (312) 554-0166, fax: (312) 554-0919.

National Organization for Victim Assistance, 1757 Park Rd. NW, Washington, DC 20010, Tel.: (202) 232-6682, fax: (202) 462-2255.

PARENT TRAINING

Peter W. Dowrick and Mary L. Osborne

Purpose: to summarize the key elements of the content and structure of parent training programs for school or other personnel who intend to set up parent training or to select and monitor effective programs to which families might be referred.

Parent training programs for parents of children with developmental disabilities are set up for families that are experiencing communicative and behavioral difficulties, compounded by developmental disabilities issues. The overall goal is to teach parents to correct maladaptive patterns occurring between themselves and their children and to promote the children's psychosocial adjustment. Children learn most of their social behaviors, positive and negative, through interactions in their environment. Parents are thus the primary educators of their children. But parents are not (usually) trained caregivers, they are emotionally involved with their children, and some of the principles involved in the teaching of skills to adults are different from those applicable to children. These issues are addressed in this chapter.

The guidelines here are not intended to be comprehensive. The actual skills that the parents will learn (e.g., problem prevention, positive reinforcement, giving instructions) are described in other chapters. Here we focus more on *how* to train the parents. The examples are drawn from extensive experience in developing such programs and from other approaches that have been rigorously developed and described in the professional literature.

DISABILITY-RELATED CONSIDERATIONS

"Parenting" is a demanding task further complicated by the presence of serious disabilities. Parents may have difficulty knowing what is reasonable behavior to expect. Sometimes it is hard to untangle a disability-related emotional reaction of anger or depression, say, from typical adolescent development. Parents may ascribe too much or too little to the disability and set inappropriate boundaries. Or parents may have difficulty knowing how to react or how to teach their child, even when they have a good sense of reasonable expectations.

All interventions need to be tailored to the developmental age of the child. Expectations for the child need to conform to his or her cognitive and physical abilities. For example, a child with motor disabilities will not learn to dress independently at the same age as another child. Parents may also need to be reminded that some social outcomes are better determined chronologically to allow better inclusion in the community with peers. For example, it is better for Julie, a 17-year-old who has mental retardation, to read fashion magazines than to read Dr. Seuss.

GENERAL PROGRAM STRUCTURE

Parent training is often done with a group of six to ten parents (including both partners when possible). Training sessions are typically one to two hours, up to three times per week, for 3 to 12 weeks. Whether training is done individually or in groups, the following format is a useful guide (adapted from Dowrick 1986, p. 35).

- Session format (typical agenda)
  1. Review of previous assignments (5–10 min.)
  2. Information and scene setting on today's topic (5–10 min.): descriptions, vignettes, role play, role reversal
  3. Solutions (about 10 min.): brainstorming, modeling, problem solving
  4. Practice (10–30 min.): rehearsal, cognitions, expressiveness, relaxation
  5. Feedback (about 5 min.): reinforcement, error correction
  6. Feedforward (about 10 min.): clarification, self-modeling, reassurance
  7. Assignments (about 10 min.): individual minigoals, self-assignments, generalization
- Program format
  1. *First session:* overview of the course; familiarization with each other, goals and concepts, videos (see below); overview of parent skills and responsibilities
  2. *Early sessions:* general skills (e.g., consistency, clarity, follow-through, caring), personal and cultural attitudes toward parenting, issues of nonverbal communication
  3. *Middle sessions:* specific target skills common to several parents (e.g., toilet training, tantrums at the supermarket)

4. *Closing sessions:* highly individual problems or complex situations (e.g., transition to a new school, self-administration of medical care)

SAMPLE COURSE

The following typical parent group intervention is adapted from Dowrick (1986, pp. 100–105). The group meets for ten weeks, once a week for 1½-hour sessions. It consists of eight single parents or five couples. One of two children sometimes attend. The children for whom the parents seek support are generally of similar age and development.

- *Session 1: Preliminaries*
  1. introductions
  2. clarification of parent's expectations of the program and of their children
  3. goals of group and anticipated efficacy
  4. developmental information for boys and girls of the age group
  5. parental description of family relevant issues; setting of individual goals
  6. assignment: discuss and revise goals with children
- *Session 2: Clarification* ("behavioral specificity")
  1. identifying behaviors and feelings that matter
  2. how to communicate objectively
  3. assignment: preliminary monitoring of behaviors that matter
- *Session 3: Monitoring* (clarification of monitoring procedures)
  1. one or two children attend this session
  2. role playing of objective observation
  3. assignment: monitor specific behaviors, antecedents, and consequences
- *Session 4: Building positively* (principles of learning, minimal jargon)
  1. positive reinforcement (see also section "Behavior Analysis" later in this chapter)

2. pragmatics of increasing good/desired/adaptive behavior

3. "Grandma's rule" and other ways to build on the positive

4. another session useful for one or two children to attend

5. assignment: observe and record positive exchanges

- *Session 5. Setting objectives, setting limits*

  1. "artificial" incentives for difficult changes of behavior

  2. task analysis (described in Chapter 9, section "School-Based Vocational Training")—breaking down large changes into manageable steps

  3. point systems and progress charts

  4. assignment: develop a charting procedure in collaboration with the child

- *Session 6: Modeling and shaping* (setting good examples; see also section "Instruction and Modeling" later in this chapter)

  1. progressing in small steps

  2. brainstorming on positive experiences of parents

  3. assignments are individually developed on this topic

- *Session 7: Settling conflicts* (expressing emotion, reducing unwanted behavior)

  1. what "punishment" means (see section "Behavior Analysis" later in this chapter)

  2. use of "time-out vs. time-in" and alternatives

  3. problem-solving techniques (see Dowrick 1986, pp. 105–108)

  4. assignment: identify any dangerous behaviors

- *Session 8: Keeping out of trouble* (parents, that is; resisting being drawn into the child's control)

  1. problems of intermittent reinforcement

  2. eliminating the problem reinforcers

3. different forms of ignoring and other diversions

4. assignment: identify patterns of failed ignoring and proposed solutions

- *Session 9: Preparing for transitions* (being less vigilant of the present, keeping eyes on the future)

  1. systematically moving from artificial incentives to natural reinforcers ("fading")

  2. plans for fading strategies

  3. plans for relapse prevention

  4. management of medical disorders, if applicable

  5. assignment: collaborate with family to revise goals

- *Session 10: Conclusion* (debriefing: closure and self-efficacy among participants)

  1. parent summaries of progress, future directions

  2. evaluations and ongoing collection of outcome data

  3. parents identified as potential future group leaders

  4. arrangements for continued support

ESSENTIAL QUALITIES OF PARENTING

A key objective of parent training is to teach the parent to act in the best interests of the child, even when taking charge. Often, being in a position of control is crucial to stabilizing the family and enabling the psychosocial development of the child. Parents often need guidance on *what* are the best interests of the child and how to promote them and their own interests at the same time. Therefore we teach parents

- *To be consistent and clear.* Parents are taught to be clearly consistent and consistently clear, across time and with different people. That is, when a rule is reasonably established, a parent stays with it, and all adults responsible for the child follow the same rule. Children thrive on structure and predictability. Parents can stick to the rules and avoid giving extra chances.

- *To convey loving.* A child should be made to feel special. Parents are encouraged to express love and warmth frequently, both verbally and nonverbally. They are taught to separate the child from the child's behavior. They learn that indulging a child is not necessarily an expression of love but can be a source of confusion.

- *To set a good example.* Children learn from what they see and hear others do. Parents are taught the important effects of their example, whether they like it or not, during positive interactions or discipline—indeed, any time the child is with them.

- *To be supportive.* Children benefit from being acknowledged, even celebrated, for what they do well—or for just trying. Also, parents are taught to engage their child as a collaborator.

- *To be fair.* Effective parenting involves setting clear and consistent consequences, including the use of reasonable discipline when necessary. Parents are taught how to explain and demonstrate fairness, especially when there are siblings for comparison.

- *To be appropriate.* Parents are taught what to expect of the child. For example, toddlers are likely to play cooperatively together only with supervision.

- *To have fun.* Parents are helped to find ways to enjoy their children: laughing, playing, tickling, teasing, talking, singing, etc.

DEVELOPING COOPERATION WITH PARENTS

The attitudes and behavior of family, teachers, or anyone who extensively interacts with a child will seriously affect the progress of training. Developing rapport with parents is an art,

for which the following guidelines will prove useful:

- Involve the parents and their supporters in as many aspects as possible in the development or running of the program. Possibilities include assessments, scheduling, assignments, and progress reports.

- Listen to their opinions, particularly specific examples of their observations. Modify the program to fit family and school circumstances.

- Make a list for each family of two or three individuals who have the most impact on the child's daily life (by virtue of authority or simple propinquity).

- Inform these people about the program, emphasizing its educational nature and its benefits to all concerned.

- Solicit specific ideas on how parents and other important individuals can facilitate supportive circumstances and change.

- Be available for suggestions and questions at any time.

ADULT LEARNING: IMPLICATIONS FOR PROGRAM DEVELOPMENT

For professionals experienced in working with children, important differences emerge when faced with teaching adults. The suggestions below were developed on the basis of experiences with packaged training models (Dowrick and Ryan-Vincek 1992 and others) and pragmatic summaries from the field, especially Zemke and Zemke (1981).

- *Overall*, adult teaching needs to be problem centered, personalized, and as self-directed as possible.
- *Motivation:* Adults can be led to the classroom but they cannot be made to learn.
  1. Adults seek learning, rather than having it thrust upon them, unless they are court referred for being at risk for child abuse; they seek learning for a purpose

related to stress (e.g., "My kid is driving me up the wall").

2. Participation is proportional to the level of stress, so attendance may drop off, ironically, as parenting improves.

3. Parents seek learning that is relevant, practical, and not just "its own reward."

4. Secondary motivators include self-esteem, power, and pleasure.

- *Curriculum:* Relevance to the learner, not the instructor, is the key.

  1. Adults appreciate single concepts, one theory, lack of controversy and choice.

  2. Facts are best received that relate to existing information, paced for focus and transition.

  3. Adults are embarrassed by risk and failure—therefore they do best with "errorless learning," feedforward, not feedback.

- *Recognition of life stages:* Adults evolve through different modes of operating. Training programs benefit from adaptations depending on the ages of individual parents in the group:

  1. 20s—creative, innovative, challenging the established methods

  2. 30s—consolidating, efficient in skills already learned

  3. 40s, 50s—suited to coordinating and supervising the skills of others

  4. 60s+—life experiences enable advising, consultation, relinquishing direct responsibility

- *Medium:* Adults do best with a good measure of self-determination and access to a range of learning media.

  1. "Adults prefer self-directed…learning projects 7 to 1 over…experiences led by a professional" (Zemke and Zemke 1981, p. 46); activities initiated by adult learners are likely to include reading, talking with qualified peers, and the involving of others.

2. Adults select "how-to" media: books, videos, interactive computers.

3. Adults enjoy lectures and short seminars when they provide interaction with experts.

4. Learners require active participation and seek to build new knowledge on old.

5. Key elements for the instructor to arrange are assignments, responsibilities, and follow-up.

- *Setting:* Adults need to be physically and psychologically comfortable.

  1. Provide short sessions and opportunities to practice.

  2. Clarify expectations at the very beginning.

  3. Create a sense of safety—build on life experiences of the participants.

  4. Present open-ended questions; do not "hold forth."

  5. The instructor controls a balance: information/ideas; debate; sharing; the clock; protection of minority opinion; diffusing of hostility; synthesizing of opinions.

USE OF VIDEO

Video is used extensively in parent training in two ways. A camcorder can be used in group sessions to support the learning of new skills. Methods include feedback and feedforward. These techniques are too complex to describe here for people not experienced in their effective use (see Dowrick 1991, especially Chapters 6 and 7). Prerecorded videos are also used for information and discussion. For example, Singer et al. (1989) use the following videotapes:

- *How To Give Clear Directions*
- *Star Chart*
- *A Child's Game* (quality time with parents)
- *Partial Participation* (children with disabilities help with family chores)

Commercial producers of videotapes especially suited for parent training include Research Press, PRO-ED, and Channing L. Bete.

REFERENCES

Dowrick, P.W. 1986. *Social survival for children: A trainer's resource.* New York: Brunner/Mazel Publishers.

Dowrick, P.W. 1991. *Practical guide to using video in the behavioral sciences.* New York: Wiley Interscience.

Dowrick, P.W., and S. Ryan-Vincek. 1992. *Statewide training for full inclusion of children with low incidence disabilities in rural classrooms.* Grant awarded by U.S.

Dept. of Education, Office of Special Education Programs.

Singer, G., et al. 1989. Expanding the focus of behavioral parent training. In *Support for caregiving families: Enabling positive adaptation to disability,* ed. G. Singer and L. Irvin, 85–102. Baltimore: Paul H. Brookes.

Zemke, R., and S. Zemke. 1981. 30 things we know for sure about adult learning. *Training/HRD* (June): 45–47.

ADDITIONAL SUGGESTED READINGS (Also see Appendix C of this book.)

Hundreds of books, booklets, and manuals have become available to address the content issues cited in this chapter. Of the recommendations that could be made, we list some materials for parenting principles and some for specific child issues in which parents can take an affirmative role.

General

Baker, B.L., and A.J. Brightman. 1989. *Steps to independence.* Baltimore: Paul H. Brookes.

Becker, W.C. 1971. *Parents are teachers: A child management program.* Champaign, Ill.: Research Press.

Blechman, E.A. 1985. *Solving child behavior problems at home and at school.* Champaign, Ill.: Research Press.

Christophersen, E. 1988. *Little people: Guidelines for commonsense child rearing.* Kansas City, Kan.: Westport Publishers.

Dangel, R.F., and R.A. Polster, eds. 1984. *Parent training.* New York: Guilford Press. Several notable chapters by different contributors.

Downey, P. 1986. *New directions for exceptional parenting.* Bethesda, Md.: Association for the Care of Children's Health.

Forehand, R., and R.J. McMahon. 1981. *Helping the noncompliant child: A clinician's guide to parent training.* New York: Guilford Press.

Patterson, G.R. 1976. *Living with children: New methods for parents and teachers.* Champaign, Ill.: Research Press.

Specific

Azrin, N.H., and V.A. Besalel. 1981. *A parent's guide to bedwetting control.* New York: Pocket Books.

Batshaw, M.L., ed. 1991. *Your child has a disability: A complete sourcebook of daily and medical care.* Boston: Little, Brown & Co.

Brill, M.T. 1993. *Keys to parenting a child with Down syndrome.* Haupager, N.Y.: Barron's Educational Services.

Dorris, M. 1989. *The broken cord.* New York: Harper Collins.

Dowrick, P.W., and S. Bayley. 1978. *Specific learning difficulties: An introduction for parents.* Wellington, New Zealand: New Zealand SpeLD (Specific Learning Difficulties) Inc.

Ferber, R. 1985. *Solve your child's sleep problems.* New York: Simon & Schuster, Inc.

Finston, P. 1990. *Parenting plus: Raising children with special health needs.* New York: Penguin Books.

Hughes, B.K. 1990. *Parenting a child with traumatic brain injury.* Springfield, Ill.: Charles C Thomas, Publisher.

Lash, M. 1992. *When your child goes to school after an injury.* Boston: Exceptional Parent.

Powers, M. 1989. *Autism.* Rockville, Md.: Woodbine House.

Schliechkorn, J. 1983. *Coping with cerebral palsy: Answers and questions parents often ask.* Austin, Tex.: PRO-ED.

Sloane, H. 1988. *The good kid book: How to solve the 16 most common behavior problems.* Champaign, Ill.: Research Press.

Teyber, E. 1992. *Helping children cope with divorce.* New York: Lexington Books.

ADDITIONAL RESOURCES

Also see Appendix C of this book.

Family Resource Center, P.O. Box 26307, Oklahoma City, OK 73126. Library of books, pamphlets, videos in nontechnical language. Families may call collect, Tel.: (405) 271-7033.

National Information Center for Children and Youth with Disabilities, P.O. Box 1492, Washington, DC 20013. Clearinghouse for parents and professionals. Tel.: (800) 695-0285.

Regional Parent Training and Information Centers. Approximately 65 programs throughout the United States to support organizations for parents and families of children with disabilities are funded by U.S. Dept. of Education.

Call the Office of Special Education and Rehabilitative Services (OSERS) in Washington, D.C., Tel.: (202) 205-5465, or one of the agencies above to locate a center in your region.

PREVENTION OF BEHAVIOR PROBLEMS DURING TRAINING

Joseph S. Lalli, Kelly Kates, and Sean Casey

Purpose: to discuss the appropriate use of proactive assessment and teaching procedures to reduce the occurrence of problem behavior during therapy, schooling, and other situations.

Episodes of problem behavior increase during task-related activities. That is, for many children with developmental disabilities, problems are more frequent during activities related to therapy and schoolwork. The tendency of children with developmental disabilities to avoid these training tasks places them at risk for increased social, emotional, and cognitive delays. Behavior analysts have developed many procedures for preventing problem behavior during task situations. Our goal is to introduce therapists to a selection of these procedures suitable for their use.

This section is in four parts. In the first part, we discuss the information obtained from pretreatment assessment procedures. This information includes the context during which problem behaviors occur and previous efforts to manage the problem behavior. We also discuss issues regarding task characteristics and the child's level of functioning in relation to the training task. In the second part, "Preventing Problems during Therapy," we discuss how to use the assessment information to intervene, provide suggestions on establishing rules for appropriate behavior and arranging the training environment, and describe various training procedures. In the third part, we provide suggestions for monitoring the prevention of behavior problems. We conclude the chapter by describing a case that incorporated most of the described procedures.

ASSESSMENT OF POTENTIAL PROBLEMS AND SOLUTIONS

Child's Case History

The first step in preventing problem behavior is to identify the situations when these behaviors are most likely to occur. The second step is to identify how adults respond to the behavior. If a child creates problems during a training task, it is very likely that the behavior allows the child to end the task. We suggest that therapists carefully review a child's records to obtain the following information:

- types of problem behaviors (e.g., aggression, property destruction)
- situations in which problem behavior is most likely to occur
- previous efforts to manage problem behavior

The prevention of behavioral problems also requires encouraging a child's appropriate behavior. A skilled therapist can prevent behavioral problems by rewarding a child for participating in the task or completing it. We recommend that therapists consider the following points when identifying and selecting potential rewards.

Identify possible rewards by interviewing the child (if appropriate), interviewing the parent(s), or observing the child playing (if possible). Remember that a child's likes and dislikes change, so keep up to date on possible rewards.

Rewards should be age appropriate (what someone his or her age may like) and individualized (not all children like the same toys or activities). Consider rewards that can be provided during a task (praise, pat on the shoulder, food or drinks), rewards that can be provided after a task (playing a video game), and rewards that a child's parent can provide at home (attending a circus or movie). Remember to select rewards that only the therapist and/or the parent has access to. This prevents the child from obtaining the rewards on his or her own.

Task Characteristics

We recommend that a therapist carefully consider the specific objective(s) of the therapy when developing a treatment. Clear objectives help clarify the following features of the task for the benefit of the therapist and the child:

- Identify training priorities.
- Identify the options available to meet the training objective.
- Provide the child with a choice from the options.
- Identify the conditions under which the task is to be completed.
- Identify the sequence of instruction.
- Identify the child's expected performance.
- Identify the criterion for evaluating the child's performance (and for providing rewards).
- Continually assess the child's performance on the objectives.
- Identify the necessary steps to complete a task.
- Identify a child's difficulties in completing a task.
- Identify adaptations required to complete the task.
- Identify options when task completion is not feasible.

Child's Functioning Level on the Task

The more difficult a task is, the more likely it is that problems will occur. Therefore we recommend that before training begins, a therapist assess the child's current skill level on the task. This information helps the therapist start training at a level that is unlikely to produce problem behavior. The assessment also may help a therapist to identify

- the most simple required motor responses
- an early response in the task that places the child in a better position (physically) to do the task
- unnecessary responses that can then be eliminated
- arrangements for instructional materials that reduce the child's unnecessary physical movement

In the next section, we provide suggestions for using the above information to prevent behavioral problems during therapy.

PREVENTING PROBLEMS DURING THERAPY

Standards for Acceptable Behavior

Rules serve as a framework for a therapist's and child's behavior during the training situation. In the rules, clearly describe the child's expected behavior. These expectations serve as the basis for the therapist to deliver rewards. Establish the rules, in part, on the basis of what level of behavioral problems can be tolerated in the training setting. Following are some suggestions for establishing and carrying out rules for acceptable behavior:

- Establish few rules.
- Establish simple rules.
- Establish different rules for different situations.
- State the "dos" rather than the "don'ts."
- Post the rules prominently.
- Actively teach the rules.
- Periodically review the rules with the child.
- Revise rules as needed.

- Have less tolerance for aggression, property destruction, or self-injury than for disruptive behavior.

Rules are most effective when combined with praise for acceptable behavior and not attending to mildly disruptive behaviors (Madsen et al. 1968). After a therapist establishes the rules, the next step in treatment development is to carefully examine the training environment to identify arrangements that encourage appropriate behavior.

Environmental Arrangement

Environmental arrangement refers to how a therapist organizes materials, equipment, desks, supplies, files, and so forth in the training setting. A skilled therapist can arrange these items in a way that reduces distractions and limits the opportunities for a child to make problems. For example:

- Place stationary bikes in an area without visual access to the waiting room.
- Place rewards to allow for easy access by the therapist but not for the child.
- Place delicate training instruments away from a disruptive child.
- Place equipment in a way that allows easy access to all pieces for children.
- Space the training stations as far apart as possible.
- Arrange the training equipment or materials in a way that allows the therapist to circulate freely to all areas of the setting.
- When training is conducted in a small-group arrangement, place children who require the greatest amount of instruction or supervision closest to the therapist.

A well-planned environmental arrangement allows a therapist to circulate efficiently within the training setting, reducing the time a child is left unsupervised and maximizing time for therapy.

Training Procedures

There are a number of ways to modify training tasks that will reduce the likelihood of problems. We recommend that therapists select procedures on the basis of their specific training situation.

Embedded Instructions

Embedding refers to presenting the task-related request during a child's preferred activity (Carr and Carlson 1993). This differs from incidental teaching because the preferred activity is not part of the task. Embedding in physical therapy may consist of interacting with the child (if that is a preferred activity) for one to two minutes before asking him or her to begin an exercise.

Providing Choices

Therapists have shown that providing individuals with a choice regarding the selection of a training task has increased task engagement and decreased problems during therapy (Cooper et al. 1992). To provide choices in a training situation, allow a child to select from the task options available. For example, a nutritionist may provide an overweight child the option of using either a treadmill or a stationary bike as part of the prescribed exercise program. We recommend the following guidelines for presenting a choice of training tasks:

- Present options in an *either* (task 1) *or* (task 2) arrangement.
- Allow a set time for a child to make a choice.
- Make the selection for the child if he or she does not choose within the set time.
- Monitor the child's choices, and stop providing options that are rarely selected.
- Rotate the order of choices across sessions.
- Continually look for additional task options to present.

Reducing Task Requirements

Reducing the task's requirements refers to presenting a task at its minimal requirement to reduce behavioral problems during therapy. A therapist can increase the requirement when a child performs the task without any behavioral problems. We recommend that therapists gradually increase the task's requirements until the entire task is completed. For example, a physical therapist can initially require a child to perform one set (or one repetition) of a specific exercise before providing a break. We recommend the following guidelines when reducing the task's requirements:

- Identify the task's minimal requirements.
- Identify the task's final requirements.
- Identify some intermediate steps.
- Establish the criteria for advancing or decreasing the task's requirements.

Predictability Signals

Many children with developmental disabilities engage in problems during training due to the uncertainty over their expected performance. A predictability signal is information that a therapist can provide a child to reduce problems during training. A therapist can provide verbal instructions or visual cues that show the task's sequence, content (i.e., the steps within the task), and duration (Lalli et al. 1994). We recommend the following guidelines when using predictability signals:

- Clearly state the expected performance.
- Clearly state the child's reward for complying with the request.
- Present the request in an "When you do...you can..." statement (e.g., "When you finish riding the exercise bike, you can sit in the whirlpool").

High-Probability (High-P) Requests Sequence

A high-p request is one with which a child will probably comply. A sequence of such requests is used to get a child started complying before asking him or her to participate in a training activity (Mace et al. 1988). With this procedure, a child may be more likely to comply with therapy-related requests because the therapist has "started the ball rolling," so to speak, with the sequence of high-p requests. For example, when teaching a child an occupational therapy task of putting on a shirt, a therapist provides the child with three to five high-p requests before asking him or her to put on the shirt. We suggest the following guidelines:

- Identify high-p requests during the interview with a child's parents.
- Select requests that are likely to be done correctly (e.g., "Give me five," "Shake my hand").
- Select requests that can be completed in a short time.
- Select three to five high-p requests.
- Provide requests within five seconds of each other.
- Provide descriptive praise after compliance with each high-p request.
- Continue administering high-p requests until the child complies with three consecutive requests.
- Provide the training task request within five to ten seconds of the last high-p request. Monitor the child's compliance with high-p requests; if the child does not comply with these requests, then they are not high-p requests.
- Vary the high-p requests during training tasks to provide novelty.

Reducing Errors during Training

The objective of reducing errors during training is to avoid behavioral problems that result from a child's frustration with the task. To reduce errors during training, a therapist can present the instructional request or provide assistance in a way that increases the chance that the child will respond correctly. For example, prior to starting training, a therapist can provide verbal instructions describing each step of the task. During training, a therapist can model the correct response after providing the instructional request. When teaching vocalizations, a speech therapist can provide the child with a model of the target sound. We recommend the following guidelines:

- Provide requests close to the child (within arm's length).
- Establish eye contact with the child before providing a request.
- Provide only the specific instruction in the request.
- Decide if the child can independently perform the target response.
- Identify the steps in the task that the child cannot perform.
- Identify the type of assistance that will be used in training.
- Practice providing the assistance before formal training begins.
- Establish criteria for gradually fading the assistance.

In the previous section, we described procedures for use with children with developmental disabilities who engage in problem behavior during training tasks. In the next section, we provide suggestions regarding the evaluation of these procedures.

MONITORING THE PREVENTION OF BEHAVIOR PROBLEMS

Therapists need to monitor a treatment closely to evaluate its effectiveness in reducing the occurrence of problem behaviors. Therefore we recommend that besides monitoring the child's progress on the training task, a therapist record the frequency of problem behavior. The therapist then has an objective basis for changing the treatment or for persevering with it when there are only slight gains. Also, a therapist should pay careful attention to the child's task-related performance to identify steps of the task in

which frequent errors occur. This information suggests ways to modify the task to prevent frustration. We recommend that therapists consider the following suggestions:

- Continuously evaluate the effectiveness of the training program.
- Individualize your assessment procedures.
- Assess the child's error patterns. For example:
  1. *Acquisition errors:* failure to learn skill to a minimum performance level
  2. *Fluency errors:* failure to perform skill with sufficient speed
  3. *Maintenance errors:* failure to perform skill after training

CASE STUDY

Amy was a 17-year-old, nonvocal girl with profound retardation, a seizure disorder, and cataracts, whose self-injury contributed to severe deterioration of self-care, feeding, and walking skills. Amy's self-injury consisted of head banging and hand mouthing. Her hand mouthing had resulted in skin breakdown and recurrent episodes of cellulitis. Amy's self-injury occurred most frequently during rehabilitative training tasks. In the following section, we describe procedures used by occupational, physical, speech, and recreational therapists to treat Amy's behavior problems.

The occupational therapist's pretreatment assessment (interviews with parent and direct observations) suggested that Amy's self-injury allowed her to avoid completely most training tasks. Before treatment, her occupational therapist broke into small steps each task involved in Amy's personal care routine (e.g., washing face and hands, brushing hair and teeth). Through the interview with Amy's parent, the therapist identified graham crackers as Amy's preferred food and sitting in her wheelchair and playing with a pop-up toy as a preferred activity. To start a training session, the therapist placed Amy in her wheelchair with her toy (embedding). The therapist provided her with a 30-second break and an edible reward only if she complied with the therapist's request. Initially, the therapist provided the break and edible reward contingent on compliance with each step in the task (reducing task requirements). The therapist gradually increased the criterion to obtain a break and edible reward to completion of the personal care routine. Results showed that Amy's self-injury decreased from an average of over 50 per hour to 7 per hour after the introduction of these procedures. Twenty-four of the 37 training sessions (65 percent) had zero rates of self-injury. By contrast, fewer than 1 percent of training sessions prior to the treatment had no occurrences of self-injury. At the end of training, Amy completed the personal care routine while seated at a table before taking a break and receiving her preferred items.

As described earlier, Amy's self-injurious hand mouthing resulted in severe skin breakdown and cellulitis. A physician ordered Amy's hands to remain open for periods of 10 minutes (four times per day) for increased air circulation to help dry her skin. Her occupational therapist developed hand cones for Amy to hold that kept her hands in an open position, thus improving the air circulation around the palms of her hands. To start a therapy session with Amy, the therapist seated Amy in her wheelchair and requested that she hold the cones for 30 seconds before taking a break. After the 30 seconds, the therapist removed the cones and provided Amy with descriptive praise, her preferred item, and an edible reward. The therapist gradually increased the amount of time that Amy held the cones until she met the prescribed criteria without self-injury occurring during these therapy sessions.

The physical therapy goal for Amy was to increase her independent walking, which had regressed due to her self-injury during training sessions. The initial physical therapy evaluation found normal muscle tone and strength and range of motion. An ophthalmological exam showed adequate vision for supervised walking. These findings suggested that Amy engaged in self-injury during physical therapy to avoid the training tasks. Pretreatment assessment showed that Amy engaged in high rates of self-injury (over 108 per hour) and did not comply with any of the therapist's requests to walk.

The physical therapist's approach to problems during walking training was similar to the procedures used by the occupational therapist during Amy's personal care routines. Walking sessions with Amy were started in her wheelchair, where she sat for approximately two minutes before the therapist requested her to walk. The initial distance was set at five meters. The therapist provided Amy access to the wheelchair for an additional two minutes contingent on her independently walking the set distance. The distance was gradually increased to 81 meters by the end of training. During training, Amy averaged approximately 19 self-injurious behaviors per hour. Ten of the 20 (50 percent) training sessions had no self-injury. Amy's compliance with the therapist's request to walk increased from 0 percent pretreatment to approximately 95 percent during training.

A speech and language evaluation indicated that Amy had no formal method of interacting with others within her environment. Amy's speech therapist decided to teach her how to request items appropriately using a picture card system (i.e., pointing to photographs of items). Training was started with items identified as preferred in the pretreatment assessment (e.g., her wheelchair, edibles). To teach appropriate requesting, the therapist provided Amy with a model of the correct response. For example, the therapist gave the instruction ("Point to the crackers") and immediately pointed to the photograph. When Amy complied (pretreatment assessments showed that she followed one-step directions), the therapist provided the requested item and descriptive praise. The therapist gradually increased the amount of time between her modeling and the request to five seconds to lessen Amy's dependence on assistance. The therapist reported that minimal self-injury occurred during training.

A recreational therapy goal for Amy was to increase the amount of time that she spent in age-appropriate leisure activities. Pretreatment assessment interviews identified sitting in her wheelchair and manipulating a pop-up toy as Amy's preferred activities. Amy's recreational therapist identified age-appropriate activities such as looking at a magazine, doing her nails, and applying makeup as activities that Amy could engage in with little assistance. To teach these activities, the therapist initially started sessions by placing Amy in her wheelchair with a preferred toy. After two to three minutes, the therapist removed the toy and provided Amy with one of the age-appropriate items and instructed her on its use. The therapist initially presented these items for 30-second intervals. At the end of training, Amy sat at a table and used the age-appropriate items for ten-minute periods.

REFERENCES

Carr, E.G., and J.I. Carlson. 1993. Reduction of severe behavior problems in the community using a multicomponent treatment approach. *Journal of Applied Behavior Analysis* 26:157–172.

Cooper, L.J., et al. 1992. Analysis of the effects of task preferences, task demands, and adult attention on child behavior in outpatient and classroom settings. *Journal of Applied Behavior Analysis* 25:823–840.

Lalli, J.S., et al. 1994. Treatment of escape-maintained aberrant behavior with extinction and predictable routines. *Journal of Applied Behavior Analysis* 27:705–714.

Mace, F.C., et al. 1988. Behavioral momentum in the treatment of noncompliance. *Journal of Applied Behavior Analysis* 21:123–141.

Madsen, C.H., et al. 1968. Rules, praise, and ignoring: Elements of elementary classroom control. *Journal of Applied Behavior Analysis* 1:139–150.

ADDITIONAL SUGGESTED READINGS

Bigge, J.L. 1982. *Teaching individuals with physical and multiple disabilities.* Columbus, Ohio: Charles E. Merrill Publishing Co.

Browder, D.M. 1987. *Assessment of individuals with severe handicaps.* Baltimore: Paul H. Brookes.

Cooper, J.O., et al. 1987. *Applied behavior analysis.* Columbus, Ohio: Charles E. Merrill Publishing Co.

Sloan, M.E., et al. 1986. *Functional skills training for day to day care of developmentally disabled individuals: A guide for respite care workers and parents.* Austin, Tex.: PRO-ED.

Snell, M.E. 1987. *Systematic instruction of persons with severe handicaps.* Columbus, Ohio: Charles E. Merrill Publishing Co.

USING SYMPTOM CHECKLISTS AND RATING SCALES TO MAKE REFERRALS

Thomas J. Power

Purpose: to discuss the advantages and limitations of checklists and rating scales in screening children with behavioral and emotional problems and to describe the variety of measures.

Symptom checklists or rating scales can be extremely useful in the screening of children with behavior and emotional problems. For instance, consider the following situation: Edwin, age nine years, is in treatment with a speech/language pathologist because of problems with language comprehension and expression. During the course of treatment, the language pathologist becomes aware that Edwin has a variety of behavioral and emotional difficulties that are contributing to problems functioning at home and school. The language pathologist decides to consult with a psychologist to assist with assessment of these concerns. In this case, the therapist may be able to use checklists (1) to determine whether Edwin needs a more intensive or comprehensive assessment, and (2) to decide whether systematic treatment of Edwin's behavioral and emotional problems is needed.

ADVANTAGES OF CHECKLISTS AND RATING SCALES

Rating scales have the following advantages:

1. *Ease of use:* Rating scales are relatively easy to administer, score, and interpret, and they can be used competently by a wide range of professionals, not just mental health specialists. Computer software is available to assist with the scoring and interpretation of several of these measures.

2. *Assessment of problem severity:* Rating scales are very useful in determining the type and severity of children's problems in various settings. For instance, special educators can use rating scales to evaluate the type and intensity of behavior problems exhibited by children with developmental problems in the school context.

3. *Ecological validity:* Rating scales typically are completed by individuals, such as family members or school personnel, who have extensive knowledge of how children function in real-life environments. Thus information derived from rating scales generally corresponds closely with how children function in naturalistic settings. In contrast, measures given in a clinic setting (e.g., projective personality tests) may have limited ecological validity (see also Chapter 7, the section "Psychoeducational Measures: Ecological Assessment").

4. *Norm referencing:* Many rating scales have been normed on boys and girls across a wide age range. Thus they are useful in determining whether the child has a problem in relation to peers of the same gender and of a similar age.

5. *Multiple informers:* Rating scales have been developed for use by parents, teachers, peers, and children themselves, so as to permit the assessment of a behavioral concern (e.g., aggression, peer rejection) from a variety of perspectives. Information from multiple informants also helps clinicians understand how a child's behavior varies across situations.

6. *Psychometric soundness:* Many rating scales have demonstrated excellent psychometric properties. For example, most of the subscales of the Child Behavior Checklist have been shown to measure the same construct (e.g., attention problems, social problems) consistently and accurately. Thus clinical and educational professionals who use psychometrically sound rating scales can have confidence that they are assessing dimensions of childhood functioning that they seek to assess.

LIMITATIONS OF RATINGS AND CHECKLISTS

Although rating scales are extremely useful, they have several limitations, including

1. *Vulnerability to rater bias:* People often vary greatly when they rate the nature and extent of behavioral and emotional problems in children. For instance, some teachers have a greater tendency to rate behavior as a problem than others. Also, mothers may have a bias to rate behavior as problematic. For this reason, psychologists recommended that ratings from two or more adults who are familiar with a child's functioning in a particular setting

(e.g., mother, father, grandparent) be obtained.

2. *Lack of information about the context of behavior problems:* Rating scales provide helpful information about the nature and extent of behavior and emotional problems, but they generally do not offer data about antecedents and consequences of maladaptive behavior, which is very useful in planning treatment. When conducting a comprehensive assessment for purposes of treatment planning, psychologists recommend that rating scales be used in conjunction with other procedures (e.g., interviews and direct observation techniques).

3. *Questionable sensitivity to cultural differences and handicapping conditions:* Most checklists have been developed to assess the problems typically manifested by children in home and school settings. They may not adequately assess the specific difficulties encountered by children with sensory impairments (e.g., hearing impairment) or severe developmental disabilities (e.g., autism). Also, most rating scales do not provide normative data that reflect the functioning of children from diverse cultural backgrounds. When choosing a rating scale, clinicians need to make certain the scale has been developed and normed for children of similar cultural background and/or handicapping condition.

ASSESSMENT PROCEDURES

Rating scales can be differentiated into measures that assess either a wide range of behavioral and emotional problems or a narrow range of functioning. Also, they can be subdivided according to the person providing the information: parent, teacher, peer, or self. See Table 18–7 for the characteristics of the rating scales described in this chapter.

Wide-Range Measures

The wide-range measure most commonly used in research and clinical practice is the *Child*

Table 18–7 Wide-Range and Narrow-Range Rating Scales

Measure	Respondent	Int.	Ext.	Peer
Child Behavior Checklist	Parent	x	x	x
Teacher Report Form	Teacher	x	x	x
Youth Self-Report Form	Child	x	x	x
Eyberg Child Behavior Inventory	Parent		x	
Conners Parent Rating Scale	Parent		x	
Conners Teacher Rating Scale	Teacher		x	
Home Situations Questionnaire	Parent		x	
School Situations Questionnaire	Teacher		x	
Manifest Anxiety Scale	Child	x		
Children's Depression Inv.	Child	x		
Self-Perception Profile	Child	x		
Peer Ratings	Peer			x
Social Skills Rating Scale	Parent			x
Social Skills Rating Scale	Teacher			x
Social Skills Rating Scale	Child			x

Note: Int. = internalizing problems, *Ext.* = externalizing problems, and *Peer* = peer relation problems.

Behavior Checklist series. This set of measures has been developed to be used by

- parents (*Child Behavior Checklist;* Achenbach 1991b)
- teachers (*Teacher Report Form;* Achenbach 1991c)
- youths 11 to 18 years of age (*Youth Self-Report Form;* Achenbach 1991d)

Each measure is an 118-item rating scale that yields scores on dimensions of

- externalizing behavior (e.g., hostile, aggressive, conduct problem)
- internalizing behavior (e.g., anxious, depressed, withdrawn)

These checklists yield scores on the following eight subscales:

- Withdrawn
- Somatic Complaints
- Anxious/Depressed
- Social Problems
- Thought Problems
- Attention Problems
- Delinquent Behavior
- Aggressive Behavior

Because each form of the *Child Behavior Checklist* yields scores on similar factors, clinicians can compare parent, teacher, and youth ratings regarding specific dimensions of functioning (see Achenbach 1991a). The integration of rating scale information from a variety of sources is a valuable feature of the Achenbach scales.

Narrow-Range Measures

Numerous rating scales are available to assess the severity of specific behavioral, emotional, and social problems. These measures can be categorized according to whether they assess externalizing behavior, internalizing functioning, or peer relation problems.

Measures of Externalizing Problems

The *Eyberg Child Behavior Inventory (ECBI;* Eyberg 1980) is a 36-item parent rating scale that assesses conduct problems and oppositional behavior of children ages 2 to 16 years. The *ECBI* yields two indices:

- a Problem score, reflecting the extensiveness of antisocial behavior
- an Intensity score, reflecting the degree of conduct problems

This measure has been used frequently in clinical practice and research.

The Conners Parent Rating Scale—Revised (Goyette et al. 1978) is a 48-item checklist that has been normed on boys and girls from ages 3 to 17 years. The *Conners Teacher Rating Scale* (Conners 1969) is a 39-item scale, standardized on a very large sample of children ages 3 to 14 years. The Conners scales have been used extensively as measures of

- conduct problems
- hyperactivity
- inattention

The *Home Situations Questionnaire (HSQ;* Barkley 1990), a parent report scale, assesses

- the extensiveness of a child's behavior problems across 16 home situations (e.g., mealtimes, bedtime)
- the severity of problems in each situation

The *School Situations Questionnaire (SSQ;* Barkley 1990) is a teacher report scale that provides information similar to that of the *HSQ* regarding behavior problems in 12 different school situations (e.g., during lectures, at lunch). The *HSQ* and *SSQ* can be completed in about two minutes and can provide information that is very useful when conducting a parent or teacher interview.

Measures of Internalizing Problems

A well-designed, easy-to-use, self-report measure of anxiety is the *Revised Children's Manifest Anxiety Scale (RCMAS;* Reynolds and

Richmond 1985). This 37-item scale has been constructed for use with children ages 6 to 17 years. The *RCMAS,* which has been normed on a very large sample of children, yields scores on the following subscales:

- Total Anxiety
- Physiological Anxiety
- Worry/Oversensitivity
- Social Concerns/Concentration
- Lie Scale

The most commonly used self-report measure of depression is the *Children's Depression Inventory* (*CDI*; Kovacs 1992), a 27-item questionnaire for children ages 7 to 17 years. The *CDI* yields an overall index of depression as well as five factor scores:

- Negative Mood
- Interpersonal Problems
- Ineffectiveness
- Anhedonia
- Negative Self-Esteem

A very useful and widely used measure of self-esteem is the *Self-Perception Profile for Children* (*SPPC;* Harter 1985). The *SPPC* is a 36-item scale designed for children in grades 3 through 8. Alternate versions of this scale have been developed for older and younger children. This scale assesses a child's perception of self in five domains:

- Scholastic Competence
- Social Competence
- Athletic Competence
- Physical Appearance
- Behavioral Conduct

Measures of Peer Functioning

The *Social Skills Rating Scale* (*SSRS*; Gresham and Elliott 1990) is a measure used to assess social functioning from multiple perspectives, including parent, teacher, and self. Separate versions of the scale are available for use with preschool, elementary, and secondary-age children. The SSRS yields scores on the following subscales:

- Cooperative
- Assertive
- Self-Control
- Empathy
- Responsibility

When possible, an assessment of peer functioning should include information from peers because peer assessments have been shown to provide different information from that provided by parents and teachers. Peer nominations are the most commonly used peer assessment method. This procedure involves asking each child to nominate three classmates whom they like the most and three whom they like the least. On the basis of this information, children can be classified as popular, rejected, neglected, or controversial. Psychologists typically view children in the rejected category as being at risk for emotional difficulties and social adjustment problems in the future.

Some psychologists have criticized peer nomination methods because of concerns about the stigmatizing effects of asking children to nominate peers whom they do not like. An alternative procedure (see Asher and Dodge 1986) is to ask each child how much they like to play with each peer on a 1 (*I don't like to*) to 5 (*I like to a lot*) scale. Rejected children tend to be those with the lowest play rating scores. Play rating scores have been shown to be highly correlated with scores derived from the peer nomination procedure.

DETERMINING CUTOFF SCORES

Establishing cutoff scores on checklists depends on the purpose for conducting a child assessment. When psychologists use checklists to diagnose or to determine eligibility for a program, they usually select a conservative cutoff score (e.g., at or above the 95th percentile). This cutoff helps to ensure that only more severe cases are classified or placed into specialized, potentially restrictive programs. When speech therapists or occupational therapists use checklists for screening, a more liberal cutoff score (e.g., at or above the 85th percentile) might be used. Setting the cutoff score lower helps to ensure that children who need additional help are not overlooked in the screening process.

CASE STUDY

With regard to the case of Edwin, previously mentioned, the speech pathologist asked his teacher and mother to complete the *Child Behavior Checklist* (see the results in Table 18–8). The most important findings were

- parent and teacher concerns about attention deficits and hyperactivity (ratings at or above the 95th percentile on the *Attention Problems Scale* for parent and teacher)
- parent and teacher concerns about noncompliant, oppositional behavior (ratings at or above the 93rd percentile on the *Aggres-*

sive Behavior Scale for both parent and teacher)

- parental concern about excessive anxiety (parent rating at the 99th percentile on the *Anxious/Depressed Scale*)

Because the parent's ratings of anxiety were so high, the speech therapist, after conferring with the psychologist, decided to administer the *Revised Children's Manifest Anxiety Scale* (see Table 18–8). This scale revealed marked elevations on the total score (95th percentile) as well as the Worry/Oversensitivity factor (96th percentile).

On the basis of this information, the speech therapist determined that this child displayed considerable evidence of attention deficits and hyperactivity, oppositional behavior, and excessive anxiety. After conferring with the psychologist, the language pathologist referred the child to the school Child Study Team for further assessment of school problems and to a clinical child psychologist for behavioral family therapy and school consultation.

Table 18-8 Percentile Scores for Edwin on the *Child Behavior Checklist* (Parent and Teacher Forms) and the *Revised Children's Manifest Anxiety Scale*

Child Behavior Checklist		
Subscale	Parent Rating	Teacher Rating
Internalizing Dimension	98	60
Externalizing Dimension	99	93
Withdrawn	50	50
Somatic Complaints	80	50
Anxious/Depressed	99	72
Social Problems	90	55
Thought Problems	75	55
Attention Problems	96	95
Delinquent Behavior	96	80
Aggressive Behavior	99	93

Revised Children's Manifest Anxiety Scale	
Subscale	Score
Total Anxiety	95
Psychological Anxiety	91
Worry/Oversensitivity	96
Social Concerns/Concentration	85
Lie Scale	17

REFERENCES

Achenbach, T.M. 1991a. *Integrative guide for the 1991 CBCL/4-18, YSR, and TRF Profiles.* Burlington, Vt.: University of Vermont, Department of Psychiatry.

Achenbach, T.M. 1991b. *Manual for the Child Behavior Checklist/4-18 and 1991 Profile.* Burlington, Vt.: University of Vermont, Department of Psychiatry.

Achenbach, T.M. 1991c. *Manual for the Teacher's Report Form and 1991 Profile.* Burlington, Vt.: University of Vermont, Department of Psychiatry.

Achenbach, T.M. 1991d. *Manual for the Youth Self-Report and 1991 Profile.* Burlington, Vt.: University of Vermont, Department of Psychiatry.

Asher, S.R., and K.A. Dodge. 1986. Identifying children who are rejected by their peers. *Developmental Psychology* 22:444–449.

Barkley, R.A. 1990. *Attention-deficit hyperactivity disorder: A clinical workbook.* New York: Guilford Press.

Conners, C.K. 1969. A teacher rating scale for use in drug studies with children. *American Journal of Psychiatry* 126:884–888.

Eyberg, S.M. 1980. Eyberg Child Behavior Inventory. *Journal of Clinical Child Psychology* 9:22–28.

Goyette, C.H., et al. 1978. Normative data on Revised Conners Parent and Teacher Rating Scales. *Journal of Abnormal Child Psychology* 6:221–236.

Gresham, F.M., and S.N. Elliott. 1990. *Social Skills Rating System.* Circle Pines, Minn.: American Guidance Service.

Harter, S. 1985. *Manual for the Self-Perception Profile for Children.* Denver, Colo.: University of Denver.

Kovacs, M. 1992. *Children's Depression Inventory.* North Tonawanda, N.Y.: Multi-Health Systems, Inc.

Reynolds, C.R., and B.O. Richmond. 1985. *Revised Children's Manifest Anxiety Scale (RCMAS).* Los Angeles: Western Psychological Services.

ADDITIONAL SUGGESTED READINGS

Mash, E.J., and L.G. Terdal, eds. 1988. *Behavioral assessment of childhood disorders.* 2nd ed. New York: Guilford Press.

Ollendick, T.H., and M. Hersen, eds. 1993. *Handbook of child and adolescent assessment.* Boston: Allyn & Bacon.

Reynolds, C.R., and R.W. Kamphaus, eds. 1990. *Handbook of psychological and educational assessment of children: Personality, behavior, and context.* New York: Guilford Press.

Shapiro, E.S., and T.R. Kratochwill, eds. 1988. *Behavioral assessment in schools: Conceptual foundations and practical applications.* New York: Guilford Press.

ADDITIONAL RESOURCES

Ordering Information for Measures Discussed

1. *Child Behavior Checklist* (Teacher Report Form, Youth Self-Report Form): T.M. Achenbach, University Associates in Psychiatry, One South Prospect St., Burlington, VT 05401-3456.

2. *Eyberg Child Behavior Inventory:* Sheila Eyberg, Ph.D., Department of Clinical Psychology, University of Florida, Box J-165, JHMHC, Gainesville, FL 32610.

3. *Conners Parent Rating Scale—Revised* and *Conners Teacher Rating Scale:* MHS, 908 Niagara Falls Blvd., North Tonawanda, NY 14020-2060.

4. *Home Situations Questionnaire* and *School Situations Questionnaire:* Barkley, R.A. 1990. *Attention-deficit hyperactivity disorder: A clinical workbook.* Available from Guilford Publications, Inc., 72 Spring St., New York, NY 10012.

5. *Revised Children's Manifest Anxiety Scale:* Western Psychological Services, Publishers and Distributors, 12031 Wilshire Blvd., Los Angeles, CA 90025-1251.

6. *Children's Depression Inventory:* MHS, 908 Niagara Falls, North Tonawanda, NY 14020-2060.

7. *Self-Perception Profile for Children:* Susan Harter, Ph.D., Psychology Department, University of Denver, 2155 S. Race St., Denver, CO 80208.

8. *Peer Ratings:* Asher, S.R., and K.A. Dodge. 1986. Identifying children who are rejected by their peers. *Developmental Psychology* 22:444–449.

9. *Social Skills Rating Scale:* American Guidance Service, Publisher's Bldg., Circle Pines, MN 55014.

Resources for Selecting Appropriate Checklists

Each school district has a consulting school psychologist, who may be helpful in determining checklists appropriate for a specific problem and population of children.

Children's hospitals generally have a team of pediatric psychologists who are knowledgeable about methods to assess children's behavior and emotional problems.

Medical schools usually employ clinical child psychologists or pediatric psychologists within divisions of child development or psychiatry who can be helpful in selecting appropriate checklists.

OVERVIEW OF BEHAVIORAL CHANGE STRATEGIES

Thomas J. Power

Purpose: to provide an overview of strategies to change undesirable behaviors in children with developmental disabilities.

A wide range of behavioral change strategies is available to assist clinicians in their work with children who have learning, behavior, and social problems. Strategies of behavioral change can be differentiated into those that are externally managed versus those that are self-managed. External management procedures require that a person other than the child (e.g., a parent, health worker, or peer) assume primary responsibility for implementation of the strategy. In contrast, self-management procedures place a high level of responsibility on the child.

Strategies for changing behavior also can be differentiated into those that are experiential, instructional, and consequential. Experiential interventions involve making changes in the child's environment to promote the desired behavioral response. Instructional strategies entail providing verbal and nonverbal training to a child regarding how to behave in a situation. Consequential interventions refer to treatments that structure the consequences that occur or are provided following a behavior performed by the child. Both externally managed and self-managed interventions can be classified according to those that focus primarily on experience versus

instruction versus consequences (see Table 18–9). The following are examples of each of these types of behavioral change strategies.

EXTERNALLY MANAGED STRATEGIES

Historically, the focus of behavioral intervention has been primarily on training supervising adults or peers in strategies to bring about change in children. This class of interventions has been applied successfully in home, school, and clinic settings.

Experiential Procedures

Environmental Planning

Children are able to learn more effectively and behave more appropriately when they function in environments that are responsive to their educational and social needs. Making changes in the child's environment often will lead to higher rates of learning and more socially appropriate behavior. For instance, if a teacher instructs children using curricular materials that are too difficult, they will be less attentive and productive in their work. Changing the curriculum so that students are being taught at their instructional levels often will improve rates of on-task behavior and productivity (Shapiro 1989). Similarly, if a

---

Table 18–9 Classifying Behavioral Change Strategies

Locus of Responsibility	Type of Intervention		
	Experiential	*Instructional*	*Consequential*
External to self	Environmental planning Systematic desensitization	Verbal instructions Modeling	Differential reinforcement/token economy Punishment
Self	Emotion management Role play and rehearsal	Self-instruction Social problem solving	Self-monitoring Self-evaluation

child has problems studying attentively when the television is on, turning off the TV might provide a context that is more conducive to concentrating.

Systematic Desensitization

Systematic desensitization is a procedure frequently used to treat children's fears and phobias. This procedure involves the inhibition of a fear response through the substitution of a response or activity that is incompatible with fear (e.g., relaxation). Systematic desensitization involves having the child work through his or her anxiety in a graduated manner, starting with the least anxiety-provoking situations related to a particular fear and proceeding to more anxiety-provoking events (Wolpe 1991). For instance, children can be taught to manage their fear of taking tests by being trained to use a relaxation response when confronted with a test-related situation. As a therapist, I would begin by focusing on low-anxiety situations (e.g., taking a quiz in a subject that is easy for the child) and then gradually proceed to higher anxiety situations (e.g., taking a major test in a more difficult course).

Instructional Procedures

Verbal Instructions

When a child does not behave in an appropriate fashion, I can give verbal instructions to train the child to respond in the desired manner. Children often misbehave in part because they do not know the rules that apply in a particular situation. A fundamental strategy to improve compliance with rules is

1. to state the rule in clear, concise terms in advance
2. to check to make certain the child understands the rule
3. to prompt the child to follow the rule when required to do so (see Forehand and McMahon 1981)

For instance, if I want my daughter to take out the trash after dinner, a good intervention would be (1) to state clearly to her that she needs to take out the trash; (2) to observe her carefully to make sure she is complying with this directive; and (3) to provide her with a reminder and warning if she does not comply within 20 seconds.

Modeling

Modeling refers to learning by observing the behavior of others, including adults and peers, either in real life or symbolically through observation of videotape. This type of learning can also occur by observing oneself through the use of video procedures, which is referred to as *self-modeling* (Dowrick 1991). Children can learn to respond more adaptively in a situation by watching coping or mastery of the same or similar circumstances. For instance, watching a film about a peer undergoing a particular surgical procedure has been shown to reduce the anxiety of children who are about to undergo a similar procedure (Parrish and Babbitt 1991). Similarly, for a boy who is nonambulatory, observing himself on videotape walking independently, through the use of video editing procedures, may be useful in increasing his motivation and skills to walk.

Consequential Procedures

Differential Reinforcement and Token Economy

Differential reinforcement refers to the systematic provision of positive reinforcement (e.g., adult attention, social praise) in response to the performance of a desired behavior (e.g., talking at the right times in a group), with the systematic exclusion of any positive reinforcement for competing behaviors (e.g., talking at inappropriate times). For instance, when speech therapists pay attention to and praise children for following classroom or clinic rules and systematically ignore misbehavior, children will behave in a more compliant manner. Similarly, as a parent I can help my child overcome her resistance to eating by praising all attempts to eat food and ignoring all behaviors designed to avoid eating.

Token systems are often used to strengthen the intensity of positive reinforcement, increasing the likelihood that a child will follow rules or become a team player. In a token system, children earn tokens or points when they perform specified target behaviors (e.g., staying in seat, paying attention, complying with an exercise procedure). Tokens are accumulated and can be exchanged for backup reinforcers (e.g., privilege of playing a video game for one-half hour; opportunity to play a preferred game with Dad for 20 minutes). Token economy systems have been shown to be very helpful in improving compliance with rules in children who are impulsive or defiant (see Barkley 1987).

Punishment

Punishment, as a technical term in psychology, refers to the application of any consequence to a behavior that reduces the likelihood of that behavior occurring again. Punishment generally occurs in one of two ways: (1) the removal of a positive reinforcer in response to failure to comply with a directive, which is referred to as *response cost*; or (2) the application of an aversive stimulus in response to the performance of an unwanted behavior. An example of response cost is the systematic removal of points, as part of a token system, when the child calls out in a group or fails to pay attention. *Time-out* is another example of response cost in that the privileges of being able to socialize with family members, play with toys, and watch television are withdrawn from the child during a time-out. An example of the application of mild aversives is the use of verbal reprimands to reduce the occurrence of disruptive behavior. Corporal punishment, which generally is not recommended, is an example of the use of a more intensive aversive procedure.

The use of punishment as a method of behavioral change is somewhat controversial. In general, psychologists recommend that consequential approaches to behavioral change consist of primarily positive reinforcement techniques. When positive reinforcement approaches are not sufficient to accomplish change and reductive techniques are considered, it is recommended that nonaversive methods that utilize the least intrusive and least restrictive methods needed to bring about change be used (e.g., privilege removal or time-out for short periods of time; see following section "Applied Behavior Analysis").

SELF-MANAGED STRATEGIES

Over the past 15 years, increased emphasis has been placed on training children in strategies to manage their own behavior. Self-management strategies also can be differentiated according to whether the focus of treatment is upon changing experiences, method of instruction, or behavioral consequences. Furthermore, this class of interventions has a wide range of applications in home, school, and clinic settings.

Experiential Procedures

Emotion Management

Emotion management or *stress inoculation* training entails teaching children strategies to cope independently with emotions (e.g., anger and anxiety) that often interfere with their ability to adapt in social and educational situations. For instance, problems coping with anger in response to provocation from peers on the playground may lead a child to become physically aggressive. Similarly, problems managing anxiety in evaluation situations may make it difficult for a child to concentrate and perform optimally when taking a test. The main components of emotion management training are (1) the reduction of emotional arousal (e.g., through relaxation training) and (2) the identification and modification of inaccurate perceptions or irrational beliefs about a situation (e.g., helping a child identify and confront his or her tendency to take comments from peers too personally; see Meichenbaum 1985).

Role Play and Rehearsal

Another way I can help a child learn new skills is by setting up a simulated experience and having the child act out one or more roles in the situation. Through repetition and rehearsal of roles, the child can refine and master specific skills. Role-play procedures have been used extensively in the training of social skills (Walker et al. 1988). For instance, if I wanted to train a child to cope better with teasing from peers, I would

1. collaborate with the child to identify a potentially helpful strategy to employ
2. set up a simulated experience in which I took the role of the bully and the student assumed the role of him- or herself equipped with a new set of procedures
3. once the child was comfortable using the strategies with me, set up another simulated experience with a peer who was trained to assume the role of a bully
4. after several opportunities to practice the new skills with a peer, encourage the child to try out the procedure by him- or herself on the playground

Instructional Procedures

Self-Instruction

Self-instruction training involves teaching verbal self-control or "self-talk" strategies to enable children to regulate their own behavior more effectively. This procedure is based upon a model of development that posits that problems with self-control are the result of deficits in one's ability to use internal language to regulate behavior. The process of training involves a gradual fading of externally provided direction, in the form of verbal instructions and modeling provided by adult or peer trainers, and a gradual increase in reliance on the child to make appropriate self-statements to direct his or her own actions (Meichenbaum and Goodman 1971). For instance, children can be taught verbally mediated strategies to organize their approach to

completing math worksheets in the following manner:

1. A peer tutor could perform the task and provide verbal instructions about how to approach the assignment in an organized manner.
2. Next, the student could perform the task while the tutor gave the instructions aloud.
3. Then the student could perform the task independently while talking aloud, and the tutor could provide guidance when needed.
4. Finally, the student could perform the task silently on his or her own.

Social Problem Solving

Training in social problem solving involves teaching children a model of problem solving and guiding them to apply this model on their own to cope with the variety of social problems they encounter (e.g., coping with teasing from peers or coping with losing when playing during competitive sports). The main steps of social problem solving training are

1. specification of the problem that needs to be addressed
2. generation of a list of alternative solutions for the problem
3. estimation of the probable consequences of each possible course of action and selection of one alternative
4. evaluation of the outcomes of the selected course of action and return to earlier steps in the process if the problem has not been resolved (Kendall and Braswell 1985)

Social problem solving is often done in groups, which can provide children with valuable insights and feedback from peers about specific social behaviors. Also, social problem-solving training is frequently conducted in conjunction with role-play techniques; the problem-solving process can help children to identify a potentially fruitful course of action, which can be tested out and practiced during role-play sessions.

Consequential Procedures

Self-Monitoring

Self-monitoring requires having a child observe him- or herself to determine whether a particular behavior has occurred. Generally, children are requested to indicate on a recording device whether a specific behavior has happened. For instance, to help a child improve his or her attention skills, I might

1. ask the child to monitor his or her ability to pay attention during a 15-minute seatwork task
2. with the assistance of an audio recorder, present a tone to the child via headphones at random intervals, with the average interval between tones being 45 seconds
3. instruct the child to observe and record whether he or she was paying attention each time the tone sounded

Interventions such as this have been found to be quite effective in improving rates of on-task behavior with children who are inattentive (Lloyd et al. 1989).

Self-Evaluation

Self-evaluation requires that the child evaluate whether he or she has complied with a specified rule (e.g., staying in seat, completion of an assigned task). The child typically is asked to indicate his or her rating on a recording sheet. Self-evaluation interventions generally include an external evaluation component in the initial stages to check that children are rating their own performance accurately. Once children demonstrate that they are able to evaluate their own behavior accurately, external validation systems are gradually faded. Self-evaluation interventions frequently are used in conjunction with token systems described earlier (Rhode et al. 1983). For instance, I could incorporate a self-evaluation procedure into a daily report card sent home from the teacher (see Exhibit 18–5) in the following way:

1. Ask the child to rate him- or herself at the end of the morning and the afternoon regarding how well he or she was able to pay attention, complete work, and work accurately, using a four-point scale.

Exhibit 18–5 Example of a Daily Report Card with a Self-Evaluation Component

DAILY REPORT CARD

Name: _____ Date: _____

Directions: At the end of the morning and afternoon, ask the child to rate his/her behavior on the following scale and then provide your ratings.

> 0 = work harder
> 1 = OK
> 2 = good
> 3 = outstanding

	Morning		*Afternoon*	
Behaviors to work on	Child	Teacher	Child	Teacher
1. Pays attention	_____	_____	_____	_____
2. Completes class work	_____	_____	_____	_____
3. Works carefully and accurately	_____	_____	_____	_____

Total Teacher Ratings _____
Total Match Points _____
GRAND TOTAL _____

Did I meet my goal today? (check one)   ___ Yes! Much better than goal. Outstanding.
___ Yes! Met goal. Good work.
___ No! Did not meet goal. Work a little harder.

2. Request that the teacher provide his or her own rating after the child rates him- or herself.

3. Request the child to bring home the report card each day to show his or her parents.

4. Ask the child to sum the teacher ratings and to sum bonus points, given for number of matches between child and teacher ratings.

5. Have the child compare his or her grand total to an established goal level to determine whether the child was eligible for a reinforcer.

6. Once the child is able to succeed consistently with this intervention, fade gradually the level of external evaluation by having the teacher provide feedback less frequently.

CONCLUSION

The clinician or therapist has a wide variety of behavioral change strategies available to assist a child who is having trouble learning or complying with medical procedures. These interventions can be classified according to a 2 (externally versus self-managed) × 3 (experiential versus instructional versus consequential) matrix. When designing behavioral change strategies, clinicians are strongly encouraged to integrate techniques from several cells of this matrix: that is, interventions should be as comprehensive as possible. For instance, interventions to improve attention in the classroom might include

- environmental manipulations to help a child concentrate better
- clear instructions to pay attention when key points are being presented
- a self-monitoring system
- a token economy procedure to reinforce attentive behavior

Through the integration of various types of procedures, intervention protocols are more likely to be effective and to achieve specified objectives.

REFERENCES

Barkley, R.A. 1987. *Defiant children: A clinician's manual for parent training.* New York: Guilford Press.

Dowrick, P.W., ed. 1991. *Practical guide to using video in the behavioral sciences.* New York: John Wiley & Sons, Inc.

Forehand, R.L., and R.J. McMahon. 1981. *Helping the non-compliant child: A clinician's guide to parent training.* New York: Guilford Press.

Kendall, P.C., and L. Braswell. 1985. *Cognitive-behavioral therapy for impulsive children.* New York: Guilford Press.

Lloyd, J.W., et al. 1989. Self-monitoring of attention versus productivity. *Journal of Applied Behavioral Analysis* 22:315–323.

Meichenbaum, D. 1985. *Stress inoculation training.* New York: Pergamon Press.

Meichenbaum, D., and J. Goodman. 1971. Training impul-sive children to talk to themselves. *Journal of Abnormal Psychology* 77:115–126.

Parrish, J., and R. Babbitt. 1991. Video-mediated instruction in medical settings. In *A practical guide to using video in the behavioral sciences*, ed. P.W. Dowrick, 166–185. New York: John Wiley & Sons, Inc.

Rhode, G., et al. 1983. Generalization and maintenance of treatment gains of behaviorally handicapped students from resource rooms to regular classrooms using self-evaluation procedures. *Journal of Applied Behavior Analysis* 16:171–188.

Shapiro, E.S. 1989. *Academic skills problems: Direct assessment and intervention.* New York: Guilford Press.

Walker, H., et al. 1988. *The Walker Social Skills Curriculum: The ACCESS Program.* Austin, Tex.: PRO-ED.

Wolpe, J. 1991. *The practice of behavior therapy.* 4th ed. New York: Pergamon Press.

ADDITIONAL SUGGESTED READINGS

Dangel, R.F., and R.A. Polster, eds. 1984. *Parent training.* New York: Guilford Press.

Kazdin, A.E. 1989. *Behavior modification in applied settings.* 4th ed. Pacific Cove, Calif.: Brooks/Cole Publishing Co.

Russo, D.C., and J.H. Kedesky, eds. 1988. *Behavioral medicine with the developmentally disabled.* New York: Plenum Press.

Shapiro, E.S., and D.L. Cole. 1994. *Behavior change in the classroom: Self-management interventions.* New York: Guilford Press.

Witt, J.C., et al. 1988. *Handbook of behavior therapy in education.* New York: Plenum Publishing Corp.

ADDITIONAL RESOURCES

To locate a provider who is skilled in the application of behavioral strategies to resolve children's learning and behavior problems, the following resources are available:

- All school districts have a division of special education and access to a school psychologist.
- Every county has a system for providing mental health services to families in their catchment area.
- The Association for the Advancement of Behavior Therapy has a referral service to help clinicians find psychologists with a behavioral orientation in their region; call (212) 647-1890.
- Parent support groups, such as Children with Attention Deficit Disorder (CHADD) can be very helpful in locating providers within a specific region who are well trained in behavior modification procedures. The national number for CHADD is (305) 587-3700.

To purchase books, videotapes, and other materials about behavior modification that have been developed for use by health care professionals, educators, and parents, the following distributors and/or publishing companies can be contacted:

- A.D.D. Warehouse, Tel.: (800) 233-9273
- MHS (Multi-Health Systems), Tel.: (800) 456-3003
- Research Press, Tel.: (217) 352-3273

APPLIED BEHAVIOR ANALYSIS

John M. Parrish, Lee Kern, and Peter W. Dowrick

Purpose: to provide an overview of behavior analysis and to present selected procedures based on consequential strategies of behavior change. We illustrate principles and procedures by way of definition and example. Our descriptions are not endorsements. We do not so much prescribe as inform, with the goal of decreasing the probability that these tactics will be misused. More in-depth resources describing the principles and procedures of applied behavior analysis are recommended at the conclusion of this chapter.

Any thoughtful behavior change strategy begins with a systematic behavior analysis. Other forms of assessment may assign a diagnosis, assign a level of urgency relative to a larger population, or secure funding for services. Behavior analysis identifies the specific circumstances in which behaviors occur so that environmental events can be modified to effect behavior change. It can also be used to characterize the skill level of the child or family member and assess the interactions among family members and other significant individuals.

The strategies described are most commonly associated with applied behavior analysis because of a strong historical link with operant research. These strategies are effective in the management of behavior problems exhibited by individuals with disabilities. Such applications are well supported by an extensive research literature. Our approach emphasizes empowerment through the learning of new skills.

BEHAVIOR ANALYSIS TECHNIQUES AND EXAMPLES

A-B-C: Antecedent-Behavior-Consequence

A basic principle of behavior analysis is that all behavior takes place following some identifiable antecedents and is maintained (or discouraged) by consequences. A behavior analysis requires the following elements (from Dowrick in press):

- The total situation is *observed firsthand.*
- The context (variously termed the *situation, stimulus,* or *antecedent condition*) is described in observable terms: e.g., "Sean is left in the kitchen with a jug half full of orange juice."
- The *behavior*—also called the *response*—currently observed or as planned as the outcome of the intervention is described in objective terms: e.g., "Sean empties the jug down the sink."
- The *consequence* (i.e., the event that results from the behavior) is described, also in observable terms: e.g., "Sean's mother tells him he is a 'bad boy.'"
- The process may be repeated a number of times to be sure behavior and surrounding events or sequences of events occur consistently.
- Any one behavior may be divided into smaller *components*, each with its context and outcome, so that analyses provide useful information.

Qualitative Specification

Example: "Sean is a nuisance around the house" is a fairly objective description. However, a better behavioral description is "When Sean finds anything half full (juice jug, washing machine, whatever), within half a minute he either empties it or fills it." This description includes

- a precipitating event

- a time interval
- a behavior
- other observable qualities

Quantitative Specification

Behavior analysis benefits from descriptions that include

- frequency
- duration
- intensity

Methods of Observation

Some methods of observation are

- *Yes/no determination:* Indication of whether a behavior occurred within a given period of time. Example: The truancy officer indicates that Tommy did not attend school on Tuesday.
- *Frequency count:* Indication of how many times a behavior occurred within a given period of time. Example: Teacher records that Judy correctly answered five questions.
- *Outcome recording:* Indication of whether desired outcome was achieved. Example: Dad notes that Philip washed the supper dishes on time.
- *Event recording:* Notation of the specific occurrence or episode of a target behavior, along with brief description of antecedent(s) and consequence(s). Example: Mom enters the following into her diary: "*Antecedent:* Mom asked Anita to add a 'please' to her curt demand for an apple. *Behavior:* Anita snapped 'No!' and reached for the apple. *Consequence:* Mom calmly removed the apple from Anita's reach."
- *Partial interval recording:* Indication of whether behavior occurred during a specified interval of time. Example: Every

minute for ten minutes, the teacher noted whether Carlos left his seat or not.

- *Frequency-within-interval recording:* Indication of the number of occurrences of a target behavior within a defined time interval. Example: During the first minute of a five-minute observation, Mom records that Julie interrupted Dad two times.

- *Time sampling:* Periodic planned observation of target behavior at times and within situations considered to be representative of longer time interval. Example: During the first five minutes of each breakfast meal, Mom records whether Susie accepts or refuses each presented spoonful of food.

Reactance

When behavior is observed, it often changes. When observations are intensive and are communicated in some form (charts, logs, etc.) to the children or family members observed, the following changes are likely:

- "Desired" behaviors increase.
- "Nondesired" behaviors decrease.
- The effects are most often temporary.
- Effects can be positive and stable for academic skills, sport skills, and social skills that are endorsed by peers.

CONSEQUENCE-BASED TECHNIQUES AND EXAMPLES

Most training techniques involving consequences are known as *contingency management.* Listed below are the core principles.

Reinforcement

Reinforcement refers to circumstances in which a behavior increases. *Positive reinforcement* is defined as the process in which consequences following a behavior result in an increase in that behavior. For example, if praising a child's attempts to walk by herself result in increased steps, positive reinforcement is said to have occurred. Positive reinforcement is often used to enhance a child's life skills. For example, when teaching a child to label objects verbally, the therapist holds a ball in front of the child and asks him to say "ball." If he says "ball," the therapist gives him the ball.

Negative reinforcement is defined as the process in which avoiding a consequence or ceasing an antecedent condition results in an increase of the behavior. For example, a child swallows a disliked food to avoid a reprimand or to escape nagging.

The *reinforcer* is the item or activity provided following a behavior that results in the increase of that behavior. An item or activity is defined as a reinforcer solely by its effect on a behavior. Reinforcers vary widely across children, and within children across time. Reinforcers must be carefully selected on the basis of each child's preferences. Reinforcers are called *primary* if they are biologically necessary or important, such as food, water, warmth, or sex. Reinforcers are called *secondary* if they have become reinforcing because they have been paired with primary reinforcers. For example, if praise is paired repeatedly with delivery of food, praise will become a secondary reinforcer.

Punishment

Punishment refers to a situation in which consequences following a behavior decrease the likelihood of that behavior. When something is taken away from the situation (e.g., a fine, loss of points), it is generally referred to as *response cost.*

Contingency

Sometimes a consequence is described not only as "following" a behavior but as *contingent* on a behavior. To say an event is contingent is to indicate a functional relationship between the behavior and the following event that strengthens or weakens it. The reinforcing value of a consequence can be intensified by clarifying the contingency. For example, instead of saying "good girl," one can give descriptive praise, such as "I like the way you shared the cake with your brother."

Planned consequences can be provided after a set number of responses have occurred (*ratio* schedule) or after a certain amount of time (*interval* schedule). Ratio, interval, or other schedules are termed *intermittent*. *Continuous* reinforcement refers to the application of a reinforcer for every occurrence of a behavior.

Strategies for Reinforcer Selection

Reinforcers vary widely for different children or for the same child across time. No assumptions (e.g., "All children like praise or candy") should be made. Reinforcers should be carefully selected based on the preferences of the child and no one else.

- *Ask the child directly* to name some items or activities that he or she would like, especially ones highly valued or not usually available.
- *Ask others* who are familiar with the child's likes and dislikes.
- *Observe the child* during natural situations, such as mealtimes or play. Observe across daily routines, over a number of days, and in different settings. Note the time the child gazes at an item or activity or the signs of distress when removed.
- *Provide reinforcer sampling:* that is, systematically expose the child to various items (e.g., toys, foods) or activities (e.g., playing outside, listening to music). Record the frequency and duration of the child's engagement with each item or activity.

Further considerations are:

- Select reinforcers consistent with child's chronological age. For example, give an adolescent opportunities to listen to music, look at magazines, or take walks. Providing age-appropriate reinforcers decreases social misperceptions about children and youth with disabilities and facilitates interactions among diverse peers.
- Select natural reinforcers. For example, when teaching a child to say "juice," provide juice as a reinforcer rather than some arbitrary reinforcer, such as a toy. Because such a reinforcer corresponds with natural daily events, it improves the likelihood of generalization.

Effectiveness of Reinforcement

Factors influencing the effectiveness of reinforcement are:

- *Degree of deprivation:* A child may prefer a particular type of soda. However, the soda is likely to be more reinforcing when he or she is thirsty.
- *Timing:* Immediate reinforcement is usually most effective. This is because it prevents intervening behaviors from inadvertently being reinforced.
- *Amount of reinforcement:* Make the amount of reinforcement proportional to the child's effort. At the beginning of a program, larger amounts of reinforcement may be needed to establish a desired behavior because more effort by the child may be required.
- *Schedules of reinforcement:* Ratio schedules are useful when the behavior being reinforced has a definite beginning and end (e.g., Marty receives reinforcement for each toy put away or for each math problem solved). Interval schedules are more suitable when behaviors are continuous or of extended duration (e.g., Juliette receives reinforcement for playing appropriately with Marty for two minutes). Continuous reinforcement is often necessary to establish new behaviors. Once a behavior is established (i.e., it occurs routinely), intermittent reinforcement may effectively maintain it.

- *Quality of reinforcer:* Reinforcers should be highly valued by the individual child. For example, Carlos will work hard for the opportunity to play Zeebo-Zeebo because that is his favorite video game. Zeebo-Zeebo may have no value to another child—or to Carlos next week.
- *Novelty of reinforcer:* Introducing new reinforcers periodically, and otherwise varying old ones, often improves their effectiveness.

Varying the Availability of Reinforcement

Planned Ignoring

Some problem behaviors (e.g., whining, demands, tantrums) are inadvertently maintained by attention in the form of reprimands or arguments given when the misbehavior occurs. Instead, ignoring these behaviors may help to decrease them. For example, when Mom is speaking on the telephone, Essie frequently seeks Mom's undivided attention by whining. Mom avoids attending to Essie in these circumstances so that Essie's whining will "extinguish." Planned ignoring can be an effective intervention for this type of nondangerous, nondestructive behavior.

Many people, however, have difficulty ignoring misbehavior consistently. It is sometimes hard because some adults feel uncomfortable allowing a child's misbehavior to go "unnoticed." Planned ignoring may also be difficult because usually the problem behavior becomes worse before it gets better.

Planned ignoring is not a recommended intervention when the child's problem behavior may place the child's or anyone else's safety at risk or may cause damage to property.

Differential Reinforcement ("Accenting the Positive")

A combination of positive reinforcement for prosocial behavior and planned ignoring for nondangerous, nondestructive misbehavior can effectively promote a child's development. Differential reinforcement is effective for teaching the child to discriminate what to do, what not to do, and when. For example:

- Dad encourages Mi to speak more clearly by responding to her requests when her speech is audible and well enunciated, while withholding attention when she mumbles.
- Differential reinforcement of *appropriate* behavior ("catch 'em being good") is illustrated by acknowledging a child's sharing, while withholding attention when he or she talks out of turn.
- *Incompatible* behaviors can be differentially reinforced, as when a child sits on her hands instead of biting her nails.
- *Low-rate* behavior can be differentially reinforced, such as responding positively to a child's low rate of television watching.
- Differential reinforcement of (any) *other* behavior occurs when the absence of a targeted inappropriate behavior (e.g., fighting) during a predetermined time interval is used as the basis for a reinforcer.

Shaping

Providing positive reinforcement contingent upon occurrence of successive approximations to targeted appropriate behavior helps a child learn new behaviors. Shaping is used to teach new behaviors by reinforcing improved attempts at a target response. Training occurs systematically in a step-by-step manner, in which each step toward a final goal is reinforced. As steps are consistently performed, they are no longer reinforced; however, reinforcement is provided for performing more advanced steps. For example, Wally, an underweight child who is being taught to self-feed, is reinforced initially for merely touching his spoon. Once Wally consistently touches his spoon, positive reinforcement is discontinued for spoon touching and provided if and only if Wally grasps the spoon. After spoon grasping has occurred consistently, Wally is required to grasp the spoon and move it to his plate to receive reinforcement, and so on.

Fading Positive Reinforcement

Systematic withdrawal of contrived reinforcement after a skill or behavior pattern is established, to allow natural or inherent reinforcement to continue, is referred to as *fading*. Fading can be accomplished by decreasing the amount of reinforcement or by requiring more occurrences of a target behavior prior to the delivery of the same amount of reinforcement. Such fading will increase the likelihood that wanted behaviors will occur spontaneously and in settings other than one(s) in which training occurred. For example, Lisa initially received the teacher's praise every time she raised her hand before asking a question. Now he quietly thanks her only at the end of each class session.

Supplementing Other Behavior Change Strategies

Prompting

Prompting is an environmental cue that can be improved with associated reinforcement. There are several types of prompts:

- *Verbal:* "Henry, open your book to page 17."
- *Gestural:* Teacher points to red construction paper and says, "Gwen, please give me a sheet of red paper."
- *Manual:* Teacher provides hand-over-hand guidance while saying, "Vicki, pick up your cup and take a sip."
- *Visual:* Teacher scores Bill's work with a red pencil and asks him to redo "the problems circled in red."
- *Auditory:* When the bell rings, Simone goes to her next class.

Instructional Training and Modeling

In instructional training and modeling, the teacher provides prompts or instructions or demonstrates what to do. She allows the child the opportunity to complete or imitate the action, then provides positive reinforcement. (Also see the section "Instruction and Modeling" later in this chapter.)

Time-In

Time-in refers to the opportunity for a child to spend time in a preferred activity. It is a recognition of the importance of enriching the environment to promote positive participation by a child, rather than disciplining unwanted behavior, since through participation a child practices skills and acquires new ones. Preferred time-in activities might be consuming a favorite snack, taking a bath, accomplishing a challenging task, or being left alone.

Some examples of time-in are:

- Oscar's friends encourage him to play "four-square" with them as long as he follows the rules.
- Wanda is given an array of preferred options from which to select. Each provides social rewards and access to objects and developmental activities.

Setting Limits and Decreasing Unwanted Behavior

Negative Reinforcement

Negative reinforcement is often confused with punishment because both are likely to include an unpleasant event. However, the effects of negative reinforcement and punishment could not be more different. If the behavior decreases in frequency, we say that "punishment" has occurred. If the behavior increases in frequency, we say that reinforcement, whether positive or negative, has occurred. For example:

- The teacher discontinues urging when John completes his work. John's work rate increases to escape the "get busy" comments.
- Li removes a pebble from her shoe. Her behavior of taking off the shoe is negatively reinforced, as she becomes more

likely to remove her shoe when she experiences the discomfort caused by pebbles.

Punishment

Punishment is a controversial and often unreliable way to decrease behavior. It is often important to avoid unintended "punishment" in the technical sense. For example, Mike suggests to Dad that they have spaghetti for supper. Dad says, "Good idea, Mike. But we're fresh out of noodles. You go to Pop's corner store and buy some for us." Given the time and effort to fetch the noodles, Mike reconsiders whether to make any other suggestion about the supper menu.

Punishment is often considered doing something "mean" to someone because that person did something "wrong." The technical meaning of *punishment* is quite different. Punishment is said to have occurred when a behavior decreases as a result of some consequence. What one individual considers an unpleasant event may not be a punisher for another, and the same event that is a positive reinforcer for one child may be another child's punisher.

Many experts contend that punishment strategies should be avoided. The selection of any intervention must follow the principle of least intrusiveness. That is, nonaversive procedures must be tried first and shown to fail. If punishment is used, mild punishers (e.g., response cost, such as contingent, temporary removal of privileges) that are effective should always be the first option.

Response Cost

Response cost is loss of access to reinforcement, contingent on a "misbehavior." It is a straightforward option when disruptive or destructive behavior occurs during an activity in which reinforcement is available. For example:

- Thomas throws an object while listening to a personal stereo; an effective consequence may be to switch off the stereo.
- Julie loses recess time, consequent to aggression in the lunch line.

Time-Out

Time-out occurs when a child is placed in an environment that is less stimulating or engaging than an alternative environment. *Exclusionary* time-out is placing a child in a physically distinct (less desirable) location. *Nonexclusionary* time-out is letting a child stay in the same location but not letting him or her engage in preferred activities.

Time-out may be effective when the child's problem behavior is maintained by time-in: that is, when there are reinforcers available for which the child will "work" to avoid or escape time-out. The effectiveness will depend on the contrasting value of the alternative environments. For example, time-out might work well to decrease a child's tantrums that have been reinforced by social attention and "giving in." However, time-out would not be effective or appropriate to decrease his or her resistance to toothbrushing.

The following are pointers for using time-out:

- "Time-in is tops": A rich schedule of positive reinforcement must be an available alternative. Otherwise time-out is most likely to fail.
- "Time-out is no fun": The amount of reinforcement available to the child during time-out is to be kept to a minimum.
- "Time-out makes sense": Problem behaviors warranting time-out should be agreed upon beforehand, with time-out administered if and only if a behavior previously identified occurs. Precise criteria for use of time-out should be clear.
- "Time-out fits the crime": Use time-out only for inappropriate behaviors that are (potentially) dangerous or destructive and that occur infrequently.
- "The sooner the better": Time-out is best applied immediately following a targeted misbehavior.
- "Let your actions do the talking": Application of time-out is to be accompanied by limited verbal exchange. The caregiver

should quickly direct the child's attention to the labeled misbehavior via a brief, matter-of-fact, and firm statement, such as "Jerry, no hitting Sam. Jerry, go to time-out." The caregiver should not talk to the child while time-out is in effect. Any reasoning or negotiating must be done at another time.

- "Keep it brief": Length of time-out should be predetermined and brief. In general, the lower the developmental age of child, the shorter the duration.

- "Don't lose focus": Upon satisfactory completion of time-out, the child is to be returned immediately to the specific situation in which the troublesome behavior occurred.

- Use time-out sparingly in response to the most challenging behavior. Do not use or recommend time-out as a frequent, first-line response to multiple problem behaviors.

The following is a procedural overview for time-outs:

1. Establish rules for time-out based on the examples above.

2. If exclusionary time-out is intended, select a site that is (1) safe but free of the child's preferred activities, (2) easily monitored by caregiver, and (3) minimally disruptive to others.

3. Practice the entire procedure during problem-free interactions marked by calm and cooperation.

4. In some cases, a warning for impending time-out may be issued, but this should be done only once.

5. Label the misbehavior immediately upon its occurrence, followed by an instruction for the child to go to time-out. If necessary, provide minimal physical guidance necessary to escort the child to the site of time-out.

6. If nonexclusionary time-out is used, preclude the child's ongoing engagement with an activity by saying, "This is time out from _____."

7. Set the timer or announce the time required (by previous agreement).

8. When time-out is successfully completed, reorient the child to the previous situation without admonishment, nagging, or threats.

9. Seek an opportunity soon after time has been served to notice and praise the child's appropriate behavior.

10. *Do not continue* attempts to use time-out if it is repeatedly unsuccessful.

A less intrusive variant of time-out is *contingent observation* ("sit and watch"). A combination of time-in, time-out, and modeling occurs when a child is asked to "sit at the sidelines" while continuing to observe an ongoing activity from which he or she has been removed. While the child is on the sidelines, he or she is instructed in what to observe as prosocial peer behaviors. Attention to those behaviors and agreement to try them are used as criteria for returning to time-in.

PROMOTING SKILL ACQUISITION

Graduated Guidance and Guided Compliance

Graduated guidance combines minimal physical guidance and fading of prompts. *Guided compliance* entails use of graduated guidance in the context of compliance training. The goal is to teach the child to initiate and complete a requested action. These techniques are particularly suitable for functional activities that are developmentally appropriate but that the child has not learned through other means—for example, daily living skills.

The following is a procedural overview for using graduated guidance/guided compliance:

1. Graduated guidance is used to teach a sequence of skills. Each time graduated

guidance is attempted, complete the entire sequence.

2. Adjust physical guidance (e.g., hand pressure) frequently, depending on the child's behavior.

3. Once the child initiates a desired action, decrease the amount of guidance (i.e., provide partial guidance or shadowing).

4. If the child resists direction of guidance, apply only the amount of pressure necessary to maintain his or her progress.

5. When the child's resistance decreases, praise him or her and reduce guidance.

6. Discontinue guidance at the point in the sequence where the child is capable of finishing, at which time both social and tangible reinforcement may be given.

For example, when teaching Trudy to put on tube socks, Mom gently places her hands over the back of Trudy's hands and guides her hands to grasp the top of one sock. Trudy's hands are guided to expand the elastic top of the sock and to fold the top outward and downward slightly. The opened sock, while still in Trudy's guided hands, is placed on Trudy's foot and pulled just past her heel. Trudy receives praise for cooperation to this point. Then Mom continues to provide guidance until the sock is fully extended past Trudy's ankle. If Trudy resists, Mom uses just enough counteracting force to ensure that Trudy proceeds with the task. Immediately upon completion of the task, Mom provides descriptive praise and perhaps a tangible reward.

When Trudy routinely permits her hands to be guided without offering any resistance, Mom reduces amount of guidance provided. For instance, Mom guides Trudy's hands using minimal physical contact, such as by touching the back of Trudy's hand with only a couple of fingers. As long as Trudy continues the task independently, Mom provides verbal praise and encouragement. Mom provides partial graduated guidance until sock is positioned on Trudy's foot just past her heel. At this point, Trudy receives a prompt to use her hands to pull sock up past her ankle. If Trudy initiates and completes this activity independently, Mom praises her immediately. If Trudy is slow to self-initiate, Mom again provides minimal graduated guidance until sock is fully extended past Trudy's ankle.

As the child's skills become increasingly reliable, the teacher or caregiver begins to shadow. That is, she keeps her hands within an inch of child's hands throughout the task. If the child ceases to complete the activity or makes a mistake, the caregiver provides only that degree of guidance necessary for the child to complete the task. During shadowing, the caregiver offers verbal prompts, as needed, and praise. Thus the child simultaneously acquires a skill, becomes more and more independent, and learns to follow verbal instructions. Use of shadowing is faded altogether by gradually increasing distance between the child's hands and the caregiver's hands.

REFERENCE

Dowrick, P.W. In press. *Strategies of behavior change.* New York: John Wiley & Sons, Inc.

ADDITIONAL SUGGESTED READINGS

Baker, B.L., et al. 1976. *Behavior problems.* Champaign, Ill.: Research Press.

Becker, W.C. 1971. *Parents are teachers.* Champaign, Ill.: Research Press.

Blechman, E.A. 1985. *Solving child behavior problems at home and school.* Champaign, Ill.: Research Press.

Christophersen, E.R. 1988. *Little people: Guidelines for common sense child rearing.* 3rd ed. Kansas City, Kan.: Westport Publishers, Inc.

Dangel, R.F., and R.A. Polster. 1988. *Teaching child management skills.* New York: Pergamon Press.

Forehand, R.L., and R.J. McMahon. 1981. *Helping the noncompliant child: A clinician's guide to parent training.* New York: Guilford Press.

Foxx, R.M. 1982. *Increasing behaviors of persons with severe retardation and autism.* Champaign, Ill.: Research Press.

Garber, S.W., et al. 1987. *Good behavior.* New York: Villard Books.

Gerring, J.P., and L. McCarthy. 1988. *The psychiatry of handicapped children and adolescents: Managing emotional and behavioral problems.* Boston: College Hill Press.

Miller, L.K. 1980. *Principles of everyday behavior analysis.* 2nd. ed. Monterey, Calif.: Brooks/Cole Publishing Co.

Swift, M.S., and G. Spivack. 1975. *Alternative teaching strategies: Helping behaviorally troubled children achieve: A guide for teachers and psychologists.* Champaign, Ill.: Research Press.

INSTRUCTION AND MODELING

Shirley A. Harris-Carlson, Mary L. Osborne, and Peter W. Dowrick

Purpose: to familiarize practitioners with some of the key components of modeling and verbal and nonverbal instruction so that they can then apply these techniques, or aid parents and others in the application of these techniques, to manage common behavior problems and teach new behaviors.

Modeling is the process in which a child learns a behavior by simply observing another individual engage in that behavior. Children also learn through other verbal and nonverbal instruction. Verbal instruction is the use of language to teach a child new ways of interacting with the environment, through exact descriptions of effective behavior options. Nonverbal instruction involves the use of gestures, facial expressions, physical guidance, or materials such as cue cards or photographs. Adaptive responding to adult directions is learned most effectively when instructions are positively framed, brief, and direct and when they highlight salient aspects of the instruction.

SPECIAL CONSIDERATIONS FOR DEVELOPMENTAL DISABILITIES

When employing any techniques to manage behavior problems, it is important to tailor interventions to the developmental level or physical limitations of the child. In general, the more salient the intervention, the faster children learn.

Instruction and modeling are particularly suited to teaching children with developmental disabilities. Many children with disabilities benefit from being shown what to do, rather than having to depend on abstract rules. If the practitioner models the correct behavior and instructs the child in the specific steps of the task, the child can learn without having to practice incorrect responses. The pace of a child's progress can be matched against his or her ability to learn.

CASE STUDY

"Emily Ward" is a seven-year-old child with mental retardation. One morning at 7:30, Emily's mother went upstairs to wake Emily for school. "Emily—time to get up. It's snowing and cold outside, so you need to wear warm clothes today." Then, remembering all the mornings that she had to keep nagging Emily to get ready for school, Mrs. Ward said, "Honey, be a good girl this morning, and start the day off right."

Emily eventually crawled out of bed and went downstairs to watch television. Emily's mother rushed through the family room and reminded her again that she needed to get dressed soon. "In a minute," answered Emily, as she flipped through the channels looking for cartoons.

Several minutes later, Mrs. Ward called to her daughter again, "Emily, can you start getting dressed? Get your warmest sweater, because it's cold out today." Emily answered, "Not yet, Mom, this is my favorite."

Several minutes later, Emily's mother came through the family room on her way to the bathroom and impatiently said, "Emily, don't watch cartoons for so long that you make me late for work."

Finally, Mrs. Ward called to Emily from upstairs, "Emily, get dressed now, please." Emily continued to stare at the TV and did not get dressed. Mrs. Ward was upstairs busy getting ready for work. Fifteen minutes later, she realized Emily was still watching TV. Angry that she was spending so much time trying to coax Emily into getting ready for school, she yelled downstairs, "Emily, do you think we have all morning? Get dressed immediately, or I'll send you to school without breakfast."

Mrs. Ward walked into the family room and turned off the television. She knelt down in front of Emily and gently cupped her hand under Emily's chin to establish eye contact. In a firm but quiet voice, she said, "Emily, it's time to get dressed. Go to the laundry room and get your red sweater." When they got to Emily's bedroom, Mrs. Ward found her black leggings hanging in the closet and got her turtleneck from the top shelf. She laid her clothes out on the bed, and told Emily to put them on. Mrs. Ward found Emily's socks and shoes, and Emily was tucking her turtleneck into her pants when her mother turned around. "Nice job, Emily," said her mother. "I'll button your sweater while you get your socks and shoes on." Emily was dressed and ready for school in five minutes.

TECHNIQUES FOR GIVING EFFECTIVE INSTRUCTIONS

As illustrated above, effective instructions often involve both verbal and nonverbal components. As such, they are included together. When delivering instructions to children, there are various points to consider that will help increase the likelihood of follow-through. Dos and don'ts of effective instructions are as follows:

- *Establish attention by securing eye contact.* It is important to obtain the child's attention—often accomplished by securing eye contact. With some children, it is sufficient to call their name. With children who are developmentally delayed or highly distractible, it is often helpful to prompt them physically to establish eye contact. A cue such as putting your hand under the child's chin can be effective, as it was with Emily and her mother.

- *Tailor directions to the child's developmental age.* Do not speak above the child's level of comprehension. The child must be able to understand the verbal direction as well as possess the necessary skills to follow the direction. For example, Mrs. Ward was finally successful in obtaining Emily's compliance when she gave simpler, more specific directions and helped with more difficult tasks such as getting the turtleneck from off the top shelf.

- *Directions should be clear, specific, and direct.* Avoid abstract directions. It is always best, regardless of the child's developmental age, to state the directions clearly in terms of specific behaviors rather than in general terms. Parents and professionals frequently fall into the trap of placing too great a demand on children's abstract thinking. Instead of telling Emily to "be a good girl," Mrs. Ward would have met with more success if she had given her a more specific direction, such as "Emily, put your sweater on, now."

- *Directions should be given in a low-key but firm voice.* Sometimes adults become so annoyed and angry that they yell and threaten when stating a direction. Stating the direction in a matter-of-fact, firm, and calm voice is much more likely to produce the desired result. Shouting at Emily did not help to gain her compliance.

- *Use positive rather than negative directions (i.e., what to do rather than what not to do).* If a child is told *not* to do something, she or he may still not know which behaviors are expected of her or him. Stating the target behavior will increase the likelihood of the child's understanding and following the direction. Telling Emily not to make her mother late for work does not tell her exactly what to do.

- *Directions are better than questions.* Giving a direction in the form of a question usually invites a choice you really do not want to give. A good rule is: "Never ask a question you do not want to hear the answer to." When Mrs. Ward asked Emily if she could start getting dressed, Emily told her "no" because her favorite cartoon was on.

- *Avoid "let's" phrases.* Using "let's" phrases when stating directions is similar to using a question form. It may create a sense of options when there are none.

- *Avoid multiple commands.* It is important not to give too much information at once, especially to preschool children. Giving a sequence of commands often leads to confusion. By the time the child completes the first direction, she or he will probably have forgotten the other two directions.

- *If a rationale is given, keep it short, and always state the command at the end.* Stating the direction last in the sequence helps to increase the likelihood that the direction will be followed. When Mrs. Ward provided a rationale for Emily to get her warmest sweater, she distracted Emily from following a specific direction that she had given at the beginning of the sentence.

- *Don't nag.* Give clear parameters with instructions. Otherwise, children learn to delay because they have learned that Mom does not really mean it until she says it the tenth time. State the expectations clearly and only once, perhaps twice to make sure they are clear, and then give an opportunity

to respond if necessary (see preceding section "Applied Behavior Analysis"). For young children, particularly those developmentally under five or six years of age, it is best to state the direction at the time the child is expected to complete the task. For example, Emily is obviously in the habit of ignoring her mother's directions to get dressed until her favorite cartoon ends!

- *Be quiet after giving a direction.* Prevent distraction, give the child space, and allow time for him or her to follow the direction. In the example, Mrs. Ward continued talking, sometimes with additional directions after giving a specific instruction.

- *Give only directions on which you are prepared to follow through.* It may be necessary to back up an instruction with a consequence such as time-out or other procedures discussed in earlier sections of this chapter. For example, Mrs. Ward would have done better not to threaten Emily that she would forfeit breakfast since she obviously did not intend to follow through.

MODELING

Modeling is the process by which an individual (the model) serves to illustrate behavior that can be imitated or adapted in the thoughts, attitudes, or overt behaviors of another individual (the observer). This definition and the key points below are adapted from Dowrick (1994). For more information, see Bandura (1986, in press).

The four components of observational learning are

- attention by the child to modeled events
- retention of what is observed
- the child's ability to imitate the modeled behavior
- motivation to reproduce those behaviors

The efficacy of modeling is influenced by the characteristics of the model, the setting, and the process.

Important characteristics of the model are

1. *Similarity:* The child will pay more attention to a similar model and be more likely to replicate the demonstrated behavior. Behavioral similarity is more important than looks, social background, and so on. Thus an adult who *behaves* similarly to the child makes a better model than another child who characteristically acts differently.

2. *Multiple models:* Two or three models demonstrating similar coping behavior are better than one. They improve the overall effect, especially generalization. But unusual models, such as clowns, can be more distracting than effective.

3. *Coping models:* To some extent, a model who is seen to struggle (and then succeed) is better than one who is slick and overly masterful. But *high-status* models, such as pop singers or school athletes, are also effective.

4. *Skill matching:* The above characteristics amount to the need to ensure that the skills demonstrated are attainable at an appropriate level of difficulty for the child who is learning.

Important characteristics of the setting are

1. *Medium:* Modeling can be demonstrated by a live performance; on video, audio tape, or other representation; or in the imagination.

2. *Location:* Events are best arranged in the place where the learned behavior is to occur. But they can be staged in a "safe" setting or pointed out wherever they naturally occur. The child may be given the task of counting instances of effective behavior in the classroom, on television, or at the mall.

3. *Consequences:* Modeling can be enhanced by two types of consequence. A positive outcome or contrived reward can be arranged for the model. Or the child can be rewarded in connection with observing and attending to important elements of the model's behavior. But beware of "negative outcome modeling," often arranged with the intention to act as a deterrent. It usually backfires, sometimes tragically. For example, televised dramatizations of teenage suicides are routinely followed by increased self-inflicted deaths in that age group.

Important characteristics of the process are

1. *Imitation:* Some children (e.g., with autism) must first be taught observational learning as a skill in itself. That is, attending to the model, remembering, practicing, and appropriately applying the response can all be taught through instruction and positive consequences.

2. *Sequence of learning:* There are many ways for a child to learn. Different approaches each have their role in a phase of development or set of new skills. Modeling is most often used early in the learning sequence: basic information, modeling, practice, feedback, and feedforward.

3. *Self as a model:* When new skills are very challenging, self-modeling may be most effective. Self-modeling videos are made by planning ways to stage an effective outcome and editing the tape to display two minutes of adaptive behavior by the child himself or herself (Dowrick 1991, pp. 109–126). This technique is most used when other forms of learning or performance are inhibited by anxiety, low self-esteem, or a poor concept of what is to be achieved.

Some key uses of modeling for psychosocial support are

1. *New skills:* Modeling and instructions are usually the methods of choice for skills for which the child has no approximations in the repertoire: for example, tying shoelaces.

2. *Appropriate use of skills:* Modeling can also be used to increase the frequency of a skill seldom used or to encourage a common response—such as interrupting, making suggestions, laughing—to occur in more useful contexts.

3. *Aggression:* Problem solving or social skills can be taught as replacements to tantrums, fighting, or other unacceptable behavior.

4. *Impulsivity:* Children can learn to wait, count to ten, or apply self-talk.

5. *Teamwork:* Cooperating with others often needs to be modeled; this would help Emily (see below).

6. *Safety:* Modeling is essential to teaching personal safety and road and home safety because the circumstances of occurrence are so rare (we hope).

7. *Daily living and motor skills:* These skills may be "new," as noted above, or they may require special adaptation for the child's disability.

8. *Preparation for treatment:* Modeling is often used to prepare children for operations, dentistry, and so on. Some videos are commercially available.

9. *Social skills:* In addition to those mentioned above, communications of all kinds, including signing and other language acquisition, benefit from or even depend on modeling.

Case Study: Modeling for Emily

Several uses of modeling could be employed to assist with Emily's situation of dawdling in the morning. Mrs. Ward could arrange for Emily to come to her mother's room and dress together. That would allow instructions, modeling, and praise to occur in combination. In a naturalistic way, an older sibling could provide a model of the steps of getting ready for school. Because Emily likes to watch television in the morning, her mother could put on a videotape of getting ready for school in place of the broadcast program. It may be best to identify specific skills that need focused modeling instruction. Getting Emily away from the television is probably best done using systematic consequences (see previous section in this chapter, "Applied Behavior Analysis," or the later section "Prevention of Behavior Problems during Training"). But if some skill of getting ready, such as buttoning or choosing the right garments, makes Emily confused or anxious, it would benefit from a modeling approach. If it were really challenging, it could be worth self-modeling. And that would give Emily something her mother would approve her watching on television.

REFERENCES

Bandura, A. 1986. *Social foundations of thought and action: A social cognitive theory.* Englewood Cliffs, N.J.: Prentice Hall.

Bandura, A. In press. *Self-efficacy: The agency of control.* New York: Freeman.

Dowrick, P.W. 1994. Behavioral modeling. In *Encyclopedia of psychology,* 2nd ed., ed. R.J. Corsini, 145–147. New York: John Wiley & Sons, Inc.

Dowrick, P.W. 1991. *Practical guide to using video in the behavioral sciences.* New York: Wiley Interscience.

ADDITIONAL RESOURCES

The ARC of the U.S. (formerly Association of Retarded Citizens), Tel: (800) 433-5255. This organization, which can refer you to your local ARC organization, can offer information and referrals for parent training.

Your local Community Mental Health Agency can often provide guidance or refer you to the appropriate source.

In seeking professional assistance, look for someone who has experience in working with children with disabilities and their families. Your school district may be able to refer you to professionals in your area, or you can contact your local community hospital or university-affiliated program for assistance.

PREVENTION OF BURNOUT IN PARENTS AND PROFESSIONALS

Symme W. Trachtenberg and Jocelyn I. Trachtenberg

Purpose: to focus on the signs, symptoms, and causes of burnout experienced by parents of children with developmental disabilities and special health care needs and the human service professionals that work with them, and to offer suggestions for prevention, intervention, and treatment.

DEFINITION OF BURNOUT

Burnout is a state of distress caused by a specific situation or daily pressures that build up and become intolerable. Burnout develops gradually in both parents and professionals, and if it remains untreated, it can cause people to lose their ability to function at their normal level. People experiencing burnout often show signs of fatigue, frustration, and dissatisfaction with their lives. In work settings, people with burnout develop negative attitudes toward their work, such as apathy, loss of caring, alienation; they withdraw from work or life in general (Cyr and Dowrick 1991; see also the Additional Suggested Readings):

- *Emotional exhaustion:* The parent or professional becomes so tired and stressed that he or she is unable to deal effectively with daily caregiving tasks or job responsibilities. Emotional exhaustion, for professionals, can be caused by intense transactions (overinvolvement) with clients (parents of children with complicated medical needs). Stressful events, hassles, and excessive work demands, insufficiently diminished by supervisor supportiveness, can lead to mental health symptoms, significantly contributing to job dissatisfaction and eventual job termination (Koeske and Kelly 1995).
- *Depersonalization:* The parent or professional begins to have negative feelings toward the child or clients. These negative feelings may cause the parent or professional to become distant and to treat the child or client as an object rather than a person, thus becoming less sensitive and jeopardizing the quality of care the child or family receives. However, Lief and Fox's work in 1963 on "detached concern" acknowledges the need for the professional to have the ability to balance professional caring with objectivity and to maintain a professional distance in order to be able to continue to work in a potentially emotionally draining environment (Koeske and Kelly 1995).
- *Feelings of lack of personal accomplishment and powerlessness:* The parent or professional feels that his or her efforts are unimportant and unnoticed. These feelings cause the person to lose confidence in his or her ability to be effective at home or at work.

Both parents and professionals exhibit emotional exhaustion, depersonalization, and lack of personal accomplishments. But differences exist in the intensity of the feelings. For example, depersonalization is more common in professionals than in parents.

SYMPTOMS OF BURNOUT

Many symptoms are common to both parents and professionals experiencing burnout. These symptoms are both emotional and physical.

Emotional symptoms are those of feeling

- depressed
- threatened
- worried
- helpless
- hopeless
- like a failure

- irritable
- unproductive
- confused
- unable to make positive changes
- forgetful
- guilty
- angry and resentful

Physical symptoms are

- tense muscles, headaches, lower/upper back pain
- high blood pressure and/or heart palpitations
- loss of appetite or overeating
- fatigue
- lowered immune system functioning
- psychosomatic disorders
- sexual problems

Some signs of burnout are specific to parents (see the References and Additional Suggested Readings at the end of this chapter):

- fatigue from chronic role strain or from constantly being responsible to provide or coordinate the child's care
- feeling stigmatized by the child with special needs, thus isolating self from family and friends
- feeling vulnerability and stress when faced with a lack of resources
- feeling depression and guilt
- reacting negatively to the child, creating a risk for child abuse
- inability to cope with demands of daily living
- overwhelming stress to the point of requesting out-of-home placement
- neglecting the child's needs (e.g., follow-up medical and therapy appointments, school)
- daily tasks and responsibilities neglected or forgotten
- lack of communication between parent and child

Some signs of burnout more specific to professionals are

- decreased personal accomplishments, frustration
- depersonalization
- increased susceptibility to accidents and to illness, absenteeism
- loss of empathy for consumers
- withdrawal and isolation
- decreased productivity and ability to help
- lack of job satisfaction
- inability to organize
- avoidance or overreliance on colleagues
- procrastination

CAUSES OF BURNOUT

Parents and professionals who live or work with children who are chronically ill and needy are often in the caregiver mode, are rarely rewarded for their work, are at great risk for burnout. How an individual reacts depends on

- past life experiences with managing stress
- personality and interpretation of stressful situations
- attitudes toward the disability
- work, environmental, and social factors

Specific possible causes of parental burnout are

- feelings of guilt that the condition could have been prevented
- child and parent feeding negatively off one another
- constant demands to center one's life on the child
- responsibilities and costs of caring for child
- inability to trust professionals for parent support or for caring properly for the child
- competing priorities
- continuous uncertainties in diagnosis, etiology, treatment, and prognosis
- no outlet for frustrations or other feelings

Specific possible causes of professional burnout are

- constant contact with children who make minimal progress
- need to deal with government officials and regulations
- lack of social recognition, lack of resources, isolation, oversized caseload for classrooms, lack of supervisory support
- conflicts over roles and values
- perceptions of unfair treatment by the employing organization or the population served
- work overload
- feeling unappreciated by demanding parents under emotional stress
- economic pressures
- changes in senior management, other personnel, and policies
- routine mundane work
- inability to use full range of skills

Professionals who emotionally overextend themselves to consumers and have an overlap of stresses between their personal life and their work are at the highest risk for burnout.

PREVENTING AND TREATING BURNOUT

The strategies below are compiled on the basis of research listed in the References and Additional Suggested Readings at the end of this chapter.

The following are some interventions for parents:

- Implement stress management programs in which parents can learn effective ways to recognize and deal with stress, promote self-awareness, and develop coping skills.
- Develop a skills training program for parents to reduce stress and depression, improve communication and problem-solving skills, and improve satisfaction with professional support.

- Locate and utilize additional resources and strategies, in support of both personal and socioecological coping skills.
- Arrange caregiver respite—another person trusted to care for the child.
- Obtain temporary respite: the use of humor is both underused and very useful.
- Make contact with other parents of children with similar diagnosis (peer support group).
- Write a diary to share with other parents or professionals.

The following are some interventions for professionals:

- Obtain peer support through confronting issues, debriefing, and expressing feelings.
- Obtain other support from colleagues, supervisors, or mentors, such as peer review or collective problem solving.
- Care for the body through exercise, diet, sleep, and relaxing activities.
- Enhance work group autonomy and opportunities to develop competence.
- Obtain help to live in the present and differentiate between long- and short-term goals; to construct a job list and set goals; to develop realistic expectations; and to limit involvement appropriately.
- Have periodic performance evaluations, including adequate supervision, skills training, and appreciation of services provided.
- Pace yourself to do/complete one project at a time to avoid a sense of being overwhelmed, out of control, and unsuccessful.
- Take time off work, take vacations with loved ones, and spend time with people who care for and support you.

SUMMARY

It is of paramount importance that professionals be able to identify the signs and symptoms of burnout in themselves, those they supervise, and the clients (parents/families of children with developmental disabilities) to whom they provide clinical services and to develop appropriate intervention. Depending on the reason for an individual's problem, a treatment plan should be developed and be put into place.

One must respect the choice of an individual who does not seek help for burnout. At times, the best that can be done is for the person to acknowledge that some difficulty exists. When individuals needing help are ready, they will either engage in some of the interventions available or remove themselves from the situation. When the symptoms are medical, a referral to a physician is essential.

Prevention programs and intervention strategies should be established and made available to avoid burnout in as many instances as possible. Prevention and treatment of burnout lead to improved health and capability to do difficult tasks and empowerment to find solutions, both in the day-to-day care of a child with developmental disabilities and the professional organization. In the workplace, prevention/treatment leads to less turnover, improved client care, a potential for a balance of caring without overinvolvement, and increased job satisfaction.

REFERENCES

Cyr, C., and P.W. Dowrick. 1991. Burnout in crisisline volunteers. *Administration and Policy in Mental Health* 18:343–354.

Koeske, G.F., and T. Kelly. 1995. The impact of overinvolvement on burnout and job satisfaction. *American Journal of Orthopsychiatry* 65:282–292.

ADDITIONAL SUGGESTED READINGS

Adams, J., ed. 1980. *Understanding and managing stress: A book of readings.* San Diego: University Associates, Inc.

Bereford, B.A. 1994. Resources and strategies: How parents cope with care of a disabled child. *Journal of Child Psychology and Psychiatry* 35:171–209.

Bourn, D.F. 1993. Over-chastisement, child noncompliance and parenting skills: A behavioral intervention by a family center social worker. *British Journal of Social Work* 23:481–499.

Burke, S.O., et al. 1991. Hazardous secrets and reluctantly taking charge: Parenting a child with repeated hospitalizations. *Image* 23, no. 1:39–45.

Canam, C. 1993. Common adaptive tasks facing parents of children with chronic conditions. *Journal of Advanced Nursing*, 18, no. 1:46–53.

Gray, D.E. 1993. Perceptions of stigma: The parents of autistic children. *Sociology of Health and Illness* 15, no. 1:102–120.

Johnson, J.T., et al. 1993. Professional burn-out among head and neck surgeons: Results of a survey. *Head and Neck* 15:557–560.

Kirkham, M.A. 1993. Two year follow-up of skills training with mothers of children with disabilities. *American Journal of Mental Retardation* 97:509–520.

Leiter, M. 1991. The dream denied: Professional burnout and the constraints of human service organizations. *Canadian Psychology* 32:547–558.

Lowenstein, L.F. 1991. Teacher stress leading to burnout: Its prevention and cure. *Education Today* 41, no. 2:12–16.

Meyer, W.J., et al. 1994. Parental well-being and behavioral adjustment of pediatric survivors of burns. *Journal of Burn Care and Rehabilitation* 15, no. 1:62–68.

Pasquali, E.A. 1991. Humor: Preventive therapy for family caregivers. *Home Health Nurse* 9, no. 3:13–17.

Pelletier, K. 1979. *Mind as healer, mind as slayer: A holistic approach to preventing stress disorders.* New York: Dell Publishing Co.

Pelsma, D.M., et al. 1989. Parent burnout: Validation of the Maslach Burnout Inventory with a sample of mothers. *Measurement and Evaluation in Counseling and Development* 22, no. 2:81–87.

Stav, A., et al. 1986. Burnout among social workers working with physically disabled persons and bereaved families. *Journal of Social Service Research* 10, no. 1:81–94.

Stevenson, R.G. 1989. Professional burnout in medicine and the helping professions. *Loss, Grief and Care* 3, nos. 1–2:33–38.

Tunali, B., and T.G. Power. 1993. Creating satisfaction: A psychological perspective on stress and coping in families of handicapped children. *Journal of Child Psychology and Psychiatry* 34:945–957.

Vaccaro, J.V., and G.H. Clark. 1987. A profile of community mental health center psychiatrists: Results of a national survey. *Community Mental Health Journal* 23:282–289.

Walton, W.T. 1993. Parents of disabled children—children burn out too: Counseling parents of disabled children on stress management. *International Journal for the Advancement of Counseling* 16, no. 2:107–118.

SIBLING SUPPORT

Karen M. Hudson, Hillary S. Domers, and Joan Rhodes

Purpose: to identify and address the specific needs of siblings of children with disabilities.

All children have special and differing needs. It is valuable to discriminate the needs of siblings in typically developing families in comparison to the needs of siblings of people with disabilities.

The birth of a brother or sister has a great impact on the family system. Siblings have a reciprocal relationship that is considerable. Sibling relationships are a microcosm of life in which the child experiences a full range of emotions and begins to master the tasks of living. The emotions that siblings experience toward each other span the spectrum of human emotion: love, hate, happiness, sadness, glee, anger, and so on. The tasks of life include friendship, companionship, loyalty, negotiating, caregiving, comforting, teaching, advising, mediating, and trailblazing.

A sibling relationship is often the longest relationship one ever experiences. When a child is born with or acquires a disabling condition, the delicate balance of the family system is thrown into chaos and creates stress for each member. Parents, unable to grasp the full significance of the disability, are often uncertain of what to report to siblings and how to tell them. Parents may have difficulty offering accurate information to siblings as they themselves struggle. As parents experience fluctuating grief, anger, loss, and denial, their emotions interfere with their ability to assimilate what they are hearing from the medical team. Therefore an inaccurate or incomplete picture may be presented to the sibling.

There is a range of opinions among professionals as to the emotional impact of having a child with a disability in the family (see Freeman and Hagen 1989; Lobato 1990; McHale et al. 1986; Tritt and Esses 1988; Seligman and Darling 1989). Factors with an impact include siblings' age at the time of onset, financial conditions of the family, and cultural values concerning disabilities. The success of interventions with siblings often depends on the involvement of the parents. Nonetheless, the adjustment needs of the healthy sibling are as important as those of the sibling with a disability.

There is some consensus on what aids overall adjustment:

1. Parents have resources to cope with the disability and can act as role models for siblings.
2. Parents can communicate openly with siblings about disability on an age-appropriate level, recognizing that the type of information needed changes across developmental stages.
3. Parents do not overburden siblings with responsibility for brother or sister with a disability.
4. Parents have a good marital relationship.
5. Parents have time for healthy siblings.

6. Siblings have exposure to other families with similar situations and mutual support.

Some guidelines to assist parent communications with the siblings of the child with disabilities are set out in Table 18–10.

INTERVENTIONS

Approaches to sibling support vary with the age of the siblings.

Early Childhood

Table 18–11 shows issues for very young siblings (0–5 years) of a disabled child.

The following case study illustrates some early childhood issues and possible interventions.

Diane W., at age four years, five months, fell into the apartment complex swimming pool. She nearly drowned but was resuscitated by efforts of the fire/rescue squad and the lifeguard on duty. Her brothers Roger (eight years) and Carl (six years) were present and witnessed the near-drowning episode of their sister. There was also a two-year-old sister, Betty. The family lived in a very small two-bedroom apartment. The mother worked full time, and the father was unemployed because of intense recurring migraine headaches.

Diane was physically and developmentally devastated. She was severely and profoundly impaired and totally dependent for her care. She was unable to communicate in any way, but she seemed to respond to music and the voices of her family. She was large for her age and difficult to handle because of her weight and the stiffness of her muscles. She took all her feedings via a gastrostomy tube. She had difficulty with her secretions and needed frequent suctioning. She was described by her parents and siblings as a previously vivacious, bright, strong-willed child who was close to her brothers and sister and friendly with all who knew her.

The parents were grief stricken and guilt ridden. The father projected his anger toward the lifeguard who did not intervene successfully enough with Diane's near-drowning, the apartment complex management, and anyone who came into his life. He expressed a desire "to hurt somebody." The mother offset her husband's an-

Table 18–10 Guidelines To Assist Parents in Communicating with Healthy Siblings

Children's Common Errors of Thinking	Ways Parents Can Correct These Errors
Children often misinterpret what they have heard.	Ask children to restate in their own words what parents have told them about sibling. By age three, children can understand the disability.
Young children have "magical thinking" and may incorrectly believe that an event they have been involved with has caused their sibling's disability.	Reinterpret child's story and stress the causal event(s), emphasizing that a bad thought or bad deed did not bring harm to the brother or sister.
Children often have a "private version" or unspoken reasons that the sibling has the disability.	Offer accurate and factual information to the sibling.
Children have a different perception of the disability and the impact on the family.	Assist children to reflect on their feelings and concurrently provide a model (e.g., it is confusing/upsetting/complicated for me too, but we'll learn/figure it out/manage).
Children may worry and become fearful or resentful about who will care for the sister or brother with a disability if something happens to parents.	Reassure siblings that as parents they can care for all their children and that the child without a disability will not be expected to care for the brother or sister with a disability.

Table 18–11 Issues and Interventions in Early Childhood for Siblings of a Child with Disabilities

Age of Sibling	Life Stage Model (Erikson 1964)	Possible Disability Issues	Family Interventions
0–5 years	Basic Trust vs. Mistrust (0–18 months)		
	Dependence on the quality of care he or she receives	Separation from family	Support and encourage family and sibling involvement at hospital
	Development of a basic trust in the environment	Inconsistent caregiving and caregivers. Inconsistencies with daily routine	Maintain consistent caregiving whenever possible
	Autonomy vs. Shame and Doubt (18–36 months)		
	Child struggles to control and master his or her environment	Altered family interactions; siblings may feel neglected	Provide social, physical, and play stimulation and interaction with the sibling with a disability
	Initiative vs. Shame and Doubt (3–6 years)		
	Effort to attain independence while maintaining self-esteem	Confusion/sadness in face of brother's or sister's illness/disability	Facilitate and validate feelings; provide role model for parents/caregivers

ger by internalizing her own emotions. The oldest sibling Robert had nightmares and was preoccupied with his sister Diane. Carl was acting out at school and not cooperating with the classroom routine.

The support at home and at school was not enough to give relief and to help both boys understand the anger, grief, guilt, and fears that were triggered by having watched their sister nearly die. Mr. and Mrs. W. took turns staying with Diane at the hospital. The older children admitted that they missed their parents. After Diane's return home, the presence of nurses staying many hours greatly changed family dynamics and diminished privacy and a normal life. Roger and Carl, questioned by peers at school, were not prepared how to talk about their sister's condition. Discussions about Diane with the other children at home were overly optimistic with the focus on what she used to be like. There was little opportunity to express confusion and sadness. The family was in need of multiple options for therapeutic support when Diane was transferred for rehabilitative services.

The family received the following interventions:

- Mr. and Mrs. W. received weekly counseling to assist their expression of anger, guilt, sadness, and confusion regarding Diane's profound delays and medical complexities. (The focus initially was to support the marital relationship so that they could in turn provide the support and guidance necessary for Diane's siblings.)

- A play therapist provided the parents and the three siblings an opportunity to express difficult concerns through roles and imagined situations.

- A social worker met several times with the family, encouraging the children to express their personal worries regarding peers with their parents present to help develop a plan to understand and cope with the siblings' issues.

- Drawings were used to bring out the children's feelings and concerns.

- A psychotherapist modeled possible responses to questions asked by peers and neighbors as examples of how the children and parents might comfortably respond.

- A social worker discussed options for residential placement as a choice for the family, given the demands of Diane's care. However, Mr. and Mrs. W. were adamantly opposed to foster care or any possible residential placement in the event that Diane's care became overwhelming to the family.

- The family was connected with a family therapist at discharge to help with Diane's transition home and related issues.

- The family life planner from the law firm handling the litigation and the health insurance case manager made certain that support services for the siblings, such as adequate housing, van transportation for Diane and her siblings, and access to public school, were in place.

- The social worker encouraged the siblings to learn about Diane's care so they could be more familiar with her equipment, medication, and medical routine. The social worker invited significant extended family to be involved in sessions to encourage appropriate balance of attention and support for Diane as well for as the siblings and parents.

- A therapist provided specific focus for the father's issues, referring him to a physician for migraines and exploring paid training in a governmental program focused on vocational rehabilitation to improve family finances.

Further interventions for this age group are

- Pen Pal Network for siblings to share feelings and common concerns
- sibling support groups available through community organizations or hospitals
- special trips and activities for siblings—for example, Children's Museum
- potluck suppers to enable social interaction among siblings from different families

- development and implementation of curriculum in schools to address feelings of children with disabilities and their siblings
- newsletter for siblings addressing feelings, concerns, and suggested ideas to organize a network of sharing and communication for mutual support

Middle Childhood

Table 18–12 shows issues for siblings who are in middle childhood (6–12 years).

The following case study illustrates some middle childhood issues and possible interventions.

Jimmy J., 11 years old, had a fraternal twin brother, Nick. The boys had been developing normally, with no significant past medical history. They were due to start sixth grade in a local school. They had an older sister, Kelly, age 17 years. Both parents worked outside the home. The family lived in a tightly knit community in a large city.

Two days prior to the start of school, the family, except the father, were traveling home when their van was struck broadside by a speeding vehicle on the passenger's side. The mother and Kelly in the front seat were not harmed. Nick was seated behind the driver and sustained only minor bruises and a broken arm. Jimmy was in the middle back seat and was found unconscious at the scene by the rescue crew. He was helicoptered to a trauma center and transferred to a neurorehabilitation unit three weeks later. He showed only generalized response to any external stimulus.

Both parents took a leave during the acute care stay. On Jimmy's admission to the rehabilitation center, Mrs. J. stayed at the bedside several nights a week. Sometimes Nick and Kelly brought their books and homework assignments to Jimmy's bedside. Nick started sixth grade by himself—of great significance to him and to his family. He and Jimmy were described as "best buddies" by their parents. Nick seemed to be quite distressed by going to school without his brother. His broken arm was a constant reminder

Table 18–12 Issues and Interventions in Middle Childhood for Siblings of a Child with Disabilities

Age of Sibling	Life Stage Model (Erikson 1964)	Possible Disability Issues	Family Interventions
6–12 years	*Industry vs. Inferiority*		
	Need to be effective and successful	Fear and confusion that sibling is "different" from peers	Adults give concrete, specific information to enable understanding of disability—reassuring sibling when realistic
	Mastery of school life	Feelings of isolation that family is dissimilar from families of peers	Use peer support and foster connections with "veteran families"
	Cultural and social identity is formed	Parent overinvolved with child with disabilities. Other sibling feels ignored and not valued at a time when family interactions are vital	Encourage balance of attention and facilitate special time and forum for other siblings and family as a whole
	Mastery of external environment	Concern with illness as a punishment for misdeed or "bad" thoughts, or "survivor's guilt"	Dissipate the fantasies by encouraging discussion of suppressed concerns and foster positive self-worth

of what had happened. Other children were asking many questions.

Because of Mrs. J.'s bedside vigils at the rehabilitation center, Nick was home in the mornings before school and back in the afternoons without his mother. He was expected to get his homework completed and manage his time by himself, although his mother was available by telephone. By his parents' report, he was sullen and moody or acting out. Sometimes Nick sought out his parents as he struggled to understand why this injury had happened to his brother. His brother was in coma, but the trauma had happened to him also.

The family received the following interventions:

- The parents were encouraged to revise their hospital visiting schedule to spend more time with Nick.
- Nick (and the rest of the family) received suggestions of how to interact with Jimmy.
- Suggestions were offered to bring in familiar objects from home that might stimulate Jimmy. Nick was empowered to take re-

sponsibility for this task (e.g., he chose objects like a favorite toy, or his pillow, and a baseball hat Jimmy liked to wear).

- It was explained to Nick that his brother could probably "hear" in spite of his deep state of coma.
- Nick and Kelly were encouraged to record their voices reading and in general conversation for Jimmy to hear.
- Nick was included in professional discussions about stages of coma. By being included in bedside meetings, Nick was able to gain factual information as well as reassurance that his brother was following a normal progression of recovery.
- Nick was provided with individual counseling sessions. He needed a forum to ask questions and to try to understand what had happened.
- The school was contacted to determine the school's understanding of Jimmy's injuries and Nick's subsequent needs. Factual information was provided about traumatic brain injury and the effects on siblings.

- Nick was encouraged to become involved in extracurricular and group activities.

Further interventions useful to this age group are

- encouraging siblings to attend workshops for healthy siblings
- encouraging reading of appropriate materials (e.g., fictional stories written about families where there is a sibling with a disability)
- encouraging activities to be enjoyed by entire family (e.g., day trips to museums or amusement parks so the family can function as a whole unit)
- encouraging ways for parents to spend individual time with healthy siblings

Teenage Years

Table 18–13 shows issues for teenage siblings.

The following case study illustrates some issues of the teenage years and possible interventions.

Marianne T. was a 16-year-old with juvenile-onset Tay–Sachs disease who had experienced a decline in intellectual functioning and activities of daily living. From her early years, she had exhibited emotional and behavioral disturbances but was able to be managed in the home and at school. She was admitted to the hospital for the development of a behavior management program to reduce her aggression.

Marianne's behavior at home and at school had become very problematic. Her moodiness and aggressive acts were puzzling, and her parents were concerned about the safety of family members and about how she had changed ("We just want our daughter back"). Previously, her parents described Marianne as lovable.

Marianne's brother Joel (7 years) and two sisters, Linda (17 years) and Rose (18 years) lived at home with their parents. Rose had graduated, was employed, and was contributing financially

Table 18–13 Issues and Interventions in Teenage Development for Siblings of a Child with Disabilities

Age of Sibling	Life Stage Model (Erikson 1964)	Possible Disability Issues	Family Interventions
13-18 years	*Identity vs. Role Confusion*		
	Identity formation associated with peer relations	Heightened power, concern, and importance of peer group judgment of teenager with a disability	Engage teenager in discussions that teach proactive ideas and techniques to influence peers toward accepting sibling
	Development of self	Parents' expectations that healthy sibling will assume responsibility and caregiving for the sibling with disabilities	Assess family functioning and advocate for appropriate understanding of the needs of the healthy sibling. Explore options for networking
	Growth of sexual identity Search for young love	Given typical adolescent issues compounded with stress of disabilities, family may experience further crisis and dysfunction	Exploration of individual and family counseling for different family members
	Creation of occupational identity Development of a sense of difference	"Parentified" sibling may worry about separation from family and future	Provide information and support for personal and occupational adult development

to the household. She was afraid to "get too close" in a romantic relationship because of her perceived responsibility for Marianne. Mrs T. was a homemaker and primary caregiver of Marianne. Mr. T. was sporadically employed and had a history of alcoholism. He was a war veteran who experienced post-traumatic stress disorder. Linda and Rose felt compromised in their lifestyles, with occasional rebelliousness.

The family received the following interventions:

- Individual, sibling, marital, and family counseling was offered on a regular basis after the admission.
- A therapist encouraged Rose and Linda to express their feelings of anger, confusion, and sadness about their sister.
- Therapists facilitated increased communication between Rose and Linda to discuss mutual concerns about their sister.
- The hospital social worker encouraged Rose and Linda to pursue ongoing friendships and close relationships.
- Rose and Linda were encouraged to pursue developmental tasks such as moving from the family home to an apartment to attend college.
- The hospital social worker referred Rose and Linda to an adult children of alcoholics support group.
- The hospital social worker encouraged communication between siblings and their parents, including some effort to examine the perceived expectation that the sisters would become Marianne's lifelong caregivers.
- Siblings were offered information about other options for Marianne, such as a group home.
- The father was encouraged to reconnect with his therapist about the post-traumatic stress disorder.

- The mother was encouraged to consider part-time employment as a way of increasing her contribution to the household and increasing self-esteem.

Further interventions useful to this age group are

- encouraging siblings to network with each other
- encouraging siblings to connect with organizations to share information and express feelings
- encouraging involvement in community and political lobbying to increase services to the affected population
- encouraging siblings to educate themselves to support medical progress

SUMMARY

The literature and our case examples—which are all factual—suggest that siblings of children with disabilities and chronic illness often have special concerns and needs that should be addressed. The concerns differ depending upon the ages of the children, the disability, and the family's willingness and ability to be open with the healthy siblings.

One lesson to be learned is that healthy siblings are special, as is their lifelong role with their sibling with a disability. The uniqueness of all children needs to be recognized by the parents and the health professionals. It is crucial to address concerns on a developmental level and allow all children to explore their needs. This attention and exploration can enhance the psychological adjustment of these siblings. It also expands the role of the team and the health care professional to provide more holistic care to the children, their siblings, and the families served.

REFERENCES

Erikson, E. 1964. *Childhood and society.* New York: W.W. Norton & Co., Inc.

Freeman, D.J., and J.W. Hagen. 1989. Effects of childhood chronic illness on families. In *Chronic illness during childhood and adolescence: Psychological aspects*, ed. W.T. Garrison and S. McQuiston. Newbury Park, Calif.: Sage Publications, Inc.

Lobato, D.J. 1990. *Brothers, sisters, and special needs.* Baltimore: Paul H. Brookes.

McHale, S.M., et al. 1986. Sibling relationships of children with autistic, mentally retarded, and nonhandicapped

brothers and sisters. *Journal of Autism and Developmental Disorders* 16:399–413.

Seligman, M., and R.B. Darling. 1989. *Ordinary families, special children: A systems approach to childhood disability.* New York: Guilford Press.

Tritt, S.G., and L.M. Esses. 1988. Psychosocial adaptation of siblings of children with chronic medical illness. *American Journal of Orthopsychiatry* 58:211–220.

ADDITIONAL SUGGESTED READINGS

Craft, M.J. 1979. Help for the family's neglected "other" child. *Maternal Child Nursing Journal* 4:297–300.

Eiser, C. 1990. *Chronic childhood disease: An introduction to psychological theory and research.* New York: Cambridge University Press.

Holland, J.C., and J.H. Rowland, eds. 1989. *Handbook of psychooncology: Psychological care of the patient with cancer.* New York: Oxford University Press.

Lobato, D. 1983. Siblings of handicapped children: A review. *Journal of Autism and Developmental Disorders* 13:347–364.

Rutter, M., and M. Rutter. 1992. *Developing minds: Challenge and continuity across the lifespan.* New York: Basic Books, Inc.

San Martino, M., and M.B. Newman. 1974. Siblings of retarded children: A population at risk. *Child Psychiatry and Human Development* 4, no. 3:168–177.

Schlecter, M.J. 1987. I'm not going to be John's baby sitter forever: Siblings, planning and the disabled child. *Exceptional Parent* (Nov–Dec):60–64.

Thibodeau, S.M. 1988. Sibling response to chronic illness: The role of the clinical nurse specialist. *Issues in Comprehensive Pediatric Nursing* 11:17–28.

Williams, P.D., et al. 1993. Pediatric chronic illness: Effects on siblings and mothers. *Maternal Child Nursing Journal* 4:111–120.

ADDITIONAL RESOURCES

Sibling Information Network, Dept. of Educational Psychology, Box U-64, the University of Connecticut, Storrs, CT 06269.

Siblings for Significant Change, Room 208, 823 United Nations Plaza, New York, NY 10017.

Sibling Information Network of South Windsor, Connecticut, offers a quarterly newsletter, a list of sibling support groups in every state, bibliographies of books about disabilities for children and adults, and guidelines on how to start a sibling group. Membership: $7 a year. Sibling Information Network, AJ Papponikou Center, 1776

Ellington Road, South Windsor, CT 06074, Tel.: (203) 344-7500.

The *NASP* (National Association of Sibling Programs) *Newsletter* is published by the Sibling Support Project, Children's Hospital and Medical Center, P.O. Box 5371 CL-09, Seattle, WA 98105-0371, Tel.: (206) 368-4911. This project supports the development of materials and programs for peer and sibling support, and it maintains a national database with support from the Maternal and Child Health Bureau.

Chapter 19

Play and Recreation

Kathleen H. Murphey

Purpose: to offer an overview of developmental play sequences, with suggestions for guiding and implementing children's play activities; to review, for each developmental level, the main characteristics of children's play, along with examples of normal play activities for that phase; and to note special considerations for children with special needs, as well as strategies for adapting play activities and materials.

A basic understanding of the form and content of age-appropriate play at various levels offers the clinician the opportunity to identify developmentally appropriate play activities for children, to use appropriate play to support and enrich treatment interventions and therapies, to introduce and promote play activities that give children pleasure and enhance quality of life, and to introduce to children and families opportunities for play and recreation in the home and community.

PLAY AND DEVELOPMENT

At the most basic level, the play of a very young child is a way of seeking out the experiences necessary to gain information about the people and things around him or her, what they look and feel like, and how they act and react. In spontaneous experiments the baby practices newly emerging skills and builds on those schemas already successfully acquired. As children mature, they experience and experiment with many different materials and circumstances, exploring their properties, creating new uses for them, and incorporating them into their repertoires. And throughout childhood, children use play to recreate parts of their world so they can explore how these various parts fit together.

For the older child, play activities help to consolidate and refine a youngster's growing sense of self and contribute significantly to the evolution of the social skills and peer relationships that are essential for success in the community beyond the home and neighborhood. And as the young person matures into adolescence, recreation and leisure help in exploring options for academic and vocational choices.

Play also helps the child to manage some of the emotional challenges and disruptions that life presents. The preventive value of play is evident when a child uses it to express emotions or urges that are not acceptable or accepted in daily life—don't kick your sister, but you can kick the beach ball around the yard all you want. In play, children can relieve themselves of the need to do things that would cause harm.

Play is also healing. Children face many kinds of trials in their lives beyond their ability to understand or to cope. From the simple separation anxiety of a toddler to the more profound fear of a preschooler facing surgery or a school-aged child dealing with the death of a grandparent, children endure circumstances that are confusing, frightening, or traumatic. Children do not think like adults, and they do not cope the same ways adults do. Where adults "talk it out," children "play it out." In their play, children examine and explore things that have upset them, enacting a more positive resolution. They try to organize and make sense of situations and episodes they do not understand and to fantasize control and mastery over things that are really out of their hands. Here children can achieve what adults reach by a different path: a way to neutralize the damaging effects of disturbing events and to cope effectively with difficult experiences.

PLAY AND CHILDREN WITH DEVELOPMENTAL DISABILITIES

Children whose lives are complicated by a disability are often in need of greater and more intense, enriched, or varied experiences available through play than other children, but their ability to initiate or sustain play independently may be compromised. For these children, it is very important that the adults understand the functions served by play and how play experiences can be structured to be accessible even to children with severely disabling conditions.

For young children with disabilities, play is often used in the service of therapeutic goals: the wise pediatric therapist knows how to use a child's play interests to help attain milestones. Yet play for its own sake has intrinsic value—being able to seek and enjoy pleasurable experiences and to engage in activities that are chosen for their own rewards is an important aspect of quality of life for all children.

PLAY AND INFANTS (BIRTH TO 12 MONTHS)

Developmental Characteristics of Play

As infants' wake time increases, so do alertness, interest, and ability to seek new experiences and explore the physical and social environment. Developmental tasks underlying much of baby's play include

- exploring and gaining control over body movements
- acquiring multiple and varied sensory experience
- forming a secure attachment to the caregiver

Exploring new sensations, abilities, and skills through play allows a baby to generalize them from familiar situations to new ones.

Caregiver responsiveness helps create rhythmic cycles of hunger/satiation, discomfort/relief, separation/reunion that are predictable, allowing the baby to trust his or her world and eventually gain control over these events. Play between infants and adults offers a shared experience of pleasure that helps the infant to feel loved and secure and the parent to feel competent and successful as a caregiver and that allows both to form a healthy attachment that serves as a crucial prerequisite for social and emotional growth.

Suggested Play Strategies

Table 19–1 shows suggested play strategies for infants.

Special Consideration for Babies with Special Needs

Parents of children with disabilities may need to spend large amounts of time and energy providing physical or medical care, leaving less time for play. Further, parents' sense of obligation to provide remedial developmental activities targeted at specific skills or deficits may

Table 19–1 Suggested Play Strategies for Infants

Play Area/Rationale	Applications	Other Considerations
Mobiles		
Patterns and movements are of great visual interest	Be sure mobile is positioned so it is easy for infant to see	Mobiles that move or play music may add interest
Baby will begin to reach when ready	Bar or dowel hung across the crib may have objects on short strings that will swing or make noise when baby bats them	Mobiles can be adapted to respond to baby's voice
	A sturdy baby gym that has objects to grasp, pull, or bat may be used as baby gains motor control	Change objects on a dowel or gym to provide a variety of different "effects"
Face Play		
Gazing at faces helps the baby recognize his or her primary caregiver	Attach a safety mirror to crib rails at baby's eye level to provide the opportunity for self-inspection	Select a crib "activity box" that includes a small mirror
Infants prefer the human face over other patterns	Use baby's name frequently during mirror play; touch or pat image in mirror	Crib panels with high contrast encourage visual inspection
	Name body parts as you touch them on baby, and then in the mirror	A small towel or scarf can be placed over child's face to play "where's baby?"
	Play hide and seek, allowing part of your body to show	
Large Motor Play		
Encourages purposeful movement	Place baby on a blanket with a few safe toys within reach	Use a play mat that has interesting toys attached to make floor play a portable activity
Develops strength and coordination	Place toys somewhat out of reach to encourage rolling, creeping, and crawling	Jingle bells sewn securely on socks or booties add auditory stimuli
	Kicking and leg thrusts get muscles ready for standing—let baby kick against your hands, a pillow, or a large ball	
Sensory Play		
A variety of sensory experiences help baby learn to discriminate between various sensations	Use rattles, squeeze toys, bells with different sounds	
	Offer baby objects with different textures: a soft plush toy, a plastic brush, a metal cup	
	Provide a small basin filled with water, beans, macaroni, sand, or other material	Use hands to splash, dig, and sift, cups to scoop and pour
Toy Fun		
Offers sensations and actions for baby to experience and experiment	Try a busy box with things to pat, push, click, clack, and ring	Toys that provide a reward for baby's action introduce cause and effect
	Plastic or cloth blocks are safe to bang, stack, or line in a row	
	Plastic pop beads can be pulled apart and, later, put together	
	Graduated cups for nesting and stacking demonstrate how things fit together	

take precedence over activities that allow spontaneous play interactions. But while parents and professionals can and should use play activities to promote growth and adaptation in the child with a disability, they should also be encouraged to spend time in play for its own sake. Selected play activities will be most enjoyable when they

• are of obvious interest to the child

• are comfortable and pleasant for the parent

- recognize the infant's abilities and limitations, allowing many opportunities for success experiences

PLAY AND TODDLERS (12–36 MONTHS)

Developmental Characteristics of Play

Physical maturation and the desire to test and exercise new physical skills greatly influence the toddler's play. Exploring the world without direct assistance from adults helps develop a sense of autonomy and self-direction. The toddler's sense of individuality and separateness from the caregiver is fueled by the power and control experienced in the play arena. Simple imitation of adults' gestures or actions evolves into more complex role imitation. The ability to pretend, or to *represent* with respect to objects or actions, permits social and interpersonal exploration and experimentation through play.

Suggested Play Strategies

Table 19–2 shows suggested play strategies for toddlers.

Special Considerations for Toddlers with Special Needs

Toddlers need many opportunities for active play to exercise whatever physical skills they have; children with disabilities may need specific adaptations in such play. Physical independence enables functional independence by allowing the toddler to run away from, or rebel against, caregivers. Control over activity and environment available in the play arena helps the toddler with a disability to assert his or her individuality and independence. Play offers the toddler a safe arena for expressing feelings of frustration, aggression, and resentment that may not be physically discharged.

PLAY AND PRESCHOOLERS (3–5 YEARS)

Developmental Play Characteristics

Growing skills and independence allow the preschooler to initiate activities and interactions for him- or herself. The desire to test physical powers and to experiment with problem-solving skills drives much of his or her voluntary activity.

The ability to *symbolize* or *represent* influences the play of preschoolers. Imitative play evolves into more complex, realistic, dramatic and sociodramatic play. Motor play, sensory play, and manipulative play continue to develop and expand; these are often incorporated in dramatizations that vary in form and content. As the preschooler's social contacts increase in the family, neighborhood and community, he or she needs to examine and understand social roles:

- In dramatic play, the preschooler "tries on" what it means to be the mommy, the doctor, or the firefighter.
- Increased social interchange brings opportunities for conflict, frustration, and anxiety; "acting out" these conflicts in play helps discharge tension, ease fears, and gain mastery over unfamiliar or threatening situations.

Suggested Play Strategies

Table 19–3 shows suggested play strategies for preschoolers.

Special Considerations for the Preschooler with Special Needs

Dramatic and sociodramatic play

- facilitates development of social skills
- encourages development of imagination and fantasy
- gives the player active role and control over situations
- requires negotiation and conflict resolution

Table 19–2 Suggested Play Strategies for Toddlers

Play Area/Rationale	Applications	Other Considerations
Large Motor Play Helps develop and practice balance and coordination Provides movement experiences Promotes spatial awareness Supports developing independence	Push toys such as a doll carriage, lawnmower, or shopping cart help to explore the environment Balls of all sizes, weights, and textures encourage different types of physical activity Riding toys enable the toddler to scoot around astride a vehicle or small tricycle Scooter boards allow children to explore lying on their stomachs, using hand or feet to propel Slides, swings, tunnels, steps, and ladders promote balance, spatial awareness, and coordination	"Shopping" or "collecting" certain types of items adds structure to this activity Balls can be rolled, tossed, kicked, thrown, or bounced alone or among several players Toddlers can be encouraged to explore different aspects and angles of the physical environment
Manipulative/ Construction Play	Plastic blocks, wooden blocks, and large cardboard blocks are all good for construction (and destruction) activity Shape sorters, pegboards, and simple puzzles all provide manipulation experience Duplo block, star builders, and stickle bricks all have different properties to examine Stringing beads on a thick lace helps hand/eye coordination Pop-up toys that require the toddler to push, slide, turn, or press something to produce a result illustrate cause and effect	Use blocks to introduce concepts: up/down, tall/short, together/apart, how many, what color The chance for the toddler to "figure it out" makes these activities interesting Beads can be used for color identification, counting, and sorting
Pretend/ Imaginative	Caring for baby—feeding, rocking, dressing—is the toddler's way of trying to be like mommy Toddlers like to mimic household activities that they frequently observe Toy cars, houses, garages, etc., may be interesting at first for their physical properties: windows open and close, cars roll down, doorbells ring	Simple, short activities like these later become elements of more extended pretend play Provide a play telephone, broom, play food, or doll high chair or cradle to allow imitative activities Later on, the child can use these toys to symbolize people and situations in imaginative play
Sensory/Perceptual	Water play or sand play can be set up in a small basin, a water table, or a small pool or sandbox Fingerpaint on paper or tabletop helps in learning what fingers and palms can do Play dough or clay can be rolled, shaped, squeezed, and molded Pasting and gluing can be done with paper scraps, buttons, ribbons, pipe cleaners, and other textural items Music tapes with children's songs introduce rhymes and rhythms	Introduce funnels, sieves, rakes, spades, cups, and molds at various times to add novelty Be sure that clay, paints, crayons, and glue are nontoxic, as many toddlers still examine new items by mouth Use simple percussion instruments to demonstrate different rhythms, and encourage the toddler to match the beat

Table 19–3 Suggested Play Strategies for Preschoolers

Play Area/Rationale	Applications	Other Considerations
Pretend Play		
Explore and elaborate on social roles	Doll play allows exploration of most familiar social roles	Dolls and dollhouse characters may reflect various racial and ethnic characteristics
Practice emerging social skills	Dollhouse play allows higher level of control and enactment of multiple roles	Provide bottles, cups, chairs, pots, and other play props
Fantasize enactment of unacceptable wishes	Dress-ups and larger play props set the stage for elaborate scenarios	Make observations or ask questions to encourage imagination
Provide opportunity for several children to pretend in mutually cooperative dramatization	Hand puppets extend dramatic play into fantasy play	Encourage older preschoolers to create a story or play to perform
	Miniature farms, schools, and stores provide for community exploration	Use preferred play themes in different areas of activity
	Animals, dinosaurs, and action figures can safely represent a child's desired or feared traits	
Manipulative/ Constructive		
Integrate various skills into one activity	Stringing beads can start as a simple task and later be used for color identification, counting, and sorting	Create a bead pattern for the preschooler to match
Provide for refinement of fine motor and visual/ perceptual skills	Different building sets (Legos, K'Nex, Lincoln Logs) use different construction strategies	Use sets with characters and other pretend play props to integrate various play schemes
Offer opportunity for concept development	Block play may become more elaborate and imaginative, with a fantasy element ·	Provide trucks, cars, planes, and other vehicles and props to incorporate into block play
Art/Crafts		
Explore properties of different media	The preschooler may begin to use markers and colored pencils as well as crayons	Ask the preschooler to tell a story to go with his or her painting
Express ideas and feelings	Easel painting with a stubby brush produces colorful, dramatic results	Cut out pictures of green things, pictures of mommies, pictures of favorite foods
Develop creativity	Cut paper into random shapes with safety scissors; move on to shapes, outlines	
Early Games		
Introduce rules, turn taking	Board games for nonreaders (Candyland, Chutes and Ladders) help match colors and shapes	Some board games combine concepts with constructive or manipulative play
	Outdoor games like "Mother May I" and "Red Light Green Light" include gross motor play along with other rules and rewards	

Children with disabilities need all these experiences in abundance because of their risk for social isolation, their diminished ability to initiate dramatic play independently, and their need to learn to negotiate more challenging social and community interactions. Adults can help by

- serving as pretend play partner
- setting up opportunities for sociodramatic play
- providing assistance with toys and props
- providing physical assistance to enact scenes or stories

PLAY AND SCHOOL-AGED CHILDREN

Developmental Characteristics of Play

School-aged children's increasing skills make play and recreation options much broader and more diverse. Exploring many different kinds of activities can help create a broad base of leisure interests.

The enlarging social world of the school-aged child offers new opportunities and requires new strategies:

- Increased social competence brings new opportunities to try out new cognitive, physical, and social skills with individuals outside of the family culture.
- More complex games introduce rules, competition, turn taking, cooperation, role taking, winning and losing, and elements of game play and sports that must be practiced and mastered.
- Social transactions learned in play and games can enhance social success and increase independence.

The school-aged child's interest in a product arises from a growing sense of industry and is evident in many types of activities, from model car kits to cooking to woodcrafts to needlework. The focus on a product, and on its correctness, completeness, and adequacy, both reflects and influences the child's feelings of competence, confidence, and self-esteem. The child who feels proud of a handmade kite or ceramic pot is likely to see him- or herself as successful and productive and to be more likely to attempt new projects or tasks.

Suggested Play Strategies

Table 19–4 shows suggested play strategies for school-aged children.

Special Considerations for the School-Aged Child with Special Needs

Children with disabilities are now more frequently included in educational settings with nondisabled children. Preventing social isolation and promoting appropriate social interaction among all children is a significant challenge. Play and recreation activities can be used to promote integration and make inclusion meaningful:

- Select activities in which disabled and nondisabled players can both participate.
- Make modifications or adaptations that allow equal participation.
- Assist with social communication and interpersonal awareness—prompt, cue, model, and reinforce appropriate social interactions.

PLAY AND ADOLESCENTS

Characteristics of Recreation and Leisure

Many adolescents have established distinct recreation and leisure preferences that have evolved from childhood and begin to resemble adult interests. Some activities are peer oriented and may be marked by social boundaries as cliques and in-groups control access to opportunities; teens may struggle to "fit in." Recreation and leisure pursuits contribute to individuals' maturing sense of identity, helping individuals both to distinguish themselves from others and to be included in a larger group. Practice of preferred pursuits and the exploration of new activities may serve in exploring occupational roles, an important task of the adolescent.

Suggested Recreation and Leisure Approaches

Table 19–5 shows suggested recreation and leisure activities for adolescents.

Special Considerations for the Teenager with Special Needs

Healthy identity development central to adolescence may be jeopardized by disability. At an age when appearance is so important and the

Table 19–4 Suggested Play Strategies for School-Aged Children

Play Area/Rationale	Applications	Other Considerations
Active Play		
Combine physical abilities with cognitive skills	Schoolyard games	The first time a child is introduced to a sport or game, he or she should be in-
Incorporate children of different ages	Red Rover	troduced to the safety equipment and practices associated with it
Provide lots of experience in moving through space	Simon Says	Children can participate in sports at vary-
Help practice and refine advancing skills in balance and coordination	Dodgeball	ing levels; some may become lifelong interests
	Tag/Freeze Tag	
	Physical/motion play	
	jumprope	
	roller skates	
	slides	
	swings	
	balls	
	bicycles	
	Individual sports	
	swimming	
	tennis	
	bowling	
	gymnastics	
	track and field	
Team sports require cooperat- ing, following rules, taking different perspectives	Team sports	
	soccer	
	volleyball	
	T-ball	
	softball	
	hockey	
Creative Arts		
Give children the chance to explore and express in concrete, malleable media	Plastic arts	Children may explore properties of the medium, or delve into technique, or fo-
	drawing, coloring, painting	cus on result
	collage	
	modeling, sculpting	
	cartooning	
Music helps create a common culture through game and jumprope songs, folks songs or children's songs learned in the classroom	Music and movement	
	songs and chants	
	percussion instruments	
	piano, electronic keyboard	
	guitar	
	movement/rhythm activities	
	dance	
Performing for others can bolster self-esteem	Dramatic arts	
Videotaping can help children see how they look to others	skits	
	plays	
	commercials	
	video productions	
	talent shows	
Games		
Require varying degrees of skill, attention, and/or luck	Connect Four	Examine the skills required—number rec- ognition, counting, predicting, following
	Monopoly	complex rules—and match the game to
	Checkers	the abilities of the players
	Scrabble	
	Pictionary	
	Card games: Old Maid, War, Go Fish, gin rummy	

continues

Table 19–4 continued

Play Area/Rationale	Applications	Other Considerations
Crafts		
Introduce different leisure skills	Sewing, needlecraft	Children with limited energy or ability can
Develop task-planning skills	Woodworking	use prepackaged craft kits for maxi-
	Bead and jewelry making	mum result with minimum effort
	Model building: cars, planes	
	Weaving and lacing	
	Pottery, ceramics	
	Leathercraft	
	Tie dye, cloth painting	
Hobbies/Collections		
Require the collector to sort,	Stamps	Encourage children to record the proper-
organize, and catalogue his	Coins	ties, features, history and special items
or her collection	Sports cards and paraphernalia	of their collections
	Matchbox cars	

Table 19–5 Suggested Recreation and Leisure Activities for Adolescents

Play Area/Rationale	Applications	Other Considerations
Sports/Athletics		
Organized team sports demand	Baseball	
integration of physical, cognitive	Football	
and interpersonal skills	Soccer	
	Tennis	
Some sports are more social in	Bowling	
nature; teens choose when and	Ping-pong	
with whom they will participate	Rollerblading	
	Swimming	
	Miniature golf	
Games	Video or computer games requiring more complex problem-solving strategies appeal to some teens	Doom, Myst are currently popular
	Some table games require the player to give an answer, action, or perform-ance, facilitating social interaction	Pictionary, Outburst, Scattegories
Creative Arts/Crafts		
Provide opportunities for self-expression	Musical instruments, voice	
	Painting, sculpture	
High-level craft products can win	Modern dance, ballet, jazz dance	
notice from peers or adults	Crafts: stained-glass work, loom weaving, string art, jewelry design	
Entertainment/Diversion		
Combine interests with independent socialization	Movies, arcade, mall, pizza shop, concerts, theater	
Hobbies		
May influence vocational choices	Photography, science inquiries, model trains, sewing, computer program-ming	Planning and structuring one's leisure time is a learned skill
		Teens can benefit from talking to adults who have made careers out of their hobbies

judgment of peers so critical, a teen who has an evident difference risks letting that become a defining characteristic. Negative identification is more likely to occur when other strong traits or features are absent. The teen who has strong family, school, and community loyalties, as well as a clear set of defining interests or abilities, has a better chance of coming to see him- or herself as a well-rounded individual with a unique and valuable place in the world—regardless of ability or disability.

ADAPTATIONS FOR PLAY

Adapting play experience for children with physical and developmental disabilities allows them to enjoy the pleasures of exploration, interaction, and achievement on their own terms. The easiest of adaptations is simply selecting play activities and materials that use a child's existing abilities and are appropriate to his or her developmental age. Adapting play experiences may require modifying materials, rules, the environment, and/or the relationship among these elements.

Adapting the Child-Environment Relationship

The child with physical mobility challenges requires special consideration for set-up at playtime. Positioning issues for children with various needs are treated extensively in Chapter 11, but a few strategies are widely pertinent. For maximum play value, the child should have

- as much freedom of movement as possible while still having enough support to carry out the activity
- ability to see as much as possible, particularly toys and play materials, as well as his or her hands (or feet, if that is what he or she is using); mirrors can help here, as can adjustable tray tables
- a good view of the social environment, in group play; place the child who can turn on his or her own in a spot where he or she can

see who is coming and going, as well as who is here
- freedom from barriers that prevent access to desired play materials
- support or restraint that prevents dysfunctional position or muscle pattern

Adapting Toys and Play Materials

Developmentally appropriate toys and play materials do not always lend themselves easily to use by children with disabilities. Toys selected for a child will ideally be suited to him or her on several dimensions:

- motor needs
- sensory needs
- developmental needs
- normalization needs

Ideal play materials

- require only the motor skills that the child can perform
- provide stimulus in sensory domains that are intact for the player
- facilitate play activity that is developmentally suited
- approximate as nearly as possible: age, gender, and cultural appropriateness

For example, a teenager with cerebral palsy and severe cognitive limitations can enjoy music that peers like and with some modifications may be able to use a tape player that resembles other teens' radios.

Musselwhite (1986) outlines specific strategies for adapting play materials for children with disabilities and gives examples (Table 19–6).

Switch Toys

For children with severe physical and cognitive limitations, switch toys offer a whole range of alternative play opportunities. At their most basic, switch toys are battery-operated, cause-

Table 19–6 Strategies for Adapting Play Materials

Strategy	Description	Example
Stabilize	Attach play materials to steady surface	Affix play house to lap tray with C-clamp
Enlarge	Enlarge materials to enhance visual perception	Use large puzzle pieces
	Enlarge key parts to enhance toy manipulation	Affix large Plexiglass "button" over small Push'n'Go button
Prosthetize	Affix part to allow access for child with physical disability	Use foam hair curlers to add grip to brush handle
Reduce required response	Minimize distance, range of motion, complexity of response	Place doll on elevated tray Use tray to keep cars within range. Use plate switch rather than on-off switch
Make more familiar	Relate to environment	Select symbols that reflect child's world
Make more concrete	Reduce abstract quality	Demonstrate activity, toy play Add cues to graphic symbols
Remove extraneous cues	Consider goal and remove unrelated cues	If the task is shape recognition, do not simultaneously color-code items to be sorted
Remove distracting stimuli	Simplify "busy" backgrounds	Use dark background behind objects being visually tracked, or as a backdrop for puzzles
Add or enhance cues	Increase visual stimuli Increase tactile stimuli	Use bright, contrasting colors Affix fabrics to adaptive switches
Improve safety and durability	Avoid sharp objects Protect objects from drool Increase strength of toys	Round off or pad corners Laminate, add nontoxic sealant Replace cardboard with triwall Replace staples or nails with screws

Source: From *Adaptive Play for Special Needs Children,* C.R. Musselwhite, 1986, Austin, TX: PRO-ED, Inc., Copyright © 1986 by Pro-Ed, Inc. Reprinted with permission.

---

and-effect toys that are activated by a special switch, initiated by a child's action—for example, a child applies pressure with her hand to a plate switch, which activates a mechanical teddy bear to play his cymbals. Types of switches and their indications are covered in Chapter 17.

The variety of switches, and the actions required to activate them, allow these toys to be individualized to the unique needs and abilities of each child. The potential for enjoyment and novelty comes from the type of "effects" that can be activated by a switch, including toys that

- make music
- light up
- perform an action or series of actions
- vibrate
- blow air
- provide other visual display

In some cases, the child can control the quality of the "effect" by altering the quality of the activation: for example, squeezing a pressure switch harder makes a toy vibrate at a higher speed. Some switches offer the child the opportunity to choose from among several effects, adding the experience of choice and control to the play experience. Switch toys are often used by therapists to help strengthen and develop specific skills—voice-activated toys to encourage vocalization, light displays to encourage visual tracking. At playtime it is important that the "target outcome" be the child's pleasure and play satisfaction. Switch toys provide an avenue for independence and control for youngsters whose situations allow them few opportunities for those experiences.

REFERENCE

Musselwhite, C.R. 1986. *Adaptive play for special needs children.* Austin, Tex.: PRO-ED, Inc.

ADDITIONAL SUGGESTED READINGS

Barnard, M.U., et al. 1981. *Handbook of comprehensive pediatric nursing.* New York: McGraw-Hill Publishing Co.

Cook, J.L., and M. Sinker. 1992. Play and the growth of competence. In *The therapeutic powers of play*, ed. C.E. Shaefer, 65–80. Northvale, N.J.: Jason Aronson, Inc.

Curry, N., and S. Arnaud, eds. 1971. *Play: The child strives toward self-realization.* Washington, D.C.: National Association for the Education of Young Children.

Erikson, E.H. 1950. *Childhood and Society.* New York: W.W. Norton & Co., Inc.

Fine, A.H. 1988. *Therapeutic recreation for exceptional children.* Springfield, Ill.: Charles C Thomas, Publisher.

Ginsburg, H., and S. Opper. 1969. *Piaget's theory of intellectual development.* Englewood Cliffs, N.J.: Prentice Hall.

Hart, R., et al. 1992. *Therapeutic play activities for hospitalized children.* St. Louis: Mosby Year Book.

Landreth, G.G. 1992. Self-expressive communication. In *The therapeutic powers of play*, ed. C.E. Shaefer, 41–63. Northvale, N.J.: Jason Aronson, Inc.

Miller, K. 1984. *Things to do with toddlers and twos.* Marshfield, Mass.: Teleshare Publishing Co. Inc.

Miller, K. 1985. *Ages and stages.* Marshfield, Mass.: Teleshare Publishing Co. Inc.

Morris, L.R., and L. Schulz. 1989. *Creative play activities for children with disabilities.* Champaign, Ill.: Human Kinetics Books.

Schaefer, C.E., ed. 1992. *The therapeutic powers of play.* Northvale, N.J.: Jason Aronson, Inc.

Schwartz, S., and J.E. Miller. 1988. *The language of toys: A guide for parents and teachers.* Kensington, Md.: Woodbine House.

Sparling, J., and L. Lewis. 1979. *Learning games for the first three years.* New York: Walker & Co.

Sutton-Smith, B. 1971. The playful modes of knowing. In *Play: The child strives toward self-realization*, ed. N. Curry and S. Arnaud, 13–25. Washington, D.C.: National Association for the Education of Young Children.

ADDITIONAL RESOURCES

Children with disabilities can and should expect to have a range of options for play in their communities. The Americans with Disabilities Act has opened up a world of play and recreation opportunities for children and families; a little research with a telephone directory can yield a menu of options for individuals of varying ages and interests.

Play Libraries

Play libraries lend toys and play materials to member families. Trained professionals assess play abilities, interests, and needs and recommend toys for loan. Parents learn and participate in guiding and encouraging play. *Lekotek* is a national organization of play libraries modeled after Scandinavian methods of early intervention with over 65 centers throughout the United States. Some Lekotek centers have *CompuPlay* programs, which offer children and families the chance to try out different types of software and computer access methods. Contact the National Lekotek Center, 2100 Ridge Avenue, Evanston, IL 60201, Tel.: (800) 366-PLAY.

Sports and Athletics

Special Olympics offers a range of programs for children and adults with developmental disabilities. Well-structured, well-supervised events are held locally, and athletes may go on to compete in regional and national games. Contact: Special Olympics International, 1325 "G" Street NW, Washington, DC 20005, Tel.: (202) 628-3630.

Wheelchair Sports USA (formerly the National Wheelchair Athletic Association) has a growing junior division that offers wheelchair users the opportunity to compete in a range of individual and team sports, including tennis, archery, track and field. Local teams are often sponsored by schools or residences for children with disabilities. Contact Wheelchair Sports USA, 3595 E. Fountain Boulevard, Suite L-10, Colorado Springs, CO 80910, Tel.: (719) 574-1150.

Adaptive sports programs offer disabled athletes opportunities and instruction for participation in a whole range of sports, including swimming, rowing, skiing, bowling, basketball, and so on.

Parks/Playgrounds

The past several years have seen a significant increase in the manufacture, construction, and availability of playground equipment that is accessible to wheelchair users and safe for children of varying abilities. Consult your local department of recreation and parks for information.

Clubs and Groups

Girl Scouts, *Boy Scouts,* and other youth groups have made active commitments to include children of all abilities in local troops. Consult your local council for information.

Camps

Camping experiences are available for many children with disabilities, chronic illness, or other specialized health care needs. Some camps serve disabled children exclusively, others offer one- or two-week encampments for special populations. The American Camping Association publishes a guide listing camps, including specialty camps, by state. Contact the American Camping Association, 5000 State Road 67 North, Marville, IN 46252-7902, Tel.: (800) 428-2267.

Music and Art

Some communities have agencies or organizations that specialize in teaching music or art to children with disabilities.

Cultural Institutions

Many museums, libraries, theaters and children's theaters, historical sites, zoos, aquariums, and other popular sites have accommodations or special programs for visitors with disabilities.

Vacation Destinations

Disneyworld, *Busch Gardens*, and other vacation destinations favored by families with children publish guides for visitors with disabilities; some note in detail relevant accessibility and safety information. Many travel agencies have quick and easy references for travellers with disabilities, including airline, hotel, and resort information.

Appendixes—Resource Directory

University-Affiliated Programs and Other National Resources

Peter W. Dowrick

This appendix lists national programs that provide resources to the developmental disabilities field in general, such as the National Center for Education in Maternal and Child Health. The programs listed are mostly in the United States, many funded by federal agencies. Programs that have a more specific focus, such as a type of disability (autism, cerebral palsy, etc.) or purpose (housing, recreation, etc.), are listed in Appendix B.

The first section is an alphabetical listing of various clearinghouses and referral centers in different parts of North America that are willing to take calls on a national (sometimes international) basis. The rest of this appendix is a listing by U.S. state of the university-affiliated programs, developmental disabilities planning councils, and protection and advocacy agencies. These programs are mandated by statute—the Developmental Disabilities Assistance and Bill of Rights (Pub.L. 100-146, etc.)—to serve all states and territories of the United States.

An effort was made in the two weeks before this book went to press to reverify and update all information. We apologize for any errors or omissions. The lists are necessarily incomplete and no endorsement should be inferred for those programs included.

CLEARINGHOUSES AND REFERRAL CENTERS

ACCENT on Information, P.O. Box 700, Bloomington, IL 61702. Tel.: (309) 378-2961; fax: (309) 378-4420. Provides information from computer databases on all major topics related to disabilities. Publishes periodicals (e.g., *Accent on Living* Magazine) and practical booklets.

American Academy of Pediatrics, 141 Northwest Point Boulevard, P.O. Box 927, Elk Grove Village, IL 60007-0927. Tel.: (708) 228-5005; fax: (708) 228-5097. Membership association for board-certified pediatricians. Provides continuing education, professional journals, national and regional conferences.

American Association for the Advancement of Science, Project on Science, Technology, and Disability, 1333 H Street, NW, Washington, DC 20005. Tel.: (202) 326-6672 (voice/tdd); fax: (202) 371-9849. Provides information, especially related to professional advancement (in science), for people with disabilities. Offers advocacy and networking.

American Association of University Affiliated Programs on Developmental Disabilities, 8630 Fenton Street, Suite 410, Silver Spring,

MD 20910. Tel.: (301) 588-8252; (301) 588-3319 (tdd); fax: (301) 588-2842; e-mail: aauapjones@aol.com. Refers individuals and organizations to regional UAPs, as listed later in this appendix. Provides information on resources from computer databases; national conference.

American Psychological Association (APA), Division 36: Mental Retardation and Developmental Disabilities. Call APA Head Office at (703) 247-7760 for the current location of the division president. Professional membership organization. Provides policy information, advocacy, and technical assistance.

Association of Birth Defect Children, 827 Irma Avenue, Orlando, FL 32803. Tel.: (800) 313-2232 (voice, 24 hr.); fax (and voice): (407) 245-7035. Clearinghouse on birth defects; produces periodicals and videos; provides networking, referrals, and advocacy.

Canadian Association for Community Living, 4700 Keele Street, Kinsman Building, York University, North York, ON M3J 1P3. Tel.: (419) 661-9611 (voice); (419) 661-2023 (tdd); fax: (419) 661-5701. Produces periodicals and other publications; provides extensive information, advocacy, and referrals. Annual conference.

Canadian Rehabilitation Council for the Disabled, 45 Sheppard Avenue East, #801, Willowdale, ON M2N 5W9. Tel.: (416) 250-7490 (voice/tdd); fax: (416) 229-1371. Produces publications and videos. Advocates, refers, and networks for Canadian providers and consumers.

Clearinghouse on Disability Information, Office of Special Education and Rehabilitation Services (OSERS), U.S. Department of Education, Switzer Building, Room 3132, 330 C Street SW, Washington, DC 20202-2524. Tel.: (202) 732-1241/-1245/-1723. Provides information on services, funding, and legislation. Maintains databases and other document retrieval. Can refer inquiries to other sources. Status uncertain under Federal reorganization. Refer to ERIC, below.

Easter Seals—see National Easter Seal Society below.

ERIC Clearinghouse on Disabilities and Gifted Education, Council for Exceptional Children (CEC), 1920 Association Drive, Reston, VA 22091-1589. Tel.: (703) 264-9474; (703) 620-3660 (tdd). Association for professionals and family members interested in children with atypical development (including giftedness), especially related to education. Gathers abstracts and indexes professional literature on disabilities and giftedness. Publishes reviews, digests, and bibliographies. Provides referrals, references, and computer searches.

Federal Information Center Program (FIC), General Services Administration, Washington, DC 20405. For local or toll-free telephone numbers, call (202) 501-1794 (Consumer Information Center). One-stop source of information on federal agencies, programs, and services.

Federation for Children with Special Needs, 95 Berkley Street, Suite 104, Boston, MA 02116. Tel.: (617) 827-2915. Provides information and advocacy, especially for parents, related to transition and inclusion issues. Four regional centers:

1. *Midwest Regional Center,* Parent Advocacy Coalition for Educational Rights (PACER), 4826 Chicago Avenue South, Minneapolis, MN 66417. Tel.: (612) 827-2966.

2. *Northeast Region Center,* Parent Information Center, P.O. Box 1422, Concord, NH 03302. Tel.: (603) 224-0402.

3. *South Regional Center*, Parent Empowerment Project, Georgia ARC, 1851 Ram Runway #104, College Park, GA 30337. Tel.: (404) 761-3150.

4. *West Regional Center*, Washington State PAVE, 12208 Pacific Highway, SW, Tacoma, WA 98499. Tel.: (206) 588-1741.

March of Dimes Birth Defects Foundation, 1275 Mamaroneck Avenue, White Plains, NY 10605. Tel.: (914) 428-7100. Provides information about birth defects and related health issues, also in Spanish. Offers grant support from genetics to parent groups.

Mobility International, P.O. Box 3551, 1870 Onyx #E, Eugene, OR 97403. Tel.: (503) 343-1284; fax: (503) 343-6812; e-mail: miusa @igc.apc.org. International exchange programs for young people with and without disabilities. (Head Office at 62 Union Street, London SE1, England; Tel. 01-403-5688.)

National Association of Developmental Disabilities Councils, 1234 Massachusetts Avenue NW, Suite 103, Washington, DC 20005. Tel.: (202) 347-1234; fax: (202) 347-4023; e-mail: nadc@paltech.com. Makes referrals to regional DD (Planning) Councils—listed later in this appendix—and to systems of service. Provides national status reports, advocacy, and networking.

National Association of State Protection and Advocacy Agencies, 900 2nd Street NE, S-211, Washington, DC 20002. Tel.: (202) 408-9514; fax: (202) 408-9520. Makes referrals to regional P&As—listed later in this appendix—and other legal support on disability (and mental health) issues. Provides legal advice, supports class actions.

National Center for Education in Maternal and Child Health, 38th and R Streets NW, Washington, DC 20057. Tel.: (202) 625-8400; fax: (202) 625-8404. Provides information, educational materials, and technical assistance to organizations, agencies, and individuals with interests in maternal and child health, including chronic illness and disabilities. Their own publications (single copies usually available at no cost) are available from the *National Maternal and Child Health Clearinghouse* (same address as above). Tel.: (202) 625-8410 or (703) 821-8955, ext. 254.

National Center for Youth with Disabilities, University of Minnesota, Box 721, 420 Delaware Street, SE, Minneapolis, MN 55455, Tel.: (612) 624-8644. Provides information, especially related to adolescent health, including recreation and transition. Maintains databases, research library.

National Easter Seal Society, 70 East Lake Street, Chicago, IL 60601. Tel.: (312) 726-6200, (800) 221-6827. Serves more than 1 million people a year through nearly 200 re-gional agencies. Produces pamphlets and other publications. Supports research and community-based health programs.

National Family Caregivers Association (NFCA) 9621 East Bexhill Drive, Kensington, MD 20895. Tel.: (301) 942-6430; fax: (301) 942-2302.

National Information Center for Children and Youth with Disabilities (NICCHY), P.O. Box 1492, Washington, DC 20013. Tel.: (800) 555-9955; tdd: (703) 893-8614. Federal agency provides information to professionals and family members. Provides referrals, information packets, publications.

National Information Clearinghouse (NIC) for Infants with Disabilities and Life-Threatening Conditions. Tel.: (800) 922-9234, ext. 210 (voice/tdd), M–F 9 am to 5 pm ET. Joint program of the Center for Developmental Disabilities, UAP, University of South Carolina, Benson Building, Columbia, SC 29208, Tel.: (803) 777-4435; fax: (803) 777-6058, and the Association for the Care of Children's Health, 7910 Woodmont Avenue, Bethesda, MD 20814, Tel.: (301) 654-6549; fax: (301) 986-4553. Provides information especially concerning the rights of infants with life-threatening conditions. The clearinghouse serves primarily family members, health care providers, and social service professionals, using computer databases and other resources. They produce fact sheets, bibliographies, articles, and other publications.

National Maternal and Child Health Clearinghouse—see National Center for Education in Maternal and Child Health.

National Organization on Disability, 910 16th Street NW, #600, Washington, DC 20006. Tel.: (202) 293-5960 (voice/tdd); fax: (202) 293-7999. Provides networking and referral, advocacy, and public awareness.

National Parent Network on Disabilities, 1600 Prince Street, #115, Alexandria, VA 22314. Tel.: (703) 684-6763. Provides networking and referral for all disabilities. Maintains databases on support groups by region and by content (e.g., diagnosis, developmental stage).

National Rehabilitation Clearinghouse, 816 West Sixth Street, Oklahoma State University, Stillwater, OK 74078. Tel.: (405) 624-7650; fax: (405) 624-0695. Publishes pamphlets and other materials. Provides information and distributes training publications.

National Rehabilitation Information Center (NARIC), 8455 Colesville Road, Suite 935, Silver Spring, MD 20910-3319. Tel.: (800) 346-2742 (voice/tdd); fax: (301) 587-1967. Provides information from computer databases and library. Publishes newsletter and several directories.

TASH (The Association for Persons with Severe Handicaps), 11210 Greenwood Avenue North, Seattle, WA 98133. Tel.: (206) 361-8870 (voice); (206) 361-0113 (tdd); fax: (206) 361-9208. Produces periodicals and videos, provides advocacy (especially full inclusion), networking, and referral. State and regional chapters; national conference.

World Institute on Disability, 510 16th Street, #100, Oakland, CA 94612. Tel.: (510) 763-4100 (voice/tdd); fax: (510) 763-4109. Produces periodicals and other publications. Provides information, referrals, and advocacy, especially on public policy and systems of service.

UNIVERSITY-AFFILIATED PROGRAMS (UAP), DEVELOPMENTAL DISABILITIES (DD) PLANNING COUNCILS, AND PROTECTION AND ADVOCACY AGENCIES (P&A)

Listed below, alphabetically by state, are programs and protection and advocacy agencies required by federal statutes to provide, improve, and protect the rights and services to children with disabilities and their families.

Alabama

UAP

Center for Developmental and Learning Disorders (CDLD), University of Alabama-Birmingham, 1720 Seventh Avenue S., Birmingham, AL 35233. Tel.: (205) 934-5471; fax: (205) 975-6330; e-mail:sramey.civitan@ civmail.circ.uab.edu.

P&A

Alabama Disabilities Advocacy Program, The University of Alabama, P.O. 870395, Tuscaloosa, AL 35487-0395. Tel.: (205) 348-4928; fax: (205) 348-3909.

DD Council

Alabama Developmental Disabilities Planning Council, 100 N. Union Street, RSA Union Building, P.O. Box 301410, Montgomery, AL 36130-1410. Tel.: (334) 242-3973, (800) 232-2358; fax: (334) 242-0797.

Alaska

UAP

Center for Human Development: UAP, University of Alaska Anchorage, 2330 Nichols Street, Anchorage, AK 99508. Tel.: (907) 272-8270; fax: (907) 274-4802; e-mail: anmre @orion.alaska.edu.

P&A

Advocacy Services of Alaska, 615 E. 82nd Avenue, Suite 101, Anchorage, AK 99518. Tel.: (907) 344-2002.

DD Council

Governor's Council on Disabilities and Special Education, P.O. Box 240249, Anchorage, AK 99524-0249. Tel.: (907) 563-5355; fax: (907) 563-5357.

American Samoa

UAP

Pacific Basin University Affiliated Satellite Program, American Samoa Site, American Samoa Community College, P.O. Box 2609, Pago Pago, American Samoa 96799. Tel.: 011 (684) 699-9155; fax: 011 (684) 699-2062.

DD Council

Executive Director of Developmental Disabilities Council, P.O. Box 3823, Pago Pago, American Samoa 96799. Tel.: 011 (684) 633-1805; fax: 011 (684) 633-1139.

Arizona

UAP

Institute for Human Development, Northern Arizona University, P.O. Box 5630, Flagstaff, AZ 86011. Tel.: (602) 523-4791; fax: (602) 523-9127; e-mail: kmh@nauvax.ucc.nau.edu.

P&A

Arizona Center for Law in the Public Interest, 363 N. First Avenue, #100, Phoenix, AZ 85003. Tel.: (602) 252-4904.

DD Council

Governor's Council on Developmental Disabilities, 1717 West Jefferson, Site Code 074Z, Phoenix, AZ 85007. Tel.: (602) 542-4049; fax: (602) 542-5320.

Arkansas

UAP

University Affiliated Program for Developmental Disabilities, University of Arkansas, 1120 Marshall Street, #306, Little Rock, AR 72202. Tel.: (501) 320-3760; fax: (501) 320-3773; e-mail: aruap@oz.ach.uams.edu.

P&A

Advocacy Services, Inc., 1120 Marshall Street, Suite 311, Little Rock, AR 72202. Tel.: (501) 371-2171.

DD Council

Governor's Developmental Disabilities Council, 4815 West Markham Street, Slot 12, Little Rock, AR 72205. Tel.: (501) 661-2589; fax: (501) 661-2399.

California

UAPs

Mental Retardation and Developmental Disabilities Program, University of California at Los Angeles, 760 Westwood Plaza, Los Angeles, CA 90024. Tel.: (310) 825-8902; fax: (310) 206-4446, e-mail: ahernandez@npimain.med sch.ucla.edu.

University Affiliated Training Program, Children's Hospital of Los Angeles, 4650 Sunset Boulevard, Los Angeles, CA 90027. Tel.: (213) 669-2300; fax: (213) 953-0439; e-mail: mbaer%smtpgate@chlais.usc.edu.

P&A

California Protection and Advocacy, Inc., 101 Howe Avenue, #185N, Sacramento, CA 95835. Tel.: (916) 488-9950, (800) 766-5746; in Los Angeles, (818) 546-1631.

DD Council

California State Council on Developmental Disabilities, 2000 "O" Street, Room 100, Sacramento, CA 95814. Tel.: (916) 443-8481; fax: (916) 443-4957.

Colorado

UAP

John F. Kennedy Center for Developmental Disabilities, University of Colorado Health Science Center, 4200 E. Ninth Avenue, #C234, Denver, CO 80262. Tel.: (303) 270-8826; fax: (303) 270-6844; e-mail: cohrsm@essex.hsc. colorado.edu.

P&A

The Legal Center, 455 Sherman Street, Suite 130, Denver, CO 80203. Tel.: (303) 722-0300; fax: (303) 722-0720.

DD Council

Colorado Developmental Disabilities Planning Council, 777 Grant, Suite 304, Denver, CO 80203. Tel.: (303) 894-2345; fax: (303) 894-2880.

Connecticut

UAP

A.J. Pappanikou Center on Special Education and Rehabilitation, A University Affiliated Program, 249 Glenbrook Road, Box U-64, Storrs, CT 06269-2064. Tel.: (860) 486-5035; fax: (860) 486-5037.

P&A

Office of Protection and Advocacy for Persons with Disabilities, 60 B Weston Street, Hartford, CT 06120-1551. Tel.: (203) 297-4300; (203) 566-2102 (tdd); (800) 842-7303 (statewide); fax: (203) 566-8714.

DD Council

Connecticut Council on Developmental Disabilities, 460 Capitol Avenue, East Hartford, CT 06106-1308. Tel.: (203) 418-6160; (203) 418-6172 (tdd); fax: (203) 418-6003; e-mail: 72322.2415@compuserv.com.

Delaware

UAP

University of Delaware UAP for Families and Developmental Disabilities, 101 Alison Hall, University of Delaware, Newark, DE 19716. Tel.: (302) 831-6974; fax: (302) 831-8776; e-mail: penny.diner@mvs.udel.edu.

P&A

Disabilities Law Program, 144 East Market Street, Georgetown, DE 19947. Tel.: (302) 856-0038.

DD Council

Developmental Disabilities Planning Council, Townsend Building, Box 1401, Dover, DE 19901. Tel.: (301) 739-3333; fax: (301) 739-6704.

District of Columbia

UAP

Georgetown University Child Development Center, 3307 M Street NW, Suite 401, Washing-ton, DC 20007-2197. Tel.: (202) 687-8635; fax: (202) 687-8899; e-mail: nolte@guvax.acc.georgetown.edu.

P&A

I.P.A.C.H.I., 330700 I Street NE, Suite 202, Washington, DC 20002. Tel.: (202) 547-8081.

DD Council

DC Human Services Developmental Disabilities Council, 801 N. Capitol Street NE, #954, Washington, DC 20002. Tel.: (202) 279-6085; fax: (202) 727-6787.

Florida

UAP

Mailman Center for Child Development, University of Miami School of Medicine, P.O. Box 016820, D-820, Miami, FL 33101. Tel.: (305) 547-6635; fax: (305) 547-6309; e-mail: tpereira @peds.med.miami.edu.

P&A

Advocacy for Persons with Disabilities, 2671 Executive Center, Circle W, Suite 100, Tallahassee, FL 32301-5024. Tel.: (904) 488-9071; (800) 342-0823, (800) 346-4127 (statewide toll-free); fax: (904) 488-8640.

DD Council

Florida Developmental Disabilities Planning Council, 124 Marriott Drive, #203, Tallahassee, FL 32301. Tel.: (904) 488-4180, (800) 580-7801; fax: (904) 922-6702.

Georgia

UAP

University Affiliated Program for Persons with Developmental Disabilities, Dawson Hall, University of Georgia, Athens, GA 30602-3622. Tel.: (404) 542-3457 fax: (706) 542-4815; e-mail: khelms@uga.cc.uga.edu.

P&A

Georgia Advocacy Office, Inc., 999 Peachtree Street NE, #870, Atlanta, GA 30309. Tel.: (404)

885-1234, (800) 537-2329; fax: (404) 607-8286.

DD Council

Governor's Council on Developmental Disabilities, 2 Peachtree Street NW, #3-210, Atlanta, GA 30303. Tel.: (404) 657-2126; fax: (404) 657-2132.

Hawaii

UAP

Hawaii University Affiliated Program for Developmental Disabilities, University of Hawaii at Manoa, 1776 University Avenue, UA4-6, Honolulu, HI 96822. Tel.: (808) 956-5009; fax: (808) 956-5713; e-mail: bisconer@uhunix.uhcc. hawaii.edu.

P&A

Protection and Advocacy Agency of Hawaii, 1580 Makaloa Street, #1060, Honolulu, HI 96814. Tel.: (808) 949-2922.

DD Council

Hawaii State Planning Council on Developmental Disabilities, 919 Ala Moana Boulevard, Room 113, Honolulu, HI 96814. Tel.: (808) 586-8100; fax: (808) 586-7543.

Idaho

UAP

Idaho Center on Developmental Disabilities, College of Education, University of Idaho, 129 W. 3rd Street, Moscow, ID 83843. Tel.: (208) 885-3559; fax: (208) 885-3628; e-mail: fifield@ uidaho.edu.

P&A

Co-Ad, Inc., 4477 Emerald Street, #B100, Boise, ID 83706. Tel.: (208) 336-5353; fax: (208) 336-5396.

DD Council

Idaho State Council on Developmental Disabilities, 280 N. 8th Street, #208, P.O. Box 83720, Boise, ID 83702. Tel.: (208) 334-2178;

(800) 544-2433 (statewide); fax: 208 (334) 3417.

Illinois

UAP

Institute on Disabilities and Human Development, 1640 West Roosevelt Road, University of Illinois at Chicago, Chicago, IL 60608. Tel.: (312) 413-1647; fax: (312) 413-1630; e-mail: u38382@uicvm.cc.uic.edu.

P&A

Equip for Equality, 11 East Adams, #1200, Chicago, IL 60603. Tel.: (312) 341-0022; fax: (312) 341-0295.

DD Council

Illinois Council on Developmental Disabilities, State of Illinois Center, 830 S. Spring Street, Springfield, IL 62704. Tel.: (217) 782-9696; fax: (217) 524-5339.

Indiana

UAPs

Institute for the Study of Developmental Disabilities: UAP, Indiana University, 2853 E. Tenth Street, Bloomington, IN 47408-2601. Tel.: (812) 855-6508; fax: (812) 855-9630; e-mail: uap@isdd.isdd.indiana.edu.

Riley Child Development Center, James Witcomb Riley Hospital for Children, Indiana University Medical Center, 702 Barnhill Drive, Indianapolis, IN 46202. Tel.: (317) 274-8167; fax: (317) 274-9760; e-mail:jdrau@indyuap.iu pui.edu.

P&A

Indiana Advocacy Services, 850 N. Meridian Street, #2-C, Indianapolis, IN 46204. Tel.: (317) 232-1150, (800) 622-4845.

DD Council

Governor's Planning Council on Developmental Disabilities, 143 West Market Street,

Suite 404, Indianapolis, IN 46204. Tel.: (317) 232-7770; fax: (317) 233-3712.

Iowa

UAP

Iowa University Affiliated Program, Division of Developmental Disabilities, University Hospital School, The University of Iowa, Iowa City, IA 52242-1011. Tel.: (319) 353-6390; fax: (319) 356-8284; e-mail: mark-moser@uiowa.edu.

P&A

Iowa P&A Service, Inc., 3015 Merle Hay Road, #6, Des Moines, IA 50310. Tel.: (515) 278-2502; fax: (515) 278-0539.

DD Council

Governor's Developmental Disabilities Council, 617 East 2nd Street, Des Moines, IA 50309. Tel.: (515) 281-9082; fax: (515) 281-9087.

Kansas

UAPs

Institute for Life Span Studies, University of Kansas, 1052 Robert Dole Human Development Center, Lawrence, KS 66045. Tel.: (913) 864-4295; fax: (913) 864-5323; e-mail: davidas@dole.isi.ukans.edu.

Child Development Unit, Kansas University Affiliated Facility, Kansas City, Children's Rehabilitation Unit-Kansas University Medical Center, 3901 Rainbow Boulevard, Kansas City, KS 66160-7340. Tel.: (913) 588-5900; fax: (913) 588-5916.

Kansas University Affiliated Facility-Parsons, 2601 Gabriel, Parsons, KS 67357. Tel.: (316) 421-6550; fax: (316) 421-1702.

P&A

Kansas Advocacy and Protection Services, 2601 Anderson Avenue, #200, Manhattan, KS 66502-2876. Tel.: (913) 776-1541, (800) 432-8276.

DD Council

Kansas Council on Developmental Disabilities, Docking State Office Building, Room 141, Topeka, KS 66612-1570. Tel.: (913) 296-2608; fax: (913) 296-2861.

Kentucky

UAP

Human Development Institute, University of Kentucky, 126 Mineral Industries Building, Lexington, KY 40506-0051. Tel.: (606) 257-1714; fax: (606) 323-1901; e-mail: middendk@uklans.uky.edu.

P&A

Office of Public Advocacy, Division for Protection and Advocacy, 100 Fair Oak Lane, 3rd Floor, Frankfort, KY 40601. Tel.: (502) 564-2967, (800) 372-2988; fax: (502) 564-7890; e-mail: swest@advocate.pa.state.ky.us.

DD Council

Kentucky Developmental Disabilities Planning Council, Dept. of MH/MR Services, 275 East Main Street, Frankfort, KY 40621. Tel.: (502) 564-7842; fax: (502) 564-3844.

Louisiana

UAP

Human Development Center, Louisiana's University Affiliated Program, School of Allied Health Professions, Louisiana State University Medical Center, 1100 Florida Avenue, New Orleans, LA 70119-2799. Tel.: (504) 942-8200; fax: (504) 942-8305; e-mail:slawso@nombs.lusmc.edu.

P&A

Advocacy Center for the Elderly and Disabled, 210 O'Keefe, #700, New Orleans, LA 70112. Tel.: (504) 522-2337, (800) 662-7705; fax: (504) 522-5507.

DD Council

LA State Planning Council on Developmental Disabilities, P.O. Box 3455, 1201 Capitol Access, 5th Floor, East Entrance, Baton Rouge, LA 70802-1970. Tel.: (504) 342-6804; fax: (504) 342-4419.

Maine

UAP

Center for Community Inclusion, UAP, 5717 Corbett Hall, University of Maine, Orono, ME 04469-5717. Tel.: (207) 581-1084; (207) 581-3328 (tdd); fax: (207) 581-1231; e-mail:annel@ maine.maine.edu.

P&A

Maine Advocacy Services, 32 Winthrop Street, P.O. Box 2007, Augusta, ME 04330. Tel.: (207) 626-2774; fax: (207) 621-1419.

DD Council

Developmental Disabilities Council, Nash Building, 139 State House Station, Augusta, ME 04333-0139. Tel.: (207) 287-4213; fax: (207) 287-8001.

Maryland

UAP

John F. Kennedy Krieger Institute, 707 N. Broadway, Baltimore, MD 21205-1890. Tel.: (410) 550-9483; fax: (410) 550-9524; e-mail: ander-jm@jhuvms.hcf.jhu.edu.

P&A

Maryland Disability Law Center, 2510 St. Paul Street, Baltimore, MD 21218. Tel.: (410) 333-7600.

DD Council

MD Developmental Disabilities Council, One Market Center, Box 10, 300 W. Lexington Street, Baltimore, MD 21201. Tel.: (410) 333-3688; fax: (410) 333-3686.

Massachusetts

UAPs

Developmental Evaluation Center/UAP, Children's Hospital, 300 Longwood Avenue,

Boston, MA 02115. Tel.: (617) 735-6509; fax: (617) 355-7940; e-mail:dove@al.tch.harvard. edu.

Eunice Shriver Center/University Affiliated Program, 200 Trapelo Road, Waltham, MA 02254. Tel.: (617) 642-0001; fax: (617) 894-9968.

P&A

Disability Law Center, Inc., 11 Beacon Street, #925, Boston, MA 02108. Tel.: (617) 723-8455; fax: (617) 723-9125.

DD Council

Massachusetts Developmental Disabilities Council, 600 Washington Street, Room 670, Boston, MA 02111. Tel.: (617) 727-6374; fax: (617) 727-1174.

Michigan

UAPs

Developmental Disabilities Institute, Wayne State University, 326 Justice Building, 6001 Cass Avenue, Detroit, MI 48202. Tel.: (313) 577-2654; fax: (313) 577-3770.

P&A

Michigan Protection and Advocacy Service, 106 Allegan, #210, Lansing, MI 48933-1706. Tel.: (517) 487-1755; fax: (517) 487-0827.

DD Council

Michigan Developmental Disabilities Council, Lewis Cass Building, 6th Floor, 200 N. Washington Street, #120, Lansing, MI 48933. Tel.: (517) 334-6123; fax: (517) 334-7353.

Minnesota

UAP

Institute on Community Integration, University of Minnesota, 150 Pillsbury SE, 102 Pattee Hall, Minneapolis, MN 55455. Tel.: (612) 624-4848; fax: (612) 624-9344; e-mail: smcconnell @vx.cis.umn.edu.

P&A

Minnesota Disability Law Center, 222 Grain Exchange Building, 323 Fourth Avenue S., Minneapolis, MN 55415. Tel.: (612) 332-7301.

DD Council

Governor's Council on Developmental Disabilities, 300 Centennial Office Building, 658 Cedar Street, St. Paul, MN 55155. Tel.: (612) 297-4018; (612) 297-9962 (tdd); fax: (612) 297-7200.

Mississippi

UAP

Institute for Disability Studies, Mississippi University Affiliated Program, University of Southern Mississippi, Southern Station, Box 5163, Hattiesburg, MS 39406-5163. Tel.: (601) 266-5163; fax: (601) 266-5114; e-mail: uap@bul.cc.usm.edu.

P&A

Mississippi Protection and Advocacy System for Developmental Disabilities, Inc., 5330 Executive Place, Suite A, Jackson, MS 39206. Tel.: (601) 981-8207, (800) 772-4057; fax: (601) 981-8313.

DD Council

Developmental Disabilities Planning Council, 1101 Robert E. Lee Building, 239 N. Lamar Street, Jackson, MS 39201. Tel.: (601) 359-1288; fax: (601) 359-6295.

Missouri

UAP

University Affiliated Program for Developmental Disabilities, University of Missouri-Kansas City, Institute for Human Development, 2220 Holmes Street, 3rd Floor, Kansas City, MO 64108. Tel.: (816) 235-1770; fax: (816) 235-1762; e-mail: cfcalkins@vax1.umkc.edu.

P&A

Missouri Protection and Advocacy Services, Inc., 925 S. Country Club Drive, Unit B-1, Jefferson City, MO 65109. Tel.: (314) 893-3333; fax: (314) 893-4231.

DD Council

Missouri Planning Council for Developmental Disabilities, P.O. Box 687, Jefferson City, MO 65102. Tel.: (314) 751-8611; fax: (314) 526-2755.

Montana

UAP

Montana University Affiliated Program, 52 Corbin Hall, University of Montana, Missoula, MT 59812. Tel.: (406) 243-5467; fax: (406) 243-2349.

P&A

Montana Advocacy Program, P.O. Box 1680, Helena, MT 59624. Tel.: (406) 444-3889; fax: (406) 444-0261.

DD Council

Developmental Disabilities Planning and Advisory Council, 111 N. Last Chance Gulch, Arcade Building, Unit C, Box 526, Helena, MT 59620. Tel.: (406) 444-1334; fax: (406) 444-5999.

Nebraska

UAP

Meyer Rehabilitation Institute, University of Nebraska Medical Center, 444 South 44th Street, Omaha, NE 68131. Tel.: (402) 559-6430; fax: (402) 559-5737; e-mail: mleibowi@unmc.edu.

P&A

Nebraska Advocacy Services, 522 Lincoln Center Building, 215 Centennial Mall South, Lincoln, NE 68508. Tel.: (402) 474-3183; fax: (402) 559-5737.

DD Council

Department of Health/Developmental Disabilities, 301 Centennial Mall South, P.O. Box 95007, Lincoln, NE 68509-5007. Tel.: (402) 471-2330; fax: (402) 471-0180/-0383.

New Hampshire

UAP

New Hampshire University Affiliated Program, Institute on Disability, 7 Leavitt Lane, Suite 101, University of New Hampshire, Durham, NH 03824-3512. Tel.: (603) 862-4320; fax: (603) 862-0032; e-mail: sue.hoopes@ unh.edu.

P&A

Disabilities Rights Center, Inc., P.O. Box 3660, Concord, NH 03302-3660. Tel.: (603) 228-0432; fax: (603) 225-2007.

DD Council

New Hampshire Developmental Disabilities Council, The Concord Center, Box 315, 10 Ferry Street, Concord, NH 03301-5022. Tel.: (603) 271-3236; fax: (603) 271-1156.

New Jersey

UAP

University Affiliated Program of New Jersey—UMDNJ, Robert Wood Johnson Medical School—Brookwood II, 45 Knightsbridge Road, P.O. Box 6810, Piscataway, NJ 08855-6810. Tel.: (908) 235-4447; fax: (908) 235-5059; e-mail: knox@umdnj.edu.

P&A

New Jersey Protection and Advocacy, Inc., 210 South Broad Street, 3rd Floor, Trenton, NJ 08608. Tel.: (609) 292-9742, (800) 792-8600; fax: (609) 777-0187.

DD Council

New Jersey Developmental Disabilities Council, 20 West State Street, CN 700, 7th Floor, Trenton, NJ 08625. Tel.: (609) 292-3745; fax: (609) 292-7114.

New York

UAPs

Rose F. Kennedy Center, Albert Einstein College of Medicine, Yeshiva University, 1410 Pelham Parkway S., Bronx, NY 10461. Tel.: (718) 430-2325; fax: (718) 892-2296; e-mail: birenbau@aecom.yu.edu.

Developmental Disabilities Center, Street Lukes, Roosevelt Hospital Center, 428 W. 59th Street, New York, NY 10019. Tel.: (212) 523-6230; fax: (212) 523-6271.

The Strong Center for Developmental Disabilities, Box 671, 601 Elmwood Avenue, Rochester, NY 14642. Tel.: (716) 275-2986; fax: (716) 275-3366; e-mail:burns@troi.cc.rochester.edu.

Westchester Institute for Human Development, 325 Cedarwood Hall, Valhalla, NY 10595. Tel.: (914) 285-8204; fax: (914) 285-1973; e-mail: slwhite@aol.com.

P&A

New York State Commission on Quality of Care for the Mentally Disabled, 99 Washington Avenue, Albany, NY 12210. Tel.: (518) 473-4057; fax: (518) 473-6296.

DD Council

New York State Developmental Disabilities Planning Council, 155 Washington Avenue, 2nd Floor, Albany, NY 12210. Tel.: (518) 432-8233, (800) 395-3372; fax: (518) 432-8238.

North Carolina

UAP

Clinical Center for the Study of Development and Learning, Biological Sciences Research Center 220H, University of North Carolina-Chapel Hill, CB#7255, BSRC, Chapel Hill, NC 27599-7255. Tel.: (919) 966-5171; fax: (919) 966-2230; e-mail: kjens@css.unc.edu.

P&A

Governor's Advocacy Council for Persons with Disabilities, 2113 Cameron Street, #218, Raleigh, NC 27605-1344. Tel.: (919) 733-9250; fax: (919) 733-9173.

DD Council

North Carolina Council on Developmental Disabilities, 1508 Western Boulevard, Raleigh, NC 27606. Tel.: (919) 733-6566; fax: (919) 733-1863.

North Dakota

UAP

The North Dakota Center for Disabilities, Minot State University, 500 University Avenue West, Minot, ND 58701. Tel.: (701) 857-3580; (800) 233-1737; fax: (701) 839-6933; e-mail: ragan@warp6.cs.misu.nodak.edu.

DD Council

North Dakota Developmental Disabilities Council, State Capitol Building, 600 E. Boulevard Avenue, Bismarck, ND 58505-0250. Tel.: (701) 224-3219; fax: (701) 328-2359.

Ohio

UAPs

University Affiliated Cincinnati Center for Developmental Disorders, Pavillion Building, 3333 Burnet Street, Cincinnati, OH 45229. Tel.: (513) 559-4688; fax: (513) 559-7361.

The Nisonger Center, Ohio State University, McCampbell Hall, 1581 Dodd Drive, Columbus, OH 43210-1296. Tel.: (614) 292-8365; fax: (614) 292-3727; e-mail: jrojahn@magnus.acs.ohio-state.edu.

DD Council

Ohio Developmental Disabilities Planning Council, Department of MR/DD, 8 East Long Street, Atlas Building, 6th Floor, Columbus, OH 43215. Tel.: (614) 466-5205; fax: (614) 466-0298.

Oklahoma

UAP

UAP of Oklahoma, University of Oklahoma, College of Medicine, P.O. Box 26901, ROB-342, Oklahoma City, OK 73190-3042. Tel.: (405) 271-4500; fax: (405) 271-1459; e-mail: valerie-williams@uokhsc.edu.

DD Council

DHS—Oklahoma Planning Council/Developmental Disabilities, Sequoya Building, Room B5, Box 25352, Oklahoma City, OK 73125. Tel.: (405) 521-4984; fax: (405) 521-6684.

Oregon

UAPs

Center on Human Development, University of Oregon-Eugene, College of Education, Clinical Services Building, Eugene, OR 97403-1211. Tel.: (503) 346-3591; fax: (503) 346-5639.

Child Development and Rehabilitation Center, Oregon Health Sciences University, P.O., Box 574, Portland, OR 97207-0574. Tel.: (503) 494-8364; fax: (503) 494-6868; e-mail: sellsc@ohsu.edu.

DD Council

Oregon Developmental Disabilities Council, 540 24th Place NE, Salem, OR 97301-4517. Tel.: (503) 945-9941; fax: (503) 945-9947.

Pennsylvania

UAPs

Children's Seashore House, Department of Pediatrics, University of Pennsylvania School of Medicine, 3405 Civic Center Boulevard, Philadelphia, PA 19104. Tel.: (215) 895-3208; fax: (215) 895-3587; e-mail:steinberga@a1.mscf.upenn.edu.

Institute on Disabilities, Temple University, Ritter Hall Annex, Room 423, 13th Street and Cecil B. Moore Avenue, Philadelphia, PA

19122. Tel.: (215) 204-1356; fax: (215) 204-6336; e-mail: dianeb@astro.ocis.temple.edu.

P&A

Pennsylvania Protection and Advocacy, Inc., 116 Pine Street, Harrisburg, PA 17101. Tel.: (215) 236-8110, (800) 692-7443.

DD Council

Developmental Disabilities Council, 569 Forum Building, Harrisburg, PA 17120. Tel.: (717) 787-6057.

Puerto Rico

UAP

Developmental Disabilities Institute: UAP, Graduate School of Public Health, Medical Science Campus, University of Puerto Rico, Box 365067, San Juan, PR 00936-5067. Tel.: (809) 754-4377; fax: (809) 759-6719; e-mail: mamiranda@rcmaca.upr.clu.edu.

P&A

Ombudsman for the Disabled, P.O. Box 5163, Hato Rey, PR 00919. Tel.: (809) 766-2333, (809) 766-2388.

DD Council

Developmental Disabilities Council, P.O. Box 9543, Santurce, PR 00908. Tel.: (809) 722-0595; fax: (809) 721-3622.

Rhode Island

UAP

Rhode Island University Affiliated Program, Institute for Developmental Disabilities, Rhode Island College, 600 Mount Pleasant Avenue, Providence, RI 02908. Tel.: (401) 456-8072; fax: (401) 456-8605.

P&A

Rhode Island Protection and Advocacy System (RIPAS), Inc., 155 Broadway Street, 3rd Floor, Providence, RI 02903. Tel.: (401) 831-3150, (800) 733-5332; fax: (401) 274-5568.

DD Council

Rhode Island Developmental Disabilities Council, 600 New London Avenue, Cranston, RI 02920. Tel.: (401) 464-3191; fax: (401) 464-3570.

South Carolina

UAP

South Carolina University Affiliated Program, University of South Carolina, Center for Developmental Disabilities, Benson Building, 1st Floor, Columbia SC 29208. Tel.: (803) 777-4435; fax: (803) 777-6058.

P&A

South Carolina P&A System for the Handicapped, Inc., 3710 Landmark Drive, #204, Columbia, SC 29204. Tel.: (803) 282-0639.

DD Council

South Carolina Developmental Disabilities Council, 1205 Pendleton Street, Room 372, Edgar A. Brown Building, Columbia, SC 29201. Tel.: (803) 734-0465; fax: (803) 734-0356.

South Dakota

UAP

South Dakota University Affiliated Program, University of South Dakota, School of Medicine, 414 East Clark Street, Vermillion, SD 57069. Tel.: (605) 677-5311; fax: (605) 677-6274; e-mail: kkathol@charlie.usd.edu.

P&A

South Dakota Advocacy Services, Inc., 221 South Central Avenue, Pierre, SD 57501. Tel.: (605) 224-8294; (800) 742-8108 (statewide); fax: (605) 224-5125.

DD Council

South Dakota Governor's State Planning Council on Developmental Disabilities, Hill

View Plaza, East Highway 34, c/o 500 East Capital, Pierre, SD 57501. Tel.: (605) 773-6415; fax: (605) 773-5483.

Tennessee

UAP

Boling Center for Developmental Disabilities, The University of Tennessee, Memphis, 711 Jefferson Avenue, Memphis, TN 38105. Tel.: (901) 448-6511; fax: (901) 448-4097; e-mail: wwilson@utmem1.utmen.edu.

P&A

Tennessee Protection and Advocacy, Inc., P.O. Box 121257, Nashville, TN 37212. Tel.: (615) 298-1080; (800) 342-1660 (statewide); fax: (615) 298-2046.

DD Council

Developmental Disabilities Planning Council, Department of MH/MR, Gateway Plaza, 10th Floor, 710 James Robertson Parkway, Nashville, TN 37243-0675. Tel.: (615) 532-6530; fax: (615) 532-6964.

Texas

UAP

Texas University Affiliated Program, University of Texas at Austin, 306 Sanchez Building (D5300), Austin, TX 78712-1290. Tel.: (512) 471-7621, (800) 828-7839, (512) 471-1844 (tdd); fax: (512) 471-7549; e-mail: pseay@mail.utexas.edu.

P&A

Advocacy, Inc., 7800 Shoal Creek Boulevard, #171-E, Austin, TX 78757. Tel.: (512) 454-4816; (800) 252-9108 (statewide voice/tdd).

DD Council

Texas Planning Council for Developmental Disabilities, 4900 N. Lamar Boulevard, Austin, TX 78751-2316. Tel.: (512) 483-4080; fax: (512) 433-4097.

Utah

UAP

Center for Persons with Disabilities, Utah State University, Logan, UT 84322-6800. Tel.: (801) 797-1981; fax: (801) 797-3944; e-mail: sharon@cpd2.usu.edu.

P&A

Legal Center for the Handicapped, 455 E. 400 South, #410, Salt Lake City, UT 84111. Tel.: (801) 363-1347, (800) 662-9080; fax: (801) 363-1437.

DD Council

Utah Governor's Council for People with Disabilities, 555 East 300 South, #201, Salt Lake City, UT 84102. Tel.: (801) 533-4128; fax: (801) 533-5305.

Vermont

UAP

UAP of Vermont, University of Vermont, 499C Waterman Building, Burlington, VT 05405-0160. Tel.: (802) 656-4031; fax: (802) 656-1357; e-mail: wfox@moose.uvm.edu.

P&A

Vermont Developmental Disabilities Law Project, 12 North Street, Burlington, VT 05401. Tel.: (802) 863-2881.

DD Council

Vermont Developmental Disabilities Council, 103 South Main Street, Waterbury, VT 05671-0206. Tel.: (802) 241-2612; fax: (802) 241-2979.

Virgin Islands

UAP

University of the Virgin Islands, #2 John Brewers Bay, Charlotte Amalie, Street Thomas, VI 00802-9990. Tel.: (809) 693-1323; fax: (809) 693-1185.

P&A

Virgin Islands Advocacy Agency, 7A Whim Street, Suite 2, Fredericksted, VI 00840. Tel.: (809) 772-1200; Street Thomas: (809) 766-4303; (809) 772-4641 (tdd).

Virginia

UAP

Virginia Institute for Developmental Disabilities Administration, Virginia Commonwealth University, Box 3020, Richmond, VA 23284-3020. Tel.: (804) 225-3876; fax: (804) 371-0042; e-mail: forelove@cabel.vcu.edu.

P&A

Department of Rights for the Disabled, James Monroe Building, 101 North 14th Street, 17th Floor, Richmond, VA 23219. Tel.: (804) 225-2042, (800) 552-3962.

DD Council

Virginia Board for People with Disabilities, P.O. Box 613, Richmond, VA 23205-0613. Tel.: (804) 786-0016; fax: (804) 786-1118.

Washington

UAP

Center on Human Developmental Disabilities, University of Washington, Box 357920, Seattle, WA 98195-7920. Tel.: (206) 543-2832; fax: (206) 543-3417; e-mail: mjgural@u.washington.edu.

P&A

Washington P&A System, 1401 E. Jefferson, #506, Seattle, WA 98122. Tel.: (206) 324-1521.

DD Council

Washington Developmental Disabilities Council, 906 Columbia Street SW, P.O. Box 48314, Olympia, WA 98504-8314. Tel.: (206) 753-3908; fax: (206) 586-2424.

West Virginia

UAP

University Affiliated Center for Developmental Disabilities, West Virginia University, 955 Hartman Run Road, Research Park, Morgantown, WV 26505. Tel.: (304) 293-4692; fax: (304) 293-7294.

P&A

West Virginia Advocates, 1524 Kanawha Boulevard. East, Charleston, WV 25311. Tel.: (304) 346-0847; statewide (800) 950-5250.

DD Council

West Virginia Developmental Disabilities Planning Council, 110 Stockton Street, Charleston, WV 25312-2521. Tel.: (304) 558-0416; fax: (304) 558-0941.

Wisconsin

UAP

Waisman Center UAP, University of Wisconsin, 1500 Highland Avenue, Madison, WI 53705-2280. Tel.: (608) 263-1656; fax: (608) 263-0529; e-mail: kuehn@waisman.wisc.edu.

P&A

Wisconsin Coalition for Advocacy, Inc., 16 N. Carroll Street, #400, Madison, WI 53703. Tel.: (608) 267-0214.

DD Council

Wisconsin Council on Developmental Disabilities, 722 Williamson Street, 2nd Floor, P.O. Box 7851, Madison, WI 53707-7851. Tel.: (608) 266-7826; fax: (608) 267-3906.

Wyoming

UAP

Wyoming Institute for Disabilities (WIND/UAP), Box 4298, University Station, University of Wyoming, Laramie, WY 82071-4298. Tel.: (307) 766-2761; fax/tdd: (307) 766-2763; e-mail: WIND.@uwyo.edu.

P&A

Wyoming Protection & Advocacy System, Inc., 2424 Pioneer Avenue, #100, Cheyenne, WY 82001. Tel.: (307) 638-7668/-3496, (800) 624-7648.

DD Council

DD Planning Council, 122 West 25th Street, Hersch Building, Cheyenne, WY 82002. Tel.: (307) 777-7230; fax (307) 777-5690.

Table A–1 State Lead Agencies Responsible for Early Intervention Programming for Children from Infancy to Third Birthday

State	Lead Agency	Telephone Number
Alabama	Education/Rehabilitation Services	(205) 242-9700
Alaska	Health and Social Services/Div. Public Health	(907) 465-3030
Arizona	Economic Security/Developmental Disabilities	(602) 542-0419
Arkansas	Human Services/Developmental Disabilities	(501) 682-1001
California	Developmental Services	(916) 654-1897
Colorado	Education	(303) 866-6710
Connecticut	Education	(203) 638-4208
Delaware	Health and Social Services/MR	(302) 739-4452
District of Columbia	Commission on Social Services	(202) 727-5930
Florida	Health and Rehabilitation Services	(904) 487-2690
Georgia	Human Resources	(404) 657-2727
Hawaii	Health/Children with Special Needs	(808) 733-9070
Idaho	Health and Welfare	(208) 334-5514
Illinois	Education	(217) 782-4321
Indiana	Mental Health/Bureau of Developmental Disabilities	(317) 232-7842
Iowa	Education	(515) 281-7844
Kansas	Health and Environment	(913) 296-6135
Kentucky	Mental Health/Mental Retardation	(502) 564-7700
Louisiana	Bureau of Interagency Coordination/Office of Special Education	(504) 763-3552
Maine	Education/Division of Special Education	(207) 287-5950
Maryland	Governor's Office of Children and Youth	(410) 333-8100
Massachusetts	Public Health	(617) 727-5089
Michigan	Education	(800) EARLY ON
Minnesota	Education	(612) 296-7032
Mississippi	Health/Bureau of Early Intervention Services	(601) 960-7427
Missouri	Education	In Missouri— (800) 873-6623 Out of state— (816) 543-4193
Montana	Social and Rehabilitation Services, Developmental Disabilities Division	(406) 444-2995
Nebraska	Education/Social Services	(402) 471-2472 (800) 742 7594
Nevada	Human Resources	(702) 687-5982
New Hampshire	Health and Human Service	(603) 271-5122
New Jersey	Department of Health/Special Child Health Services	(609) 777-7734
New Mexico	Health/Developmental Disabilities	(405) 521-3351
New York	Public Health/Early Intervention, Child, and Adolescent Program	(518) 473-7016
North Carolina	Human Resources/MH-DD-SAS	(919) 733-7672
North Dakota	Human Services	(701) 224-2310
Ohio	Health/Bureau of Early Intervention	(614) 644-8389
Oklahoma	Education/Department of Special Education	(405) 521-3351
Oregon	Education	(503) 378-3598
Pennsylvania	Public Welfare/Office of Mental Health/Mental Retardation	(717) 783-8302
Rhode Island	Health	(401) 277-2312
South Carolina	Health and Environmental Control	(803) 737-0395
South Dakota	Education/Office of Special Education	(605) 773-3678

Table A–1 Continued

State	Lead Agency	Telephone Number
Tennessee	Education/Division of Special Programs	(901) 741-2851
Texas	Interagency Council on Early Childhood Education	(512) 502-4900
Utah	Health/Baby Watch—Early Intervention	(801) 584-8226
Vermont	Education/Office of Special Education	(802) 828-3141
Virginia	MH/MR/SAS, Office of Prevention and Children's Resources	(804) 786-1530
Washington	Social and Health Services, Department of Children and Family	(206) 721-4115
West Virginia	Health and Human Resources	(304) 558-0684
Wisconsin	Health and Social Services	(608) 266-9622
Wyoming	Health and Social Services/Developmental Disabilities	(307) 777-7731

Organizations and Associations

Symme W. Trachtenberg and Peter W. Dowrick

This appendix is designed to assist families and professionals in locating service information, referrals, written materials, and technical and emotional support through knowledge of national organizations, many with local chapters. The list is arranged alphabetically under headings of diagnosis or the type of support that might be required.

In addition to the national resources listed below, pediatric hospitals and general hospitals with pediatric units are a resource for parents and professionals. Local phone books also have *Blue Pages* with a Guide to Human Services. One should focus attention on the sections entitled "Health," "Disabilities" (or synonyms, such as "Handicapped Children"), "Education," "Information and Referral Services," "Mental Health and Mental Retardation," "Hearing Impairments," and "Vision Impairments."

We made every effort to contact all listed phone numbers immediately before going to press to verify the information as current. We regret any errors or omissions and do not imply any endorsement of listed services.

ACCESSIBILITY

Adaptive Environments Center, 374 Congress Street, Suite 301, Boston, MA 02210. Tel.: (617) 695-1225 (voice/tdd). A not-for-profit organization offering consultation, workshops, courses, conferences, and resource materials on accessible and adaptive design and accessibility legislation, standards, and guidelines. The center's library contains a comprehensive collection of materials on accessible design.

Architectural and Transportation Barriers Compliance Board, 1331 F Street NW, Suite 1000, Washington, DC 20004-1111. Tel.: (202) 272-5434 (voice/tdd), (800) 872-2253; fax: (202) 272-5447. An organization created by

Adapted from a compilation by Marge Rose and Symme W. Trachtenberg, M.S.W., Children's Seashore House for Batshaw, Mark L., & Perret, Yvonne M. *Children with disabilities: A medical primer* (3rd ed). Baltimore: Paul H. Brookes, 1992, updated and verified by Symme Trachtenberg, M.S.W., Peter W. Dowrick, Ph.D., Jennifer Euster, M.S.W., Libby Pollak, M.S.W., Ross and Jocelyn Trachtenberg, and others.

Section 504 of the Rehabilitation Act of 1973 to enforce the Architectural Barriers Act of 1968 (Pub.L. 90-480). Offers free publications and answers to technical questions about accessibility.

Barrier-Free Design Centre, 444 Young Street, College Park, Toronto M5B2H4, Canada. Tel.: (416) 977-5010; fax: (416) 977-5121. A not-for-profit organization providing information, referral, and direct services for individuals, organizations, and professionals seeking expert advice on how to make facilities accessible to people at every level of ability.

In Door Sports Club, Inc., 1145 Highland Street, Napoleon, OH 43545. Tel.: (419) 592-5756. Educates the public to promote and support opportunities that provide accessibility for people with disabilities interested in opportunities for rehabilitation and employment.

The Research and Training Center for Accessible Housing, North Carolina State University School of Design, Box 8613, Raleigh, NC 27695-8613. Tel.: (919) 515-3082, (800) 647-6777; fax: (919) 515-3023; e-mail: cahd @ ncsu.edu. Provides publications and information to parents and professionals concerning accessible housing design and financing issues. Referrals are made to local organizations.

AIDS

National AIDS Information Clearinghouse, P.O. Box 6003, Rockville, MD 20849-6003. Tel.: (800) 458-5231; tdd: (800) 243-7012; fax: (301) 738-6616; e-mail:cdcnac.aspensys. com. A comprehensive information service for health professionals, including public health managers and officials at the state and local level and health care providers. The clearinghouse offers free government publications and information about resources.

National AIDS Hotline. Tel.: (800) 342-AIDS (342-2437); (800) 344-SIDA (344-7432; Spanish access); (800) AIDS-TTY (243-7889; tdd). A 24-hour service, seven days a week, that provides confidential information, referrals, and educational materials to the public. The hotline offers information on transmission, prevention, testing, and local referrals.

Project STAR, 1800 Columbus Avenue, Roxbury, MA 02119. Tel.: (617) 442-7442; fax: (617) 442-1705. Multidisciplinary services and referral for schools and families of children who are HIV-positive.

ATTENTION-DEFICIT DISORDER

CHADD National, 499 NW 70th Avenue, Suite 101, Plantation, FL 33317. Tel.: (305) 587-3700; fax: (305) 587-4599. Support group for parents of children with attention-deficit disorders. Provides continuing education for both parents and professionals, serves as a community resource for information, and advocates for appropriate educational programs.

AUTISM

Autism Services Center/National Autism Hotline, The Prichard Building, 605 Ninth Street, P.O. Box 507, Huntington, WV 25710-0507. Tel.: (304) 525-8014; fax: (304) 525-8026. Provides direct care services (group homes, supervised apartments, etc.), information, advocacy, training, consultation, and seminars for individuals with autism and other developmental disabilities.

Autism Research Institute, 4182 Adams Avenue, San Diego, CA 92116. Tel.: (619) 281-7165; fax: (619) 563-6840. Information, referral, and newsletter for parents, teachers, physicians, and students working with children who have autism or related disabilities.

Autism Society of America, 7910 Woodmonte Avenue, Suite 650, Bethesda, MD 20814. Tel.: (301) 565-0433; fax: (301) 657-0869. Provides information about autism and about various options, approaches, methods, and systems available to parents of children with autism, family members, and the professionals who work with them. Advocates for rights and needs of individuals with autism and their families.

CAREER COUNSELING

ERIC Clearinghouse on Disabilities and Gifted Education, 1920 Association Drive, Reston, VA 22091-1589. Tel.: (703) 264-9474. Provides information on disabilities and gifted education, including published and unpublished documents.

Higher Education and Adult Training for People with Disabilities (HEATH Resource Center), 1 Dupont Circle NW, Suite 800, Washington, DC 20036-1193. Tel.: (800) 54-HEATH, (202) 939-9320; fax: (202) 833-4760; e-mail: heath@ace.nche.edu. Operates as a national clearinghouse on postsecondary education for individuals with disabilities. Provides informational exchange about educational services, policies, procedures, adaptations, and opportunities on American campuses, vocational and technical schools, independent living centers, and transition and training programs after high school.

Job Accommodation Network (JAN), 918 Chestnut Ridge Road, Suite 1, P.O. Box 6080, Morgantown, WV 26506. Tel.: (800) 526-7234; in Canada, (800) 526-2262; fax: (304) 293-5407. Information and resources to make the workplace accessible to those with disabilities. Offers information on the ADA.

CEREBRAL PALSY

American Academy for Cerebral Palsy and Developmental Medicine, 6300 N. River Road, Suite 727, Rosemont, IL 60018. Tel.: (708) 698-1635; fax: (708) 823-0536. Multidisciplinary scientific society that fosters professional education, research, and interest in the problems associated with cerebral palsy. Provides information to the public.

United Cerebral Palsy Associations, Inc., 1660 L Street NW, Suite 700, Washington DC 20036. Tel.: (202) 842-1266, (800) 872-5827; fax: (202) 776-0414. Direct services to children

and adults with cerebral palsy that include medical diagnosis, evaluation and treatment, special education, career development, counseling, social and recreational programs, and adapted housing for people with disabilities.

CHILD ABUSE

Covenant House Hotline, 346 West 17th Street, New York, NY 10011. Tel.: (800) 999-9999. A national toll-free hotline for young people and parents requiring crisis intervention and referrals throughout the country.

National Committee To Prevent Child Abuse, P.O. Box 2866, Chicago, IL 60690. Tel.: (312) 663-3520. Provides information on parenting and child abuse prevention.

CLEFT LIP AND PALATE

Cleft Palate Foundation, 1218 Grandview Avenue, Pittsburgh, PA 15211. Tel.: (412) 481-1376, 800-24-CLEFT; fax: (412) 481-0847. Professional organization that educates and assists the public regarding cleft lip and palate and other craniofacial anomalies and that encourages research in the field. Provides information and referrals, including parent support groups. Distributes brochures, fact sheets, and a quarterly newsletter.

COMPUTERS

Trace Research and Development Center, 1500 Highland Avenue, S-151, Madison, WI 53705-2280. Tel.: (608) 262-6966, (608) 263-5408 (tdd); fax: 608-262-8848. Conducts research and development in the areas of communication and computer access for individuals with disabilities. Offers information and a reprint service.

CORNELIA DE LANGE SYNDROME

Cornelia de Lange Syndrome Foundation, Inc., 60 Dyer Avenue, Collinsville, CT 06022. Tel.: (203) 693-0159; fax: (203) 693-6819.

Supports parents and children affected by Cornelia de Lange Syndrome. Promotes research and publishes a newsletter and informational pamphlets.

CRI DU CHAT

The 5p-Society (Cri Du Chat) Parent Support Group, 11609 Oakmont, Overland Park, KS 66210. Tel.: (913) 469-8900. Offers information, networking, and advocacy.

CYSTIC FIBROSIS

Cystic Fibrosis Foundation, 6931 Arlington Road, Bethesda, MD 20814. Tel.: (301) 951-4422, (800) FIGHT CF (344-4823); fax: (301) 951-6378. Provides referral for diagnostic services and medical care, offers professional and public information, and supports research and professional training.

DOWN SYNDROME

Association for Children with Down Syndrome, 2616 Martin Avenue, Bellmore, NY 11710. Tel.: (516) 221-4700; fax: (516) 221-4311. Information and referral services, including free publication list and workshops for parents, teachers, and children that provide hands-on experience with computers; has a library of catalogs, articles, and books that relate to computers, disability, and special education. Supports parent self-help.

National Down Syndrome Congress, 1605 Chantilly Drive, Suite 250, Atlanta, GA 30324. Tel.: (404) 633-1555; fax: (404) 633-2817; e-mail: ndsc@charitiesusa.com. Provides an information and referral system in the United States and 40 foreign countries; publishes two journals, newsletter, etc. Serves as a clearinghouse on all aspects of Down syndrome; monitors research. Provides legislative awareness and pursues public awareness.

National Down Syndrome Society, 666 Broadway, Suite 800, New York, NY 10012. Tel.: (800) 221-4602, (212) 460-9330; fax: (212) 979-2873. Conducts research, promotes public awareness and education, and provides services to families about Down syndrome.

DWARFISM (ACHONDROPLASIA)

Dwarf Athletic Association of America, c/o Janet Brown, 418 Willow Way, Lewisville, TX 75067. Tel.: (214) 317-8299. Develops, promotes, and provides quality amateur athletic preparation, coaching, training, and competitive sports opportunities for athletes who are dwarfs.

Little People of America, Inc., P.O. Box 9897, Washington, DC 20016. Tel.: (800) 24-DWARF (243-9273). Nationwide, voluntary organization dedicated to helping people of short stature. Provides fellowship, moral support, and information to "little persons" affected with dwarfism. Provides information on organizations, products, services, and medical services nearest to caller.

EDUCATION—BEST PRACTICES (Also See "Legal Rights")

Association for Childhood Education International, 11501 Georgia Avenue, Suite 315, Wheaton, MD 20902. Tel.: (301) 942-2443; fax: (301) 942-3012. Professional membership organization provides workshops, publishes periodicals and books.

Association on Higher Education and Disability (AHEAD), P.O. Box 21192, Columbus, OH 43221-0992. Tel.: (614) 488-4972 (voice/tdd); fax: (614) 488-1174. Professional organization committed to full participation in higher education for persons with disabilities.

Council for Exceptional Children, 1920 Association Drive, Reston, VA 22091. Tel.: (703) 620-3660; fax: (703) 264-9494. Provides information to teachers, administrators, and others concerned with the education of children who have disabilities and those who are gifted. Maintains a library and database on literature in special education. Provides professional membership and legislative advocacy.

Education Testing Service/College Board, ATP Services of Handicapped Students, P.O. Box 6226, Princeton, NJ 08541-6226. Tel.: (609) 771-7143; fax: (609) 771-7681. Develops and administers standardized testing systems. Publishes testing-related materials.

National Association of Private Schools for Exceptional Children, 1522 K Street NW, Suite 1032, Washington, DC 20005. Tel.: (202) 408-3338; fax: (202) 408-3340. National organization of private schools that promotes communication among these schools and informs the public about schools across the country. Publishes a comprehensive directory.

National Information Center for Educational Media (NICEM), P.O. Box 40130, Albuquerque, NM 87196. Tel.: (505) 265-3591, 800-926-8328; fax: (505) 256-1080. Provides database of educational audiovisual materials including video, motion pictures, filmstrips, audio tapes, slides.

IN*SOURCE, Indiana Resource Center for Families with Special Needs, 833 Northside Boulevard, Building #1—Rear, South Bend, IN 46617. Tel.: (219) 234-7101; statewide (800) 332-4433; fax: (219) 234-7279; e-mail: jgross@vines.iusb.edu. Coalition of concerned parents, professionals, and consumers dedicated to the rights of all children, including those with disabilities, to a free, appropriate public education.

TASH: The Association for Persons with Severe Handicaps, 29 W. Susquehanna Avenue, Suite 210, Baltimore, MD 21204. Tel. (410) 828-8274; (410) 828-1306 (tdd); fax: (410) 828-6706. Advocates high-quality education for children (and adults) with disabilities. Disseminates research findings and practical applications for education and habilitation; national conferences.

EPILEPSY

Epilepsy Foundation of America, 4351 Garden City Drive, Landover, MD 20785. Tel.: (301) 459-3700, (800) 332-1000; fax: (301) 577-2684. Provides programs of information and education, advocacy, support of research, and the delivery of needed services to people with epilepsy and their families.

FRAGILE X

National Fragile X Foundation, 1441 York Street, Suite 303, Denver, CO 80206. Tel.: (800) 688-8765, (303) 333-6155; fax: (303) 333-4369. Promotes education in diagnosis, treatment, and research in Fragile X syndrome and provides referral to local resource centers. Sponsors biannual conference. Offers extensive audiovisual and teaching aids.

GENERAL INFORMATION (Also See Appendix A)

National Information Center for Children and Youth with Disabilities (NICHCY), P.O. Box 1492, Washington, DC 20013. Tel.: (800) 999-5599 (outside Washington, DC area); (703) 893-6061 (Washington, DC area); (703) 893-8614 (tdd). NICHCY is a federally funded project mandated by section 633 of the Individuals with Disabilities Act (IDEA) under Pub.L. 101-476. NICHCY collects and shares information and ideas that are helpful to children and youth with disabilities and the people who care for and about them. The center answers questions; links people with others who share similar interests; publishes fact sheets, newsletters, and papers; and generally assists the flow of information from those who have it to those who need it. Single copies of NICHCY publications are available free of charge. Some are available in Spanish or alternative formats.

GENETICS

National Society of Genetic Counselors, 233 Canterbury Drive, Wallingford, PA 19086. Tel.: (610) 872-7608; fax: (610) 872-1192. Professional organization of genetic counselors. Provides referral to nearest source for genetic counseling and services. This office does not provide or disseminate information about specific genetic disorders.

GUILLAIN-BARRÉ

Guillain-Barré Syndrome Foundation, International, P.O. Box 262, Wynnewood, PA 19096. Tel.: (610) 667-0131; fax: (610) 667-7036. Provides emotional support to patients and their families. Fosters research and public education, develops nationwide support groups, and directs people with this syndrome to resources, meetings, newsletters, and symposia.

HEARING, SPEECH, AND LANGUAGE

Alexander Graham Bell Association for the Deaf, 3417 Volta Place NW, Washington, DC 20007. Tel.: (202) 337-5220 (voice/tdd). Umbrella organization for International Organization for the Education of the Hearing Impaired (IOEHI), International Parents Organization, and Oral Hearing Impaired Section. Provides information and referrals. Encourages improved communication, better public understanding, and detection of early hearing loss. Provides scholarships and training opportunities.

American Academy of Audiology, 1735 N. Lynn Street, Suite 950, Arlington, VA 22209. Tel.: (800) 222-2336. Provides information regarding audiology services, hearing loss, and amplification.

American Society for Deaf Children, 814 Thayer Avenue, Silver Spring, MD 20910. Tel.: (800) 942-2732; (301) 585-5401 (tdd), fax: (916) 482-0121. Provides information and support to parents and families with children who are deaf or hearing impaired.

American Speech-Language-Hearing Association, 10801 Rockville Pike, Rockville, MD 20852. Tel.: (301) 897-5700 (voice/tdd), (800) 638-8255; fax: (301) 897-7348. Professional and scientific organization; certifying body for professionals providing speech, language, and hearing therapy; conducts research in communication disorders; publishes several journals. Provides consumer information and professional referral.

Hearing Aid Helpline, 20361 Middlebelt Road, Livonia, MI 48152. Tel.: (800) 521-5247; fax: (810) 478-4520. Information on how to proceed when hearing loss is suspected; free consumer kit, facts about hearing aids, and a variety of literature on hearing-related subjects is available.

National Information Center on Deafness, Gallaudet University, 800 Florida Avenue NE, Washington, DC 20002. Tel.: (202) 651-5051; (202) 651-5052 (tdd); fax: (202) 651-5054. Provides information related to deafness; has a multitude of resources and experts available for individuals with hearing impairments, their families, and professionals. Collects information about resources around the country.

Captioned Films and Videos for the Deaf/Modern Talking Picture Services, 4707 1400 Street, Clearwater, FL 34622. Tel.: (800) 237-6213; fax: (800) 538-5636. Government-sponsored distribution of open-captioned materials to eligible institutions and families. Application sent upon request.

Deafpride, 1350 Potomac Avenue SE, Washington, DC 20003. Tel.: (202) 675-6700 (voice/tdd); fax: (202) 547-0547. Information gathering and distribution, and advocacy programs for the rights of deaf people. Also offers community-based services for people who are deaf involving AIDS awareness, substance abuse issues, maternal and child health issues, and sign language classes.

Self Help for Hard of Hearing People (SHHH), 7800 Wisconsin Avenue, Bethesda, MD 20814. Tel.: (301) 657-2248; (301) 657-2249 (tdd); fax: (301) 913-9413. Educational organization assisting those who are committed to participating fully in society. Publishes journal and newsletter and provides advocacy and outreach programs.

INDEPENDENT LIVING

National Center for Youth with Disabilities, Box 721-UMHC, Harvard Street at East River Road, Minneapolis, MN 55455. Tel.: (800)

333-6239. An information and resource center focusing on adolescents with chronic illnesses or disabilities and the issues associated with making the transition to adult life.

National Council on Independent Living, 2111 Wilson Boulevard, Suite 405, Arlington, VA 22201. Tel.: (703) 525-3406; fax: (703) 525-3409. Provides referral to local Centers for Independent Living, which will facilitate achievement of maximum independence in the community.

LEARNING DISABILITIES

Learning Disabilities Association of America, 4156 Library Road, Pittsburgh, PA 15234. Tel.: (412) 341-1515; fax: (412) 344-0224. Encourages research and the development of early detection programs, disseminates information, serves as an advocate, and works to improve education for individuals who are learning disabled.

National Center for Learning Disabilities (NCLD), 381 Park Avenue, Suite 1420, New York, NY 10016. Tel.: (212) 545-7510; fax: (212) 545-9665. Promotes public awareness of learning disabilities. Provides computer-based information and referral services to consumers and professionals on learning disabilities. Publishes a magazine for parents and professionals.

Orton Dyslexia Society, Chester Building, #382, 8600 LaSalle Road, Baltimore, MD 21286. Tel.: (800) 222-3123, (410) 296-0232; fax: (410) 321-5069. Publishes periodicals. Makes referrals to local chapters and other resources; national conference.

Dyslexia Research Institute, 4745 Centerville Road, Tallahassee, FL 32308. Tel.: (904) 893-2216; fax: (904) 893-2440. Training, workshops, and seminars for professionals; literature sent on request.

LEGAL RIGHTS

American Civil Liberties Union, Children's Rights Project, 132 W. 43rd Street, New York, NY 10036. Tel.: (212) 944-9800, ext. 714; fax: (212) 921-7916. Nationwide test-case litigation program designed to protect and expand the statutory and constitutional rights of children, especially the rights of children in foster care.

American Bar Association Center on Children and the Law, 740 15th Street NW, 9th Floor, Washington, DC 20005. Tel.: (202) 662-1720; fax: (202) 662-1032. Offers information and advocacy to professionals and parents of children and adolescents with disabilities.

Children's Defense Fund, 25 E Street NW, Washington, DC 20001. Tel.: (202) 628-8787; fax: (202) 662-3510. Provides information about legislation in health care, child welfare, and special education. Publishes a guide for parents and advocates to the rights under the Individuals with Disabilities Education Act.

Disability Rights Education and Defense Fund (DREDF), 2212 Sixth Street, Berkeley, CA 94710. Tel.: (510) 644-2555; fax: (510) 841-8645. Law and policy center to protect the rights of people with disabilities. Referral and information regarding rights of people with disabilities, especially the Americans with Disabilities Act. This organization educates legislators and policy makers on issues affecting the rights of people with disabilities.

Mental Health Law Project, 1101 15th Street NW, Suite 1212, Washington, DC 20017. Tel.: (202) 467-5730; fax: (202) 223-0409. Legal advocacy program that works to define, establish, and protect the rights of children and adults with developmental disabilities using test-case litigation, federal policy, advocacy, training, and technical assistance for attorneys and other advocates nationwide.

National Center for Law and the Deaf, 800 Florida Avenue NE, Washington, DC 20002. Tel.: (202) 651-5373 (voice/tdd); fax: (202) 651-5381. Provides a variety of legal services to the deaf and hard-of-hearing community including representation, counseling, information, and education.

MENTAL RETARDATION

American Association on Mental Retardation, 444 N. Capital Street NW, Suite 846, Washington, DC 20001. Tel.: (202) 387-1968; fax: (202) 387-2193. Professional organization that promotes cooperation among those involved in services, training, and research in the field of mental retardation. Encourages research, dissemination of information, development of appropriate community-based services, and the promotion of preventive measures to reduce the incidence of mental retardation.

The ARC of the United States (formerly Association for Retarded Citizens), 500 East Border Street, Suite 300, Arlington, TX 76010. Tel.: (817) 261-6003; fax: (817) 277-3491. National advocacy organization working on behalf of individuals with mental retardation and their families; has local chapters across the United States.

The Joseph P. Kennedy, Jr. Foundation, 1325 G Street NW, Suite 500, Washington, D.C. 20005. Tel.: (202) 393-1250; fax: (202) 824-0351. Promotes public awareness, provides seed grants for scientific research, and provides new models of service for persons with mental retardation. Also sponsors the Kennedy Foundation International Awards in Mental Retardation.

National Association of State Mental Retardation Program Directors, 113 Oronoco Street, Alexandria, VA 22314. Tel.: (703) 683-4202; fax: (703) 684-1395. Organization consisting of one representative from each state. Publishes two newsletters; provides information on state and national trends, statistics, and programs in the field of developmental disabilities.

MUSCULAR DYSTROPHY

Muscular Dystrophy Association, 3300 East Sunrise Drive, Tucson, AZ 85718-3208. Tel.: (602) 529-2000; fax: (602) 529-5300. Volun-

tary health care agency that fosters research and direct care for individuals with muscular dystrophy; concerned with conquering muscular dystrophy and other neuromuscular diseases.

NEUROFIBROMATOSIS

The National Neurofibromatosis Foundation, Inc., 95 Pine Street, 16th Floor, New York, NY 10005. Tel.: (212) 344-6633; fax: (212) 747-0004; e-mail: nnff@aol.com. Supplies information to public and professionals. Offers genetic counseling and support groups throughout the United States.

OCCUPATIONAL THERAPY

The American Occupational Therapy Association, Inc., 4720 Montgomery Lane, P.O. Box 31220, Bethesda, MD 20824-1220. Tel.: (301) 652-2682; fax: (301) 652-7711. Professional organization of occupational therapists; services provided include accreditation of educational programs, professional publications, public education, and continuing education for practitioners.

OSTEOGENESIS IMPERFECTA

Osteogenesis Imperfecta Foundation, Inc., 5005 W. Laureo Street, # 210, Tampa, FL 33607. Tel.: (813) 282-1161; fax: (813) 287-8214. Supports research on osteogenesis imperfecta and provides information to those with this disorder, their families, and others.

PARENTS

Compassionate Friends, P.O. Box 3696, Oak Brook, IL 60522-3696. Tel.: (708) 990-0010; fax: (708) 990-0246. National and worldwide organization that supports parents and siblings in the positive resolution of the grief experienced upon the death of their child.

The Exceptional Parent, 1170 Commonwealth Avenue, Boston, MA 02134-4645. Tel.: (617)

730-5800; fax: (617) 730-8742. This magazine, published since 1971, covers straightforward, practical information for families and professionals; many articles are written by parents.

PACER Center, Inc. (Parent Advocacy Coalition for Educational Rights), 4826 Chicago Avenue, S., Minneapolis, MN 55417-1098. Tel.: (612) 827-2966 (voice/tdd); statewide, (800) 53PACER; fax: (612) 827-3065. Provides education and training to help parents understand the special education laws and to obtain appropriate school programs for their children. Topics include early intervention, emotional disabilities, and health services. Also provides disability awareness puppet program for schools, child abuse prevention program, services, newsletters, booklets, extensive written materials, videos. Services and workshops for parents are free of charge.

Parent Educational Advocacy Training Center, 10340 Democracy Lane, #206, Fairfax, VA 22030. Tel.: (703) 691-7826; fax: (703) 691-8148. Professionally staffed organization that helps parents to become effective advocates for their children with school personnel and the educational system.

Team of Advocates for Special Kids (TASK), 100 W. Cerritos Avenue, Anaheim, CA 92805. Tel.: (714) 533-TASK; fax: (714) 533-2533. Promotes services to enable children with disabilities to reach their maximum potential. Offers training, education, support, information, resources, and community awareness programs.

PHYSICAL THERAPY

American Physical Therapy Association, 1111 N. Fairfax Street, Alexandria, VA 22314. Tel.: (800) 999-APTA (999-2782); fax: (703) 684-7343. Professional membership association of physical therapists, assistants, and students. Operates clearinghouse for questions on physical therapy and disabilities. Publishes bibliographies on a wide range of topics.

RECREATION AND SPORTS

American Alliance for Health, Physical Education, Recreation and Dance, 1900 Association Drive, Reston, VA 22091. Tel.: (703) 476-3400; fax: (703) 476-9527. Association of professionals in physical education, sports and athletics, health and safety education, recreation and leisure, and dance. Supports and disseminates research, promotes better public understanding of these professions, and supports professional growth of members.

American Athletic Association of the Deaf, 3607 Washington Boulevard, Suite 4, Ogden, UT 84403. Tel.: (801) 393-8710; (801) 393-7916 (tdd); fax: (801) 393-2263. Promotes sports competition on a local, national, and international level for people who are deaf and hearing impaired.

American Camping Association, 5000 State Road, Marville, IN 46252-7902. Tel.: (800) 428-2267. Publishes a guide listing camps by state. Listing includes specialty camps that offer camping experiences to children with disabilities, chronic illness, or specialized health care needs.

Boy Scouts of America, Scouting for the Handicapped Division, 1325 W. Walnut Hill Lane, P.O. Box 152079, Irving, TX 75015-2079. Tel.: (214) 580-2000; fax: (214) 580-2502. Provides educational, recreational, and therapeutic resource programs through the Boy Scouts of America.

Disabled Sports USA, 1145 19th Street, #717, Washington, DC 20036. Tel.: (202) 393-7505; (301) 652-0119 (tdd); fax: (301) 652-0790. Provides year-round sports and recreational opportunities to children (and adults) with orthopedic, spinal cord, neuromuscular, and visual impairments through a national network of local chapters.

Girl Scouts of the USA, 420 5th Avenue, New York, NY 10018. Tel.: (212) 852-8000; fax: (212) 852-6509. Open to all girls ages 5 through 17 (or kindergarten through grade 12). Runs camping programs, sports and recreational activities, and service programs.

Mainstreams children with disabilities into regular Girl Scout troop activities.

National Lekotek Center, 2100 Ridge Avenue, Evanston, IL 60201. Tel.: (800) 366-PLAY. National organization of play libraries modeled after Scandinavian methods of early intervention. At Lekotek centers, trained professionals assess play abilities, interests, and needs and recommend toys and play materials that are available for loan to member families.

Wheelchair Sports, USA, 3595 East Fountain Boulevard, Suite L-10, Colorado Springs, CO 80910. Tel.: (719) 574-1150; fax: (719) 574-9840; e-mail: wheelchis@aol.com. Governing body of various sports of wheelchair athletics. Publishes a newsletter for paid members.

Special Olympics International, 1325 G Street, NW, Suite 500, Washington, DC 20005-3104. Tel.: (202) 628-3630; fax: (202) 824-0200. Largest organization to provide year-round sports training and athletic competition for children and adults with mental retardation. Sanctioned by the U.S. Olympic Committee. Local, state, and national games are held throughout the United States and in over 140 countries.

Special Recreation, Inc., 362 Koser Avenue, Iowa City, IA 52246-3038. Tel.: (319) 337-7578. Serves the recreational needs, rights, and aspirations of people with disabilities, in all age groups, whether in treatment, in institutions, or in communities. Publishes a compendium of 1,500 resources and other guides. Provides information and referral on employment in recreation, education, grants, international resources, research, training, etc.

REHABILITATION ENGINEERING

RESNA, 1101 Connecticut Avenue NW, Suite 700, Washington, DC 20036. Tel.: (202) 857-1199. RESNA is an organization concerned with the maximization of science and technology in the rehabilitation process so that people with disabilities can live independently to the fullest extent possible. Publications and a newsletter are available for a fee, discounted to members.

REHABILITATION PRODUCTS AND EQUIPMENT (Also See Appendix C)

ABLEDATA, National Rehabilitation Information Center (NARIC), 8455 Colesville Road, Suite 935, Silver Spring, MD 20910-3319. Tel.: (301) 588-9284, (800) 346-2742. A public database containing information on commercially available rehabilitation products, including personal care and educational aids.

Accent on Information, Inc., P.O. Box 700, Bloomington, IL 61702. Tel.: (309) 378-2961. A computerized retrieval system containing information on products and devices that assist people with physical disabilities. It also provides "how-to" information in such areas as eating, bathing, grooming, clothing, furniture, home management, toilet care, sexuality, mobility, and written and oral communication.

Independent Living Aids, Inc., 27 E. Mall Street, Plainview, NY 11803. Tel.: (516) 752-8080; fax: (516) 752-3135. Free catalog of aids for sale that make daily tasks easier for those with physical disabilities. For those with visual problems offers clocks, calculators, magnifying lamps, and E-Z-to-see and talking watches.

RETT SYNDROME

International Rett Syndrome Association, Inc., 9121 Piscataway, Clinton, MD 20735. Tel.: (301) 856-3334, (800) 818-RETT; fax: (301) 856-3336. Provides information and referral, support to families, and links with professionals. Facilitates research on Rett syndrome; annual conference for parents and professionals.

SCOLIOSIS

National Scoliosis Foundation, Inc., 72 Mt. Auburn Street, Watertown, MA 02172. Tel.:

(617) 926-0397; fax: (617) 926-0398; e-mail: scoliosis@aol.com. Provides information about scoliosis. Promotes early detection and treatment of scoliosis; publishes the newsletter *Spinal Connection.*

Scoliosis Association, Inc., P.O. Box 51353, Raleigh, NC 27609. Tel.: (800) 800-0669. Educates the public about scoliosis; provides support groups; publishes the newsletter *Backtalk.*

SENSORY INTEGRATION THERAPY

Sensory Integration International, P.O. Box 9013, Torrance, CA 90508. Tel.: (301) 320-9986; fax (310) 320-9934. A not-for-profit organization devoted to developing awareness, knowledge, skills, and services in sensory integration. Provides educational and training programs, information, and support of research activities. Also publishes a directory of occupational and physical therapists who have been certified in the administration and interpretation of the *Sensory Integration and Praxis Tests.*

SERVICE DOGS

Canine Companions for Independence, 1215 Sebastopol Road, Santa Rosa, CA 95407. Tel.: (707) 528-0830. Provides trained service, hearing, and social dogs for children with disabilities. Service dogs perform such tasks as turning on/off light switches, pulling a wheelchair, or retrieving items. Hearing dogs alert people with hearing impairments to critical sounds such as a telephone, smoke alarm, or baby's cry. Social dogs are provided to children with disabilities for any situation in which supervision of a third party is required.

SIBLINGS

The Sibling Information Network, A.J. Pappanikou Center, 249 Glenbrook Road, Box U64, Storrs, CT 06269-2064. Tel.: (203) 344-7500. Assists individuals and profession-

als interested in serving the needs of families of people with disabilities; disseminates bibliographic material and directories. Provides networking and a newsletter written for and by siblings and parents.

Sibling Support Project, Children's Hospital and Medical Center, P.O. Box 5371 CL-09, Seattle, WA 98105-0371. Tel.: (206) 368-4911. This project publishes the *National Association of Sibling Programs (NASP) Newsletter* and supports the development of materials and programs for peer and sibling support. It also maintains a national database with support from the Maternal and Child Health Bureau.

SICKLE-CELL DISEASE

Howard University Center for Sickle Cell Disease, 2121 Georgia Avenue NW, Washington, DC 20059. Tel.: (202) 806-7930; fax: (202) 806-4517. Screening and counseling for sickle-cell disease; provides services to both adults and children, including medical treatment and psychosocial intervention.

National Association for Sickle Cell Disease, Inc., 200 Corporate Point, Suite 495, Culver City, CA 90230-7633. Tel.: (310) 216-6363; (800) 421-8453; fax: (310) 215-3722. Provides education, screening, genetic counseling, technical assistance, tutorial services, vocational rehabilitation, and research support in the United States and Canada.

SPINA BIFIDA

Spina Bifida Association of America, 4590 Macarthur Boulevard NW, Suite 250, Washington, DC 20007. Tel.: (800) 621-3141; fax: (202) 944-3295. Provides information and referral for new parents and literature on spina bifida; supports a public awareness program; advocates for individuals with spina bifida and their families; supports research; conducts conferences for parents and professionals.

SOTO SYNDROME

Soto Syndrome Support Association (SSSA), c/o Lisa Cruse, 1288 Lughborough Court, Wheaton, IL 60187. Tel.: (708) 682-8815. Provides information, referral, networking, and advocacy to families.

TAY–SACHS

The National Tay–Sachs and Allied Diseases Association, 2001 Beacon Street, #204, Brookline, MA 02146. Tel.: (617) 277-4463; fax: (617) 277-0134. Promotes genetic screening programs, maintains international listing of Tay–Sachs prevention centers. Provides educational literature to public and professionals; peer group support for parents.

TOURETTE SYNDROME

Tourette Syndrome Association, 42-40 Bell Boulevard, Bayside, NY 11361. Tel.: (800) 237-0717, (718) 224-2999; fax:(718) 279-9596; e-mail: tourette@ix.netcon.com. Offers information, referral, advocacy, education, research, and self-help groups to those affected by this syndrome.

TRAUMA

American Trauma Society, 8903 Presidential Parkway, Suite 512, Upper Marlboro, MD 20772. Tel.: (800) 556-7890; fax: (301) 420-0617. Organization dedicated to the prevention of trauma and the improvement of trauma care. Provides prevention programs and materials related to prevention of injury.
Brain Injury Association, 1776 Massachusetts Avenue NW, Suite 100, Washington, DC 20036. Tel.: (800) 444-6443, (202) 296-6443; fax: (202) 296-8850. Provides information to educate the public, politicians, businesses, and schools about head injury: its effects, causes, and prevention.

TREACHER–COLLINS SYNDROME

Treacher–Collins Foundation, c/o Hope Charkins-Drazin and David Drazin, P.O. Box 683, Norwich, VT 05055. Tel.: (802) 649-3050, (800) TCF-2055. Organization of families, professionals and others interested in pursuing knowledge and experience about Treacher–Collins syndrome and related disorders. Provides networking, educational material, newsletter, video, and referral information.

TRISOMY 18, 13, AND RELATED DISORDERS

Support Organization for Trisomy 18, 13, and Related Disorders, c/o Barb Van Herreweghe, 2982 S. Union Street, Rochester, NY 14624. Tel.: (716) 594-4621. Provides support and family packages with a newsletter and appropriate literature underscoring the common problems for children with Trisomy 13 and Trisomy 18. There are chapters in most states. A yearly conference for families and professionals is held.

TUBEROUS SCLEROSIS

National Tuberous Sclerosis Association, 8000 Corporate Drive, Suite 120, Landover, MD 20785. Tel.: (800) 225-NTSA, (301) 459-9888; fax: (301) 459-0394; e-mail: ntsa@aol.com. Provides information to newly diagnosed individuals, their families, and professionals. Referrals are made to support groups located in most states. Funds research through membership fees and donations.

VISION

American Foundation for the Blind, Inc., 11 Penn Plaza, #300, New York, NY 10001. Tel.: (212) 502-7600; fax: (212) 502-7777. Cooperates with other organizations and schools to offer services to people who are blind and visually impaired. Provides consultation, public education, referrals, information, talking books, and adaptation of equipment for people who are visually impaired.

American Printing House for the Blind (APH), P.O. Box 6085, Louisville, KY 40206-0085. Tel.: (502) 895-2405; fax: (502) 895-1509. Publishing house for people who are visually impaired; books in braille, large type, and recordings are available. A wide range of aids, tools, and supplies for education and daily living is also available.

Association for Education and Rehabilitation of the Blind and Visually Impaired, 206 N. Washington Street, #320, Alexandria, VA 22314. Tel.: (703) 548-1884; fax: (703) 683-2926; e-mail: aernet@laser.net. In-service training primarily through conferences and publications for educators and those involved in rehabilitation of people who are blind or have low vision.

National Association for Visually Handicapped, 22 West 21st Street, 6th Floor, New York, NY 10010. Tel.: (212) 889-3141; fax: (212) 727-2931. Provides informational literature, guidance and counsel, referral services for parents of children who are partially sighted and those who work with them. Publishes free large-print newsletter.

National Braille Association, Inc., 3 Townline Circle, Rochester, NY 14623. Tel.: (716) 427-8260; fax: (716) 427-0263. Produces and distributes braille reading materials for people who are visually impaired. Collection consists of college-level textbooks, technical materials, and some materials of general interest.

National Federation of the Blind, 1800 Johnson Street, Baltimore, MD 21230. Tel.: (410) 659-9314; fax: (410) 685-5653. Goal is the complete integration of people who are blind into society on a basis of equality. Offers advocacy in housing, insurance, etc. Operates a job referral and an aids and appliances department. Offers college scholarships, monthly and quarterly publications.

National Library Service for the Blind and Physically Handicapped, Library of Congress, 1291 Taylor Street NW, Washington, DC 20542. Tel.: (202) 707-5100; fax: (202) 707-0712. Administers a free library program of braille and recorded books for eligible readers who are visually impaired and physically handicapped throughout the United States and for American citizens living abroad.

Prevent Blindness America, 500 East Remington Road, Schaumburg, IL 60173. Tel.: (800) 331-2020; fax: (708) 843-8458. Committed to the reduction of cases of needless blindness. Provides information to the public, people who are blind, and professionals working with them.

Recording for the Blind, 20 Roszel Road, Princeton, NJ 08540. Tel.: (609) 452-0606, (800) 221-4792; fax: (609) 987-8116. Provides tapes and discs, including the classics, for people who are visually impaired, physically disabled, and learning disabled, from fourth grade through graduate school.

WILLIAMS SYNDROME

Williams Syndrome Association, P.O. Box 297, Clawson, MI 48017-0297. Tel.: (810) 541-3630; fax: (810) 541-3631. General information, newsletter, and networking for parents.

Appendix C

Product Resources

Lisa A. Kurtz

This appendix is designed to assist families and professionals in locating products referenced within this volume. In Table C–1, the companies are listed alphabetically, with the righthand column indicating categories for which they provide products. We made every effort to contact all companies shortly before going to press to verify the information. We regret any errors or omissions and do not imply any endorsement of listed services.

Table C–1 Companies Listed Alphabetically, with Product Categories

	Activities of Daily Living	Assistive Technology	Books/Periodicals/Audiovisuals	Hearing and Vision Impaired	Medical/Nursing Supplies	Rehab/Exercise Equipment	Seating/Positioning/Mobility	Splinting/Orthotics	Sports/Recreation	Teaching/Therapy Media	Tests/Assessment Materials	Toys/Games
3M Health Care 3M Center, Building 275-4E-01 St. Paul, MN 55144-1000 (800) 228-3957, (612) 736-0111 fax: (800) 772-2547								x				
AbleNet, Inc. 1081 Tenth Avenue SE Minneapolis, MN 55414-1312 (800) 322-0956 fax: (612) 379-9143		x										
Academic Therapy Publications High Noon Books, Ann Arbor Publications 20 Commercial Boulevard Novato, CA 94949-6191 (800) 422-7249, (415) 883-3314 fax: (415) 883-3720			x							x	x	
Access Industries 4001 E. 138th Street Grandview, MO 64030 (800) 925-3100, (816) 763-3100 fax: (816) 763-4467	x											
Access to Recreation, Inc. (Don Krebs) 2509 E. Thousand Oaks Boulevard, Suite 430 Thousand Oaks, CA 91362 (800) 634-4351 fax: (805) 498-8186		x										
Accessible Environments 111 Cedar Street New Rochelle, NY 10801 (800) 285-2525 fax: (914) 632-1357	x											
Achievement Products for Children P.O. Box 9033 Canton, OH 44711 (800) 373-4699 fax: (216) 453-0222	x	x				x	x			x		x
AdaptAbility P.O. Box 515 Colchester, CT 06415-0515 (800) 243-9232 fax: (800) 566-6678	x	x			x	x						

continues

Table C–1 continued

	Activities of Daily Living	Assistive Technology	Books/Peridicals/Audiovisuals	Hearing and Vision Impaired	Medical/Nursing Supplies	Rehab/Exercise Equipment	Seating/Positioning/Mobility	Splinting/Orthotics	Sports/Recreation	Teaching/Therapy Media	Tests/Assessment Materials	Toys/Games
Adaptive Design Shop 12847 Pt. Pleasant Drive Fairfax, VA 22033 (800) 351-2327, (703) 631-1585 fax: (703) 631-1585	x											
Adaptive Engineering Lab, Inc. 4493 Russell Road, Suite 113 Mukilteo, WA 98275 (800) 327-6080 fax: (206) 348-6299							x					
Adrian's Closet P.O. Box 9930 Rancho Santa Fe, CA 92067 (800) 831-2577 fax: (619) 759-0578	x											
Alimed, Inc. 297 High Street Dedham, MA 02026 (800) 225-2610 fax: (617) 329-8392	x	x				x	x	x				
Allyn & Bacon 160 Gould Street Needham Heights, MA 02194 (800) 278-3525, (617) 455-1250 fax: (617) 455-1294			x								x	
American Guidance Service 4201 Woodland Road, P.O. Box 99 Circle Pines, MN 55014-1796 (800) 328-2560, (612) 786-4343 fax: (612) 786-9077			x							x	x	
American Printing House for the Blind 1839 Frankfort Avenue, P.O. Box 6085 Louisville, KY 40206-0085 (800) 223-1839, (502) 895-2405 fax: (502) 895-1509			x	x								
American Psychological Association 750 First Street, NE Washington, DC 20002-4242 (202) 336-5500			x								x	

continues

Table C–1 continued

	Activities of Daily Living	Assistive Technology	Books/Peridicals/Audiovisuals	Hearing and Vision Impaired	Medical/Nursing Supplies	Rehab/Exercise Equipment	Seating/Positioning/Mobility	Splinting/Orthotics	Sports/Recreation	Teaching/Therapy Media	Tests/Assessment Materials	Toys/Games
American Wheelchair Products 2862 N. Larken Avenue Clovis, CA 93612 (209) 291-1863 fax: (209) 291-1867							x					
Amigo Mobility International 6693 Dixie Highway Bridgeport, MI 48722-0402 (800) 248-9130 fax: (517) 777-8184							x					
Andover Medical Publishers 125 Main Street Reading, MA 01867 (617) 944-8242			x									
Ann Morris Enterprises, Inc. 890 Fams Court East Meadow, NY 11554 (516) 292-9232 fax: (516) 564-9692		x										
Apple Computer, Inc. 1 Infinite Loop, Consumer Relations Dept. Mail Stop 72-P Cupertino, CA 95014 (800) 776-2333		x										
Apt Technology, Inc. 8765 Township Road 513 Shreve, OH 44676-9421 (216) 567-2001 fax: (216) 567-9217		x										
Aquatic Access, Inc. 417 Dorsey Way Louisville, KY 40223 (800) 325-5438 fax: (502) 425-9607	x								x			
Arjo, Inc. 8130 Lehigh Avenue Morton Grove, IL 60053 (800) 323-1245 fax: (708) 967-9546	x				x							

continues

Table C–1 continued

	Activities of Daily Living	Assistive Technology	Books/Peridicals/Audiovisuals	Hearing and Vision Impaired	Medical/Nursing Supplies	Rehab/Exercise Equipment	Seating/Positioning/Mobility	Splinting/Orthotics	Sports/Recreation	Teaching/Therapy Media	Tests/Assessment Materials	Toys/Games
Aspen Publishers 200 Orchard Ridge Drive Gaithersburg, MD 20878 (301) 417-7500 fax: (301) 417-7550			x								x	
Atlantic Rehabilitation, Inc. 81 Rumford Avenue Waltham, MA 02254 (617) 894-0069							x					
Attainment Company, Inc. P.O. Box 930160 Verona, WI 53593-0160 (608) 845-7880 fax: (608) 845-8040		x								x		
Augmentative Communication Consultants, Inc. 280-B Moon Clinton Road Moon Township, PA 15108 (412) 264-6121 fax: (412) 269-0923		x										
Bailey Manufacturing Co. P.O. Box 130 Lodi, OH 44254 (216) 948-1080 fax: (216) 948-4439						x	x					
Barrier Free Lifts P.O. Box 4163 Manassas, VA 22110 (800) 582-8732, (703) 361-6531 fax: (703) 361-7861	x											
Bernell Corporation 750 Lincoln Way East, P.O. Box 4637 South Bend, IN 46601 (800) 348-2225, (219) 234-3200 fax: (219) 233-8422				x								
Best Priced Products, Inc. P.O. Box 1174 White Plains, NY 10602 (800) 824-2939, (914) 472-1006 fax: (800) 356-8587, (914) 472-2715	x				x	x	x	x		x	x	

continues

Table C–1 continued

	Activities of Daily Living	Assistive Technology	Books/Peridicals/Audiovisuals	Hearing and Vision Impaired	Medical/Nursing Supplies	Rehab/Exercise Equipment	Seating/Positioning/Mobility	Splinting/Orthotics	Sports/Recreation	Teaching/Therapy Media	Tests/Assessment Materials	Toys/Games
Blind Children's Center 4120 Marathon Street Los Angeles, CA 90029 (800) 222-3566, (213) 664-2153 fax: (213) 665-3828				x								
Brunner/Mazel Publishers 19 Union Square West New York, NY 10003 (800) 825-3089, (212) 924-3344 fax: (212) 242-6339			x									
Bruno Independent Living Aids, Inc. 1780 Executive Drive P.O. Box 84 Oconomowoc, WI 53066 (800) 882-8183, (414) 567-4990 fax: (414) 567-4341							x					
Carapace 12626 East 60th Street, #110 Tulsa, OK 74146 (800) 223-5463 fax: (918) 254-0965								x				
Carnation Nutritional Products Division Nestle Food Company 800 N. Brand Boulevard Glendale, CA 91203 (818) 545-9141 fax: (818) 549-6952					x							
Carolyn's Products for Enhanced Living P.O. Box 743 Brookfield, WI 53008-0743 (800) 648-2255	x											
Charles C Thomas, Publisher 2600 South First Street Springfield, IL 62794-9265 (800) 258-8980 fax: (217) 789-9130			x									
Childcraft, Inc. P.O. Box 29149 Mission, KS 66201-9149 (800) 367-3255 fax: (913) 752-1095												x

continues

Table C–1 continued

	Activities of Daily Living	Assistive Technology	Books/Peridicals/Audiovisuals	Hearing and Vision Impaired	Medical/Nursing Supplies	Rehab/Exercise Equipment	Seating/Positioning/Mobility	Splinting/Orthotics	Sports/Recreation	Teaching/Therapy Media	Tests/Assessment Materials	Toys/Games
Cleo, Inc. 3957 Mayfield Road Cleveland, OH 44121 (800) 321-0595, (216) 382-9700 fax: (216) 382-1934	x					x	x					
Clintec Nutrition Company Three Parkway North, Suite 500 Deerfield, IL 60015-0760 (800) 388-0300, (708) 317-2800 fax: (708) 317-3186					x							
Columbia Medical Manufacturing Corp. Dept. E5, P.O. Box 633 Pacific Palisades, CA 90272 (800) 454-6612, (310) 454-6612 fax: (310) 305-1718	x						x					
Communication Skill Builders 555 Academic Court San Antonio, TX 78204 (800) 866-4446 fax: (800) 232-1223		x	x							x	x	
Concepts ADL, Inc. P.O. Box 339 Benton, IL 62812-0339 (800) 626-3153 fax: (618) 435-3110	x					x	x	x		x		
Concepts To Go, Early Childhood Activities P.O. Box 10043 Berkeley, CA 94709 (510) 848-3233 fax: (510) 486-1248										x		x
Consumer Care Products, Inc. 810 North Water Street, P.O. Box 684 Sheboygan, WI 53082-0684 (414) 459-8353 fax: (414) 459-9070							x					
Convaid Products, Inc. P.O. Box 2458 Ranchos Palos Verdes, CA 90274 (310) 539-6814 fax: (310) 539-3670	x						x					

continues

Table C–1 continued

	Activities of Daily Living	Assistive Technology	Books/Peridicals/Audiovisuals	Hearing and Vision Impaired	Medical/Nursing Supplies	Rehab/Exercise Equipment	Seating/Positioning/Mobility	Splinting/Orthotics	Sports/Recreation	Teaching/Therapy Media	Tests/Assessment Materials	Toys/Games
Council for Exceptional Children 1920 Association Drive Reston, VA 22091 (800) 328-0272, (703) 620-3660 fax: (703) 264-9494			x								x	
Craftime, Inc. P.O. Box 93706 Atlanta, GA 30377 (800) 849-8463 fax: (404) 874-5148										x		
Creative Rehabilitation Equipment 609 N.E. Schuyler Street Portland, OR 97212 (800) 547-4611 fax: (503) 288-8817							x					
Crestwood Company 6625 N. Sidney Place Milwaukee, WI 53209-3259 (414) 352-5678 fax: (414) 352-5679	x	x								x		x
Damaco 5105 Maureen Lane Moorepark, CA 93021 (800) 432-2434 fax: (805) 532-1836							x					
Danmar Products, Inc. 221 Jackson Industrial Drive Ann Arbor, MI 48103 (800) 783-1998, (313) 761-1990 fax: (313) 761-8977	x					x	x	x				
Denver Developmental Materials P.O. Box 6919 Denver, CO 80206-0919 (800) 419-4729, (303) 295-6379 fax: (303) 355-5622											x	
Developmental Test Materials 389 Myrtle Avenue Albany, NY 12208 (800) 724-5028 fax: (518) 262-6316											x	

continues

Table C–1 continued

	Activities of Daily Living	Assistive Technology	Books/Peridicals/Audiovisuals	Hearing and Vision Impaired	Medical/Nursing Supplies	Rehab/Exercise Equipment	Seating/Positioning/Mobility	Splinting/Orthotics	Sports/Recreation	Teaching/Therapy Media	Tests/Assessment Materials	Toys/Games
Don Johnston, Inc. 1000 North Rand Road, Building 115 Wauconda, IL 60084 (800) 999-4660, (708) 526-2682 fax: (708) 526-4177		x										x
Dow Chemical Corporation P.O. Box 1206 Midland, MI 48641 (800) 441-4369 fax: (517) 832-1465							x					
Dynamic Systems, Inc. 46 Sunlight Drive Leicester, NC 28748 (704) 683-3523 fax: (704) 683-3511							x					
E-Z-On Products of Florida 500 Commerce Way West, Suite 3 Jupiter, FL 33458 (800) 323-6598, (407) 747-6920 fax: (407) 747-8779							x					
Electric Mobility 1 Mobility Plaza Sewell, NJ 08088 (800) 662-4548 fax: (609) 468-3426							x					
Enduro/Wheel Ring, Inc. 199 Forest Street Manchester, CT 06040 (203) 647-8596 fax: (203) 647-7517							x					
Equipment Shop P.O. Box 33 Bedford, MA 01730-0033 (617) 275-7681 fax: (617) 275-4094						x	x					
Evenflo Juvenile Furniture Co. 1801 Commerce Drive Piqua, OH 45356 (800) 233-5921 (parts), (513) 773-3971 fax: (513) 778-5410							x					

continues

Table C–1 continued

	Activities of Daily Living	Assistive Technology	Books/Peridicals/Audiovisuals	Hearing and Vision Impaired	Medical/Nursing Supplies	Rehab/Exercise Equipment	Seating/Positioning/Mobility	Splinting/Orthotics	Sports/Recreation	Teaching/Therapy Media	Tests/Assessment Materials	Toys/Games
Everest & Jennings 1100 Corporate Square St. Louis, MO 63132 (800) 235-4661 fax: (800) 542-3567							x					
F.A. Davis Co. 1915 Arch Street Philadelphia, PA 19103 (800) 523-4049, (215) 568-2270 fax: (215) 568-5065			x									
Filmmakers Library 124 East 40th Street New York, NY 10016 (212) 808-4980 fax: (212) 808-4983			x							x		
Flaghouse, Inc. 150 North MacQuesten Parkway Mount Vernon, NY 10550 (800) 793-7900 fax: (800) 793-7922				x		x	x		x	x	x	x
Foundation for Knowledge in Development (MAP) 1901 W. Littleton Boulevard Littleton, CO 80120-2058 (303) 794-1182 fax: (303) 798-2526											x	
Franklin Electronic Publishers 122 Burrs Road Mt. Holly, NJ 08060 (800) 762-5382, (609) 261-4800 fax: (609) 261-1631		x										
Fred Sammons, Inc. P.O. Box 386 Western Springs, IL 60558-9900 (800) 631-7277 fax: (800) 323-5547	x	x	x			x	x	x		x	x	
Freedom Designs, Inc. 2241 Madera Road Simi Valley, CA 93065 (800) 331-8557 fax: (805) 582-1509							x					

continues

Table C–1 continued

	Activities of Daily Living	Assistive Technology	Books/Peridicals/Audiovisuals	Hearing and Vision Impaired	Medical/Nursing Supplies	Rehab/Exercise Equipment	Seating/Positioning/Mobility	Splinting/Orthotics	Sports/Recreation	Teaching/Therapy Media	Tests/Assessment Materials	Toys/Games
Gallaudet University Book Store 800 Florida Avenue NE Washington, DC 20002 (800) 451-1073, (202) 651-5380 fax: (202) 651-5489			x	x							x	
Guardian Products 4175 Guardian Street Simi Valley, CA 93063 (800) 255-5022 fax: (800) 548-6396	x					x						
Guilford Publications, Inc. 72 Spring Street New York, NY 10012 (800) 365-7006, (212) 431-9800 fax: (212) 966-6708			x									
Gunnell, Inc. 8440 State Street Millington, MI 48746 (800) 551-0055 fax: (517) 871-4563							x					
Harper Collins Publishers Inc. (formerly Harper & Row) 10 East 53rd Street New York, NY 10022 (800) 242-7737, (212) 207-7000 fax: (800) 242-7737			x								x	
Hartley Courseware, Inc. 3451 Dunckel Road, Suite 200 Lansing, MI 48911 (800) 247-1380 fax: (517) 394-9899		x										
Haworth Press 10 Alice Street Binghamton, NY 13904 (607) 722-5857 fax: (607) 722-1424			x									
Imaginart Communication Products 307 Arizona Street Bisbee, AZ 85603 (800) 828-1376 fax: (520) 432-5134										x		

continues

Table C–1 continued

	Activities of Daily Living	Assistive Technology	Books/Peridicals/Audiovisuals	Hearing and Vision Impaired	Medical/Nursing Supplies	Rehab/Exercise Equipment	Seating/Positioning/Mobility	Splinting/Orthotics	Sports/Recreation	Teaching/Therapy Media	Tests/Assessment Materials	Toys/Games
IntelliTools 55 Leveroni Court, Suite 9 Novato, CA 94949 (800) 899-6687, (415) 382-5950 fax: (415) 382-5950		x										
Invacare 899 Cleveland Street Elyria, OH 44035 (800) 333-6900, (216) 329-6696 fax: (216) 366-0709							x					
J.A. Preston Corporation P.O. Box 89 Jackson, MI 49204-0089 (800) 631-7277 fax: (800) 245-3765	x					x	x			x		
James Stanfield Co., Inc. P.O. Box 41058 Santa Barbara, CA 93140 (800) 421-6534 fax: (805) 897-1187			x							x		
Jay Medical, Ltd. P.O. Box 18656 Boulder, CO 80308 (303) 442-5529 fax: (303) 442-3855							x					
Jesana, Ltd. P.O. Box 17 Irvington, NY 10533 (800) 443-4728 fax: (914) 376-0021		x					x		x			x
Johnson & Johnson P.O. Box 4000 New Brunswick, NJ 08903 (800) 225-2500, (908) 524-0400 fax: (908) 562-2212								x				
Kapable Kids P.O. Box 250 Bohemia, NY 11716 (800) 356-1564 fax: (516) 563-7179		x										x

continues

Table C–1 continued

	Activities of Daily Living	Assistive Technology	Books/Peridicals/Audiovisuals	Hearing and Vision Impaired	Medical/Nursing Supplies	Rehab/Exercise Equipment	Seating/Positioning/Mobility	Splinting/Orthotics	Sports/Recreation	Teaching/Therapy Media	Tests/Assessment Materials	Toys/Games
Kaye Products, Inc. 535 Dimmocks Mill Road Hillsborough, NC 27278 (919) 732-6444 fax: (800) 685-5293	x						x					x
Kushall of America 708 Via Alondra Camarillo, CA 93012 (800) 654-4768 fax: (805) 987-9844							x					
L.C. Technologies, Inc. 9455 Silver King Court Fairfax, VA 22031 (800) 733-5284, (703) 385-7133 fax: (703) 385-7137		x										
LaBac Systems, Inc. 8955 South Ridgeline Boulevard Highlands Ranch, CO 80126 (800) 445-4402 fax: (303) 791-2847							x					
Laureate Learning Systems, Inc. 110 East Spring Street Winooski, VT 05404-1837 (800) 562-6801, (802) 655-4755 fax: (802) 655-4757		x										
Lighthouse Low Vision Products 36-02 Northern Boulevard Long Island City, NY 11101 (800) 453-4923, (800) 829-0500, (718) 937-6959 fax: (718) 786-0437				x								
Little, Brown & Co. Book Division 200 West Street Waltham, MA 02254 (800) 759-0190, (617) 890-2125 fax: (617) 890-0875			x									
Little, Brown & Co. Medical Subscriptions P.O. Box 7671 Riverton, NJ 08077-7671 (800) 628-9089, (609) 786-9089 fax: (617) 859-0629			x									

continues

Table C–1 continued

	Activities of Daily Living	Assistive Technology	Books/Peridicals/Audiovisuals	Hearing and Vision Impaired	Medical/Nursing Supplies	Rehab/Exercise Equipment	Seating/Positioning/Mobility	Splinting/Orthotics	Sports/Recreation	Teaching/Therapy Media	Tests/Assessment Materials	Toys/Games
LMB Hand Rehab Products, Inc. P.O. Box 1181 San Luis Obispo, CA 93406 (800) 541-3992, (805) 541-3992 fax: (805) 541-1839								x				
McGraw-Hill Publishers 1221 Avenue of the Americas New York, NY 10020 (800) 722-4726, (212) 512-2000			x									
Mead Johnson Nutrition Co. 1211 West 22nd Street, Suite 900 Oak Brook, IL 60521 (708) 572-0919 fax: (708) 572-0953					x							
Mobility Plus 215 North 12th Street P.O. Box 391 Santa Paula, CA 93060 (805) 525-7165 fax: (805) 933-1082							x					
Modern Learning Press and Programs for Education P.O. Box 167, Dept. 335 Rosemont, NJ 08556 (800) 627-5867, (609) 397-2214 fax: (609) 397-3467			x							x	x	
Modern Signs Press, Inc. P.O. Box 1181 Los Alamitos, CA 90720 (310) 596-8548, (310) 493-4168 (voice or tdd) fax: (310) 795-6614				x								
Modular Medical Corporation 1513 Olmstead Avenue Bronx, NY 10462 (718) 829-2626 fax: (718) 430-0914							x					
Mosby Co. 11830 Westline Industrial Drive St. Louis, MO 63146 (800) 325-4177, ext. 4554, (314) 872-8370 fax: (800) 535-9935			x									

continues

Table C–1 continued

	Activities of Daily Living	Assistive Technology	Books/Peridicals/Audiovisuals	Hearing and Vision Impaired	Medical/Nursing Supplies	Rehab/Exercise Equipment	Seating/Positioning/Mobility	Splinting/Orthotics	Sports/Recreation	Teaching/Therapy Media	Tests/Assessment Materials	Toys/Games
Mulholland Positioning P.O. Box 391 Santa Paula, CA 93060 (800) 543-4769, (805) 525-7165 fax: (805) 933-1082							x					
Multi-Health Systems, Inc. 908 Niagara Falls Boulevard North Tonawanda, NY 14120-2060 (800) 456-3003, (416) 424-1700 fax: (416) 424-1736											x	
National Association for Parents of the Visually Impaired P.O. Box 317 Watertown, MA 02272-0317 (800) 562-6265, (617) 972-7441 fax: (617) 972-7444				x								
National Association for the Visually Handicapped 22 West 21st Street, 6th Floor New York, NY 10010 (917) 899-3141				x								
National Center for Vision and Child Development, The Lighthouse, Inc. 111 E. 59th Street New York, NY 10022 (212) 821-9200 fax: (212) 821-9707				x								
National Federation of the Blind 1800 Johnson Street Baltimore, MD 21230 (410) 659-9314 fax: (410) 685-5653				x								
National Library Service for Blind and Physically Handicapped Library of Congress 1291 Taylor Street NW Washington, DC 20542 (800) 424-8567, (202) 707-5100 fax: (202) 707-0712			x	x								
NFER Publishing Company, Ltd. Darville House 2 Oxford Road East Windsor, Berkshire SL4, 1DF, England 011-44-753-858-961 fax: 011-44-753-856-830				x							x	

continues

Table C–1 continued

	Activities of Daily Living	Assistive Technology	Books/Peridicals/Audiovisuals	Hearing and Vision Impaired	Medical/Nursing Supplies	Rehab/Exercise Equipment	Seating/Positioning/Mobility	Splinting/Orthotics	Sports/Recreation	Teaching/Therapy Media	Tests/Assessment Materials	Toys/Games
NOIR Medical Technologies 6155 Pontiac Trail, P.O. Box 159 South Lyon, MI 48178 (800) 521-9746, (313) 769-5565 fax: (313) 769-1708				x								
North Coast Medical, Inc. 187 Stauffer Boulevard San Jose, CA 95125-1042 (800) 821-9319 fax: (408) 283-1950	x					x	x					
Orthokinetics W220 N507 Springdale Road, P.O. Box 1647 Waukesha, WI 53187 (800) 824-1068, (414) 542-6060 fax: (414) 542-4258							x					
OT Ideas, Inc. 124 Morris Turnpike Randolph, NJ 07869 (201) 895-3622 fax: (201) 895-4204										x		x
Otto Bock Orthopedic Industry, Inc. 3000 Xenium Lane North Plymouth, MN 55441 (800) 228-4058, (612) 533-9464 fax: (612) 553-9472							x					
Paul H. Brookes Publishing Co. P.O. Box 10624 Baltimore, MD 21285-0624 (800) 638-3775, (410) 337-9580 fax: (410) 337-8539			x									
PDP Products 12015 North July Avenue Hugo, MN 55038 (612) 439-8865 fax: (612) 439-0421			x									
Permobil, Inc. 6B Gill Street Woburn, MS 01801 (617) 932-9009 fax: (617) 542-4258							x					

continues

Table C–1 continued

	Activities of Daily Living	Assistive Technology	Books/Peridicals/Audiovisuals	Hearing and Vision Impaired	Medical/Nursing Supplies	Rehab/Exercise Equipment	Seating/Positioning/Mobility	Splinting/Orthotics	Sports/Recreation	Teaching/Therapy Media	Tests/Assessment Materials	Toys/Games
Pin Dot Products 2840 Maria Avenue Northbrook, IL 60062 (800) 451-3553 fax: (708) 508-2818							x					
Pocket Full of Therapy, Inc. P.O. Box 174 Morganville, NJ 07751 (800) 736-8124 fax: (908) 290-0711										x		x
Prentke Romich Co. 1022 Heyl Road Wooster, OH 44691 (800) 262-1984 fax: (216) 263-4829		x										
Pro-Ed 5341 Industrial Oakes Boulevard Austin, TX 78735 (512) 892-3142 fax: (512) 451-8542			x							x	x	
Psychological and Educational Publications, Inc. 1477 Rollins Road Burlingame, CA 94010 (800) 523-5775, (415) 340-9669 fax: (800) 447-0907										x	x	
Psychological Assessment Resources, Inc. P.O. Box 998 Odessa, FL 33556 (800) 331-TEST, (813) 968-3003 fax: (800) 727-9329		x								x	x	
Psychological Corporation, Harcourt, Brace & Co. 555 Academic Court San Antonio, TX 78204-2498 (800) 228-0752 fax: (800) 232-1223		x									x	
Q'Straint 3085 Southwestern Boulevard Orchard Park, NY 14127 (716) 675-2222 fax: (716) 675-2270							x					

continues

Table C–1 continued

	Activities of Daily Living	Assistive Technology	Books/Peridicals/Audiovisuals	Hearing and Vision Impaired	Medical/Nursing Supplies	Rehab/Exercise Equipment	Seating/Positioning/Mobility	Splinting/Orthotics	Sports/Recreation	Teaching/Therapy Media	Tests/Assessment Materials	Toys/Games
Quickie Designs 2842 Business Park Avenue Fresno, CA 93727-1328 (800) 456-8168 fax: (800) 456-8167							x					
Rehabco 1513 Olmstead Avenue Bronx, NY 14202 (718) 829-3800 fax: (718) 430-0914							x					
Rehabilitation Designs, Inc. 901 Watso Avenue, Suite 102 Madison, WI 53713 (800) 783-1734, (608) 274-6702 fax: (608) 274-6706							x					
Research Press Dept G, P.O. Box 9177 Champaign, IL 61826 (217) 352-3273 fax: (217) 352-1221			x							x	x	
Rifton Equipment Box 901 Rifton, NY 12471-0901 (800) 374-3866, (800) 777-4244 fax: (800) 336-5948							x					
Right Start Catalogue, Right Start Plaza 5334 Sterling Center Drive Westlake Village, CA 91361 (800) 548-8531 fax: (800) 762-5501												x
Riverside Publishers 8420 Bryn Mawr Avenue Chicago, IL 60631 (800) 767-8378			x								x	
ROHO, Inc. 100 Florida Avenue Belleville, IL 62221-9990 (800) 851-3449 fax: (618) 277-6518							x					

continues

Table C–1 continued

	Activities of Daily Living	Assistive Technology	Books/Peridicals/Audiovisuals	Hearing and Vision Impaired	Medical/Nursing Supplies	Rehab/Exercise Equipment	Seating/Positioning/Mobility	Splinting/Orthotics	Sports/Recreation	Teaching/Therapy Media	Tests/Assessment Materials	Toys/Games
Ross Product Division, Abbott Laboratories 625 Cleveland Avenue Columbus, OH 43215-1724 (614) 624-7677					x							
S & S Arts & Crafts P.O. Box 513 Colchester, CT 06415-0513 (800) 243-9232 fax: (800) 566-6678										x		x
Sandoz Nutrition 5100 Gamble Drive St. Louis Park, MN 55416 (800) 999-9978, (612) 925-2100 fax: (612) 593-2087					x							
Science Products Box 888 Southeastern, PA 19399 (800) 888-7400, (610) 296-2111 fax: (610) 296-0488				x								
Scott Designs 14375 Saratoga Drive, Suite J Saratoga, CA 95070 (408) 867-7447 fax: (408) 867-7851							x					
Sentinel Systems Technology, Inc. 2100 Wharton Street Pittsburgh, PA 15203 (800) 344-1778, (412) 381-4883 fax: (412) 381-5241		x										
Sherwood Medical 1915 Olive Street St. Louis, MO 63103-1642 (314) 621-7788 fax: (800) 325-7472					x							
Singular Publishing Group, Inc. 4284 41st Street San Diego, CA 92105 (619) 521-8000, (800) 521-8545 fax: (800) 774-8398			x									

continues

Table C–1 continued

	Activities of Daily Living	Assistive Technology	Books/Peridicals/Audiovisuals	Hearing and Vision Impaired	Medical/Nursing Supplies	Rehab/Exercise Equipment	Seating/Positioning/Mobility	Splinting/Orthotics	Sports/Recreation	Teaching/Therapy Media	Tests/Assessment Materials	Toys/Games
Slack Incorporated 6900 Grove Road Thorofare, NJ 08086-9447 (800) 257-8290 fax: (609) 853-5991			x									
Slosson Educational Publications, Inc. P.O. Box 280 East Aurora, NY 14052 (800) 828-4800, (716) 652-0933 fax: (800) 655-3840											x	
Smith & Nephew Rolyan N104 West 13400 Dongesbay Road Germantown, WI 53022 (800) 228-3693 fax: (800) 545-7758					x			x				
Snug Seat, Inc. 10810 Independence Point Parkway P.O. Box 1739 Matthews, NC 28105 (800) 336-7684, (704) 847-0772 fax: (704) 847-9577							x					
Southpaw Enterprises, Inc. 109 Webb Street, P.O. Box 1047 Dayton, OH 45401-1047 (800) 228-1698, (513) 252-7676 fax: (513) 252-8502						x					x	x
Special Clothes for Special Children P.O. Box 333 Harwich, MA 02645	x											
Special Designs, Inc. P.O. Box 130 Gillette, NJ 07933 (908) 464-8825 fax: (908) 464-8251							x					
Special Health Systems, Ltd. 90 Englehard Drive Aurora ON L4G 2V2, Canada (800) 263-2223, (905) 841-1032 fax: (905) 841-6162							x					

continues

Table C–1 continued

	Activities of Daily Living	Assistive Technology	Books/Peridicals/Audiovisuals	Hearing and Vision Impaired	Medical/Nursing Supplies	Rehab/Exercise Equipment	Seating/Positioning/Mobility	Splinting/Orthotics	Sports/Recreation	Teaching/Therapy Media	Tests/Assessment Materials	Toys/Games
Sportime Abilitations One Sportime Way Atlanta, GA 30340 (800) 283-5700 fax: (800) 845-1535						x	x		x	x		
SRA/DLM Macmillan-McGraw-Hill P.O. Box 543 Blacklick, OH 43004-0543 (800) 843-8855 fax: (614) 860-1877			x									
Stoelting Company 620 Wheat Lane Wood Dale, IL 60191 (708) 860-9700 fax: (708) 860-9775			x								x	
Stroller-Pack P.O. Box 707 Juneau, AK 99802 (800) 487-9652 fax: (907) 463-4889							x					
Stryker Corporate Instruments 4100 East Milham Avenue Kalamazoo, MI 49001 (800) 253-3210 fax: (800) 999-3811								x				
Sunburst Communications 101 Castleton Street, P.O. Box 100 Pleasantville, NY 10570-0100 (800) 321-7511 fax: (914) 747-5349		x										
Susquehanna Rehab Products RD 2, Box 41, 9 Overlook Drive Wrightsville, PA 17368 (800) 248-2011 fax: (717) 252-1768	x					x	x					
TASH, Inc. Unit 1, 91 Station Street Ajax, Ontario, Canada L1S 3H2 (905) 686-4129, (800) 463-5685 fax: (905) 686-6895		x										

continues

Table C–1 continued

	Activities of Daily Living	Assistive Technology	Books/Peridicals/Audiovisuals	Hearing and Vision Impaired	Medical/Nursing Supplies	Rehab/Exercise Equipment	Seating/Positioning/Mobility	Splinting/Orthotics	Sports/Recreation	Teaching/Therapy Media	Tests/Assessment Materials	Toys/Games
TFH (USA), Ltd. 4537 Gibsonia Road Gibsonia , PA 15044 (800) 467-6222, (412) 444-6400 fax: (412) 444-6411				x						x		x
Theradapt Products, Inc. 17W163 Oak Lane Bensenville, IL 60106 (708) 834-2461 fax: (708) 834-2478							x					
Therapy Skill Builders c/o Psychological Corporation P.O. Box 839954 San Antonio, TX 78283-3954 (800) 866-4446, (210) 299-1061 fax: (800) 323-1223			x								x	
Things from Bell 230 Mechanic Street, P.O. Box 206 Princeton, WI 54968 (800) 543-1458, (414) 642-7337 fax: (800) 432-2842									x	x		
Toys for Special Children 385 Warburton Avenue Hastings-on-Hudson, NY 10706 (800) 832-8697, (914) 478-0960 fax: (914) 478-7030		x										x
Toys To Grow On P.O. Box 17 Long Beach, CA 90801 (800) 874-4242 fax: (310) 537-5403												x
Troll Learn and Play 100 Corporate Drive Mahwah, NJ 07430 (800) 247-6106, (800) 542-8338 (orders) fax: (800) 451-0812												x
University of Illinois Press 1325 South Oak Street Champaign, IL 61820-6903 (217) 333-0950, (800) 545-4703 (orders) fax: (217) 244-8082			x								x	

continues

Table C–1 continued

	Activities of Daily Living	Assistive Technology	Books/Peridicals/Audiovisuals	Hearing and Vision Impaired	Medical/Nursing Supplies	Rehab/Exercise Equipment	Seating/Positioning/Mobility	Splinting/Orthotics	Sports/Recreation	Teaching/Therapy Media	Tests/Assessment Materials	Toys/Games
Vort Corporation P.O. Box 60880 Palo Alto, CA 94306 (415) 322-8282 fax: (415) 327-0747			x							x	x	
Western Psychological Corporation 12031 Wilshire Boulevard Los Angeles, CA 90025-1251 (800) 648-8857, (310) 478-2061 fax: (310) 478-7838			x								x	
Wheel Ring, Inc. 199 Forest Street Manchester, CT 06040 (203) 647-8596 fax: (203) 647-7517							x					
Wiley Interscience 604 Third Avenue New York, NY 10158-0012 (212) 850-6000 fax: (212) 850-6088 (professional/reference/ trade), (212) 850-6591 (education)			x									
Williams & Wilkins 428 East Preston Street Baltimore, MD 21202 (800) 638-0672, (410) 528-4423 fax: (800) 447-8438			x									
Wolverine Sports 745 State Circle, Box 1941 Ann Arbor, MI 48106 (800) 521-2832 fax: (313) 761-8711									x			x
Woodbine House, the Special Needs Collection 6510 Bells Mill Road Bethesda, MD 20817 (800) 843-7323 fax: (301) 897-5838			x									
Wyeth-Ayerst Laboratories 31 Morehall Road Frazer, PA 19355 (610) 644-8000					x							

Source: Children's Seashore House. Updated and verified by Nancy Moritz and others.

Index

Note: Page numbers in *italics* denote figures and exhibits; those followed by "t" denote tables.